Early Childhood Experiences in Language Arts

Early Childhood Experiences in Language Arts 11e

EARLY LITERACY

Jeanne M. Machado

Emerita, San Jose City College

CENGAGE
Learning·

Australia • Brazil • Canada • Mexico • Singapore • United Kingdom • United States

***Early Childhood Experiences in Language Arts:
Early Literacy,* Eleventh Edition**
Jeanne M. Machado

Product Director: Marta E. Lee-Perriard

Product Manager: Mark Kerr

Content Developer: Kassi Radomski

Product Assistant: Julia Catalano

Content Project Manager: Samen Iqbal

Art Director: Marissa Falco

Manufacturing Planner: Doug Bertke

IP Analyst: Jennifer Nonenmacher

IP Project Manager: Brittani Hall

Production Service/Project Manager:
Charu Khanna, MPS Limited

Photo Researcher: Nazveena Begum Syed,
Lumina Datamatics Ltd.

Text Researcher: Punitha Rajamohan, Lumina
Datamatics Ltd.

Text and Cover Designer: Jeanne Calabrese
Design, Inc.

Cover Image Credit: Large photo of boy in
striped shirt (front cover): Blend Images –
JGI/Jamie Grill/Getty Images Three small
photos appear on front and back cover:
(children using letters on floor) Paul Burns/
Getty Images (two children reading a book)
JGI/Jamie Grill/Getty Images (teacher
reading to students) Purestock/Getty Images

Compositor: MPS Limited

© 2016, 2013, Cengage Learning

WCN: 01-100-101

ALL RIGHTS RESERVED. No part of this work covered by the copyright
herein may be reproduced, transmitted, stored, or used in any form or by
any means graphic, electronic, or mechanical, including but not limited to
photocopying, recording, scanning, digitizing, taping, Web distribution,
information networks, or information storage and retrieval systems, except
as permitted under Section 107 or 108 of the 1976 United States Copyright
Act, without the prior written permission of the publisher.

For product information and technology assistance, contact us at
Cengage Learning Customer & Sales Support, 1-800-354-9706.

For permission to use material from this text or product,
submit all requests online at **www.cengage.com/permissions.**
Further permissions questions can be e-mailed to
permissionrequest@cengage.com.

Library of Congress Control Number: 2014943033

Student Edition:
ISBN: 978-1-305-08893-1

Loose-leaf Edition:
ISBN: 978-1-305-49688-0

Cengage Learning
20 Channel Center Street
Boston, MA 02210
USA

Cengage Learning is a leading provider of customized learning solutions with
office locations around the globe, including Singapore, the United Kingdom,
Australia, Mexico, Brazil, and Japan. Locate your local office at
www.cengage.com/global.

To learn more about Cengage Learning Solutions, visit **www.cengage.com.**

Purchase any of our products at your local college store or at our preferred
online store **www.cengagebrain.com.**

Brief Contents

Contents

Preface

Early Childhood Experiences in Language Arts: Early Literacy is a teacher-training text designed to help those working in the early childhood education field provide an opportunity-rich program full of interesting, appropriate, and developmental language arts activities that reflect current standards. It is both a practical "how-to" manual and a collection of resources that includes numerous classic, tried-and-true activities.

Because a comprehensive, dynamically planned early childhood language arts curriculum consists of four broad interrelated areas—speaking (oral), listening, writing, and reading—each is fully explored and described in separate chapters. Visual literacy is also covered, as it is closely tied to the other language arts areas, and because young children today have frequent interactions with visual technology.

The text recommends early childhood education students create, design, and prepare classroom activities and environments based on newborn through kindergarten-age children's assessed needs, interests, developmental level, and potential. Beginning teachers are urged to use their own unique teaching talents, skills, and creativity—along with their past memories of the enjoyed childhood language-related experiences—to help guide their instruction. It is hoped that the confidence and skills gained by readers will help to provide young children with enthusiastic, knowledgeable teacher-companions who enjoy and encourage children in their discovery of the language arts.

Organization and Content

Section 1
In Section 1, the first three chapters present a detailed account of language acquisition, young children's early communicative capacities, growth milestones, and age-level milestones (infancy through preschool), along with suggested professional techniques to promote each child's self-esteem and potential. In Chapter 1, the characteristics of attuned and sensitive caregiver behaviors have been highlighted to emphasize their significance. Infant and toddler chapters (Chapters 1 and 2) increase the reader's ability to both tailor and individualize his or her own actions, comments, and activity plans to suit the needs of diverse children. Educators become better equipped to identify child progress or suspected lags in language use and growth. Toddlers' physical development and concurrent mushrooming verbal skills appear in a predictable, yet individual, pattern. Chapter 3 provides the reader with an accurate portrait of preschoolers' emerging language and literacy accomplishments, and also covers other concurrently developing growth systems that affect language and literacy. These are physical, cognitive, perceptive, and socioemotional areas. Finding a typical or average preschooler may be an impossible task, as preschoolers, like adults, display infinite variety. The well-known and well-documented characteristics of the preschool-aged child are presented.

Section 2
Special attention is paid to second-language learners and children with special needs in Chapter 4, *Understanding Differences*. With the number of second-language learners and children with special needs continuing to grow, it has become more critical than ever for early childhood teachers to create language-rich environments and interact as enthusiastic, supportive, and observant companions and collaborators. Chapter 5 covers the basics of developing language arts programs based on identified goals, as well as assessment strategies, and includes information about children's literacy portfolios. Specific teaching strategies are addressed in Chapter 6, *Promoting Language and Literacy*, and Chapter 7, *Developing Listening Skills*, to aid a teacher's knowledge and practice of professional responses and interchanges in daily conversation and discussions. Tips and suggestions are designed to get the most "literacy-developing mileage" possible from daily happenings. Since listening well is a learned skill, Chapter 7 does not leave it to chance, but promotes the teacher's role as cultivator of each child's growing ability.

Section 3
Children's literature is introduced in Chapter 8 and begins with a brief history of picture book development and change over time. Readers are

urged to discover new and older classics and skillfully share them with children in a way that increases each child's love of story and joy in acquiring new knowledge and skill. This chapter is extensive and alerts readers to the many types of books available and their appeal to young listeners. Text discussions include teacher techniques that build children's comprehension of stories and also their understanding of books' connection to writing (print), viewing, reading, and oral expression. During book readings, educators are directed to share their thinking aloud and to define new words to increase children's vocabulary, analysis, and problem solving abilities.

Chapters 9, 10, and 11 concentrate on developmentally appropriate vehicles to widen children's background and knowledge and experience in storytelling, poetry, and flannel board activities. Teacher skill in the presentation of these language arts subsections is recommended, and suggested stories, poems, and flannel board sets give beginning teachers an initial collection to immediately try out and enjoy with young children. The use of puppetry and classroom dramatization is also included in these chapters.

Section 4

In order to increase children's ability to express their ideas and dramatize real life or fantasy experience, Chapter 12 discusses an early childhood educator's promotion of children's oral expression and symbolic (dramatic) play. The beginning teacher's ability to plan, conduct, and manage small and large groups in a competent and professional manner is the subject of Chapter 13, which also focuses upon the language and literacy producing aspects of children's group experiences. Again many circle time hints are provided, along with suggested games and activities, such as finger plays, poems, songs, chants and choruses, and body movements connected to words.

Section 5

Quality language arts programs in early childhood centers are increasingly focused on the promotion of each child's ability to learn to read with ease when formal reading instruction begins. The alphabetic principle, orthographic and print awareness, sight reading, and invented spelling are clearly explained in Chapter 14, *Print—Early Knowledge and Emerging Interest*. This chapter introduces and outlines the probable sequence of events that proceed a child's printing his first alphabet letter. Using the appropriate form of printscript letters is emphasized as teachers model and write alphabet letters. A number of print-related child activities are included, as well as sample print alphabets with construction arrows. Print-rich and print-appropriate classroom environments are suggested. Children's natural curiosity and their innate ability aids their emergence as competent readers when formal instruction begins in kindergarten. Chapter 15 describes the desirable skills, knowledge, and abilities that promote children's progress in learning to read. The differences in reading instruction methodology are discussed so that early childhood educators become aware of what types of instruction are used in the first grades of school.

Section 6

Chapter 16 looks at the physical features and equipment needed to enhance learning in a literacy-based classroom. Chapter 17 discusses the critical importance of increasing a family's ability to partner with their children's school and teachers. Suggestions are included to increase the beginning teacher's ability to establish fruitful school-home relationships. Parent tips to extend language and provide literacy-enriched home environments and activities are listed. The text urges educators to honor children's homegrown literacy knowledge and skills. Well-prepared educators recognize that families may use various and diverse vocabulary- and literacy-building strategies. Cultural differences are increasingly commonplace in America's classrooms, and each child's unique difference is respected and dignified as teachers promote the English language arts.

New Features

The eleventh edition includes a number of new features to aid the student's mastery of each chapter's content.

- **NEW Learning Objectives** at the beginning of each chapter now correlate with main headings within the chapter and the Summary at the end of the chapter. The objectives highlight what students need to know to process and understand the information in the chapter. After completing the chapter, students should be able to demonstrate how they can use and apply their new knowledge and skills.

- **NEW and improved integration of early childhood professional standards** helps students make connections between what they are learning in the textbook and the standards. This edition now contains a list of standards covered at the beginning of each chapter, including NAEYC's Early Childhood Program Standards and Accreditation Criteria, 2007; Developmentally Appropriate Practice (DAP): Focus on Infants and Toddlers (2013); and Common Core Standards for English language arts and literacy. These standards are called out with icons throughout the text; a complete list of the standards can be found in the standards correlation chart on the inside front and back covers.

- **NEW TeachSource Digital Downloads** are downloadable and sometimes customizable practical and professional resources, which allow students to immediately implement and apply the textbook's content in the field. Students can download these tools and keep them forever, enabling preservice teachers to begin building a library of practical, professional resources. Look for the TeachSource Digital Download label that identifies these items.

- **New MindTap for Education** is a first-of-its kind digital solution that prepares teachers by providing them with the knowledge, skills, and competencies they must demonstrate to earn an education degree and state licensure, and to begin a successful career. Through activities based on real-life teaching situations, MindTap elevates students' thinking by giving them experiences in applying concepts, practicing skills, and evaluating decisions, guiding them to become reflective educators.

- **NEW Brain Connection** boxes place additional emphasis on brain-based learning practices.

- **Updated coverage of technology and literacy learning** including information about the joint position statement from NAEYC, the Fred Rogers Center for Early Learning, and Children's Media at St. Vincent College.

- **Additional attention to children's oral language experience** has been included to help beginning teachers increase children's conversation and expression of ideas and discoveries.

- **Newly described teacher interaction behaviors** (Chapter 8) are used in the discussion of children's comprehension of storybook read-alouds and the promotion of their development of analytical thinking while enjoying literature.

Other Features

- **TeachSource Videos**—The TeachSource Videos feature footage from the classroom to help students relate key chapter content to real-life scenarios. Critical-thinking questions following each video provide opportunities for in-class or online discussion and reflection.

- **Discussion Vignettes**—Discussion Vignettes introduce chapters with real-life classroom teaching situations that promote student analysis. The Questions to Ponder that follow promote reflection and class discussion.

- **Additional Resources**—This section follows each chapter's summary. It presents readings for students wanting further depth, reinforcement of chapter topics, and/or pursuit of special interests. Resources such as commercial educational materials, professional organizations in which further information can be obtained, and helpful websites are also included.

- In addition to current research, the eleventh edition continues to use classic findings and recommendations.

Supplements

- **NEW MindTap™, The Personal Learning Experience, for Machado's *Early Childhood Experiences in Language Arts: Early***

Literacy, **Eleventh Edition**, represents a new approach to teaching and learning. A highly personalized, fully customizable learning platform, MindTap, helps students to elevate thinking by guiding them to:

- Know, remember, and understand concepts critical to becoming a great teacher;

- Apply concepts, create tools, and demonstrate performance and competency in key areas in the course;

- Prepare artifacts for the portfolio and eventual state licensure, to launch a successful teaching career; and

- Develop the habits to become a reflective practitioner.

As students move through each chapter's Learning Path, they engage in a scaffolded learning experience designed to move them up Bloom's Taxonomy from lower- to higher-order thinking skills. The Learning Path enables preservice students to develop these skills and gain confidence by:

- Engaging them with chapter topics and activating their prior knowledge by watching and answering questions about TeachSource videos of teachers teaching and children learning in real classrooms;

- Checking their comprehension and understanding through *Did You Get It?* assessments, with varied question types that are autograded for instant feedback;

- Applying concepts through mini-case scenarios—students analyze typical teaching and learning situations and create a reasoned response to the issue(s) presented in the scenarios; and

- Reflecting about and justifying the choices they made within the teaching scenario problem.

MindTap helps instructors facilitate better outcomes by evaluating how future teachers plan and teach lessons in ways that make content clear and help diverse students learn, assessing the effectiveness of their teaching practice, and adjusting teaching as needed. The

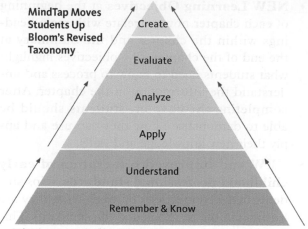

Anderson, L. W., & Krathwohl, D. (Eds.). (2001). *A taxonomy for learning, teaching, and assessing: A revision of Bloom's taxonomy of educational objectives.* New York: Longman.

Student Progress App makes grades visible in real time so students and instructors always have access to current standings in the class.

MindTap for *Early Childhood Experiences in Language Arts*, Eleventh Edition, helps instructors easily set their course because it integrates into the existing Learning Management System and saves instructors time by allowing them to fully customize any aspect of the learning path. Instructors can change the order of the student learning activities, hide activities they don't want for the course, and—most importantly—add any content they do want (e.g., YouTube videos, Google docs, links to state education standards). Learn more at www.cengage.com/mindtap.

Online Instructor's Manual with Test Bank

An online Instructor's Manual accompanies this book. It contains information to assist the instructor in designing the course, including: sample syllabi, discussion questions, teaching and learning activities, field experiences, learning objectives, and additional online resources. For assessment support, the updated test bank includes true/false, multiple-choice, matching, short-answer, and essay questions for each chapter.

PowerPoint® Lecture Slides

These vibrant Microsoft® PowerPoint lecture slides for each chapter assist you with your lecture by providing concept coverage using images, figures, and tables directly from the textbook.

Cognero

Cengage Learning Testing Powered by Cognero is a flexible online system that allows you to author, edit, and manage test bank content from multiple Cengage Learning solutions; create multiple test versions in an instant; and deliver tests from your LMS, your classroom, or wherever you want.

Professional Enhancement Book

A new supplement to accompany this text is the Language Arts and Literacy Professional Enhancement booklet for students. This book, which is part of Cengage Learning's Early Childhood Education Professional Enhancement series, focuses on key topics of interest to future early childhood teachers and caregivers. Students will keep this informational supplement and use it for years to come in their early childhood practices.

About The Author

The author's experience in the early childhood education field has included full-time assignment as community college instructor and department chairperson. Her duties included supervision of early childhood education students at two on-campus laboratory child development centers at San Jose City College and Evergreen Valley College, as well as child centers in the local community. Her teaching responsibilities encompassed early childhood education, child development, and parenting courses.

She received her Master's Degree from San Jose State University and her community college life credential with coursework from the University of California at Berkeley. Her experience includes working as an elementary school teacher, preschool owner/director, work experience instructor/advisor, early childhood and family studies community college and university instructor, and an education consultant in public, private, and parent cooperative programs. Ms. Machado is an active participant in several professional organizations concerned with the education and well-being of young children and their families. She is a past president of California Community College Early Childhood Educators (CCCECE) and the Peninsula Chapter of the California Association for the Education of Young Children. In addition to *Early Childhood Experiences In Language Arts*, she co-authored with Dr. Helen Meyer-Botnarescue a text for student teachers called *Student Teaching: Early Childhood Practicum Guide*, Seventh Edition, ©2011. She also co-authored *Employment Opportunities in Education: How to Secure Your Career*, ©2006, with Romana Reynolds. Ms. Machado consults with parents, teachers, and administrators, and interacts with young children in classrooms in Cascade, Idaho, and San Jose, California.

Acknowledgments

The author wishes to express her appreciation to the following individuals and agencies.

The students at San Jose City College, AA Degree Program in Early Childhood Education

Arbor Hill Child Care Center, Albany, NY

San Jose City College Child Development Center's director and teachers

Evergreen Valley College Child Development Center's director and staff members, San Jose, CA

James Lick Children's Center, Eastside High School District, San Jose, CA

Kiddie Academy, Albany, NY

Piedmont Hills Preschool, San Jose, CA

Pineview Preschool, Albany, NY

St. Elizabeth's Day Home, San Jose, CA

W.I.C.A.P. HeadStart, Donnelly, ID

Cascade Elementary School – Pre-K Class, Cascade, ID

The staff at Cengage Learning

In addition, special appreciation is due the reviewers involved in the development of this edition

Cecile Arquette, Bradley University

Katrin Blamey, DeSales University

Johnny Castro, Brookhaven College

Roseann Chavez, Warren County Community College

Tina Dekle, Vance-Granville Community College

Deirdre Englehart, University of Central Florida

Randa Gamal, Central New Mexico Community College

April Grace, Madisonville Community College

Jeanne Helm, Richland Community College

Annemarie Hindman, Temple University

Colleen Lelli, Cabrini College

Jeannie Morgan-Campola, Rowan Cabarrus Community College

Crystal Stephens, Western Piedmont Community College

Maria Vazquez, Florida International University

Wendy Fletcher, Wiregrass Georgia Technical College

Karen Ray, Wake Technical Community College

To The Student

Because you are a unique, caring individual who has chosen an early childhood teaching career or who is currently working with children, this text is intended to help you discover and share your developing language arts gifts and talents. Create your own activities using your college coursework and life experiences and an assessment of what would be valuable growing opportunities for the children you teach. Design and base your activities on an understanding of current research and theory. Consider the wisdom you have gained through your past experiences with children. Share your specialness and make your classroom memorable as a place where literature and communication thrive.

In this text, I urge you to become a skilled teacher who interacts, converses, and collaborates, and acts as "a subtle opportunist," getting the most possible out of each child–adult interaction. Make your joy in the language arts the children's joy. You can make a difference in young children's lives. Ideally, this text will help you become the kind of teacher who does. Because I am growing, too, I invite your suggestions and comments, so that in future editions I can refine and improve this text's value.

1 Beginnings of Communication

Objectives

After reading this chapter, you should be able to:

1-1 Discuss the reciprocal behaviors of infants, parents, and caregivers.

1-2 Name four important influences that may affect an infant's language growth and development.

1-3 Compare two theories of human language emergence.

1-4 Name two areas of particular importance to infant care addressed in Developmentally Appropriate Practice (DAP) guidelines.

1-5 Discuss the behaviors and vocalizing efforts that infants use to communicate their needs and desires.

1-6 Describe what caregiver actions should take place when infants develop joint attentional focus.

1-7 Name and comment upon early reading and writing activities in late infancy.

1-8 Identify how infant centers monitor each infant's language and communicating behaviors.

naeyc NAEYC Program Standards

1A05 Teacher shares information with families about classroom expectations and routines.

1B01 Teaching staff foster children's emotional well-being by demonstrating respect for children and creating a positive emotional climate as reflected in behaviors, such as frequent social conversations, joint laughter, and affection.

1B11 Teaching staff engage infants in frequent face-to-face social interactions each day.

1B14 Teaching staff quickly respond to infants' cries or other signs of distress by providing physical comfort and needed care.

DAP Developmentally Appropriate Practice (DAP)

1A2 The infant's primary caregiver comes to know the child and family well, and so is able to respond to that child's individual temperament and needs and cues, and to develop a mutually satisfying pattern of communication.

1B1 Caregivers talk in a pleasant, calm voice, making frequent eye contact.

1C1 Caregivers often talk about what is going on with the infant.

1D2 Caregivers observe and listen and respond to sounds the infant makes.

1D3 Caregivers frequently talk to, sing to, and read to infants.

3B3 Appropriate games are played with interested infants.

COMMON CORE Common Core State Standards for English Language Arts and Literacy

L.CCR 3 Apply knowledge to understand how language functions in different contexts.

A New Sign

Noah, 10 months, had a new sign for "cracker" that he had used a few times during the day at the infant center. He was very pleased when his "sign" resulted in someone bringing him a cracker. At pick-up time, one of the staff believed it important to talk to Noah's dad. Mr. Soares did not really understand what the teacher, Miss Washington, was talking about when she said "signing." Miss Washington gave Mr. Soares a quick explanation. He smiled proudly and then said, "That's great. I'll talk to his mom and let her know."

Questions to Ponder

1. Miss Washington had a new language-related topic for the next staff meeting. What would you suspect it was?

2. Did this episode tell you something about the language-developing quality of the infant center?

3. What do you know about male infants and their signing ability compared with that of female infants? Could you describe infant signing behavior?

(If you are hesitating, this chapter provides answers.)

In this chapter the reader is acquainted with those elements in an infant's life that facilitate optimal growth in communication and language development. Socioemotional, physical, cognitive, and environmental factors that influence, promote, or deter growth are noted. Recommended interaction techniques and strategies are supported by research and reflect accepted appropriate practices and standards. As foundational aspects of infant communication are presented, *boxed* descriptions of the attuned and reciprocal behaviors caregivers make with infants are provided. Caregivers establish a relationship with each infant in their care, and the quality of that relationship serves to motivate each infant to engage in learning (McMullen & Dixon, 2006). Higher levels of warmth are connected to positive caregiver sensitivity. Gerber, Whitebook, & Weinstein (2007) note that the quality of caregiver practices has been linked to children's brain development and cognitive functioning.

For you to become the kind of educator children deserve, one who enhances language growth, you should begin by believing that most infants are able and natural communicators from birth onward unless some life circumstance has modified their natural potential. Infant care facilities with well-planned, positive, and growth-producing environments—that are staffed with skilled, knowledgeable, and well-trained adults who offer developmentally appropriate activities—provide a place where infants can and do thrive.

Each infant is a unique combination of inherited traits and environmental influences. Structural, hormonal, and chemical influences present before birth may have affected the growth and development of the fetus (Gould, 2002). Newborns seem to assimilate information immediately and are interested in their surroundings. Some suggest an infant possesses "the greatest mind" in existence and is the most powerful learning machine in the universe. During the third trimester of pregnancy, most mothers notice that their babies kick and move in response to music or loud noises. The sound of speech may draw a less spirited reaction, but there is little question that fetuses hear and react to a wide variety of sounds and seem to recognize the rhythm of their mother's voice.

Technology can now monitor the slightest physical changes in breathing, heartbeat, eye movement, and sucking rhythm and rates. Babies begin learning how to carry on conversations quickly and sucking patterns produce a **rhythm** that mimics that of give-and-take dialogues. Infants respond to very specific maternal signals, including tone of voice, facial changes, and head movements.

Greenspan (1999) suggests what may happen when interacting with a one- or two-month-old baby at a relaxed time after a nap or feeding:

> ... when you hold him at arm's length and look directly into his eyes with a broad smile on your face, watch his lips part as if he's trying to imitate your smile. (p. 31)

Babies gesture and make sounds and seem to hold up their ends of conversations, but, at times, they appear to suppress output and channel their energy into seeing and hearing. Their eye contact with their caregivers, called **gaze coupling**, is believed to be one of their first steps in establishing communication. Infants can

---

rhythm — uniform or patterned recurrence of a beat, accent, or melody in speech.
gaze coupling — infant-mother extended eye contact.

shut off background noises and pay attention to slight changes in adult voice sounds.

An attuned adult responds with sensitivity and accuracy based on an understanding of an infant's (child's) cues.

an **ATTUNED** adult would:

- notice infant actions, including gestures, body positioning, noisemaking, eye gazing, and any shift from listening to watching.
- make face-to-face contact frequently.
- display admiration, affection, and pleasure and smile frequently.
- provide verbal and nonverbal communication.
- seek to maintain and prolong eye contact. <

McMillen (2013) posits babies are captivating, wondrous, and beguiling beings coming into the world fully equipped to enchant and draw us in. The qualities an infant inherits from parents and the events that occur in the child's life help shape the child's language development. Gender, temperament, and a timetable for the emergence of intellectual, emotional, and physical capabilities are all genetic givens. In the short four to five years after birth, the child's speech becomes purposeful and similar to adult speech. This growing language skill is a useful tool for satisfying needs and exchanging thoughts, hopes, and dreams with others. As ability grows, the child understands and uses more of the resources of oral and recorded human knowledge and is well on the way to becoming a literate being.

The natural capacity to categorize, to invent, and to remember information aids the child's language acquisition. Although unique among the species because of the ability to speak, human beings are not the only ones who can communicate. Birds and animals also imitate sounds and signals and are believed to communicate. For instance, chimpanzees exposed to experimental language techniques (American Sign Language, specially equipped machines, and plastic tokens) have surprised researchers with their language abilities. Some have learned to use symbols and follow linguistic rules with a sophistication that rivals that of some two-year-olds. Researchers continue to probe the limits of their capabilities. However, a basic difference between human beings and other species exists.

It is the development of the cerebral cortex that sets humans apart from less intelligent

TeachSource Video 1-1

© 2016 Cengage Learning®

Observing and Monitoring Language Development in Infants: The Importance of Assessment

This video provides an example of a body motion play that is taking place with infants.

1. How long were the infants able to attend to the body play before they started turning away?
2. The babbling of a consonant was demonstrated by a child; do you know which consonant?
3. Did you notice infants imitating teacher actions?
4. Did teachers really understand why toddlers were distressed or did they have to guess?

animals. Our advanced mental capabilities, such as thought, memory, language, mathematics, and complex problem solving, are unique to human beings. Humans have the unique species-specific ability to test hypotheses about the structure of language. They can also develop rules for a particular language and remember and use them to generate appropriate language. Within a few days after birth, human babies recognize familiar faces, voices, and even smells and prefer them to unfamiliar ones.

Infant research has advanced by leaps and bounds to reveal amazing newborn abilities. Long before they can talk, for example, babies remember events and solve problems. They can recognize faces, see colors, hear voices, discriminate speech sounds, and distinguish basic tastes. When you combine the psychological and neurological evidence, it is hard not to conclude that babies are just plain smarter than adults. This is especially true when it comes to learning something new.

Begley (2009) urges teachers to be aware that a child's genes (inherited DNA) in themselves do not determine intelligence or any other complex human trait. An infant or child's appearance and temperament may elicit particular parent and teacher behaviors. These can include the adult's responsiveness and ability to pay attention to, interact with, speak with, and provide intellect-building interaction to the child. naeyc

1-1 Infant Actions Prompt Caregiver Behaviors naeyc

The human face becomes the most significantly important communication factor for the infant, and the facial expressions, which are varied and complex, eventually will influence infant body reactions (interior and exterior). Caregivers strive to understand the infant's state of well-being by interpreting the infant's face and postures, as infants also search faces in the world around them.

Figure 1-1 identifies a number of signals infants use and their probable meanings. Response and intentional behavior become apparent as infants age and gain experience. Infants initially respond with various preprogrammed gestures, such as: smiling, intent and interested

Photo 1-1 "Wow, that is interesting!"

© 2015 Cengage Learning®

looking, crying, satisfied sucking, and snuggling. Soon these behaviors are followed by active demanding and attention-seeking patterns in which attempts to attract and solicit caregiver attention rapidly become unmistakable and intentional.

Researchers are studying the roles of facial expressions, gestures, and body movements in human social communication (Photo 1-1). Early expressions that look like smiling may occur minutes after birth and are apparent in the faces of sleeping babies, whose facial expressions seem to constantly change. When studying infant smiling during an infant's first week of life, observers note that infants smile during brief alertness periods, when drowsy, in active and quiet sleep, and randomly when nothing seems to provoke it. Many parents have noticed that smiling most often occurs in deep sleep.

Caregivers observe that infants search for the source of the human voice and face. An infant may become wide-eyed and crane his neck and lift his chin toward the source. His body tension increases as he becomes more focused and somewhat inactive. Most caregivers respond to these signals by picking up the infant and cuddling him. The National Association for the Education of Young Children in a 2013 publication, *Developmentally Appropriate Practice: Focus on Infants and Toddlers*, points out that it is a caregiver's responsibility to cultivate children's (infants' and toddlers') delight in exploring and understanding their world. They believe early childhood should be a time of laughter, love, play, and great fun.

Figure 1-1 Born communicators.

Infant Acts	Probable Meaning
turning head and opening mouth	feeling hungry
quivering lips	adjusting to stimuli
sucking on hand, fist, thumb	calming self, feeling overstimulated
averting eyes	tuning out for a while
turning away	needing to calm down
yawning	feeling tired/stressed
looking wide-eyed	feeling happy
cooing	feeling happy
appearing dull with unfocused eyes	feeling overloaded, needing rest
waving hands	feeling excited
moving tongue in and out	feeling upset/imitating

an **ATTUNED** adult would:

- be aware of opportunities to soothe and touch and engage in some way with an infant.
- pick up and hold an infant gently while providing firm support.
- note an infant's well-being and comfort.
- attempt to interpret an infant's facial and body signals. <

1-1a Definitions

Language, as used in this text, refers to a system of intentional communication and self-expression through sounds, signs (gestures), or symbols that are understandable to others. Language also refers to a symbol-based, rule-governed, multidimensional system that is used to represent the world internally and to others through the process of communication (Pence, Justice, & Wiggins, 2008). The language-development process includes both sending and receiving information. Input (receiving) comes before output (sending); input is organized mentally by an individual long before there is decipherable output.

Communication is a broader term, defined as giving and receiving information, signals, or messages. A person can communicate with or receive communications from animals, infants, or foreign speakers in a variety of ways. Even a whistling teakettle sends a message that someone can understand. Infants appear to be "in tune," focused on the human voice, hours after birth.

Speech is much more complex than simple parroting or primitive social functioning. The power of language enables humans to dominate other life forms. The ability to use language secured our survival by giving us a vehicle to both understand and transmit language and to work cooperatively with others. Language facilitates peaceful solutions between people.

1-2 Influences on Development

A child's ability to communicate involves an integration of body parts and systems allowing hearing, understanding, organizing thoughts, learning, and using language. Most children accomplish the task quickly and easily, but many factors influence the learning of language.

Research suggests that babies instinctively turn their heads to face the source of sound and can remember sounds heard before birth. This has prompted mothers to talk to, sing to, and read classic literature and poetry to the unborn. Research has yet to document evidence of the benefits of these activities.

Of all sounds, nothing attracts and holds the attention of infants as well as the human voice—especially the higher-pitched female voice. "Motherese," a distinct caregiver speech, is discussed later in this chapter. Dietrich, Swingley, and Werker (2007) note:

> Infants begin to acquire their language by learning phonetic categories. At birth, infants seem to distinguish most of the phonetic contrasts used by the world's languages. However, over the first year, this "universal" capacity shifts to a language-specific pattern in which infants retain or improve categorization of native-language sounds but fail to discriminate many non-native sounds. (p. 16030)

Rhythmic sounds and continuous, steady tones soothe some infants. A number of commercial sound-making products that attempt to soothe can be attached to cribs or are imbedded in plush stuffed animals. Most emit a type of static or heartbeat sound or a combination of the two. Too much sound in the infant's environment, especially loud, excessive, or high-volume sounds, may have the opposite effect. Excessive household noise can come from televisions or other sources. Many have described sensory-overload situations when infants try to turn off sensory input by turning away and somehow blocking that which is at the moment overwhelming, whether the stimulus is mechanical or human. This blocking includes falling asleep.

Although hearing ability is not fully developed at birth, newborns can hear moderately loud sounds and can distinguish different pitches. Newborns' auditory systems are better developed than their sight systems, so the importance of language and voices to children's development is evident from the start (Galinsky, 2010). During the last weeks of pregnancy, a child's auditory system becomes ready to receive and remember sounds.

---

language — the systematic, conventional use of sounds, signs, or written symbols in a human society for communication and self-expression. It conveys meaning that is mutually understood.

communication — the giving (sending) and receiving of information, signals, or messages.

Photo 1-2 Sound-making toys attract attention.

Auditory acuity develops swiftly. Infants inhibit motor activity in response to strong auditory stimuli or when listening to the human voice, and attempt to turn toward it. Some researchers see this as an indication that infants are geared to orient their entire bodies toward any signal that arouses interest (Photo 1-2). Infants' body responses to human verbalizations are a rudimentary form of speech development (Figure 1-2).

Sensory-motor development, which involves the use of sense organs and the coordination of motor systems (body muscles and parts), is vital to language acquisition. Sense organs gather information through seeing, hearing, smelling, tasting, and touching. These sense-organ impressions of people, objects, and life encounters are sent to the brain, and each **perception** (impression received through the senses) is recorded and stored, serving as a base for future oral and written language.

Newborns and infants are no longer viewed as passive, unresponsive "mini-humans." Instead, infants are seen as dynamic individuals, preprogrammed to learn, with functioning sensory capacities, motor abilities, and a wondrous built-in curiosity. Families and caregivers can be described as guides who provide opportunity and act *with* newborns, rather than *on* them.

1-2a Beginning Socialization

A child's social and emotional environments play a leading role in both the quality and the quantity of beginning language. Many researchers

Figure 1-2 Auditory perception in infancy.

Age	Appropriate Hearing Behaviors
birth	awakens to loud sounds
	startles, cries, or reacts to noise
	makes sounds
	looks toward then looks away from environmental sounds
0–3 months	turns head to hear parent's or others' speech
	reacts to speech by smiling
	opens mouth as if to imitate adult's speech
	coos and goos
	seems to recognize a familiar voice
	calms down when adult's voice is soothing
	repeats own vocalizations
	seems to listen to and focus on familiar adults' voices
4–6 months	looks toward environmental noise (e.g., barking, vacuum, doorbell, radio, TV)
	attracted to noise-making toys
	babbles consonant-like sounds
	makes wants known with voice
	seems to understand "no"
	reacts to speaker's change of tone of voice
7–12 months	responds to own name
	may say one or more under-standable but not clearly articulated words
	babbles repeated syllables or consonant- and vowel-like sounds
	responds to simple requests
	enjoys playful word games like Peak-a-boo, Pat-a-cake, etc.
	imitates speech sounds frequently
	uses sound making to gain others' attention

© 2015 Cengage Learning®

---

auditory — relating to or experienced through hearing.

acuity — how well or clearly one uses the senses; the degree of perceptual sharpness.

sensory-motor development — the control and use of sense organs and the body's muscle structure.

perception — mental awareness of objects and other data gathered through the five senses.

describe communicative neonatal behaviors that evoke tender feelings in adults. Human children have the longest infancy among animals. Our social dependency is crucial to our individual survival and growth. Much learning occurs through contact and interaction with others in family and social settings. Basic attitudes toward life, self, and other people form early, as life's pleasures and pains are experienced. The young child depends on parents and other caregivers to provide what is needed for growth and **equilibrium** (a balance achieved when consistent care is given and needs are satisfied). This side of a child's development has been called the **affective sphere**, referring to the affectionate feelings—or lack of them—shaped through experience with others (Photo 1-3). Most experts believe that each time an infant takes in information through the

Photo 1-4 An infant who feels comfortable and whose needs are satisfied is alert to the world.

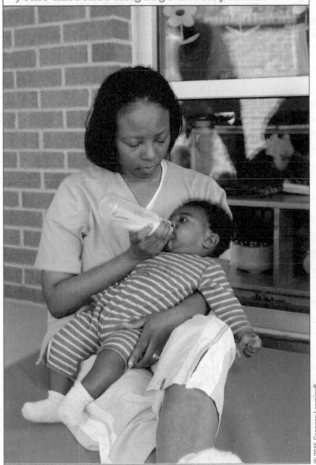

Photo 1-3 Care and attention in the early years influence language development.

senses, the experience is double-coded as both a physical/cognitive reaction and as an emotional reaction to those sensations.

Textbooks often speak indirectly about the infant's need to feel loved consistently, using words like *nurturance, closeness, caring,* and *commitment*. The primary goal of parents and caregivers should be handling the infant and satisfying the child's physical needs in a way that leads to mutual love and a bond of trust (Photo 1-4). This bond, often called **attachment**, is an event of utmost importance to the infant's progress. A developmental milestone is reached when a baby responds with an emotional reaction of his own by indicating obvious pleasure or joy in the company of a parent or caregiver (Figure 1-3). Attachment is formed through mutual gratification of needs

---

equilibrium — a balance attained with consistent care and satisfaction of needs that leads to a sense of security and lessens anxiety.

affective sphere — the affectionate feelings (or lack of them) shaped through experience with others.

attachment — a two-way process formed through mutual gratification of needs and reciprocal communication influenced by the infant's growing cognitive abilities. It is sometimes referred to as bonding or a "love affair" relationship.

Figure 1-3 Milestones in developing language behavior.

Infant's Age	Stages of Language Development
before birth	Listens to sounds. Reacts to loud sounds.
at birth	Birth cry is primal, yet individual—vowel-like. Cries to express desires (for food, attention, and so on) or displeasure (pain or discomfort). Makes eating, sucking, and small throaty sounds. Hiccups. Crying becomes more rhythmic and resonant during first days. Shows changes in posture—tense, active, or relaxed.
first days	Half cries become vigorous; whole cries begin to take on depth and range. Coughs and sneezes.
1 month	Three to four vowel sounds apparent. Seems to quiet movements and attend to mother's voice. Eating sounds mirror eagerness. Sighs and gasps. Smiles in sleep.
2–3 months	Coos and makes pleasurable noises (babbling) and blowing and smacking sounds. Most vowel sounds are present. Open vowel-like babbles may begin. Consonant sounds begin, usually the following—*b, d, g, h, l, m, n, p, t*. Markedly less crying. Smiles and squeals and may coo for half a minute. Peers into faces. Adults may recognize distinct variations in cries (i.e., cries that signal fear, tiredness, hunger, pain, and so on). Focuses on mother's face and turns head to her voice. May be frightened by loud or unfamiliar noise. May blow bubbles and move tongue in and out.
4–5 months	Sound play is frequent. Social smiling more pronounced. Can whine to signal boredom. May laugh. Reacts to tone of voice. Seems to listen and enjoy music. Likes adult vocal play and mimicking. Favorite people seem to induce verbalness. Babbles several sounds in one breath. Body gestures signal state of comfort or discomfort. Attracted to sounds. Approaching six months of age, may start to show understanding of words often used in household. Turns head and looks at speaking family members. Consonant sounds more pronounced and frequent.
6–8 months	Increased babbling and sound making; repeats syllables; imitates motions and gestures; uses nonverbal signals; vocalizes all vowel sounds; reduplication of utterances; more distinct intonation. Increases understanding of simple words. Enjoys making noise with toys and household objects. Repeats actions to hear sounds again. May blow toy horn. Delights in rhythmic vocal play interchange, especially those that combine touching and speaking. Twists and protrudes tongue, smacks, and watches mother's mouth and lips intently. May look at picture books for short period or watch children's television programs.
9–10 months	May make kiss sounds. Increasing understanding of words like *no-no, mommy, daddy, ball, hat,* and *shoe*. May play Pat-a-cake and wave bye-bye. May hand books to adults for sharing. Uses many body signals and gestures. May start jargonlike strings of sounds, grunts, gurgles, and whines. Listens intently to new sounds. Imitates.
11–14 months	Reacts to an increasing number of words. Speaks first word(s) (usually words with one syllable or repeated syllable). Points to named objects or looks toward named word. Makes sounds and noises with whatever is available. Imitates breathing noises, animal noises (like dog's bark or cat's meow), or environmental noises (like "boom" or train toot). Uses many body signals, especially "pick me up" with arms outstretched and reaching for another's hand, meaning "come with me." May understand as many as 40 to 50 words. At close to 15 months, one word has multiple meanings. Jargonlike strings of verbalness continue. The child's direction of looking gives clues to what the child understands, and the child may have a speaking vocabulary of 10 or more words. Uses first pretend play gestures such as combing hair with a spoon-shaped object, drinking from a pretend cup, pretending to eat an object, and pretending to talk with another on a toy telephone.

and reciprocal communication influenced by the infant's growing cognitive ability. The two-way nature of the attachment process is also referred to as bonding. The infant develops a beginning mental picture of the way people in his life interact with one another in systematic and loving relationships. Bardige (2009) describes early bonding in this way:

> Call it chemistry, natural attraction, or falling in love—babies lure adults from the start, and adults who tune in are easily lured. Bonding begins when parent and baby see each other for the first time—and it's a two-way street. With their large eyes and sweet expressions, babies are as cute as they are helpless. Adults naturally soften in their presence, and soon baby and parent are gazing into each other's eyes and forging a connection. (p. 20)

The special feelings an infant develops for a main caregiver later spread to include a group of beloved family members. If an attachment bond is evident and consistent care continues, the child thrives. Social interaction with an empathic and attuned caregiver plays the major role in the growth and regulation of the child's nervous system, and it helps the infant develop the strength needed to become socially competent (Gould, 2002).

Newborns seem to have an individual preferred level of arousal, a **moderation level**, neither too excited nor too bored. They seek change and stimulation and seem to search out newness. Each human may possess an optimal level of arousal—a state when learning is enhanced and pleasure peaks. Mothers and experienced caregivers try to keep infants at moderate levels of arousal, neither too high nor too low. One can perceive three states during an older infant's waking hours: (1) a state in which everything is all right and life is interesting; (2) a reactive state to something familiar or unfamiliar, when an observer can see an alert "what's that?" or "who's that?" response; and (3) a crying or agitated state. One can observe a switch from feeling safe or happy to feeling unsafe or unhappy in a matter of seconds (Photo 1-5). Loud noises can startle the infant and elicit distressed crying. Infants control input and turn away or turn off by moving their eyes and head or body and by becoming fussy or falling asleep.

Greenspan (1999) urges parents and caregivers of infants to improve their observational skills.

Photo 1-5 With tears still wet, this infant has moved on to observing another feature of his environment.

© 2015 Cengage Learning®

As you sharpen your observational skills and pay attention to the times when your baby seems to have more trouble becoming calm and sharing attention with you, you'll begin to assemble a truly revealing developmental profile of your child. You'll start recognizing whether an unpleasant smell, an unexpected hug or cuddle, or a piercing noise overwhelms your child. Don't forget, though, that even a crying, finicky baby is capable of a lot of looking and listening. You may receive some very expressive looks from your three-month-old when he's got a gas bubble in his stomach! If you rub his back while murmuring sympathetically, he may be encouraged to keep his looking and listening skills even when he's not feeling so good. He may be able to use your soothing sounds and touches to calm him. Practicing under slightly stressful conditions will make him into a stronger looker and listener later on. (p. 201)

an **ATTUNED** adult would:

- observe closely.
- assess infants' needs and work to satisfy them.
- notice reactions to room sounds—sound intensity or rhythm or other features.
- calm infants when necessary by trying a variety of strategies.
- use an attention-getting voice, voice variety, and/or high-pitched tones. ◄

---

moderation level — an individual preferred state of arousal between bored and excited when learning and pleasure peak.

1-2b Parent and Caregiver Attitudes and Expectations

As mentioned earlier, research indicates that parent and caregiver attitudes and expectations about infants' awareness and sensory abilities may be predictive of developmental growth.

> Certainly there are many possible explanations for developmental differences. But the fact remains: The earlier a mother thought her baby would be aware of the world, the more competent her baby grew to be. Why was this so? It is because the mothers treated the babies according to their expectations. In home visits, researchers observed that mothers who knew more about their infants' abilities were more emotionally and verbally responsive to their babies. They talked to them more. They provided them with more appropriate play materials and initiated more stimulating experiences. And they were more likely to allow their babies to actively explore the world around them. (Acredolo & Goodwyn, 2000, p. 102)

How we perceive children (infants) shapes how we treat them and therefore what experiences we give them (Begley, 2009). Eliot, a neuroscientist and author of *Pink Brain, Blue Brain* (2009), believes there is little solid evidence that sex differences exist in young children's brains. She maintains the sex differences in adult brains are the result of parent actions and expectancies and life experiences in infancy and childhood.

Eliot points out baby boys are often more irritable than girls, making parents less likely to interact with their thought-to-be nonsocial sons. She notes that, at four months, infant boys and girls differ in amount of eye contact, sociability, emotional expressivity, and verbal ability they exhibit. This, she feels, is not an innate trait but a self-fulfilling prophecy arising from an expectation that males are nonverbal and emotionally distant. Eliot entreats educators to not act in ways that make these perceived characteristics come true.

1-2c Growing Intellect

Other important factors related to the child's mental maturity or ability to think are ages, stages, and sequences of increased mental capacity that are closely related to language development. Language skill and intellect seem to be growing independently, at times, with one or the other developing at a faster rate. The relationship of intelligence and language has been a subject of debate for a long time. Most scholars, however, agree that these two areas are closely associated. Researchers suspect the mind's most important faculties are rooted in emotional experiences from very early in life.

The natural curiosity of humans requires discussion here. Curiosity can be defined as a compulsion (drive) to make sense of life's happenings. Over time, exploring, searching, groping, and probing by infants shift from random to controlled movements. At approximately eight months of age, infants begin to possess insatiable appetites for new things—touching, manipulating, and trying to become familiar with everything that attracts them. Increasing motor skill allows greater possibilities for exploration. Skilled caregivers of infants are kept busy trying to provide novelty, variety, and companionship while monitoring safety. The curiosity of infants seems to wane only when they are tired, hungry, or ill, but even then they are learning. Galinsky (2010) notes:

> Some people think babies aren't learning about talking until they start to babble or say actual words, but that couldn't be farther from the truth. (p. 112)

Cultural Ideas Concerning Infant Communication. Cultural and social forces affect language acquisition. They influence young lives through contact with group attitudes, values, and beliefs. Some cultures expect children to look downward when adults speak, showing respect by this action. Other cultures make extensive use of gestures and signaling. Still others seem to have limited vocabularies or believe that engaging in conversations with infants is inappropriate.

1-3 Theories of Language Emergence

Many scholars, philosophers, linguists, and researchers have tried to pinpoint exactly how language is learned. People in major fields of study—human development, linguistics, sociology, psychology, anthropology, speech-language pathology, and animal study (zoology)—have contributed to current theory. The following are major theoretical positions.

1-3a Behaviorist/Environmentalist (or Stimulus-Response) Theory

As parents and main caregivers reward, correct, ignore, or punish the young child's communication, they exert considerable influence over both the quantity and quality of language usage and the child's attitudes toward communicating. Under this theory, the reactions of the people in a child's environment have an important effect on a child's language development. In other words, positive, neutral, and negative reinforcement play a key role in children's emerging communicating behaviors.

The child's sounds and sound combinations are thought to be uttered partly as imitation and partly at random or on impulse, without pattern or meaning. The child's utterances may grow, seem to reach a standstill, or become stifled, depending on feedback from others (Photo 1-6). This theory is attributed to the work of B. F. Skinner, a pioneer researcher in the field of learning theory.

1-3b Maturational (Normative) Theory

This theory represents the position that children are primarily a product of genetic inheritance and that environmental influences are secondary. Children are seen as moving from one predictable stage to another, with "readiness" the precursor of actual learning. This position was widely accepted in the 1960s, when linguists studied children in less-than-desirable circumstances and discovered consistent patterns of language development. Using this theory as a basis for planning instruction for young children includes (1) identifying predictable stages of growth in language abilities and (2) offering appropriate readiness activities to aid children's graduation to the next higher level.

1-3c Predetermined/Innatist Theory

Under this theory, language acquisition is considered innate (a predetermined human capacity). Each new being is believed to possess a mental ability that enables that being to master any language to which he has been exposed from infancy. Chomsky (1968), a linguistic researcher, theorizes that each person has an individual language acquisition device (LAD). Chomsky also theorizes that this device (capacity) has several sets of language system rules (grammar) common to all known languages. As the child lives within a favorable family climate, his perceptions spark a natural and unconscious device, and the child learns the "mother tongue." Imitation and reinforcement are not ruled out as additional influences.

Chomsky notes that two- and three-year-olds can utter understandable, complicated sentences that they have never heard. More current theory also suggests that young children are equipped with an implicit set of internal rules that allows them to transform the sequences of sounds they hear into sequences of ideas—a remarkable thinking skill. Theorists who support this position note the infant's ability to babble sounds and noises used in languages the child has never heard.

1-3d Cognitive-Transactional and Interaction Theory

Under a fourth theory, language acquisition develops from basic social and emotional drives. Children are naturally active, curious, and adaptive and are shaped by transactions with the people in their environment. Language is learned as a means of relating to people. Others provide social and psychological supports that enable the child to be an effective communicator. L. S. Vygotsky's major work, *Thought and Language* (1986), suggests

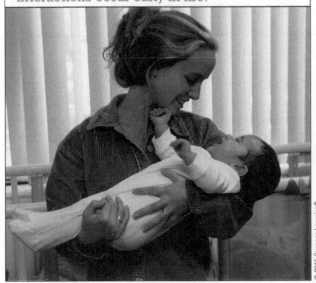

Photo 1-6 Enjoyable conversational interactions occur early in life.

© 2015 Cengage Learning®

that children's meaningful social exchanges prepare them for uniting thought and speech into "verbal thought." This inner speech development, he theorizes, promotes oral communication and is the basis for written language. Drives stem from a need for love and care, and the need prompts language acquisition.

Children are described as reactors to the human social contact that is so crucial to their survival and well-being. They are natural explorers and investigators. The adult's role is to prepare, create, and provide environments and events. Children's views of the world consist of their mental impressions, which are built as new life events are fit into existing ones or as categories are created for new events. Language is an integral part of living; consequently, children seek to fit language into some pattern that allows understanding. With enough exposure and with functioning sensory receiving systems, children slowly crack the "code" and eventually become fluent speakers. There is a wide acceptance of this theory by early childhood professionals.

Vygotsky (1980) argues that language learning is, in part, biological, but that children need instruction in the zone between their independent language level and the level at which they can operate with adult guidance. The early childhood practitioner adopting Vygotsky's ideas would believe both the teacher's behaviors and the child's active physical manipulation of the environment influence and mediate what and how a young child learns or "constructs" mentally. In other words, without the teacher's social interaction, a child does not learn which characteristics are most important or what to notice and act upon. The teacher's role is to find out through thoughtful conversation, observation, and collaboration what concept a child holds during a jointly experienced happening and to aid the child to further mental construction(s). Consequently, under Vygotskian theory, teachers can affect young children's cognitive processes—the way they think and use language. Other individual and societal features that affect children's thinking are family, other children and people in their lives, and society at large, including language, numerical systems, and technology. Children learn or acquire a mental process by sharing or using it in circumstances with others, and then move forward in an independent manner.

1-3e Constructivist Theory

Proponents of constructivist theory propose that children acquire knowledge by constructing it mentally in interaction with the environment. Children are believed to construct theories (hypothesize) about what they experience and then put happenings into relationships. Later, with more life experiences, revisions occur and more adequate explanations are possible. Constructivists point to young children's speech errors in grammar. Internal rules have been constructed and used for a period of time, but with more exposure to adult speech, these rules change and speech becomes closer to adult forms. The rules young children used previously were their own construct and never modeled by adult speakers.

Planning for language development and early literacy using a constructivist perspective would entail offering wide and varied activities while emphasizing their interrelatedness. Teachers and parents are viewed as being involved jointly with children in literacy activities from birth onward. The overall objective of a constructivist's approach is to promote children's involvement with interesting ideas, problems, and questions. Teachers would also help children put their findings and discoveries into words, notice relationships, and contemplate similarities and differences. Children's hands-on activity is believed to be paired with mental action. A secure, unstressed environment encourages the development of children's ability to cooperate, respect one another, exercise curiosity, gain confidence in themselves, and figure things out on their own. They become autonomous learners.

1-3f Other Theories

There is no all-inclusive theory of language acquisition substantiated by research. Many relationships and mysteries are still under study. Current teaching practices involve many different styles and approaches to language arts activities. Some teachers may prefer using techniques in accord with one particular theory. One goal common among educators is to provide instruction that encourages social and emotional development while also offering activities and opportunities in a warm, language-rich, supportive classroom, center, or home.

Educators believe children should be included in talk and treated as competent language partners.

This text promotes many challenging activities that go beyond simple rote memorization or passive participation. It offers an enriched program of literary experience that encourages children to think and use their abilities to relate and share their thoughts. The text is based on the premise that children's innate curiosity, their desire to understand and give meaning to their world, and their predisposition equip them to learn language. Language growth occurs simultaneously in different-yet-connected language arts areas and all other curriculum offerings. Children continually form, modify, rearrange, and revise internal knowledge as experiences, activities, opportunities, and social interactions are encountered. Children's unconscious mental structuring of experience proceeds in growth spurts and seeming regressions, with development in one area influencing development in another.

1-4 Developmentally Appropriate Practice— Infant Care DAP

The National Association for the Education of Young Children's (NAEYC) 2013 Developmentally Appropriate Practice (DAP) guidelines for infants and toddlers are consistent with available research and have the acceptance and the consensus of most early childhood educators. The practice guidelines address the six areas of particular importance to young children's optimum development. These include: (1) relationships between caregivers and children, (2) environment, (3) exploration and play, (4) routines, (5) reciprocal relationships with families, and (6) policies. These guidelines have tried to capture the major aspects of practice that one might see in an excellent program rather than in a program that has not reached that level. Almost all recommended practice mentioned in the material affects young children's language development in some way. The author suggests teachers in training study the complete publication (NAEYC, 2013).

1-4a Research on Infants' Brain Growth naeyc

Researchers of **neurolinguistics** are making new discoveries about infants' and young children's brain growth and their early experience with their families and caregivers. Although awed by the brain's exceptional malleability, flexibility, and plasticity during early years and its ability to "explode" with new **synapses** (connections), scientists also warn of the effects of abuse or neglect on the child's future brain function. It is estimated that at birth, each neuron in the cerebral cortex has approximately 2,500 synapses, and the number of synapses reaches its peak at two to three years of age, when there are about 15,000 synapses per neuron.

A discipline called cognitive science unites psychology, philosophy, linguistics, computer science, and neuroscience. New technology gives researchers additional tools to study brain energy, volume, blood flow, oxygenation, and cross-sectional images. Neuroscientists have found that throughout the entire process of development, beginning even before birth, the brain is affected by environmental conditions, including the kind of nourishment, care, surroundings, and stimulation an individual receives. The brain is profoundly flexible, sensitive, and plastic and is deeply influenced by events in the outside world. The new developmental research suggests that humans' unique evolutionary trick, their central adaptation, their greatest weapon in the struggle for survival, is precisely their ability to learn while they are babies and to teach when grown-ups (Gopnik et al., 1999).

Early experience has gained additional importance and attention. New scientific research does not direct families to provide special "enriching" experiences to children over and above what they experience in everyday life. It does suggest, however, that a radically deprived environment could cause damage. Gould (2002) reports that various types of unpredictable, traumatic, chaotic, or neglectful environments can physically change the infant's brain by overactivating and/or stressing the brain's neural pathways. According to Gould, these changes may include a change in the child's muscle

---

neurolinguistics — a branch of linguistics that studies the structure and function of the brain in relation to language acquisition, learning, and use.

synapses — gap-like structures over which the axon of one neuron beams a signal to the dendrites of another, forming a connection in the human brain. They affect memory and learning.

tone, profound sleep difficulties, an increased startle response, and significant anxiety. Life experiences are now believed to control both how the infant's brain is "architecturally formed" and how intricate brain circuitry is wired. Infant sight and hearing acuity need to be assessed as early as possible given this new information. If a newborn's hearing disability is diagnosed and treated within six months, the child usually develops normal speech and language on schedule (Spivak, 2000). With new technology, hearing tests are far more accurate and can pinpoint the level of hearing loss in babies who are only a few hours old. (The American Academy of Pediatrics recommends that all infants be examined by six months of age and have regular checkups after age three.)

Infants are also far more sophisticated intellectually than we once believed. Babies, as young as four months old, have advanced powers of deduction and an ability to decipher intricate patterns. They have a strikingly nuanced visual palette, which enables them to notice small differences, especially in faces. This is an ability that adults or older children lose. Until a baby is three months old, he can recognize a scrambled photograph of his mother just as quickly as a photograph in which everything is in the right place.

Older debates about nature (genetic givens) versus nurture (care, experiential stimulations, parental teaching, and so on) are outdated (Figure 1-4). Nature and nurture are inseparably intertwined. Genetics lays out our neurological blueprints, but parents and life experiences wire infants' brain (Raftery, 2009).

Many scientists believe that in the first few years of childhood there are a number of critical or sensitive periods, or "windows," when the brain demands certain types of input. If a child's brain is not stimulated during a specific window of time, consequences occur. For example, researchers posit vision will not be normal if by approximately six months, an infant is not seeing things in the world around him. In neurobiological literature, these special periods are described as "critical periods" or "plastic periods," and they are believed to be one of nature's provisions for humankind to be able to use environmental exposure to change the anatomy of the brain and make it more efficient. A span of time from about nine months of age to roughly five years of age is believed to be a period when a natural human opportunity to acquire new skills and use higher cognition exists. This includes learning a second language. This silent and invisible infant language ability is used when a mother or family is bilingual and converses consistently in both languages around the infant. As the child ages he or she may become a functioning bilingual. Increasingly research is showing that the brains of people who know two or more languages are different from monolinguals. Bilinguals can be better at reasoning, multitasking, and grasping and reconciling conflicting ideas (Kluger, 2013). Kluger believes bilinguals are not smarter, they just have more flexible and resourceful brains.

Explosive language growth takes place during the early years and is scattered throughout the brain, but as early as toddlerhood, a pruning

Figure 1-4 Rethinking the brain.

Old Thinking . . .	New Thinking . . .
How a brain develops depends on the genes you are born with.	How a brain develops hinges on a complex interplay between the genes you are born with and the experiences you have.
The experiences you have before age three have a limited architecture impact on later development.	Early experiences have a decisive impact on the architecture of the brain and on the nature and extent of adult capacities.
A secure relationship with a primary caregiver creates a directly favorable context for early development and learning.	Early interactions do not just create a context; they affect the way the brain is "wired."
Brain development is linear: the brain's capacity to learn and change grows steadily as an infant progresses toward adulthood.	Brain development is nonlinear: there are prime times for acquiring different kinds of knowledge and skills.
A toddler's brain is much less active than the brain of a college student.	By the time children reach age three, their brains are twice as active as those of adults. Activity levels drop during adolescence.

Brain Researchers' Recommendations

- Providing excellent child care for working parents.
- Talking to babies frequently.
- Cuddling babies and using hands-on parenting.
- Using **parentese**, the high-pitched, vowel-rich, sing-song speech. The way we typically talk to infants—speaking more slowly, enunciating words, pausing between sounds, and varying the pitch of our voice—makes learning language much easier (Galinsky 2010).
- Giving babies freedom to explore within safe limits.

- Providing safe objects to explore and manipulate.
- Giving babies regular eye examinations and interesting visual opportunities.
- Providing loving, stress-reduced care for the child's emotional development.
- Believing an infant's brain is actively seeking meaning in speech sounds and is trying to understand the actions, intentions, and behaviors of others.

---

or scaling back action happens, making the brain more cognitively and categorically efficient. This is a "use it or lose it" phenomena and is important to bilingual parents who speak a language other than English. They should be continuing to use their native language around their children if they wish them to become true bilinguals. Many educators support programs for early second language learning. Second language learning creates new neural networks that increase the brain's capacity for all sorts of future learning, not just language learning.

Gopnik (2013) notes the newest research suggests infants and toddlers are designed to be especially open to experience and are not encumbered by the executive function of older children's and adults' brains. This makes very young children vividly conscious of every common sight that habit has made invisible to adults. Babies and toddlers are enchanted with the world around them, including things the adult doesn't find the least bit fascinating, like a water bottle, or a butterfly, or the sound of a small horn. Educators and families agree that infant care should be provided by knowledgeable adults who realize that early experiences and opportunities may have long-term developmental consequences (Photo 1-7). Caregivers should also provide rich, language-filled experiences and opportunities and recognize delayed development. Experts describe possible infant learning difficulties related to brain function:

- 0–3 months: Infant does not turn head toward a speaker or try to make vocal sounds.

- 4–6 months: Infant does not respond to *no* or note changes in other's tone of voice. Does

not search for sources of sounds or babble and make consonant-like sounds.

- 7–12 months: Infant does not react to his name; imitate speech sounds, or use actions or sounds to gain attention.

Photo 1-7 Knowledgeable teachers respond with attention and warmth.

---

parentese — a high-pitched, rhythmic, singsong, crooning style of speech. It is also known as motherese or baby talk.

Greenspan's (1999) observations suggest that certain kinds of emotional nurturing propel infants and young children to intellectual and emotional health and that affective experience helps them master a variety of cognitive tasks. He states:

> As a baby's experience grows, sensory impressions become increasingly tied to feelings. It is the **dual coding** of experience that is the key to understanding how emotions organize intellectual capacities and indeed create the sense of self. (p. 78)

Coles (2004), a reviewer of brain research, also points out that growing evidence suggests that thinking is an inseparable interaction of both **cognition** and emotion (feelings, desires, enthusiasms, antipathies, etc.). Interactive emotional exchanges with caregivers and their reciprocal quality are increasingly viewed as being critical to human infants' growth and development, including language development. Early childhood caregivers realize:

> . . . the adult a baby will someday become is the end result of the thousands of times a parent or caregiver comforted her when she cried, helped her to play well with others in the sandbox and sang just one more lullaby before she finally closed her eyes for the night. Each of these seemingly simple acts gently shapes a child's growing sense of self. (Kantrowitz, 2000, p. 6)

The importance of environmental feedback is considerable. Feedback by caregivers includes giving words of approval and providing caregiver attention, and it promotes the emotional satisfaction an infant feels when he is successful in doing something he set out to do.

Some developers of infant materials, equipment, books, and services suggest they can speed brain development. Families may feel they need to find ways to accelerate early childhood experiences and believe that it is up to them to find products and services. Most educators believe this is unnecessary and suggest spending time with infants and providing natural parenting, such as playing, engaging in reciprocal talk, and simply putting plastic mixing bowls on the floor. Honig (2007) concurs and points out that when an infant shakes a bell or pulls a toy on a string to make it move, he is delightedly learning he can get a specific effect. She notes scientists use these same strategies in their laboratories every day.

1-5 Communicative Abilities in Infancy

Newborns quickly make their needs known. They cry and their parents or caregivers respond. Adults feed, hold, and keep infants warm and dry. The sounds of footsteps or voices or a caring touch often stops infants' crying. Babies learn to anticipate. The sense perceptions they receive begin to be connected to stored impressions of the past.

Infants are very powerful in shaping relationships with significant caregivers. They are a wonderful combination of development, potential development, and cognitive flexibility. An infant can perceive from caregivers' behavior a willingness to learn from the infant and respond to his patterns of behavior and rhythms of hunger. This is accomplished by a caregiver's close observation of the infant's vocal and body clues, which indicate the child's state of being. At some point, the caregiver notices that a pattern of mutual gazing is established. Then a type of proto-conversation begins with caregiver vocalizations followed by infant response and noisemaking. Two important developmental tasks that confront infants are: learning to regulate and calm themselves, and learning to interact and "play" with caregivers. The first may be difficult for some infants, but the second seems to come naturally.

The infant is a noisemaker from birth. The child's repertoire includes sucking noises, lip smacking, sneezes, coughs, hiccups, and, of course, different types of cries. As an infant grows, he makes vocal noises, such as **cooing** after feeding. During feeding, slurping and guzzling sounds indicate eagerness and pleasure. Cooing seems to be related to a child's comfort and satisfaction. Cooing consists of relaxed, low-pitched vowel sounds that are made in an open-mouthed way; for example, *e* (as in see), *e* (get), *a* (at), *ah*, and *o, oo, ooo*. The infant appears to be in control of this sound making. Discomfort, by comparison, produces consonant sounds, made in a tense manner with the lips partly closed and

---

dual coding — the belief that infants' experiences and emotions influence cognition.

cognition — the process that creates mental images, concepts, and operations.

cooing — an early stage during the prelinguistic period in which vowel sounds are repeated, particularly the *u-u-u* sound.

the tongue and the ridge of the upper or lower jaw constricting airflow.

Families who attend to infant crying promptly and who believe that crying stems from legitimate needs rather than attempts to control, tend to produce contented, trusting infants. Advice for families of colicky babies consists of holding and carrying the infant more frequently in an effort to soothe. Infants differ in numerous ways from the moment of birth. In speaking to parents about the unique differences in infants, Greenspan (1999) notes the following:

> For most babies, swaddling (gently but firmly bundling the baby's arms and legs in a receiving blanket wrapped around their bodies) is soothing. Other babies enjoy a body massage in which their limbs are gently flexed and extended.

> Up until recently, scientists assumed that all human beings experienced sensations in similar ways. We now know that individuals perceive the same stimulus very differently. Your feathery touch could feel tickly and irritating on your newborn's skin, while another baby might take delight in the same caress. (p. 91)

The individual pace of development varies. Whether an infant reaches developmental milestones on the early or late side of normal seems to bear little relation to either cognitive skills or future proficiency (Raymond, 2000). However, in most cases, milestones in language development are reached at about the same age and in a recognizable sequence (Figure 1-5 and Photo 1-8).

Babies learn quickly that communicating is worthwhile because it results in action on the part of another. Greenspan (1999) warns that unless a child masters the level we call two-way intentional communication, normally achieved by an eight-month-old infant, the child's language, cognitive, and social patterns ultimately develop in an idiosyncratic, piecemeal, disorganized manner. There is a high degree of relationship between a caregiver's responsiveness and a child's language competence. By 9 to 18 months of age, the more responsive mothers promoted greater language facility and growth.

Infants quickly recognize subtle differences in sounds. This helps infants to calm down and pay attention—in other words, to listen. Infants move their arms and legs in synchrony to the rhythms of human speech. Random noises, tapping sounds, and disconnected vowel sounds do not produce this behavior.

Figure 1-5 Examples of the typical order of emergence of types of nonword vocalizations in the first year.

Age	Nonword Vocalizations
newborn	cries
1–3 months	makes cooing sounds in response to speech (*oo, goo*) laughs cries in different ways when hungry, angry, or hurt makes more speechlike sounds in response to speech
4–6 months	plays with some sounds, usually single syllables (e.g., *ba, ga*)
6–8 months	babbles with duplicated sounds (e.g., *bababa*) attempts to imitate some sounds
8–12 months	babbles with consonant or vowel changes (e.g., *badaga, babu*) babbles with sentencelike intonation (expressive jargon/conversational babble) produces protowords

Photo 1-8 Infants often babble to toys: especially ones that make noise.

© 2015 Cengage Learning®

There is a difference between people in an infant's life. Some talk and touch. Others show delight. Some pause after speaking and seem to wait for a response. The child either "locks on" to the conversationalist, focusing totally, or breaks eye contact and looks away. It is almost as though the infant controls what he wants to receive. Of course, hunger, tiredness, and other factors also influence this behavior and may stop the child's interest in being social.

The special people in the infant's life adopt observable behaviors when "speaking" to him or her, just as the infant seems to react in special ways to their attention. Talking to babies differs from other adult speech in that the lyric or musical quality of speech seems more important than words. Infants listening to these long, drawn-out vowels experience an increase in heart rate. At the same time, it speeds up the brain's ability to recognize connections between words and objects. Educators believe "baby-talk" speech modifications can vary among cultures. The attention-holding ability of this type of adult speech may help the infant become aware of the linguistic function of vocalizations (Sachs, 1997). Mothers sometimes raise voice pitch to a falsetto, shorten sentences, simplify syntax and vocabulary, use nonsense sounds, use a slower tempo, and use longer pauses than in adult conversations. They maintain prolonged eye contact during playful interchanges. Most infants are attracted to high-pitched voices, but a few infants seem to overreact and prefer lower speech sounds. Infants can pick up higher-pitched sounds better than lower-frequency ones, which may be why they are entranced by the high-pitched coos and singsong nature of parent talk. Parents' voices when talking to their infants can be described as playful, animated, warm, and perhaps giddy. Falk (2004) proposes that parent talk forms a scaffold for infants' language acquisition, and caregivers often use vocal means to placate and reassure. They attempt to control their infant's state of well-being. Falk notes that vowels are lingered over, phrases are repeated, and questions carry exaggerated inflections.

A mutual readiness to respond to each other appears built-in to warm relationships. The infant learns that eye contact can hold and maintain attention and that looking away usually terminates both verbal and nonverbal episodes. They learn a great deal about language before they ever say a word. Most of what they learn at a very early age involves the sound system of language.

1-5a Crying

Crying is one of the infant's primary methods of communication. Cries can be weak or hearty, and they provide clues to the infant's general health. Crying may be the only way an infant can affect his situation of need or discomfort. Infants begin early in life to control the emotional content of their cries. Many parents believe they can recognize different types of crying, such as sleepy, frightened, hungry, and so on, especially if infant body actions are observed concurrently. Researchers have discovered that parents do indeed accurately infer the intensity of an infant's emotional state from the sound of the cry itself, even if the baby is not visually observed. Even adults inexperienced with infants seem to possess this ability.

Child development specialists advise adult alertness and responsiveness to minimize crying. Crying will take place in the best of circumstances, and research has indicated that there are some positive aspects of crying, including stress reduction, elimination of toxin in tears, and reestablishment of physical and emotional balance. However, although crying may have its benefits, it is not recommended that infants be left to cry, but rather that adults continue to attempt to soothe and satisfy infants' needs. Narvaez (2012) believes the "cry it out" strategy adopted by some parents and sometimes endorsed by infant pediatricians can have negative effects on a child's moral and cognitive development. She suggests the practice can threaten the child's sense of safety and security. Stepping in to comfort a crying infant every two or so minutes allows a child a period to calm down. This has been called the "every few minutes approach." It may result in reducing stress that allows sleep—a preferred alternative to crying it out. Most caregivers check for conditions that might cause discomfort or distress periodically as a preventative measure.

A baby's crying may cause strong feelings in some adults, including anger, frustration, irritation, guilt, and rejection. Successful attempts at soothing the infant and stopping the crying give the infant and the caregiver satisfaction, feelings of competence, and a possible sense of pleasure.

Photo 1-9 A child may fall asleep while being soothed.

When out-of-sorts infants cease crying, alertness, attentiveness, and visual scanning usually happen and/or the infants fall asleep (Photo 1-9). Infant-caregiver interaction has been described as a rhythmic drama, a reciprocal dance, and a family melody. All of these touch on the beauty and coordination of sound-filled moments between the adult and child.

Emotions are expressed frequently in crying as the infant nears his first birthday. Fear, frustration, uneasiness with novelty or newness, separation from loved ones, and other strong emotions can provoke crying through childhood and beyond. Infant care providers in group programs engage in frank staff discussions concerning infant crying. Normal and natural staff feelings concerning crying need to be openly discussed so that strategies can be devised in the best interests of both the infants and the staff members. Many techniques exist to minimize crying and also to monitor the crying

levels of individual infants so that health or developmental problems can be spotted quickly.

1-5b Smiling and Laughing

True smiling can occur before six months of age and is usually associated with a caretaker's facial, auditory, or motor stimuli. Laughter may occur as early as four months of age and is believed to be a good predictor of cognitive growth. Some developmental experts suggest that the earlier the baby laughs, the higher the baby's developmental level is. In the second half of the first year, infants smile at more complex social and visual items. Laughter at this age may be full of squeals, howls, hoots, giggles, and grins. Incongruity may be noticed by the infant, and laughter follows. If an infant laughs when he sees the family dog in the driver's seat with its paws on the wheel, the child may be showing recognition of incongruity—the child has learned something about car drivers.

Responsive caregivers promote infant smiling. Ainsworth and Bell (1972) concluded that **responsive mothers**, those who are alert in caring for the infants' needs, had babies who cried less frequently and had a wider range of different modes of communication (Photo 1-10). These responsive mothers created a balance between showing attention and affording the infant autonomy (offering a choice of action within safe bounds) when the infant became mobile. They also provided body contact and involved themselves playfully at times.

Photo 1-10 A quick adult response to crying is appropriate and recommended.

---

responsive mothers — mothers who are alert and timely in responding to and giving attention to infants' needs and communications.

an **ATTUNED** adult:

- notices infant reactions to auditory stimuli.
- is aware of infant preferences.
- notices if an infant has an attachment to a caregiver and/or expresses pleasure in another's company.
- seeks to help the infant maintain a state of balance and a comfort level.
- is attentive and consistent in recognizing and satisfying a child's needs.
- has sufficient energy and seeks to engage frequently with an infant.
- monitors an infant's health and safety and observes closely.
- provides a variety of experience and sensory materials for exploration.
- uses words to accompany child and adult actions.
- records milestones in development and uses them to guide caregiver interactions.
- is playful, gives attention, and provides feedback to an infant's efforts. <

1-5c Infant Imitation and Babbling

Acredolo and Goodwyn (2000) suggest that infants as young as one or two days old may imitate parent head movements and facial behaviors; they explain:

> This inborn push to mimic others gets babies into a problem-solving mode from the very beginning. And as we mentioned earlier, babies thrive on problem solving. The payoff is such a pleasant one—Dad sticks around to interact some more, and baby is amused. Imitation is such an important developmental component that Mother Nature has not left it up to chance. She has made sure that each of us begins life's journey with a necessary tool in hand. (p. 185)

Early random sound making is often called **babbling**. Infants the world over babble sounds they have not heard and that they will not use in their native language. This has been taken to mean that each infant has the potential to master any world language. Close inspection shows repetitive sounds and "practice sessions" present. Babbling starts at about the fourth to sixth month and continues in some children through the toddler period. However, a peak in babbling is usually reached between 9 and 12 months. Periods before the first words are spoken are marked by a type of babbling that repeats syllables, as in *dadadada*. This is called **echolalia**. Infants seem to echo themselves and others. Babbling behavior overlaps the stages of making one and two or more words, and may end for some children at about 18 months of age.

Infants who are deaf also babble. In play sessions, they will babble for longer periods without hearing either adult sound or their own sounds, as long as they can see the adult responding. However, these children stop babbling at an earlier age than do hearing children. It is not clearly understood why babbling occurs, either in hearing or hearing-impaired children, but it is thought that babbling gives the child the opportunity to use and control the mouth, throat, and lung muscles. Researchers trying to explain babbling suggest that infants are not just exercising or playing with their vocal apparatus. Instead, they may be trying out and attempting to control their lips, tongues, mouths, and jaws to produce certain sounds. A child's babbling amuses and motivates the child, acting as a stimulus that adds variety to the child's existence. Meltzoff et al. (2009) suggest the language background of the home is continually being collected, digested, sorted, and analyzed by the infant's computer-like brain. Consequently, it is forming patterns of sounds that may be practiced or reproduced during later babbling periods.

In time, the child increasingly articulates clear, distinct vowel-like, consonant-like, and syllabic sounds. *Ba* and *da* are acquired early because they are easy to produce, whereas *el* and *ar* are acquired late because they require a sophisticated ability to articulate sounds. Although babbling includes a wide range of sounds, as children grow older, they narrow the range and begin to focus on the familiar language of the family. Other sounds are gradually discarded.

Physical contact continues to be important. Touching, holding, rocking, and engaging in other types of physical contact bring a sense of security and a chance to respond through sound making. The cooing and babbling sounds infants make may also draw caregivers into "conversations." Babies learn to wait for the adult's response after they have vocalized, and both infants and adults are constantly influencing

---

babbling — an early language stage in sound production in which an infant engages in vocal play with vowel and consonant sounds, including some sounds not found in his or her language environment.

echolalia — a characteristic of the babbling period. The child repeats (echoes) the same sounds over and over.

Photo 1-11 Infants' vocal and playful interactions with caregivers are the precursors of conversation.

one another in establishing conversation-like vocal interactions (Photo 1-11).

Bardige (2008) points out babies need to hear everyday language during their babbling period. She suggests adults talk about what the baby and they themselves are doing and continue to make language part of their daily care as they bathe, change, feed, play, and soothe the infant.

The active receiving of perceptions is encouraged by warm, loving parents who share a close relationship. Secure children respond more readily to the world around them. Children who lack social and physical contact or those who live in insecure home environments fall behind in both the number and range of sounds made; differences start showing at about six months of age. Sound imitation eventually becomes syllable imitation, and short words are spoken near the end of the child's first year.

1-5d Stages of Vocalization

There is a definite progression of infant production and vocalization ability that early educators focusing on their development notice. Progress may include a blending of steps as infants move forward. The reflective vocalizations of infants during their first few months include sound making such as fussing, crying, burping, miscellaneous sounds, and a few vowel like sounds that meld into a stage of sound production that indicates a mellowing during comfort and feeding satisfaction situations. This can include cooling,

giggles, and laughs. In the next few months a wider repertoire of vocalization emerges. It is full of voice changes indicating a playful nature exists. Loud and soft sounds happen during the day along with squeals of delight and what seems to be vowel – making episodes. This is typical in the months before and infants' first half year of age.

The appearance of babbling takes hold next. This period produces an increase in the variety of sound making and includes sequences of both consonant and vowel blended episodes. Parents and educators may believe they recognize a few almost words in infants sound making. Deaf infants can appear to be limited in their babbling efforts while infants with normal hearing ability may be reinforced by the vocal enjoyment they share with others and increase babbling. Real words, though few at first, begin to appear.

1-5e A Shared Developmental Milestone

Almost immediately after birth, infants display a critical cognitive skill. It is their ability to focus their attention on the features of their environment, especially to voices and sounds. By the last half of the first year, children begin to take part in a new type of interaction with their caretakers. They share attention given to objects with another person by following that individual's gaze or pointing, responding to the individual's emotional reaction to an event, and imitating that person's object-directed actions (Nelson & Shaw, 2002). This gives adults who notice this behavior a chance to pair words with objects, actions, events, and people. First words or sounds are usually simple associates of objects or situations. The infant simply voices a shared reference. Nelson and Shaw note that the leap from shared reference associations to meaningful language requires the child to integrate skills with communicative patterns and conceptual knowledge. The child is then standing on a first communicative step.

1-5f Infant Signing (Signaling) and Beginning Understanding

At a few months of age some infants realize that some of their simple actions cause caregivers to focus their attention on them. Waving arms, kicking legs, and banging objects may promote adult reactions, such as speaking to them. During the latter part of the first year, alert caregivers notice hand and body positions that suggest the child is attempting to communicate. Researchers suggest that parents pair words with easy-to-do gestures. At the age of one year, children cannot gain enough mastery over their tongues to form many words. Gesturing with their fingers and hands is simpler. For example, infants as young as seven months may bang on a window to get a family cat's attention or reach out, motion, or crawl toward something or someone they want. The use of signs continues until the child's ability to talk takes off. Some educators believe **signing** may spark other critical thinking skills and lead to better intelligence quotient (IQ) scores when testing begins. This has led to overeager commercial advertisers making unproven assertions and claims concerning signings' present and future educational advantages. Most educators believe that promoting the practice isn't harmful, in fact it seems to give infants confidence and satisfaction. They recognize that many parents are enthusiastic proponents. Only further research can substantiate signing benefits.

Toward the end of the child's first year, pointing becomes goal oriented—the infant will point to a desired object. As time progresses, more and more infant body signaling takes place. Signals are used over and over, and a type of sign language communication emerges. It can be a "signal and sound system" understood by caregivers. When caregivers respond appropriately, the infant easily progresses to word use and verbal aptitude. Signing by infants and young toddlers is believed to stimulate brain development, particularly brain areas involved in language, memory, and concept development.

Some studies of communication gestures note that infants with more advanced gestures have larger vocabularies and that girls seem slightly more advanced in gesturing than do boys. (This paragraph offered an answer to one of the questions in this chapter's beginning vignette. The next paragraph answers another.)

Well-meaning parents or caregivers may choose not to respond to infant gestures and signals, thinking this will accelerate or force the use of words. The opposite is thought to be true. Alert parents who try to read and receive signals give their infant the message that communication leads to fulfillment of wishes. Successful signaling becomes a form of language—a precursor of verbal signals (words). Some experts believe baby signers by age two are better at both expressing themselves and understanding others' speech and, on average, have slightly larger vocabularies than their peers who do not sign. Sitting down at the child's level at times when the infant is crawling from one piece of furniture to another may facilitate the adult's ability to pick up on signaling. Watching the infant's eyes and the direction the infant's head turns gives clues. Infants about eight months old seem fascinated with the adult's sound-making ability. They often turn to look at the adult's lips or want to touch the adult's mouth.

Early childhood educators employed by infant-toddler centers need to know their center's position regarding expected educator behaviors. Most centers expect educators to actively pair words with adult or child signs, encourage child use of signs, and learn and respond to each child's individual sign language.

Most babies get some idea of the meaning of a few words at about six to nine months. At about 10 months of age, some infants start to respond to spoken word clues. Somewhere between eight and 13 months, the child's communication, whether vocal or a type of gesture, becomes intentional. The child makes a connection between his behavior and the parent's or early childhood educator's response (Photo 1-12). Children seem to recognize a prime caregiver's change of voice tone and also that some of their caregiver's nonverbal behaviors may communicate a message. Infants are becoming aware of adult actions that may affect them. A game such as Pat-a-cake may start the baby clapping, and "bye-bye" or Peek-a-boo brings about other imitations of earlier play activities with the parents. The child's language is called passive at this stage, for he primarily receives (or is receptive). Speaking attempts will soon become active (or expressive). Vocabulary provides a small portal through which adults can gauge a little

---

signing — a body positioning, sound, action, gesture, or combination of these undertaken by an infant in an effort to communicate a need, desire, or message.

Photo 1-12 This infant has learned to respond to the adult's pointing gestures.

of what the child knows. There is a point at which children expand nonverbal signals to true language.

Older infants still communicate with their caregivers through many nonverbal actions; one common way is by holding up their arms, which most often means, "I want to be picked up." Other actions include facial expression, voice tone, voice volume, posture, and gestures such as "locking in" by pointing fingers and toes at attention-getting people and events.

Although infants at this stage can respond to words and changes in caregivers' facial expressions, voice tone, and voice volume, actions and gestures also carry feelings and messages important to infants' well-being. Understanding the tone of caregivers' speech comes before understanding the words used.

Gopnik et al. (1999) describe what happens when infants are about one year old.

> One-year-old babies know that they will see something by looking where other people point; they know what they should do to something by watching what other people do; they know how they should feel about something by seeing how other people feel. (p. 243)

Research suggests infants at 20 months have what Galinsky (2010) calls *language sense*. This means they can detect statistical patterns in which speech sounds go together in their native language (or languages) to determine the beginnings and endings of words (p. 2). She also suggests new research theorizes another infant sense, *people sense*, exists in infancy as infants focus on people's intentions rather than seeing what people do as random movements.

1-5g First Words

Before an understandable, close approximation of a word is uttered, the child's physical organs need to function in a delicate unison and the child must reach a certain level of mental maturity. Close to 12 months of age, the speech centers of the brain have developed the capacity to enable the infant to produce his first word—a great accomplishment and milestone. The child's respiratory system supplies the necessary energy. As the breath is exhaled, sounds and speech are formed with the upward movement of air. The larynx's vibrating folds produce voice (called **phonation**). The larynx, mouth, and nose influence the child's voice quality (termed **resonation**). A last modification of the breath stream is **articulation**—a final formation done through molding, shaping, stopping, and releasing voiced and other-than-voiced sounds that reflect language heard in the child's environment.

Repetition of syllables such as *ma*, *da*, and *ba* in a child's babbling occurs toward the end of the first year. If *mama* or *dada* or a close copy is said, parents and caregivers show attention and joy. Language, especially in the area of speech development, is a two-way process; reaction is an important feedback to action.

The term *protoword* is often used for the invented words a child may use during the transition from prespeech to speech. During this transition, a child has acquired the difficult concept that sounds have meaning and is unclear only about the fact that one is supposed to find out what words exist instead of making them up.

Generally, first words are nouns or proper names of foods, animals, or toys; vocabulary may also include *gone*, *there*, *uh-oh*, *more*, and *dat* ("what's that?"). Greetings, farewells, or other social phrases, such as *peek-a-boo*, are also among the first recognizable words.

Monolingual (one-language) children utter their first words at approximately 11 months of age; the range is from about 9 months to about 16 months. At about a year and a half, the child learns approximately one new word every three days. Most experts believe that talking alone shows no link to mental development at age two, but a child's comprehension of words is paramount. Experts conclude that there is little scientific evidence to suggest that late talkers will become less fluent than early talkers. Some children acquire large numbers of object names in their first 50 to 100 words. The first spoken words usually contain *p*, *b*, *t*, *d*, *m*, and *n* (front of the mouth consonants), which require the least use of the tongue and air control. They are shortened versions, such as *da* for "daddy," *beh* for "bed," and *up* for "cup." When two-syllable words are attempted, they are often strung together using the same syllable sound, as in *dada* or *beebee*. If the second syllable is voiced,

the child's reproduction of the sound may come out as *dodee* for "doggy" or *papee* for "potty."

At this stage, words tend to be segments of wider happenings in the child's life. A child's word *ba* may represent a favorite, often-used toy (such as a ball). As the child grows in experience, any round object seen in the grocery store, for instance, will also be recognized and called *ba*. This phenomenon has been termed *over-extension*. The child has embraced "everything round," which is a much broader meaning for ball than the adult definition of the word.

Following is a list of words frequently understood between 8 and 12 months of age: *mommy*, *daddy*, *bye-bye*, *baby*, *shoe*, *ball*, *cookie*, *juice*, *bottle*, *no-no*, and the child's own name and names of family members.

A child finds that words can open many doors. They help the child get things and cause caregivers to act in many ways. Vocabulary quickly grows from the names of objects to words that refer to actions. This slowly decreases the child's dependence on context (a specific location and situation) for communication and gradually increases the child's reliance on words—the tools of abstract thought. Children learn very quickly that words not only name things and elicit action on another's part but also convey comments and express individual attitudes and feelings.

an **ATTUNED** adult:

- nurtures infant curiosity.
- uses words and gestures in communication.
- builds a sign language relationship with infants.
- tries to judge the intensity of infants' emotions.
- offers a choice of child actions and explorations within safe limits.
- responds to and promotes reciprocal communication.
- pairs words with actions and objects.
- observes the direction of infants' gazes for clues to infants' moment to moment interests.
- continues to be at eye level when possible.
- expects and recognizes invented words.
- encourages first word use by repeating word back to child and connecting the child's word to objects or actions as appropriate.
- guesses frequently about a child's meaning in communication.
- works toward a child's success at using words to fulfill his desires, needs, and interests. <

---

phonation — exhaled air passes the larynx's vibrating folds and produces "voice."

resonation — amplification of laryngeal sounds using cavities of the mouth, nose, sinuses, and pharynx.

articulation — the adjustments and movements of the muscles of the mouth and jaw involved in producing clear oral communication.

Figure 1-6 Approximate frequency of child utterances from 6 to 12 months.

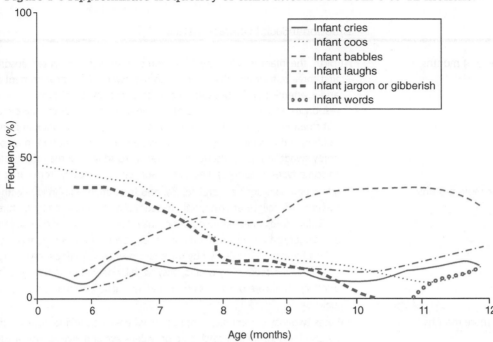

Toddlerhood begins, and the child eagerly names things and seeks names for others. The child's single words accompanied by gestures, motions, and intonations are called **holophrases**. They usually represent a whole idea or sentence.

While the child is learning to walk, speech may briefly take a backseat to developing motor skill. At this time, the child may listen more intently to what others are saying. The slow-paced learning of new words (Figure 1-6) is followed by a period of rapid growth. The child pauses briefly, listening, digesting, and gathering forces to embark on the great adventure of becoming a fluent speaker.

1-6 Implications for Infant Center Staff Members

The importance of understanding the responsive, reciprocal nature of optimal care-giving in group infant centers cannot be overestimated. The soothing, calming, swaddling, rocking, sympathizing, and responding behaviors of infant care specialists help infants maintain a sense of security and a relaxed state, calmness, and equilibrium.

The emotional well-being of infants has been given increased attention as research on infant development uncovers its importance. Physician Chet Johnson (2005) points out:

The research shows how powerful emotional well-being is to a child's future health. A baby who fails to meet certain key "emotional milestones" may have trouble learning to speak, read, and later, do well in school. By reading emotional responses, doctors have begun to discover ways to tell if a baby as young as three months is showing early signs of possible psychological disorders, including depression, anxiety, learning disabilities and perhaps autism. Instead of just asking if they're crawling or sitting we're asking more questions about how they share their world with their caregivers. (p. 35)

See Figure 1-7 for infants' emotional milestones.

At about four months, babies begin to gaze in the direction in which caregivers are looking. Caregivers are able to follow the line of vision of babies as well. Well-trained caregivers will naturally comment and offer language labels and a running commentary. This process is known as *joint attentional focus*. When adults know that the infant does not yet understand language,

---

holophrases — the expression of a whole idea in a single word. They are often found in the speech of children at about 12 to 18 months of age.

Figure 1-7 Emotional milestones and social skill characteristics.

Age	Emotional/Social Characteristics
Birth to around 3–4 months	At birth, the infant is able to feel fear and contentment and is self-absorbed. During first three to four months, infant becomes aware of the environment around him and is attentive and interested; seems able to calm self at times; develops deliberate responses; focuses on the faces of people and smiles at them; eyes may widen in anticipation; may react to strong scents or odors; has a developing sense of security; holding and touching may reduce stress, and rhythmic motion may soothe; may enjoy swaddling; pays attention and reacts to sounds (some infants are oversensitive to some types of sounds). Reacts to visual cues, especially from care provider's face.
Around 5–6 or more months	Displays emotions such as surprise, joy, and frustration. Falls in love with care provider; beams with delight at times; able to see the pattern formed by features on care provider's face; smiles in recognition; may display sorrow and annoyance; builds a stronger relationship with primary care provider; begins to realize he can make things happen; is comforted by physical closeness; develops feelings of being loved, valued, and esteemed by others; easy to tell when infant is happy; sense of self is a reflection of care provider's emotional interactions with infant; may experience jealousy.
Around 10 or more months	Initiates two-way communication; notices where care provider looks and often follows by also looking; tries to catch care provider's eye and gives physical cues to others to obtain a desired action, such as being held; may use signs and signals to make things happen; may respond to rhythm with rhythmic movements; expects his action will prompt a reaction; may mimic gestures; may express fear, anger, anticipation, caution, and surprise with strangers; responds to name, words, and sounds, and attempts to imitate them; Is curious and perhaps assertive and negative at times; May experience a sense of loss at something removed; May show fear if care provider looks angry, frowns, or stares (not recommended). Seeks pleasure and enjoys stimulating self (for example, touching toes and participating in adult-infant games that involve moving or touching body parts, such as "This Little Piggy." Note: This is not intended to be a complete inventory of emotional milestones; research in identifying infant emotional development and capacity is still in its infancy. Notice social skill and emotional response is intertwined and dependent on environmental and human experience.

most adults behave as if the child's response is a turn in the conversation. Adult caregivers need to read both nonverbal and vocalized cues and react appropriately (Photo 1-13). They need to be attentive and loving. Learning to read each other's signals is basic to the quality of the relationship. Liberal amounts of touching, holding, smiling, and looking promote language and the child's overall sense that the world around him is both safe and fascinating. Recognizing the child's individuality, reading nonverbal behaviors, and reacting with purposeful actions are all expected of professional infant specialists, as is noticing activity level, mood, distress threshold, rhythms of the body, intensity, sense of adventure, distractibility, adaptability, and attention span.

There are many skills that well-trained caregivers possess, beginning with holding the infant firmly yet gently and making soft, gentle sounds while moving smoothly and holding the infant close. Gillespie and Hunter (2011) suggest caregivers' laughter helps children form connections and signal a safe and loving environment. Leong and Bodrova (2012) note that as infant educators interact and react to infant's growing communication ability, emotional bonds form. Educators, consequently, prepare infants to learn from them. Adults in early childhood centers become play partners and perhaps become an infant's first play mentor other than their family members. Other caregiver skills are identified in the following list.

Photo 1-13 It is easy to tell these infants are focused and eager activity participants.

© 2016 Cengage Learning®

an **ATTUNED** adult:

- talks in a pleasant, soothing voice; uses simple language; and makes frequent eye contact.
- emphasizes and expects two-way "conversation"; hesitates; and pauses for an infant response.
- makes a game out of the infant's smiles, sounds, and movements when the infant is responsive.
- speaks clearly.
- explains what is happening and what will happen next.
- is consistently attentive.
- does not interrupt the infant's vocal play, jargon, or self-communication.
- engages in word play, rhyme, chants, and fun-to-say short expressions.
- is an animated speaker and a responsive companion.
- may, with an older infant, attempt to offer simple finger plays.
- plans real and concrete participatory activities with textures, sights, and sounds.
- encourages sound making and provides noisemaking and musical toys.
- labels objects, happenings, actions, and emotions.
- uses highly intonated speech that may be high pitched at times with very young infants.
- speaks distinctly with clear enunciation to help children identify phonemes.
- emphasizes, at times, one word in a sentence.
- uses repetition but avoids overdoing it.
- gives feedback by responding with both words and actions.
- creates and pursues game-like strategies and techniques.
- serves as a co-explorer. ◄

Being playful and initiating singing conversations with infants can be enjoyable and may lay the foundation for later musical activities. Both recorded and live musical sounds are part of an auditory-rich environment for infants. For identified early childhood goals and additional caregiver activities, see Figure 1-8.

Williams (2008) urges caregivers to explore the world outside the classroom or home with older infants and toddlers. Children are born with a desire to understand the environment around them, and they possess incessant curiosity that compels them to explore it (Medina, 2008). Their discoveries can bring joy. Like an addictive drug, Medina believes, exploration creates the need for even more discovery. Think about watching or feeling raindrops, experiencing mud, touching a caterpillar, smelling flowers, or hearing birds. The reality and beauty of natural landscapes surrounds us, and there are multiple ways to experience it safely.

Remember that infants are alike yet uniquely different. Some sensitive infants may appear overwhelmed and require little stimuli to maintain equilibrium. Others will thrive in an environment that provides a multitude of people, sights, sounds, and new activities. Each infant provides a challenge one must "puzzle out" to decide best courses of action—what works, what does not work, and what is best. Bardige (2009) suggests adult-infant connection may not always go smoothly.

> Some babies are fussy and hard to soothe, some are so sensitive that they have to be approached carefully and given lots of support before they can engage, and some are challenged in one modality (e.g., hearing or sight) but hyperacute in another. Some babies are flexible by nature, but others are fearful or feisty. Babies also differ in their natural activity levels and in their rates of development. Some babies give clear signals when they need food or play or comfort or rest; others are much harder to read. (p. 23)

Figure 1-8 Adult goals and activities for language development during infancy.

Age	Adult Goals	Adult Activity
birth to 2 months	1. to create a trusting, intimate relationship 2. to take pleasure in the reciprocal infant-adult interactions 3. to help infant calm and regulate himself 4. to verbally communicate and promote a two-way pattern of responses 5. to maintain eye contact and spend time face to face 6. to seek to create an appropriate environmental moderation level	1. anticipate and satisfy infant needs 2. show interest and provide positive reactions and joy in the infant's presence and communicative attempts 3. provide sights, sounds, touches, and playful companionship 4. talk, croon, whisper, sing, and mimic infant gesture 5. repeat infant sounds 6. provide a comfortable environment that satisfies the child's needs
2–6 months	1. to keep alert to infant attempts to communicate distress or needs 2. to strengthen growing bond of enjoyment in adult-infant "together time" and explorations 3. to recognize child individuality, moods, likes and dislikes, uniqueness 4. to encourage "you talk" and "I talk" behaviors 5. to see infant gestures as possibly purposeful 6. to hold child's eye contact when speaking and gain child's attention with animated speech 7. to use clear and simple speech	1. provide adult-infant play time and joint new experiences 2. provide infant exploring of sights, sounds, music, and play materials and indoor and outdoor environments 3. offer "talking" opportunities with others 4. name child's actions, toys, happenings while changing, bathing, and feeding 5. play baby games such as Pat-a-cake 6. use talk and touch as a reward for the child's communication attempts 7. repeat child sounds and gestures
6–12 months	1. to pursue infant interests, tailoring your talk to child focus 2. to promote the idea that language is used for naming and describing 3. to play with rhythm and rhyme in adult-infant communications 4. to speak clearly, emphasizing new words when appropriate 5. to show delight in child's verbal and physical accomplishments 6. to pair your words with actions, happenings, and objects 7. to recognize and respond appropriately to child signaling and words 8. to make sure sound level and noise is appropriate 9. to listen for intent, not perfection 10. to provide safe environment conducive to child exploring and action	1. expand the child's world with neighborhood trips, people, playthings, and experiences 2. name and describe happenings, emotions, actions, and environments as things take place 3. introduce and read board books to the child, letting child explore them himself 4. sing songs, perform finger plays, play word games with visual and touching actions 5. listen and pause for infant response 6. name body parts, colors, and objects 7. tell simple stories 8. delight in the world and its joyful pursuits with the child

Because infants' first sensory experiences are part of emotional relationships with caregivers, caregivers' efforts to provide developmental care go hand in hand with providing positive emotional support in daily reciprocal exchanges between the child and adult. The terms *child-centered* and *child-focused* need to be coupled with reactive, observant, playful, and nurturing adult behaviors. This type of infant care is nearly impossible when adult-infant ratios are inadequate.

Generally, the types of adults who promote language are those who are alert to the child's achievements, notice them, and enjoy interacting, as well as adults who can offer novelty, assistance, and enthusiasm in addition to focusing on the child's interests. Mangione (2010) believes the emotional security infants derive from positive caring relationships with primary and secondary care providers, provides infants with a buffer for the negative stresses he might encounter in daily experiences.

1-6a Baby Games and Explorations

Almost daily, infants seem to increase the ways they can explore and enjoy verbal-physical games. Birchmayer, Kennedy, and Stonehouse (2008) urge caregivers to explore creative ways to communicate with infants to sustain their interest.

> For very young children, spoken language can be extended through face and body games and rhymes. Though infants still will not understand many or even most words used, they will nevertheless enjoy the sound, rhythm, and tone of the language and other creative elements of the experience. (p. 31)

Most adults know that holding an infant and singing or dancing with him are good ways to comfort the fussy child or to foster interest in place of boredom. Since some infants are newly experiencing game play at a center, watching for stress signs and tenseness is important. Some infants adapt readily and enjoy immediately. Others are more cautious and need a slow introduction to any bouncing or other baby movements. Infants may also register boredom or tiredness when the game is no longer fun signaling they will need a new activity or rest.

Infant educators create their own games and activities that are enjoyable to both infants and caregivers. They become aware of their infants' focus and reactions. Games that deal with child anticipation often elicit smiles or giggles. Playing classics such as Peek-a-boo or Johnny Jump Up or hiding an object under a cloth has delighted generations of children. More newly devised activities include tying a soft tinkling bell to the wrist or leg of an infant or connecting a soft ribbon from an infant's ankle to an overhead mobile (under adult supervision).

Experts recommend that, from a baby's earliest days, caregivers begin with simple imitation games during face-to-face interaction, making sure to pause long enough for the infant to take in the information and mount a response. The best distance for these games is 8 to 12 inches away from the child's face. Imitation of the baby's movement or vocal efforts is also suggested, as is rewarding the baby's effort with attention or smiles.

The following classic language and body action play has brought delight to generations of infants. The most enjoyed play activities include tickling, bouncing, and lifting with accompanying words and rhymes.

This Little Piggy

(Each line is recited while holding a toe, moving toward the pinkie.)

This little pig went to market. This little pig stayed home. This little pig had roast beef. This little pig had none. This little piggy cried, "Wee, wee, wee, wee!" all the way home.

(First published in 1728.)

Pat-a-Cake

(Recited while helping the child with hand clapping.)

Pat-a-cake, pat-a-cake, baker's man.

Bake me a cake as fast as you can.

Pat it and prick it and mark it with a "B."

And put it in the oven for baby and me.

So Big

Say, "Look at you—so big!" Slowly raise both of the infant's arms up, extending them over the child's head while saying, "[child's name] is so-o-oh big" and then slowly bring the arms down.

Repeat.

Say the child's name slowly as you raise the infant close to your face at eye level. Then say, "So-o-oh big." Then gently say, "Wow, wow, wow—what a baby. A so-o-oh big baby!" with a big smile.

1-6b Musical Play

Music, singing, and musical expression appear to be a central part of the crucial interaction that occurs between caregivers and infants as infants develop over the first year of life. Two types of musical or singing interaction take place: (1) a soothing go-to-sleep lullaby-style interaction and (2) a playful, upbeat adult behavior that might be described as rhythmic and joyful. The first style is seen as caregivers attempt to regulate or promote a particular infant state (such as relaxation, contentment, or sleep), and the second style, the communication of emotional information (such as mutual enjoyment and love of music).

Experts believe babies as young as three months can distinguish between certain melodies. Musical infant babbling has been described as tonal and rhythmic babble. Tonal babble is babbling in a single pitch, the babble sounding like a monotone singer. In rhythmic babble the child's body or voice displays a rhythmic beat or quality. Geist, Giest, and Kuznik (2013) believe research implies that even the youngest children have the potential to inherently respond to music and also mathematical constructs. Music contains beats, rhythm, tempo, and steady beats, which often make up a rhythmic pattern that infants and toddlers pay attention to. Often caregiver's rock infants to soothe them using an accompanying music or song. This can involve simple to complex musical patterns. These patterning experiences support later literacy learning, it is believed.

Nursery, cultural, and folk tunes can be introduced in intimate and pleasant settings. Simple, safe musical instruments are enjoyed, and moving to music is natural to young children. Wolf (2000) suggests that educators start with songs they love, ones sung to them as children. Others suggest using children's music recorded by well-known performers. Some educators recommend Bach preludes and Vivaldi's *Springtime* Symphony along with other classical pieces. Yet others recommend popular children's bouncy selections. Two benefits of musical activities for some older preschoolers and primary children are believed to be enhanced abstract reasoning and **spatial-temporal reasoning**.

Scientists are finding that the human brain may be "prewired" for music. They suspect that some forms of intelligence are heightened by music. Although controversial at present, some researchers believe learning musical skills in childhood can help children do better at mathematics.

Schmid (2010) confirms the beliefs of many educators.

> Words and music are such natural partners that it seems obvious they go together. Now science is confirming that those abilities are linked in the brain, a finding that might even lead to better stroke treatment. (p. A6)

Only more studies with more children will prove whether music produces specific or lasting benefits in cognition.

See Additional Resources at the end of this chapter for favorite musical and movement activities and song books.

1-7 Early Reading and Writing Practices

Common Core State Standards in the English Language Arts and Literacy in History/Social Studies, Science, and Technical Subjects (2010) are affecting language and literacy instruction at all educational levels and may modify or change how caregivers interact with children in Pre-K programs, as well as the curriculum to be planned for them. Although the standards are designed for grade levels K–12, they are sure to prompt Pre-K programs to examine how they align to preschool practices. The standards have been adopted by most states and the recommended instructional goals are being exercised in almost all curriculum areas, including the English language arts.

Giving young children the idea that they are capable communicators starts with alert infant caregivers who provide attention to and are aware of the infant's nonverbal communicative actions. What is at first an infant caregiver's guesswork concerning an infant's state of being, be that

---

spatial-temporal reasoning — the mental arrangement of ideas and/or images in a graphic pattern indicating their relationships over time.

hunger, tiredness, or distress or well-being, leads to the adult's ability to spot infants' communicating behaviors and act effectively and in a reciprocal manner. The infant soon begins to understand that he can influence how others (mother and teachers) interact with him. He becomes even more successful at communicating his wants or needs.

Educators' and early childhood caregivers' goals include more than teaching language and literacy. They aim to create a child's learning habit and disposition that develops from the joy and excitement of learning. This is encouraged by the exploring, engaging, and discovering that happens in activities and experiences during his early years. Hopefully, a love of learning will be retained in future schooling. Many early childhood centers are developing new ways to equip children to be successful when they enter common core kindergarten classrooms.

1-7a Reading to Infants

Some parents read books aloud during a mother's later stages of pregnancy, believing the practice will produce some positive results. Some infants remember and give greater attention to stories read to them before their birth. Conclusive research evidence has yet to verify this. Zambo and Hansen (2007) suggest that from birth to three months, read-alouds are purely an emotional connection between the infant and caregiver.

> Being held, feeling good, and having a familiar, comforting voice are more important than the kind of book or the content of the story. Lullabies, singsong stories, and other repetitive, rhythmic experiences bring joy and comfort to infants and establish a special time together for child and caregiver. (p. 34)

Between 6 and 12 months, some infants will sit and look at a picture book with an adult. It is the sound of the reader's voice that gets the young child's attention, even before the child's focus shifts to the pictures. The warmth and security of being held and the reader's voice make for a very pleasurable combination.

The child may want to grab pages and test the book in his mouth or try to turn pages. His head may swivel to look at the adult's mouth. If the child has brought a book to the adult, he will usually want to sit on the adult's lap as both go through the book. Children get ever more adept at turning pages as their first birthday nears (Photo 1-14). Familiar objects in colorful illustrations set on white or plain backgrounds and large faces seem to be particularly fascinating. Infants seem to respond well to and enjoy the rhyme they hear.

Photo 1-14 Ryan is trying to turn a page.

Adult-reading to infants younger than 12 months of age is increasingly recommended, for researchers believe the infant is learning about the sound patterns in words and how words are formed. Book-reading techniques include reading something the adult enjoys with average volume and expression, using gesturing or pointing when called for, promoting child imitation, letting the child turn sturdy pages, and making animal or sound noises. A good rule of thumb is to stop before the child's interest wanes. Adults may find that many infants enjoy repeated reading of the same book. Some parents are very adept at sharing picture books. These parents find **cues** in book features, such as familiar objects, events depicted, sounds, colors, and so on, that give the infant pleasure, as may be evidenced by the adult saying, "It's a dog like our Bowser!" Skilled early childhood educators realize it is the colorful illustrations that attract, so they name and point to features and when possible relate words to like objects found in the classroom. They also attempt to make illustrations relevant to the child's past experience.

Colorful books with sturdy or plastic-coated pages or cardboard books are plentiful. Books of cotton fabric and ones with flaps to lift and peek under, soft furry patches to feel, rough sandpaper to touch, and holes to look through or stick a finger through are books that include enjoyable sensory exploration. Homemade collections of family photographs have delighted many young children. Faces and common household objects in illustrations catch infants' attention. Picture books with simple, large illustrations or photos that are set against a contrasting background and books that are constructed to stand on their own when opened are also popular.

There are a number of literary classics (although not all experts agree to the same titles) that most children in our culture experience. Many of these involve rhyme and rhythm. They have, over time, become polished gems passed onto succeeding generations.

1-7b Recordings

Growing numbers of CDs, tapes, tablet activities, and videos are being produced for infants. Infants watch, listen, and sometimes move their bodies rhythmically. Research has yet to confirm the educational or language-developing benefits claimed by manufacturers of audios or visuals. In *The Journal of Pediatrics*, Interlandi (2007) reports on a new study that included a group of 1,000 families and reviewed the use of infant DVDs; this report suggests that babies who watch recordings fared worst with DVDs than with several other types of programming in terms of educational or language-developing benefits.

> Exposure to educational shows, like "Sesame Street," and noneducational ones, like "Sponge-Bob SquarePants," had no net effect on language, researchers said—but for every hour that infants 8 to 16 months spent watching the baby DVDs, they understood six to eight fewer words, out of a set of 90, than infants who didn't watch. (p. 14)

1-7c Early Experiences with Writing Tools

As early as 10 to 12 months, infants will watch intently as someone makes marks on a surface or paper. They will reach and attempt to do the marking themselves. Large chalk, thick crayons, or large crayon "chunks" are recommended for exploring, but caregivers are reminded to supervise closely because of infants' tendency to put small objects in their mouths. Large-sized paper (for example, torn flat grocery brown bags) taped at the edges to surfaces and chalkboards work well. The child may not realize the writing tool is making marks but may imitate and gleefully move the whole arm. Many believe it is simply not worth the effort to supervise very young children during this activity and save this activity until the children are older.

1-8 Monitoring Infant Development

Stark, Chazen-Cohen, and Jerald (2002) point out that normal paths of development within various domains serve as reference points to assess infant competence. Infant assessments undertaken by educators try to identify strengths and developmental areas where the infant and/ or family may need supportive assistance to

---

cues — prompts or hints that aid recognition, such as a parent pointing to and/or saying "teddy bear" when sharing a picture book illustration. This is done because the infant is familiar with his own teddy bear.

promote optimal infant growth. Maternal health histories sometimes provide clues, as do home visits and daily or periodic educator-family interactions. An examination of whether the school's schedules, activities, staff, and curriculum need to change or adapt takes place frequently so that each child's individual needs have every chance of being met.

Infants should be observed daily with an eye toward assessing developmental milestones and mental and physical health, and educators must be knowledgeable of ages and stages. In a busy center, making dated notes for individual files is suggested as new, questionable, or important behaviors are observed. A notepad in a handy pocket is recommended. Frequent staff meetings should discuss individual infant language behaviors and development. This is followed by planning sessions that create individual learning plans and family consultation when necessary.

Eiserman and associates (2007) note that hearing loss may be an "invisible" condition. Dramatic improvements in hearing screening technology and growth in the number of hospitals that do at-birth screenings have occurred in the past 10 years.

1-8a Implications for Families

Family attitudes about their infant's communicating abilities may influence the infant's progress, in part by affecting how the family responds to the infant. These attitudes are the early roots of the critical partnership between adult and child and the child's sense of feeling lovable and powerful. Consequently, they influence the child's self-assessment.

Special infant projects to promote later school success have provided information in this area. Positive home factors mentioned include the following:

- a lot of attention by socially responsive caregivers
- little or no disruption of bonding attachment between the infant and his primary caregiver during the first year
- availability of space and objects to explore
- good nutrition
- active and interactive exchanges and play time
- parent knowledge of developmental milestones and the child's emerging skills

- parent confidence in infant handling
- maintenance of the child's physical robustness
- positive attention and touching in play exchange

Parent (or family) stress and less-than-desirable quality in child-parent interactions seem to hinder children's language development. Because most families face stress, a family's reaction to stress, rather than stress itself, is the determining factor. In today's busy families, time spent interacting and talking to infants and young children needs to remain a family priority.

Good advice for families includes not worrying about teaching as much as creating a rich and emotionally supportive home atmosphere. A rich atmosphere is one that offers opportunity and companionship rather than expensive toys and surroundings. Current research indicates that families who spontaneously speak about what the child is interested in and who zoom in and out of the child's play as they go about their daily work are responsive and effective families. Also, families should know early and late "talkers" usually show little difference in speaking ability by age three. The variation between children with respect to the onset and accomplishment of most human characteristics covers a wide range when considering what is normal and expected.

Munir and Rose (2008) describe healthy social behavior in infancy, as well as infants who display possible early autistic behaviors.

> Healthy infants as young as six or eight months do communicate and respond nonverbally to social cues. Most look up or turn at the sound of their name. By 12 months, they typically babble and point at objects. By 16 months, they say single words; by 24 months, two-word phrases. In contrast, children with autism seldom make meaningful eye contact or respond to familiar voices. They may never speak. Their play is often repetitive and characterized by limited imagination. Others may simply flap their hands in excitement or disappointment.
>
> On their own, none of these signs means a child has autism or another development disorder. Nevertheless, if a child has any of these signs, he or she merits evaluation. (p. 64)

Regardless of the setting, the experts agree the primary need of infants and toddlers is emotional connection (Lloyd-Jones, 2002). Human relationships are the key, and emotional development is critical for growth. Children of the poor, who are considered to be at-risk, may escape at-risk status if they share the following commonalities. They live in large, extended families that provide supportive language stimulation and encouragement, and they have no other social or biological risks present. Their families manage to safeguard their infants' and older children's health. Intervention and social service programs may also be accessible. It is the isolated poor families with multiple risk factors, including abusive home environments, whose children are the most negatively affected.

Summary

1-1 Discuss the reciprocal behaviors of infants, parents, and caregivers.

Caregivers and other adults observe and interpret an infant's state of well-being, try to understand both general and specific behaviors. They identify child signals and clues and are responsive and alert companions who interact, communicate, and provide consistent care. Caregivers attempt to provide language and intellect-building comments during daily routines and play periods.

Infants search adult faces for facial expression and gain information through their sense organs. Basic attitudes form through contact and interactions. With consistent, affectionate care that satisfies infant needs, attachment bonds form. This is a two-way process. The quality and quantity of caregiver attention becomes an important factor in infant communication and language growth.

1-2 Name four important influences that may affect an infant's language growth and development.

Important influences in infant language growth and development include the care and attention infants' experience, the integration of their bodies' growth systems, the growing cognitive ability and intellectual understandings they possess, their sensory organ development, their emerging ability to recognize language-specific patterns in the speech they hear around them, and also whether they make early attempts to categorize speech sounds. The social and emotional environment can influence the achievement of equilibrium and attachment in infants. Adult attitudes and expectations may affect infant language growth along with other cultural and social factors.

1-3 Compare two theories of human language emergence.

In comparing two theories of human language growth mentioned in the text one would have to display a knowledge of the identifying characteristics of two of the following theoretical positions: Behaviorist/Environmentalist theory, Maturational (Normative) theory, Predetermined/Innatist theory, Cognitive – Transactional (Interaction) theory, or Constructivist theory.

1-4 Name two of the areas of particular importance to infant care addressed in Developmentally Appropriate Practice (DAP) guidelines.

The six areas of particular importance addressed in developmentally appropriate practice are: (1) relationships between caregivers and children, (2) the environment, (3) exploration and play, (4) routines, (5) reciprocal relationships with families, and (6) policies.

1-5 Discuss the behaviors and vocalizing efforts that infants use to communicate their needs and desires.

Infant behaviors and vocalizing efforts start with crying, body movements, and body positions. They develop mutual gazing behavior and early proto-conversations with caregivers begin. Infants respond with noisemaking and eye contact. Infant noises include sucking, sneezing, coughing, and feeding noises. Later these early noises are accompanied with cooing and vowel-like sounds or discomfort noises and sounds. Infants usually display a pleasure in engagement with others and an eagerness to communicate. Infants find their actions and vocalizations can result in caregiver attention and sometimes action.

1-6 Describe what caregiver actions should take place when infants develop joint attentional focus.

When infants gain the ability to focus jointly with caregivers, their caregivers are responsive and seek reciprocal interactions. Caregivers seek to offer optimal opportunities for speech and language development. This includes teacher pointing, pairing and connecting words with objects or events, and perhaps imitating an infant's object-directed actions. Emotional reactions to an event are shared and noted by teachers. Shared reference associations lead to eventual meaningful language usage. First words or sounds are usually simple associates of objects or situations.

1-7   Name and comment upon early reading and writing activities in late infancy.

Early reading activities in late infancy include teacher activities, such as reading books, offering lullabies, songs, storytelling experiences, and other language developing experiences. The text suggested that reading material and activities should contain repetitive, musical, and rhythmic features to attract older infants. Reading books aloud is also designed to promote child enjoyment and social–emotional togetherness. When possible book features were to be related to chil-

dren's life experiences and naming illustrative features and pointing to objects together was suggested. Early writing activities mentioned in the text included safe writing tools and sturdy taped-down paper for a child to scribble upon.

1-8   Identify how infant centers monitor each infant's language and communicating behaviors.

Infant centers monitor each child's progress in a number of ways, including: conducting assessments, creating health histories, and continually observing if each infant's developmental needs have been met. Developmental milestones are recorded and individual growth files are developed. The center's program and schedules are adjusted and reviewed during planning sessions to assure quality care is offered each infant. Continual communication with parents and families is undertaken and the school encourages positive home language growth—producing features, activities, and experiences.

Additional Resources

Readings

Anderson, N. A. (2007). *What Should I Read Aloud? A Guide to 200 Best-Selling Picture Books*. Newark, DE: International Reading Association.

Bjorklund, D. F. (2011). *Children's Thinking: Cognitive Development and Individual Difference*. Belmont, CA: Cengage Learning.

Karp, H. (2002). *The Happiest Baby on the Block*. New York: Bantam Dell.

Murray, C. G. (2007). *Simple Signing with Young Children: A Guide for Infant, Toddler, and Preschool Teachers*. Beltsville, MD: Gryphon House.

Infant Books

Aston, D. H. (2006). *Mamma Outside, Mama Inside*. New York: Henry Holt.

Bauer, M. D. (2003). *Toes, Ear, and Nose*. New York: Little Simon.

Boyton, S. (2004). *Moo Baa, La La La!* New York: Simon & Schuster.

Hindley, J. (2006). *Baby Talk: A Book of First Words and Phrases*. New York: Candlewick Press.

Intrater, R. G. (2002). *Hugs and Kisses*. New York: Scholastic.

Saltzberg, B. (2004). *Noisy Kisses*. San Diego: Red Wagon.

Infant Play Games

Silberg, J. (2012). *125 Brain Games for Babies*. Beltsville, MD: Gryphon House

Infant Music, Movement Activities, and Song Books

Beaton, C. (2008). *Playtime Rhymes for Little People*. Cambridge, MA: Barefoot Books (CD and book).

Charmer, K., Murphy, M., & Clark, C. (2006). *The Encyclopedia of Infant and Toddler Activities*. Beltsville MD: Gryphon House.

Long, S. (2002). *Hush Little Baby*. San Francisco: Chronicle Books.

Helpful Websites

Better Brains for Babies

http://www.fcs.uga.edu

Current research in infant brain development.

National Parent Information Network

http://npin.org

Contains readings and parenting resources.

Sensory Awareness Foundation

http://www.sensoryawareness.org

Lists available infant experiences.

The Program for Infant/Toddler Care

http://www.pitc.org

Responsive care guides.

2 The Tasks of the Toddler

Objectives

After reading this chapter, you should be able to:

2-1 Name four conventions of the English language that toddlers are learning about speaking.

2-2 Describe how toddlers move from using first words to using sentences.

2-3 Identify three common characteristics of toddler language.

2-4 State two criteria for selecting books and describe four recommended techniques when reading books to toddlers.

2-5 Identify three suggestions for toddler teachers and parents concerning toddler opportunities to explore and experience their environment.

naeyc NAEYC Program Standards

1C02 Support children's development of friendship; provide opportunities for children to play and learn from each other.

1B13 Adjust interactions to toddlers' various states and levels of arousal.

1B15 Talk frequently with children and listen to children with attention and respect.

1B15 Use strategies to communicate effectively and build relationships with every child.

2E02 Toddlers have varied opportunities to experience books, songs, rhymes, and routine games.

DAP Developmentally Appropriate Practice (DAP)

1A2 Know the child and family well and respond to child's individual temperament, needs, and cues and develop a mutually satisfying pattern of communication with child and family.

1B1 Caregivers use pleasant, calm voices as well as simple language and nonverbal cues.

1B3 Caregivers frequently read to toddlers and sing, do finger plays, and act out simple stories and folktales with children participating actively.

1B6 To satisfy toddlers' native natural curiosity caregivers give simple, brief, accurate responses.

1C1 Adults initiate conversations with a toddler giving ample time to respond. They attentively listen and respond verbally.

COMMON CORE Common Core State Standards for English Language Arts and Literacy

L.CCR 4 Determine or clarify the meaning of unknown and multiple meaning words and phrases.

The Toddler Teacher

Kelsa (26 months) and her grandfather entered the classroom. He drew me aside after his granddaughter had run off to the housekeeping area. With a smile he shared what Kelsa had done and said to him. "We were watching TV, and I commented on something," he said. "She got up and stood right in front of me. Next, she cupped my cheeks with her hands and said, 'Look at me when you say words.'" He laughed. I explained, "Sometimes with toddlers we can understand their words only if they speak right into our face."

Questions to Ponder

1. Is this a teacher strategy that helps toddlers?
2. Was the teacher's explanation to Kelsa's grandfather sufficient, or would a longer explanation have been better?
3. Is Kelsa's language acquisition advanced or about average for her age?

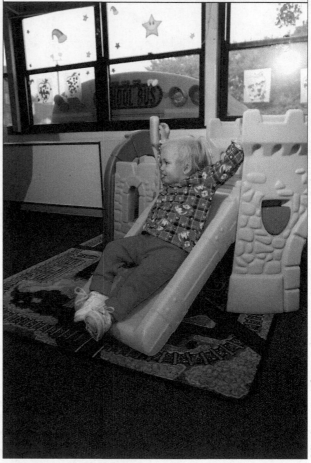

Photo 2-1 Exploring a small slide is a toddler adventure.

© 2015 Cengage Learning®

If you were amazed at the infant's and the one-year-old's ability, wait until you meet the toddler! Toddlerhood marks the beginning of a critical language-growth period. Never again will words enter the vocabulary at the same rate; abilities emerge in giant spurts almost daily. When children stop and focus on things, from specks on the floor to something very large, concentration is total—every sense organ seems to probe for data.

Toddlerhood begins with the onset of toddling (walking), a little before or after the child's first birthday. The toddler is perched at the gateway of a great adventure, eager to proceed, investigating as she goes, and attempting to communicate what she discovers and experiences (Photo 2-1). "The bags are packed" with what has been learned in infancy. The child will both monologue and dialogue as she ages, always knowing much more than can be verbally expressed. During toddlerhood she uses words whose meanings have been rooted in social acts and may have significance.

Toddlers are action-oriented. They simultaneously act on and perceive the environment around them. Toddlers' thoughts become a sensorimotor activity. As they age higher-level thinking happens, and toddlers begin to think first and then act.

By the age of two, toddlers' brains are as active as those of adults. The metabolic rate keeps rising, and by the age of three, toddlers' brains are two and a half times more active than the brains of adults—and they stay that way throughout the first decade of life (Shore, 1997). One can compare the working rate of a toddler's mind to an adult's mind as that of supercomputer to an abacus.

An important milestone during the toddler period occurs when the toddler uses symbolic (speech) communication rather than communicating primarily through body actions and gestures. This is made possible by the child's growing mental capability and the richness of the child's affective and life experiences.

Many experts believe that a warm, close relationship with a caregiver promotes the child's communication ability and provides satisfaction in itself. Experts agree that the primary need of toddlers (and infants) is emotional connection.

From a few spoken words, the toddler will move to purposeful speech that gains what is desired, controls others, allows personal comments, and accompanies play. It becomes evident that the toddler recognizes the give and take of true conversation. She also realizes the difference between being the speaker and being the one who listens and reacts—the one who persuades or is persuaded, the one who questions or is questioned. Toddlers become aware that everything has a name and that playfully trying out new sounds is an enjoyable pursuit. The child's meanings for the few words she uses at the start of the toddler period may or may not be the same as common usage. As children age, they will continually and gradually modify their private meanings of the words in their speaking vocabulary to conform to public meanings.

Cambourne (1988) describes the enormous complexity of learning to talk:

> When one has learned to control the oral version of one's language, one has learned literally countless thousands of conventions. Each language spoken on the Earth today (some three or four thousand) comprises a unique, arbitrary set of signs, and rules for combining those signs to create meaning. These conventions have no inherent "rightness" or "logic" to them, just as driving on the right or left side of the road has no intrinsic rightness or logic to it. Yet each language is an amazingly complex, cultural artifact, comprising incredibly complex sets of sounds, words, and rules for combining them, with equally numerous and complex systems for using them for different social, personal, and cognitive purposes. (p. 252)*

Even though toddlers have an innate predisposition for learning to communicate, they face four major tasks in learning the rule systems of language: (1) understanding phonology (the sound system of a language); (2) learning syntax (a system of rules governing word order and combinations that give sense to short utterances and sentences, often referred to as *grammar*); (3) learning semantics (word meanings); and (4) learning pragmatics (varying speech patterns depending on social circumstances and the context of situations). The understanding of these rule systems takes place concurrently—one area complementing and promoting the other. Rule systems form without direct instruction as toddlers grope to understand the speech of others, to express themselves, and to influence others both verbally and nonverbally. We can think

of the toddler as one who tests many hypotheses—the kind of thinker who over time can unconsciously discover and formulate the rules of language.

Language emergence is but one of the toddler's achievements. Intellectually, toddlers' process, test, and remember language input. They develop their own rules, which change as they recognize what are and are not permissible structures in their native language. Other important developmental achievements intersect during late toddlerhood as children increasingly shift to symbolic thinking and language use. Gains in social, emotional, and physical development are apparent, as are issues of power and autonomy.

2-1 Learning the English Language naeyc DAP COMMON CORE

Toddlers learn the **phonology** of their native language—its phonetic units and its particular and sometimes peculiar sounds. This is no easy job! An enormous growth in phonology learning occurs between birth and age five. The young language learner must sort sounds into identifiable groups and categories while she is possibly experiencing the speech of a variety of people in various settings. Because spoken language is characterized by a continuous flow of word sounds, this makes the task even more difficult.

After the child learns sounds, she learns sound combinations. It is prudent to point out here that not every sound in one language exists in another. Consequently, English language learners may be unfamiliar with new sounds in English.

A **phoneme** is the smallest unit of sound that distinguishes one utterance from another—implying a difference in meaning. Standard American English has approximately 39 phonemes; of these 15 are vowels and 24 are consonants. Not all experts agree on these numbers. Language from a phonetic perspective might be conceived as a continuous sequence of sounds produced when air is pushed through the throat and mouth, and then received and recognized by sensitive ear structures.

Languages are divided into vowels and consonants. When pronouncing vowels, the breath stream flows freely from the vocal cords; when pronouncing consonants, the breath stream is blocked and molded in the mouth and throat

---

* From Brian Cambourne, *The Whole Story*. Copyright ©1988.

---

phonology — the sound system of a language and how it is represented with an alphabetic code.

phoneme — the smallest unit of speech that distinguishes one utterance from another.

Figure 2-1 Average age of consonant sound production.

Learned by	
Age 1 to 3 = h, m, n, p, w.	
Age 2 to 4 = b, d, g, k.	
Age 2-1/2 to 4 = f, y.	
Age 2 to 6 = t, ng.	
Age 3 to 6 = r, l.	
Age 3 to 8 = s, z.	
Age 3-1/2 to 7 = ch, sh.	
Age 4 to 7 = j.	
Age 4 to 8 = v.	
Age 4-1/2 to 7 = th (unvoiced).	
Age 5 to 8 = th (voiced).	
Age 6 to 8 = zh.	

area by soft tissue, muscle tissue, and bone, with the tongue and jaw often working together. The child focuses on those sounds heard most often. The toddler's speech is full of repetitions and rhythmic speech play. Toddler babbling of this type continues and remains pleasurable during early toddlerhood. Sounds that are combinations of vowels and consonants increase. Vowel production is reasonably accurate by age three. Low, unrounded vowels (that is, *i, o, u*) are favored during infancy. Consonant sounds that are difficult to form will continue to be spoken without being close approximations of adult sounds until the child reaches five or six years of age or is even slightly older (Figure 2-1). Early childhood teachers realize that, in many instances, they will have to listen closely and watch for nonverbal clues to understand child speech.

It is a difficult task for the child to make recognizable sounds with mouth, throat, and breath control working in unison. Perfecting the motor control of speech-producing muscles is a sophisticated skill that comes ahead of many other physical skills. It requires precise and swift movements of the tongue and lips. This is all but fully developed when most other mechanical skills are far below levels of their future accomplishment.

Much of early speech has been described as unintelligible or gibberish. The toddler seems to realize that conversations come in long strings of sound. Rising to the occasion, the child imitates the rhythm of the sound but utters only a few understandable words.

Toddlers hear a word as an adult hears it. Sometimes, they know the proper pronunciation but are unable to reproduce it. The child may say "pway" for *play*. If the parent says "pway," the child objects, showing confusion and perhaps frustration. Toddler talk represents the child's best imitation, given present ability. Parents and teachers are urged to look at toddlers' speech mistakes as evidence that children are learning in an intelligent way.

Adult-to-child talk can be defined as "child-directed speech," that is, a set of speech modifications commonly found in the language adults use to address young children. Most speech researchers divide adult-child language into five main categories: pedagogy, control, affection, social exchange, and information. The pedagogy mode is characterized by slow adult speech that is over enunciated or overemphasizes one or two words. This type of adult speech is "tailor-made" for one- or two-year-olds trying to segment the speech stream into comprehensible units. Many adults tend to label happenings and objects with easy-to-learn, catchy variations, such as *choo-choo*, *bow-wow*, and so forth. Additional parental language techniques include the following:

1. Labeling themselves as "Mommy" or "Daddy," instead of "I" or "me" in speech.

2. Limiting topics in sentences.

3. Using short and simple sentences.

4. Using repetition.

5. Expanding or recasting children's one-word or unfinished utterances. If the toddler says "kitty," the parent offers "Kitty's name is Fluff."

6. Using a wide range of voice frequencies to gain the child's attention and initiate a communication exchange.

7. Carrying both sides of an adult-child conversation. The adult asks questions, and then answers them too. This technique is most often used with infants but is also common during the toddler period. The adult is modeling a social exchange.

8. Echoing a child's invented word. Many toddlers adopt a special word for a certain object (Photo 2-2). The whole family may use the child's word in conversational exchanges also.

Photo 2-2 The teacher's comments concentrate on the hat when the hat is the object of children's attention.

© 2015 Cengage Learning®

▶❚❚ **TeachSource Video 2-1**

© 2016 Cengage Learning®

Observing and Monitoring Language Development in Toddlers: The Importance of Assessment

This displays a toddler classroom in action and teacher behaviors to increase child language.

1. Would you describe most of the teachers in this video as being at eye level when they're talking with children?

2. Were the demonstrations teachers were providing toddlers along with words effective?

3. Did you notice teachers tending to talk about the children's agendas and follow their interests?

4. Would you say that toddlers were understandable in their speech some of the time or most of the time?

When adults feel infants and toddlers are able communicators, it is reflected in their actions and speech. This can, and usually does, increase children's communicative abilities and opportunities. Early childhood educators believe caregivers should treat toddlers as communicating children, and avoid childlike or cutesy expressions. They offer simple forms of speech and easy-to-pronounce words whenever possible, especially when they introduce new words.

Views on adult use of baby talk after the infancy period stress the idea that the practice may limit more mature word forms and emphasize dependency. On the other hand, adults may offer simplified, easily pronounced forms, such as *bow-wow* for a barking poodle. They later quickly switch to harder-to-pronounce forms when the child seems ready. In the beginning, though, most adults automatically modify their speech when speaking with toddlers by using short sentences and stressing key words.

Children progress with language at their individual rates and with varying degrees of clarity. Some children speak relatively clearly from their first tries. Other children, who are also progressing normally, take a longer time before their speech is easily understood. All basic sounds (50, including diphthongs) are perfected by most children by age seven or eight.

2-1a Morphology

A **morpheme** is the smallest unit of language standing by itself with recognized meaning. It can be a word or part of a word. Many prefixes (*un-*, *ill-*) and suffixes (*-s*, *-ness*, *-ed*, *-ing*) are morphemes with their own distinct meanings. The study of morphemes is called **morphology**. There are wide individual differences in the rates toddlers' utter morphemes. It is unfortunate if early childhood teachers or families attempt to compare the emerging speech of toddlers or equate greater speech usage with higher ability, thus giving the quiet toddler(s) perhaps less of their time. Between the ages of two and four years, children gradually include a variety of different morphemes in their

---

morpheme — the smallest unit in a language that by itself has a recognizable meaning.
morphology — the study of the units of meaning in a language.

spontaneous utterances. There seems to be a common sequence in their appearance.

2-1b Syntax

Languages have word orders and rules, and young children speak in word order and follow the rules of their native tongue. Children typically acquire the rules of grammar in their native language, with little difficulty, from normal communicative interactions with adults.

The rules for ordering words in sentences do not operate on specific words, but on classes of words such as nouns, verbs, and adjectives, and a relatively small number of syntactical rules can account for the production of a very large number of sentences. In some languages, the subject of a sentence follows the verb; in other languages, it precedes the verb.

Modifiers (descriptive words) in some languages have gender (male and female forms), but in others they do not. Plurals and possessive forms are unique to each language. Young speakers will make mistakes, but adults marvel at the grammar the child does use correctly, having learned the rules without direct instruction. One can compare children's mastery of **phonetics** to their mastery of **syntax**. The child's mastery of phonology is gradual, but the child's use of correct syntax is almost completely mastered from early beginning attempts.

By age two, and sometimes as early as 18 months, children begin to string together two or more holophrases and have thereby arrived at the telegraphic stage. All telegraphic speech consists of acceptable grammatical sequences that are the precursors of the sentence.

From all the perceptions she has received and the words spoken to and about her, the child has noted regularities and has unconsciously formed rules, which are continually revised. Chukovsky (1963) describes this task:

> It is frightening to think what an enormous number of grammatical forms are poured over the poor head of the young child. And he, as if it were nothing at all, adjusts to all the chaos, constantly sorting out in rubrics the disorderly elements of words he hears, without noticing as he does this, his gigantic effort. If an adult had to master so many grammatical rules within so short a time, his head would surely burst. (p. 31)

Grammar involves the way sounds are organized to communicate meaning. With grammatical knowledge, the young child can produce and understand a wide range of new, novel, grammatically correct, and meaningful sentences. As the child learns to talk during preschool years, she may construct many ungrammatical sentences and use words in unusual ways. The errors of the two-year-old disappear as the child gains more control over language, but new kinds of errors appear in three-year-olds, who are trying new forms of expression. An understanding of the general rules of grammar develops before an understanding of the exceptions to the rules. Correct grammar forms may change to incorrect forms as the child learns new rules. *First past tenses of the irregular verbs may have been correct. Then when a child starts using and adding -ed endings for regular verb past tenses, her "came" may become "camed," or her "broke" to "broked it," or her "went" to "wented." The child has replaced the correct irregular past tense form with an incorrect **over-generalization**. The child may not return to correct forms until she ages and hears more English spoken around her. Even though the correct forms may have been practiced for several months, they are driven out of the child's speech by* **overregularization**.

In later years, during elementary school, the child will formally learn the grammar rules of the English language. What the child has accomplished before that time, however, is monumental. The amount of speech that already conforms to the particular syntactical and grammatical rules of language is amazing. The child has done this through careful listening and by mentally reorganizing the common elements in language that have been perceived. The toddler's growing use of

---

modifiers — words that give a special characteristic to a noun (e.g., a large ball).

phonetics — pertaining to representing the sounds of speech with a set of distinct symbols, each denoting a single sound.

syntax — the arrangement of words as elements in a sentence to show their relationship.

grammar — the rules of a specific language that include both written and spoken utterances and describe how that specific language works and the forms of speech that conform to the rules that well-schooled speakers and writers observe in any given language.

over-generalization — the act of presuming something to be true of all members of a particular class of words.

overregularization — the tendency on the part of children to make the language regular, such as using past tenses like -ed on verb endings.

Photo 2-3 Mara's teacher knows the child frequently does not maintain eye contact when speaking.

intonation and **inflections** (changes in loudness of voice) adds clarity, as do nonverbal gestures. The child is often insistent that adults listen.

The toddler's system of nonverbal signals, body postures, and motions that were used in late infancy continues and expands, becoming part of the toddler's communication style (Photo 2-3). Many signals translated by mothers or care providers to strangers leave strangers bewildered as to how the mother or another adult could possibly know what the child wants. It may seem impossible based on what the stranger observed and heard.

English sentences follow a subject-verb-object sequence. The three fundamental properties of sentences are verb-object, subject-predicate, and modification, and almost all human languages have rules for these basic sentential structures. Learning grammar rules helps the toddler express ideas, and her understanding of syntax

helps the child to be understood. Our knowledge of the rules of combination determines how we construct and understand an infinite number of sentences from a finite vocabulary. Syntax gives language its power.

A person who listens closely to the older toddler will sometimes hear the child self-correct speech errors. Toddlers talk to themselves and to their toys often. It seems to aid the storage of words and memory. The toddler understands adult sentences because the child has internalized a set of finite rules or combinations of words.

2-1c Semantics

Semantics is the study of meanings and acquisition of vocabulary. It probes how the sounds of language are related to the real world and life experiences. The toddler absorbs meanings from both verbal and nonverbal communication sent and received. The nonverbal refers to expressive associations of words, such as rhythm, stress, pitch, gesture, body position, facial change, and so on. Adults perform important functions in the child's labeling and concept formation by giving words meaning in conversations.

The toddler who comes from a home that places little emphasis on expressing ideas in language may be exposed to a relatively restricted range of words for expressing conceptual distinctions. Every early childhood center should offer opportunities for children to learn a rich and varied vocabulary to refer to various experiences and to express ideas (Photo 2-4).

Photo 2-4 Toddlers begin to engage in social interactions with others.

---

inflections — the grammatical "markers," such as plurals. Also, a change in pitch or loudness of the voice.

semantics — the study of meanings associated with words and the acquisition of vocabulary.

In toddler classrooms, teachers have many opportunities to name objects and happenings as the day unfolds. Using teacher gesturing along with words (or pointing to illustrations and photographs in simple picture books or classroom signs) helps the toddler form a connection between what is seen and heard. Repeating words with voice stress can be done in a natural way while monitoring whether the child is still interested.

Word meanings are best learned in active, hands-on experiences rather than "repeat-after-me" situations. Meanings of words are acquired through their connotations, not their denotations, that is, in situations that consist of feelings and verbal and nonverbal messages with physical involvement. The word *cold* for instance, means little until physically experienced. Toddlers assume that labels (words) refer to wholes instead of parts (the creature, not the tail) and to classes instead of items (all horses, not one horse) (Cowley, 2000).

When an older infant is first learning to talk, the same sound often serves for several words; for instance, *bah* can mean "bottle," "book," "bath," and "bye." And sometimes infants use one sound to name an object and also to express a more complicated thought; for example, a child may point to a ball and name it, but later may say the same word and mean, "I want to play with the ball. Roll it to me."

The child's **concept** building is an outgrowth and result of a natural human tendency to try to make sense of the surroundings. Attending to and pondering about the relationships, similarities, and differences in events and happenings, and mentally storing, remembering, and retrieving those ideas and impressions are important aspects of concept development. With young children's innate curiosity, drive, and desire to explore and experience, concepts are continually being formed, reformed, and modified.

Examples of toddler behavior demonstrate that conceptual conclusions happen daily in group and home care settings. When a child blows a whistle-shaped toy, licks and bites a plastic fruit, tightly clings to an adult when a dog barks, or says "hot" when pointing to a water faucet, one can see past experiences are basic to the child's concept development.

To understand how concept development is individual and based on life experiences, ask yourself what makes a cup a cup. How many distinguishing features can you list? Ask another adult to do the same. You will both probably list some of the following characteristics:

- has a handle
- holds liquids and substances
- is often round on top, tapering to a smaller round base or can be cylindrical
- is used as a standard measurement in cooking (8 ounces)
- is made from clay, plastic, glass, metal, or other solid substances
- can be used to drink liquids

Adults speaking about cups understand one another because they usually recognize the same distinguishing characteristic(s). If asked to get the cup on the shelf, they won't get a glass. A toddler using the word cup often means his personal drinking cup.

A toddler may overuse concepts in new situations. Perhaps a bandage on the tip of a brother's finger will be called a thimble. For a short time, all men are daddies, a cow may be called a big dog, and all people in white are feared. As mental maturity and life experiences increase, concepts change; small details and exceptions are noticed. Toddlers may use a word to refer to a smaller category than would adults. An example of this phenomenon is the toddler's use of the word *dog* only in reference to the child's pet rather than all dogs encountered.

Concepts, often paired mentally with words, aid categorizing. Concept words may have full, partial, or little depth of meaning. The toddler's level of thought is reflected in speech. When counting to three, the toddler may or may not know what "three" represents. Words are **symbols**. Young children acquire word meaning and also begin to understand the symbolic nature of words. The meaning of a word is known and learned from other speakers of a common language. A word is a sign that signifies a referent. Infants' first words are almost always nouns that are common, familiar objects or people. In an English-speaking family a one year old infant who becomes familiar with hearing the word "doggie" being used when

---

concept — a commonly recognized element (or elements) that identifies groups or classes; usually has a given name.

symbols — things that stand for or suggest (such as pictures, models, word symbols, and so forth).

referring to the hairy, little critter who barks, will use the word doggie when she speaks about it or calls it. The dog is the referent. If the same dog is given away to a Spanish speaking family and lives around that family's infant and becomes a familiar object, it is still a referent, but the word the child uses will be that family's word for the dog. This arbitrary relationship between the referent and the sign for the word is symbolic. A few words in English are not arbitrary but have a sound associated with its referent such as hiss, tinkle, and woof.

A toddler's firsthand sensory experiences are very important. Stored mental perceptions are attached to words. Words are only as rich as the experiences and depth of understanding behind them. The activities and experiences found in subsequent chapters will help the early childhood teacher enrich the child's concepts by providing deeper meanings in a wide range of language arts. Every activity for young children—a total school program—gives them a language arts background full of opportunities to explore by handling, tasting, using their bodies, smelling, and touching, as well as by seeing and listening.

2-1d Common Core State Standards and Children's Vocabulary

A rich and varied vocabulary will be necessary if kindergartners are to function successfully and reach the expectations of the *Common Core State Standards for English language arts & literacy in history/social studies, science, and technical subjects-K-12*, (National Governors Association Center for Best Practices and Council of Chief State School Officers, 2010). It has been adopted in most state school systems. Without words learned in the toddler-preschool period, the ideas found in kindergarten books and early readers may escape children's comprehension. Children will also need an abundant repertoire of content words gained through an early childhood curriculum that not only built language, literacy skills, and background knowledge, but also promoted a specific and detailed vocabulary in other core domains.

In picture book readings, toddler teachers emphasize and explain, as simply as possible, new words and how they relate to toddlers' past experiences. Educators will also need to clarify and review words enough times for children

to become familiar with them and understand their meanings. Word learning will not be left to chance, but rather will be teacher promoted.

2-1e Pragmatics

The subtleties of our language are multifaceted. **Pragmatics** is the study of how language is used effectively in a social context, or the practical aspect of oral communication. It is the study of who can say what, in what way, where and when, by what means, and to whom (Figure 2-2). Language is a tool in questioning, ordering, soothing, ridiculing, and engaging in other social actions. One can request quiet in the form of a question such as, "Can't anyone get a peaceful moment around here?" or talk longingly about the candy in a store for the purpose of obtaining it without making a direct request, as in, "Oh, they have my favorite kind of chocolate bar!"

The language that young children use to express desires, wishes, concerns, and interests becomes a reflection of their social selves. When a toddler communicates effectively, the toddler receives feedback from others. Many times, a sense of well-being elicited by positive events helps the child shape a feeling of competency and self-esteem. Not yet socially subtle in speech, the toddler has not learned the pragmatically useful or appropriate behaviors of older children. Toddlers seem to have just one goal: to get messages across by gaining adult attention regardless of

Figure 2-2 Pragmatic skills.

Pragmatic Skills
1. taking turns in a conversation with another
2. knowing you are supposed to answer when a question is asked
3. noticing nonverbal body cues, signals, gestures, and signs and then responding
4. introducing a topic in a conversation for the listener to understand
5. having the ability to stay on the subject of a conversation
6. maintaining the right amount of eye contact; not staring or turning away too frequently
7. using different communicative styles that suit different communicative partners
8. learning that in certain situations talking is inappropriate

pragmatics — the study of how language is used effectively in a social context; varying speech patterns depending on social circumstances and the context of situations.

who is present and in what situation. The world, from the toddler's perspective, revolves around the toddler and her need to communicate.

2-2 Attachment and Development of Language Skills

Attachment problems can slow communicative development. Observers describe infants and toddlers in less-than-adequate care situations as fearful, apathetic, disorganized, and distraught. If responsive social interaction and adult feedback exchanges are minimal, limited, frightening, or confusing, the infant or toddler may display a marked lack of interest in holding or obtaining adult attention. During toddlerhood these children can fall behind in speech development. Lally (1997) describes the importance of toddler social interaction:

> Infants and toddlers develop their sense of who they are from the adults who care for them. They learn from their caregivers what to fear, what behaviors are appropriate, and how their communications are received and acted upon. They learn how successful they are at getting their needs met by others, what emotions and intensity levels of emotions to safely display, and how interesting others find them. (p. 288)

Toddlers are sometimes shy with newcomers, so caregivers cast their eyes to the side rather than searching a toddler's face at first meeting. They bend or squat to toddler eye level. When more comfortable conversing takes place, teachers comment on toddler movements while watching for child wariness and/or acceptance. They react and respond to all of toddlers' verbal overtures including babble, gestures, miscellaneous sound making, hand or body signs, or words. Teachers are enthusiastic and joyful companions celebrating toddler accomplishments with attentive and appreciative feedback. They explain what is happening between themselves and the toddler and also what is occurring in the environment around them. naeyc DAP

2-2a First Words

Any time between 10 and about 22 months is considered within the normal range for first words. A vocabulary growth spurt happens around 18 to 22 months (Strickland & Schickedanz, 2004).

Photo 2-5 Gestures often indicate a child's desire or need.

© 2015 Cengage Learning®

First words and content words carry a lot of meaning. They usually consist of names of important people or objects the toddler encounters daily and include functional words such as *up*, *out*, *night-night*, and *bye-bye* used in social contexts (Photo 2-5). Easy-to-pronounce words are more likely to be included in toddlers' early expressive vocabularies.

Single words can frequently go further than naming by representing a meaningful idea (a holophrase). The task of the adult includes both being responsive and guessing the child's complete thought. This may sound simple, but many times it is difficult and frustrating. Many factors influence the degree of adult responsiveness and talkativeness, particularly in child center settings—room arrangements, adult-child ratios, level of staff training, and other emotional and environmental factors. The greatest inhibitor of adults' speaking and responding to children seems to be adults' talking to one another instead of the children. Professionals save chatting for breaks and after school meetings. The nature of the work in a group care program can easily be described as emotion packed and demanding, in addition to rewarding and challenging. On the surface, the general public may not see or understand skilled verbal interactions taking place between toddlers and caregivers. What seems to be random, natural playfulness and verbal responsiveness can be really very skilled and professionally intentional behavior. The same, of course, is true regarding family behavior.

Adults sometimes question the practice of responding to toddlers' grunts and "uhs"; instead they respond only to toddlers' spoken words. Many toddlers seem to understand everything said to them and around them but get by and satisfy most of their needs with sounds and gestures. The points for adults to consider are that the child is performing and learning a difficult task and that speech will soon follow. The message that responsive adults relay to children when rewarding their early attempts with attention is that children can be successful communicators and that further attempts at speech will get results.

2-2b From Egocentric Speech to Inner Speech

During the toddler period, observers notice that words or short phrases spoken by adults are remembered and spoken out loud. The toddler's "hot," "no," "kitty," or similar words accompany the child's actions or a simple viewing of objects at hand. Vygotsky (1986) has called this "egocentric" speech, which is ultimately and usefully tied to the toddler's thinking.

As the child matures, this type of speech slowly becomes **inner speech**; part of the child's thinking process. Egocentric speech is regulatory, that is, useful in helping the child regulate (manage) her own behavior. As adults, we see examples of this regulatory function when we talk ourselves through particular perplexing situations. For example, "First the key goes in the lock, then turn the handle, and the bar moves to the left."

2-2c Symbolic Gesturing

It is old-fashioned to believe that real communication does not exist before a child's first words. Researchers have helped us understand that gestures and signs (signals) occur in tandem with early vocalizing. Young toddlers can possess a rich repertoire of signals, and female infants tend to rely on or produce them with slightly greater frequency than male infants. Signs have been defined as nonverbal gestures symbolically representing objects, events, desires, and conditions that are used by toddlers to communicate with those around them. They literally can double a young toddler's vocabulary.

Toddlers' interest in learning hand signals (signing) varies greatly. Conducting an infant-toddler program in which signing is a regular part of the curriculum has become popular. Some toddlers may use 20 or more signs for various objects, feelings, and needs; other toddlers mixed only a few gestures with their beginning words. Both would be displaying normal development.

The use of words and symbols to influence other people in predictable ways requires the child to represent mentally the relationship between the symbol (word or gesture), the *meaning* for which it stands, and the intended effect on the other person. A symbol—a word, a picture, a dance—exists because of human intention to infuse some tangible form—a sound, a mark, a movement—with meaning and thereby to comment on or take action in the social world.

Various researchers have studied a child whose parents felt that their child was capable of learning nonverbal as well as verbal labels. The parents informally concocted hand or body signs on the spot for new events without any reference to a formal sign language system. Figure 2-3, from a study by Acredolo and Goodwyn (1985), describes the signs and gives the age the signs appeared in the child's communicative behaviors and the age the child said the word represented by the sign. The list of signs includes the signs the child learned with and without direct parent teaching.

Gestures are integral companions of toddler verbalizations. Adults may have modeled the gestures in their adult-child interactions. A family's signals are "read" by toddlers, and a hand held palm up is usually read as "give it to me." Toddlers show their understanding by behaviors. Toddlers can and do invent new gestures; consequently, signing is not simple, imitative behavior. Pointing is probably the most commonly used gesture of toddlers. Eventually, words are preferred and gesturing remains as an accompaniment of speech. We have all slipped back into a gesturing mode as we search for words in conversation, and hand gestures are used automatically to convey the word(s) that we cannot quite express.

Early childhood educators employed by infant-toddler centers need to know their centers' position regarding expected language-developing behaviors. Most centers expect educators to pair words with adult hand signs, to encourage toddler use of signs, and to learn and respond

---

inner speech — mentioned in Vygotsky's theory as private speech that becomes internalized and is useful in organizing ideas.

Figure 2-3 Symbolic signs, in order of acquisition, produced by case study subject.

Signs	Description	Age of Sign Acquisition (Months)	Age of Word Acquisition (Months)
flower	sniff, sniff	12.5	20.0
big	arms raised	13.0	17.25
elephant	finger to nose, lifted	13.5	19.75
anteater	tongue in and out	14.0	24.0
bunny	torso up and down	14.0	19.75
Cookie Monster	palm to mouth plus smack	14.0	20.75
monkey	hands in armpits, up-down	14.25	19.75
skunk	wrinkled nose plus sniff	14.5	24.00
fish	blow through mouth	14.5	20.0
slide	hand waved downward	14.5	17.5
swing	torso back and forth	14.5	18.25
ball	both hands waved	14.5	15.75
alligator	palms together, open-shut	14.75	24.0
bee	finger plus thumb waved	14.75	20.00
butterfly	hands crossed, fingers waved	14.75	24.0
I dunno	shrugs shoulders, hands up	15.0	17.25
hot	waves hand at midline	15.0	19.0
hippo	head back, mouth wide	15.0	24.0
spider	index fingers rubbed	15.0	20.0
bird	arms out, hands flapping	15.0	18.5
turtle	hand around wrist, fist in-out	15.0	20.0
fire	waving of hand	15.0	23.0
night-night	head down on shoulder	15.0	20.0
X-mas tree	fists open-closed	16.0	26.0
mistletoe	kisses	16.0	27.0
scissors	two fingers open-closed	16.0	20.0
berry	"raspberry" motion	16.5	20.0
kiss	kiss (at a distance)	16.5	21.0
caterpillar	index finger wiggled	17.5	23.0

to each child's individual sign language. To do this, teachers must be alert to children's cues, in particular noticing what in the environment attracts them so that words can be supplied and the children's intentions can be "read." Teachers' behaviors should reflect their awareness, intentional efforts, and attention to toddlers' efforts to communicate. Their continual goal is to establish a warm, emotionally fulfilling connection to each child in their care.

Toddlers are very interested in exploring. Teachers should hang back when toddlers interact with other toddlers and try not to interrupt play. Becoming social with peers is given priority and promoted. Teachers of toddlers do a lot of word modeling. They attempt to be both calm and fun companions. Most will tell you that after a full day with toddlers they look forward to conversing with adults.

2-2d First Sentences

The shift from one word to a two-word (or more) stage at approximately 18 months is a milestone. At that time, the toddler has a speaking vocabulary of about 50–75 words; by 36 months, upward of 1,000 words. It is crucial in talking about vocabulary to acknowledge that children not only acquire new words as they get older but also expand their understanding of old words.

If one looks closely at two-word utterances, two classes of words become apparent. The smallest group of words is made up of what are called "pivot words." Examples of toddlers' two-word sentences, with pivot words underlined, are shown in Figure 2-3. Pivot words are used more often than other words, and seem to enter the vocabulary more slowly, perhaps because they are stable and fixed in meaning. In analyzing two-word toddler comments, one finds they are both subject-predicate and topic-comment in nature. Frequently stressed syllables in words and word endings are what toddlers' first master, filling in other syllables later. At times, toddlers use -um or -ah as placeholders for syllables and words. They replace these with correct syllables and words as they age.

Understanding of grammar rules at this two-word stage is displayed even though many words are missing. Toddlers frequently use a simple form and, almost in the same breath, clarify by expansion (by adding another word). The invention of words by toddlers is common. One 18-month-old had her own private word for "sleep," consistently calling it "ooma." Families trying to understand their toddlers get good at filling in the blanks. They then can confirm the child's statement and can add meaning at a time when the child's interest is focused.

2-2e Toddler – Adult Conversations

Toddlers control attending or turning away when interacting with others, as do infants. At about one year, they understand many words and begin to display turn-taking in conversation, with "you talk, I answer" behaviors. **Joint attention** starts around nine- to 10-months of age. At this time infants develop intentional communication and willingly share emotions, intentions, and interest in the outside world. To do this, the child has to be sure that both she (the speaker) and her intended receiver is focused on the same thing. She does this by capturing another's attention, establishing the topic of conversation, and maintaining attention on the topic by looking back and forth. Her communication usually consists of one or more of the following: looking, pointing, gesturing, showing, giving, making sounds, and changing her facial expression.

Toddlers learn that speech deserves attention and that speech is great for getting adults to notice them. They seem to revel in the joint-endeavor aspect of conversations. Toddlers are skillful communicators. They converse and correct adult interpretations, gaining pleasure and satisfaction from language exchanges. The following incident shows more than toddler persistence:

> A first-time visitor to the home of a 20-month-old toddler is approached by the toddler. The visitor eventually rises out of his chair, accompanies the toddler to the kitchen, gets a glass of water, and hands it to the child. The toddler takes a tiny drink, and returns, satisfied, to the living room. Parents were not involved. Thirst, itself, was unimportant. The pleasure gained by the child seemed to motivate her actions.

For the child to accomplish her ends, the following actions occurred. The visitor:

1. focuses attention on child.
2. realizes a "talking" situation is occurring.
3. listens and maintains a receiver attitude.
4. corrects his own behavior, guesses at the child's meaning, and tries new actions.
5. realizes the conversation is over.

While the toddler:

1. stands in front of visitor; searches face to catch eye; makes loud vocalization, dropping volume when eye contact is made; observes visitor behavior.
2. repeats first sound (parents understand, visitor does not) and observes visitor reaction.
3. grabs visitor's hand, vocalizes loudly, and looks in visitor's eyes.
4. tugs at hand, uses insistent voice tone, and gestures toward the kitchen.
5. pulls visitor to sink and uses new word (visitor does not understand); corrects through gestures when visitor reaches for the cookie jar.
6. corrects visitor's guess (milk), gestures toward water, and holds out hand.
7. drinks a small sip and hands back the glass, smiles, and walks away.

---

joint attention — child's awareness that he or she must gain and hold another's focus during communicational exchanges to get his or her message understood.

Photo 2-6 Children seek out people willing to show interest in what they are doing.

This type of behavior has been called *instrumental expression* because vocalization and nonverbal behaviors were used to obtain a certain goal. The toddler seeks people willing to listen and learns from each encounter (Photo 2-6). Toddlers' subject matter in conversations is commonly concerned with recent memorable happenings in toddler's lives. Adults modify and adapt their speech based on the abilities they observe in the child. This is done intuitively by use of shorter and less complex comments, and it changes when adults notice increased capacity.

Many experienced caregivers describe a time when some toddlers in their care remain very close. During this time, the toddler's behavior is characterized by clinging to a primary caregiver, watching adult lips intently, showing decreased interest in toys or playing independently, frequently bringing objects to the caregiver, and attempting to say words. The duration and appearance of these behaviors is unique to each toddler, and some do not display them at all. Families can worry about spoiling the toddler, if these behaviors persist, and educators urge families to satisfy children's needs for increased attention and language input. Usually the child will emerge with a longer attention span and branch out to explore a wider world.

2-3 Characteristics of Toddler Language

The speech of young children speaking in two-word, or longer, sentences is termed **telegraphic** and **prosodic**. It is telegraphic because many words are omitted because of the child's limited ability to express and remember large segments of information; the most important parts of the sentence are usually present. Prosodic refers to the child's use of voice modulation and word stress with a particular word or words to give special emphasis and meaning. Telegraphic speech can be defined as utterances that are devoid of function words and resemble messages sent by telegraph, for instance, "Jimmy truck" could represent "That truck belongs to Jimmy" or "Give me my truck." Meanings often depend on context and intonation of the utterance. For additional toddler language characteristics that may appear before the child's third birthday, see Figure 2-4.

No discussion of older toddlers' language would be complete without mentioning the use of "no." There seems to be an exasperating time when children say "no" to everything—seemingly testing whether there is a choice. Young children first use "no" to indicate nonexistence. Later it is used to indicate rejection and denial. Even when the child can speak in sentences longer than three words, the "no" often remains the first in a sequence of words. A typical example is "No want go bed." Soon, children insert negatives properly between the subject and the verb into longer utterances, as sentence length increases. Of all speech characteristics adults remember, toddlers' use of negatives and their avid energetic demands to be "listened to" stick in the memories of their caregivers.

2-3a Aids to Toddler Speech Development

The swift rate of new words entering toddlers' vocabularies indicates that educators caring for them should begin to become increasingly specific with descriptive terms in their speech. If a truck is blue, a comment like "The blue truck rolled in the mud" is appropriate. If an object is

---

telegraphic speech — a characteristic of young children's sentences in which everything but the crucial word or words are omitted, as if for a telegram.

prosodic speech — the child's use of voice modulation and word stress to give special emphasis and meaning.

Figure 2-4 Toddler language characteristics.

Toddler Language Characteristics

- Uses two- to five-word sentences.
  "Baby down."
  "Baby boom boom."
  "No like."
  "No like kitty."
  "Me dink all gone."
  "See me dink all gone."
- Uses verbs.
  "Dolly cry."
  "Me going."
  "Wanna cookie."
- Uses prepositions.
  "In car."
  "Up me go."
- Adds plurals.
  "Birdies sing."
  "Gotta big doggies."
  "Bears in dat."
- Uses pronouns.
  "Me big boy."
  "He bad."
- Uses articles.
  "The ball gone."
  "Gimme a candy."
- Uses conjunctions.
  "Me and gamma."
- Uses negatives.
  "Don't wanna."
  "He no go."
- Runs words together.
  "Allgone," "gotta," "gimme," "lookee."
- Asks questions.
  "Wa dat?"
  "Why she sleep?"
- Does not use letter sounds or mispronounces spoken words.
  "Iceam," "choo" (for shoe), "member" (for remember), "canny" (for candy).
- Sings songs.
- Tells simple stories.
- Repeats words and phrases.
- Enjoys word and movement activities.

on the bottom shelf, in the top drawer, or under the table, those words can be stressed. A color, number, or special quality, like fast or slow, big or little, or many other adjectives and adverbs, can be inserted in simple comments. Playing detective to understand toddlers will always be part of adults' conversational style. Teachers may request that toddlers look directly at them when they communicate so that teachers can better hear each word and determine intent.

Many experts offer adults advice for providing an optimal toddler environment for language stimulation. The following are some specific tips.

- Expose the child to language with speech neither too simple nor too complex, but just slightly above the child's current level (Photo 2 - 7).
- Stay in tune with the child's actual abilities.
- Omit unreasonable speech demands, yet encourage attempts.
- Remember that positive reinforcement is a more effective tool than negative feedback.
- Accept the child's own formulation of a language concept.
- Provide a correct model.
- Make a point of being responsive.
- Follow the child's interest by naming and simple discussion.

Photo 2-7 "I see you found a green block!"

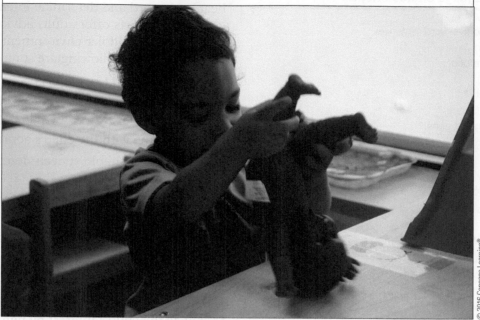

Photo 2-8 Shea croons and repeats "up, down, up, down," as he turns the doll upside down and then turns it to an upright position again.

Other suggested pointers follow.

- Explain what you are doing as you work.
- Describe what is happening.
- Display excitement for the child's accomplishments (Photo 2-8).
- Talk about what the child is doing, wanting, or needing.
- Pause and listen with ears and eyes after you have spoken.
- Encourage toddler imitation of gestures and sounds.
- Imitate the child's sounds playfully at times.

Language and self-help skills blossom when two-year-olds have opportunities to participate in "real" activities, such as cutting bananas (using a plastic knife), emptying baskets, sponging off the table, and helping sweep the floor.

The following selected passages of recommended adult behaviors are included in developmental appropriate practices identified by the National Association for the Education of Young Children (NAEYC) in *Developmentally Appropriate Practice: Focus on Infants and Toddlers* (Copple, Bredekamp, & Charner, 2013). A few others were listed on this chapter's first page.

- Caregivers spend most of the day in one-to-one, face-to-face conversations with toddlers. The tone of the interactions is warm and caring: caregivers use pleasant calm voices as well as simple language and nonverbal cues. [*p. 67*]
- Caregivers learn each toddler's cues and respond consistently in ways that are caring and specific to each child, which lets the child explore, knowing he can trust the adults to be there for help or comfort as needed. [*p.67*]
- Caregivers frequently read to toddlers—to one child individually or to groups of two or three—always in close physical contact. Caregivers sing with toddlers, do finger plays, and act out simple stories or folktales, with children participating actively. [*p.68*]
- Caregivers create an emotionally and physically inclusive classroom. They give every toddler warm, responsive care. They make sure that spatial organization, materials, and activities are planned such that all children can participate actively (e.g., a child with a physical disability eats at the table with other children). [*p.68*]
- To satisfy toddlers' natural curiosity, caregivers give simple, brief, accurate responses when children stare at or ask questions about a person with a disability or other differences. [*p.68*]

- Caregivers respect toddlers interest in objects—to carry objects around with them, collect objects, move them from one place to another, and to roam around or sit and parallel play with toys and other objects. [*p.69*]

- An adult initiating a conversation with the toddler gives the child ample time to respond. Caregivers also listen attentively for children's verbal initiations and respond to these. [*p.70*]

- Caregivers label or name objects, describe events, and reflect feelings ("Youre angry that Yvette that took the block.") to help children learn new words. Caregivers simplify their language for toddlers who are just beginning to talk. Then as children acquire their own words, caregivers expand on the toddler's language (Child: "Mark sock." Adult: "Oh, that's Mark's missing sock, and you found it"). [*p.70*]

- Caregivers ask the family what sounds, words, and nonverbal cues their toddler uses to better understand what the child means when she uses beginning speech or a home language that is not understood by the caregivers. [*p.70*]

- Caregivers learn what each child's cries mean (e.g., fear, frustration, sleepiness, pain) and when to wait (e.g., to see if the child solves his own problem) or take action. They respond promptly to toddler's cries or other signs of distress.[*p.70*] (NAEYC, 2013)

The above passages are from a larger body of material and selected because of their relationship to toddler's language and literacy growth. Teachers aware of developmentally appropriate practice put it in action during the course of a toddler's day as they interact and participate in a wide range of both planned and unplanned teacher activities. Toddler teacher actions that commonly take place in centers can include:

- setting out two or three familiar objects and asking the child to get one.
- calling attention to interesting things you see, hear, smell, taste, or feel.
- showing and labeling your facial features and the child's in a mirror.
- labeling and pointing to objects around a room.
- verbally labeling items of clothing as the child is dressing and undressing.
- labeling the people in the toddler's world.

Frequent teacher-child exchanges using language and movement play are recommended by many experts. One classic play activity follows.

Take Your Little Hands

Take your little hands and go clap, clap, clap.

Take your little hands and go clap, clap, clap.

Take your little hands and go clap, clap, clap.

Clap, clap, and clap your hands.

Take your little foot and go tap, tap, tap.

Take your little foot and go tap, tap, tap.

Take your little foot and go tap, tap, tap.

Tap, tap, and tap your foot.

Take your little eyes and go blink, blink, blink.

Take your little eyes and go blink, blink, blink.

Take your little eyes and go blink, blink, blink.

Blink, blink, and blink your eyes.

Take your little mouth and go buzz, buzz, buzz.

Take your little mouth and go buzz, buzz, buzz.

Take your little mouth and go buzz, buzz, buzz.

Buzz like a bumblebee.

Take your little hand and wave bye, bye, bye.

Take your little hand and wave bye, bye, bye.

Take your little hand and wave bye, bye, bye.

Wave your hand bye-bye.

2-3b Language with Music

Toddlers are music lovers. If a bouncy melody catches their ear, they move. They obtain plenty of joy in swaying, clapping, or singing along. Young children can anticipate a pattern when a song is familiar. They usually first recognize its rhythm or beat and then its words. Often children watch others first before joining in. With teacher encouragement and enough repetitions they learn the song and actions completely and may improvise and make additions.

Many can sing short, repeated phrases in songs, and some toddlers will create their own repetitive melodies (Photo 2-9). Adult correction is not necessary or appropriate. Playful singing and chanting by adults is a recommended language-development technique.

Photo 2-9 Making music is a popular preschool activity.

© 2015 Cengage Learning®

Educators can encourage young children's creativity with music. If teachers always focus on everyone singing the same words and/or doing the same actions, they may not be using music to promote creative expression. Fortunately, with the uninhibited and exuberant toddler this is not a problem; teachers are going to see some fantastic "moves" and hear some unique lyrics and takeoffs on songs and dances. The author remembers the time a two-year-old composed his own song: "Zipper your do da."

The social component in musical games is also a language facilitator. Joining the fun with others gradually attracts even the youngest children (Photo 2-10). A toddler can be introduced to the joy of moving to a new song with others; mutual musical listening and participation in music experiences at small group times add new avenues for language growth.

One technique educators frequently engage in with music is to verbally describe how a particular child is moving to music. ("Johnny is lifting his knee high up to his tummy.") This encourages children's movement to music and should be used when appropriate. The adult can extend two index fingers for the shy or wobbly child to grip, thereby creating a dance partnership. This allows the child to release

at any time. Gently swaying or guiding movements to the music may increase the child's enjoyment.

The following criteria for selecting sing-along songs, recorded music, and songbook selections are recommended. Choose a short selection for toddlers, repetitive phrases, reasonable, range (C to G or A), and simple rhythms. Try to find pieces that represent the ethnic and cultural diversity of attending children and include folk music.

2-3c Symbolic Play

What often looks like random play during the toddler period is actually experimentation that may produce new understandings. Children's cause and effect knowledge can be enhanced by manipulating features of the environment. For toddlers this might be pots and pans, toys, art materials, large rocks, or about anything they have gained access to. Objects can be sorted, lined up, and classified in some manner during play and particular attributes of playthings may be noticed. An alert teacher can casually or purposefully supply fitting words, labels for objects, or simple action words describing child action as they enjoy toddler's company.

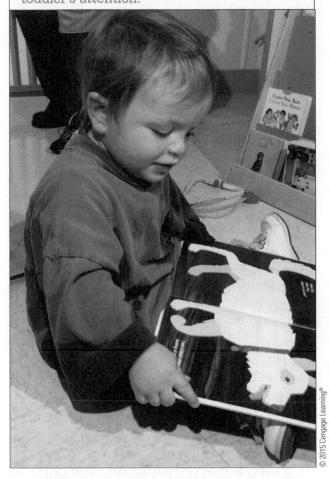

Photo 2-10 The right book can hold a toddler's attention.

© 2015 Cengage Learning®

At approximately 12 to 15 months, toddlers will begin to engage in symbolic (pretend) play. This important developmental leap allows the child to escape the immediate and firsthand happenings in her life and use symbols to represent past experiences and imagine future possibilities. Medina (2008) explains:

> Symbolic reasoning is a uniquely human talent. It may have arisen from our need to understand another's intentions and motivations, allowing us to coordinate within a group. (p. 47)

The acts of toddler pretend play observed by adults are widely diverse and depend in part on the child's life experiences. Greenspan (1999) describes a parent observing a young toddler's symbolic play:

> . . . he tenderly puts his teddy bear to be inside an empty shoe box, and the parent recognizes the child is starting to grasp that one thing can stand for, or symbolize, another. Because he can picture what a bed looks and feels like in his mind, he is able to pretend that a hollow, rectangular box is

really a symbol for a bed. When the parent comments that his teddy bear "is sleeping in his bed," he will eventually comprehend that the word "sleeping" stands for the bear's activity in the bed. As soon as he can articulate the sounds, the toddler will himself use the word symbol "sleeping" to describe an elaborate pattern of behaviors that he has observed. (p. 200)

One can always find toddlers who will talk into toy phones, spank dolls, grab the wheel of toy vehicles, and accompany motor movements with sounds, speech, and *vrooms*. Some reenact less common past experiences that are puzzling to their teachers. Gowen (1995) suggests the teacher techniques listed in Figure 2-5.

2-3d Making Friends

Toddlers seem to have a strong need for both individual identity and autonomy and social connectedness. At times they display the ability to help others and are sympathetic or empathetic. They may venture out toward peers and retreat back to the security, closeness, physical comfort of caring adults. They are constantly learning from their first contacts and relationships with "other small people" and new adults.

Wittmer (2008) believes that teachers cannot underestimate the importance of their relationships with toddlers. Social competence and emotional control development predict school readiness. Caring adults can be instrumental in helping toddlers figure out, experiment with, and understand new ways to interact and communicate with peers and also in learning the rules of physical contact and socialization.

Each toddler entering group care differs not only in personality, capability, culture, and gender but also in past human relationships, memories, and their expectations of others. Past experience may or may not include attachment to significant adults or positive social interactions with other like-age children. Some toddlers may avoid peers, or express hostility and aggression, or ignore them. Toddler communication skills also vary. Vocal ability can range from utter silence to being a chatterbox.

Often, toddler play is side-by-side play. A toddler may watch what a neighboring peer is doing and may sometimes imitate the peer's actions. However, two toddlers playing cooperatively in an organized, shared-goal play situation is infrequent. Toddlers are usually in-their-own-

Figure 2-5 Teacher's response to toddlers' symbolic play.

1. Mirror the child's sounds, words or actions.
   (Child is rocking a doll while humming.)
   Teacher picks up a doll, rocks it, while saying "Go to sleep, baby."
   (Child is putting blocks together.)
   Teacher sits with child and puts one block on top of another and says "Blocks."

2. Describe the child's actions.
   (Child is climbing stairs.)
   Teacher says "One foot on the step, two feet on the step."
   (Child feeds doll with toy bottle.)
   Teacher says "You are giving your baby a drink of milk. Um, um, that tastes good."
   "Your ball is bouncing up, and down, up and down. Down it goes; up it goes. You picked up the ball, Will."

3. Suggest a child action.
   (Child has rolled a toy car across the rug.)
   Teacher says "Let's push our cars under the table and park them," as she grabs another toy car pushes it and parks it.
   (Child has picked up small floor pillows and is carrying them.)
   Teacher says "I'll get the wagon so you can put the pillows inside."

4. Request or suggest an action or vocalization.
   (Child is putting a plastic bowl on his head.)
   "Robin (child's name) has a new hat." teacher says.
   Then sitting next to him and picking up another bowl, she says,
   "Teacher needs a new hat too. Put it on my head, please."

5. Make a positive statement.
   (Child pats doll's back putting it upon her shoulder.)
   Teacher says "Your dolly feels better now. What a good mommy you are."
   (Child puts pretend play iron over the play ironing board.)
   "You are ironing your family's clothes so they look neat and pretty.
   (Child tries to feed teacher a plastic apple.)
   Teacher says "That apple tastes good. I was hungry. Thank you very much."

6. Model an action or word(s) for the child to copy.
   With stuffed dog and baby blanket, teacher says,
   "My dog is cold today. I'm going to wrap him up so he can take a nap."
   While on the play yard a loud airplane has attracted children's attention overhead.
   "I'm an airplane flying to grandma's house."
   Teacher pretends to fly.

world-of-discovery people, but they do at times pick up play ideas from one another. Social graces may be absent, yet some beginning empathy for others may be apparent when one toddler communicates by patting or hugging a crying peer or handing over a toy. Poole (1999) describes the difficulties toddlers face in building peer friendships:

> It's hard work for toddlers to learn how to play with one another. At first, some may examine their playmates as if they were inanimate objects, such as a doll or a ball, pinching and poking without understanding that their actions can hurt. Toddlers also don't always have control over their strong emotions.
>
> It takes time to learn not to hug too hard or to say "Hello" rather than swipe at a friend's face. Even when toddlers begin to sense that such behavior is frowned upon, they may continue testing the limits. (p. 37)

Wittmer (2008) reminds teachers that it takes time for toddlers to become interested in peers, feel comfortable playing with them, and develop their growing ability to be a caring friend.

> Children's sense of *self* and other, which they bring to their interactions with peers, begins to develop in their first relationships with significant adults. A self that is full of confidence, capable of being intimate with others, and convinced that others are likely to be enjoyable and responsive (or not) emerges from these first relationships. Infants and toddlers develop their beginning sense of other as kind, trustworthy, helpful, and fun in the embrace and enfolding (figuratively and literally) of the mother, father, and other special adults. (p. 10)

By 15 to 18 months of age, many toddlers participate in joint physical activities and may more fully enjoy others' company. By age two, they often pair off with a peer and have favorite companions. Young toddlers' emotions may erupt when sharing classroom playthings, causing friendships to change quickly. It is then, at age two, that words can help children attract companions and repel others. Two-year-olds mimic increasingly and use words a friend uses.

Early childhood teachers are better able to identify accelerated, normal (average), and delayed speakers at about 18 months of age. What causes diversity is too complex to mention here, but some factors can be inferred, and others have been previously mentioned. Families' and caregivers' responses to children's nonverbal and verbal attempts to communicate toward the end of the first year and into the second year can be a determining factor. **naeyc**

Birckmayer, Kennedy, and Stonehouse (2010) urge caregivers to observe and discover each child's particular way of communicating, which may be crying, smiling, making noises, hand and body actions, or other behaviors that the child employs to convey thoughts and feelings. Then responsive caregiver feedback should occur so the toddler learns making sounds and/ or other overtures prompts the receiver (adult) to make sounds and/or actions back.

Language growth differences, in particular their vocabulary growth, can relate to a child's temperament. Temperament can affect interactions with peers and adults. A number of temperament traits become somewhat stable during toddlerhood and catch the teacher's eye. A child's activity level might range between highly active to relaxed. A child's typical behavior can appear cautious or withdrawn when faced with new activities or people. Teacher may notice moodiness, even temper, or a positive or negative attitude developing toward certain classroom activities. Persistence and sticking to a new task varies in children. When faced with a problem or hurdle some children may give up quickly while others do not. Individuality can enhance toddlers' learning opportunities or block them. They may also cause caregivers to limit or modify their own verbal interaction. A teacher's attitude or expectations can change. Well-trained early educators when recognizing child temperaments that are in some way affecting language growth and development act after gathering more information to confirm their observations. They try to discover if the behavior is new, only happens under certain circumstances, or is typical and somewhat stable behavior. In other words, they assess the situation and act accordingly using strategies and techniques that might facilitate the child's language growth in a positive way. Actions might include attempting to increase a child's social integration, social competence, play skills, or his group inclusion. Children's general well-being is observed and monitored by all staff involved. Children are not labeled, but studied. Teachers analyze their own attitudes and child

expectations always aware of how their verbal comments, teaching behaviors, and program planning might produce the best educational results for each child.

2-4 Introducing Toddlers to Books and Other Activities

Toddlers show an interest in simple, colorful books and pictures and enjoy adult closeness and attention. Pointing and naming can become an enjoyable game. Sturdy pages that are easily turned help the toddler. A scrapbook of favorite objects mounted on cardboard individualizes the experience. Clear contact paper and lamination will add life and protection.

Board books (usually stiff, coated, heavy cardboard) for toddlers allow exploratory play and may offer colorful, close-up photographs or illustrations of familiar, everyday objects. These books promote the child's naming of pictures and active participation at book-reading times.

Toddler books are plentiful, and school collections include both fiction and nonfiction. Experts and librarians recommend volumes that are colorful, simple, inviting, realistic, and contain opportunities that encourage child involvement. With durable, glossy, wipe-clean page coating and smaller-than-average picture-book size, board books allow small and sometimes sticky hands to explore without tearing sturdy covers or pages. Oversized and big books with giant illustrations can also be enjoyable.

Because a toddler may move on quickly to investigating other aspects of the environment, adults offering initial experiences with books need to remember that when interest has waned, it is time to respect the search for other adventures (Photo 2-11).

Other hints concerning the introduction of books, from Kupetz and Green (1997), are as follows:

- Do not expect to quiet a rambunctious toddler with a book.
- Pick a time when the child seems alert, curious, and interested.
- Establish a special reading time (although books can be read anytime).

Photo 2-11 Toddlers often name what they see in book illustrations.

Photo 2-12 Certain toys promote early scribbling behavior.

- Use your voice as a tool to create interest.
- Be responsive.
- React positively to all of the child's attempts in naming objects, turning pages, or attempting any form of verbalization (Photo 2-12).

Toddlers with past experiences with picture books may have certain expectations for adult-child book sharing. They may want to cuddle with a blanket, sit in adult laps, turn pages for themselves, point to and question book features, name objects, watch the adult's mouth during reading, and so on. Exhibiting flexibility and following the child's lead reinforces the child's social enjoyment of the book.

Educators should be cautioned about the practice of requiring a group of toddlers to sit and listen to a story together. The key words are group and require. Toddler group times are of short duration and planned for active child participation. As toddlers age, they maintain focus for longer periods. Educators of toddlers might try sharing a picture book with a few children. When they do so, they endeavor to keep the experience warm, comfortable, and intimate.

Jalongo (2004) suggests the following when reading to a small group:

- Choose developmentally appropriate titles with simple text, larger size, familiar objects, and with available child "join in" opportunities.
- Adjust your expectations of toddler behavior. Coach patiently and offer needed support as they settle down.
- Use a routine signal to begin story time and be aware the shared reading time (or looking time) may be some children's initial experience. Slow down and urge assisting adults to offer the comfort of a lap.
- Pace reading to maintain child focus.
- Alternate active movement and quiet times during group time by using singing, finger play, or physical movement, which is suggested by oral or textual material (p. 122).

What can toddlers begin to understand during the reading of picture books? Besides knowing that photographs and illustrations are between the covers of books, the toddler gathers ideas about book pleasure. As the child touches pictured objects, the child may grasp the idea that the objects depicted are representations of familiar objects. The toddler can notice that books are not handled as toys. According to Cohen (2013), research suggests reading aloud to toddlers may dramatically increase their receptive and expressive language abilities. These are pre-reading skills necessary for success when reading instruction begins.

Very young children's reading-like behaviors may surprise their teachers especially when they observe the independent activity of toddlers with their favorite books. Almost as soon as the older toddler becomes familiarized with particular books through repetitive readings, he begins to play with them in reading-like ways. Attracted by the familiar object with which she has such positive associations, the toddler picks up the book, opens it, and begins attempting to retrieve some of the language and its intonations. Almost unintelligible at first, this reading-like play rapidly becomes picture-stimulated, page-matched, and story-related.

Near two years of age, the toddler probably still names what is pictured but may understand stories. The toddler may grasp the idea that book characters and events are make-believe. If a particular book is reread to a child, the child can know that the particular stories in books do not change, and what is to be read is predictable. Sometimes the toddler finds that she can participate in the telling by singing, repeating character lines, and making physical motions to represent actions; for example, "knocking on the door" and saying "moo."

2-4a Selecting Toddler Books

Books for toddlers should be:

- repetitive and predictable.
- rhythmical.
- illustrated with simple, familiar, easy-to-identify colorful objects, animals, toys, and so on.
- fiction or nonfiction.
- filled with feel, touch, and smell opportunities.
- sturdy, with easy-to-turn pages.
- set with few words on each page.
- relatively short, with simple, concise story lines about common, everyday life and environmental experiences.
- full of common, everyday activities toddlers can imitate such as waving goodbye, tooth brushing, face washing, using a spoon, wiping

face with napkin, door knocking, stair climbing, or movement activities such as kissing, blowing, clapping, bouncing, stepping, jumping, stretching, and so on.

- simple and illustrate elementary concepts such as black and white, big and little, on and off, up and down, over and under, large and small, inside and outside, and so on.
- formatted with illustrations matched to the text on each page.

Bardige (2009) suggests selecting toddler books that include big, noisy things, such as garbage trucks, airplanes, farm and zoo animals, or small intriguing things such as birds, bugs, butterflies, baby animals, and balls. This type of book often offers specific content vocabulary.

Additional desirable features of toddler-appropriate books often include simple, uncomplicated storylines; colorful, well-spaced illustrations or photographs; opportunities for the toddler to point and name familiar objects; sensory features; predictive books (ones allowing the child to guess or predict successfully); and strong, short rhymes or repetitive rhythms. "Touch and feel" books are particularly enjoyed, as are sturdy, heavy board pages. Novelty books that make noise, pop-up books, and books with easy-to-use moving parts capture a toddler's attention. Now is the time to also share the strong rhyming rhythms of Mother Goose and introduce two classics: *Mary Had a Little Lamb* and *Pop Goes the Weasel*.

Adults sing with toddlers, do finger plays, act out simple stories like *The Three Bears* with older toddlers participating actively, or tell stories using a flannel board or magnetic board, and allow children to manipulate and place figures on the boards. This is an age when book-handling skills begin. This includes how to hold a book, where to look for illustrations, and how to open it. These skills can be modeled and discussed while adults point, ask questions, gesture, stress words, follow child interest or note lack of it, and enthusiastically enjoy the shared book experience.

2-4b Electronic Books

Books with electronic features provide another way to engage toddlers with stories and print. Each book differs, but many have colorful illustrations that move, flash, "talk," or make musical sounds and noises. Pressing an area, button, icon, or symbol activates prerecorded features. But the research of Zimmerman and Christakis (2007) alerts early childhood educators to possible ill effects of early media exposure, particularly children's media viewing before the age of three. Their study conclusions note that viewing of either violent or nonviolent entertainment television before age three was significantly associated with subsequent attention problems in school five years later. The viewing of any content type at ages four to five was not associated with attentional problems. Another research study by the same researchers (Christakis and Zimmerman, 2007) examined violent television viewing during preschool years and its associated increased risk of children's antisocial behavior during school-age years. Other researchers (Dworak et al., 2007) have concluded that a link exists between television and computer game exposure and children's sleep patterns, diminished verbal cognitive performance, and their learning and memory abilities. Dworak and associates' research was conducted with a small group of school-age children. More extensive research is needed to probe preschoolers' entertainment viewing and their educational game playing.

Most educators and parents agree that electronic books, games, and television programs do attract toddlers, but that interest usually wanes quickly unless the media is shared with a responsive adult. Educators understand how easily clever television commercials and television programs sometimes capture and engage toddlers. They advise families to limit or omit toddler viewing time. Toddlers may respond to catchy tunes, animation, and flashing colorful images with physical movement such as singing, dancing, and clapping. It looks like toddlers are learning, but the television program can't interact, build on a child's response, or expand interest with language-developing feedback. Overexposure to the medium actually crowds out and subtracts from time spent in more positive human contact and/or conversation in which language is really learned. Chapter 16 includes a discussion on a joint position statement developed by the National Association for the Education of Young Children and the Fred Rogers Center for Early Learning and Children's Media (2012). This publication offers current and well-respected recommendations for early childhood educators.

2-4c Scribbling

In most home environments, toddlers see others writing and want to try it themselves. Large, chunky crayons and nontoxic markers are easily manipulated by toddlers at about 18 months of age. They usually grasp them in their fist and use a scrubbing motion. They have some difficulty placing marks where they might wish, so it is best to use very large sheets of sturdy paper taped to a tabletop. Brown bags cut flat or untreated shelf paper work well. The act of scribbling can serve several useful purposes, including enhancing small muscle coordination, exercising cognitive abilities, promoting social interaction, and allowing emotional release. It can also be seen as a precursor to an interest in symbols and print. An important point in development is reached when the child moves from linear scribbles to enclosed shapes and at a later age begins realistic, representational drawing. Some Asian families may place a high emphasis on drawing activities for young children, and their children's work at school often reflects more comfort and experience with art materials and writing tools.

During toddlerhood, some children gain general knowledge of books and awareness of print. This is viewed as a natural process, which takes place in a literate home or early learning environment. Immersing toddlers in language activities facilitates their literacy development. It is possible to establish a positive early bonding between children and book-sharing times—a first step toward literacy. Some toddlers, who show no interest in books will, when exposed to books at a later time, find them as interesting as other children. Parents need to understand that a literary interest can be piqued throughout early childhood. The fact that a toddler may not be particularly enamored with books or book-sharing times at a particular stage is not a matter of concern. It may simply be a matter of the child's natural, individual activity level and her ability to sit and stay focused in an environment that holds an abundance of features to explore.

2-4d Musical Activities

Musical play with toddlers can help promote literacy skills. Activities can include:

- focused listening experiences.
- play that focuses on or highlights discrimination of loud and soft and fast and slow, rhythms, repeated patterns, tones, words, and so on.
- the use of repetitive beats, catchy melodies or words, clapping, tapping, rocking, galloping, marching, motions, and body actions.

- coordination of movement and music in some way.
- creative and imaginative opportunities.
- experiences with a variety of simple, safe musical instruments.
- the singing of age-appropriate songs.

Music activities often can be used to create an affectionate adult-child bond. Singhal (1999) describes toddlers participating in adult and child music activities:

> Toddlers are beings in motion, and music is the perfect vehicle for directing and freeing their movements. They feel and internalize the steady beat of adult motions. Contrary to popular belief, toddlers can also be excellent listeners. They are fascinated by sound, whether it's a bee buzzing or a clarinet melody. The different shapes, feel, and sounds of simple rhythm instruments also mesmerize toddlers. Being able to make a steady sound on his own on an instrument such as the drum is very empowering to a young child who wants to "do it myself!"
>
> Even though at this age children may not be willing to echo back chanted tonal and rhythm patterns, it is still important that they hear them. The patterns are being "recorded" in their minds for future reference.
>
> Singing, listening, and music-making are a completely natural and enjoyable part of a young child's being. (p. 22)

2-4e Toys

Certain types of toys have a strong connection to toddlers' emerging language development (Photo 2-12). Musical toys, dolls, and stuffed animals that make noises or talk, and alphabet toys, including magnetic alphabet letters, can be described as language-promoting toys. Noise-making toys or recordings, both audio and visual, capture the toddler's attention. Manipulative toys for toddlers are becoming increasingly available.

2-5 Freedom to Explore

Greenspan (1999) emphasizes how toddler problem solving develops and describes its relationship to "freedom to explore" (within supervised limits).

An ability to solve problems rests on the even more basic skill of seeing and deciphering patterns. It is the ability to understand patterns that lets a toddler know if she takes two steps here and two steps there that she'll be able to reach her favorite toy. She becomes a successful navigator not only because her muscles are coordinated, but also because her growing brain now enables her to understand patterns. Toddlers learn to recognize how one room leads to another, and where you are in relation to them. They can meaningfully explore the world long before they are able to express their wishes and thoughts in words.

2-5a The Comical Toddler— Exploring Humor

Adults may not realize that children begin honing their own comedic skills at impressively early ages. They point out that a child's reaction to physical stimuli, seen in activities such as tickling and bouncing, take a new form sometime after the first birthday by becoming visual or oral rather than tactile. Toddler silliness or "joking" behavior can be seen as rudimentary attempts at humor and can be appreciated as child-initiated attempts to get others' reactions to the ridiculous and unexpected. They may playfully mimic adult words or actions, wear a pot for a hat, make a funny face, or wholeheartedly enjoy participating in an "All Fall Down" activity.

2-5b Advice to Toddler Teachers

Bardige (2009) concludes that the quality of care, especially language-developing care, for toddler-to-three-year-olds in the United States needs improvement.

> At the critical age for language learning, public investments in children's education are lower than they will be at any time during childhood. Caregivers and teachers on the frontlines, who are doing their best to provide safe, loving, growth-promoting care, are not doing enough talking. (p. 219)

She concludes that with appropriate supports, caregivers and teachers will be able to maintain language-rich environments and provide care attuned to the needs of the individual child and the group as a whole. Under these conditions children will thrive, but more financial program support is necessary.

Brain Connection

Brain Growth Approach

Teaching involves the active engagement of the child's mind using purposeful teaching strategies based on principles derived from research and neuroscience. Teachers and caregivers are encouraged to consider the nature of the brain to make better decisions concerning instructional methods useful in reaching more learners. **DAP**

Teachers using a brain growth approach realize the brain is a mass of highly connected areas with one brain area affecting others. The brain is also a whole entity that is highly adaptable and designed to respond to environmental input.

Early childhood educators have made special efforts to plan and equip classrooms that provide language and literacy opportunities that are both functional and responsive to the developmental needs of children's bodies and minds. Carefully designed classrooms help teachers to fulfill job duties while promoting children's full potential.

Young children's brains are busy routing and filtering environmental input gained through their sensory organs. Input is sent to specific brain areas for processing. If the information gathered is deemed by the brain to be of sufficient importance, it is organized and indexed and stored. There is no single brain pathway, but rather different shared and unique pathways for different types of learning, such as emotional, social, spatial, vocabulary, and other brain areas. This statement should remind the reader of the work of Howard Gardner (1993), a well-known theorist and psychologist, whose work focused on multiple intelligences.

No discussion of brain activity can exclude the fact that there are different types of brain cells. A brain neuron is a basic structural and processing unit of the nervous system. It continuously fires, integrates, and generates information across gaps called *synapses* linking one cell to another and acts as a conduit for information. As a rule, the more connections one's cells make, the better (Jensen, 2008, p. 13). A two-year-old has twice the number of neurons as an adult.

Toddlers may seem cute and naïve when they refer to all males as daddy or when they attempt to bite a toy that resembles a banana. Their behavior illustrates toddler global (macro) thinking prior to their further experience when they notice details and exceptions that refine their understandings. The brain can be thought of as acting like a muscle. The more activity that takes place, the larger and more complex it can become. What a child experiences intellectually and physically changes what his/her brain looks like. The brain can wire and rewire depending on environment, life choices available, and also the individual choices that are made, such as choosing to learn to play a musical instrument or learning how to move the body to play a physical sport (Medina, 2008, p. 58).

2-5c Consulting with Families

Verbally responsive and playful people, and a "toddler-proof" home equipped with objects and toys the toddler can investigate, will help facilitate a toddler's emerging language skills. An adult sitting on the floor or on a low chair near a toddler at play can promote toddler communication and also help the adult see things from the child's vantage point.

Objects and toys need not be expensive and can be designed and created at home. Social contact outside the home is important also. Toddlers enjoy branching out from the home on excursions into nature and community with caring adults. Local libraries may offer toddler story hours, and play groups are increasingly popular and sponsored by a wide number of community groups. Exposing the toddler to supervised toddler play groups gives the child "peer teachers" and promotes social skills. Typically, toddlers play side-by-side rather than cooperatively, but beginning attempts at sharing and short give-and-take interactions take place.

Some toddlers may frequently ask for the names of things and can be insistent and impatient about demands. Words will be learned during real events with concrete (real) objects. Children continue to generate language when their early efforts are accepted and reinforced. Situations that involve positive emotions and those that involve multiple sensory experiences also evoke child language production.

Regularly involving toddlers in educative conversations with educational toys and simple books prompts language growth. Patience and interest—rather than heavy-handed attempts to teach—are best. Getting the most from everyday experiences is a real art that requires an instructive yet relaxed attitude and the ability to talk about what has captured the child's attention. A skilled adult who is with a toddler who is focused on the wrapping paper rather than the birthday present will add comments about the wrapping paper. Or at the zoo, in front of the bear's cage, if the child is staring at a nearby puddle, the adult will discuss the puddle. Providing words and ideas along the child's line of inquiry, and having fun while doing so, becomes second nature after a few attempts.

Skilled adults tend to modify their speech according to the child's ability. They speak clearly, slowly enunciate and slightly exaggerate intonation, and pause between utterances. They may end their sentences with the "focused-on" new word and emphasize it in pitch and stress. They

also add to sentence length and complexity, providing that which is just a little beyond the child's level. Parent talk that sensitively and effectively suggests and instructs primes the child's language growth. If the home language is not English, supporting children's development of that language by using it extensively around the home is a wise course of action for it serves as a foundation for the later learning of a second language (in this case, English). This is aided by a strong school-home partnership and the families' active role in their child's education (Figure 2-6).

Parents may need to become aware of the consequences that can result from home or center environments where toddlers experience chaos,

Figure 2-6 Checklist for working with non-English speaking families.

Do	Don't
Make sure parents know it is acceptable to stay with their toddlers for an adjustment period before leaving the toddler on his/her first day or week.	constantly push English word learning by turning most of your teaching interactions or handling of a toddler into an English lesson.
Encourage parents to tour the early childhood center and stay a few hours before enrollment. This allows the child and parent to feel more comfortable.	neglect the importance of promoting the family's use of home language and their feeling of pride in their culture.
Secure a volunteer or a staff member who speaks the toddler's home language. Hearing the home language bolsters the toddler's sense of security.	forget to invite parents to share cultural songs, poetry, and stories at school or record them for school use.
Create a welcoming display or bulletin board outside the classroom, which uses print and photos of non-English-speaking communities, neighborhoods and neighborhood activities. Print captions in multiple languages.	
Find family members or seek volunteers who can develop a key word vocabulary list in the home language of all attending children with words such as "mama," "hello," "help," "bathroom," "drink," "no more," "bottle," "water," "yes," "no," etc. for teacher use.	
Learn to be an expert at reading children's gestures, cues, body positions, state of well-being, or distress, etc.	
Stress key English words calmly and simply and use gestures often to accompany words or phrases. Simple teacher gestures if repeated this way become a visual clue to what is happening next.	
Repeat a nonverbal gesture in the child's home language, for example, pretend to drink while saying water. The toddler will eventually connect the word water with your pretend gesture.	
Invite parents to volunteer and use their native language at school. They become great teachers for teachers trying to learn a child's language.	

unpredictability, violence, and frightening experience as a daily reality. Honig (1999) describes these toddlers as quick to be startled, aroused, angry, defiant, fearful, or withdrawn. She describes the chemical activity in their brains as abnormal. Building intimate, warm, trusting relationships is the best way to teach a child's brain that it need not send the body messages to release high levels of stress hormones. Experts recommend that nurturing providers offer each child interpretable, orderly, soothing, and loving experiences daily to support optimal brain development.

Summary

2-1 Name four conventions of the English language that toddlers learn about speaking.

Toddlers are sorting the sounds they hear in spoken words around them. They attempt group and categorize spoken sounds and develop beginning understandings of, the phonology of their native language. An understanding of the rules of grammar is also happening with exposure to oral speech experiences and listening to others while observing their actions. Grammar rules form and reform as the child gets closer to reproducing mature speech patterns. Toddlers are learning about word order in sentences (syntax). Toddlers also learn the meanings of some words and nonverbal communications. Morphemes enter toddler speech. They are learning to notice regularities and the meanings of words and gestures (semantics). They gain new vocabulary. Pragmatics, the study of how language is used effectively in social contexts, begins to be understood by toddlers. This promotes the toddler's ability to express his needs, wants, ideas, and concerns successfully.

2-2 Describe how toddlers move from using first words to using sentences.

Toddler's first words relate to significant and important people, and objects in their daily lives. Parents and caregivers conversations with toddlers together with firsthand exploration using their sense organs provides depth and meaning to toddlers' new words. Toddlers are active in conversations, speaking and listening, sometimes correcting themselves when trying to get their message across to whomever will listen. Sentences are barely recognizable at first but gain more and more clarity as children age.

Functional action words used in social exchanges appear. Toddlers talk to themselves and their toys in one-word and then two-word (or more) sentences. Easy to pronounce words are added and gestures accompany words adding clarity. One word in a two word sentence is often a pivot word. Toddler sentences become condensed containing only important words or parts of words because of their limited vocabulary and ability to express them (telegraphic and prosodic speech). Understanding the child's meaning often depends on context and the child's voice intonation. Longer sentences appear when children add more verbs, and prepositions, pronouns, articles, and conjunctions.

2-3 Identify three common characteristics of toddler language.

- Toddlers use telegraphic and prosodic speech at times and sentences may be devoid of function words.
- Two to five word sentences are typical.
- Verbs, prepositions, plurals, pronouns, articles, and conjunctions begin to appear in speech.
- Negatives are used.
- Words are often run together and mispronounced alphabet letter sounds are commonplace.
- Gestures accompany many words.
- Toddlers initiate conversations with others and use verbalization to gain adult attention.
- Egocentric speech is frequent and commonplace.
- Toddlers understand much more than they can express.

2-4 State two criteria for selecting books and describe four recommended techniques for reading books to toddlers.

Simple and colorful illustrations or photographs of familiar, everyday objects and situations are appropriate in toddler books. Durable coatings on board books extend use and paperweight facilitates the toddler's handling and page turning. Both fiction and nonfiction books are to be considered. Books containing sensory items to explore were recommended and also books with content that allowed toddlers to interact in some way. Recommended toddler teacher presentation techniques include:

- Select a reading time when a child is curious.
- Don't attempt to use books as a focusing mechanism or a calming down tool during high activity periods.
- Use teacher enthusiasm to entice child interest.
- React by providing recognition for children's positive behaviors such as page turning, naming, or pointing.
- Expect occasional or frequent loss of toddler focus during reading times, for interest may wane quickly and switch to something else.
- Set a special reading time and location for book readings.

2-5 Identify three suggestions for toddler teachers and parents concerning toddlers' opportunities to explore and experience their environment.

- Toddler problem solving is encouraged when toddlers are able to explore and experience their environment with adult supervision.
- Toddlers' growing brains allow them to observe and understand patterns and relationships before they are able to express or describe them.
- Social interactions, playfulness, experiencing instances of cause-and-effect, and investigating objects and people expand children's mental capabilities and verbal skills.
- A language-rich environment with interesting objects coupled with verbally responsive adults promotes speech growth and development.
- Skilled adults modify their comments to a toddler's ability and they speak clearly. An adult may focus upon and emphasize new words that are important aspects of any situation at hand that is interesting to the child.
- Toddlers are able to thrive in and out of the classroom, in nature, and in the community when adults arrange supervised excursions and play groups.

Additional Resources

Readings

Barbro, J. (2013). *Foundations of Responsive Caregiving: Infants, Toddlers, and Twos.* St. Paul, MD: Redleaf Press.

Falasco, D. (2010). *Teaching Twos and Threes: A Comprehensive Curriculum.* St. Paul, MN: Redleaf Press.

Pan, B. A., Rowe, M. L., Singer, J., & Snow, C. E. (2005). Maternal correlates of toddler vocabulary production in low income families. *Child Development.*76 (4), 765–782.

Toddler Books

Cowley, J. (1999) *Mrs. Wishy-Washy.* East Rutherford, NJ: Philomel Books. (Board book.)

Davenport, Z. (1995). *Toys.* New York: Ticknor & Fields. (Common toys and objects.)

Elya, S. M. (2006). *Beebe Goes Shopping.* New York: Harcourt.

Fleming, D. (2006). *The Cow Who Clucked.* New York: Henry Holt. (Sounds and silliness that delight.)

Kindersley, D. (2003). *Are Lemons Blue?* New York: Author. (Playful.)

Low, W. (2009). *Machines Go to Work.* New York; Henry Holt.

Manushkin, F. (2009). *The Tushy Book.* New York: Macmillan.

Oxenbury, H. (1988). *Tickle, Tickle.* New York: Macmillan.

Priddy, R. (2002). *My Big Animal Book.* New York: St. Martin's Press.

Wattenberg, J. (2007). *Mrs. Mustard's Baby Faces.* San Francisco: Chronicle Books.

Whitford, R. (2005). *Little Yoga: A Toddler's First Book of Yoga.* New York: Holt, Henry Books for Young Readers. (Expect to try yoga positions with toddlers.)

Helpful Website

National Parent Information Network

http://npin.org

Provides related websites for parents and teachers.

3 Preschool Years

Objectives

After reading this chapter, you should be able to:

3-1 Identify three characteristics of younger preschoolers' speech and communication.

3-2 Describe three pieces of recommended advice to a family concerned about a preschooler's speaking abilities.

3-3 Describe conversational skills necessary for an older preschooler to maintain a true conversation.

3-4 Discuss older preschoolers' manipulation and playful use of words.

3-5 List reasons for planning sensory, motor skill activities; cognitive, building activities; or social, emotional growth activities, to promote language development.

naeyc NAEYC Program Standards

C03 Teaching staff support children as they practice skills and build friendships.

1F01 Teaching staff actively teach children social, communication, and emotional regulation skills.

1F02 Teaching staff help children use language to communicate needs.

2A10 The curriculum guides teachers to incorporate content, concepts, and activities that foster language and literacy.

DAP Developmentally Appropriate Practice (DAP)

1A2 Teachers help children learn how to establish positive, constructive relationships with others.

2B3 Teachers help children acquire new skills and understandings using a range of strategies.

2B6 Teachers frequently engage children in planning or reflecting on their experiences, discussing past experiences, and working to represent them.

2B7 Teachers promote children collaborating to work through ideas and solutions.

2D2 Teachers use verbal encouragement and acknowledge effort with specific comments.

3G2 Teachers make sure that children have plenty of opportunities to use large muscles.

3G4 Teachers provide for fine motor skill development.

COMMON CORE Common Core State Standards for English Language Arts and Literacy

L.CCR 5 Demonstrate understanding of figurative language, word relationships, and nuances in meaning.

SL.CCR 4 Present information, findings, and supporting evidence such that listeners can follow the line of reasoning and the organization, development, and style that are appropriate to task, purpose, and audience.

R.CCR 7 Integrate and evaluate content presented in diverse media and format, including visually and quantitatively, as well as in words.

On And On And On . . .

Wilford is four and eager to speak in groups. He rambles, goes on and on, and both bores and loses his audience. Renee, his teacher, waits, patiently listening, but occasionally interrupts him to say, "Thank you, Wilford, for sharing with us." Sometimes this stops him, but often it does not.

Questions to Ponder

1. Is this "stream of consciousness" talking typical of four-year-olds? Is this a behavior found in some adults?
2. What teacher strategies might help Renee?
3. Describe three program activities that might help Wilford.

The preschool child's speech reflects sensory, physical, and social experiences, as well as thinking ability. Teachers accept temporary limitations, knowing that almost all children will reach adult language levels. During the preschool years, children move rapidly through successive phases of language learning. By the time youngsters reach their fifth year, the most challenging hurdles of language learning have been overcome.

An understanding of typical preschool speech characteristics can help the teacher interact skillfully and provide appropriate learning opportunities and activities, as does classroom experience and child study. This chapter pinpoints language use during preschool years. Although speech abilities are emphasized, growth and change in other areas, as they relate to speech, are also covered. In addition to school, the child's home environment and playing with other children are major factors influencing language development. Finding friends in his age group is an important benefit of attending an early childhood center. In a place where there are fascinating things to explore and talk about, language abilities blossom (Photo 3-1).

It is almost impossible to find a child who has all of the speech characteristics of a given age group, but most children possess some age-typical characteristics. There is a wide range within normal age-level behavior, and each child's individuality is an important consideration. For simplicity's sake, the preschool period is divided into two age groups: young, or early,

Photo 3-1 Children often share their ideas concerning how or what they might play.

© 2015 Cengage Learning®

preschoolers (two- and three-year-olds) and older preschoolers (four- and five-year-olds).

3-1 Young Preschoolers

Preschoolers communicate needs, desires, and feelings through speech and action. Close observation of a child's nonverbal communication can help uncover true meanings. Raising an arm, fiercely clutching playthings, or lying spread-eagle over as many blocks as possible may express more than the child is able to put into words. Stroking a friend's arm, handing a toy to another child who has not asked for it but looks at it longingly, and following the teacher around the room are behaviors that carry other meanings. One can expect continued fast growth and changing language abilities, and children's understanding of adult statements is surprising. They may acquire six to 10 new words a day. Figure 3-1 displays children's stunning vocabulary growth from ages one to seven.

Figure 3-1 Vocabulary growth.

Vocabulary Growth

10–14 months	first word	First words are usually nouns instead of verbs.
12–18 months	two words a week; close to 50 by 18 months	Child looks at something (or someone), points, and then says one or two words. Mispronunciations are common.
18–24 months	200 words	Some toddlers constantly ask "What dat?" or just "Dat?" They want objects named.
2–3 years	500 words	Questions, questions, questions! Mispronunciations still happen, and consonants may be substituted for one another in some words.
3–4 years	800 words	Preschoolers start to use contractions ("won't," "can't") as well as prepositions ("in," "on") and time expressions ("morning," "afternoon"). They may also make up words.
4–5 years	1,500 or more words	Children speak with greater clarity, can construct five- and six-word sentences, and make up stories.
5–7 years	11,000 words	Children retell and discuss stories. They have many words at hand and will know more than 50,000 as adults.

Squeals, grunts, and screams are often part of play. Imitating animals, sirens, and environmental noise is common. The child points and pulls to help others understand meanings. Younger preschoolers tend to act as though others can read their thoughts because, in the past, adults anticipated what was needed. A few children may have what seems to be a limited vocabulary at school until they feel at home there.

A difference between the child's **receptive** (or **comprehension**) **vocabulary** and his **expressive** (or **productive**) **vocabulary** is apparent, with the productive vocabulary lagging behind the receptive vocabulary. The receptive vocabulary requires that the child hears a word and anticipates or reacts appropriately; the production of a word means the child speaks the word at an appropriate time and place.

Children begin to acquire the more complex forms of grammar during this time period, including past tenses, embedded clauses, and passive constructions. Creative mistakes happen, such as "he breakeded my bike," which indicates that the child is noticing consistent patterns and applying them to the language system as he understands it.

The words used most often are nouns and short possessives: *my, mine, Rick's*. Speech focuses on present events, things are observed in newscaster style, and "no" is used liberally.

As preschoolers progress in the ability to hold brief conversations, they must keep conversational topics in mind and connect their thoughts with those of others. This is difficult for two-year-olds, and true conversational exchange with playmates is brief, if it exists at all. Although their speech is filled with pauses and repetitions in which they attempt to correct themselves, early preschoolers are adept at conversational turn taking. Talking over the speech of another speaker at this age occurs only about five percent of the time.

Speech may be loud and high-pitched when the child is excited, or it may be barely audible and muffed when the child is embarrassed, sad, or shy. Speech of two- and three-year-olds tends to be uneven in rhythm, with comments issued in spurts rather than in an even flow like the speech of older children (Photo 3-2). There seems to be an important step forward in the complexity of content in children's speech at age two. They may begin making comments about cause and effect and sometimes use conjunctions, such as *'cause, 'ah,* and *'um,* between statements. Young preschoolers' talk is self-focused and mostly concerned with their intentions and feelings. Why they wanted or did not want to do certain things, or what they wanted other people to do. Statements such as "I'm painting" or "I'm not climbing!" are commonplace.

---

receptive (comprehension) vocabulary — the comprehension vocabulary used by a person in listening (and silent reading).

expressive (productive) vocabulary — the vocabulary a person uses in speaking and writing.

Much of the time very young preschoolers' play focuses on recreating the work of the home and family—cooking, eating, sleeping, washing, ironing, infant care, and imitations of family events and pets (Photo 3-3). Play of slightly older preschoolers is more interactive. The child continues self-play and also explores other children, adults, environments, and actions. Eventually, most preschoolers understand that it is usually worth their while to share toys and take turns because when other playmates are around it is more fun. Two-year-olds may believe, as one preschooler remarked to his teacher, that "share means you give it away." When children begin exploring these other play options, "what's happening" in play becomes a speech subject, along with brief verbal reactions to what others are saying and doing.

Photo 3-2 Speech can be limited when children are very interested.

A desire to organize and make sense of their experiences is often apparent in young preschoolers. Colors, counting, and new categories of thought emerge in their speech. There is a tendency for them to live out the action words they speak or hear in the speech of others. An adult who says "We won't run" may motivate a child to run; in contrast, an adult who says "Walk" might be more successful in having the child walk. This is why experienced teachers tell children what they want children to do rather than what they do not want them to do.

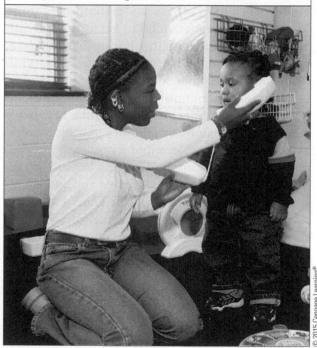

Photo 3-3 Teachers encourage the verbalizations of preschoolers.

3-1a The Subdued Two-Year-Old

In any given group of young children, a few may appear subdued and quiet, having a tendency toward what many might call shyness. These children may possess a natural inclination that tends to inhibit spontaneous speech. Strong emotions can cause muscle tension, including tension in the larynx. Some adults asked to speak in front of a group experience this phenomenon. It can also affect speech volume. Most preschool teachers have worked with children whose speech was difficult to hear. Often, these children seem restrained when faced with unfamiliar situations. As older preschoolers, they may become more outgoing and talkative or may continue to be less talkative and somewhat subdued when compared with their more boisterous counterparts. Teachers respect these children's natural inclinations and tendencies, but try to build the children's trust and their play opportunities with others.

3-1b Verb Forms

In English, most verbs (regular forms) use *-ed* to indicate past tense. Unfortunately, many frequently used verbs have irregular past-tense forms, such as *came, fell, hit, saw, took,* and *gave.* Because the child begins using often-heard words, early speech contains correct verb forms. With additional exposure to language, children realize that past events are described with *-ed* verb endings. At that point, children tack the *-ed* on regular verbs as well as on irregular verbs, creating words such as *broked, dranked,* and other charming past-tense forms. This beautiful logic often brings inner smiles to the adult listeners. Verbs ending with *-ing* are used more than before. Even auxiliary verbs are scattered through speech—"Me have," "Daddy did it." Words such as *wanna, gonna,* and *hafta* seem to be learned as one word, and stick in children's vocabulary, to be used over and over.

A term for children's speech behavior that indicates they have formed a new internal rule about language and are using it is **regularization**. As children filter what they hear, creating their own rule systems, they begin to apply the new rules. An expected sequence in forming rules for past-tense verb usage follows.

- Uses irregular tense endings correctly (e.g., *ran, came, drank*).
- Forms an internal rule when discovering that *-ed* expresses past events (e.g., *danced, called, played*).
- Over-regularizes; for example, adds *-ed* to all regular and irregular verbs that were formerly spoken correctly (e.g., *camed, dided, wented, goed*).
- Learns that both regular and irregular verbs express past tense, and uses both.

In using plural noun forms, the following sequence is common.

- Remembers and uses singular forms of nouns correctly (e.g., *ball, dog, mouse, bird*).
- Uses irregular noun plurals correctly (e.g., *men, feet, mice*).

- Forms an internal rule that plurals have "s" or "z" ending sounds.
- Applies rule to all nouns (e.g., *balls, mens, dogs, feets, birds, mices,* or *ballsez, dogsez, feetsez*).
- Achieves flexible internal rules for plurals, memorizes irregular plural forms, and uses plurals correctly.

3-1c Key-Word Sentences and Questioning

The two-year-old omits many words in sentences, as does the toddler. The remaining words are shortened versions of adult sentences in which only the essentials are present. These words are key words and convey the essence of the message. Teachers attempt to relate questionable child utterances to concurrent child activity to grasp a child's meaning. Sentences at this stage are about four words long. Some pronouns and adjectives, such as *pretty* or *big*, are used. Very few, if any, prepositions (*by, on, with*) or articles (*a, an, the*) are spoken. Some words are run together and are spoken as single units, such as "whadat?" or "eatem," as are the verb forms mentioned earlier. The order of words (syntax) may seem jumbled at times, as in "outside going ball," but basic grammar rules are observed in most cases.

Pronouns are often used incorrectly and are confused, as in "Me finish milk," and "him Mark's." Concepts of male and female, living things, and objects may be only partly understood, as shown in the example of the three-year-old who says of a special toy she cannot find, "Maybe it is hiding!" This probably indicates she hasn't yet learned that hiding can be done only by an animate object.

Questions (where, what, why, who) begin to appear in the speech of the young preschooler. During the toddler period, rising voice inflection and simple declarative utterances such as "Dolly drink?" are typical. At this stage, questions focus on location, objects, and people. Occasionally, their questions display a special interest in causation (why), process (how), and time (when). This reflects more mature thinking that probes purposes and intentions in others. Encouraging children's questions is an important job skill and allows early childhood teachers to at times to answer 'I don't know." A teacher might say, "That's

---

regularization — a child's speech behavior that indicates the formation and internalization of a language rule (regularity).

Figure 3-2 Question development.

Age	
age 2	raises voice pitch at sentence ending: "Me go?" "All gone?"
	uses short "what" and "where" questions: "Whas dat?" "Where kitty?"
age 3	asks yes-no questions
	begins to use "why" questions
	begins to use auxiliary verbs in questions: "Can I have gum?" "Will you get it?"
	begins to use "how" questions: "How you do that?"
age 4	adds tag endings: "Those are mine, okay?" "You like it, huh?" "That's good, isn't it?"
	inverts auxiliary verbs in questions: "Why are you sad?" "Why aren't we staying with gramma?"
	begins to use complex and two-part questions and statements: "I will tell him how to do it if you like."
	"What can I do when he won't come?" "I don't know what to do." "Why does it fall down when the door slams?"

a good question," or if speaking with a younger preschooler, they can follow the child's question with an open ended question of their own such as "what happened?" This can lead to seeking the answer together. Teachers often call attention and point to features purposefully letting children in on their thoughts and observations. Sometimes this practice prompts children's questions. Nurturing children's questions can increase their sense of wonder and curiosity leading to further vocabulary development and support for a further search for answers or solutions. Figure 3-2 shows one child's question development. Questions are frequent, and the child sometimes asks for an object's function or the causes of certain events. It is as if the child sees that things exist for a purpose that in some way relates to him. The answers adults provide stimulate the child's desire to know more. Questions about words and word meanings appear, such as "Why is his name Ang?" Vocabularies of the young preschooler range from 250 to more than 1,000 words (Figure 3-3). An average of 50 new words enters the child's vocabulary each month.

3-1d Categories in Children's Thinking

Children organize a tremendous amount of sensory data and information gained though life experiences by forming mental categories. Studies point out that young children can be quite sophisticated in how they group objects and think about their groupings. Young preschoolers' categories differ from those of older children. The

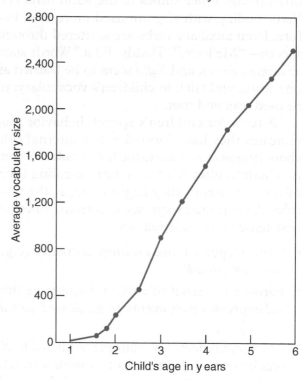

Figure 3-3 Growth of vocabulary.

young preschooler tends to focus on superficial properties such as the "look" of something and where it is found. A younger child may focus on the teacher's fuzzy sweater by wanting to touch and rub it and saying "soft." An older preschooler may talk about its number of buttons, or patterns, or its similarity to his own sweater or other sweaters he has seen. Preschoolers often put items together in terms of their visual similarities rather than grouping items according to more fundamental likenesses.

Figure 3-4 Common overextensions used in a child's first three years.

First Word	Word Was Used to Identify an Object, Person or Event	Later Word Was Applied to
dada	daddy	store clerk, doctor, mailman, football player, teenager.
moo	moon	cookie, melon, letter O, clock, pizza pan, button.
ah	soft	fuzzy sweater, dog's fur, flower petal, plush doll.
em	worm	pasta, caterpillar, licorice ropes, string, rice.
wh	sound of train	vacuum cleaner, mixer, wind, fast vehicles. motor noise.
ba	ball	oranges, meatballs, yarn, coconut, overhead light, lollypop, bubbles.

Younger preschoolers commonly call all four-footed furry animals "dog," and all large animals "horse." This reflects **overextension**, in which the child has overextended and made a logical conclusion because these animals have many of the same features, can be about the same size, and therefore fit the existing word. This phenomenon is seen in the examples given in Figure 3-4.

Concept development, defined in Chapter 2 as the recognition of one or more distinguishing features or characteristics, proceeds by leaps and bounds during preschool years and is essential to meaningful communication. The details, exceptions, and discrepancies are often discussed in four-year-olds' conversations. The younger preschooler can be described as a "looker and doer" who engages in limited discussion of the features of situations. The excitement of exploration and discovery, particularly of something new and novel, is readily apparent in preschool classrooms. Children typically crowd around to see, touch, experience, and make comments about objects and events. Teachers notice the all-consuming focusing and the long periods of watching or touching, usually followed by verbalizing and questioning an event or experience.

As they age, young children can find that learning not only brings them pleasure, but also perhaps mastery and satisfaction. Medina (2008) suggests this breeds the confidence it takes to take intellectual risks. A young preschooler who learns to button his sweater, tie his shoe, ride a bike, or count to five, usually wants to share his accomplishment with anyone who will listen and will repeat the physical actions over and over just to prove he can do them.

3-1e Running Commentaries and Repetition

As children play, their actions are sometimes accompanied by a running self-commentary or "stream of consciousness" talking concerning what they are doing or what is happening (Figure 3-5). It can be described as a kind of verbal thought process, like mentally talking to oneself such as "Now, where did I put that key?" It seems to increase in complex play situations as the child problem solves and talks it through.

Researchers suggest multiple reasons for preschoolers' private speech. These include the following: (1) talking to themselves is a way of giving themselves directions for their intended actions, (2) they need a sensorimotor activity as a reinforcer or "crutch" because their cognitive schemes are not yet well developed, and (3) it is more efficient for them to talk their ideas through in words rather than silently.

Self-talk may help children sequence actions, control their own behavior, use more flexible modes of thinking, and manipulate the goals they are trying to achieve in their play. Talking to self and talking to another can occur alternately. Toys, animals, and treasured items still receive a few words. Statements directed to others do not usually need answers. Private speech rarely considers another's point of view. A conversation between young preschoolers may sound like two children

---

overextension — in the early acquisition of words and their meanings, the application of a word to include other objects that share common features, such as "water" being used to describe any liquid.

Figure 3-5 Conversation during play activity.

Situation: Four- and five-year-old girls playing with water

	Commentary	Characteristic
Debbie:	"Two of those make one of these." (playing with measuring cups)	Talking to self.
Debbie:	"Two cups or three cups . . . whoops it went over."	Talks about what happened.
Tifine:	"Stop it or else I'll beat you up." (said to Debbie)	Does not respond to another's speech.
Debbie:	"This is heavy." (holding the 2-cup measuring container full of water)	Describes perception.
Christine:	"Is it hot?" (Christine just dropped in)	
Debbie:	"Feel it and see." "It's not hot." (feeling the water)	Hears another; answers appropriately. Child talking to self.
Debbie:	"I'm finished now. Oh this is awfully heavy—I'm going to pour it into the bottle."	Talking about what she perceives and what she is doing.

talking together about different subjects. Neither child is really listening or reacting to what the other says. When a very young preschooler does wish to talk directly to another child, it is sometimes done through an adult. A child may say, "I want truck," to an adult, even if the child playing with the truck is standing close by.

Other researchers who have examined self-talk suggest a number of possible developmental benefits. These include:

• practicing newly recognized language forms (Photo 3-4).

• obtaining pleasure through play with word sounds.

• exploring vocal capacities.

• reliving particular significant events.

• creating dialogue in which the child voices all participants' parts, perhaps helping the child later fit into social settings.

• experimenting with fantasy, thereby accommodating the creative urge.

• attending objectively to language.

• facilitating motor behavior in a task or project.

Photo 3-4 Trying to put the peg into the hole, Valerie utters, "Goes in."

Whatever its benefits, self-talk is natural, common behavior. By the age of five, the child's self-talk is observed infrequently. As children approach the age of three, both dialogue and monologue are apparent. Observers of play conversations find it difficult to determine just how much of each is present.

Teachers who conduct group times with younger preschoolers are familiar with children who ramble on and on; the teachers deal with this behavior by using a variety of techniques. Teachers try to encourage "my turn, your turn" behaviors. Kitchen timers, a ping-pong paddle held by one speaker and then passed to another, or a turned-on flashlight used to signal a child that his speaking turn is over are strategies teachers have devised. Teachers also try to draw focus back to the subject at hand by saying, "Amy, yes, dogs do use their tongues when they drink. It is Jeremy's turn to tell us about his dog now."

Repetition in speech is common. Sometimes it happens randomly at play, and at other times it is done with a special purpose. A young child may repeat almost everything said to him. Most young preschoolers repeat words or parts of sentences regularly. Children's growing language skills allow them to create repetitions that rhyme, as in "oogie, woogie, poogie bear," which greatly please them. They quickly imitate words that they like; sometimes, excitement is the cause. Rhyming words or rhyming syllables may promote enjoyable mimicking and younger preschoolers are particularly fascinated and attracted to words that rhyme. Repetition of rhyming words seems to help children remember things such as "Get up at eight and you won't be late." Free associations (voiced juggling of sounds and words) occur at play and at rest and may sound like babbling. Many times, it seems as though, having learned a word, the child must savor it or practice it, over and over (Photo 3-5).

3-1f Lack of Clarity

About one in every four words uttered by the young preschooler is not readily understandable. This lack of clarity is partially caused by an inability to control the mouth, tongue, and breathing and an inability to hear subtle differences and distinctions in speech. Typically, articulation of all English speech sounds, especially some **consonant** blends, is not accomplished until age seven or eight. Young preschoolers are only 40 to 80 percent correct in their articulation of words. This lack of intelligibility can be partly attributed to the complexity of the task of mastering the sounds. Although children may be right on target in development, their speech may still be difficult to understand.

Photo 3-5 Elsa Beth calls this "bussing" her teeth.

© 2015 Cengage Learning®

The young preschooler may have difficulty with the rate of speech, phrasing, inflection, intensity, syntax, and voice stress. Faulty articulation and defective sound making can also contribute to the problem. The child who attempts to form the longest utterances is the one who is hardest to understand. The child who omits sounds is less clear than the one who distorts them. As a rule, expect omissions, substitutions, and distortions in the speech of two- and three-year olds, for they will be plentiful.

By three years of age, children's pronunciation patterns are not yet fully like those of adults, but the basic features of the adult phonological system are present. Most children can produce all of the **vowel** sounds and nearly all of the consonant sounds in at least a few words, but their productions are not 100 percent accurate.

Young children typically omit sounds at the ends of words, saying, for example, *ba* for "ball." Middle consonants in longer words are also passed over lightly—*ikeem* for "ice cream" or *telfone* for "telephone." Even beginning sounds may be omitted, as in *ellow* for "yellow."

Substitutions of letter sounds are also common, for example, *aminal* and *pasghetti*. Until the new sound is mastered, one consonant may even

---

consonant — (1) a speech sound made by partial or complete closure of the vocal tract, which obstructs air flow; (2) an alphabet letter used in representing any of these sounds.

vowel — (1) a voiced speech sound made without stoppage or friction of air flow as it passes through the vocal tract; (2) an alphabet letter used in representing any of these sounds.

▶❚❚ TeachSource Video 3-1

Preschool: Communication Development through Language and Literacy Activities

The video focuses on preschoolers' dramatic play and role playing as well as songs, stories, and prewriting opportunities that are language and literacy-building.

1. What dramatic play scenarios might be commonly initiated by a full classroom of preschoolers living in a rural farm community? And how might their teachers plan to accommodate it? How about a classroom full of inner-city urban preschoolers?

2. In what way might early childhood educators connect alphabet letter recognition or print awareness opportunities with preschoolers' dramatic play?

take the place of another; *wabbit*, *wun*, and *wain* are common examples. Children who cannot yet produce all of the speech sounds accurately can generally hear the differences such as the difference between *w* and *r*, or *t* and *th*, when they are pronounced by others.

Short play sequences that involve acting or imitating the behavior of family begin at home and school. Speech usually accompanies the reenactments. Although young children at this age play side-by-side, most of this dramatic play starts as solitary activity. Common play themes include talking on the phone, caring for a baby, or cooking. Dolls, toys, and dress-up clothes are usually part of the action and may serve to initiate this type of play. Observers of two- and three-year-olds in classrooms find it hard to determine whether children are engaged in joint planning

of play or are simply playing in the same area with the same kinds of playthings. Preschools purposely purchase multiple dolls so that many children can feed and rock "their babies" when they see others doing it.

3-2 Advice for Families and Early Childhood Educators **DAP**

Families sometimes fret about a child who stops, stammers, or stutters when speaking. Calling attention to this speech and making demands on the child cause tension, making the situation worse. All children hesitate, repeat, stop, and start in speaking—it is typical behavior. Searching for the right word takes time, and thoughts may come faster than words. Adults need to relax and wait. Speech is a complex process of sending and receiving. Maintaining patience and optimism and assuming a casual "I'm listening" stance is the best course of action for the adult. Many schools routinely send home informational material to alert families to age-level speech characteristics and the need to check child's hearing frequently due to colds and upper respiratory infections.

Teachers frequently encounter child statements that are seemingly illogical and they suspect, if they acknowledge them, that the child will soon provide more information. Child logic is there, but teachers know that they are not privy to inner thought processes or children's past experiences. With more information, what at first appeared illogical turns out to have beautiful logic.

Frequently, a listening teacher will feel on the edge of understanding what a child is trying to say. This happens with both younger and older preschoolers struggling at times to put into words what they are thinking (Photo 3-6). Acceptance and interest are appropriate.

Attentive interaction with positive feedback is recommended for adults who live or work with two- and three-year-olds. Reacting to the intent of the child's message is more helpful than concentrating on correctness. In other words, focus on what is said rather than the way it is said. A lot of guessing is still necessary to determine what the child is trying to say. The adult's model of speech will override temporary errors as the child hears more and more of it.

Photo 3-6 "Me eatem!"

© 2015 Cengage Learning®

By simply naming objects, adults can encourage children to notice how different items are similar and can help children gain new information about the world. Helping children see the details and relationships in what they encounter is useful if done in a matter of fact rather than a pressured way or an "I'm trying to teach you something" manner. Connecting past events to present events may aid their understanding.

3-2a Books for Younger Preschoolers

Many picture books are available for younger preschoolers. Experts suggest books for this age group that have:

- themes, objects, animals, or people that are familiar and within their range of life experience.
- clarity of content and story line.
- clear, simple illustrations or photographs with backgrounds that do not distract from the intended focus.
- themes concerning everyday tasks and basic human needs.

Most two- and three-year-olds enjoy actively participating in story reading, but they can be very good listeners as well. Participation can include pointing, making noise, repeating dialogue, or performing imitative body actions. Books that are repetitive and predictable offer the enjoyment of anticipating what will come next. For children who are used to being read to at bedtime,

the calming effect of listening to the human voice becomes very apparent during story reading when heads nod or children act sleepy. Chapter 8 covers the topic of introducing preschool children to literature.

3-3 Older Preschoolers

As younger preschoolers get older, adults can expect the following:

- longer sentences with more words per sentence
- more specificity
- more "ing" endings on verbs
- increased correctness in the forms of the verb "to be"
- use of more auxiliary verbs
- more facility with passive-voice verbs, including "did" and "been"
- changes in negative sentences, from "No want" to "I don't want"
- changes in question forms, from "Car go?" to "Where did the car go?"
- changes in mental categories
- additional clarifications in articulation of speech sounds

By the time they are between four and five years of age, most preschoolers' speech is similar to adult use; their sentences are longer, with almost all words present rather than only key words (Photo 3-7).

Preschoolers' play is active and vocal, and they copy each other's words and manner of speaking. A word such as "monster," or more colorful words, may swiftly become of interest and spread rapidly from child to child. Remember the joy that both younger and older children exhibited with the phrases: "zip-a-dee-doo-dah," "bibbidi-bobbidi-boo," "scoobidoobi-do," "blast off," "fuzzy-wuzzy," and "ooey-gooey"? Every generation of preschoolers seems to have their own favorite sayings, and new ones are constantly appearing.

The older preschooler's social speech and conversations are heard and interpreted to a greater degree by others of the child's age. The child learns and practices the complexities of social conversation, including (1) gaining another's attention by making eye contact, touching, or using words or catch-phrases like "Know what?"; (2) pausing and listening; (3) correcting himself; (4) maintaining attention and word flow by not pausing, so as not to let another speaker jump in; (5) taking turns in conversing by developing patience and trying to listen while still holding in mind what he wants to say. Being more social

now, four- and five-year-olds' self-talk has almost completely disappeared. He now plans, monitors ideas, and evaluates silently, but he has yet to stop talking about his accomplishments and discoveries and still displays a "look at me" need.

3-3a Friendships and Group Play

The young preschooler may develop a new friend or find another he prefers to play near or with. At ages two and three, friendships are usually temporary, changing from day to day. Friendships of older preschoolers are more stable and lasting. By ages four and five, there seems to be a desire to remain compatible and work out differences, therefore creatively maintaining a type of play acceptable to both. Negotiation, clarification, and open-mindedness flourish during play. A friend's needs and requests are handled with sensitivity, and flexibility characterizes conversations. Needless to say, spats, "blowups," and the crushed feelings accompanying rejection sometimes occur. Verbal interaction between children adds a tremendous amount of verbal input and also promotes output.

Joint planning of play activities and active make-believe and role-playing take on new depth in older preschoolers. Most four- and five-year-olds' main concern seems to be interacting with age-mates. Twosomes and groups of play companions are typical in older preschoolers' classrooms and play yards (Photo 3-8). As speech blossoms, friendships blossom and disintegrate (Photo 3-9). Speech is used to discourage and disallow entrance to play groups when running from newcomers is impossible. Speech is found to be effective in hurting feelings, as in statements such as "I don't like you" or "No girls." Children find that verbal inventiveness may help them join play or initiate play.

In group play, pretending is paramount. Make-believe play appears to be at its zenith. Many children grow in the ability to (1) verbally suggest

Photo 3-7 Rene is explaining why she selected a certain puzzle piece.

Photo 3-8 Twosomes may become stable or disintegrate.

new directions and avenues of fantasy, (2) engage in verbal negotiation, (3) compromise, (4) argue, and (5) become a group's leader by using the right words. Popular children seem to be those who use speech creatively and become enjoyable companions to others. Violent statements such as "I'm going to shoot you" or "cut you up" are sometimes heard, and these tend to reflect television viewing or media drama. The reality-fantasy dividing line

may become temporarily blurred in some play situations, causing some children considerable anxiety.

Older preschoolers talk "in character" as they elaborate their dramatic play. If a scenario calls for a mother talking to a baby or teenagers talking, preschoolers routinely adopt appropriate speech. Imitations of pop singers or cartoon characters are common. Role-taking is an important skill in mature communication, indicating that

Photo 3-9 Group play encourages social development and social connectiveness.

social and dramatic play and improvisation are effective means of facilitating growth in communicative competence.

Four-year-olds seem to boast, brag, and make lots of noise. However, apparently boastful statements such as "Look what I did" may just be the child's attempt to show that he is capable and to share his accomplishments. Although preschoolers enjoy being with their peers, they quickly and easily engage in quarreling and name-calling. Sometimes, they do battle verbally. Typically, three- to five-year-olds disagree over possession of objects or territory, and verbal reasons or verbal evidence may help them win arguments. Many conflicts are resolved and lead to continued play. Speech helps children settle their affairs with and without adult help.

As a child develops an enhanced sense of humor, giggling becomes part of the noise of play. Silliness often reigns. One preschool boy thought it hilarious to go up to a teacher named Alice and say, "What's your name, Alice?" and then run off laughing—quite mature humor for a four-year-old! Preschoolers may distort and repeat what a caregiver says, making changes in sounds and gleefully chanting the distorted mes-

sage. Teachers who want to cultivate children's ability to understand and appreciate humor try to plan activities and present materials that challenge children's ability to interpret humor. Getting a joke often depends on understanding a play on words or ideas. Slapstick humor is still the most popular form with older preschoolers.

Argument, persuasion, and statements aimed at controlling others are frequently heard during play. Older preschool children are able to state reasons (Photo 3-10), request information, give explanations, utter justifications for their behavior, and verbally defend themselves. At times, establishing authority in disagreements seems paramount to compromising.

3-3b Exploring the Conventions of Conversation

Children learn language by reinventing it for themselves, not by direct instruction. They crack the code through exposure and opportunities to converse. They actively, although unconsciously, ingest and discover the rules of the system. Their speech errors often alert adults to the inner rules of language being formed.

Conversations have unwritten rules and expectations, the "you-talk-I-talk" sequence being the most apparent. Some preschoolers (three- and four-year-olds) may delight in violating or "playing" with the conventions of conversation. Sometimes preschoolers deliberately mislead (usually to tease playfully) or use "taboo" bathroom talk, nonsense talk, or unexpected tone when they are capable of verbally responding at a more mature level. Most teachers sense the child may be asserting independence by rejecting conversational convention. One teacher termed this "going into the verbal crazies"—to reject what another child or adult is saying, therefore attempting to change or control the situation. By violating conversational convention, children may clarify how conversational interaction should take place.

Photo 3-10 Look at what I caught!

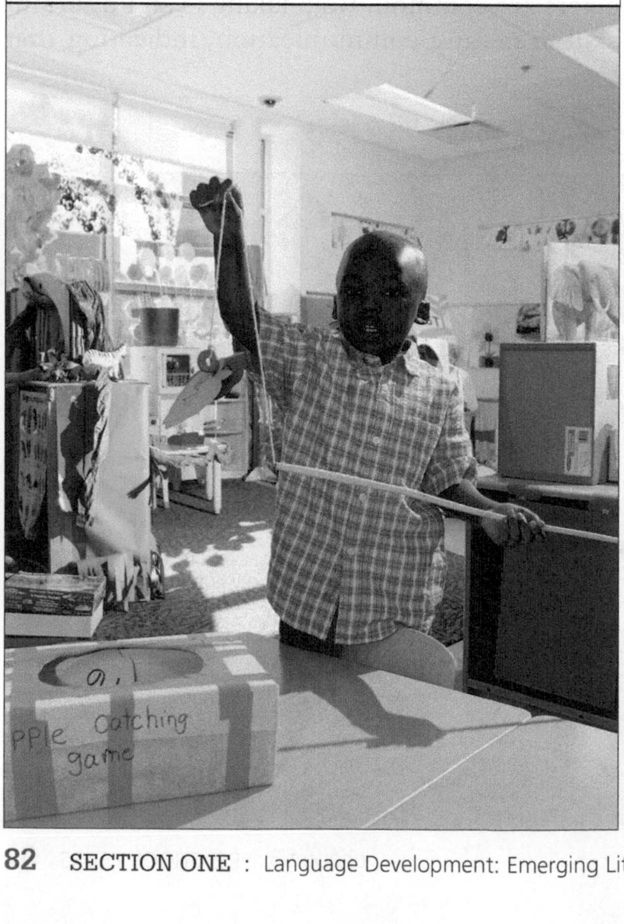

© 2015 Cengage Learning®

3-3c Relational Words

More and more relational words appear as the child begins to compare, contrast, and revise stored concepts with new happenings. The following teacher-recorded anecdote during a story-telling activity shows how the child attempts to relate previously learned ethics to a new situation.

During storytelling Michael repeated with increasing vigor, "He not berry nice!" at the parts of the story when the wolf says, "I'm going to blow your house down." Michael seemed to be checking with me the correctness of his thinking based on his internalized rules of proper moral conduct. (Machado, 2011, p. 16)

Perhaps because adults stress bad and good or because a young child's inner sense of what is and what is not proper is developing, teachers notice that preschoolers often describe feelings and people within narrow limits. One is pretty or ugly, mean or nice. Shades of meaning or extenuating circumstances seem yet to be understood. Preschoolers are focused on the here and now. Their senses actively probe by touching, smelling, observing, and listening to sounds. Around age four, conceptual dimensions begin to be understood, and they question the function and use of items, make comparisons, and discover relationships. They are beginning to categorize their environment differently:

> Although the words "big" and "little" are commonly used by preschoolers, they are overused. Many other comparison words give children trouble, and one hears "biggerer," "big-big-big," and "bestus one" to describe size. Time words elicit smiles from adults as children wrestle with present, past, and future, as in "zillion days" or "tomorrower." Number words are difficult for some children to handle, and expressions such as "whole bunches" and "eleventeen" are sometimes heard.

Although four-year-olds are able speakers, many of the "plays on words," double meanings, and connotative language subtleties that are important in adult speech are beyond children's understanding. Their creative uses of words at times seem metaphoric and poetic and are valiant attempts to put thoughts into words. Half-heard words and partially or fully learned words are blended together and are, at times, wonderfully descriptive. The author still laughs about the four-year-old who called her "Mrs. Eye Shadow."

3-3d Creative, Impact Words and Vocal Manipulation

There is tremendous variety in the ways children can modify their voices, and they may speak in a different pitch or rhythm when speaking to different people. They can whine, whisper, change volume, and distort timing and pronunciation. Some children discover that by increasing volume or changing tone they can affect others' behavior. They find that speech can show anger or sarcasm and can be used aggressively to hurt others.

Preschoolers may mimic the speech of "bad guy" media characters. Acts of aggression, clothed in the imitated speech and actions of a movie, television, or video character, can become part of this type of play. Purposeful echoing or baby talk can irritate or tease. Excessive talking is sometimes used to get one's way, and "talking back" may occur. Some children find that silence can get as much attention from adults as loud speech. Tattling on another may simply be a way of checking for correctness, or it can be purposeful.

Through trial and error and feedback, the child finds that words can hurt, gain friends or favor, or satisfy a wide range of needs. Because preschoolers are emotion-packed human beings, their statements range from expressions of "you're my buddy" to "you're my enemy" within a matter of minutes. What may appear to be violent statements may be just role-playing or make-believe competition. To some adults, preschooler speech may appear loud and wild. Their speech seems overly nasal and full of moisture that sprays outward. A young child may have frequent nasal colds and congestion during this period. Preschoolers tend to stand close to others and their volume increases when they feel strongly about their subjects.

Impact Words. Not all speech used by older preschoolers is appreciated by adults. Name-calling and offensive words and phrases may be used by active preschoolers to gain attention and reaction from both adults and children. Children discover that some phrases, sentences, and words cause unusual behavior in others. They actively explore these and usually learn which of these are inappropriate and when they can be used. Children recognize that most of this type of talk has "impact value." If certain talk makes people laugh or gives the children some kind of positive reward, it is used over and over.

Bathroom words seem to be explored and used as put-downs and attention getters. As every parent and teacher knows, young children experiment with language related to the body, and particularly to the private parts, going to the bathroom, and sexuality. In fact, children's use of sexual words can make it seem as if they know more than they do. Giggles and uproarious laughter can ensue when these words are used, adding to the child's enjoyment, and new teachers may not know how to handle these situations. The school's policy regarding this matter can be a subject for staff discussion. Generally, newly spoken bathroom talk should be ignored unless it is hurtful, or the child should be told that the place to use the word is in the bathroom. This often remedies the behavior because the child's enjoyment of it is spoiled without an audience. Alternatively, it might suffice to firmly say, "That's a word that hurts. His name is Michael," or in a calm but firm voice, "That kind of talk is unacceptable." Preschoolers love using forbidden words, especially when they play together. What parents and teachers can control is what is said in their presence.

Sound Words. In our culture, children are particularly fond of repeating conventionalized sounds reputedly made by animals ("arf-arf," "meow," "baa") as well as action sounds for toy vehicles ("putt-putt," "beep," "varoom"). When a child is playing the baby in home reenactment dramatic play, "wa-wa" will be heard frequently. Rough-and-tumble outside play may be accompanied by cartoon-strip sounds like "pow," "bam," and "zap." In addition, a good number of four-year-olds can distinguish rhyming words, and they enjoy creating them.

Created Words. Created words such as "turner-overer" for pancake turner, "mudpudders" for rain boots, or "dirt digger" for spade are wonderfully descriptive and crop up occasionally in child speech, perhaps as a means of filling in gaps in their vocabularies. Many cite young children's fascination with the functions of objects in their environment as the reason such words are created. Children enjoy nonsense words, and may revel in their newly gained abilities to use them.

Displaying Creativity. Being creative is not a problem for most preschoolers. Most display their growing ingenuity and imaginative thought and see relationships outside of conventional categories as they manipulate, discover, and investigate their environment and the new experiences their teachers plan and introduce. Many school activities are carefully rigged for children's manipulation and first-hand exploration. In classrooms where children have learned their ideas are welcomed and listened to, discussion can lead to clarification and further dialogue. In an activity planned to

help children cross a street safely, a teacher will no doubt get many practical and illogical suggestions including asking an adult for help, looking and listening carefully, and perhaps creative solutions such as riding an elephant borrowed from the zoo.

3-4 Word Meanings naeyc DAP COMMON CORE

During later preschool years children often become focused on what words mean and they begin to think and wonder about words. They begin to understand that words are arbitrary symbols with no intrinsic connection to their meaning but rather are representatives of meaning. The young child who says, "Templeton has a big name; my name is small," is displaying a recognition of word length or number of syllables.

3-4a Reality, Nonsense, and Speech Myths

Some preschool children can enjoy the absurd, nonsensical, and ridiculous in their experiences and find humor in the unexpected. Others, at a different stage in their cognitive development with another orientation, insist on knowing the right way—the real, the accepted, the "whys and wherefores"—and will see no humor in what confuses them or contradicts the "usual order of things." A number of preschoolers view life and surroundings seriously, literally. Others can "play" in speech with the opposite of what they know to be true. We know this is true in some adults also. Some simply do not seem to enjoy what most of us may find humorous.

There is considerable "language play" in nursery rhymes, fairy tales, and classic stories and children discover wonderful, fun ways to repeat things that story characters say. They may gleefully stomp up a hallways saying, "Fee, fi, fo, fum, here I come!" They may build bridges with blocks and make play figures "trip, trap, trip, trap" across them. Teachers are careful not to suppress a child's delight in absurdity by insisting on exact or literal renditions of things. Teachers encourage nonsense play by appreciating a child's inventions or nonsensical propositions. They may model some silliness or nonsense themselves. For example, the teacher might invert words in a sentence well known to the children to evoke child laughter by saying, "And the dogs go meow and cats say bowwow." And then the teacher would hope the children would either correct her or join in the game, producing their own inversions.

A large and mature vocabulary at this age may lead teachers to think a child has superior intelligence. Making conclusions about children based on language ability at this age has inherent pitfalls considering the many factors that could produce limited or advanced vocabulary, particularly when one considers cultural differences, bilingualism, and the child's access to "language-rich environments." At later ages language usage does seem to be related to school success.

3-4b Common Speech Patterns of Older Preschoolers

Four-year-olds often rhyme words in their play and speech, as previously mentioned. Older preschoolers engage in less frequent self-chatter. They continue to make errors in grammar and in the use of the past tense of verbs ("He didn't caught me"), adjectives ("It's biggerer than yours") (Figure 3-6), time words ("The next tomorrow"), and negatives ("I didn't did it"). But preschoolers' skills increase, and their use of forms of the irregular verb "to be" improves such as "I am so," or "Mine are hot, and yours are cold." Sentence structure comes closer to adult usage, including use of relative clauses and complex and compound sentence forms. Articulation of letter sounds is still developing; about 75 percent of English letter sounds are made correctly. Omissions of letter sounds (*'merca* for "America") and substitutions (*udder* for "other") are still present.

Older preschoolers may have a vocabulary larger than 1,500 words. They are learning new words and new concepts while they also enrich and solidify their knowledge of known words by establishing multiple links among words and concepts. Four-year-olds' attention and memory improve as they gain a greater understanding of concepts, strategies, and relationships that are associated with their first-hand manipulation and real experiences (Thomlinson & Hyson, 2009).

Many older preschoolers are very concerned about the correct names of things and detect errors in the speech of others. Being an active explorer, his questions can indicate his interest in natural phenomena such as "Why is the moon in the sky?" The four-year-old becomes a problem solver and tends to explain things through visually noted attributes; for example, "A cow is called that 'cause of its horns."

Additional speech and language characteristics include:

- Preschoolers may not be able to talk about their solutions to problems. Although they can respond to and solve questions posed verbally, they may not be able to explain their thinking.
- Four-year-old children enjoy books, stories, and more of their time is spent on them leading to a greater interest in words.
- A best friend's speech or his nonverbal gesturing might be copied for a period of time.
- Older preschooler's basic mental categories become elaborated as experience and details and specifics are noticed and understood. The basic category animals eventually includes a subcategory, cats, and then may include a smaller category such as Persian or Siamese.

A wide range of individual speech behavior is both normal and possible. Some younger preschoolers may have the speech characteristics of older preschoolers, whereas some older preschoolers have the characteristics of younger preschoolers or kindergarteners. Each child is unique in his progress and rate of acquiring language skills.

3-4c Standards & Early Childhood Special Needs

As early as 15 months, environmental factors, including the socioeconomic group in which the child resides, may have depressed the child's vocabulary development. By age three, there may be a significant and noticeable gap in the number of words in a child's vocabulary. This may only widen before the child enters kindergarten. Since preschool years are the years of the highest vocabulary growth, it is a crucial time to intervene and use instructional vocabulary building strategies and other planning to increase both quantity and quality of children's receptive and expressive vocabulary. *The Common Core State Standards in English Language Arts and Literacy in History/Social Studies, Science, and Technical Subjects* (2010) (CCSS), only identifies what language arts' outcomes kindergartners should attain, but does not do so for the preschool years. If one was to decide what experiences and

Figure 3-6 Developmental language-related milestones at ages two through five.

Child's Age		
2–2½ years	joins words in sentences of two or more words knows name has vocabulary of more than three words understands long spoken sentences and simple commands begins using plurals and past tense changes pitch and/or loudness for specific meaning begins using forms of verb "to be" uses a few prepositions uses "I," "me," and "you"	uses about 25 phonemes articulates about 10 to 12 vowel types and about 12 to 15 consonants points to and names objects in pictures names five to eight body parts enjoys rhythm in words, nursery rhymes, finger plays, and simple stories understands and responds to almost all of adult speech generalizes by calling round objects ball, and so on
2½–3 years	begins to use negatives, imperatives, and commands shows variety in question types adds as many as two to three words to vocabulary daily names items in signs and books uses three- or four-word sentences enjoys fun with words	follows simple directions points to body parts when asked names many common objects uses an increasing number of nouns, verbs, and pronouns draws lines and circular forms in artwork knows words or lines from books, songs, and stories
3–4 years	asks why, what, where, how, and when questions loves word play makes closed figures in art begins using auxiliary verbs tells sex and age utters compound sentences with connecting "and . . . er . . . but," and so on engages in imaginary play with dialogue and monologue says full name follows two- and three-part requests relates ideas and experiences uses adverbs, adjectives, and prepositions answers who, what, and where questions names some colors and is interested in counting	looks at books while alone and enjoys reading times talks about relationships memorizes a short song, poem, finger play, or story repeats three digits and two to three nonsense syllables if asked uses adjectives and pronouns correctly can copy a recognizable circle or square well if shown a model can imitate a clapping rhythm starts to talk about the function of objects can find an object in group that is different can find missing parts of wholes can classify using clear, simple distinctions knows names of common shapes
4–5 years	has vocabulary of more than 1,500 words uses sentences of five to six (or more) words may use impact, shock, and forbidden words may use words of violence argues, convinces, and questions correctness shares books with friends acts out story themes or recreates life happenings in play has favorite books likes to dictate words notices signs and print in environment uses etiquette words, such as "please," "thank you," and so on enjoys different writing tools knows many nursery rhymes and stories	may add alphabet letters to artwork creates and tells long stories can verbally express the highlights of the day knows many colors can repeat a sentence with six or more words may pretend to read books or may actually read others' name tags holds writing tools in position that allows fine control traces objects with precision classifies according to function asks what words mean is familiar with many literary classics for children knows address and phone number can retell main facts or happenings in stories uses adultlike speech

Metalinguistic Awareness and Brain Growth

Metalinguistic awareness is a child's knowledge of the nature of language as an object. Children begin to notice words as objects and later become able to manipulate them to learn to read and write and to accomplish a host of other ends, such as using metaphors, creating puns, and using irony. Pan and Gleason (1997) observe:

> Before children can engage in flexible uses of words, they must have an implicit understanding that words are separate from their referents. Young children often consider the name of an object another of its intrinsic attributes. They believe, for instance, that if you called a horse a cow, it might begin to moo. Later children learn that words

themselves are not inherent attributes of objects, which allows them to move beyond literal word use and adopt a metaphoric stance. (p. 327)

A critical restructuring of the brain begins at about age four, when a surge in learning is happening. The brain is beginning to eliminate weak connections but is still eagerly seeking information from the senses. Early childhood educators and many researchers are urging that a national emphasis and priority be given to early childhood education, especially in the key areas of language learning, mathematics, music education, and problem-solving skill development.

---

activities should be offered to children identified as needing special instruction to equip them to enter a CCSS kindergarten, the author's recommendations are found in the Appendix.

3-5 Additional Growth Systems Affect Language Development

All body systems need a minimum level of movement (exercise) to keep the body in good working order and to stimulate brain growth. Food, living conditions, and emotional security can also affect a child's acquisition of language. A preschool center intent on developing language skills focuses on satisfying both physical and emotional needs, while offering intellectual opportunity and challenge.

3-5a Physical Growth

Early childhood teachers are aware of fundamental physical changes that take place in young children. Physical development can affect children's perceptions of themselves, as well as the way they are treated by others. A slightly taller, physically active, strong, and well-coordinated child who can ride a two-wheel bike and dropkick a football may be admired by peers. These two skills are not

often witnessed during preschool years, but occasionally a child accomplishes these physical skills. A wide range of physical abilities in individual children exists within any preschool group.

Preschoolers grow at a rate of two to three inches in height and add three to four pounds in weight a year. At about 18 to 24 months, the child's thumb is used in opposition to just one finger. The ability to use some tools and drawing markers with a degree of skill emerges. The nutritional quality of the child's diet exerts an influence on both body and neural development. Illness during an accelerated growth period may produce conditions affecting language development if it damages necessary body systems. Hearing loss and vision difficulties can also impair the child's ability to receive communications and learn a native language.

3-5b Planned Physical Activities

Planned physical movement opportunities and activities prepare children for academic learning. Movement stimulates learning physiologically, and helps young children experience concepts so they can process them cognitively. Teachers often offer children opportunities to solve movement problems by urging them to invent their own solutions and activities. Abstract concepts like over and under are made concrete if the teacher asks children to physically

---

metalinguistic awareness — a conscious awareness on the part of a language user of language as an object in itself.

Brain Connection

Physical Movement and Cognition

Brain-based learning advocate, Eric Jensen (2008), emphasizes the benefits and needs of physical movement for children. He believes exercise triggers the release of a brain-derived factor that enhances cognition by boosting the ability of neurons to communicate with one another. Jensen urges early childhood educators to:

- facilitate hand movements each day with clapping games, dancing, puzzles, and manipulative objects.

- engage learners in cooperative activities and group work.
- offer novel activities in a variety of learning locations, and plan child activities and choices connected to the learning that require moving the body in some way. (p. 39).

---

experience them. Teachers can urge children to talk aloud about a motor task at hand while they are performing it. According to a study by Winsler, Manfra, and Diaz (2007), both kindergarteners and preschoolers respond to a teacher's speech instructions and "performance on motor sequencing and counting tasks improved when children are able to speak out loud" (p. 28).

3-5c Perception and Perceptual Skills

Seeing and trying to touch or act upon the environment are the work of infancy. This early physical stage precedes and develops into the child's **mental image** of his world, and this makes later verbal labeling and speech possible. As the child matures, perceptual acuity increases; finer detail is seen. Most children achieve 20/20 vision (adult optimum) at age 14. From ages two to five, vision is in the 20/45 to 20/30 range. It is estimated that 20 to 25% of preschoolers have some eye problem that, if uncorrected, could delay learning or cause vision loss. Experts advise watching for an eye that slightly turns in or out, squinting, eye closing, or head turning when the child is focusing, avoidance of coloring activities or books, and clumsiness or frustration during play. Vision tests should be performed by professionals.

Young children are noted for their desire to get their hands on what they see that interests them. If a new child with a particularly noticeable hair style joins a group, hands and fingers are sure to try to explore its texture. If a teacher wears bright or shiny jewelry, some children will want to touch it. Perceptions are gathered with all sense organs. Experts believe the main purpose of receiving, organizing, and interpreting what one encounters perceptually is to achieve constancy—a stable, constant world. Development involves changes or shifts in the way a person organizes experience and copes with the world, generally moving from simpler to more complex, from single to multiple and integrated ways of responding.

Young children, as they age, get better at focusing on one aspect of a complex situation. They become selective in focusing their attention, and they ignore the irrelevant and distracting. Individual differences exist in the way children explore their environment and react to it.

Visual Literacy. The process of visual perception involves several basic parts, including the sensing of information along dual pathways in the brain. An understanding of this process is essential to realizing the power of visual images to move us emotionally and behaviorally and to influence our conscious thought. Visual literacy is a basic human capacity that aids learning and problem solving and is useful across many educational disciplines. It involves young children's understanding and use of symbolic representation. It refers to a group of vision competencies. The development of these competencies is fundamental to normal human learning. When developed, they enable a visually literate person to discriminate and interpret the visible actions, objects, and symbols that the person encounters in the environment.

Literacy in the 21st century is primarily visual—pictures, graphics, images of every kind—and students must learn to process both words and pictures and shift back and forth between

---

mental image — a "perceptual representation" or mental picture of a perceptual experience, remembered or imagined.

them. Teachers can help children become more knowledgeable and more skilled in their use of verbal communications, and can also help them gain skill in using and understanding visual images. Children will need to know how to make meaning, not just from text, but also from vast amounts of information conveyed through images.

Perceptual-Motor Skills. Perceptual-motor, or sensory-motor, intelligence has been defined as an action-oriented knowledge, not to be confused with the intelligence that invokes thinking and logic. Intelligence grows during preschool years and beyond when children think about and know without acting out in a physical way. During preschool years, the development of motor skills is as important as the development of language skills. Just as there is gradually increasing control over language, movement, and body control in the preschool years, there is also a similar continuing increase in the ability to scan new material, organize one's perception of it, remember it, and perhaps refer to it by some label or assign meaning in some other way. The close ties between motor activities and thought processes indicate that the child needs motor activity involving the five sense organs, as well as large muscle use. Figure 3-7 describes perception activities that promote perception skills.

Figure 3-7 Perceptual activities.

Experiences Dealing with	Possible Materials and Equipment
Visual Discrimination	
long, longer, longest	felt or paper strips; sticks; ribbons
small, smaller, smallest	nested boxes; blocks; buttons; measuring cups
big, little	blocks; jars; buttons; balloons; toys
tall, short	felt figures; stuffed toys
wide, narrow	pieces of cloth and paper; scraps of wood; boxes
high, low	jump rope; small ball; see-saw made from small board with tiny block in middle
above, below	felt pieces to place above and below a box with colored stones
Auditory Discrimination	
quiet, noisy	two boxes: one containing something that rattles (such as stones or beads) and one containing cloth or paper
bell sounds	bells of varying shapes and sizes for a variety of tones
falling sounds	feather; leaf; stone; block of wood; cotton
shaking sounds	maracas; baby rattle; pebbles inside coffee can
musical sounds	variety of rhythm instruments
Tactile Discrimination	
textures	sandpaper; tissue; stone; waxed paper; tree bark; velvet; wool; fur; cotton
outline of shapes	thin wooden circle, square, triangle, rectangle; letters cut from sandpaper
recognition of objects	four different-shaped objects, each tied in end of sock—children guess what each is by feeling it (change objects often)
hard, soft	handkerchief; rock; cotton batting; nail; sponge
Taste Discrimination	
identifying food: sweet, salty, sour	small jars: filled with salt, sugar, unsweetened lemonade
trying new foods	variety of vegetables children may not know; samples of fruit juices; honey, molasses, maple syrup
Smell Discrimination	
identifying object by smell	cake of soap; vial of perfume; pine sprig; onion; vials of kitchen spices; orange
Kinesthetic Discrimination	
lifting, racing downhill, swinging, throwing, running, jumping, climbing, bending, stretching, twisting, turning, spinning, balancing	yard and motor play materials

3-5d Motor Skill Development and Activities

Motor skills develop in an orderly, predictable head to toe fashion. Neck, head, and upper body muscles are controlled first (large muscles before small muscles), and center-of-body muscles are coordinated before extremities (fingers and toes). Handedness (left or right) is usually stable by age five or six. Child limitations can occur if motor and sensory motor experience is limited. A child who has had limited experience may not be prepared for the finer adjustments that are required in the motor skills of eye movement and hand-eye coordination in the early grades of school. Many educators who study the Montessori approach (1967) to early childhood education are influenced by her ideas. Montessori believed an obvious advantage was to be obtained by enlarging children's perception skills. She suggested that intellect is built by experience, firsthand contact, and other exploration of the environment.

Preschools are full of appealing equipment (Photo 3-11), and programs offer planned approaches to the development of sensory motor skills. They are seen as integral parts of the curricula. There seems to be no clearly accepted or definite separate place within the preschool curriculum for sensory skill development. Yet almost all centers include them in their instructional goals and identify a series of sequential activities and label them perceptual or sensory motor activities. Every activity in which the child moves can be classified as an activity that develops perceptual-motor skill. Commonly, music activities and physical games are so classified, for they often deal with physical coordination and endurance.

Early childhood programs often plan for perceptual-motor activities within their language arts curriculum. What remains important is that this type of emphasis is part of every center's program. The following list of objectives (goals) is designed to promote and refine perceptual-motor skills. It is drawn from a number of schools' and centers' goal statements.

- awareness of self in space
- awareness of self in relation to objects
- flexibility
- body coordination
- posture and balance
- awareness of spatial relationships
- rhythmic body movements
- ability to identify objects and surfaces with the eyes closed
- awareness of temperatures by touch
- ability to trace form outlines with fingers
- ability to discriminate color, shapes, similar features, different features, sizes, textures, and sounds

Photo 3-11 Bicycles are a popular outside play equipment choice.

© 2016 Cengage Learning®

- ability to match a wide variety of patterns and symbols
- ability to identify parts of figures or objects when a small part of a whole is presented
- eye-hand coordination
- familiarity with the following terms: same, different, long, longer, longest, small, smaller, smallest, big, little, tall, short, wide, narrow, high, low, above, below, on, in, hard, soft, sweet, salty, sour
- ability to identify food by tasting
- ability to identify smells of various items
- ability to identify common sounds

3-5e Cognitive Development

There are opposing views concerning the link between language and thought. One view holds that language is the foundation of thought and vital to a person's awareness of the world. Another view suggests that language is dependent on thinking; as intelligence grows, language grows, reflecting thoughts. Most educators agree that language and thought are closely associated. Educators also tend to agree that preschool children are much more capable of learning than previously believed. Therefore, educators attempt to provide a variety of experiences and opportunities for children's self-discovery, and they encourage thoughtful classroom discussions and teacher-child interactions.

Experience changes the brain, but then those very changes alter the way new experience affects the brain. Children who have lived in unfortunate circumstances and have been passive viewers of life rather than active listeners, explorers, and conversationalists, may lack both auditory analysis skill and logical and sequential reasoning skills. The idea that the reciprocal emotionally charged interactions between young children and caregivers influence their cognitive development is not new, but increasingly it is given close attention by anyone working with the young.

Problem-solving ability has been associated with the preschool literacy experiences that come before conventional reading and writing. Once children become higher-level symbolic thinkers, they are able to piece together the mental processes used in everyday problem solving with the symbols needed for reading and writing. As mentioned previously, intellect is rooted in each particular child's stored perceptual and sensory-motor experiences. Each child interprets happenings and attempts to connect each to what she already knows. If it fits, the child understands and it all falls together. Children classify what they encounter, including events, people, and objects before they have words for them. Each mental grouping is distinguished by a set of distinct features, and objects yet to be classified are examined for the presence of these features. Later, a word or language symbol can be attached to a class or category, which makes it possible for the child to communicate about what the class or category means to the child or how the child feels about it. Preschool teachers observe differences between the feelings and meanings expressed by each child. For example, the way that a child reacts when meeting a new large animal may demonstrate what she knows and feels about large animals. One child's reaction might be entirely different from another's.

Putting events and experiences into classes and categories is innate—a natural mental process. The motivation to engage actively with the environment—to make contact, to have an impact, and to make sense of experience—is built into human beings. The mind yearns for order and knowledge is built within from what is experienced. Children construct theories or hypotheses about objects and phenomena by putting things into relationships. A child's knowledge is constantly changing, for children are curious and are constantly searching for a variety of experience, and to fight boredom. A new or novel idea or event may greatly affect a child by adding to or changing all a child knows and feels on a particular subject.

As a child's language ability develops, mental classes, categories, and concepts are represented symbolically by words. Words become an efficient shortcut that eliminates the need to act out by gesturing or signaling to make something known to another. Thoughts can be analyzed and evaluated internally as the child grows older. If a common language system exists between the child and others, it can be used to reveal the child's unique self.

Piaget's (1952) terms **assimilation** and **accommodation** describe what happens when children experience something new. Each individual

---

assimilation — the process that allows new experiences to merge with previously stored mental structures.

accommodation — the process by which new experiences or events change existing ideas or thought patterns.

unconsciously structures (internally builds and organizes) what is perceived. If a new experience or event is perceived, it is assimilated into what already mentally existed. If it changes or modifies those existing structures, the new is accommodated. In other words, children attend to features that make sense to them, and learning involves adding to what is already known or modifying what is known. The brain structures of some children may be developing more slowly than those of others, which might affect their ability to learn and cause teachers to compare them unfairly with children of the same age who have developed more quickly. Figure 3-8 lists children's emerging intellectual skills.

What a teacher may at first consider an error in thinking, may, upon deeper analysis, be seen as quite mature and understandable and not just random guesses. When a child says a camel is a horse with a hump, the child should be given credit for seeing the similarity, rather than being merely corrected. "It has four legs like a horse, but this animal has a hump on its back and it is called a camel" a teacher can say.

3-5f The Teacher's Role

The teacher's role in intellect building not only includes the teacher's provision of materials and equipment that promote exploring and experiencing, but also involves teacher interactions.

Figure 3-8 The child's emerging intellectual skills.

1. seeking information (focusing)
2. seeking word labels (concept building)
3. naming, classifying, categorizing, and grouping experiences mentally—objects, ideas, etc. (general to specific; revising concepts)
4. responding and remembering (memorizing and recalling)
5. comparing and contrasting information (abstracting)
6. making inferences and predicting in general ways (predicting)
7. generalizing (inductive thinking)
8. applying known information to new situations (transferring)
9. making hypotheses (educated guesses) and predicting in specific ways (deductive thinking)

A "zone of proximal development" is what Vygotsky (1980) calls the area between what a child can solve alone when faced with the problem or experience, and what a child can possibly solve or come to know with the help of a teacher or another. When adults name and explain happenings and talk about relationships, this is seen as a stimulant to both language and mental growth. It is also important that adults know when not to interrupt children's thoughts when they are deeply engaged, but rather show interest and wait for the child to put happenings into words. Dialogue makes much more sense when children seek adult help or when teachers are companions in activities. Teachers can talk about both meaning and feelings. Each intellect-building encounter and interaction starts with supportive acceptance and caring. Teachers promote further discovery, and they listen and observe closely. Listening may expose aspects of the child's thinking, logic, concepts, and feelings. Children can ask many questions on any given day. Teachers may sometimes answer a question with a question and often provide answers the child cannot discover herself. Skillful questioning and sensitive responses preserve children's feelings about expressing worthwhile ideas and make a child more willing to speak, share, and ask again. Teachers can also support children as they converse by encouraging them to step outside their own perceptions to become aware of larger, more generalized patterns in the things they observe. The process of questioning, predicting, and testing possibilities can be learned firsthand as children solve their own problems. Early childhood educators facilitate children's ability to come to their own conclusions and relate those conclusions to observable evidence when possible. A teacher may also ask children to compare their ideas with one another in group conversations (Photo 3-12).

Children may gain **metalinguistic skills** during their preschool years. They are then able to think about language as a separate entity, and some children make comparisons between spoken and written words or analyze words into individual parts. Some may also judge what correct word usage is and what it is not, or playfully manipulate words.

---

metalinguistic skills — the ability to think about language as a separate entity.

Photo 3-12 A teacher attempts to extend children's discussion of a discovered bug in the sandbox.

3-5g Social and Emotional Growth and Connectedness

Interaction with other people is always a major factor in a child's language learning. Children who have positive feelings about themselves—feelings of self value and security—tend to speak frequently. New contacts with adults or children outside of the home can run smoothly. Gallagher and Mayer (2008) suggest the school day should begin with feelings of warmth and comfort as children transition from family. This is a time when responsive teachers make an effort to recognize each child's individual presence by welcoming and greeting them.

How to be in a relationship may be the most important skills children learn (Gallagher and Mayer, 2008). Research suggests children able to form high-quality and secure relationships display better language usage, Problem-solving ability, **social connectedness**, and they acquire harmonious play skills. Young children watch and learn from their teachers and others. The tone set in a caring and supportive school environment can lead to feelings of acceptance. Each child should feel he or she is a valued member of a group of others. Social connectedness has been

defined as a characteristic of people with stable and secure lives, supportive families and friends, and close ties to community. They are accepted as a worthy individual part of a group. They are the children who seem to be able to weather life's stresses and possess a sense of individual identity.

During preschool years, children form ideas of self-identity. It becomes difficult for children to believe in themselves, or their language abilities, if self-esteem is constantly undermined. A teacher's behavior and response when communicating with children can promote a variety of social skills (Figure 3-9). Social development must not be ignored when planning and conducting language activities or in trying to manage groups. Structure and rules are necessary for group living. An individual child's status in the eyes of the group can be enhanced through the sharing and appreciation of the child's ideas and accomplishments and by providing frequent opportunities for the child to lead or help lead the group in activities, at times. This is almost always a confidence- and status-building experience.

Through activities, preschoolers begin to learn labels for feelings, such as happy, sad, jealous, fearful, and so on, and many begin to think of others' feelings. The conscience is forming, and interest

---

social connectedness — a term associated with the following human characteristics: is stable and secure, develops close relationships with others, has supportive family and friends, and is deemed a worthy individual by others. Often seen by others as able to transcend stress and possess an individual identity.

Figure 3-9 Teacher behaviors that are helpful to the child's social growth.

In communication, the teacher:
- cares and is ready to give of self.
- listens, intent on understanding.
- adds simple words when the child cannot.
- does not correct speech when this might break down willingness to speak further.
- is available for help in clarifying ideas or suggesting new play and exploring possibilities.
- senses child interests and guides to new real experiences.
- is available when problems and conflicts happen.
- enjoys time spent in child activities.
- establishes friendships with each child.
- talks positively about each child's individual uniqueness.
- is an enthusiastic and expressive communicator.
- offers friendly support while redirecting undesirable social behavior or stating rules.
- notices and respects each child's work.

Photo 3-13 Being left out feels like the end of the world.

© 2015 Cengage Learning®

in right and wrong is being expressed. Teachers who speak of their own feelings as adults set an example and provide a classroom climate in which children's feelings are accepted and understood.

Most children explore social actions and reactions. They want to have friends (Photo 3-13). In play, they learn to make plans, negotiate, and communicate. Strong emotions accompany much of children's behavior; their total being speaks. When a child feels left out, life becomes an overwhelming tragedy; on the other hand, a party invitation may be a time to jump for joy. It is through symbolic and pretend play that young children are most likely to develop both socially and intellectually, so many play opportunities and room areas are set up for it. Planned play periods are a daily event. Play activities can also help children develop a sense of self.

The following is a list of social ability goals that serve as a strong foundation for future schooling. These are promoted throughout a school's day. Children should be able to

- get and hold the attention of adults in a variety of socially acceptable ways.

- express affection or mild annoyance to adults and peers when appropriate.
- use adults as resources after determining that a task is too difficult to handle alone.
- show pride in achievement.
- both lead and follow children of the same age.
- compete with age mates.

Teachers strive to supply a center atmosphere in which a sense of trust and security thrives. Children need to learn to trust people in their world, or else they reject all that these people want to teach them. They need to have faith in those who respect them and accept their feelings, and also learn to trust themselves. Whether young children see themselves as valued identities depends on their interactions with others.

Summary

3-1 Identify three characteristics of younger preschoolers' speech and communication.

Younger preschoolers' speech is often unclear, but close teacher observation may uncover meaning. Frequent gestures and body motions accompany words. Young children understand teacher's speech with apparent ease and they daily acquire new vocabulary. Vocal noises often accompany their play and they may limit speech output when adjusting to new situations. Younger preschoolers possess receptive and expressive vocabulary and are acquiring more complex forms of English grammar. They are noticing consistent speech patterns and applying them to their developing language system. Their most frequently spoken words are nouns. And "no" is liberally used. They engage in short conversations and their speech can be uneven with pauses and repetitions. At times, they correct their own speech. Excitement elevates their speech volume and pitch, but some may be shy, using a barely audible voice. Cause-and-effect statements are appearing. Self-talk is commonplace and often reflects what they are physically performing. Their short sentences may include only key words. Questions are frequently asked, and their new words may be practiced and repeated over and over.

3-2 Describe three pieces of recommended advice to a family concerned about their preschooler's speaking abilities.

1. Calling a child's attention to his speech or making demands causes child tension, making the situation worse rather than better. Families were advised to wait and relax. A child often needs time to speak the words he wishes to.
2. Speaking is a complex process, so families were advised to remain patient and optimistic while assuming an "I'm here to listen" stance.
3. Children's illogical comments in conversations are frequently cleared up when the child adds more information. Families were advised to gain more information by asking questions. Advice implied this is an age level characteristic.
4. Families were advised to be accepting and interested as a child struggles to express himself.
5. Families were advised to react to the intent of the child's messages, rather than his word usage.
6. Families were advised to help children see the details and relationships.

3-3 Describe conversational skills necessary for an older preschooler to maintain a true conversation.

In a functional conversation, a child needs skill in gaining the attention of the listener, turn taking, pausing to listen to the speaker, which encourages the conversational partner to talk, correcting himself if necessary, maintaining word flow and not pausing long enough for the other to jump in, and holding in mind what he wants to say or answer as he continues listening.

3-4 Discuss older preschoolers manipulation and playful use of words.

Some preschoolers may enjoy absurd, nonsensical, and ridiculous word use. They may repeat catchy phrases or words that are funny to them. They may use silly or nonsense words in their play or invert words in sentences or state the opposite of what they know to be true. Words in nursery rhymes may delight them because they are fun to say. These children see humor in using words unconventionally.

3-5 List reasons for planning sensory, motor skill activities; cognitive, building activities; or social, emotional growth activities to promote language development.

1. Motor activity involves the five sense organs. Educators believe a strong connection exists between the development of mental and physical skill development. The sharpening of perceptual-motor skill offers a solid foundation for intellectual growth. A preschool child with limited perceptual-motor skill may not be as successful in the small motor skills necessary for the eye movement and hand-eye coordination called for in kindergarten.

2. Language growth is viewed by many educators as being dependent on or related to a child's thinking. As language grows, intelligence grows. Offering children problem solving associated with literacy experiences, aids learning to read and write. Preschoolers classify life experiences and add words to them. This can take place in an early childhood center through teacher interaction and planned activities. Teachers supply activity materials and verbal comments during activities to promote child exploration and discovery. Discussing classroom happenings and relationships that exist in any given situation stimulates both language and mental growth.

3. Teachers start the day by welcoming and greeting individual children and they try to create a classroom of comfort and warmth for the child. They realize that young children are forming a self-image partially based on how they are treated in the classroom. Planned activities have built in social rules for group living. Teachers offer activities that provide labels for feelings and model feelings of their own. They promote each child's status in the group and give attention to children's ideas and accomplishments. Teachers are aware of each child's social connectedness and promote it whenever possible. Play activities are offered, particularly pretend play experiences, and room area furnishings are set up to encourage child participation.

Additional Resources

Readings

Christ, T., & Wang, X.C. (2012). Supporting preschoolers' vocabulary learning: Using a decision making model to select appropriate words and methods. *Young Children, 67*(2): 74–80.

Sharapan, H. (2013). From STEM to STEAM: How early childhood educators can apply Fred Rogers' approach. In C. Copple, S. Bredekamp, D. Loralek, & K. Charner (Eds.). *Developmentally Appropriate Practice: Focus on Preschoolers*. (pp.158–163). Washington, DC: National Association for the Education of Young Children.

Siegler, R. S., & Alibali, M.W. (2005). *Children's Thinking*. Upper Saddle River, NJ: Prentice Hall.

Helpful Websites

National Child Care Information Center

http://nccic.org

Staff will research your questions and connect you with information on young children's language and literacy.

National Network for Child Care

http://www.nncc.org

Ages and stages of three-and four-year-olds is provided. Select Articles & Resources and then select Child Development.

International Visual Literacy Association

http://www.ivla.org

Contains articles and information on research and conferences.

National Child Care Information Center

http://www.nccic.org

Lists ages and stages of growth.

4 Understanding Differences

Objectives

After reading this chapter, you should be able to:

4-1 Describe a safe and sensitive classroom environment for children with language or cultural differences.

4-2 Discuss the similarities and differences between Standard English and American dialects.

4-3 Identify common strategies second-language learners use to learn Standard English on their own.

4-4 Discuss program planning for second-language learners.

4-5 Name two common school program types for second language learners.

4-6 Identify young children's common speech problems.

4-7 Name at least four characteristics of language-advanced preschoolers.

 NAEYC Program Standards

2A02 The curriculum allows for adaptations and modifications to ensure access for all children.

2D03 Children have varied opportunities to develop competence in verbal and nonverbal communications by responding to questions, communicating needs, thoughts, and experiences, and describing things and events.

2D04 Children have varied opportunities to develop vocabulary through conversations, experiences, field trips, and books.

2A04 The curriculum can be implemented in a manner that reflects responsiveness to family home values, beliefs, experiences, and language.

2D02 Children are provided opportunities to experience oral and written communications in a language their family uses or understands.

DAP Developmentally Appropriate Practice (DAP)

3H5 Teachers support dual language learners and their home language as well as promoting their English.

3H4 Teachers attend to the particular needs of dual language learners and children behind in vocabulary and other aspects of language learning.

3H7 Teachers help children use communication and language as tools for thinking and learning.

A Problem Solved

It was the first song at circle time.

> Good morning, I like the shoes you've got on. / In fact, I like 'em so much, I'm gonna put 'em in a song. / In a song, in a song, / I'm gonna put you and your shoes in a song.

A boy asked if we could put hair in. "Good morning, I like the hair you've got on. . . ." The boy stopped singing. We finished the verse. The boy leaned toward me and said quietly, "But what about Mr. Baker?" "Who's Mr. Baker?" I asked. The boy lifted one hand from his lap and pointed to his left. I saw Mr. Baker, one of the father volunteers who came to tell stories. He was totally bald and trying not to laugh. None of the children found it funny. To leave Mr. Baker out was not funny. A girl whispered loudly to the boy, "Say skin." He leaned toward me and said, "Sing skin this time." The cloud left the boy's face. . . . and Mr. Baker gave him a thumbs-up, as if to celebrate another problem solved (Hunter, 2003).

Questions to Ponder

1. What is this reading an example of? What do you like about this song activity?

2. Could this vignette's song be used in a planned unit of study on diversity? If so, explain how?

The United States is a multicultural society. It is a vast array of people of different backgrounds and ethnicities. Members of families may be married, remarried, single, gay, straight, birth parents, adoptive parents, and/or unrelated individuals.

Children's families also differ substantially in size, resources, values, goals, languages spoken, educational attainment, child-raising practices, past experiences along with immigration status, countries of origin, and length of time in the United States. Families have broken almost all traditional rules for what makes a family, but continue to affirm the most basic definition of family: a bond reinforced by love and caring.

Experienced teachers throughout the United States report that the children they teach are more diverse in their backgrounds, experiences, and abilities than were those they taught in the past. Projections suggest that by the year 2025, more than half of the children enrolled in America's schools will be members of "minority" groups, not of European-American origin. Diversity is the new norm and immigrant families are widely dispersed. Garcia and Jensen (2009) note two to three million children, ages birth to eight in the United States are learning English as a second language. Many reside in families with culturally different backgrounds. Early childhood programs and elementary grade levels are enrolling more Spanish-speaking and non-English speaking children in parts of the country with little or no history of ethnic or racial diversity. This trend is stronger at early childhood levels where Hispanic preschoolers under age five account for over 20 percent of the preschool population (Collins & Ribeiro, 2004).

Some young children enter school with addictions, diseases, and disorders, such as fetal alcohol syndrome, and without having had sufficient sleep, food, or supervision at home. Teachers have found themselves virtually unprepared to deal with the vastly different linguistic and life experiences and abilities of language-diverse children (Photo 4-1).

Early childhood educators recognize that **DAP** extra efforts made early in some young children's lives can prevent problems with learning to read. Children who are poor and nonnative speakers are considered much more likely to fail to learn to read adequately. As with other educators, you will be searching for ways to meet young children's varied educational needs. Since play opens children to expression, it will be an integral part of any early childhood program.

Barrett (2003) reviewed research concerning preschool enrollment and later reading achievement. His findings led him to believe that:

- Preschool programs can have an important short-term impact on general cognitive development and academic abilities including reading achievement.

- Effects appear to be larger for intensive, high-quality educational programs targeting children in poverty.

- School success (primarily grade repetition and special education placement) is dependent on verbal

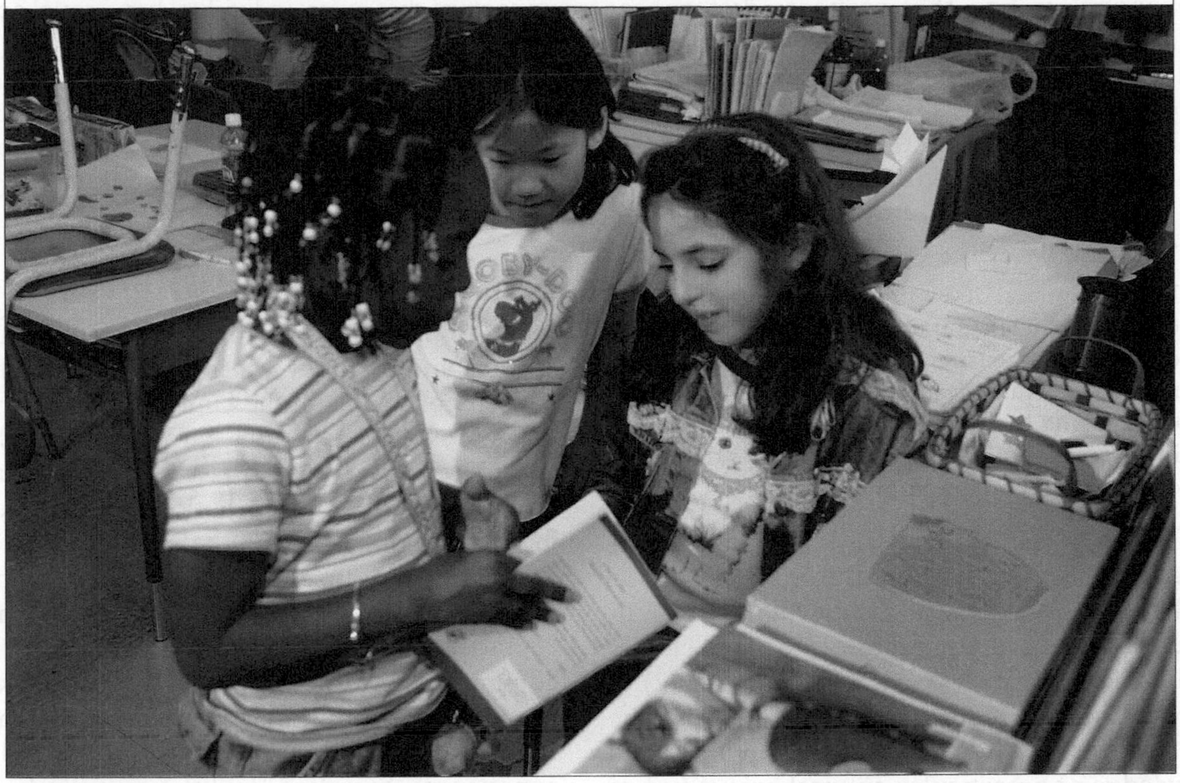

© 2015 Cengage Learning®

abilities; in particular, reading plays an important role in accessing new knowledge from textbook readings and other schoolwork. (p. 57)

Barrett concluded that preschool education in a variety of forms improves general cognitive abilities during early childhood and produces long-term increases in reading achievement.

4-1 Child-Focused and Child-Sensitive Approaches

Au (2006) describes what is important to consider when a classroom includes children of diverse backgrounds. Establishing positive relationships with children is key:

> It may be helpful for the teacher to have an understanding of the students' cultural backgrounds and the values they bring to school. Once positive relationships and open communication have been established, students will accept the teacher as a role model and as a model of literate behavior. (p. 197)

Program planners are experimenting and refining instructional models. These new approaches are described as child-focused and child-sensitive approaches (Figure 4-1). A child focused-approach is based upon the individual child observations and inferences the teacher makes concerning a child's learning style, needs, classroom interactions, and the attitudes a child possesses that tend to promote learning and school success. Child-sensitive approaches are similar but primarily involve a teacher's knowledge of what is respectful and appropriate in light of a child's cultural and experiential background.

Figure 4-1 Wall chart.

Kids Are Different

Kids are different
They don't even look the same
Some kids speak different languages
They all have a different name
Kids are different
But if you look *INSIDE* you'll see
The one with brown hair, black hair, red hair
    or blond hair,
Is just like you and me.

Author Unknown

A safe classroom environment using these approaches is one that respects differences and uniqueness and energizes young children's ability to communicate desires, fears, and understandings.

In 1996 the NAEYC recognized and recommended the following child-sensitive suggestions that have continued to gain increased importance:

> For the optimal development and learning of all children, educators must accept the legitimacy of children's home language, respect (hold in high regard) and value (esteem, appreciate) the home culture, and promote and encourage the active involvement and support of all families, including extended and nontraditional family units. (p. 42)

Teachers realize that children whose language skills or patterns are different are just as intelligent and capable as those who speak Standard English. An early childhood educator's goal is (1) to help all young children and (2) to help in such a way that it will not actually make matters worse. The teacher's sensitivity to and knowledge of a particular cultural group and its different language patterns can aid a particular child's growth. Preserving the child's feelings of adequacy and acceptance is the teacher's prime goal; moving the child toward the eventual learning of standard forms is a secondary goal.

Early childhood educators strive, through professional associations, individual efforts, and attention to standards, to increase program quality. In doing so, each center needs to examine its program to ensure language learning is not seen as occurring only at language time but from the moment teachers greet each child at the beginning of the day. Every child-adult interaction holds potential for child language learning. The key question is whether each child is receiving optimum opportunity during group care to listen and speak with a savvy adult skilled in natural conversation that reinforces, expands, and extends.

Language acquisition is more than learning to speak; it is a process through which a child becomes a competent member of a community by acquiring both the linguistics and sociocultural knowledge needed to learn how to use language in that particular community. It is particularly important that every individual have equal access to educational and economic opportunity, especially those from groups who have consistently been found on the bottom of the educational, social, and economic heap: African-Americans, Latinos, and Native American people.

4-2 Standard English

Standard English is the language of elementary schools and textbooks. It is the language of the majority of people in the United States. Increasingly, preschool programs enroll children whose speech reflects different past experiences and a cultural (or subcultural) outlook. When attending a preschool or center, these children become aware of the group's values, attitudes, food preferences, clothing styles, and so on, and gain acceptance as group members by practicing and copying the enrolled group's way of speaking. Some theorize that group membership influences children's manner of thinking about life's experiences. Standard English usage is advantageous and a unifying force that brings together cultures within cultures, thereby minimizing class differences.

Dialect, as used here, refers to language patterns that differ from Standard English. Dialects exist in all languages and fall into two categories: (1) regional and geographical and (2) social and ethnic. Dialect is a regional or social variety of language distinguished by pronunciation, grammar, or vocabulary, especially a variety of speech differing from the standard literary language or speech pattern of the culture in which it exists. Diverse dialects in the United States include African-American English, Puerto Rican English, Appalachian English, and varieties of Native American English, Vietnamese English, and others. Dialects are just as highly structured, logical, expressive, and complex as Standard English.

Boser (2006) notes that experts have been predicting the imminent demise of American dialects for decades because of increased mass media exposure, but the opposite seems true. Boser notes his conclusion is drawn from the work of expert linguists who are compiling a multi-volume

---

Standard English — substantially uniform formal and informal speech and writing of educated people that is widely recognized as acceptable wherever English is spoken and understood.

dialect — a variety of spoken language unique to a geographical area or social group. Variations in dialect may include phonological or sound variations, syntactical variations, and lexical or vocabulary variations.

reference North American English called the *Dictionary of Regional English*. This reference, which plots all major speech patterns in the continental United States and Canada, shows that regional dialects have become more pronounced. Boser points out that although mountains of data have been collected on *how* dialects are changing, understanding of *why* they change remains elusive.

African-American preschoolers who speak **Black English** (African-American English) use advanced and complex syntax, such as linking two clauses, as do their Standard English-speaking peers. Black English is a systematic, rule-governed dialect that can express all levels of thought. African-American English, Black English, and the term **Ebonics** refer to a grammatically consistent speech whose key features include not conjugating the verb "to be" and the dropping of some final consonants from words (Figure 4-2). In the past, many debated whether African-American English is a distinct language or a dialect; the controversy still exists today. Elevating African-American English to the status

Figure 4-2 Some features of African-American vernacular English.

1. extreme reduction of final consonants ("so" for "sold," "fo" for "four," "fin" for "find," "ba" for "bad")

2. phonological contrasts absent, such as -th versus -f at word endings ("baf" for "bath," "wif" for "with")

3. "l" or "r" deleted in words ("pants" for "parents," "doe" for "door," "he'p" for "help")

4. verb "be" used to indicate extended or continuous time ("I be walkin")

5. deletion of some "to be" verb forms ("He sick" or "She talk funny")

6. deletion of s or z sounds when using third person singular verbs ("He work all the time" or "She say don't go")

7. elimination of s in possessives ("Mama car got crashed")

8. use of two-word subjects ("Ben he be gone")

9. use of "it" in place of "there" ("It ain't none pieces left" for "There are no pieces left")

of a language has evoked emotional reaction nationwide from both African-Americans and others. Early childhood professionals have mixed opinions.

Many educators believe that the professional teacher's primary task is to preserve children's belief that they are already capable speakers and that teachers also should provide the opportunity for children to hear abundant Standard English speech models in classrooms. Linguists and educators do agree on the desperate need to teach some African-American children Standard English, but there is little agreement on how best to do so. Although it has long been suggested that the dialectic features of African-American vernacular English and its phonology create additional challenges for learning to read English, limited efforts to test this hypothesis have been undertaken. It should also be made clear that many African-American children speak Standard English, not African-American English.

Relatively minor variations in vocabulary, pronunciation, and grammatical forms are apparent in most dialects. Speakers of a particular dialect form a speech community that reflects the members' lifestyles or professional, national, family, or ethnic backgrounds. Certain common features mark the speech of the members, and no two members of a particular community ever speak exactly alike because each person's speech is unique. Unfortunately, to some, the term dialect can connote less-than-correct speech. Speech accents differ in a number of ways and are fully formed systems. Children from other than mainstream groups enter school with a set of linguistic and cultural resources that in some respects differ from, and even conflict with, rather than resemble, those of the school culture.

Individuals react to dialects with admiration, acceptance, ambivalence, neutral feelings, or rejection based on value judgments. Many Americans have just a superficial acquaintance with stereotypes of American Southern or New York varieties of English. People make assumptions about an individual's ethnicity, socioeconomic status, and competence based on the way he or she speaks, and unfortunately discrimination is not uncommon.

Black English — a language usually spoken in some economically depressed African-American homes. A dialect of non-Standard English having its own rules and patterns, it is also called African-American English.

Ebonics — a nonstandard form of English, a dialect often called Black English that is characterized by not conjugating the verb "to be" and by dropping some final consonants from words.

Just as a child who meets another child from a different part of the country with a different **accent** might say, "You sound funny!" Others may think of dialectic speech as crude or reflecting a lack of education. Early childhood teachers are trained to remain nonjudgmental and accepting. Dialect-speaking teachers, aides, and volunteers (working with children and families of the same dialect) may offer children a special degree of familiarity and understanding (Photo 4-2). A Standard English-speaking teacher may sound less familiar, but affords the child a model for growth in speaking the dominant language of our society, which is important to his life opportunities.

Although a dialect (or accent) may be an advantage in one's community, it may be a disadvantage outside of that community. When someone begins to learn English, others may feel betrayed because they feel the individual has denied his or her identity and joined forces with those who are rejecting group values.

4-2a The Teacher's Role: Working with Dialect-Speaking Families

Many early childhood centers employ **DAP** staff members who have dialects that the children can easily understand so that children feel at home. Teachers who speak the children's dialect may be eagerly sought and in short supply. Additional insight into the child's culture and the particular meanings of their words is often an advantage for teachers who have the same dialect as the children. They may be able to react to and expand upon ideas better than a Standard English-speaking teacher.

It is important for teachers to know whether the children are speaking a dialect and to understand dialectic differences. The four most common dialectic differences between Standard English and some common dialects occur in verb forms. These differences occur in the following areas:

- Subject-verb agreement
- Use of the verb "to be"
- Use of present tense for past tense
- Use of "got" for "have"

In some areas where a language other than English is spoken, part of the rules of the second language may blend and combine to form a type of English different from the standard. Two examples of this are (1) English spoken by some Native American children and (2) English spoken in communities close to the Mexican-American border.

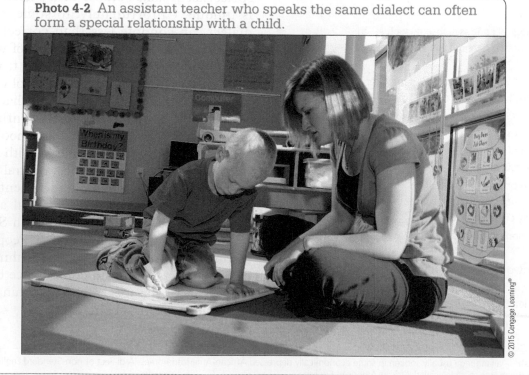

Photo 4-2 An assistant teacher who speaks the same dialect can often form a special relationship with a child.

---

accent — prominence or emphasis given to a word or syllable through one or more of the following factors: loudness, change of pitch, and longer duration (Harris & Hodges, 1995).

There are differing opinions about the teaching of preferred Standard English in early childhood centers. In most centers, however, preserving the child's native dialect, while moving slowly toward Standard English usage, is considered more desirable than providing immediate, purposeful instruction in standard forms. Joint family and center discussions can help clarify program goals.

Understanding dialectic differences is important to the teacher's understanding of each child. To give young children the best model possible, the early childhood teacher should speak Standard English. The federal government mandates that all children attending American public schools learn English, and instruction in English always begins at some point during the elementary school years.

Many successful teachers have speech accents and also possess other characteristics, abilities, and useful techniques that aid young children's development of language and literacy. It matters very little to children whether the teacher speaks a bit differently from the way they speak. The teacher's attitude, warmth, and acceptance of the dialect and the children themselves are very important considerations (Photo 4-3).

Teachers are in a unique position to build bridges rather than walls between cultures. Teachers' essential task is to create new and shared meanings with the children—new contexts that give meaning to the knowledge and skills being taught. The challenge is to find personally interesting and culturally relevant ways of creating new contexts for children, contexts in which school skills are meaningful and

Photo 4-3 A teacher builds a warm relationship with each child.

© 2016 Cengage Learning®

rewarding. Competence is not tied to a particular language, dialect, or culture. Professional educators realize that language instruction or any other part of the planned curriculum should not reject or be designed to be a replacement of children's language or culture, but rather be viewed as language expansion and enrichment.

Early childhood teachers may receive little instruction (teacher training) in the types of language behaviors to expect from diverse speakers; training in how to affect growth in language competencies also may be lacking. Teachers themselves will need to do their own classroom observation and research to identify cultural variations and differences that affect attending children's speech growth and development. Young preschoolers have learned the social speech expectations of their homes and possibly their communities. They know when to speak and when to be silent. At school they infer what is appropriate based on what they hear and observe there. When children begin to use a second language or second dialect, they tend to use words in syntactic constructions found in their native speech or dialect. Because many cultures, including Asian and some Native American communities, expect children to learn from listening, young children from these cultures may be relatively silent compared with children encouraged to be verbal from birth. Hawaiian children observed by researchers often did not like to be singled out for individual attention and tended to give minimal answers when questioned. In some cultures, children may be encouraged to use "yes" and interrupt adult speech to signify that they are in tune with the speaker.

Some facial expressions or gestures acceptable in one culture may be highly insulting in another. Even the acceptable distance between speakers of different languages varies. Teachers may interpret various child language (or lack of it) as disrespectful without considering cultural diversity. Misunderstandings between children, humorous as they may be to teachers, require sensitive handling.

A child may be a very good speaker of his particular dialect or language, or he may be just a beginner. Staff members working with the young child respect the child's natural speech and do not try to stop the child from using it. The goal is to promote the child's use of natural speech in his native dialect. Standard English can be taught by having many good speaking models available at the center for the child to hear. Interested adults, play activities, other children, and a rich language arts program can provide a setting where children listen and talk freely. Teachers refrain from correcting children's oral language errors and look for meaning and intention. They stress cooperation, collaboration, and frequent conversation.

The teacher should know what parts of the center's program are designed to increase the child's use of words. Teachers can show a genuine interest in words in their daily conversations with the children. Teachers can also use the correct forms of Standard English in a casual way, using natural conversation. Correcting the children in an obvious way could embarrass them and stop openness and enthusiasm.

Delpit (1995) points out that constant teacher correction and a focus on correctness impedes the child's "unconscious acquisition" of a language by raising the child's anxiety level and forcing him to cognitively monitor his every word. She provides an example of one four-year-old's resistance to being taught to answer the teacher's morning greeting with a specific "I'm fine, thank you" response. Delpit's example (1995) follows.

Teacher: Good morning, Tony. How are you?

Tony: I be's fine.

Teacher: Tony, I said, How are you?

Tony: (with raised voice) I be's fine.

Teacher: No Tony, I said, How are you?

Tony: (angrily) I done told you I be's fine. I ain't telling you no more. (p. 94)

Careful listening, skillful response, and appropriate questions during conversations help the child learn to put thoughts into words. The child thinks in terms of his own dialect or language first and, in time, expresses words in Standard English. Delpit (1995) recommends that teachers provide students with exposure to an alternative form and allow children the opportunity to practice that form in contexts that are not threatening, have real purpose, and are intrinsically enjoyable.

Preschool teachers must face the idea that children's language and appearance may unconsciously affect their attitudes about those children and, consequently, teacher behaviors. A new or unsure teacher may tend to seek out and communicate with children whose speech and appearance is most similar to her or his own. Extra effort may be necessary to watch this tendency and converse and instruct all attending children. Staff-parent meetings and additional planning are musts to meet the needs of children with diverse language patterns. Pronunciation guides helping teachers say children's names correctly are gathered from families at admitting interviews. This is just a small first step.

Sensitive, seasoned teachers will not put some children on the spot with direct questions or requests at group times. They may include additional storytelling or demonstration activities with young children whose native cultures use this type of approach. "Rappin" and words-to-music approaches may appear to a greater extent in some child programs. Drama may be a way to increase language use in other classrooms. To be sure, with the great diversity in today's early childhood classrooms, teachers will be struggling to reach and extend each child's language competence. This is not an easy task. Teachers who work with other than mainstream children learn that their own views of the world, or ways of using language in that world, are not necessarily shared by others.

Accepted instructional strategies used when working with dialect speaking children and families include:

1. Treating individual dialects with immediate acceptance and avoiding any pressure to hurry children toward Standard English usage. Over time, as exposure increases and children explore and gain experience, their speech will change.

2. Recognizing that trial and error are a part of the learning process. Children should be able to practice language skills on their own and have teachers who both listen and converse.

3. Realizing new language skills are added to existing linguistic skills while young children retain their native dialect and culture.

4. Providing a stimulating language environment full of the functional uses of language and meaningful social interactions. Grammar will improve over time.

5. Using teacher observations to guide the children or adults learning a language other than their native language, their speech is planning of program activities,

a teacher should guard against:

- correcting children in a way that makes them doubt their own abilities.
- giving children the idea that they are not trying hard enough to correct or improve their speech.
- discouraging children's speaking.
- allowing teasing about individual speech differences.
- interrupting children who are trying to express an idea.
- hurrying a child who is speaking.
- putting children on stage in an anxiety-producing way.

4-3 Second-Language Learners

Non-English-speaking children, like nonstandard dialect speakers, tend to come from lower socioeconomic backgrounds and attend schools with disproportionately high numbers of children in poverty; however, many will not fit this description. A large group of professional, foreign-born technology workers' families reside in some urban areas. In the world today, in many countries it is "natural" to grow up speaking more than one language. More than 70 percent of the world's population does so.

Second-language learners are children who speak their native language in social and cultural contexts out of school and have developed the necessary communicative competence. Second-language learners are also referred to as **bilingual** learners, English as a second-language students, students with limited English proficiency, language-minority learners, English-language learners, dual language learners, cultural learners, and linguistically diverse students.

Second-language learners are being introduced, in substantive ways, to another language. In this discussion, it is English. Cummins (2011) suggests it usually takes about two years for students to become reasonably fluent in conversational English. When second-language learners their speech is characterized by high-frequency vocabulary words and common grammatical constructions. A child is usually described as "balanced bilingual" when she possesses age-appropriate competence in both languages.

How many years will it take a child to gain second-language proficiency? The answer depends on whether oral or academic proficiency is being assessed. Hakuta, Goto Butler, and Witt (2000) calculate two to three years for oral proficiency, and four to seven years for academic English proficiency with school-age children. Most seasoned early childhood teachers will estimate fewer years for preschoolers who seem to learn English at an amazing rate.

There are two main categories of second-language learners who speak no or very little English. The first category consists of those children who come to this country at a very young age or are born here to immigrants who have lived in areas of the world where language as well as the culture, systems of government, and social structures are quite unlike those of the United States. The second group of learners is native born, such as Native Americans or Alaskan native born children, but speak a different language and are members of a different culture than the mainstream American culture.

4-3a Bilingual learners

A bilingual child can be described as a child younger than three who learns two (sometimes more) languages at the same time, or a child who learns a second language after age three. Sequential acquisition describes what occurs when a child starts to learn a second language after the first language is only partially established—such as when a young child enrolls in a school where his native language is not spoken.

Many researchers believe that some individuals may have a natural aptitude for learning language (Photo 4-4). Research emphasizes that the experience of becoming bilingual *itself* may make learning an additional new language easier (Marian, 2009). A bilingual advantage is also likely to be generalized beyond word learning to other kinds of language learning and an ability to better maintain verbal information.

---

bilingual — refers to an individual with a language background other than English who has developed proficiency in the primary language and a degree of proficiency in English.

Photo 4-4 Arianne speaks Spanish, German, and English.

© 2015 Cengage Learning®

It is not unusual to find enrolled preschool children who are learning English and also possess different degrees of proficiency in two or more other languages (Photo 4-4). Bilingual children initially might have smaller vocabularies when each language is considered separately. But when one considers that the memory capacity of young children is limited and this restricts their rate of vocabulary acquisition, it is understandable. Bilingual children have two sets of vocabularies to learn. At any particular point during development, one would expect them to know fewer vocabulary items in each language but approximately the same number when both languages are considered.

Many experts suggest that if more than one language is spoken in the home and both languages are spoken well, the infant should be exposed to both from the beginning. However, if, as is so often the case, the first language is spoken exclusively in the home, research indicates the child should be encouraged to develop expertise in a wide range of language functions in the first language with the expectation that these will easily transfer to the second language (English). Learning his native language allows the child's phonemic sensitivity to develop, which may allow him to gain an alphabetic insight that is needed for learning to read with ease.

4-3b Assessing Second-Language Learners

The most immediate question the teacher of a bilingual child must face is deciding how well the child is progressing in all of the languages the child is learning. A full language assessment with respect to the child's first language and with respect to the child's knowledge of English will probably show that the child's difficulties are limited to the acquisition of English. The testing of young children in multicultural and economically diverse classrooms is a growing practice. **DAP**

Teachers attempt to continually gauge if children are learning new vocabulary and gaining concept knowledge. Gaining a clear picture of each child's progress is, at times, difficult. Neuman and Wright (2013) note that second-language learners are likely to go through a silent period that indicates a lack of comfort in trying out new words.

Simple game-like testing after planned activities can reveal a lack of vocabulary learning or concept knowledge, which may indicate the need for more repetition of new vocabulary and content. One teacher's assessment game consisted of giving children a small flag on a stick to wave when they heard their teacher make a mistake. It was an assessment game that the children enjoyed. Objects and photos were among teacher's props for this game. "This is a turkey because it has colorful feathers," the teacher said. The teacher was showing a photo of a parrot. "You're waving flags, why?" the teacher asked. Another example is when the teacher said, "I'm holding a small shovel. You are waving because you don't think I can't dig a hole with this. How can I use it?" (The teacher was holding a small rake.) "Wave your flag if this is called a rake as Brooke has just told us." Both examples are a fast visual check to assess what wasn't retained and who didn't profit from instruction. The examples given suited children with English language ability. The game-like assessment might also be used for the names of common classroom or environment words or objects that second-language learners are learning.

Tests of language always reflect aspects of culture, so it is impossible to construct a single test that is absolutely culturally sensitive and incorporates aspects of all cultures to which children belong. The phrase "culturally sensitive" refers to whether a test is responsive to social and cultural differences among test takers. Any intelligence test with many questions about farm animals would be considered insensitive if one was trying to test the knowledge of inner city preschoolers.

When working with English language learners it is important that the learner receives input that is not only comprehensible, but that is just slightly beyond his or her current level of competence. Knowing common strategies that young children use to learn English as a second language helps teachers. Children may:

- assume that what people are saying is directly related to the ongoing situation.
- learn a few stock expressions or formulaic speech and start to talk.
- search for patterns that recur in the language.
- make the most of the language they already have.
- spend their major effort on getting across meaning and save refinement for later.

Recommended strategies that teachers of language learners use follow. Teachers:

- should build on what the child already knows.
- should not rush instruction, but rather should go slow enough to aid understanding.
- should use scaffolding and combine new words with some kind of gesture or action.
- design room area hideaways that provide child comfort and safety.
- plan frequent activities with no or minimal expectations of a child having to speak.
- encourage English-speaking children by suggesting ways to communicate with second-language peers.
- expand and extend children's limited word use.
- talk about present and at hand classroom happenings.
- restate their comments in more simplified terms at times and offer consistent routines.
- ensure children's inclusion by inviting a child by name to small-group activities.

Most educators realize it will take time for most second-language learners to become competent users of English and children will also need to develop a knowledge and mastery of formal schooling practices. Educators believe all children can attain high levels of achievement if provided with a rich, challenging curriculum and appropriate forms of assistance.

An effective early childhood curriculum for second-language should provide for frequent and diverse opportunities for speaking and listening that offer **scaffolding** to help guide the child through the learning process. The curriculum also should encourage children to take risks when speaking, construct meaning, and reinterpret knowledge within comfortable social contexts. Pairing students as language partners and coworkers in projects is being given increased classroom emphasis.

The dilemma that second-language learners may face in early school experiences is likened to a situation in which you can't win. To learn the new language, one needs to be socially accepted by those speaking the language; however, to be socially accepted, one has to be able to speak the new language. Young children often hurdle this bind by using various strategies, including gestures to invite others to play and accept their company. Crying, whimpering, pointing, miming, and making other nonverbal requests may also be tried. Children collect information by watching, listening, and speculating. They may talk to themselves and experiment with sounds or rehearse what they have heard. Telegraphic and formulaic language develops and they may say "Hey!" or "Lookit" over and over to gain attention.

Preschool dual language learners (DLLs) may exhibit temporary disruptive, challenging or inappropriate coping behaviors in classrooms. These behaviors may occur as a reaction to the difficulty or stress of learning languages both at home and school. Educators routinely examine all children's behaviors and possible causes that might be responsible for new or persistent behavior that can interfere with learning. They use informal and varied professional assessments and conduct family consultations to develop instructional planning strategies and individual plans that may affect a change of unwanted behaviors.

Monolingual and bilingual speakers make inferences about social and linguistic appropriateness based on continued interaction in diverse

---

scaffolding — a teaching technique helpful in promoting languages, understanding, and child solutions. It includes teacher-responsive conversation, open-ended questioning, and facilitation of children's initiatives. Also defined as instruction in which a teacher builds upon what the child already knows to help the child accomplish a task and/or suggests breaking a task down into simpler components to promote accomplishment.

According to Schwartz (2011), regular high-level use of more than one language may actually improve early childhood brain development He notes:

> According to several different studies, command of two or more languages bolsters the ability to focus in the face of distraction, decide between competing alternatives, and disregard irrelevant information. These essential skills are grouped together, known in brain terms as executive function. The research suggests they develop ahead of time in bilingual children, and are already evident in kids as young as 3 or 4." (p. 26)

---

social situations. Learning a second language includes a number of difficult tasks. The child must:

- produce sounds that may not be used in the native language.
- understand that native speech sounds or words may have different meanings in the new (second) language.
- learn and select appropriate responses.
- sort and revise word orders.
- learn different cultural values and attitudes.
- control the flow of air while breathing.

Experts have identified four stages in learning English: (1) home language use, (2) an observational and listening period, (3) telegraphic and formulaic speech, and (4) fluid language use. Many factors may have an impact on how quickly young children acquire a second language: motivation, exposure, age, personality, aptitude, consistency, attitude, learning style, opportunity and support, and the individual characteristics of the home and family environment. Snow (2011) states research is clear. Children who are dual-language learners show the best gains in English when their teacher uses their home language in conjunction with English. An important technique—admitting and recognizing that a child is a classroom resource when it comes to explaining other ways of naming and describing objects or other ways of satisfying human needs—should be utilized by educators. Printed word cards in both languages can be added to the classroom to reinforce this idea.

Bilingual youngsters have not encountered a lifelong setback, but instead, they may be more imaginative, better with abstract notions, and more flexible in their thinking than monolingual children. They also have been described as more creative and better at solving complex problems. Compared with monolingual children, bilingual children may develop more awareness concerning the nature of language and how it works. Horz (2012) suggests that being bilingual enhances cognitive development. He posits bilinguals are better able to pay attention, identify spoken syllables, and display an enhanced working memory.

Some English-only parents, particularly more affluent ones, seek tutors or early childhood programs that offer their monolingual children the opportunity to become second-language learners. Nationally many legislators believe bilingual programs should be available for all children, but this is yet to become a national priority.

Youngquist and Martinez-Griego (2009) conclude that when a *strong foundation* is developed in a child's native language, he will learn to read, write, and speak in English faster than a child without one. These authors emphasize the importance of involving families and community to support the school's efforts. This *has* become a national priority recognized by professional associations, such as NAEYC and the International Reading Association (IRA). It is also considered a priority in Head Start programs and the No Child Left Behind legislation, and it is mentioned in most state standards that promote quality.

Pandey (2012) suggests functional bilingualism strengthens children's interpersonal and academic skills, and their understanding of people and customs (p. 96). In Pandey's 2010 publication, *The Child Language Teacher*, she states that familiarity with more than one language enhances children's academic and problem-solving skills and helps them maintain healthy, confidence-boosting ties with at least two communities. On the other hand, some educators worry that a young child's bilingualism may cause family distress. Educators have raised concerns about placing young English-language learners in English-only preschools and believe that this may result in the children losing the ability to communicate effectively in their native language. This, they feel, may adversely affect family relationships and the young child's conceptual development.

4-4 Program Planning for Second-Language Learners

Educators urge program planners who provide second-language learning opportunities to realize that the child's exposure, comfort level, motivation, familiarity, and practice in real communicative contexts are all important considerations. Curriculum developers in early childhood programs that enroll other-than-English-speaking children will have to decide their position on the best way to instruct. A debate rages. One end of the debate espouses native language use, native cultural instruction, and academic learning in the child's native language before instruction in English begins. At the other end, advocates would present English on the child's first day of schooling, with minimal use of the child's native language. Those on this side of the argument believe that the earlier English is introduced and confronted, the greater the child's linguistic advantage. Others disagree, saying no research evidence supports the idea that there is a neural window on second-language learning, and deferring instruction for a year or two is not a disadvantage. Policy recommendations put forth by the National Institute for Early Education Research in 2006 say that support for English language learners should be provided in both the home language and English, where feasible.

Educators note the different points of view concerning English language learners, but may choose to create their own programs by using innovative curricula and other instructional techniques because no comprehensive studies clearly chart the right path for educators to take when teaching preschool ELLs (English language learners) (Freedson-Gonzales, 2008). Each teacher and each educational leader must decide what will work for the children they have enrolled in the context of the curriculum they use and the standards that guide them (Nemeth,

2009). Nemeth and Endosi (2013) note some programs schedule home language times and English-only times each school day. This might mean English-only during play times and home language during meals and snack times. They recommend teachers use props, a tone of voice, body language, pictures, and visuals to clarify new word meanings.

Above all, most educators agree that other-than-English-speaking children need to be perceived as intellectually able, and their teachers should hold high achievement and academic expectations for them as they do for all enrolled children. Teachers are aware that planning well for each child means gathering and knowing as much as one can about the child's culture, home environment, family, and community.

Au (2006) recommends that in any curriculum approach, educators need to realize that one factor that handicaps the academic advancement of English language learners is some teachers' tendency to be overly concerned about the surface features of language, such as correct pronunciation of English, rather than the content of the ideas students are trying to communicate. She also points out that if students believe that what they have to say is important, they will have the confidence to learn the language needed to express those ideas. Most programs approach the differences existing between home and school cultures by promoting children's biculturalism. This allows children to have successful experiences both in their families, where one set of values and behaviors prevails, and in school, where another set of values and behaviors may be expected. In a culturally sensitive approach, early childhood professionals would use modeling with culturally diverse children and slowly introduce and increase the practice of teaching via direct inquiry, particularly using verbal questions while they continue to use modeling. This practice would help increase children's verbal skills and their ability to follow directions.

Planned activities that relate to the experiences of children's everyday lives are also important. For example, cooperative learning activities that involve a small group of young children working together helps develop social skills and positive group relations. Jones and Shue (2013) describe how one preschool teacher's approach to instruction evolved from her desire to implement a classroom project approach. The project was to be interesting enough to engage all children attending. Noticing that native English-speaking children spoke and played with only others like themselves and Spanish-speaking children did the same, the teacher believed a project approach could integrate her group: particularly the hands-on activities planned when the class endeavored to create a classroom pizza parlor. Both groups had home and community pizza experiences in common. The pizza project she planned became an effective method of introducing a curricular topic where joint problem-solving and teamwork occurred. This was done by both child consulting and planning meetings and resulting exploration of hands-on activities that promoted cooperation, language use, and vocabulary. Concept development opportunities occurred frequently.

Early childhood educators working with enrolled English language learners have studied the *Common Core State Standards for English Language Arts* (2010), which is used in all but a few states. They realize kindergarten outcomes will be a huge challenge for English language learners. Educators, therefore, are re-examining how best to increase children's attainment of these ambitious expectations with appropriate preschool-level instruction. Kindergarten curriculum outcomes aim to ensure children can demonstrate a beginning level of Standard English grammar and its conventions when speaking or writing at the end of the school year.

Photo 4-5 The introduction of English picture books benefit second-language learners.

© 2015 Cengage Learning®

4-4a Classroom Activities

The importance of opportunities for English language learners to engage in pretend play early in their preschool attendance period is emphasized by Roskos and Christie (2007) and Cheatham and Ro (2010). Teacher support can promote and extend children's play periods. When reading and writing play materials are suggested and supplied by a teacher during child-selected (or teacher suggested) play scenarios, child play has a chance for added literacy depth. Many read-alouds lead naturally to possible pretend play and reenacting of the story. Role-playing, whether based on book characters or child-chosen scenario characters, provides an additional benefit resulting in higher measures of child creativity and enhanced ability to analyze situations from different perspectives (Bronson & Merryman, 2010).

The value of exposing second-language learning children to quality books cannot be overlooked (Photo 4-5). Story times and one to-one, adult-child book readings can supply vocabulary and meaning in a way that conversational models alone cannot accomplish. Songs and music can also present language-learning opportunities. Print use in the center environment is another vehicle to promote literacy development. Above all, opportunities for abundant play and interaction with English-speaking children are critical. The most successful methods for teaching a second language include the same techniques mentioned in the monolingual child's learning of his first language—warm, responsive, articulate adults involved with children's everyday, firsthand exploration of the environment.

Additional suggested teacher strategies and techniques follow.

- Provide a safe, accepting classroom environment.
- Respond to meaning, rather than speech technicalities or specifics.
- Promote sharing and risk taking.
- Make classroom activities inviting, interesting, meaningful, and successful.

- Emphasize and repeat key words in sentences.
- Point at objects or touch them while naming them, when possible.
- Learn how to correctly pronounce the child's name.
- Include the child in small groups where there are other child models to follow.
- Help the child realize he is unique and special, exactly "as is."
- Learn a few useful words in the child's language (for example, *bathroom*, *eat*, *stop*, *listen*).
- Gesture and use objects and pictures that give children additional clues, such as a picture-based daily schedule.
- Provide activity choices in which the child does not have to interface with others—so-called safe havens.
- During activity times, provide enough staff so that teachers can work closely with children and materials.
- Use a running commentary technique in interactions. "Serena is painting with red paint." "I'm pinning a name tag on your sweater."
- Choose predictable books to share.
- Work with a small group at story-reading times.
- Use repeated presentations of the same songs at group times.
- Link up English-speaking "partners" in noncompetitive games.
- Take the time to look children in the eye, showing you value your interaction (Nemeth, 2009).
- Check classroom noise levels to assure English-language learners will have no difficulty distinguishing English speech sounds.

When teachers work with second-language learners, they make adjustments similar to those families make when talking to their very young children; these include organizing talk around visual references (real objects, actions, happenings, people, and so on), using simple syntax, producing many repetitions and paraphrases, speaking slowly and clearly, checking often for comprehension, and expanding and extending topics introduced by the child. The teacher can develop a list of survival words in both English and the native language of attending children such as eat, help, bathroom, play, rest, and so on for her own and the children's use. Figure 4-3 is a list of some survival words in Spanish. Professional education associations recommend that teachers faced with many different languages in their classrooms consider grouping together, at specific times during the day, children that speak the same or similar languages so that children can construct knowledge with others who speak their home language.

Playmates of second-language learners can be encouraged not only to be aware and accepting of other children but to approach and invite them to play. Through discussion, example, and modeling, children can learn to use gestures, to use simple sentences, to speak slowly, and to repeat themselves or use different words when they think their "friends" do not quite understand. Teachers stress that these new classmates may need help. One classroom regularly scheduled a short picture book reading time when family members shared a book in a language other than English. Children could choose whether to attend. The book would then

Figure 4-3 Survival words and phrases in English and Spanish.

English Word or Phrase	Spanish Word or Phrase
Hello	Hola
Teacher	la maestra
Bathroom	el baño
Eat	comer
Play	jugar
Drink	beber
Wash	lavar
Please sit down	Siéntese, por favor
Welcome to school	Bienvenidos a la escuela
Take a rest	Tome un descanso
Do you need help?	¿Necesita ayuda?
My name is	Mi nombre es…
Join us, please	Por favor, únase a nosotros.
We are friends	Somos amigos
Does that hurt?	¿Te duele?
Pleased to meet you	¡Mucho gusto!
Let's go outside	Salgamos fuera
Are you cold?	¿Está frío?
Time to clean up	Momento de la limpieza
Time to pick up	Hora de recogida
Thank you	Gracias
Your mom will be here soon.	Tu mamá volverá pronto.

be repeated in English by their regular teacher, and a discussion period examined how children both attempted to understand and felt during the first reading.

Second-language learners can be ignored and left out of peer play. Even when trying to communicate nonverbally, they can be treated as "babies" or as invisible. They may be cast as the infant in dramatic play situations or be the object of a mothering child's attention—perhaps unwanted attention. Other children may speak to them in high-pitched voices and in shortened and linguistically reduced forms as they have observed adults sometimes do with very young children who are learning to speak. Teachers should monitor these peer behaviors and discourage them if necessary.

4-4b Reaching Families

Home-school instructional support programs have provided books, electronic media, "borrowed" materials and equipment, and "take home" suggestions for homes with limited access to English-language models and storybooks. Encouraging families to continue to maintain their first language and their home language literacy activities, and perhaps increase everyday conversations, is a common practice. Schools usually ask families questions about what types of language exposure a child has had since birth and what types of literacy experiences have been associated with them. Designing room features and planning curriculum activities that welcome a family's participation in classroom activities are both important considerations. **naeyc** **DAP**

Early childhood educators who speak more than one language and are culturally knowledgeable are an invaluable resource in the early childhood setting. Many experts and researchers advocate recruiting teacher assistants and classroom volunteers who speak children's native tongue. A classroom interpreter may frequently be necessary and considered an invaluable staff member in many programs.

Teachers can expect a Spanish-speaking child to have a problem producing consonant sounds that do not exist in his native language, such as *d, j, r, v, sh, th*, and *s*; beginning-of-word blends, such as *st, sp*, and *sm*; and word endings of *r* blends, such as *-rd, -rt*, and *-rs*. A few other word sounds also will be difficult.

Second-language learners may reach a stage when they seem to repeat words, focus intently, and rehearse words. This happens not for the purpose of communication, but rather so the child can practice through repetition, which is reminiscent of younger preschoolers' private speech or self-talk during play situations. These rehearsing behaviors are usually done at a low volume. The first unintelligible utterances that second-language learners issue may be sound experimentation.

4-4c Providing Targeted Support

English language learners are just as unique as native speakers, and they often profit from the targeted supportive assistance teachers offer. Motivation to learn a new language when separate from family overwhelms some children, and they may have a problem initiating play with others. The social actions and reactions of teachers and other children can help or impact their desire to learn the classroom's language. Teachers should design activities, environments, and classroom situations that attempt to increase children's motivation in a number of ways. Capturing a child's curiosity, enhancing children's feelings of acceptance and safety, or developing trust helps. Most teachers get clever when offering targeted teaching strategies to influence a child's adjustment and ability to choose to participate and engage. Teaching a child a few common English vocabulary words and gestures can be a first positive step in the child's ability to communicate his needs and desires. Beginning vocabulary words are usually labels for objects and people or short social phrases such as "Hi," "Play," and "Please." The child's receptive vocabulary grows at a faster pace as she understands additional words to name things in both languages. Noticing Alfaro's minimal understanding of English words, his teacher planned targeted support activities and one-on-one instruction.

Teachers can plan more effectively if they have background information concerning the second-language learners. Getting the answers to the following questions would help. Answers and information is gained through observation at school and by interviewing parents and families during intake interviews or at a later time:

- Is there any special speech (either native or English) that the child uses during the school day? If so, when, where, and with whom?

- Does the child participate in nonverbal play with peers?
- Does the child seek out native-speaking peers or native-speaking adults in the classroom that the child feels comfortable with?
- Do parents describe the child as talkative at home? Or verbally limited or having a recognized problem speaking with neighborhood children?
- Is the child being ignored, teased, or laughed at during school?
- When does the child appear happy at home and at school?
- Are there times of day when the child speaks more often or that are particularly difficult for the child at school?
- Does the child use any headsets for listening activities at school?
- Are there people who use his home language at school?
- Will the child join in during a song in his home language at school or home?
- If given a sign or signal to use to gain help, will the child use it at school?
- Has using a school buddy system had any success?
- When was the child's last eye and ear physical exam?

- At school, how many English directions does the child follow? When?
- What classroom areas or materials interest him the most?
- Does he use nonverbal communication at home or school? Is it successful?

4-5 Promoting Cultural Awareness

Teachers interested in studying the cultures of enrolled children can start by identifying components of culture. These components include family structure; definitions of stages, periods, or transitions during a person's life; roles of adults and children; their corresponding behavior in terms of power and politeness; discipline; time and space; religion; food; health and hygiene; history; traditions; holidays; and celebrations (Photo 4-6).

In some cultures it is believed that children are not appropriate conversational partners for adults. Children may not be encouraged to initiate conversations about themselves or their interests, and adult talk may not be child-centered. Children may have learned that it is impolite to look directly at adults when talking. Some children grow up learning that cooperation is more highly valued than competition; others do not.

Photo 4-6 Children's food preferences are often discussed with parents.

TeachSource Video 4-1

© 2016 Cengage Learning®

Multicultural Lessons: Embracing Similarities and Differences

Shelley Outwater, a literacy coach, discusses her philosophy for helping her students become aware of cultural similarities and differences in her classroom.

1. Discuss how multicultural learning and language learning can go hand-in-hand in a classroom such as Shelly's classroom or in a preschool classroom.

2. In the video's read-aloud segment, what teacher techniques and strategies are used in the adult-child conversation to increase child understanding and comprehension?

Cultures are complex and changing, so understanding cultural similarities and differences can be a life's study in itself. **Culture** is defined here as all the activities and achievements of a society that individuals within that society pass from one generation to the next.

Ethnic origin is often a basic ingredient in subcultural groupings. **Subculture** is defined as other than a dominant culture. Class structure also exists in societies consisting of upper, middle, and lower income groups. Often, patterns of child-rearing vary between cultures and classes.

Practitioners may have to field questions from children about another child's speech. Answering in an open, honest fashion with accurate information gives the adult an opportunity to affirm diversity and perhaps correct a child's biased ideas. Negative stereotypes can be diminished or

dismissed. Before answering, it is a good idea to clarify what the child is really asking. Examples of teacher statements follow:

"Yes, Paloma speaks some words you don't understand. Her family comes from Guatemala and they speak the Spanish language. Paloma is learning lots of new words at school in the language of her new country—English."

"Quan doesn't talk to you because he doesn't know our words yet. He speaks a different language at his house. He is listening, and one day he will speak. While he is listening and learning words to speak, he wants to play. Show him with your hands and words what you want him to do. He will understand."

Teachers working with culturally diverse children need to watch and listen closely. Children's behavior and movements will give clues to their well-being and feelings of safety in the group. Teachers may need to ease into situations in which unpleasant remarks or actions are directed at a newly enrolled child who speaks a different language and express sadness, such as: "Ricardo has heard some unkind and unfriendly words from you boys in the loft. He is new at school and doesn't know what our school is like. I'm going to try and help Ricardo enjoy his first day in our room."

An adult's inability to modify their speech to a child's level, neutral or negative environments, family arrangements that require children to be alone for long periods, frequent situations in which children are expected to be quiet or cannot gain adult attention, and a lack of books or early reading experiences are all factors that can affect speech growth. Families are the primary language teachers during the early years, and language competence grows out of familiar situations, such as seeking help or establishing joint attention—situations that provide frameworks in which children learn to make their intentions plain and to interpret the intentions of others.

4-5a Planning Cultural Awareness Language Activities

In planning language activities of all types, every effort must be made to make children aware of cross-cultural similarities while exploring

---

culture — all the activities and achievements of a society that individuals within that society pass from one generation to the next.

subculture — an ethnic, regional, economic, or social group exhibiting characteristic patterns of behavior sufficient to distinguish it from others within an embracing culture or society.

differences. Language arts programming should draw on the linguistic, cultural, and personal experiences of language-diverse children. When planning instructional activities, it is important to provide opportunities that are familiar to children from their family and community life. Parents and extended family members can be invited to share family stories and artifacts relating to theme units, learning centers, or other program components.

Young children can be exposed to the idea that people eat, sleep, wear clothing, celebrate, dance, sing, live in groups, and speak to one another in common languages, and that they do these things in ways that may be either the same as or different from the ways their families do these things. Planned activities can make comparisons, treating diversity with the dignity it deserves. Skin color, hairstyles, food preferences, clothing, and music are starting points for study. Modeling friendship and cooperation between cultures and planning activities showing dissimilar individuals and groups living in harmony is a good idea. Stories exist in all languages and in most dialects. Some centers ask children and parents to contribute family photos to use to construct a classroom "My Family" book. Each child is asked to dictate a caption for each family photo. The book is permanently placed in the class library collection. When a new child enrolls, new family photos are added. (Identifying quality multicultural and multiethnic picture books is discussed in Chapter 8.) Room displays, bulletin boards, and learning centers should also reflect the cultural diversity of attending children.

It is important to plan language arts programs that incorporate different cultural styles of dramatic play, storytelling, and chanting. Librarians can help teachers discover picture books and other materials written in dialects or two-language translations.

4-5b Families as Partners

A strong connection between home and school should exist with families playing a role in program planning and as assistants or teachers in classrooms. When family literacy rates are depressed, teachers have to proceed carefully with suggestions concerning reading to children. Wordless books and parent's oral stories are alternatives. Reading books aloud at home in a bilingual child's primary language is also recommended. (Family literacy programs are discussed in Chapter 18.)

Volk and Long (2005) have the following suggestions, which can help educators honor children's home and school literacy resources.

- Guard against a **deficit perspective** that distorts the educator's vision when working with marginalized families.
- Gain the perspective that homes, families, cultures, and communities possess "funds of knowledge," that is literacies and individuals with valuable skills.
- Understand that children become literate in many ways.
- Recognize that most families value education and believe it is important.
- Recognize that families may use different yet various and effective methods to support literacy.
- Believe that children participate in many literacy interactions at home (Figure 4-4).
- Realize that children may be surrounded by abundant human and literary resources including networks of support and people of varying ages and abilities.
- Recognize that peers help each other and may clarify the teacher's statements.

4-5c Program Types

Controversy exists concerning which type of program is best suited to the child learning English as a second language. There are various program types, such as

- Bilingual programs: Two languages are used for instruction.
- Transitional bilingual programs: Children's first language is used as a medium of instruction until they become fluent enough to receive all of their instruction in English.
- Newcomer programs: Recent immigrant children are provided a special academic environment for a limited period. They provide a welcoming classroom environment and use instructional strategies to orient children to American life and culture. Bilingual staffs are secured when possible.
- Developmental bilingual programs: Equal status is given to English and another language,

---

deficit perspective — an attitude or belief that attributes children's school failures to children themselves, or to their family or culture.

Figure 4-4 How families can increase child literacy with home activities.

Dear Families,

Many parents ask how they can help develop their child's literacy skills at home.

A families' daily activities can be literacy-building and might include:
- Reading letters from their country of origin together.
- Consulting on children's homework.
- Jointly reviewing school assignments.
- Reading all school-home written communication with children.
- Reading and discussing all kinds of books such as phone book, dictionaries, encyclopedias, address books, recipe books, and reference books in their home language or English.
- Practicing new school skills or family skills that require reading such as instruction manuals, bills, announcements, advertisements, junk mail, milk and cereal cartons, and so on.
- Reading age-level appropriate books to their child in English or home language and discussing narrative, or naming actions or objects in illustrations.
- Discussing electronic or digital media they experience it together. Selecting educational content when possible.
- Playing games with and without electronic media especially games with cards, numbers, alphabet letters and rules.
- Participating in writing, singing, listening, viewing activities connected to their home or the American culture.
- Reading or listening to material concerned with the family's religious orientation and experience.
- Providing writing and art materials in a home area that is comfortable and supplied with a variety of paper, notebooks, coloring books, etc. and different kinds of writing tools—pens, markers, crayons, etc.
- Talking about print in the neighborhood such as street signs, house numbers, window ads, posted ads and announcements, menus, and so on.
- Enacting books, plays, events, or common and important family occasions with role playing.

Sincerely,
Your child's teacher

Digital Download

promoting full proficiency in two languages. Mixing and translating language is avoided but acceptable at social times.

- Two-way immersion programs: This type of program provides integrated language and academic instruction for native English speakers and native speakers of another language. This enables English speakers to develop second-language proficiency. Both groups' families must have an interest in bilingualism.
- Tutor-assisted programs: A special tutor (or teacher) works with a child for a portion of the school day.
- Full-immersions: A full-immersion program offers an age-appropriate curriculum in a language foreign to the child. August and Shanahan (2006) point out full immersion in English that gives no attention to children's native language has not been shown to offer any advantage for later academic schooling.

Frequently mentioned features of successful English-language learner programs include:

- ongoing and guided parental involvement.
- professional development for early childhood educators.
- the promotion of growth and proficiency in both first and secondary languages.
- the use of assessment that is linked to instructional objectives to inform instructional planning and delivery.
- developmentally appropriate and culturally sensitive curriculum.
- high standards for language acquisition and academic achievement.
- strong staff joint planning and leadership.
- sheltered instruction, an approach that integrates language and content instruction.
- academic instruction in English.
- the adoption of strategies to make content (in activities) meaningful and comprehensive.

In addition, visuals and images (pictorial representations) used while the teacher is interacting improves student listening comprehension and may reduce recall errors.

4-6 Assessment and Types of Special Needs DAP

Assessment is usually undertaken when teachers suspect that a child has difficulty communicating and could profit from specialized instruction. The goal is to identify whether a child's language is more or less advanced than that of other children his age (delayed language) or is deficient when compared with performance on social and/or intellectual tasks (language deficit) or whether the child fits other categories. Screening tests should be conducted by trained professionals.

The California State Department of Education (2009) suggests teachers should team up with professionals knowledgeable about second-language acquisition to sort out which child behaviors are caused by second-language learning and other causes. Behaviors that can be misinterpreted include the following:

- speaks infrequently
- speaks excessively (either in home language or in English)
- refuses to answer questions
- confuses similar sounding words
- is unable to tell or recall stories
- has poor general recall
- uses poor pronunciation
- uses poor syntax and grammar
- does not volunteer information (p. 64)

4-6a Types of Special Needs and Language Development

Special language-development preschool centers with expert personnel are available in most communities for children with easily identifiable communication deficiencies, such as hearing loss, visual impairment, and obvious speech impairments. Other children in need of special help may not be identified at the preschool level and may function within the wide range of children considered to be average or typical for preschool ages. In language arts, learning disability is a term that refers to a group of disorders manifested by significant difficulties in the acquisition and use of listening, speaking, reading, or writing. Most programs are reticent to label children as having language learning problems because of their lack of expertise to screen and evaluate children in a truly professional manner. Referral to speech-language pathologists or local or college clinics is suggested to families when a question exists concerning a particular child's progress. Early childhood teachers are not speech or language pathologists and therefore should not be expected to diagnose language problems or prescribe therapy. Communication disorders are usually divided into two main categories—**hearing disabilities** and speech and language disabilities.

Speech and language disabilities can affect the way people speak and understand; these range from simple sound substitutions to not being able to use speech and language effectively. Many children in the United States have experienced some kind of expressive speech problem, delay, or disability; the most common problems involving articulation, language, voice, and fluency disorders, or a combination of these. Most articulation problems not caused by physical, sensory, or neurological damage respond to treatment. Nonorganic causes of problems include:

- lack of stimulation.
- lack of need to talk.
- poor speech models.
- lack of or low reinforcement.
- insecurity, anxiety, crisis.
- shyness or lack of social confidence

4-6b Language Delay

Language delay may be connected to syntax, semantics, morphology, pragmatics, vocabulary, and remembering and discussing happenings in the right order. Language delay is characterized by a marked slowness in the development of the vocabulary and grammar necessary for expressing and understanding thoughts and ideas. It may involve both comprehension and the child's expressive language output and quality. It is wise for families to consult a speech-language pathologist if the delay is more than six months, so language therapy begins if recommended.

---

hearing disabilities — characterized by an inability to hear sounds clearly. This may range from hearing speech sounds faintly or in a distorted way, to profound deafness.

speech and language disabilities — communication disorders that affect the way people talk and understand; range from simple sound substitutions to not being able to use speech and language at all.

A complete study of a child includes first looking for physical causes, particularly hearing loss, and then examining other structural (voice-producing) conditions. Neurological limitations come under scrutiny, as do emotional development factors. Home environments and family communication styles are also examined.

A language-delayed child may have a small vocabulary and may use short and simple sentences with many grammatical errors. He may have difficulty maintaining a conversation and may often talk about the immediate present rather than future happenings. He can have difficulty understanding others and in making himself understood. Besides linguistic problems, a language-delayed child may have problems classifying objects and recognizing similarities and differences. He also may ignore opportunities to play with others.

Additional behaviors a teacher might notice in a language-delayed child include:

- less variety in sentence structure
- simple two- and three-word sentences
- less frequent speech
- frequent occurrence of playing alone
- less adept participation in joint planning with classmates

Early childhood educators concerned about the speech and socialization of "late talkers" should discuss their suspicions with their teaching team and supervisors. Teachers might readily agree with the following sample description of a language-delayed child: "Speaks markedly less well than other children of the same age and seems to have normal ability in intellectual, motor, sensory, and emotional control areas, but may be rejected by peers."

The quantity of parent talk with their young children can differ greatly between two families—a child from one family could hear 700 utterances each day while a child from another family hears 11,000 utterances. Children in the first category can seem to possess lower-level language skills not caused by any innate problem, but rather by an environmental situation.

Teachers working with language-delayed children use the following interactive techniques:

- gaining attention with tempting, interest-catching activities
- being at eye level, face-to-face, if possible

- establishing eye contact
- displaying enthusiasm and playfulness
- establishing a play activity involving "my turn, your turn" interaction
- verbalizing single words, short phrases, or short sentences, depending on the child's verbal level
- pausing, waiting, and looking expectantly, encouraging the child's turn to talk
- repeating teacher statements and pausing expectantly
- copying the child's actions or verbalizations
- following the child's focus of interest with joint teacher interest
- probing the child's interest with logical questions
- maintaining close, accepting physical contact and a warm interactive manner

A few children may make a conscious decision not to try to learn Standard English or a new language when they are confronted with a language other than their native language or dialect. A number of reasons for their choice are possible. If others enrolled or teachers speak their native language, they may believe it is not necessary or simply not worth the effort. Families may not give a high priority to learning the new language, or children's enrollment may consist of only a few mornings a week. A child's decision can be temporary or long-term.

Cloistered Children. Some teachers and educators describe children with inadequate language due to lack of human interactive environments. To be "cloistered" connotes isolation, separation, limited experience, meager human contact, a narrow view of the world, small or sparsely furnished living quarters, and perhaps a time-consuming devotion to spiritual contemplation and prayer. In the cloistered child, spiritual contemplation and prayer is replaced with the passive pursuit of hours and hours of never discussed screen watching. The cloistered child often displays language delay and may also display one or many of the following characteristics:

- limited attention span.
- inability to express ideas.
- limited language and vocabulary.
- inability to draw on past knowledge.

- inability to listen.
- impulsiveness (says first thing that pops into mind).
- lack of perseverance ("It's work. It's too hard.").
- blunted interest and curiosity.
- disorganization.
- impatience, inability to wait.
- poor conversation skills.

To develop what is seen as "missing language and missing experience," experts recommend a curriculum that includes lots of talk, active involvement, time and play with others, and exposure to literature. Some educators recommend opportunities to play with peers and plan actions, which facilitate the child's seeing himself in control, along with the promotion of child resourcefulness in seeking help from others.

Overstressed Children. There are many different reasons why some children have stressful living situations. When young children's stress is connected to new adults, new situations, groups of peers, books and book-reading times, or conversations with an adult, teachers will notice child anxiety, aversion behavior, and reluctance in speaking out in groups. O'Leary, Newton, Lundz, Hall, O'Connell, Raby, and Czarnecka (2002) describe degrees of stress and possible causative factors teachers should avoid.

> Mild stress enhances conscious learning, but too much stress, especially for too long a time, prevents it. Stress speaks primarily to the emotional learning system, and there it works primarily in a negative way.

> Extreme stress, caused by too much different information, unrelated information, or information too rapidly introduced or presented within too short a space of time, adds to a negative emotional reaction and clicks in a fear response. This memory is engraved below the level of awareness and becomes conscious as an attitude toward or feeling about the situation or topic. (p. 46)

Fortunately, when no pressure and stress exist and a safe school environment is experienced, many children who display an initial aversion to certain school activities, including language arts activities, venture forth slowly and their attitudes change. Most early childhood teachers have been acquainted with children who avoid book-sharing times, yet listen from another area in the classroom. After a period, they move closer, and eventually they join the read-aloud group.

4-6c Expressive and Receptive Language Difficulties

Educators begin suspecting problems in language development when they observe attending children in a variety of classroom situations, including group times, play times, adult-child exchanges, and social interactions. In lower elementary school grades, including kindergarten, the following characteristics are cause for concern:

1. limited use of language.
2. trouble starting and/or responding to conversation.
3. heavy reliance on gesture or nonverbal communication.
4. limited or nonspecific vocabulary.
5. inappropriate grammar.
6. difficulty in sequencing rhymes or stories.

Teachers handling preschoolers may think many of these characteristics are typical of younger preschoolers and that they will be corrected as the child approaches kindergarten age. Their program planning and teacher-child interactions aim to erase difficulties, and they would be concerned if growth in a preschooler's language ability and skill was not observable and apparent over time.

4-6d Articulation

Articulation disorders involve difficulties with the way sounds are formed and strung together, usually characterized by substituting one sound for another, omitting a sound, or distorting a sound. If consonant sounds are misarticulated, they may occur in the initial (beginning), medial (middle), or ending positions in words. It is prudent to point out again that normally developing children do not master the articulation of all consonants until age seven or eight.

Most young children (three- to five-years-old) hesitate, repeat, and re-form words as they speak. Imperfections occur for several reasons:

(1) a child does not pay attention as closely as an adult, especially to certain high-frequency consonant sounds; (2) the child may not be able to distinguish some sounds; or (3) a child's coordination and control of his articulation mechanisms may not be perfected. For example, the child may be able to hear the difference between *Sue* and *shoe* but cannot pronounce them differently. About 60 percent of all children with diagnosed articulation problems are boys.

Articulation characteristics of young children include the following.

- Substitution: One sound is substituted for another, as in "wabbit" for "rabbit" or "thun" for "sun."

- Omission: The speaker leaves out a sound that should be articulated. He says "at" for "hat," "ca" for "cat," "icky" for "sticky," "probly" for "probably." The left out sound may be at the beginning, middle, or end of a word.

- Distortion: A sound is said inaccurately, but is similar to the intended sound.

- Addition: The speaker adds a sound, as in "li-it-tle" for "little" and "muv-va-ver" for "mother."

- Transposition: The position of sounds in words is switched, as in "hangerber" for "hamburger" and "aminal" for "animal."

- Lisp: The *s*, *z*, *sh*, *th*, *ch*, and *j* sounds are distorted. There are two to 10 types of lisps noted by speech experts.

Articulation problems may stem from a physical condition, such as a cleft palate or hearing loss, or they can be related to problems in the mouth, such as a dental abnormality. Many times, articulation problems occurring without any obvious physical disability may involve the faulty learning of speech sounds. Some children will require special help and directed training to eliminate all articulation errors; others seem to mature and correct articulation problems by themselves.

Teacher behavior that helps a child with articulation problems includes not interrupting or constantly correcting the child and making sure that others do not tease or belittle. Modeling misarticulated words correctly is a good course of action. Simply continue your conversation and insert the correctly articulated word in your answering comment.

4-6e Voice Quality and Fluency Disorders

Teachers sometimes notice differences in children's voice quality, which involves pitch, loudness, resonance, and general quality (breathiness, hoarseness, and so on). The intelligibility of a child's speech is determined by how many of the child's words are understandable. One can expect 80 percent of the child's speech to be understandable at age three.

Stuttering and cluttering are categorized as fluency disorders. Stuttering involves the rhythm of speech and is a complicated, many-faceted problem. Stuttering speech is characterized by abnormal stoppages with no sound, repetitions, or prolonged sounds and syllables. There may also be unusual facial and body movements associated with efforts to speak. This problem involves four times as many males as females and can usually be treated. All young children repeat words and phrases, and this tends to increase with anxiety or stress. It is simply typical for the age and is not true stuttering. A teacher should wait patiently for the child to finish expressing himself and should resist the temptation to say "slow down." An adult talking at a slow, relaxed rate and pausing between sentences can give a child time to reflect and respond with more fluency. Keeping eye contact and not rushing, interrupting, or finishing words is also recommended. Classmates should be prohibited from teasing a peer who stutters.

Trautman (2003) identifies the following causes of stuttering:

- *Genetics*: approximately 59 percent of all people who stutter have family members who stutter.

- *child development*: children with speech, language, cognitive, or development delays are more likely to stutter.

- *neurophysiology*: research has shown that some people who stutter process speech and language in different areas of the brain than people who do not stutter.

- *family dynamics*: fast-paced lifestyles and high expectations can contribute to stuttering.

Trautman notes that most stuttering starts between the ages of two and four, and about 20 percent of children in that age group are affected. Many others in this age group go through a temporary lack of fluency and outgrow it. She points out that if stuttering lasts longer than three months and begins after age three, the child will likely need therapy to correct it. Most children make a full recovery. The disorder continues in a few, affecting about one percent of the adult population. Studies suggest that genetics plays a role in about half of stuttering cases (Rubin, 2010). A speech-language pathologist is the appropriate person to evaluate and plan improvement activities. The National Stuttering Association provides support, education, advocacy, and current research information.

Cluttering involves the rate of speaking, and it includes errors in articulation, stress, and pausing. Speech seems too fast with syllables and words running together. Listener reaction and good speech modeling are critical aspects of behavior for teachers when a child lacks fluency. Adults who work with a young child refrain from criticizing, correcting, acting negatively, or calling a speech problem to the child's attention. They create a warm adult-child relationship if possible, and try to eliminate any factors or conditions that increase problems in fluency. They work to protect the child's expectation of normal fluency and build the child's self-confidence as a speaker.

Approximately 25 percent of all children go through a stage of development during which they seem to stutter or clutter when excited or are searching for a word to express their thoughts. This may be temporary lack of fluency associated with learning to speak. Only a minority persists in early childhood stuttering, whereas in the majority of cases, stuttering is temporary and an often short-lived disorder that disappears without formal intervention, apparently on its own.

4-6f Selective (Elective) Mutism

Occasionally, early childhood teachers encounter silent children. Silence may be temporary or lasting, in which case it will be a matter for teacher concern. Children with **selective (elective) mutism** are described simply as children who can speak but do not. They display functional speech in selected settings (usually at home) and/or

choose to speak only with certain individuals (often siblings or same-language speakers). Researchers believe selective mutism, if it happens, commonly occurs between ages three and five years. Because child abuse may promote delayed language development or psychological disorders that interfere with communication, such as selective mutism, teachers need to be concerned. School referral to speech professionals leads to assessment and individual treatment programs. School administrators prefer that families make appointments and usually provide families with a description of local resources.

Teachers can help professionals by providing observational data to describe the child's behavior and responses in classroom settings. Many factors can contribute to a particular child's silence or reduced speech. Consequently, teachers are cautioned to avoid a mutism diagnosis. A child's teasing or any other action that causes the embarrassment of a child with a language or speech difference should be handled swiftly and firmly by preschool staff members. DAP

4-6g Other Conditions

Frequent crying. Occasionally, frustrated children will cry or scream to communicate a need. Crying associated with adjustment to a new situation is handled by providing supportive attention and care. Continual crying and screaming to obtain an object or privilege, on the other hand, calls for the following kinds of teacher statements:

"I don't understand what you want when you scream. Use words so I will know what you want."

"Sara does not know what you want when you cry, Ethan. Saying 'Please get off the puzzle piece' with your words tells her."

These statements let the child know what is expected and help him see that words solve problems.

Avid talkers and shouters. Occasionally, children may discover that talking incessantly can get them what they want. In order to quiet children, others sometimes give in. This is somewhat

---

cluttering — rapid, incomplete speech that is often jerky, slurred, spoken in bursts, and difficult to understand; nervous speech.

selective (elective) mutism — a behavior that describes child silence or lack of speech in select surroundings and/or with certain individuals.

different from the common give and take in children's daily conversations or children's growing ability to argue and state their cases.

Language for these children becomes a social weapon instead of a social tool. A child may find that loudness in speech can intimidate others and will out-shout the opposition. If a child behaves this way, it is prudent to have the child's hearing checked. Teachers often change this type of behavior through discussions of "inside" (the classroom) voices and "outside" voices (which may be used on the playground), and also by mentioning how difficult it is to hear a "too loud" voice.

Questioners.

At times, children ask many questions, one right after another. This may be a good device to hold or gain adults' attention: "Why isn't it time for lunch?" or "What makes birds sing?" or "Do worms sleep?" The questions may seem endless to adults. Most of the questions are prompted by the child's natural curiosity or an attempt to gain attention. Educators' help children find out as much as possible and strive to fulfill the needs of the individual child. Along the way, there will be many questions that may be difficult or even impossible to answer.

Learning Disabilities.

Children with learning disabilities may exhibit the following in their language use and behavior. They may:

- start talking later than other children
- have pronunciation problems
- display slow vocabulary growth; be unable to find the right word
- have trouble learning numbers, the alphabet, the days of the week
- display difficulty rhyming words
- seem extremely restless and easily distracted
- have trouble with peers
- exhibit poor ability to follow directions or routines
- avoid puzzles, drawing, and cutting activities

Experts point out that the sooner a problem can be identified and treated, the better the outcome is likely to be. Most programs handling children with learning difficulties strive to pinpoint causative factors, and to assess children's present level of functioning. Then programs and/or professional consultants develop individual learning plans (IEPs).

Hearing Problems and Hearing Disabilities.

A screening of young children's auditory acuity may uncover hearing loss. Rones (2004) estimates that two to three infants of every 1,000 are born with significant and/or permanent hearing loss and about 70 percent get their ears checked before leaving the hospital. The seriousness of hearing loss is related both to the degree of loss and the range of sound frequencies that are most affected. Because young children develop ear infections frequently, schools alert families when a child's listening behavior seems newly impaired.

Hearing disabilities are characterized by an inability to hear sounds clearly. Disabilities range from the ability to hear faint sounds to profound deafness. Approximately one out of every 300 children is born with permanent loss (Eiserman, Shisler, Foust, Buhrmann, & White, 2007). Appropriate intervention before the age of six months can significantly improve language and cognitive development in some milder cases of loss. The American Speech-Language-Hearing Association is a recommended teacher and family resource.

Otitis media is a medical term that refers to any inflammation of the middle ear. There are two types of otitis media: (1) a fluid-filled middle ear without infection and (2) an infected middle ear. Researchers believe that otitis media may affect babbling and interfere with an infant's ability to hold on to a string of utterances in working memory long enough to draw meaning. Many preschoolers have ear infections during preschool years, and many children have clear fluid in the middle ear that goes undetected. Even though the hearing loss caused by otitis media may be small and temporary, it may have a serious effect on speech and language learning for a preschool child. The common cold outranks child ear infection, and a teacher can expect one child in three to be affected on any given day during some seasons of the year.

---

otitis media — inflammation and/or infection of the middle ear.

If undetected hearing distortion or loss lasts for a long period, the child can fall behind. Children who have a history of middle ear disease are often enrolled in speech and language treatment programs. General inattentiveness, wanting to get close to hear, trouble with directions, irritability, or pulling and rubbing of the ear can be signs a teacher should heed. Other signs to look for include:

- difficulty hearing word endings such as -*ed*, -*ing*, and -*s*.
- problems interpreting intonation patterns, inflections, and stress.
- distractibility.
- inattentiveness.
- asking adults to repeat.
- confusion with adult commands.
- difficulty repeating verbally presented material.
- inappropriate responses to questions.
- watching for cues from other children.
- complaints about ears.
- persistent breathing through the mouth.
- slowness in locating the source of sounds.
- softer or "fuzzier" speech than others.
- aggressiveness.
- loss of temper.*

Preschool staff members who notice children who confuse words with similar sounds may be the first to suspect **auditory processing** difficulties or mild to moderate hearing loss.

Mild hearing impairment may masquerade as:

- stubbornness.
- lack of interest.
- a learning disability.

With intermittent **deafness**, children may have difficulty comprehending oral language. Severe impairment impedes language development and is easier to detect than the far more subtle signs of mild loss. Most infected ears cause considerable pain, and parents are alerted to the need for medical help. However, if the ear is not infected or if the infection does not cause pain, the problem is harder to recognize.

4-6h Suggestions and Strategies for Working with Children with Disabilities and Special Needs

The following suggestions and strategies are useful with typically developing children, but also help children with disabilities and special needs. They apply to educators, administrators, and families.

- Investigate whether a child is receiving supportive services at school and/or at an out-of-school location.
- Investigate equipment and media used or developed for specific problems or needs.
- Create and provide visual aids that depict or clarify instructional intent, such as posters and signs with pictures, drawings, or photographs.
- Use gestures that clarify words.
- Place children next to others who can provide help.
- Use cues such as a flashing light or music to gain attention, if necessary.

The Individuals with Disabilities Education Act, through federal and state mandates, ensures that children who have educationally significant hearing loss and certain other disabilities receive free, appropriate, public education. Programs develop a team approach that includes families or others familiar with the child's personality and interests, and professionals who are knowledgeable. This group creates individualized learning plans. Classroom environments are designed to promote learning and child comfort (Katz & Schery, 2006).

If a child's speech or language lags behind expected development for the child's age, school staff members should observe and listen to the child closely to collect additional data. When speech is unusually difficult to understand—rhythmically conspicuous, full of sound distortion, or consistently difficult to hear—this may indicate a serious problem. Professional help is available to preschool programs and families through a number of resources. Most cities have speech and hearing centers and public and

---

auditory processing — the full range of mental activity involved in reacting to auditory stimuli, especially speech sounds, and in considering their meanings in relation to past experience and to their future use.

deafness — hearing is so impaired that the individual is unable to process auditory linguistic information, with or without amplification.

private practitioners specializing in speech-language pathology and audiology. Other resources include:

- city and county health departments.
- universities and medical schools.
- state departments of education offices.
- the American Speech-Language-Hearing Association, as mentioned previously.

Experts give the families of hearing-impaired children the following advice:

- Help the child "tune in" to language.
- Talk.
- Provide stimulation.
- Read picture books.
- Enroll the child in an infant-stimulation program during infancy.
- Schedule frequent doctor examinations.
- Join parent organizations with a hearing-impairment focus.
- See the child simply as a child, rather than "a hearing-impaired child."

4-7 Advanced Language Achievement

Each child is unique. A few children speak clearly and use long and complex sentences at two, three, or four years of age. They express ideas originally and excitedly, enjoying individual and group discussions. Some may read simple primers (or other books) along with classroom word labels. Activities that are commonly used with kindergarten or first-grade children may interest them. Although educational experts' suspect eight to 15 percent of young children might be identified as displaying significantly advanced abilities, it is estimated that only two to three percent are recognized by teachers in the early grade of schooling (McGee & Hughes, 2011). These advanced abilities may or may not be connected to language giftedness.

Singson and Mann (1999), researchers exploring possible factors associated with precocious reading ability, found that phonological awareness and parent's emphasis on letter sounds were significant predictors of early childhood ability. A few early readers may be sight readers with an exceptional memory for words. Educators aware of current research believe young children's knowledge of both alphabet letter names and sounds will aid their reading instruction.

Just as there is no stereotypical average child, language-talented children are also unique individuals. Inferring that these language-precocious children are also intellectually gifted is not at issue here. Young children with advanced language development may:

- attend to tasks in a persistent manner for long periods.
- focus deeply or submerge themselves in what they are doing.
- speak maturely and use a larger-than-usual vocabulary.
- show a searching, exploring curiosity.
- ask questions that go beyond immediate happenings.
- demonstrate an avid interest in words, alphabet letters, numbers, or writing tools.
- remember small details of past experiences and compare them with present happenings.
- read books (or words) by memorizing pictures or words.
- prefer solitary activities at times.
- offer ideas often and easily.
- rapidly acquire English skills, if bilingual, when exposed to a language-rich environment.
- tell elaborate stories.
- show a mature or unusual sense of humor for age.
- possess an exceptional memory.
- exhibit high concentration.
- show attention to detail.
- exhibit a wide range of interests.
- demonstrate a sense of social responsibility.
- show a rich imagination.
- possess a sense of wonder.
- enjoy composing poems or stories.
- use richly descriptive expressions in talking
- be highly attentive listeners who remember exceptionally well.
- read print in the classroom environment.
- write recognizable words or combinations of words.

- have sophisticated computer skills.
- express feelings and emotions, as in storytelling, movement, and visual arts.
- use rich imagery in informal language.
- exhibit originality of ideas and persistence in problem solving.
- exhibit a high degree of imagination.

According to Spencer and Stamm (2008), characteristics of possible giftedness in children under age three include:

- meeting verbal milestones early (speaking full sentences by 18 months, for instance).
- a long attention span (30 minutes is long for toddlers).
- being able to do complicated mental tasks early (like putting together puzzles with many pieces).
- creativity in thinking and problem solving.
- an early, avid interest in books.
- responsiveness to music.
- an interest in sorting, organizing, and seeing patterns.
- asking lots of questions.
- memory for detail and how to get to many locations.
- creative play (both in art and imaginative play, including having imaginary friends).
- a preference for older children.
- a marked interest in people.
- a less-than-typical need for adult help and guidance in activities.

Preschoolers may recognize letters early and show an early focus on printed matter. They may be interested in foreign languages and also exhibit correct pronunciation and sentence structure in their native language. Young children may show an advanced vocabulary and may begin reading before they start preschool.

Unfortunately, young children who may be quiet, noncompetitive, and nonassertive; who are slow to openly express feelings; who rarely make direct eye contact, ask questions, or challenge something they know is incorrect; and who are acting appropriately according to their home culture may not be identified as gifted or talented. Native American and Alaskan native children may be more likely to fall into this category.

Most experts recommend planning activities within the regular curriculum that promote advanced children's creative thinking. Suggestions include providing the following opportunities:

- Fluency. Promoting many different responses, for example, "What are all the ways you can think of to . . ."
- Flexibility. Having the facility to change a mind-set or see things in a different light, for example, "If you were a squirrel how would you feel . . ."
- Originality. For example, "Make something that no one else will think of."
- Elaboration. Embellishing of an idea or adding detail, for example, presenting a doodle or squiggle and asking, "What could it be?"

Some educators believe that teachers can help ward off problems for advanced students by grouping language-advanced children with others of high ability or shared interests. Other educators feel doing so robs peers of the sparkle and insight some peers possess. Arranging situations in which the child's gifts or talents are seen as a group asset is another tactic, as is promoting individual special assignments and varied projects.

If teachers believe, as does Gardner (1993, 2000), in the theory of multiple intelligences (one of which is linguistic intelligence) and in the occurrence of "crystallizing experiences," those teachers will notice the young children who take particular interest in and react overtly to some attractive quality or feature of a language arts activity. These children will tend to immerse themselves and focus deeply. This may be the child who loves to act in dramatic play, collects words, is fascinated with books or alphabet letters, creates daily rhymes, or displays similar behaviors. The child may persist and spend both time and effort on his chosen pursuit and displays a definite intellectual gift.

Summary

4-1 Describe a safe and sensitive classroom environment for children with language or cultural differences.

The classroom will:

- have program goals that reflect the needs and interests of diverse children.
- use Standard English in instructional and planned activities.
- design activities that respect language and cultural differences.
- preserve children's feelings of adequacy and acceptance and value children's home culture.

4-2 Discuss the similarities and differences between Standard English and American dialects.

- Standard English is the language of America's elementary schools and its textbooks. It is the majority language in the United States. Dialects refer to the language patterns used in regional or geographical locations or those having social and ethnic variety. Dialects are distinguished by pronunciation, grammar, vocabulary, and especially a variety of speech differing from the standard literary language or speech patterns of the American culture. Widely recognized dialects are a Southern accent, the speech of some speakers in New England, and some African-American English speakers (Black English).

4-3 Identify common strategies second-language learners use to learn Standard English on their own.

- Commonly second language learners believe what is being said around them refers to the ongoing present classroom situation they find themselves in. They learn to use gestures and use a few familiar conversational phrases or words in their interactions. They begin to recognize language patterns that recur in daily speech and try to communicate their intended meanings with their limited English vocabulary using a major effort to do so. They use gestures frequently.

4-4 Discuss program planning second-language learners.

- Second-language instruction may differ from school to school depending upon the belief of the teaching staff, the administration, and the school sponsors.

4-5 Name two common school program types for second-language learners.

- Bilingual programs, transitional programs, newcomer programs, developmental bilingual programs, two-way immersion programs, tutor-assisted programs, and full immersion programs are common program types used for child instruction in Standard English.

4-6 Identify young children's common speech problems.

- Common childhood speech problems include poor pronunciation, limited vocabulary or speech output, poor syntax or grammar, poor hearing, unintelligible speech, language delay, poor articulation, and stuttering.

4-7 Name four characteristics of language advanced preschoolers.

- Advanced language achievement may be present when a child displays long and complex sentences, mature idea expression, reading ability, persistent attention to tasks, deep focus, and may know all letter names and sounds. Other characteristics include being highly creative with words, having an extensive vocabulary, having an excellent memory for words, displaying a vivid imagination, preferring older mature children as playmates, demonstrating an interest in words and numbers, and during testing exceeds age level norms.

Additional Resources

Readings

Alanis, I. (2011). Learning from each other: Bilingual pairs in dual language classrooms. *Dimensions of Early Childhood. 39*(1), 21–28.

Gadrikowski, A. (2013, May). Differentiation strategies for exceptionally bright children. *Young Children, 68*(2), 8–14.

Helm, J. H. & Katz, L. G. (2011). *Young Investigators: The Project Approach in the Early Years.* New York: Teachers College Press, & Washington, DC: National Association for the Education of Young Children.

Helpful Websites

American Educational Research Association (AERA)

http://www.aera.net

Information on the academic achievement of second-language learners (search Publications).

The Association for the Gifted (TAG)

http://www.cectag.org

Assists parents and professionals with advanced children.

*From Center for Research on Education, Diversity, & Excellence. (2001). Some program alternatives for English language learning. Practitioner's Brief #3.

Objectives

After reading this chapter, you should be able to:

5-1 Define literacy.

5-2 Describe common teaching practices in the United States in the early twentieth century.

5-3 Compare two known theories of literacy instruction.

5-4 Name two pieces of federal legislation that have substantially affected preschool language instruction.

5-5 Discuss how language growth takes place in all curriculum areas.

5-6 Describe the program and lesson planning process.

5-7 Name three areas of the preschool language arts that are commonly part of a school's written goal statements.

5-8 Explain what is entailed if a school uses a thematic approach to instruction.

naeyc NAEYC Program Standards

2A05 Curriculum goals and objectives guide teachers' ongoing assessment of children's progress.

2G02 Children are provided varied opportunities to learn key concepts and principles in science.

2G03 Children are provided varied opportunities and materials that encourage them to use the five senses to observe, explore, and experiment with scientific phenomena.

2J01 Children are provided varied opportunities to gain an appreciation of art, music, drama, and dance in ways that reflect cultural diversity.

DAP Developmentally Appropriate Practice (DAP) Preschool

13A1 Curriculum addresses key goals in language and literacy.

3A2 Curriculum is consistent with high quality, achievable, and challenging early childhood learning standards and recommendations of the relevant professional organizations.

3A5 Teachers integrate ideas and content from multiple domains and disciplines through themes, projects, play opportunities, and other learning experiences so that children are able to develop an understanding of concepts and make connections across content areas.

COMMON CORE Common Core State Standards for English Language Arts and Literacy

W.CCR. 7 Conduct short as well as more sustained research projects based on focused questions, demonstrating understanding of the subject under investigation.

Questionable Language

A group of Asian, English-language-learning boys often played only with each other. I was continually attempting to help them branch out and play with other children. It was slowly happening. At pick-up time, Mrs. Vu, Tan's mother, asked to speak with me. She had brought her neighbor with her as an interpreter. Moving out of the children's range of overhearing our conversation, her neighbor expressed Mrs. Vu's concern. Some of the Asian boys were using very inappropriate words in their native tongue, laughing, and then running away. They had been careful in avoiding this activity when Phan, the bilingual assistant, was near. After assuring Mrs. Vu that we shared her concern and would monitor the children's behavior, I thanked her. Fortunately, we had an impending family meeting.

Questions to Ponder

1. Could some kind of planned child activity be used to address this problem?
2. What words would you use if you "caught" the boys in this behavior?
3. Should this behavior be discussed at a family meeting or is this a private matter?

This text divides language arts into four interrelated areas—listening, speaking, writing, and reading—and also discusses **visual literacy** (viewing) as a primary, basic human capacity closely related to the other language arts areas. Increasing the child's understanding of how language arts combine and overlap in everyday preschool activities helps increase language use and **literacy**. Early childhood teachers realize that when children are taught to read or when a few children begin reading on their own before kindergarten, the learning of reading is dynamically concerned with the *interrelatedness* of the literacy skills of listening, speaking, and print (writing). Learning to read with ease happens more readily when young children listen, converse easily, think with and about words, and have rich vocabularies they have used to express their ideas.

To that end, a unified and balanced approach is recommended, one in which the teacher purposefully shows and stresses connections between areas (Figure 5-1). Past

Figure 5-1 Interrelations of early childhood language arts.

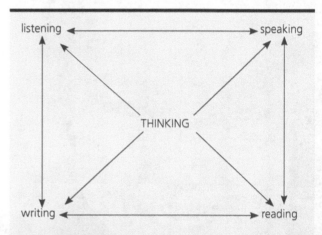

Listening (receptive language)
   One hears speech.
   One can listen to another reading orally.
   One can listen and write what one hears.

Speaking (oral expressive language)
   One can speak to a listener.
   One can put speech into written form.
   One can read orally.

Writing
   One can write what is spoken and heard.
   One's writing can be read.
   One's writing can be read and spoken.

Reading
   One can read written words.
   One can listen to another reading.
   One can read speech when it is written.

---

visual literacy — the ability to interpret and communicate with respect to visual symbols in the media other than print.

literacy — involves complex cognitive interactions between readers and their texts and between background knowledge and new information. It involves both skill and knowledge and varies by task and setting. Different types of literacy are described—prose, document, quantitative, academic, workplace, and functional.

practice and program planning in schools attempted to promote literacy by dividing (segmenting) language arts into separate skills. Educators now believe separate, but integrated, skill activities can be part of a balanced language arts program.

The ages of the children and their past life experiences will decide the literacy activities a teacher plans and presents and the techniques and adult-child interaction the educator deems appropriate. Classes may include children who have been in group settings for three or four years, children with identified disabilities, children with exceptional abilities, children who are already independent readers, and children just beginning to acquire some basic literacy. Literacy knowledge grows and develops within human relationships with responsive adults and the other children.

5-1 Literacy Goals—Skill and Knowledge

In this book, literacy is defined as a demonstrated competence in communication skills that enables the individual to function, appropriately to age, independently of society, and with a potential for movement in society. Literacy can be conceptualized as a relatively narrow domain of academic inquiry and educational practice (as in reading), or it can be viewed as an encompassing way of being that involves all forms of communication, including mathematical, scientific, and artistic forms. Literacy definitions change and reflect different historical, cultural, and technological development. New technology is enabling students to access the best information in the shortest time, which allows them to identify and solve problems and communicate this information to others. Reading and writing are but the initial layers of the richer and more complex forms of literacy required in Internet use.

Young children usually progress by developing knowledge of literacy that includes oral language skill and awareness that written (graphic) marks and words carry meaning. Early superficial understandings about picture books and reading aloud lead to a much deeper understanding of the purpose of reading. Psycholinguistic theory focuses on the unique nature of human language—humans' innate search for order, structure, and meaning. Using this theory as a basis, educators can see how children will initiate their own first steps toward literacy when

exposed to language-rich environments in which positive attitudes develop toward language arts activities.

Cambourne's definition of literacy (1988) stresses one's ability to use language in daily life.

> .... Literacy is the word which describes a whole collection of behaviors, skills, knowledge, processes and attitudes. It has something to do with our ability to use language in our negotiations with the world... Reading and writing are two linguistic ways of conducting these negotiations. So are speaking, listening, reflecting, and a host of other behaviors related to cognition and critical thinking. (p. 29)

Cultural literacy can be defined as the possession of the basic information needed to thrive in the current world. Children from poor and illiterate circumstances tend to remain poor and illiterate unless educational opportunities are available. Another definition states that an individual needs to be socialized to literacy and also to develop behaviors such as knowing how and when to ask questions, how to hold a book or listen to a story, and when and how to participate.

5-1a Visual Literacy Goals

The goals of instruction in the visual literacy area involve promoting children's visual perception skills. This includes attending behavior, discrimination, identification, analysis, classification, sorting, and categorization of visual images. In other words, a conscious noting of differences in visual characteristics would be undertaken. These characteristics include line, shape, color, number, texture, movement, and dimension, as well as other features. This area of study referred to in professional readings as visual thinking, visual intelligence, visual awareness, visual sensitivity, and visual arts. It specifically relates to a child's perception of the world; how he reacts to viewed images; how he sees, feels, and interprets emotions evoked; and how he arrives at insights concerning visual media.

Visual literacy, based on the idea that visual images are a language, is defined as the ability to understand and produce visual messages. The sense of sight is the most important and basic source of information concerning one's surroundings (Stieglitz, 2008). It involves not only the eye but also the brain. Elements of the visual

---

cultural literacy — literacy that reflects a culture's knowledge of significant ideas, events, values, and the essence of that culture's identity.

perception process are light, the visual stimulus and its characteristics, eye receptors, the individual's past experiences, previous knowledge and ideas, and the individual's purposes, interests, and feelings at a particular time.

Morrow and Asbury (2003) suggest that the visual literacy area should be integrated with writing, listening, reading, and speaking. They also suggest using instruction that is spontaneous, is authentic, and involves children in problem solving. Instruction, they believe, should be direct, explicit, and systematic.

Telling stories using a photograph or drawing, listening to children's ideas about story content after viewing a picture book's cover, and discussing children's creative art and the details therein or the emotions they feel give teachers insights into what children are thinking. These activities also reveal children's abilities to read visual cues and symbols. O'Neil (2011) points out that children's full comprehension of picture books depends upon the ability to read pictures as well as listen to the text. She believes preschool teachers can assist children's development of visual literacy skill. Illustrations convey meaning through color, line, size, and shape as well as through other elements. Usually visual images relate or interact in some way with the text to increase children's understanding and enjoyment. Illustrations can enhance and reinforce a text message and provide greater detail or might even present a discrepancy between a book's words and what is pictured. Children can become adept at decoding the implications of illustrations. Early childhood teachers might ask children to examine a character's gestures, facial and body expressions, actions, or other book features for clues to a character's nature, personality, intentions, or mood.

When children and adults are in the process of viewing an image or living an event, they are not involved in the process of critical analysis. Rather, they are absorbing those images and events and actively seeking meaning. This would account for children's barrage of questions if they are interested in a new classroom animal and also explains a good number of their other questions.

When children are encouraged to express their learning through the medium of graphic arts, they are "documenting" their understandings. Children are encouraged to do this in the Reggio Emilia approach and, at times, in almost all curriculum areas. Children trace and revisit their discoveries and actions, making them visible. This exercise is an instrument for reflection and language development as the children discuss their creations. Reflection can lead to a refinement of ideas and further search and discovery. It can be likened to a scientist writing the results of her inquiry, which then leads to further questions.

5-1b What is Early Literacy?

The term **early literacy** refers to young preschool children's language arts behaviors, concepts, and skills that precede and can develop into a literacy that includes reading, conventional writing, and a larger body of literary knowledge at later ages. It considers change over time in how the child thinks about literacy and the strategies the young child uses in her attempts to comprehend or produce oral or written language.

The act of printing shapes with an underlying logic and children's "pretending to read" behaviors are viewed as early forms of reading and writing. Many educators believe that additional research is necessary to understand exactly "what clicks into place" when young children make the transition from early reading and writing to conventional reading and writing. Instructional strategies and behavioral techniques based on that knowledge and the identification of what children understand, and which skills aided that transition, enhance a school's planning ability. Early literacy learning happens best in an atmosphere of social collaboration with peers and others who are more literate.

Emergent literacy skills usually found in the program goal statements in early childhood classrooms include phonological awareness, alphabet knowledge, the concept of words in print, invented spellings, environmental print recognition, and print awareness. These skills are widely recognized as being predictive and critical to children's literacy growth. They are precursors of successful reading and writing accomplishment in kindergarten and beyond.

Early home-life activities start children's literacy development by providing early experiences, including parent and family models and attitudes. A home environment can be stimulating or drab, rich in literate activities or deficient. Children actively search for meaning, and many have lives in

---

early literacy — speaking, listening, print awareness, and writing behaviors, reading of alphabet letters and words, and other skills that evolve and change over time, culminating in conventional literacy.

Photo 5-1 Teachers are trained to encourage child speech during daily interactions and conversations.

which print surrounds them and picture books are familiar. If children have observed and participated in home reading or writing activities, they often enter group care with interest, a positive attitude, and an early head start in literacy. They are able to enjoy symbolic dramatic play and eventually attempt symbolic representation in art, block building, and a variety of other preschool pursuits. They communicate ideas, discuss meanings, and probe adults and other children for information. Preschoolers' growing awareness and "knowledge of literacy" is evident and can include all language arts areas—reading, writing, speaking, listening, and visual representing.

Becoming literate is an extension and companion of language arts skill. Most children acquire spoken language without sit-down instruction; they all become speakers, although at different rates, unless disease, illness, or trauma interferes. Literacy, on the other hand, is not attained unconsciously or by all in our society. Literacy requires a shared body of understanding, much of which involves a common exposure to oral and written material and a level of proficiency in listening, speaking, reading, and writing. Literacy acquisition involves a commitment of time and mental energy plus opportunity. At the preschool level, this involves a teacher's commitment to promote both language arts skills and literacy understanding appropriate to preschoolers. Literacy today is still seen by some as only referring to reading and writing, but many researchers and early childhood educators are concerned with the taproots of literacy, which may be developed during the preschool period (Photo 5-1).

5-2 Historical Roots of Language Arts Instruction

In examining the historical roots of language arts instruction, we will start with the seventeenth-century theorist René Descartes (1596–1650), a French philosopher, who theorized that God was responsible for the innate knowledge in children's minds, and the English philosopher, John Locke (1632–1704), who expressed a contrasting position that children's minds at birth were blank and unfilled. Locke (1974) also emphasized the importance of experience in learning.

In the eighteenth century, Johann Pestalozzi (1846–1827) of Switzerland and Friedrich Froebel (1782–1852) of Germany presented yet another theory based on their personal interactions with young children. Both Pestalozzi (Rusk & Scotland, 1979) and Froebel (1974) recommended providing "natural environments" in which sensory experiences produce learning and a natural unfolding. Play, they suggested, was the route to learning and intellectual development along with social, emotional, and physical development. Froebel introduced the notion of treating children with kindness, caring, and compassion. Many schools of the day offered sparse, sterile classroom environments with young children seated in rows or at desks. In these schools there was little or no play time, and teachers required rote memorization, repetition, imitation, and strict adherence to rules.

5-2a The Twentieth Century

At the turn of the twentieth century in the United States, schools for very young children imitated primary school practices, which included memorization and recitation by children, or they simply offered custodial care. Disciples of Froebel began to influence educators along the eastern seaboard. In the Midwest, John Dewey (1916) began experimenting with young children's educational environments. His beliefs promoted a curriculum of teacher-selected topics, themed units of study, and theme-influenced play areas. His ideas affected language arts instructional practices. Dramatic play and book (library) areas are still with us today, and theme instruction has not disappeared. Formal skill-building activities were avoided, but on-the-spot recognized learning moments (teachable moments) were capitalized upon.

Gesell (1940) was also influential. He suggested that developmental "norms" existed, and he believed that child growth and development were based on maturation. For teachers to be effective, they needed to determine children's readiness for learning on a child-by-child basis.

Maria Montessori (1967a), a physician-educator who in 1907 started her experiment by bringing education to children in a deprived area of Rome, captured the attention of some American early educators. Ideas concerning children's learning through sequenced manipulative materials and special teacher-child interactions were recognized. Some group lessons were believed necessary, but primarily, children self-selected from offered activities and decided their own pace, followed their own interests, and worked independently. Montessori instruction stressed order and self-contained tasks. Activities (tasks) had definite beginnings and endings, which included returning materials to shelves. Many of Montessori's activities approached learning in a sensory way; some were color-coded.

In the 1930s and 1940s, it was widely believed that early exposure to formal reading instruction should wait until the necessary skills had been achieved, which was believed to be somewhere around the age of six-and-a-half (Morphett & Washburne, 1931). These prerequisite skills included auditory and visual discrimination, visual motor skills, and large motor skills.

A change occurred in early educational practice during the 1960s and the 1970s. Children were beginning to be seen as constructing their own knowledge of language from their experiences. Rather than moving children to higher levels of development, teachers were to match experiences to children's current levels. Piaget, a Swiss psychologist noted for his observations of his own children, studied children's cognitive growth. Piaget (1952a) theorized that a child passed through several sequential stages and was unable to move to a higher stage unless she had mastered the stage before it. Learning took place as the child made sense of her environment through exploration and manipulation.

Chomsky (1968), who in his early works was concerned with language development, believed that acquiring language was a matter of the child's gaining facility with the rules that govern language. These rules were not learned, but rather ingested as the child matured and interfaced with more mature speakers. Chomsky theorized that the human brain was uniquely equipped with a language facilitator that he called the "language acquisition device" (LAD).

Vygotsky (1978), considered a sociocultural theorist, suggested that learning took place through social contact and the development of what he termed "private speech." He emphasized the development of socially shared cognition with adults and peers. Adults (or others) assist the child to move ahead in development by noticing what the next logical step might be.

Morrow and Asbury (2003) have listed how different early constructivist approach theorists and philosophers influenced language arts program planning:

• Use of prepared and natural environments for learning.

• Equal emphasis on social, emotional, physical, and intellectual development.

- Supportive adults who encourage social interaction to aid learning.
- A focus on learning rather than teaching.
- Awareness that children must be actively involved to learn.

Research in the twentieth century provided educators with additional data focusing on oral language, early writing attempts, development of early reading skills, and alphabet learning and/or alphabet sound learning. It emphasized early reading behaviors. This supported the idea that literacy began at birth. Educators tended to believe that a rich literary environment with activities that aided the development of literacy skills did more to promote children's natural interests than direct reading-readiness instruction did. The whole-language movement promoted young children's access to quality literature together with listening, discussion, and active participation in dramatizing, storytelling, poetry, and picture-book times. Early writing and print-related language arts activities gained wide acceptance.

The focus shifted to developmentally appropriate practice in the 1990s, and educators became aware of instructional strategies to prevent reading difficulties through the development of early skills during the preschool years. Much of early childhood language arts instruction changed. Many programs are working toward a balanced approach to programming, combining a developmental environment and appropriate literacy experiences with research-based, skill-building activities that equip children to make smooth transitions from nonreader to beginning reader to reader.

5-2b In the Present

Currently the public eye has been more intently focused on children's reading and writing achievement and instruction because of mandated state standards. The quest for effective preschool practices and curricula that improve literacy and school readiness and help change persistent reading achievement gaps in American schools is at an all-time high (Powell & Diamond, 2012). The National Reading Panel Report in 2000 urged an organized and systematic instructional approach with highly qualified teachers. Morrow and Asbury (2003) describe a comprehensive approach to early childhood literacy:

This type of instruction is characterized by meaningful literacy activities that provide children with both the skills and the desire to achieve proficiency and lifelong literacy learning. Teaching literacy skills and providing opportunities for learning literacy skills are appropriate for young children as long as the teaching methods are appropriate to the child being taught. In such a program, teachers provide numerous literacy experiences that include the integration of reading, writing, listening, speaking, and viewing. (p. 233)

Early childhood instruction may now include the task of assessing developing skills and making instructional plans based on assessment data.

Teachers rely on assessment to gain additional information on both the individual growth of students and the overall success of their instructional approach. Evidence is collected, analyzed, and used continually as teachers work toward improvement and excellence in quality programs. Teachers and teaching team members attempt to offer a language arts program tailored to better meet the language strengths necessary for attending preschoolers who will enter kindergartens that are guided by *Common Core State Standards for English language arts and literacy in history/social studies, science, and technical subjects* (2010). These standards have promoted a movement toward an organized and systematic approach to kindergarten instruction provided by highly qualified teachers who know how to use assessment to improve their program and prepare children to achieve more academic outcomes. Common Core State Standards can be obtained on the Common Core State Standards website.

Increasingly early childhood programs are being asked to be accountable by providing data that show young children's progress in the language arts and prove that children have reached desired outcomes in a prescribed time frame. The quest to identify the most appropriate and effective instructional programs to promote children's literacy development is but one factor that has promoted state standards. Standards may describe desired outcomes, but not the how of getting there. In current professional literature the phrase *emergent literacy* has been replaced by *early literacy*. From this perspective, literacy begins at birth, is ongoing, and is influenced and interpreted by the surrounding sociocultural context. What we do know is that preschool educators will encounter children

---

assessment — a broad repertoire of behaviors involved in noticing, documenting, recording, and interpreting children's behaviors and performances. Testing is a subset of assessment behaviors in which performances are controlled and elicited in standardized conditions.

who arrive with research-identified risk factors, including: living in poverty, residing in single-parent homes, having a parent with low educational attainment, and having a home language other than English (Rimm-Kaufman, Pianta & Cox, 2000). Early childhood educators will face the challenge of providing preschool experiences and activities that prepare children for kindergarten success in the crucial area of language arts. Children will especially need a background that ensures learning to read with ease when formal reading instruction begins. Although there is no consensus about how much of each language skill should be stressed, a successful literacy program addresses all skills in sufficient depth and breadth to promote literacy growth in the earliest and later years.

There is wide agreement that **phonological awareness** is an important aspect of being ready to learn to read, but educators may not have received enough instruction and training to promote it. Phonological awareness can be taught in a number of ways, such as in activities involving speaking or listening, poetry, rhyming experiences, or with chants, songs, and so on. Proponents of strong phonics and phonological awareness training recommend a different set of practices than do those who emphasize the more contextual uses of literacy. Most early childhood educators search for meaningful and functional literacy activities, but many are introducing phonological skill-developing opportunities that encourage children to generate rhymes and segment phonemes within meaningful activities.

The joint position statement of the International Reading Association (IRA) and the National Association for the Education of Young Children (NAEYC), *Learning to Read and Write* (1998), serves as a guide for some early childhood language arts program development. It describes developmentally appropriate language arts activities in infancy through the early primary grades. Recommended teaching practices and activities are categorized according to children's age levels. It promotes nurturing adult-child relationships; print-rich environments; daily reading and discussion of high-quality books; oral opportunities that focus on sounds and meaning; phonemic awareness activities; play that includes play with literacy tools; exposure to print, icons, and words in computer games; and first-hand activities that expand knowledge and vocabulary. No one teaching method or approach is likely to be the most effective for all children, according to the position paper. A variety of teaching strategies suited to child diversity and individuality is recommended.

The National Early Literacy Panel. The National Early Literacy Panel has studied literacy research findings extensively. McCardle (2006) points out the report of the National Reading Panel (NRP), National Institute of Child Health and Human Development (2002) identified five research-based elements that need to be present in any reading approach or program for children whose first language is English to develop the skills necessary to become successful lifelong readers. These are phonics, phonemic awareness, reading fluency, vocabulary, and reading comprehension. In 2007, the National Early Literacy Panel identified variables essential for children to succeed in early literacy, including:

- expressive and receptive oral language development.
- knowledge of alphabetic code (alphabet knowledge, phonological and phonemic awareness).
- writing with the use of invented spelling.
- print knowledge (can read some environmental print).
- can write his or her name.
- can demonstrate the ability to do or use the following skills: rapid naming of letters and numbers, visual memory, and visual perception.

The panel believes that building young children's literacy skill is possible. The challenges facing early childhood educators are considerable. In using the predictors, the panel cautions that other predictors may yet be discovered when additional research becomes available.

5-2c Putting Theories in Categories

Binding similar theories loosely together may help language arts program planners realize the theoretical basis for their language program decisions. The **nativists** believe in the natural unfolding of children without direct teaching from

---

phonological awareness — the whole spectrum from primitive awareness of speech sounds and rhythms to rhyme awareness and sound similarities; at the highest level, awareness of syllables or phonemes.

nativists — those who adhere to the theory that children are born with biological dispositions for learning that unfold or mature in a natural way.

adults. These thinkers led later scholars and researchers to propose maturational theories with ages, stages, and normative behaviors.

Psychosocial theory stresses stages of human development. Erikson's psychosocial theory stressed specific tasks to be resolved during stages of human development. The major tasks of toddlers and preschoolers were autonomy and initiative. Theory, along this line of thinking, may have evolved into a philosophy of child-directed learning, such as traditional Montessori.

A **nurturist** philosophy can be seen as a precursor of highly didactic preschool practices, although it also advocates offering children experiences to promote learning. Program models promote teachers as dispensers of knowledge, but activities might also be presented. These programs are based on the theory of **behaviorism**.

Interactionists view child development and learning as taking place between children and their environment. Program planners promoting this view subscribe to the **constructivist theory**, believing in children's creation of their own internal knowledge as they interact in both social and environmental pursuits. Vygotsky's **social constructivist theory** would emphasize the importance of language and socially shared cognition. He would recommend promoting assisted and scaffolded learning and encouraging children to use private speech to aid them in solving problems.

Although these theories differ in important ways, they share an emphasis on considering children as active learners who are able to set goals, plan, and revise. They recognize that children's cognitive development, which is so closely tied to language development, evolves gradually as children acquire strategies for remembering, understanding, and problem solving (Machado & Botnarescue, 2008).

5-3 Philosophies of Literacy Instruction

A variety of approaches to literacy instruction, representing different philosophical positions, have emerged, resulting in practices using widely diverse teaching techniques, materials, and assessment methods. Theorists do not all agree about what learning is or how it happens (Phillips & Soltis, 2009). Contrasting points of view will probably continue as they have in the past. Currently, educators debate the efficacy of academically oriented versus **child-initiated curricula**. Whole-language versus teacher-directed phonics instruction has also received considerable ongoing attention. Out of these debates the "balanced," "eclectic," "natural," and "centrist" philosophical positions have evolved and become recommended positions.

In a child-initiated model of instruction, children's self-directed actions are facilitated by a teacher. A teacher facilitates learning by (a) providing children with a wide variety of experiences, (b) encouraging children to choose and plan their own learning activities, (c) engaging children in active learning by posing problems and asking questions that stimulate and extend learning, (d) guiding children through skill acquisition activities as needed, and (e) encouraging children to reflect on their learning experiences.

The staff of each early childhood center drafts a program based on the unique mesh of the staff's personal theories about what they believe is appropriate and effective. If a language arts program focuses on the correct form(s) of language, such as the planned and sequential learning of letter names, sounds, and so forth, the program could

---

psychosocial theory — the branch of psychology founded by Erik Erikson; development is described in terms of eight stages that span childhood and adulthood.

nurturist — one who adheres to the theory that the minds of children are blank or unformed and need educational input or direct instruction to develop and "output" knowledge and appropriate behavior.

behaviorism — the theoretical viewpoint, espoused by theorists such as B. F. Skinner, that behavior is shaped by environmental forces, specifically in response to reward and punishment.

interactionists — those who adhere to the theory that language develops through a combination of inborn factors and environmental influences.

constructivist theory — a theory such as that of Jean Piaget, based on the belief that children construct knowledge for themselves rather than having it conveyed to them by some external source.

social constructivist theory — such as Vygotsky's emphasis on the importance of language and socially shared cognition in exchanges between adult and child when scaffolding was used, and encouraging children's use of private speech to aid problem solving.

child-initiated curricula — a basic tenet underlying this type of curriculum is the belief that true growth occurs when children are free to develop intrinsic interests naturally.

be described as traditional, or conventional. This text urges an approach to teaching language arts that is meaning-based, brain research compatible, functional for children, literature-rich, and taught in a balanced and interrelated fashion. This type of program approach believes child knowledge and skill in language arts are reinforced and made meaningful when the reading, writing, listening, and speaking aspects of daily activities are encountered concurrently. A developmentally appropriate program first considers the unique group of children enrolled, their needs, their abilities, their interests, and their families' wishes concerning desirable educational outcomes.

Preschools and child centers have given special attention to updated infant, toddler, and preschooler developmentally appropriate practice guidelines published in 2013 by the NAEYC. In designing programs for young children, developmentally appropriate practice has twelve principles that rest on an extensively researched base. Many centers depend on developmentally appropriate practice to form a framework for curriculum and adult interactions with children. Deeply embedded in developmentally appropriate practice is the idea that children have a natural disposition toward learning and actively construct their own knowledge through exploration and interaction with materials, peers, and adults. Educators also realize that low-achieving students often need planned and systematic instruction to acquire skills that will enable them to progress and eventually learn to read with ease.

Developmentally appropriate program planning may aim to strengthen what a child already knows and can do and/or may promote what a child can potentially discover or know or can newly accomplish. This requires observing and studying children to enable the educator to provide challenges that are achievable.

Researchers trying to identify the effect of developmentally appropriate practice on children's cognitive development conclude that children's receptive language was better in programs with higher-quality literacy environments and when developmentally appropriate activities were more abundant. Many educators believe that outdated views, including extensive whole-group instruction and intensive drill and practice of isolated language arts skills, are not suitable or effective with preschoolers. In terms of cognitive development, the use of developmentally appropriate instructional strategies appears to facilitate

children's creativity, is associated with better verbal skills and receptive language, and contributes to higher levels of cognitive functioning.

Not all educators are enthusiastic about developmentally appropriate practice and feel that what children are capable of learning is simply not a function of age or grade level. Rather they contend early learning is contingent upon rich educational experiences and young children's opportunities to learn (Neuman and Wright, 2013). These researchers point to studies suggesting that

Figure 5-2 Possible sequence in language learning.

Child has experiential background observing and participating in a rich language arts school environment.

↓

Child gives attention to classroom activities, demonstrations, behaviors modeled by others, new happenings, teacher presentations, or other classroom events. Child perceives activity to be useful, interesting, or worthwhile.

↓

Child feels comfortable and safe in this situation and feels capable and likely successful. Child understands that teacher expects appropriate classroom behavior.

↓

Child continues focus and concentration on activity that is unfolding and progressing.

↓

Child gathers and selects information and data; develops beginning ideas; may ask questions; and looks, listens, touches as if investigating or trying to find out.

↓

Child may see or state relationships and form hypotheses or conclusions and may discuss points of view.

↓

Child may test ideas or check ideas with teacher or others present.

↓

Child may receive feedback from teacher and/or other children. Child may be uncertain or puzzled.

↓

Child may develop a definite idea and "fit" the newness experienced in the activity into what she already knows. Learning occurs.

Digital Download

educators may have misjudged how early young children can conceptually grasp new learnings.

Seasoned early childhood teachers have known preschoolers who have absorbed a tremendous amount of detailed and in-depth knowledge along with mature concepts on a subject of interest and importance to them (often dinosaurs or trains). Their families had provided a rich learning environment sustaining their child's advanced learning. This seems to suggest a theory of an individual learning continuum: a process rather than a developmentally appropriate age level for most children. Figure 5-2 offers a possible sequence of children's language learning in both planned and spur-of-the-moment classroom activities.

5-4 Federal Legislation and State Standards

The federal No Child Left Behind (NCBL) Act (U.S. Department of Education, 2002) sections dealing with guidelines for reading are designed to improve children's reading in publicly funded schools from kindergarten through third grade. The legislation, which is now over a decade old, was a shift toward accountability displayed by measurable gains (Webley, 2012). It asked educators to gather detailed demographic data on student performance and it promoted teacher training and development activities. Pushing formal reading instruction into preschool classrooms was not recommended and was not the legislation's intent. The idea that literacy experiences during preschool years are critical for successful learning during elementary school years was a central concern.

The assessment of preschool children and programs recommended in the NCLB Act was a "hot button" topic at the time for many early childhood educators. Educators and professional teacher organizations worried that testing labeled very young children, and they were concerned about assessment validity and unfair judgments of programs working with disadvantaged children or second-language learners.

The NCBL Act's provision that federal grants be contingent on the fact that all enrolled children at primary schools make "adequate yearly progress" in reading created shock waves throughout public educational systems. As a result, regional areas, states, cities, local communities, school districts, and professional organizations and groups have made attempts to identify age-level literacy characteristics. They have also developed standards and goal statements, pinpointing the literacy skills gained in the early years that may ease children's learning to read. Reading scores for elementary school students, including minority students, didn't budge in 2009 according to the National Assessment of Education Programs (NAEP) and achievement gaps among white, African-American, and Hispanic students has changed only slightly since 2007 (Toppo, 2010b).

Early childhood centers attempt to design curricula that are culturally relevant. Child observation and documentation activities are now part of the teacher's responsibility in many preschools as well as elementary schools. Child journals, child portfolios, teacher checklists, testing sessions, recording, and observations are commonplace as teachers struggle to identify the literacy growth of each child. Getting schools in the habit of collecting and sharing data is the NCLB law's most enduring legacy (Webley, 2012).

Many educators are involved in debates concerning the wisdom of some or all of the practices that are a result of this federal legislation. Most commonly, they express fears and frustrations involving "pushed down" curriculum formerly introduced in higher grades, literacy or academic activities "crowding out" playtime or other curricular activities, bilingual instructional techniques, and "fairness" in testing. Multiple studies show many children from low-income families enter kindergarten a year to a year and a half, on average, behind middle-class children in their language development, as well as other cognitive skills. This is a gigantic lag that dramatically affects children's success in the first grades of primary school and perhaps their entire educational future.

Arne Duncan, U.S. Secretary of Education criticizes the effectiveness of NCLB because he believes some states have "dumbed" down their Standards of Proficiency (Will, 2009). Guernsey (2009) points out that academic kindergarten practices have developed in the wake of new science. She suggests that all children, not just a select few children of above-average and advantaged circumstances, are able to learn earlier than once believed. She advocates the following: (1) training teachers to blend play with learning in planned activities, (2) making preschool affordable for working families, (3) encouraging full-day kindergarten (as 10 states do), and (4) building a bridge between preschool and kindergarten.

▶❚❚ **TeachSource Video 5-1**

© 2016 Cengage Learning®

Preschool: Guidance

The teacher in the video is conducting a teacher-led activity about feelings, personal space, good and not good touches, and seeking help when the child's efforts fail. Although this could be classified as a guidance lesson, it was also a language lesson.

1. How did the teacher personalize the activity?

2. Were new vocabulary words reinforced visually and physically? In other ways, also?

3. Could you comment on the clarity of this teacher's words, her eye contact, and her speech pacing during her presentation of new concepts?

5-4a Standards and Frameworks

According to Kendall and Marzano (2004), at least three principal reasons exist for the development of standards. These are (1) to establish clarity of curriculum content; (2) to raise expectations for achievement; and (3) to ensure accountability for public education. Most states have state initiatives and standards aimed at preparing preschoolers for kindergarten. Many states have developed accountability programs that they hope will indicate how well children in individual programs are performing relative to the skills and behaviors identified by the state as prerequisites for effective kindergarten performance. Prerequisite prereading skills and behaviors include phonological awareness, letter knowledge, and vocabulary; numeracy; and social-emotional competence.

Curriculum planners and developers in early childhood schools and centers keep standards in mind while preparing a school's program of activities if they receive public funds. Standards adopted at a particular school represent what that school and its teachers expect children to recall, replicate, manipulate, understand, or demonstrate at some point in time—in this case, prior to kindergarten entry.

Early childhood programs nationwide, depending on their state's decision to mandate or recommend their standards, may not be able to design their program of activities, for they may be spelled out in law. Some written standard statements provide examples of child behaviors teachers can observe that indicate child accomplishment or progress toward mastering a particular standard statement. Many state standard statements are in draft or final written form and are available on the Internet or available by contacting a state's Department of Education. Privately funded programs may be able to ignore state standards for publicly funded programs. Common Core State Standards, if adopted by a state, leave the how to get to prescribed outcomes open to an individual schools' discretion.

Head Start, reauthorized by Congress in 1998, augmented its Head Start Performance Standards, a document that guided language arts program planning along with other curricular areas. In 2000, the Administration for Children and Families (ACF) issued guidelines for devising and implementing outcome-based education plans. Consequently, the Head Start Child Outcomes Framework (U.S. Department of Health and Human Services, 2003) was developed. An updated and renamed version of the original framework entitled the *Head Start Child development and Early Learning Framework* (2010) again outlines the essential early childhood learning areas of three- to five-year-olds. The Improving Head Start for School Readiness Act of 2007 requires that programs' goals align with school readiness goals. To this end, the framework has 11 domains, 37 domain elements, and over 100 examples. Domains of particular interest to students of early childhood language arts and early childhood educators are language development, literacy knowledge and skills, and English language development, but since all learning areas involve language and communication reading, the complete document is suggested. The framework can be used to guide an early childhood language arts curriculum. Head Start programs are required to follow Head Start performance guidelines, but states may implement higher standards.

The National Association for the Education of Young Children's *Standards and Accreditation Performance Criteria for Early Childhood Programs* (2007) was developed through a

Figure 5-3 Questions useful in the development of standards

Speaking and Vocabulary Goals

Does your program intend to help children:
— use language for functional purposes and expression?
— increase the length of their sentences?
— use grammatical constructions of increasing complexity?
— express and orally relate personal narratives?
— question what they observe and experience?
— create stories using logical sequences?
— increase their vocabulary and oral speaking abilities?

— gain new words frequently?
— gain knowledge and refine their word meanings?
— increase their listening vocabulary?
— recognize differences in word sounds?
— discriminate between different sounds?
— gain the ability to voice letter sounds correctly?
— use words or sounds creatively or playfully?

Listening Goals

Does your program intend to help children:
— develop the ability to attend and listen?

— understand and respond to oral directions?
— hold up one end of conversations by listening closely?

Letter Knowledge and Phonological Awareness

Does your program intend to help children:
— associate alphabet letters with their shapes?
— achieve the ability to correctly point out or name 1–10 letters?
— recognize beginning letter sounds in words?
— be able to match sounds to letters?

— obtain a sight word vocabulary?
— recognize rhyming words?
— notice beginning sounds in words?
— separate words into syllables?
— play with words by switching or substituting sounds?

Print and Writing Awareness

Does your program intend to help children:
— develop the concept that reading and writing are related and connected?
— understand that books, printing, and writing hold information and perhaps enjoyment?
— know that their thoughts and ideas can be written down?
— realize that visuals and illustrations carry meaning?

— understand the difference between alphabet letters and numerals?
— understand authorship and left to right and top to bottom progression on a page?
— examine the structure and construction of books?
— write or dictate messages to be put in print?
— understand basic print conventions?

Reading Goals

Does your program intend to help children:
— develop an interest and positive feelings toward written materials and books?
— enjoy book experiences and select books as a chosen activity?

— ask adults to read picture books?
— make beginning attempts to both write and read print and books?

national effort to improve early childhood degree-granting teacher training programs. *The 2010 NAEYC Standards for Initial and Advanced Early Childhood Preparation Programs* may affect college students seeking a degree at a college that is in the process of applying for or has received accreditation from the NAEYC. These standards express a national vision of preparation and training excellence for early childhood professional educators and encompass initial (associate degree) and advanced (baccalaureate and graduate level) degree training programs. Based upon educational research and evidence, the standards contain a core set of values that are important to excellence. They are widely accepted.

Figure 5-3 is checklist of questions useful in identifying early childhood language and literacy goals and standards. A classroom where you are employed may use its own created set of standards or ones mandated by the federal government, a state department or licensing agency. Some local school district standards have been developed using standards recommended by a national organization such as NAEYC or IRA (The International

Reading Association). Private school standards are often developed through a joint home, school, and community consultation and agreement.

5-4b Common Core State Standards

The National Governor's Association Center for Best Practices and the Council of Chief State School Officers (CCSSO) has developed the latest vision of what standards should be used for the education of children in grades kindergarten through grade 12 in public schools. Their publication is called the *Common Core State Standards for English Language Arts & Literacy in History/Social Studies, Science, and Technical Subjects (2010)*. This was a joint state effort rather than a federal one. The core standards for English language arts are an attempt to universalize skills that all kindergarten through twelfth grade students will learn.

The major domains identified in the standards are literature, informational texts, foundational skills, writing, reading, speaking and listening, language, technology, and assessment. These standards articulate what it means to be a literate person and provide a clear understanding of what students are expected to achieve in each grade. It enables teachers and parents to know what knowledge and skill is expected at the end of the school year. The standards, adopted in most states, are expected to dramatically impact literacy instruction and assessment. These standards are focused on preparing exiting high school graduates to enter college and/or the workforce. They require that educators provide intentional and rigorous instruction beginning in kindergarten.

What is the importance of these common core standards to early childhood educators? They represent a major shift and not just a revision of past standards. They present qualitatively different outcomes for the education of America's children and will require changes in educational practices. There are different ways educators will help children reach these standard's expectations in language arts. Early childhood educators will be scrambling to equip children with the language arts knowledge and skills necessary to meet the challenging tasks and new demands they will face in kindergarten. The standards don't prescribe the use of certain teaching methods.

Many educational practitioners and experts have worried about how local, state, or national standards will affect the quality of their early childhood instructional programs. Some have adopted a pro-standards stance, while others feel there are inherent dangers in predetermined standards that are mandated and forced upon them. They may feel others are unaware of the needs and characteristics of their particular child group.

Pro-standards advocates frequently mention what they think are the positive benefits resulting from standards' use. These include:

- Recognized standards have been developed using the best information and research available by well-known and respected groups of educators.
- Standards identify clear and explicit goals for early childhood programs.
- Standards are designed to prepare enrolled children with the abilities and skills necessary to enable them to learn to read with ease when formal instruction in reading begins.
- With all or most schools using the same standards, transferring from school to school is not a problem.
- Teachers and teaching staffs are provided with guidelines for planning curriculum and daily activities.
- Standards' use is bound to add status to the early childhood teaching profession as well as to the programs themselves.
- Families can examine school standards and determine if the program meets their needs.
- National standards promote uniformity of instruction nationwide.
- Standards at preschool level may more easily meld into kindergarten standards.

Disadvantages cited by those who oppose standards include:

- Standards' use may promote adopting teaching practices that emphasize passing assessments or tests that measure standards' accomplishment.
- Early childhood curriculum areas that encompass art, music, or other more creative pursuits will be slighted.
- Physical development and exercise will be given a lower priority.
- Some schools will be labeled "failure factories."
- Emphasis on standards may cause teachers to ignore the individual and unique talents of some children while they concentrate on "strugglers."

- Teaching methods may not be identified in standards.
- Increased public pressure on schools and teachers may take place.
- Children's socio-emotional development may take a back seat to intellectual and academic growth.

Stott believes that standards in the field of early education are an essential first step for designing a more effective preschool curriculum.

5-5 Language use in all Curriculum Areas DAP

Every planned preschool activity uses language in some way. Past experience is basic to all language arts because a child's success often depends on her understanding of what is happening. Language helps children learn, retain, recall, and transmit information. Messages are received through words and nonverbal means. The teacher's speech, behavior, and use of words in planned activities are discussed in the following chapters.

In addition to the early childhood center's planned program, the daily sequence of activities, play with peers, and unplanned happenings also stimulate language. Teachers use every opportunity to add meanings in a natural, conversational way during the preschool day. This generally begins with the teacher's personal greeting or affectionate physical contact as the child enters the center. The "hello" and comments are part of the rituals in preschools that aim to recognize each child's presence each arrival time.

Daily routines are the regular features of a school's program that occur about the same time every day—snacks, toileting, and group activities—in which language is an associate function. Language-related activities are included in both small and large group times; these activities can range from short announcements to literacy-oriented activities the teacher presents or prepares.

Planned activities should have a purpose children can understand and in some way connect to what they already know (Photo 5-2). Most, if not all, learning can be made applicable to the child's life. Early childhood practitioners provide real, hands-on experiences in their classrooms when possible. Secondhand activities are second best. If classroom charts, posters, and graphic representations are used, teachers consider using bold colors.

Concrete vivid images are most influential. Neuroscientists theorize that this is because (1) the brain has an attentional bias for high contrast and novelty; (2) 90 percent of the brain's sensory input is from visual sources; and (3) the brain has an immediate and primitive response to symbols, icons, and other simple images. (Jensen, 2008, p. 56)

Photo 5-2 Many new words can be connected to an activity with growing plants.

© 2015 Cengage Learning®

With real object exploration in children's activities, the learner's brain may be focusing upon location, property differences, color, form, weight, and other unique properties. According to Rochman (2013), research shows that early mathematic skills are a better predictor of academic success than reading ability. Think about all of the times during teaching interactions and conversations with children that a teacher could consciously and consistently add basic number words and terms, such as more, less, count, long, short, and so on, or discuss simple age-appropriate math problems.

In an activity, planting spring seeds, signs, or labels adjacent to planted seeds have a practical purpose. The teacher could read the seed packet instructions to the children to find out about planting particulars. If individual planting pots are used, the children and/or teacher could number them and print children's names to label them.

Educators are encouraged to use number and measurement terms in preschool activities in which counting, comparing, adding, or taking away is encountered in planned or unplanned daily happenings. Participation in preschool activities that touch on math knowledge and terminology helps to reduce the disparities in educational achievement between children from low-income and middle-income families

5-6 Language Arts Programming

Preplanned language arts programs develop from identified goals: the knowledge, skills, and attitudes that the school intends to teach (Photo 5-3). Early childhood teachers also base teaching techniques on what they believe is best, right, appropriate, and prudent. This, in turn, is connected to views they hold about how, what, when, and where children learn to communicate and use language. The following views about language learning are commonly expressed or implied by staff members involved in planning language arts programs.

- Language permeates all planned and unplanned activities.

- A dynamic, rich-in-opportunity classroom stimulates communication and exchanges of ideas.

- Real experiences are preferred to vicarious ones when practical and possible.

- The reciprocal nature of exploring and discovering together should be promoted by teachers.

Photo 5-3 The school's staff meets often to assess whether the school's program is achieving standards and serving each child's individual needs.

© 2015 Cengage Learning®

- Play provides many opportunities to learn language (Photo 5-4).

- Teachers' instructional techniques should be skilled and alert to child readiness.

- Stressing relationships between objects, events, and experiences is a useful teaching technique.

- Individual planning, as well as group planning, is desirable.

- Program activities should center on the children's interests.

- Literary classics (preschool level) are an important planned-program component.

- The entire teaching staff should be committed to and enthusiastic about their planned program and should understand the stated objectives.

- An integrated approach to language arts instruction helps children experience the "connectedness" of language arts areas.

- Reading and writing is better conceptualized as a developmental continuum.

The best type of planned literacy-promoting program is one that is captivating enough to hold the imagination, engaging enough to sustain active involvement for a period of time, and stimulating enough to motivate further literacy exploration.

Early childhood teachers realize that goals for attending children may be much different than families' goals. Rather than telling families what they ought to be doing, it is the school's job to support and complement families' efforts. There is sometimes a need to find community translators to help bridge the gap between home and school.

Photo 5-4 Outdoor play can also provide language-learning opportunities.

© 2016 Cengage Learning®

One can envision an ideal language arts curriculum starting at birth and continuing throughout the child's lifetime. The author sees it as a program of home and life experiences supporting learning and self-discovery in which colorful, interconnected strands of language arts knowledge and skill thread through early childhood and come together in an "'aha' rainbow" when the child successfully decodes her first word, first sentence, or first book. The child then passes through a door equipped to move on into a vast amount of stored human knowledge, discovery, inspiration, creativity, and fantasy. These milestones in development are hopefully accompanied by understanding, rich personal life experiences, natural inquisitiveness, and a belief in the child's own ability and self-worth.

The ideal early childhood curriculum in language arts offers quality child-relevant speaking, listening, early writing, and reading activities in addition to literature opportunities. These activities encourage, sustain, and provide growth,

ensuring the necessary foundational knowledge and skill for an easy transition to school and a successful kindergarten year and beyond.

Common Core State Standards include a focus on academic vocabulary and language development. Early childhood educators will attempt to use developmentally appropriate terminology and phrases that are as academically accurate as possible to promote vocabulary specific to each content area. They will also build on words children already know and will use academically correct terminology at preschool level. It will be challenging, but educators will find that children savor new words, big or small, and with repetition and understandable examples, they will add them to their vocabularies. Words such as cocoon, motorized, or abdomen are learnable. Common core strategy suggests educators recognize key ideas, details, and new concepts in their instructional planning and also promote the integration of knowledge and ideas into what children already know or have experienced.

5-6a Teacher Training

Your classes in early childhood education, self-study, and your life experiences will influence the early childhood literacy program you will attempt to offer young children. Many times, your ideas will be incorporated into a teaching team's effort to design a planned curriculum.

Your training should have encouraged you to continually improve instructional practice and to analyze what is working and what is not. Questioning and researching are parts of the joy of teaching and can lead to new techniques and insights. When looking for program ideas, be open-minded and look inside to remember what inspired your own literacy development. Do not discount your ability to really focus on children and discover their agendas or your ability as an "innovator" of a language arts program that addresses the needs and interests of each child. The specific teaching behaviors that an early childhood educator working toward language arts and literacy goals should possess are listed below. They include both knowledge and skills. Research has identified the following "critical" teacher behaviors:

- using new words with children.
- extending children's comments through questioning.
- focusing children's attention on an analysis of books read to them.

- engaging in intellectually challenging conversations.
- placing an importance on child engagement during group time.
- obtaining and maintaining children's attention.
- believing academic and social goals are both important.
- providing literacy-learning opportunities and being intentional in instructional efforts to stretch children's thinking.
- supporting children's writing attempts.
- providing knowledge, promoting phonological sensitivity, and instilling child familiarity with the basic purposes and mechanisms of reading, especially to preschoolers with less prior knowledge and skill (at-risk children).
- giving individual children adequate time to speak.
- planning and implementing small group activities.
- engaging in extensive conversations.
- joining individual children or small groups in the library or writing areas.
- creating a literacy-rich classroom environment with accessible materials.
- ensuring careful organization and management of materials.
- providing opportunities for children to practice skills taught.
- giving guidance in structured lessons for acquisition of skills.
- providing opportunities for children to work independently or in collaborative groups.

5-6b Culturally Diverse Musical Experience

The songs and music of childhood are a part of our cultural heritage. The folk songs and ballads that have survived to the present day and the regional tunes parents and teachers offer are part of each child's cultural literacy. Early childhood programs attempt to provide the music of various ethnic groups. Most of these musical experiences give young children the opportunity to form beginning ideas concerning the music and language of diverse peoples.

Musical activities have gained new status and are viewed as language-developing activities.

Studies suggest that in cultures in which musical play is actively encouraged, children acquire heightened competencies in motor and communication skills at early ages. Neuroscientists agree that information set to music is among the easiest information to remember (Mitchell, 2013).

5-6c Classroom Environment

Classrooms should be designed to reflect the rich literate environments in which children are immersed outside of school. The use of teacher-made signs that label children's materials, furnishings, or equipment or areas where children store their belongings and books are helpful, but other educators feel labeling is not an effective practice if labels are not talked about or if there is no recognized purpose for labeling items. Available paper in various sizes, shapes, and colors that children can write on in their theme play or their independent-time activities encourage child use. All learning experiences should be organized so that they invite children to participate in literacy events.

Authentic literacy events need to become the focus of the school day as children:

- are signed in daily so that the teacher knows who has arrived in school;
- put away their materials in an appropriate setting, using the signs in the room or their names on their cubbies;
- read recipes and menus as they cook, eat, and learn about healthy nutritional activities;
- write prescriptions at the play hospital or take phone messages in the house corner; and
- read storybooks, write letters, and record observations.

Creating a warm, cozy, friendly environment where children are in a state of relaxed alertness is the goal of educators.

5-6d Determining Program Effectiveness

Goals pinpointed through staff meetings and solicited parent input can be finalized in written form to serve as a basis for planning. For one child or many, goals are achieved when teachers and staff plan interesting and appropriate activities for daily, weekly, monthly, or longer periods. In addition to the actual program, materials, and classroom equipment and arrangement, teacher techniques and interactions and other resources aid in goal realization.

Teacher observation and assessment instruments—both commercial instruments and those designed by teachers—add extra data that help in planning programs. Assessment may be defined as an ongoing process of gathering evidence of learning in order to make informed judgments about instructional practice. Many educators believe assessment of children's growth and development is an essential component of all high-quality preschool programs.

> Assessment allows teacher and parents to see how a child is progressing and helps teachers to prepare instruction for their students' ever-changing language development and literacy needs. (p. 2)

Carefully planned, recorded, and well-conducted teacher observation is an assessment tool that is hard to beat. Standardized tests all too often do not tell observant teachers anything they do not already know about children. Some assessments attempt to determine ability and accomplishment in a number of language and communication areas; others may be limited to one language skill.

School assessment and testing strategies can include collecting daily performance or work samples, making anecdotal observations, using checklists, identifying benchmarks or milestones a child has accomplished, or conducting testing with norm or criterion-referenced instruments. Literacy portfolio development is initiated in many programs to begin a documented and ongoing collection of child performance.

Standard tests are defined as tests in which a prepared script is read verbatim to the one tested. Commercial publishers also offer screening checklists besides teacher administered tests that cover language and communication skills for different age level groups. Published tests are usually referenced to a select and accepted set of norms or standards. See the Appendix for a list of well-known testing instruments. Norms reflect the average accomplishments or performances of a large group of children at a particular age or grade level. Standardized tests may cover a wide range of topics, such as listening skill, auditory memory, and vocabulary, but rarely test all skills, knowledge, and ability associated with emergent literacy or early reading ability.

Many early childhood centers test children so they can both individualize their instruction and find out if attending children are progressing by being exposed to their standards-based planned curriculum and their staffs' guidance and teaching strategies. How is a teacher otherwise to know if she and the curriculum are effective? Great teachers are always excited about learning new ways they can help students (Canada, 2010).

> At successful schools there is a constant focus on getting real information about students' performance early and often, using data to have a much better picture of student's ability and then creating an action plan to target individual students' deficiencies. . . (Canada, 2010, p. 19).

5-6e Child Literacy Portfolios

A number of centers and programs create individual literacy portfolios in an effort to track individual children's literacy development and to complement the school's standardized assessment and reporting methods. A first step is identifying educational goals and purposes that a portfolio might satisfy. Usually this deals with both school and home language arts activities and opportunities. What types of items might be collected is next considered, and then home-school collaboration particulars. Often literacy portfolio development is a joint project undertaken by both teachers and families. Items are collected over time and dated. These can include child work samples, child-dictated text, artwork with recorded comments, photographs of child work or dramatic play, a favorite book list, adult-child interviews, child-created stories or dictation, early writing attempts, alphabet-related examples, word lists; in short, records of child activities related to speaking, listening, pre-reading and reading skill development, print awareness, or any activities concerned with child literacy growth.

Child portfolios systematically follow children's development over time and aid a teacher's recognition of children's individuality and particular rate of growth. It allows multiple ways to demonstrate children's knowledge and vocabulary. It is also the easiest way to alert parents to a child's growth or lack of it.

The portfolio usually travels from school to home and back. This activity informs families about what is happening at school and affords families a review and then insertion of home-collected items. Often children's portfolios become a special book from which children and their families derive pride and pleasure in a child's accomplishments and progress.

Large, album-sized binders are used to accommodate children's artwork in some programs, and many schools use page protectors or clear plastic kitchen storage bags to protect inserts. Items are filed in chronological order when dated. Reviewing a child's portfolio with the child generates considerable interactive conversation and promotes feelings of accomplishment. Some schools create digital files of students' work.

5-6f Teacher Observation

Many child care centers encourage teachers to continually observe the language skills of attending children. Each child and group may have different needs, and the center attempts to fulfill needs and offer a language arts program that will be growth producing and enriching. Many different observation methods and instruments can be used. Some may be school-designed; others may be commercially produced.

A teacher who is a keen observer and listener gathers information, which guides teacher actions and planning. In their efforts to make an activity relevant, teachers observe attending children's needs, desires, and interests and make individual judgments regarding children's already acquired knowledge, attitudes, and language skills. Educators believe that assessing beyond children's level of performance by looking at ways children learn and interact provides a much richer portrait of children than just identifying levels of skill. As teachers observe, some try to answer the following questions:

- What individual language characteristics are present?
- How can activities be planned that capture and hold children's interest and enthusiasm?
- How do my actions and behaviors affect the children's language arts behaviors?
- Which children are interested in which indoor and outdoor areas?
- What patterns of language behavior have I noticed?
- What do children seem eager to talk about or explore?
- What can I do to provide experience or exploration just beyond what they already know?
- Which children readily express their ideas?

- Which children are socially adept and learn language in play with others?

Assessment is a continual, ongoing process. Observation information is confidential and often useful in program planning. Running accounts of child conversations are difficult to obtain because an adult's presence may affect a child's spontaneity. Also, the child's attention span and mobility make it almost impossible to capture more than a few minutes of speech with preschoolers. Many teachers note a few phrases or speech characteristics on a writing pad they carry with them throughout the day. For many teachers, having time just to observe children is considered a luxury. However, observation is important and can be considered an ongoing teacher responsibility in all areas of instruction. Observation is a daily tool to collect a point-in-time snapshot both of children's interests and progress. Observation is good for catching patterns of behaviors and noticing atypical ones. It often provokes a teacher's questioning of practice and can lead to insights.

Anecdotal observations record the details present when a child's behavior is significant and displays a developmental happening. This might include a particular child's interest in writing alphabet letters at the art easel, or a child's seemingly bored behavior during a read-aloud while peers find it very interesting, or a child's writing his name for the first time, or a child's sharing a first created oral story. Teachers carry small notebooks or use other technologies such as cell phone pictures to record.

Many programs make decisions concerning what classroom language activities, opportunities, and experiences will be offered to a specific group of children on any given day by first determining through ongoing teacher and staff observation and child assessment what focused support is necessary for language development and growth. They then identify what intentionally designed lessons, activities, and interactions will capitalize on children's existing knowledge and also systematically foster language growth and development. Educators combine the information they gain from both formative and summative assessments. Formative assessments' goal is to better understand unique student individuality and their immediate needs. Summative assessments' goal is to discover children's literary performance level by examining whether age level benchmarks are displayed in their actions, behaviors, and products. What are closely assessed in relation to a preschooler's ease of learning to read when reading instruction begins is their understandings and competencies in the areas of print concepts, phonological awareness, phonics, word recognition, and fluency. To ensure a language program's quality, plans may be changed and updated. Keeping a planned language arts program vital, dynamic, appealing, and appropriate requires continual revision and overhaul.

5-7 Goal Statements

A particular center may have many or few goal statements, which can be both general and specific. If standards exist and affect an early childhood program, goals are often identified and listed. Privately funded early childhood programs in most states may choose to look at standards statements, but some schools may decide not to incorporate them into their planned program goals and instead to develop their own.

5-7a Goals for Children's Writing Development naeyc DAP

In the process of literacy development, young children can profit from an understanding of the role of the printed word. The uses of writing, including recording and transmitting information, recording self-authored creations, and providing entertainment, are important to the quality of human life. Knowing and understanding how writing is used may lead to a realization of the value of learning to read. Writing and reading open each individual to the thoughts, creations, and discoveries of multitudes of people, living and deceased. This discussion is not intended to promote formal early printing instruction, but rather to point out that there are basic ideas about writing that must be considered when planning a language arts curriculum that promotes literacy. Photo 5-5 shows a table arrangement that introduces children to print. Chapter 15 covers print and writing development and programming ideas in detail.

There is a strong connection between the child's familiarity with books (and her book-reading experiences) and literacy. Illustrations of the reasons for writing and how writing can satisfy everyday needs can be incorporated into any center's goals for promoting literacy growth. Most schools concentrate on exposing children

Photo 5-5 Printed words may accompany new objects in early childhood classrooms.

© 2015 Cengage Learning®

to printed words rather than beginning actual writing skill practice in alphabet letter formation.

5-7b Pre-reading Goals

Reading skills are multiple and complex and they often involve the coordination of other skills and abilities. Some reading goals that will facilitate later reading skills include :

- Reads pictures
- Shows an interest in and enjoyment of stories and books
- Is able to arrange pictures in a sequence that tells a story
- Finds hidden objects in pictures
- Guesses at meanings based on contextual cues
- Reads own and others' names
- Predicts events
- Recognizes letters of own name in other words
- Senses left-right direction
- Guesses words to complete sentences
- Chooses favorite book characters
- Treats books with care
- Authors own books through dictation
- Sees finely detailed differences
- Understands the reason for reading
- Has the ability to decode a few small words
- Uses visual perception abilities
- Shows interest in the sounds of letters
- Watches or uses puppets to enact simple stories

- Has background in traditional literature appropriate for age and ability
- Develops phonemic awareness
- Has knowledge of the alphabet code that includes alphabet knowledge and phonological awareness
- Displays writing with the use of invented spelling
- Has print knowledge and can read some environmental print
- Can write her name
- Demonstrates the ability to rapidly name alphabet letters and numbers
- Possesses expressive and receptive oral language development
- Is acquainted with digital literacy devices

5-7c Early Literacy Goals

Preschool teachers planning and conducting programs that promote language development in young children try to provide a "classic" literary experience, featuring appropriate age-level materials collected from many cultures and eras. Such a curriculum would serve as a basis of human cultural understanding and would include a wide range of oral and listening materials and activities: books, poetry, language games, puppetry, and storytelling. Most teachers believe that early exposure to and familiarity with literary classics can help the child understand what might be encountered later in literature, media, or schooling. Mother Goose stories are undisputed classics. Two other agreed-upon classic stories are *Goldilocks and the Three Bears* and *Peter Rabbit*. Whether a story, play, rhyme, or song is considered a "classic," however, is usually a matter of judgment by individual teachers.

5-7d Sociocultural Language Goals

A language arts curriculum should include language activities that celebrate cultural diversity. Family and community literacy activities are important considerations. Family stories and literacy-promoting activities and events can be included in center planning. Collaboration with parents reinforces the unique contributions families and neighborhoods make to child literacy growth. Early childhood educators can lay the groundwork and monitor attitudes and feelings that in any way degrade other-than-mainstream-language speakers. To accomplish this, teachers may want to consider the following goals:

- Goal #1: All students are able to communicate effectively with all persons within a multicultural, diverse society.
- Goal #2: All students learn to value linguistic diversity and celebrate the cultural expressions of those who are different from themselves.
- Goal #3: All students see the value of language and literacy for their own lives.

5-8 Language Arts Curricula

Many early childhood **curriculum models** exist. Models usually provide well-defined frameworks to guide program implementation. Child development theories are their underlying foundation. Whether a particular model, a combination of models, or an eclectic model is used, early childhood educators are constantly challenged to examine, reflect, and improve children's daily language arts experiences.

Schools and centers differ widely in **curriculum** development; however, two basic approaches can be identified. In the first, a unit or thematic approach emerges from identified child interest and teacher-selected areas, such as families, seasons, animals, and so on. Using this approach, some centers use children's books or classic nursery rhymes as their thematic starting topic. Others introduce a proposed theme (unit) topic to small discussion groups of children. This offers input from attending children and lets teachers explore children's past experience, knowledge, and interests. Questions children ask and vocabulary used may aid teachers' thematic unit development. Staff and parent group discussion can also uncover attitudes and resources. Goals are considered, and activities are then outlined and scheduled into time slots. Many teachers believe this type of program approach individualizes instruction by providing

---

curriculum models — refers to a conceptual framework and organizational structure for decision making about educational priorities, administrative policies, instructional methods, and evaluation criteria.

curriculum — an overall plan for the content of instruction to be offered in a program.

many interrelated and, consequently, reinforced understandings while also allowing the child to select activities.

The second common instructional approach is to pinpoint traditional preschool subject areas, such as language arts, science, mathematics, art, cooking, and so forth, and then plan how many and what kind of planned activities will take place. This can be done with or without considering a unifying theme. Some teachers believe that this is a more systematic approach to instruction. In both approaches, the identification of goals comes before curriculum development. Ages of children, staffing ratios, facility resources, and other particulars all affect planning. After planned curriculum activities take place, teachers evaluate whether goals were reached and modifications and suggestions are noted. Additional or follow-up activities may be planned and scheduled for groups or individual children.

5-8a Thematic Inquiry Approach to Language Instruction

Imagine a classroom turned into a pizza parlor or a flower garden. There would be a number of activities occurring simultaneously—some for small groups, others for large groups, and some for individuals. Teachers would be involved in activities, and classroom areas might be set up for continuous, or almost continuous, child exploration. Art, singing, number, movement, science-related, health-related, safety-related, and other types of activities would (or could) be preplanned, focusing on the two themes mentioned previously. Bintz (2010) reminds teachers that singing has long been used as an instructional strategy in literacy development.

The sensory activities could be included so that children could experience the smells, sounds, sights, tastes, and so on, associated with each theme. Planning language arts instruction using this approach allows teachers to use creativity and imagination. It is an integrated approach to curriculum that takes advantage of the natural relationship between developmental domains and between content areas (Koralek, 2008). Koralek explains,

> When curriculum is integrated, children can explore a theme in depth, achieve early learning standards, and apply their knowledge in meaningful ways. They learn facts related to a specific

topic, ways to find information, and how content areas are related. p. 10.

Theme instruction requires planning time to gather and set up material that might not be found in the school storeroom or supply area. It is easy to see that there could be many opportunities for children's use of speech, listening, reading, and writing, and the natural connection among these activities might be more apparent to the children. Most teachers believe that using a thematic approach is an exciting challenge that is well worth teacher time and effort. They see this approach as one that encourages child-teacher conversations and consequently expands children's language usage and knowledge.

Teachers should not limit their program to traditional themes, but should explore and discover beyond the familiar. Teachers can follow children's curiosity and their own childhood interests. Many centers believe that real teaching is found when each staff member gives children what she individually has to offer from the heart as well as the mind.

Considerable brainstorming and discussion among staff members takes place when deciding which theme topics are suitable, feasible, appropriate, and educationally advantageous for their particular child group and facility.

In constructing a theme, the following steps are usually undertaken:

1. Observe and record a child's interest and/or teacher drawing from past experience.
2. Identify a topic. (It could be a book, poem, drama, or another category.)
3. Try to discover what children know and want to know.
4. Imagine possible activities (in and out of school).
5. Decide on attempted goals of instruction.
6. Pinpoint range, scope, vocabulary, main ideas, and activities.
7. Discuss room environment, staffing, visitors, and helpers. (What will take place in the classroom or yard or learning centers?)
8. Make specific plans for individual and group activities.
9. List the necessary materials and supplies.
10. Decide on a culminating activity (usually a recap or "grand finale").
11. Set a timetable if necessary. (Daily schedules may be prepared.)
12. Pinpoint evaluation criteria.

Brain Connection

Brain Development and Theme Instruction

What should teachers keep in mind while using a theme instruction approach, traditional approach, or a brain development learning approach?

1. Periodic repetition of theme information and ideas can aid children's learning. Medina (2008) suggests reviewing newly learned material.

2. Talking about an event *immediately* after it has occurred helps children's memory of the event. Teachers can promote children's recollections by suggesting they talk about a discovery or learning event that has just occurred.

3. Offer real objects or—second-best—pictures that accompany new vocabulary words during theme instruction. Students learn better with pictures or real objects present than from words alone (Medina, 2008).

4. It is best not to interrupt a child trying to complete a task. Wait until a child looks for help or there is a level of frustration to intervene.

5. Children need time to digest information, especially when there is lots of new information. Providing time to think things over is a good idea, then revisit new learning.

6. The brain is unable to pay attention to two things at once. Learning stations, centers, or separate room areas can be the best ways to prepare the learning environment. Eliminate visual and sound room distractions when child focus or concentration is expected.

7. Create attention-attracting activities or centers. Children do not pay attention to boring things.

8. Planning for children's sensory involvement in activities is a good idea. Children learn best if their senses of sight, hearing, touching, feeling, and even their sense of smell are present. In other words, teachers should consider stimulating several senses at once (Medina, 2008).

Nemeth (2009) suggests pinpointing key vocabulary words in any instructional theme. A key word list (with a pronunciation guide) can then be compiled in each attending child's home language. This is a daunting task, but doing so enables the teacher to connect words a child already knows to new English words.

Williams (1997) uses a four-step child-teacher interactive process to jointly plan unit (theme) activities for a group of four-year-olds.

1. The teacher asks, "What do you wonder?" or "What do you want to know about—(a particular topic, example: the ocean)?" Then the teacher records each child's answer or question in a different color on a wall chart that is posted at the children's eye level. Then the teacher adds her own questions.

2. The teacher asks, "What can we do to find out?" Then the teacher records the children's ideas on a second piece of chart paper. If no one responds, that is acceptable. The teacher instead develops a list of children's questions or ideas that might come up while the unit is in progress, and these are added to the chart.

3. The teacher asks, "What materials do we need?" on a prepared third chart. Materials suggested by the children that do not seem directly related are gently probed by teacher.

A child may have a connection to the topic of study not readily seen by the teacher.

4. The teacher asks, "What will you bring (do)?" and "What would you like me to bring (to do)?" The teacher checks with parents about objects and materials suggested by their child. A parent newsletter invites parents to share or bring in additional topic-related items to the classroom.

To promote literacy, teachers think about how each theme activity involves listening, speaking, reading, and writing and how to logically connect these areas during ongoing activities.

With current public and educator interest in standards and accountability, an increasing number of programs must document theme goal attainment and identify successful instructional strategies. Although this can be done many ways, it most frequently involves the collecting and recording of multiple pieces of evidence of theme activities, lessons, events, and classroom experiences. Children's work samples and participation might be captured using a variety of strategies including the technology available. Before, during, and after photos, videos, slides, movie, and artifacts, together with teacher observations of groups and individual children may illustrate children's engagement and learning. Seitz (2008) defines a documenter as a researcher, collecting as much information as possible to paint a picture of progress and outcomes. He believes that often the documentation provides insights into children's thinking and helps drive further curriculum planning.

5-8b Standards Can Affect Theme Plans

Early childhood educators are attempting to offer instruction that encourages children's in-depth learning and comprehension by pursuing extended themes of longer time duration and by adding more intentional (scaffolded), explicit, and purposefully planned teacher-child instructional interactions. Being influenced by higher standards and focused upon higher levels and more complex thinking skills, educators believe some themes are more basic and important than others, namely those that offer a challenge and encourage children to predict, observe, compare, and contrast ideas. Themes that promote academic or basic vocabulary used in science, social studies, mathematics, and the arts are deemed more valuable. Nonfiction picture books have consequently gained status and will be made available along with the many fiction picture books already provided in early childhood program instruction. Many educators feel this is already happening in early childhood theme instruction, but a theme's topic of study can be more thoughtfully planned and expanded to emphasize how the theme relates to all other disciplines or areas of early childhood curricular study.

5-8c Curriculum Webs and Theme-Based Instruction

The use of curriculum webs (or **webbing**) in program planning is popular with some preschool teachers. A web can be thought of as a graphic overall picture of what might be included in a theme or unit approach to instruction. (See the Appendix for an example of a web based on a picture book about trains by Donald Crews.) To create a plan a staff chooses an idea, brainstorm hands-on activities, and puts them on a tentative web. This gives a sort of road map. It's a process rather than a product. Figure 5-4 shows a skeleton web designed for the study of dogs. Under the box "care & needs" one can think of a number of items

Figure 5-4 Topic web—dog(s).

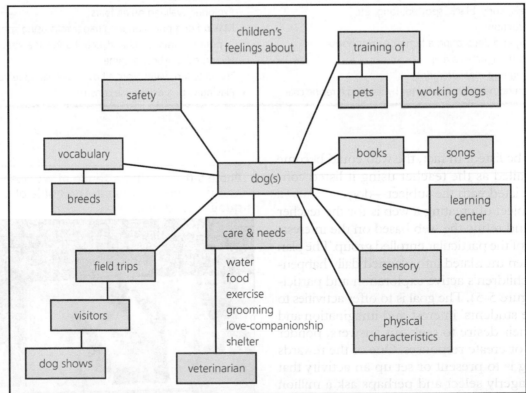

webbing — a visual or graphic method of mapping a possible course of study.

Figure 5-5 One-day plan during a weekly theme study of dogs (four-year-olds' classroom).

OPENING: Choose One Dog Sticker for Your Name Tag or Take-Home File (Stickers of Dog Breeds)

Large-group Instruction

a. Discussion
  Update and review of theme findings
    and discoveries so far
b. Chart introduction
  Different dog breeds have names
  Checking opening stickers
  Finding similarities and differences

c. Composing
  Writing an invitation to a guest speaker—the dog groomer
  Requesting a description and, when possible, a
    demonstration of the dog-care techniques and tools.
d. Song: "Bingo"
  Chant: "The Diners in the Kitchen" by James
    Whitcomb Riley
  Poem: "My Puppy" by Aileen Fisher

Small-group Instruction

a. Story time: "Harry the Dirty Dog" by G. Zion or "Dogs" by Dorling Kindersley (2005)
  Discussion
    Care of dogs
    Can dogs do small jobs or work?
    Working dog photos

Discovery Time Choices

a. Art
  Construct a dog and label using clay or body-
    part cutouts to paste and label them with the
    teacher's help
b. Sorting
  Assorted dog bones by color, size, and shape
c. Science
  How do dogs differ from one another? Examining hair
    from a variety of dogs and giving each a descriptive
    label—curly, black, spotted, long, etc.
d. Construction
  Making and decorating a large-box doghouse
    with the teacher's help
e. Cooking and measurement
  Making homemade dog bones by reading a recipe chart

f. Writing center
  Dictation of a story about a dog, or choosing to
    do a naming-seven-puppies activity
g. Listening Center
  Firehouse dog story on tape
  "Bert the Bird Dog" recording
h. Library Center
  A selection of books about dogs
i. Yard activities
  Exploring walking on all fours
  Making dog prints on long paper rolls using sponges or
    potato prints (teacher directed and supervised)
  Hiding-rubber-bones game
  Trying to lap water from a bowl (teacher supervised)
  Playing with a doghouse construction

---

that could be listed. In fact, the web could become highly detailed as the teacher using it listed concepts associated with the subject—dogs.

The object of creating a web is for the teacher to define and refine the web based on the interests and needs of the particular enrolled group. The plan (web) is then translated into planned daily happenings with children's active exploration and participation (Figure 5-5). The goal is to offer activities to engage the students' interest and imagination and to spark their desire to seek out answers, ponder questions, or create responses. One of the rewards of teaching is to present or set up an activity that children eagerly select and perhaps ask a million questions about; in other words, one that has "captured" them and engaged their minds (Photo 5-6).

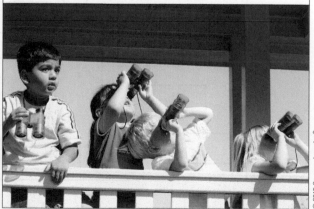

Photo 5-6 Creating a sense of wonder and discovery is among the goals of a quality program.

© 2015 Cengage Learning®

Figure 5-6 Multiple-goal approach.

NOTE: This is a portion of a longer description. The words in italics show how the teacher works toward a variety of goals.

This episode is an account of a sequence of planned activities culminating in a cooking experience for four four-year-old children. Part 1 of the episode details the preparation in the classroom for the purchase of the food and the group's trip to a local store. Part 2 describes the cooking.

The fresh pears at lunch evoked the excited comment "Apples!" from Spanish-speaking Fernando.

"Well, this is a fruit," said Miss Gordon, encouragingly, "but it has another name. Do you remember the apples we had last week?"

"They were hard to bite," said Joey.

"And we made applesauce," said Rosina.

"This fruit is called a pear, Fernando; let's taste this pear now. We'll have apples again."

The teacher responds to what is correct in the child's response, valuing his category association. First, she wants to support communication and willingness to experiment with language; later she gives the correct name. The children strengthen the experience by relating it to previous experience in which they were active.

"Mine's soft," said Joey.

"Can we make applesauce again?" begged Rosina.

The teacher replied, "Perhaps we could do what Janice wanted to do. Remember? To take some home to her family?"

"To my mommy, and my grandma, and Danny."

"Not to my baby," said Rosina. "He's too little. Him only drink milk."

"Tomorrow we'll buy lots of apples," said Miss Gordon.

The teacher is building a sense of continuity by recalling earlier intentions that had been expressed by the children.

She rarely corrects use of pronouns for four-year-olds. She knows the child will learn through greater social maturity and hearing language.

After rest, Miss Gordon asked the children how they could take home their applesauce. "What can we put it in?"

Rosina ran to the house corner and returned with two baby food jars. "I bringed lots," she said. Miss Gordon remembered that Rosina had come to school lugging a bag full of baby food jars, many of which she had put away. "A good idea! And your mommy said she would keep more for us. Let's write a note to tell her we need them tomorrow."

Rosina dictated a note: "I got to bring bunches of jars to school. We are going to make applesauce. I love you, Mommy." Rosina painted her name with a red marker.

The teacher helps children to think ahead to steps in a process.

The use of a tense form, although incorrect, represents learning for the child. The teacher does not correct at this moment, when she is responding to the child's pleasure in solving the practical problem that had been posed. She is strengthening the connection between home and school.

The teacher helps the children learn that writing is a recording of meaning and a way of communicating.

The next day was jar washing and arranging time. Each of the four children put his or her jars on a tray on which there was a large card with the child's name.

Janice put on one jar for her mother, one for her grandmother, one for her brother, and after a pause, one for herself.

Rosina changed her mind. "My baby can have a little tiny bit," she said. So she needed a jar for her father, her mother, her baby, and herself.

Joey and the teacher figured out that he needed six, and that Fernando needed nine!

The children are actively involved in the steps preparatory to the planned activity—an experience in organization that has personal meaning.

The teacher's plan calls for recognition of one's own name and one-to-one counting of family members.

The teacher turned their attention to a chart near the cooking corner. She had made a recipe chart, pasting colored (magazine) pictures next to the names of the items they would need to make the applesauce and had taped a stick of cinnamon to the chart.

Miss Gordon said, "Let's look at the recipe chart. I have a list so we can remember to buy everything."

The children said, "Apples."

Miss Gordon checked her list.

Then, "Sugar."

The children were silent as they looked at the stick of cinnamon taped to the chart.

Miss Gordon suggested, "Smell it. Have we had it before?"

Joey remembered: "Toast! What we put on toast!"

"Yes," said Miss Gordon, and then gave the word, "cinnamon."

The children are having a dual experience—pictorial representation and formal symbol usage.

The teacher supplies the word after the children have revived their direct experience with the phenomenon.

(Biber, Shapiro, & Wickens, 1977).

Translating a web into a week by week teaching overview or plan is the next step and is unique to each program. If daily lesson plans are developed, activities or lessons would be written in greater detail and could include the following steps:

- Naming the activity
- Naming the curriculum area
- Identifying room location and set up necessary
- Identifying the number of children and teaching staff present
- Listing necessary preparation
- Identifying a goal or objective or standard involved (an example of a multiple goal approach is seen in Figure 5-6)
- Identifying the developmental skills necessary for child success

Figure 5-7 Sample activity plan form.

Language Activity Plan Guide

1. Language activity title _____
_____

2. Materials needed _____
_____
_____

3. Location of activity (to be used when plan is developed for a particular classroom or area) _____
_____

4. Number of children _____
5. Language goal or objective _____
_____

6. Preparation (necessary teacher preparation, including getting materials or objects, visual aids, etc., ready) _____
_____
_____

7. Getting started (introductory and/or motivational statement) _____
_____
_____

8. Show and explore (include possible teacher questions or statements that promote language ability) _____
_____
_____
_____
_____

9. Discussion of key points, discoveries, conclusions, subjects for further study (what vocabulary and/or concepts might be included?) _____
_____
_____
_____
_____
_____

10. Apply (include child practice or application of newly learned knowledge or skill when appropriate) _____
_____
_____

11. Transition statement (needed if activity plan is to terminate or if a second activity immediately follows) _____
_____
_____
_____

12. Evaluation: (1) activity; (2) teacher; (3) child participation; (4) other aspects such as setting, materials, outcomes, etc. _____
_____
_____
_____
_____
_____
_____

Digital Download

- Describing opening teacher statements
- Describing key concepts, facts, skills, vocabulary, etc.
- Describing how the activity will proceed to conclusion
- Describing how practice or applying or reinforcing learning might take place

- Planning clean up
- Planning a transition
- Describing how the activity, teacher or child learning might be assessed or evaluated.

To examine a sample language activity planning form see Figure 5–7.

Theme planning needs to take into account the English-language learners in the class. Nemeth (2009) urges teachers to allow extra theme days for children not only learning new theme words, concepts, and skills, but also English. She points out themes can contribute to the scaffolding of language learning while also encouraging the use of English. She suggests adding home language words to classroom labels by color coding them, such as Spanish words in red ink, Chinese in green, and so on. This system of coding by color, Nemeth suggests, can also be used with stickers in the classroom book storage and reading areas to identify other than English-only books.

5-8d The Project Approach

The project approach involves integrated teaching and learning. It encourages meaningful, first-hand, relevant study of child-teacher–developed and child-teacher–chosen activities. This program approach is valued by teachers for its flexible and creative aspects, which fit diverse child groups and geographical communities. Children are involved in decision making, program planning, implementation, and evaluation through active teacher-child shared discussion, brainstorming, and project outlining. Teachers also plan activities and experiences. Children are urged to explore and investigate and become testers of ideas as individuals and in study groups. Teachers using thematic unit instruction may feel the project approach best suits kindergarten and elementary-aged children. Others have incorporated projects into preschool curriculum.

5-8e Daily Activity Plans (Lesson Plans)

Recognizing children's interests stimulates activity-planning ideas based on what captures and holds the children's attention. Part of the challenge and excitement of teaching is finding ways to be creative in daily activity planning and targeted instruction. Although two staff members work toward the same goal, they may approach the task in different ways. Lesson plans are more frequently used in schools using approaches other than the thematic (unit) approach described earlier, but can also be used for individual teacher-conducted activities within theme planning. Lesson plans are used most often in preschools when a skills-based approach is part of a planned school curriculum. Teachers focus children's attention on a skill and provide specific helpful information. A lesson plan usually involves objectives for a planned activity. It identifies where the activity will take place, and when the activity will take place, and its duration. The educator then devises instructional strategies, develops teaching procedures, sequences the skill into steps, and provides a time for practice and review. In early childhood, pre-reading skills may be called reading readiness skills. Since research confirms at-risk children profit most from skill-based instruction, most accredited and recognized quality preschools offer explicit skill instruction to help children catch up to their more advantaged peers and to succeed in kindergarten.

Lesson plans (or **activity plans**) enable teachers to foresee needs—settings, materials, and staffing. The time that children spend waiting can be minimized. Some teachers pinpoint exactly what words and concepts will be emphasized or what questions asked; other teachers prefer a more spontaneous approach. Some activities in language arts may require teacher practice beforehand. Others may require visual aids or materials that must be gathered in advance. Planning time is time well spent. Preparation reduces teacher tension and results in child activities that run smoothly.

Teachers must strive to be always aware of child safety and comfort. They must also try to maintain a reasonable level of stimulation somewhere between not very interesting and overly exciting activities so that children are encouraged to process information in a manner that is both pleasurable and efficient. Experienced teachers know when children are interested and are actively participating. Many teachers say this is one of the greatest joys of teaching.

Group size is an important factor in planning. It is easier for teachers to plan for an entire class group, and sometimes staffing demands it. However, many teachers have explored ways to keep children occupied and supervised while working with small groups. Small groups allow greater intimacy, conversational depth, and opportunity for feedback. Research substantiates the idea that both children and adults feel

---

activity plans — written, detailed, step-by-step teaching plans, often including an evaluation section.

more comfortable sharing their thoughts when in small groups. "Instant replays" with small groups can be planned and coordinated. Beginning preschool teachers may not have seen many small group activities modeled by other teachers, but this text recommends them.

Teachers strive to maintain children's attention during activities. Teachers realize that attention is mediated by specific parts of the brain and that neural systems fatigue quickly. After three to five minutes of sustained activity, children need to rest, but they can recover within minutes, too. In a familiar and safe classroom, if a child hears factual information for only four to eight minutes and a teacher is not providing novelty, the brain seeks other stimuli. Perry (2000) recommends adding "emotional seasoning" like humor and empathy to teacher presentations and linking facts to related child concepts during activities, in addition to taking advantage of the novelty-seeking property of the human brain. He believes this is a challenging task for teachers of all-aged students. Medina (2008), the author of *Brain Rules*, urges educators using lesson plans to cover and explain one core concept at a time in clear and explicit terms and later connect details during the activity or discussion. He suggests presenting key ideas in a hierarchical fashion and forming details around larger concepts. See Step 9 in Figure 5-7.

Brain research suggests educators provide down time lasting a few minutes in cognitive activities. This could be physical movement such as stretching, deep breathing, or other movement (Jensen, 2008). Teachers should plan to do so when planned activities requiring focusing and concentration go beyond planned time estimates.

Activities based on teacher enthusiasm for life and growth, skills, talents, hobbies, and pursuits can fit beautifully into language arts goals. Family and community resources, including borrowed items and field trips, increase the vitality of programs.

5-8f Evaluation

Thinking back over planned activities helps teachers analyze the benefits and possibly leads to additional planning along the same line or with the same theme. Oversights in planning frequently occur, and activities may develop in unexpected ways. Hindsight is a useful and valuable tool in evaluating activities (Figure 5-8).

Figure 5-8 Thinking back.

What I planned and how I went about it:

What effect my actions had:

What I could have done:

What effect this action would have had:

What I will do differently next time:

Digital Download

Often, centers evaluate their planned programs by asking themselves questions such as the following:

- Do children share personal interests and learning discoveries with teachers and/or other children?
- Can teachers enter conversations without diminishing children's verbal initiative?
- Do children become involved in planned activities and room centers?
- Are there times when children listen with interest?
- Are language arts areas (speaking, writing, reading, and listening) connected in a natural way during daily activities?
- Is child talk abundant?

Teachers may attempt to ascertain whether their lesson plan's goals of instruction have been achieved: particularly key vocabulary and concepts. They may implement a game review a while after the activity information has been allowed to sink in. One such teacher game is a Thumbs Up Game in which children are asked to put their thumbs up for yes, or thumbs down for no. The teacher's questions or statements might be similar to the following:

"Did a mosquito make the honey that we spread on toast?"

"A butterfly has an antenna that alerts it to the fact that a flower is nearby."

"Your thumb is down Evan. Can you tell us why you didn't think that was true?"

Currently, the accountability of a program's quality and value has become an issue and has resulted in the development of content and performance standards. Consequently, programs are frequently required to develop some type of formalized method of assessment. The example just given was an informal assessment.

Summary

5-1   Define literacy.

Literacy is a distinct domain related to language and refers to the ability to produce and comprehend written language. It involves complex cognitive interactions between readers and reading material (text, books, etc.) and between a reader's background knowledge and new information. Skill varies by task and setting.

5-2   Describe common teaching practices in the United States in the early twentieth century.

American preschools in the early twentieth century imitated primary school practices. This included memorization and recitation. Other schools offered only custodial care. John Dewey influenced changes that promoted a curriculum with educational components such as theme study and promoted planned classroom play areas. Before the mid-century Gesell introduced the idea of developmental norms, a theory that highlighted children's readiness for learning.

5-3   Compare two known theories of literacy instruction.

One might make comparisons between nativist, psychosocial theory, nurturist, interactionist, constructivist, or social constructivist theory.

5-4   Name two pieces of federal legislation that have substantially affected preschool language instruction.

Federal legislation has resulted from national concern over children's inability to master reading in the first grades of public elementary school. Legislation focused on both reading instruction and what precedes and prepares young preschoolers. The NCLB Act of 2002 and Head Start, reauthorized in 1998, are federally funded examples.

5-5   Discuss how language growth takes place in all curriculum areas.

Every planned activity uses language in some way. A school's daily routines, planned program and activities, hands-on experiences, classroom environment, and displays can promote language growth. Planned preschool activities cover many domains, including science, mathematics, health and safety, nutrition, art, language arts, and other domains with their own terminology and content.

5-6   Describe the program and lesson planning process.

A school's identified goals serve as the basis for program planning. Teaching techniques and strategies are used based upon what staff members feel to be best practices learned during teacher training or experience. Planning considers children's special needs, knowledge, past experiences, and cultural diversity. Daily planned activities, lessons, and experiences result from teacher observation and assessment that provides information that ascertains children's present abilities and needs, accomplishments, and skills. Plans are then designed to target needs, or the growth of literacy, language arts, or knowledge and skills, or a combination of these.

5-7   Name three areas of the preschool language arts that are commonly part of a school's written goal statements.

A center may write goal statements aligned with standards. Privately funded schools may choose goals unrelated to standards but related to what the school is attempting to teach. Children's writing, literacy and language development, language arts, pre-reading, and sociocultural goals are mentioned in the text along with goals concerning children's knowledge of and familiarity with books, particularly literary classics. Goal statements usually also include children's oral speech and listening development.

5-8   Explain what is entailed if a school uses a thematic approach to instruction.

The thematic approach to instruction may be based upon a topic that emerges from teacher identified child interests or classic literature. It can also result from a teacher investigating and probing a proposed theme topic by initiating a children's discussion group and recording child comments and input. Another way to arrive at a selection of a theme is to select a traditional preschool subject area, such as language arts, science, mathematics, art, cooking, or other domain and then pick a topic related to the domain.

Planning would then proceed to teacher brainstorming and identifying a number of possible simultaneously occurring classroom experiences.

This may include small group work, large group work, or individual activities that might appropriately take place during the theme's estimated timeframe. Webbing the proposed topic was suggested. It involves creating a graphic overall picture of what might be studied or offered.

Children's ability to explore facets of a topic is an important planning consideration. Thematic instruction is an integrated approach that takes advantage of the natural relationships between developmental domains and also suits the varying abilities of enrolled children.

When constructing a theme, the following steps were discussed: (1) observe and record; (2) identify topic; (3) discover children's knowledge level and questions; (4) imagine activities; (5) pinpoint goals; (6) pinpoint range, scope, vocabulary, main ideas, and activities; (7) discuss staffing needs; (8) adopt specific plans; (9) list materials and supplies; and (10) plan a culminating ending.

Additional Resources

Readings

Lonigan, C. J., & Shanahan, T. (2010). Developing early literacy skills: things we know and don't know. *Educational Research (39)*, 248–262.

Strickland, D. S. (Ed.) (2010). *Essential Readings on Early Literacy*. Newark, DE: International Reading Association.

Helpful Websites

National Association for the Education of Young Children

http://www.naeyc.org

Includes extensive information about standards and program planning.

National Governor's Association Center for Best Practices & Council of Chief State Officers

http://www.corestandards.org

Contains Common Core State Standards—English Language Arts.

International Reading Association

www.reading.org

Check out publications and position statements.

*From Goldenberg, C. (2002). Making schools work for low-income families in the 21st century. In S. Neuman & D. Dickinson (Eds.), Handbook of Early Literacy Research. Copyright © 2002 Guilford Press.

6 ⟩ Promoting Language and Literacy

Objectives
After reading this chapter, you should be able to:

6-1 List three roles of a teacher in early childhood language instruction.

6-2 Discuss ways teachers model positive language behaviors.

6-3 State three reasons why teachers should use specific and detailed speech.

6-4 Describe how and why a teacher uses extension techniques to build child language.

6-5 Discuss two ways a teacher acts as a balancer.

naeyc NAEYC Program Standards

3G04 Teachers support and challenge children's learning during interactions or activities that are teacher initiated and child initiated.

3G07 Teachers use their knowledge of content to pose problems and ask questions that stimulate children's thinking.

3G07 Teachers help children express their ideas and build on the meaning of their experiences.

DAP Developmentally Appropriate Practice (DAP)

3A8 Teachers draw on their knowledge of the content, awareness of what is likely to interest children of that age, and understanding of the cultural and social contexts of children's lives.

3A9 Teachers plan curriculum that is responsive and respectful to the specific context of children's experiences.

3A11 Teachers connect curriculum topics with children's interests and with what children already know and can do.

COMMON CORE Common Core State Standards for English Language Arts and Literacy

SL.CCR 3 Evaluate a speaker's point of view, reasoning, and use of evidence in rhetoric.

Children's Literacy Portfolios

Miss Powell, a kindergarten teacher, planned a home visit to each entering child in her fall kindergarten class. At one home, a mother proudly shared the child's preschool literacy portfolio. Miss Powell was able to sit with both her soon-to-be student and the child's mother as they both commented on items in the binder. She found the child was reading a few words and had a huge interest in cats. Although she knew her district would test each child after school started, she was delighted with this home visit.

Questions to Ponder

1. How can Miss Powell put to good use the information she now has about this child?

2. Would you suggest that a child literacy portfolio be part of this child's kindergarten experience also?

A good description of a skilled early childhood educator is a "responsive opportunist" who is enthusiastic, who enjoys discovery, and who is able to establish and maintain a warm, supportive environment. An educator is also one who tries to build language, literacy, brain power, and emotional connection (Bardige, 2009). When a reciprocal relationship between a child and teacher is based on equality, respect, trust, and authentic dialogue (real communication), child language learning is promoted. Speech is at the foundation of a child's learning life. Teachers need to create a classroom atmosphere where children can expect success, see the teacher as a significant person, are allowed choice, and are able to make mistakes. Ideally, children should join in planned activities eagerly. These activities should end before the child's capacity to focus is exhausted. The child should be able to expect the teacher to listen and respond to the child's communication in a way that respects the child's sense of the importance of the communication.

In whatever preschool activities and learning experiences a child encounters, the following is taking place.

> There are events happening in the individual "cognitive apparatus" (child's mind) of the learner as he or she struggles to understand and remember the subject that is being learned; but it is also the case that much, if not most, effective learning occurs in social settings, as learners communicate or engage in collaborative activity with other individuals. Furthermore, when a person learns, or develops, or changes cognitively, these individual and social domains are intimately interrelated (Phillips & Soltis, 2009, p. 66).

Early childhood language arts foundational skills educators should keep in mind during daily activities and adult-child interactions include the child's growing

- phonological awareness.
- phonemic awareness and word recognition ability.
- comprehension of the world around him.
- ability to collaborate with others.
- conversational success.
- question-asking ability.
- expression of thoughts and ideas.
- Standard English usage.
- vocabulary.
- engagement success.

Studies examining the quality of language environments in American preschools found that many preschools serving poor children scored in the inadequate range. High-quality group book experiences, cognitively challenging conversation, and teacher use of a wide vocabulary were associated with quality environments and young children's subsequent language and literacy development. It is impossible to overemphasize the importance of adult-child *interaction*. In schools and centers of questionable quality, some children may rarely interact with a preschool teacher and may receive little or no individualized attention. They may be unable to make a socially satisfying and trusting emotional connection to the teacher or peers. These schools fail the children who most need a quality literacy environment to prepare them for later schooling. Teacher behaviors conducive to the development of positive teacher-child relationships identified in research include providing responsive individualized attention, being consistent and firm, supporting children's positive behaviors, and incorporating elements of children's culture and language in planned activities (Gillanders, 2007).

6-1 Teaching Strategies and Behaviors

Three specific teaching functions that encourage the development of language arts and literacy are discussed in this chapter.

Photo 6-1 Lucia is showing her teacher that she can make a big smile by pulling her cheeks up as her teacher has done herself to help define the word "smile."

© 2015 Cengage Learning®

1. The teacher serves as a *model* of everyday language use. What is communicated and how it is communicated are important.

2. The teacher is a *provider* of experiences. Many of these events are planned; others happen in the normal course of activities.

3. The teacher is *one who facilitates (interacts)*. She creates sharing experiences and builds a trusting connection with the children while encouraging conversation (Photo 6-1).

These three functions should be balanced, relative to each child's developmental level and individual needs. The teaching role requires constant decision making: knowing when to supply or withhold information to help self-discovery and when to talk or listen (Figure 6-1). Basically, sensitivity can make the teacher the child's best ally in the growth of language skills. The importance of teachers' attitudes toward children's talk and teachers' recognition of children's thinking is critical. Researchers studying teacher-child interactions have found that teachers with more education are more responsive and sensitive. Teachers interested in maximizing each child's language development and potential will

- try to increase each child's language usage so language serves needs, desires, and well-being.

Figure 6-1 Range of teaching styles.

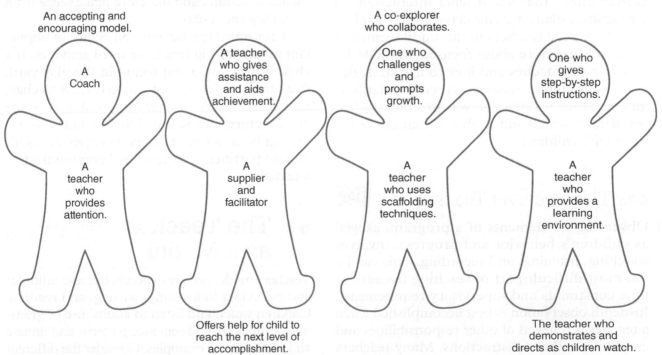

An accepting and encouraging model.

A co-explorer who collaborates.

A Coach

A teacher who gives assistance and aids achievement.

One who challenges and prompts growth.

One who gives step-by-step instructions.

A teacher who provides attention.

A supplier and facilitator

A teacher who uses scaffolding techniques.

A teacher who provides a learning environment.

Offers help for child to reach the next level of accomplishment.

The teacher who demonstrates and directs as children watch.

- encourage children's exploration and experimentation with language.

- promote children's use of language for a variety of different purposes.

- encourage child conversations and word usage with others.

- encourage the child's ability to share personal experiences and stories.

- strive to supply words and their definitions when necessary to promote a child's vocabulary growth.

- encourage curiosity, imagination, and the child's questioning ability, speaking ability, and the ability to relate what he has discovered by putting it into his own words.

- thoughtfully use sentences of increasing length and complexity offering a little above what each child might accomplish on his own.

Newer, stricter licensing regulations and standards regarding the training of early childhood educators in most states aim to improve the quality of teacher-child interactions. Zaslow and Martinez-Beck (2006) studied five teacher training models designed to build literacy expertise and enhance a teacher's ability to support children's early childhood literacy development. Their findings suggest as new teachers gain classroom experience and management skills they move around their classrooms and engage children in productive conversations that link teacher interactions to curriculum planning and classroom organization. Preschool teachers in the study seemed to want to learn more about focused and didactic learning approaches and how to use strategies that foster literacy using accepted standards as guides. Teacher reflection was promoted when teachers recorded and analyzed their conversations with children.

6-1a The Observer Teacher

Observing all elements of a program, as well as children's behavior and progress, involves watching, listening, and recording. This can be the most difficult part of teaching because of time constraints and supervisory requirements. In-depth observation is best accomplished when a teacher is relieved of other responsibilities and can focus without distractions. Many teachers who do not have duty-free observation time must observe while on duty. Observation often unearths questions regarding children's difficulties, talents, and a wide range of special needs that can then be incorporated into plans and daily exchanges.

Learners are most likely to remember and understand what they are learning if they are challenged to make the connection to their own lives (Burman, 2009). Your role as the teacher is to provide experiences that challenge young learners' thinking so new connections can be made. In the best situations, the teacher has background knowledge about each child's unique prior experience and knowledge so instruction can be individualized. Knowing children's interests, present behaviors, and emerging skills helps the teacher perform the three aforementioned functions, based on group and individual needs. Teachers must be part detective and part researcher, sifting through the clues children leave, collecting data, testing hypotheses, and examining the way children really are to make a credible record of their growth and development.

Listening intimately is highly advisable. Providing an environment that is conducive to growth depends partially on being on a child's or group's wavelength. Conversations are more valuable when teachers try to converse and question based on the child's line of thought. Activities provided should increase children's ability to think and rethink and therefore make sense from what they encounter.

Unplanned teacher talk can be just as important as talk during teacher-guided activities. If a child brings you a leaf found in the play yard, that's the time for both of you to discuss its characteristics, where or how he found it, or some other features of the leaf. The listening and observing behavior of teachers increases the quality and pertinence of teachers' communicative interactions.

6-2 The Teacher as a Model

Teachers model not only speech, but also attitudes and behaviors in listening, writing, and reading. Children watch and listen to adults' use of grammar, intonation, and sentence patterns and imitate and use adults as examples. Consider the different

Figure 6-2 Adult verbal styles.

Example A

Child:	"It's chickun soup."
Teacher:	"That's right."

Example B

Child:	"It's chickun soup."
Teacher:	"Yes. I see chicken pieces and something else."
Child:	"It's noodles."
Teacher:	"Yes, those are long, skinny noodles. It's different from yesterday's red tomato soup."
Child:	"Tastes good. It's 'ellow."
Teacher:	"Yellow like the daffodils in the vase." (Pointing.)

Example C

Child:	"Baby cry."
Adult:	"Yes, the baby is crying."

Example D

Child:	"Baby cry."
Adult:	"You hear the baby crying?"
Child:	"Uh-huh."
Adult:	"Maybe she's hungry and wants some milk."
Child:	"Wants bottle."
Adult:	"Let's see. I'll put the bottle in her mouth."
Child:	"Her hungry."
Adult:	"Yes, she's sucking. The milk is going into her mouth. Look, it's almost gone."

and similar ways teachers verbally interact with young children by examining Figure 6-2. Can you see how examples B and D offer the child more language growth?

An early and classic study by Bernstein, who studied British families in 1962, concluded that a recognizable style of verbal interaction based on social class exists. Children living in poverty, depressed economic circumstances, or in homes with significantly less enriching, educative, communicative encounters may have families that use a type of speech providing limited speech specificity and short conversational interchanges. These families' speech characteristics may be

- specific to a current physical context.
- limited.
- stereotyped.
- condensed.
- inexact.
- nonspecific.
- short in sentence length.
- vague and indefinite.

Middle-class families, on the other hand, more typically use speech that elaborates and is more differentiated, more precise, not specific to a particular situation or context, and affords opportunities for more complex thought.

Speakers' styles of communication can be powerful factors in the young child's development of cognitive structures and modes of communication, and they can result in educational advantages or disadvantages in school settings in which a different type of speech predominates. The major assumption behind this view is that middle-class ways of talking with children support literacy. Children profit when the adults in their lives engage in conversational exchanges that offer opportunities to draw conclusions, infer cause-and-effect relationships, plan together, evaluate consequences, evaluate happenings, and at times label things, provide information, and promote children's close observation. These are strategies you will want to use.

It is suggested that early childhood teachers who aim to be good speaking models focus on studying their ability to use **explanatory talk** in child-teacher verbal exchanges. Explanatory talk consists of conversations concerning some connection between objects, events, concepts, and/or conclusions that one speaker is pointing out to another (Photo 6-2). Teachers typically explain their intent and actions to children and provide explanations in response to child comments and questions. This is a preferred behavior in early childhood teachers' verbal interactive exchanges. Some examples follow.

- "The blocks go on the shelf. We will know where to find the blocks when we want to use them again, and no one will trip on them."
- "The window was open, and the wind blew into our classroom. It knocked over the small cups where our seeds were planted."
- "I'm putting my snack dish in the tub on the table when I'm finished. Mrs. Gregorio will come and get the tub after snack time."

---

explanatory talk — a type of conversation characterized by a speaker's attempt to create connections between objects, events, concepts, or conclusions to promote understanding in the listener.

Photo 6-2 This teacher is using explanatory talk to make connections as the children listen.

Photo 6-3 The teacher comments on skills she observes once work has been successfully completed.

This explanatory style sometimes carries over into teachers' personal lives. Teachers report family members often say to them, "Yes, I know why you're doing that!"

Adults should use clear, descriptive speech at a speed and pitch easily understood. Articulation should be as precise as possible. However, keep in mind that a good model involves more than merely speaking clearly, slowly, and appropriately. A good model uses a variety of facial expressions and other forms of nonverbal communication; associates talking with understanding and affection; provides happy, pleasant experiences associated with talking; and takes advantage of various timely situations. **DAP**

Teachers also need to be sure that reward in the form of attention is present in their teaching behavior as they deal with young children's attitudes, skills, and behaviors in language arts activities (Photo 6-3). Developmentally appropriate practice lists teacher acknowledgment among their excellent teaching strategies (Copple, Bredekamp, Koralek, Charner, 2013b). Most of us remember a teacher who did so by using positive comments, or a smile, or a thumbs up from across the classroom. Doing so perfectly suits the needs of preschoolers who want badly to share their discoveries and accomplishments and frequently utter "look at me" statements.

Educators should use language patterns with which they feel comfortable and natural and should analyze their speech, working toward providing the best English model possible. Familiar language patterns reflect each teacher's personality and ethnic culture. Knowing what kind of model one presents is important, because

knowing that there is room for improvement can help a teacher become more professional.

Modeling the correct word or sentence is done by simply supplying it in a relaxed, natural way rather than in a corrective tone. The teacher's example is a strong influence; when a teacher adds courtesy words ("please" and "thank you," for instance), these words appear in children's speech. Finishing an incomplete word by adding an ending or beginning may be appropriate with very young speakers. (The child may say "na na"; the teacher would provide "banana.") Completing a phrase or offering complete sentences in Standard English suits older speakers. Although adult modeling has its limits in facilitating spontaneous language, it is an essential first step in learning language.

After hearing corrections modeled, the child will probably not shift to correct grammar or usage immediately. It may take many repetitions by teachers and adults over time. What is important is the teacher's acceptance and recognition of the child's idea within the verbalization and the addition of pertinent comments along the same line.

To build children's vocabulary knowledge, the classroom needs to introduce and expose children to new words, and to provide these words in the context of situations. Definitions are offered using terms that are understandable and relate when possible to children's past experience. Opportunities will arise because of children's innate curiosity and interest in the world around them. As children mature, they develop independent strategies to figure out a word's meaning. Dictionary use is introduced and educators provide assistance and are interested word collectors themselves. Being "word conscious" happens when children's interest is piqued and they seek new word meanings (Christ & Wang, 2010). Christ and Wang point out knowing a word's meaning includes knowing what the word refers to and gaining the ability to use the word in accurate examples.

When adults focus on the way something was said (grammar) rather than the meaning, they miss opportunities to increase awareness and extend child interest. Overt correction often ends teacher-child conversation. Affirmation is appropriate; the teacher should emphasize the child's intended message.

Adults can sometimes develop the habit of talking and listening to themselves rather than to the children; it is hypnotic and can be a deterrent to really hearing the child. If one's mind wanders or if one listens only for the purpose of refuting, agreeing, or jumping to value judgments, it interferes with receiving communication from others. Teachers need not be afraid of silences and pauses before answering. The following listening suggestions are recommended:

- Work as hard to listen as you do to talk.
- Try to hear the message behind the words.
- Consciously practice good listening.

One teaching technique that promotes language skill is simple modeling of grammar or filling in missing words and completing simple sentences. This is called **expansion**. It almost becomes second nature and automatic after a short period of intentional practice. When using an expansion, the adult responds to the child by expanding the syntactic composition of the child's utterance. For example, the child's "It is cold" might be followed by "The window pane felt cold when you pressed your nose against it." The teacher's expansion is contingent and responsive, focusing on what the child was experiencing. Although using the strategy of expansion is a widely accepted and practiced teacher behavior, Crawford (2005) notes there is little research evidence that it has any positive effect. Evidence showing a negative effect is also yet to be found. Even without research validating the technique, many educators believe that the practice is still valuable, and when additional research takes place it will confirm their actions. While using

expansion, the teacher can also promote wider depth of meaning or spark interest by contributing or suggesting an idea for further exploration. Additional conversation usually occurs.

The teacher is a model for listening and speaking. Children will copy words, expressions, pronunciations, and gestures, too. A quiet teacher may have a quiet classroom; an enthusiastic, talkative teacher (who also listens) may have a classroom where children talk, listen, and share experiences. The way children feel about themselves is reflected in their behavior. When teachers listen closely, children come to feel that what they say is worthwhile.

Modeling good printing is also important. Children seem to absorb everything in their environment, so it is necessary to provide correctly formed alphabet letters and numerals on children's work, charts, bulletin boards, and any displayed classroom print. This is discussed at length in Chapter 14. Teachers' use and care of books are modeled, as are their attitudes toward story and nonfiction book experiences. Through their observations of teachers' actions, children begin to develop ideas about how books should be handled and stored. One teacher who wanted to model storytelling of personal stories divided a large paper into eight sections; in each section she drew a picture of different stages in her life. She showed this to her class and asked them to pick a picture, which she then related in storytelling. Teachers also model poetry reading and its use, dramatization, puppet play, and many other language arts activities.

What we are communicates far more eloquently than anything we say or do. This is an old saying that was not written expressly for teachers of young children; nonetheless it is a good addition to this discussion. A teacher models attitudes and ways of approaching a problem. If teacher says "Let's take a closer look at this problem," she is modeling an attitude that is catching. According to Au (2006), teachers must demonstrate the kind of literacy they want students to show. They must see themselves as readers and writers and convince students of the value of reading and writing. In doing so, they help young children gain an appreciation for literacy in their own lives. With picture books, some of the ways this is accomplished is

---

expansion — a teaching technique that includes the adult's (teacher's) modeling of words or grammar, filling in missing words in children's utterances, or suggesting ideas for child exploration.

by selecting and sharing books with an obvious enjoyment factor, by building on children's interests, and by discussing enjoyed book sections as these relate to individual children. An educator on any teaching day can model his or her thinking by talking aloud to promote children's thinking along the same lines. This is often done when sharing a book, but there are many additional opportunities.

- "Today we have three boys sitting together in our circle whose names start with the letter 'J' . . . Jacob, Joseph and Joshua."

- "You made a new color when your yellow paint touched the blue paint."

- "I hear the same sound at the end of Emma, Olivia, and Isabella's names—Emma, Olivia, Isabella. And in Isabella's name I hear the sound two times."

- "If I pour too much juice into this cup, it will spill. I don't want to do that so I'll stop a little way below the top."

6-3 The Teacher as Provider

As providers, preschool teachers strive to provide experiences that promote literacy. Fortunately, the number of interesting language arts activities one can offer children is almost limitless. Teachers rely on both their own creativity and the many resources available to plan experiences based on identified goals and what they observe and feel is necessary for child growth and needs. Early childhood resource books, other teachers, teacher magazines, workshops, the Internet, and conferences all contribute ideas.

Many beginning teachers gather activity ideas and store them in a personal resource file, so they can keep track of all of the activity ideas they come across. An activity file can include new or tried-and-true activity ideas. Developing a usable file starts with identifying initial categories (file headings) and then adding more headings as the file grows. Whatever the file size, teachers find that files are very worthwhile when it comes to daily, weekly, and monthly planning. Often, files are helpful when ideas on a certain subject or theme are needed or when a child exhibits a special interest. A file collection is not used as the basis for activity planning, but rather as a collection of good ideas or ideas one might like to try that might suit the particular needs of a group of children. Many activity ideas are presented in following chapters. Your creativity can produce many others.

As a provider of materials, a teacher must realize that every classroom object can become a useful program tool to stimulate language. From the clock on the wall to the doorknob, every safe item can be discussed, compared, and explored in some way (Photo 6-4). Because most school budgets are limited, early childhood teachers

Photo 6-4 Madison has an interest in insects so her teacher supplies both opportunity and equipment.

© 2015 Cengage Learning®

find ways to use available equipment and materials to their fullest.

Most teachers are pleasantly surprised to see how avidly their classes respond to their personal interests. When the teacher shares enthusiasm for out-of-school interests, hobbies, projects, trips, and individual talents, she can help introduce children to important knowledge. Almost anything appropriate can be presented at the child's level. Whether the teacher is an opera buff, scuba diver, gourmet cook, stamp collector, or violin player, the activity should be shared in any safe form that communicates special interest and love of the activity, and the specific vocabulary and materials relating to the activity should be presented. Enthusiasm is the key to inspired teaching.

6-3a Providing for Abundant Play

Abundant opportunities for play are important to the child's language acquisition. Play is usually divided into four types: motor play, pretend play, construction play, and games. All involve varying kinds of language usage and can overlap and combine with children's constantly changing play scenarios. Child's play is more complex than it is commonly believed. It provides a rich variety of experiences: communication with other children, verbal rituals, topic development and maintenance, turn taking, intimate speech in friendships, follower-leader conversations, and many other kinds of language exchanges. Except when the children's safety is in question, children's natural ability to pretend should be encouraged, and the flow of this kind of play, if safe, should proceed without the teacher's interference. Children will want to talk to teachers about their play, and the teacher's proper involvement is to show interest and be playful themselves at times.

According to Burman (2009), intellectual conflict, when something conflicts with a learner's existing schema and shakes up thinking, is a necessary requirement for learning. Teachers see preschool peers in frequent serious discussions. When this happens, children may shift their understanding because a playmate has offered an alternate perspective or a different idea. In the playhouse area this might be as simple as a child saying "Daddies don't cook!" and a peer replying "My dad cooks pancakes." They may even check the validity of their new understanding by running it by teacher for confirmation and/or further discussion.

If a child has chosen to engage a teacher in conversation instead of play or during play, the teacher should be both a willing listener and a competent, skillful conversationalist. As young children talk about their experiences, the talking itself aids their organization of thoughts. At times, younger children monologue in our presence. They are not really asking for our reaction, but rather, they are listening to themselves think while they also enjoy our physical closeness.

Young children explore constantly. They want to do what they see others doing. Play opportunities usually involve manipulating something. When deeply involved in play, children may seem to be momentarily awestruck in their search for meanings, but soon they will approach others with questions or comments.

They gain skills in approaching other children and asking if they can play or just nonverbally joining a play group in progress. They begin to understand what attracts others to them, how to imitate another child's actions or words, how to express affection or hostility, how to assume a leadership role, how to negotiate, and how to follow or refuse playmates' requests. These and other play skills help them stay engaged in a play group for a longer period of time. Preschoolers at play may even argue over correct language use. Some observers believe that the majority of language teaching that takes place in the four-year-olds' classroom is child-to-child teaching.

A resourceful teacher will strive to provide a variety of play by regarding all of a center's area (and furnishings) as a possible place (or object) for safe and appropriate play. Creative use can be made of each foot of floor space. Children need large blocks of uninterrupted time to construct knowledge and actively explore their problem-solving options in an environment thoughtfully and carefully prepared by the teacher.

6-3b Outside Play and Literacy

Interacting to promote literacy during outdoor play challenges educators, but it is possible to offer some materials and activities that include a literacy feature. Probably the most common way is to try to read books on a blanket, in the shade, in the playhouse, or under a tree. Sidewalk chalk activities and games can be fun and might include printing names to jump on or over, or printing simple directions that read "Stamp your feet" or "Follow this line." Snapping instant photos and writing captions with the photographed child is a favorite activity. Occasionally labeling bikes A, B, C, etc. with hang-on cards might improve letter recognition, but caution is needed here. Overzealous teachers whose aim is to "teach on all occasions" should skip this discussion because children need lots of undirected time and freedom to pursue their own agendas, particularly when out of doors and using their own creative play ideas.

Trawick-Smith (2012) notes a preschool curriculum that encourages children's pretend play through adult introduction and child-child play interactions promotes higher scores on language and literacy measures. Teacher can support this type of play by providing ideas, suggestions, physical props and materials, and, at times, companionship. Teacher actions and behaviors can supplement child play scenarios rather than directing or dominating them. Not inhibiting the free flow of children's play choices, with the exception of safety concerns, is important. Not all young children are able to play independently; and regardless of the cause of this behavior, teachers should realize adult help and involvement can model how to pretend and make believe. This helps make the same behavior appear in the child (p. 264).

6-3c Providing Accurate and Specific Speech in All Content Areas

Although this text concentrates on teacher-child interactions in the subject field of language arts, other content areas, such as mathematics (numbers), social studies, health and safety, art, music, movement, and so on, will be subjects of teacher-child conversations and discussions. The same teacher techniques that are useful in building children's language competence and vocabulary in language arts are equally useful for other content areas. Every subject area has its own vocabulary and common terms that can overlap other fields of study. For example, teacher comments will include number words whether children are focused on the number of muffins on a tray or on whether there are enough scissors to go around.

There are more than two schools of thought concerning an educator's role in offering vocabulary to preschoolers. It is possible for an educator to use both of the strategies mentioned next.

The first emphasizes a teacher's use of rich, specific, and sometimes unusual words in daily instruction and conversation that are a little above children's common daily usage. Children adopt and savor them and incorporate them into their working vocabulary. If the teacher has an extensive knowledge of flowers, their names, care, and other information, she could add considerable vocabulary in a natural way without overdoing it. The second strategy involves consciously using or planning to use vocabulary root words or key words found in read-aloud books and themes. Root words are words or parts of words that children will encounter in early readers when their reading instruction begins. These are words identified as being words that are frequently used in beginning reading primers. Several high frequency word lists have been published over time, such as those developed by Dolch (1948) or Biemiller and Slonim (2001). Kindergarten teachers can also be good resources for beginning word lists. See Figure 6-3 for additional tips for increasing vocabulary.

Teacher comments should be as accurate and specific as possible in light of what the teacher believes the children might already know or have experienced. Purposeful teacher conversation adds a little more information than the children already know, and reinforces and adds depth to words already in the children's vocabulary. When working with numerals or other subjects, the teacher should use terminology that is appropriate to the subject area but at a level the children will understand. For example, the teacher might say "Let's count the muffins" or "The tool in your hand is a wire whip" or "The metal cylinder attached to the wall is a fire extinguisher. Fire extinguishers have something inside that can be sprayed out to put out fires." In movement or music activities, many descriptive terms can be added to teacher directions and conversations, such as hop, jump, stretch, soft, loud, high, and low. These are easily understood while the child is in the process of experiencing them. The quality of the words children hear is crucial for their later school and language performance (Kalmar, 2008). Children build meaning as adults and teachers make comments, provide information, comfort them, guide them, praise and encourage their efforts, and display excitement and enthusiasm for the world around them. Sometimes, teachers are reluctant to use big, new words such as the word *hibernate* (Neuman & Roskos, 2007). Neuman and Roskos

Figure 6-3 Teaching tips for vocabulary instruction.

Instruction Method	Teaching Tip
Provide purposeful exposure to new words	**Teach thematically to provide multiple exposures to words throughout the day, through read-alouds, conversations, centers, and projects.** • Select books for read-alouds in which illustrations and text provide clues to word meanings. • Use an interactive read-aloud style and engage children in cognitively challenging discussions about books. • Create media centers where children view DVDs, explore electronic books, and listen to interactive read-alouds on DVD that use new vocabulary.
Intentionally teach word meanings	**Use a variety of direct teaching strategies.** • Ask eliciting and noneliciting questions during readalouds to prompt children to think about new words and their meanings. • Provide an embedded definition when exposing children to a new word whose meaning is important for them to understand. • Use extended instruction to help children gain a nuanced understanding of a word's meaning.
Teach word-learning strategies	**Teach word-learning strategies while reading aloud.** • Use the three steps for strategy instruction: model, guide, and practice. • Select books in which both text and illustrations give clues to a word's meaning.
Offer opportunities to use newly learned words	**Provide a variety of opportunities for children to use newly learned vocabulary.** • Use concept-mapping activities to organize pictures and props related to a classroom theme or project. • Have children retell, buddy read, or act out texts that have been read in the classroom. • Write down stories dictated by children that are related to a classroom theme or project. • Develop art and craft projects in which children can apply newly learned concepts. • Engage in inquiry projects related to the curricular theme. • Provide props related to the theme that may elicit theme-related vocabulary use.

Digital Download

urge educators to remember that teacher words and phrases are one of the main sources for giving children new knowledge. They stress giving explanations and examples:

> "When an animal goes to sleep for the winter, we say it is hibernating."
>
> Then, provide opportunities for children to practice their new language by saying "Do you remember what we call it when animals go to sleep for the winter? We call it hibernating." (p. 10)

The teacher prompts children's use of the words that the teacher provides. Most of the time, a teacher is careful to define new words immediately after using them. In number activities, number words are used in the presence of a corresponding number of objects. In movement activities, types of movement are discussed with quick demonstrations.

It is important to introduce new terms in a natural conversational tone rather than within the framework of an obvious lesson. Leading a child or groups of children to new discoveries offers the teacher an opportunity to use specific and accurate terms and also makes children feel like partners in the discoveries. A theme on birds could include many terms and specific names that a teacher might need to research. Also, keep in mind that students need multiple, daily opportunities to talk about what they are learning, to confirm what they know, and to ask questions (Risko, 2011). In these conversations, a teacher can emphasize the importance and relevance of a child's comments and provide opportunities for children to explain their thinking. A teacher can provide time for children to elaborate on their ideas, to make connections to concepts, or to express further conclusions. Frequently, young preschoolers state and rethink their misconceptions or reasons for their thinking during discussions and sometimes teach their peers what they know.

The preschool classroom's character has a lot of influence on young children's vocabulary development. Kucan (2012) suggests providing a verbal environment in which words are not only noticed and appreciated but also savored and celebrated. Since a small vocabulary affects later reading comprehension, and the young child's vocabulary growth is highly impacted by adult input, a teacher's vocabulary-promoting ability becomes important for a child's success.

Pandey (2012) suggests teachers can provide or elicit synonyms, illustrations, examples, and verbal definitions when a new vocabulary word is encountered in a learning context. When the new word "itty-bitty" is used in a song or cooking recipe activity, a teacher might say:

"Itty-bitty means tiny."

"Can you think of another word that means very little?"

"If I just put a few seeds in my hand that would be an itty-bitty pile of seeds."

"A mark made by a pen, like this, would be an itty-bitty mark."

"Itty-bitty means a very, very small amount in our recipe."

"Hold out your hand if you would like an itty-bitty pile of sand in your hand."

A teacher might also explore word parts in itty-bitty that rhyme or that it is a hyphenated word. Pandey notes vocabulary words enable children to learn more words and—through time—content. Words are powerful content capsules (p. 26).

6-4 The Teacher as a Facilitator

A teacher encourages conversation on any subject the child selects, is never too busy to talk and share interests and concerns, and listens with the intent to understand. Understanding the child's message makes the teacher's response more educationally valuable. Time is purposely planned for daily conversations with each child. When teachers talk about what they are doing, explain why particular results occur, and let children ask questions about procedures and results, children will have more exposure to and experience with extended forms of discourse. These private, personal, one-on-one encounters build the child's feelings of self-worth and open communications. Conversations can be initiated with morning greetings such as the following:

- "Alphonse, I've been waiting to talk to you."
- "Tell me about your visit to Chicago."
- "How is your puppy feeling today, Andrea?"
- "Those new blue tennis shoes will be good for running in the yard and for tiptoeing, too."

Educators are aware of the "reciprocal opportunity" that is always present in work with young children. Teachers try to really hear verbal communications and sense nonverbal messages. They give their undivided attention whenever possible, which shows interest in children's ideas and also rewards their efforts to use language and initiate social contact. A teacher can respond skillfully, first clarifying what the teacher thought she heard and then adding to the conversation and attempting to stimulate more verbal output, child discovery, some new feature or detail, or a different way of viewing what has captured the child's interest. Children's verbal expression of their thoughts, feelings, requests, or other intent is corrected only if it is socially unacceptable speech.

Teachers can emphasize the symbolic component of an activity ("These words that you see on the handles say hot and cold.") and help children identify problems or dilemmas by suggesting that children put their ideas into words ("Adam, you wanted to give your scissors to Evan but couldn't. What happened?") Teachers may need to raise their own awareness of their interactions with children, in other words, to rate themselves on their ability to expand children's verbal output and accuracy (Photo 6-5). Recording daily conversations and analyzing them at times is recommended—even experienced teachers periodically do so.

It is wise to be aware of and up-to-date on topics of special interest to preschoolers. Current popular toys, cartoon figures, community happenings, sports, recording artists, movies, and individual family events may often be the focus of young children's conversations. When a teacher has background knowledge, such as what current Disney characters are popular or familiar to her students, or which children have a new infant sibling at home, her responses when children discuss these items could be more pertinent and connected to the reality of enrolled children's lives. Sharapan (2012) mentions Fred Rogers (Mr. Rogers), a well-known and beloved children's television show host, who took advantage of everyday moments to talk out loud

Photo 6-5 Teachers' comments are based on their knowledge of individual children.

© 2015 Cengage Learning®

about what was happening around him. He would draw attention to features and details that might be missed and offered children his developmentally sensitive thoughts, questions, and observations.

Early childhood educators use a technique called **extension**. Building on a child's statement, the teacher adds information, factual data, or additional meaning, and prompts the child to elaborate. This can add vocabulary and clarify some aspect or concept encountered in the conversational interchange. The child's "It spilled" might be answered with "Yes, Quan's hand knocked the cup over. I think maybe there was a time when you spilled something, too."

Many teachers have used a conversational interaction technique called **closure**. It involves pausing, specifically, hesitating in the middle of a sentence or at sentence endings. It is a technique that prompts guessing by the child, and the teacher is willing to accept any guess. Most often, children's guesses are logical, but may not be what the teacher expected. Those children with a sense of the ridiculous may offer off-the-wall guesses equally acceptable to the teacher. It often promotes further dialogue. The teacher's saying "The sun disappeared behind a . . ." might elicit "hill," "mountain," "building," "tree," "cloud," or other possibilities from the child. The teacher's

saying "Coats are hung in the . . . by the front door" is an example of middle-of-the-sentence closure or a fill-in statement. Using closure within a familiar context, like a well known story or song ("And he blew the house. . .?") is fun, and gives the teacher a chance to say "Emma, you guessed the *word* that I left out was 'down.' Yes. It is the word." Teachers often also made lists of guessed words immediately so the children see the written word they guessed.

In looking at individual children, Covey (1989) reminds us of what we know in our hearts to be true, fair, and compassionate. Each child is to be valued for his identity as a person and for his unique individuality, separateness, and worth. Comparisons between children cloud our view. Traits teachers may see as negative can be fostered by the environment we offer and our own perceptions of correct student behavior. An educator's job, according to Covey, is to recognize potential, then coddle and inspire that potential to emerge at its own pace.

Waiting for a child's response is sometimes difficult for some teachers. When you wait, you give the child time to initiate or to get involved in an activity. You are, in effect, giving her this message: "You're in control—I know you can communicate, so you decide what you want to do or

---

extension — a teaching strategy in which an adult expands the child's information by adding new, additional, related information or meaning.

closure — a conversation technique that prompts children to verbally guess and complete or fill in a teacher's sentence. The teacher pauses or hesitates, which prompts the child to finish a teacher verbalization.

say. I'll give you all the time you need." Studies of adult-child interactions have shown that adults give children approximately one second in which to respond to a question. After one second, the adult repeats and rephrases the question or provides the answer. One second! Most children need much longer than one second to process the question and figure out their response.

Adult speech containing a relatively high proportion of statements or declaratives has been associated with accelerated language development in young children. Adult-child conversations tend to last longer if adults add new relevant information. If adults verbally accept and react to children's statements with "oh, really?" or "I see," when they are trying to grasp a child's meaning, additional conversation seems to be promoted.

When a teacher answers a child by showing interest, this rewards the child for speaking. Positive feelings are read internally as an automatic signal to continue to do what we are doing. Many experts suggest that teachers should guide and collaborate to promote children's independent problem solving in any given situation. Most often, teachers show their attention by listening to, looking at, smiling at, patting, or answering a child, or by acting thoughtfully to what a child has said or done.

Experienced teachers know that children often will silently look for teacher's attention and approval across a busy classroom when they have accomplished a task or a breakthrough. They search to see if the teacher noticed. A busy teacher might give a thumbs up or smile in response, if they can't offer words just then. The child by his behavior has indicated that he feels this is a teacher who cares about me.

Dangel and Durden (2010) urge educators to challenge children to think beyond the moment and analyze and conjecture. They suggest teachers use thoughtful questions and comments during teacher-child verbal exchanges that promote children's labeling, describing, or connecting the prior ideas and knowledge they possess to what is on hand or occurring during an activity. A teacher's questions might also prompt child hypotheses, imaginations, or opinions. All involve higher level thinking skills. Teachers trying to determine their questioning skills can test themselves using Figure 6-4.

Teachers often act as interpreters, especially with younger preschoolers. The child who says "Gimme dat" is answered with "You want the

Figure 6-4 Assess your questioning and responding abilities.

Answer the following using A = always, S = sometimes, N = need to work on this, or U = unable to determine.

1. Do I respond to child-initiated comments 100 percent of the time? _____

2. Do I keep to the child's topic and include it in my response? _____

3. Do I ask questions that prompt children to see or discover an aspect that they might not have perceived or discovered? _____

4. Am I aware of the favorite subjects and interests of individual children and ask questions along these lines? _____

   Are my questions appropriate in light of the children's development levels? _____

5. Do I often answer a child's comments using teacher echolalia?
   Child: "I went to the zoo."
   Teacher: "Oh, you went to the zoo."
   Or would my answer more likely be, "What animals did you see?" _____

6. Are my questions usually open ended? _____

7. Are my questions thought-inducing, or are they merely seeking correct answers? _____

8. Do I provide a specific response to children's questions? _____

9. Do my questions take place in the context of mutual trust and respect, based on my genuine friendliness, unconditional acceptance, warmth, empathy, and interest? _____

10. Do many of my questions seem to put a child "on-the-spot" or fluster a child? _____

---

red paint." Do not worry about faulty teacher interpretations! Most children will let teachers know when they have interpreted incorrectly by trying again. Then the teacher has the opportunity to say, "You wanted the blue paint, Taylor."

Consider the dialogue of the language-developing teacher below. Did the teacher's speech interactions accomplish the goal?

Goal #1: Use language slightly more complex than the child's.

Child: "Those are cookies."

Teacher: "Yes, they're called Gumdrop Mountains because they come to a point on the top."

Goal #2: Speak with young or limited-language children by referring to an action, object, person, and/or event that is currently happening.

Teacher: "You're climbing up the stairs."

Goal #3: Base your reactive conversation on the meaning the child intended. There are two ways to do this: (1) repetition ("Pet the dog" to child's "Pet dog"); (2) expansion (the child says, "play bath," and the teacher expands with, "You want to play with your toys in the bath tub").

Goal #4: Use recasting. (The child says, "You no get in," and the teacher responds, "No, I can't get in, can I?")

Goal #5: Use "I see," "Yes," or a similar expression to indicate you are listening.

Encouraging children to tell about happenings and how they feel is possible throughout the preschool day (Photo 6-6). A teacher may find it harder to interact verbally with quiet and shy children or the ones that rarely stay in one place or sit down, but they keep on trying.

Teachers shift to more mature or less mature speech as they converse with children of differing ages and abilities. They try to speak to each according to his level of understanding. They use shorter, less complex utterances and use more gestures and nonverbal signals with speakers trying to learn English. Whenever possible, it is professionally appropriate to interact in a way that displays a belief that all preschoolers are capable thinkers that are able to weigh complex ideas, and at times, use abstract reasoning as they strive to make sense of what happens around them.

The teacher who interacts in daily experiences can help improve the child's ability to see relationships. Although there is current disagreement as to the teacher's ability to promote cognitive growth (the act or process of knowing), attention can be focused and help provided by answering and asking questions. Often, a teacher can help children see clear links between material already learned and new material. Words teachers provide are paired with the child's mental images that have

Photo 6-6 Bending or kneeling puts adults at an appropriate level to engage in intimate conversation.

come through the senses. Language aids memory because words attached to mental images help the child retrieve stored information. Intellectually valuable experiences often involve the teacher as active participant in tasks with the child.

Pica (2007) urges teachers to combine concepts and words with active physical movement and/or involvement. She believes young children still need to experience concepts physically, when possible, to fully understand them. Her book, *Jumping into Literacy,* abounds with early learning activities that promote language and literacy through music and movement. **DAP**

The teacher facilitates by supplying words to fit situations. It should be remembered that a new word often needs to be repeated in a subtle way. It has been said that at least three repetitions of a new word are needed for adults to master the word; young children need more. In some cases, when a new word is very salient and the child is highly motivated, a child may acquire the word after a single, brief exposure. This is called *fast mapping,* and children also more readily learn new words that are conceptually similar to words they already know (Wasik, 2006). Repeated exposure to a new word in the same and other meaningful contexts is still recommended in most situations. An example of a teacher reinforcing vocabulary and conceptual learning is presented in Figure 6-5. The teacher is conducting a summary review that

Figure 6-5 Teacher review narrative with pantomime actions.

"We gathered all the ingredients necessary to follow our bread recipe chart directions. We set the oven temperature at 350°. The flour, eggs, water, salt, yeast, sugar, milk, and butter were put on the table in our work area. We needed the yeast to make our bread texture fluffy. Then we lined up all the cooking utensils, pans, bowls, and a large, flat, breadboard. After washing our hands, each ingredient was added to our bowl. Each ingredient added something to the taste of our baked bread. We used measuring cups and measuring spoons and made sure the correct amount was level with the edge. We stirred and made dough. We kneaded the dough on the breadboard. We formed a loaf. Then we lifted it into the loaf pans and then I put them into the hot oven which said the temperature was 350°. The yeast in the bread recipe made it grow bigger and bigger. Because the recipe directions told us to leave the bread in the oven for 45 minutes I took the bread out using an oven mitt. We sat and ate large slices after spreading the soft, textured bread with butter. Yum Yum.

(Note: new vocabulary words are underlined.)

---

includes newly introduced words after a cooking activity. She has asked the group to reenact (pantomime) their cooking experience as she speaks.

Walley, Metsala, and Garlock (2003) researched the ease with which children learn new words. They note that new words that are phonologically similar to a known word are also easier to acquire. If the child's vocabulary contains *hat*, *mat*, and *cat*, which contain similar morphemes, similar words may be learned readily.

Teachers often hear the child repeating a new word, trying to become familiar with it. To help children remember a new word, Bennett-Armistead, Duke, and Moses (2005) suggest making sure the words you say around the new word give clues to the word's meaning. For example, instead of saying "That is a fox," say "It is a furry animal called a fox. It looks like a small dog and has a big, fluffy tail." The best way to make a new word *real* to young children is to relate the new word to the child's own experiences and ideas.

There are times when a teacher chooses to supply information in answer to direct child questions. There is no easy way for the child to discover answers to questions such as "What's the name of today?" or "Why is that man using that funny stick with a cup on the end?" A precise, age-level answer is necessary; such as "Today is Monday, May 9" and (while demonstrating) "It's a tool, called a plunger. It pushes air and water down the drain and helps open the pipes so that the water in the sink will run out." As a provider of information, the teacher acts as a reference and resource person, providing the information a child desires. If the teacher does not wish to answer a question directly, she may encourage the child to ask the same question of someone else or help the child find out where the answer is available.

Child: "What's lunch?"

Adult: "Come on, we'll go ask the cook." *or* "Let's look at the menu. It lists all the food being served today. I'll read it to you."

Can teachers promote children's curiosity about words? By being aware that children sometimes ask about words they do not understand, educators can reward the child's interest with attention. Statements might include the following:

"You now have another word for car. It is the word automobile."

"I'm happy you asked what 'slick' means Josie."

"A new word in this book will be fun to say. The word is skedaddle and it means to move very quickly."

"When you hear a word that puzzles you, raise your hand. Ask about it, please."

"What a wonderful word that is!"

The teacher's reaction supplies children with feedback. The teacher is responsible for reinforcing the use of a new word and gently ensuring that the children have good attitudes about themselves as speakers.

Every day, the teacher can take advantage of unplanned things that happen to promote language and speech. Being able to make the most of an unexpected event is a valuable skill. Moving into a situation with skill and helping the child discover something and talk about it is part of promoting word growth (Photo 6-7).

6-4a Teachable Moments

You have probably run across the phrase "teachable moments" in your training and perhaps have become adept at using this strategy. It involves a four- to five-step process.

1. Observe a child or a child group's self-chosen actions and efforts.

2. Make a hypothesis about exactly what the children are pursuing, exploring, discovering, and playing with, and so on.

3. Make a teacher decision to intervene, act, provide, extend, or in some way offer an educational opportunity to further growth or knowledge related to the child-chosen agenda. This can be done in a number of ways, so this step often involves teacher contemplation.

4. Determine exactly what you will do or provide. Take action. Often, this can be as simple as asking a question such as, "You are putting small pieces of torn paper in Andy's cage. What do you think Andy is going to do with them?" or by silently providing wedge-shaped blocks to a group of children racing small cars down a ramp. Or perhaps you decide to let a child who has been watching the kitchen helper hand-whip eggs try the hand-whip himself.

5. As a final step, consider having the children tell, act out, communicate, dictate, or in some way represent what has been experienced, if this is appropriate.

A watchful teacher, who is working to promote early literacy skills may easily connect teachable moments to relevant opportunities involving literacy skills.

6-4b Time Constraints

Comments such as, "You finished," "That's yellow," "How colorful," "It's heavy," "I like that, too," or "A new shirt," may give attention, show acceptance, provide encouragement, and

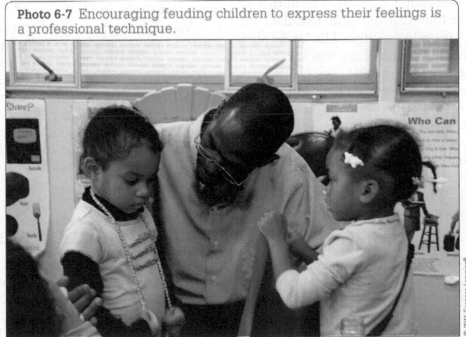

Photo 6-7 Encouraging feuding children to express their feelings is a professional technique.

reinforce behavior. They feel like suitable and natural comments or responses, and they slip out almost unconsciously. In a busy classroom, they often are said in haste when the teacher may have no time for an extended conversation because she is supervising a group of children. In other words, the best a teacher can do, time permitting.

Consciously trying to be specific and expanding takes focus, effort, and quick thinking, but with practice, it can become second nature with teacher statements such as, "You pushed your chair in under the table," "In your drawing I see red and blue," "You helped your friend Alejandra by finding her book," "Those are shoes with lights," "Tell me more about your kitten," and "Returning your crayons to the box helps others find them." Teachers' specific and/or descriptive comments promote literacy.

6-4c Scaffolding

Scaffolding is a teaching technique that combines support with challenge. This includes responsive conversation, open-ended questions, and facilitation of the child's initiatives. Adults estimate the amount of necessary verbal support and provide challenging questions for child growth in any given situation. The idea is to promote the child's understanding and solutions. The adult attempts to build upon what a child already knows to help the child accomplish a task or may suggest breaking down the task into simpler components. As the child ages, his autonomous pursuit of knowledge will need less adult support. The author is reminded of the four-year-old who described the workings of a steam locomotive. His knowledge of trains and related terminology was way above that of other children his age and even his teacher. Someone in this child's life had supplied the type of "scaffolding" (support with challenge) that allowed the child to follow an interest in trains.

It is believed that children need experiences and educational opportunities with adults who carefully evaluate, think, and talk daily occurrences through. What specific teacher verbalizations and behaviors are suggested in scaffolding? They include comments that offer responsive and authentic conversation and facilitate child initiative. Educators ask open-ended questions. They prompt and promote language by modeling slightly more mature language forms. They help children express thoughts and feelings in words. An educator attempting to scaffold

- promotes longer, more precise child comments.
- invites divergent responses.
- offers specific word cues in statements and questions that help children grasp further information, for example, *what, who, why, because, so, and, next, but, except, if, when, before, after,* etc.
- provokes lively discussions and quests for knowing more about subjects that interest children.
- increases collaborative communication with adults and other children.

Scaffolding is not as easy as it first may appear to teachers. What is opportunity and challenge for one child may not be for the next. In scaffolding, teacher decision making is constant and complex. An educator using scaffolding believes understanding, discovery, and problem solving can be guided. Rather than always being dependent on adults for help, the child actually is moved toward becoming an independent thinker, advocates believe. Adults who accompany children at home or at school can use a scaffolding approach to talk through and plan activities as simple as setting the table, cleaning the sink, getting an art area ready for finger painting, or taking care of the needs of the school pet.

What is right or wrong becomes less important than the child's expression of his own conclusions. The child is encouraged to verbalize the "whys" of his thinking. For example, "Royal thinks the rabbit eats paper because he saw Floppy tearing paper into small pieces inside the cage."

Valuable teacher collaboration with children sustains the momentum of the search, actions, or exploration. Small group projects are often a natural part of children's block area play and can also be promoted in other aspects of daily play and activities. For example, a lemonade stand can be managed by a small group, or a present or card can be designed for a sick classmate at home and then completed and mailed by a small group of children.

6-5 Teacher as Balancer

A central task for the educator is to find a balance between helping a child consolidate new understanding and offering challenges that will promote growth. Some educators believe that there are two teaching styles—transmission and interpretation.

Transmission teaching is the traditional style, in which children's knowledge is thought to be acquired through the teacher talking, sharing books, and explaining classroom events and experiences. Interpretation teaching, on the other hand, is based on the understanding that children reinterpret information for themselves, and consequently, the teacher's role involves dialogues that support the children's efforts to verbalize their ideas and actual experiences.

One can easily see how easy it is to become a transmission teacher. It may have been modeled at some point in your own schooling. An interpretation teacher really listens and does not monopolize conversations by a display of what the teacher knows. Achieving balance between these two styles is the key. Educators both transmit and interpret.

In promoting developing language arts and literacy in early childhood, an interpretation style would not only help children talk about what they know but also would help them put ideas and impressions in print by offering to take dictation or by using some other form of expression. The teacher's role is to provide the occasions, resources, and enabling climate for the pursuit of individual meaning.

Teachers can be fun-filled and playful companions at times, exhibiting their love and enthusiasm for life and the child's company. This side of teachers comes naturally to some adults and less easily to others. Perhaps many of us remember adults from our own childhood years that were able to engage themselves in adult-child interactions that could be described as joyful playing or companionable give and take. Teachers also pay deliberate attention to their own actions and words in both classrooms and play areas, and notice how their own behavior helps children make connections, comparisons, contrasts, bridges to past experiences and prior knowledge, and discoveries. Why? Because an effective teacher realizes she can be adept at promoting higher level thinking skills.

6-5a Handling Interruptions

Young children rarely limit their questions or modify their responses to the teacher for the purpose of hiding their ignorance, as older children sometimes do. During conversations, most young children intent on answers will probe enthusiastically for what they want to know. Teachers actively promote guesses and appreciate

error making in an atmosphere of trust. They interact in conversations by focusing child attention, posing questions, discussing problems, suggesting alternatives, and providing information at the teachable moment.

Children often interrupt adults during planned activities. When an idea hits, they want to share it. Their interruptions can indicate genuine involvement and interest, or they can reflect a variety of unrelated thoughts and feelings.

Teachers usually acknowledge the interruption, accept it, and may calmly remind the one who interrupts that when one wants to speak during group activities, one should raise one's hand first. Other teachers believe preschoolers' enthusiasm to speak is natural and characteristic. These teachers believe asking children to raise their hands during group discussions is a practice best reserved for a later age. Interruptions give the teacher an opportunity to make a key decision that affects the flow of the activity. Will the interruption break the flow of what is going on, will it add to the discussion, or is it best discussed at a later time? The teacher may decide to defer a comment, or accept being sidetracked and briefly digress from the main subject, or develop the interruption into a full-blown teacher-group discussion. Examples follow:

Situation: The teacher is telling a flannel-board story about a squirrel preparing for winter by hiding nuts in a tree.

Child: "My cat climbs trees."

Teacher: "Michael, I've seen cats climb trees."

(a short acknowledgment)

Teacher: "Michael's cat climbs trees, and the squirrel is climbing the tree to hide the nuts he is storing away for winter."

(The teacher acknowledges, but refers listener back to the story line.)

Teacher: "Michael, you can tell me about your cat that climbs trees as soon as we finish our story."

(The teacher defers discussion until later.)

Because preschoolers are action-packed, they enjoy activities that include an opportunity to perform the action words they encounter in books, discussions, or daily happenings (Figure 6-6). Teachers can promote "acting out" words with their own behaviors. Some action words that are easily enacted include *pounce*, *stamp*, *sneak*, *slither*, *creep*, and *slide*. *Enormous*, *droopy*, *sleepy*, *tired*, and other descriptive words can be connected to real examples or visual reproductions.

Incorporating the children's ideas and suggestions into group conversations and giving children credit for their ideas make children aware of the importance of their expressed ideas such as

"Kimberly's idea was to . . ." and

"Angelo thinks we should . . ." or

"Christal suggests that we . . .".

6-5b Using Sequential Approaches to Instruction

Teachers need a clear understanding of how children learn words and concepts. Figure 6-7 includes guidelines for the teacher's words and actions to accompany the child's progress toward new learning. Sequential instruction can be described as teacher interactions that are explicit, intentional, and built on children's existing skills. One approach to teacher interaction during structured, planned, or incidental activities, described by Maria Montessori (1967b), is called three-stage interaction. It shows movement from the child's sensory exploration to showing understanding, and then to verbalizing the understanding. An example follows.

Figure 6-6 Sample teacher interaction verbalization.

Common Teacher Statement	Possible Consequences
"Tell me more."	expands
"Did you mean . . . ?"	clarifies
"Where did you see . . . ?"	specifying
"Who said . . . ?"	
"When did the bike . . . ?"	
"Whose name shall I write on . . . ?"	specifying possession
"This belongs to . . . ?"	
"Please tell Juan . . ."	conversing with others
"Choose one person to help you."	
"Can you show . . . ?"	provides information
"Tell me again . . ."	rephrase or repeat
"What would happen if . . . ?"	guessing or problem solving
"Thang thinks . . ."	valuing others' ideas
"Taylor says . . ."	
"What could we try . . . ?"	problem solving
"Where should we put . . . ?"	creative thinking
"What's a good name for . . . ?"	
"Who had the last turn to talk . . . ?"	turn taking
"Show me with your hands."	clarifies
"What will you need to . . . ?"	specifies
"What will you do first . . . ?"	
"Do you have a question for me?"	clarifies
"Did something happen that I didn't see?"	
"Did anyone hear a sound?"	listening skill
"Show me your hand when you want to tell us something."	turn taking

*This is not meant to be a complete or comprehensive listing. Each language exchange with children is a challenge and opportunity.

Figure 6-7 Language learning and teacher interaction.

Child Activity	Teacher Actions
• focuses on an object or activity	• Name the object, or offer a statement describing the actions or situation. (supplies words)
• manipulates and explores the object or situation using touch, taste, smell, sight, and sound organs	• Try to help the child connect this object or action to his past experience through simple conversation. (builds bridge between old and new)
• fits this into what he already knows; develops some understanding	• Help the child see details through simple statements or questions. (focus on identifying characteristics) • Use "Show me . . . " or "Give me . . . " prodding statements that call for a nonverbal response. (prompting) • Put child's action into words. (Example: "John touched the red ball.") (modeling) • Ask the child for a verbal response. "What is this called?" "What happened when . . . ?" (prompting)
• uses a new word or sentence that names, describes, classifies, or generalizes a feature or whole part of the object or action	• Give a response in words indicating the truth factor of the response. "Yes, that's a red ball" or "It has four legs like a horse, but it's called a cow." (corrective or reinforcing response) • Extend one-word answers to full simple sentence if needed. (modeling) • Suggest an exploration of another feature of the object or situation. (extend interest) • Ask a memory or review question. "What did we discover when . . ." (reinforcing and assessing)

Digital Download

Step 1: *Associating Sense Perception with Words.* A cut lemon is introduced, and the child is encouraged to taste it. As the child tastes, the adult says, "The lemon tastes sour," pairing the word sour with the sensory experience. Repetition of the verbal pairing strengthens the impression.

Step 2: *Probing Understanding.* A number of yellow fruits are cut and presented. "Find the ones that taste sour," the teacher suggests. The child shows by his actions his understanding or lack of it.

Step 3: *Expressing Understanding.* A child is presented with a cut lemon and grapefruit and asked, "How do they taste?" If the child is able to describe the fruit as sour, he has incorporated the word into his vocabulary and has some understanding of the concept.

When using the three-step approach, Montessori (1967b) suggests that if a child is uninterested, the adult should stop at that point. If a mistake is made, the adult remains silent. The mistake indicates only that the child is not ready to learn—not that he is unable to learn. This verbal approach may seem mechanical and ritualistic to some, yet it clearly illustrates the sequence in a child's progress from not knowing to knowing.

The following example of a variation of the Montessori three-step approach includes additional steps. In this teaching sequence, the child asks the teacher how to open the tailgate of a dump truck in the sandbox.

TEACHER INTENT:	TEACHER STATEMENTS:
1. Focus attention.	"Look at this little handle."
2. Create motivation, defined as creating a desire to want to do or want to know (note that in this situation this is not necessary because the child is interested).	"You want the tailgate to open." (Pointing)
3. Provide information.	"This handle turns and opens the tailgate." (Demonstrating)

4. Promote child's attempts or practice.

"Try to turn the handle."

5. Give corrective information, feedback, or positive reinforcement.

"The handle needs to turn." "Try to push down as you turn it." (Showing how) Or, "You did it; the tailgate is open."

Steps 1 through 5 are used in the following situation in which the teacher wants the child to know what is expected in the use of bathroom paper towels.

1. "Here's the towel dispenser. Do you see it?"

2. "You can do this by yourself. You may want to dry your hands after you wash them."

3. Demonstration: "First take one paper towel. Dry your hands. Then the towel goes into this wastebasket."

4. "You try it."

5. "That's it. Pull out one towel. Dry your hands. Put the towel in the wastebasket."

"Now you know where the dirty paper towels go. No one will have to pick up your used towel from the floor. You can do it without help now like some of your classmates."

Statements of this kind help the child learn both the task and the vocabulary. The ability to provide information that the child needs, without talking too much, is one of the skills required of a really excellent teacher. Most theorists believe that the successful completion of a task is a reward in itself. Others believe that an encouraging verbal pat on the back is in order.

The same dump truck scene detailed earlier could be handled using a discovery approach, instead of a teacher-directed sequence, with the following types of questions. "Did you see anyone else playing with this dump truck? Is there a button to push or a handle to turn that opens the tailgate? What happens if you try to open the tailgate with your hand?"

The goal of prompting in a child-adult conversation is to encourage the child to express ideas perhaps more precisely and/or specifically. It is used slightly differently with younger preschoolers, as shown in the following examples:

Young preschooler: "Cookie."

Adult: "You want a cookie?"

Child: "Dis cookie."

Adult: "You want this brown cookie?"

Older preschooler: "I want that cookie."

Adult: "You want one of these cookies. Which one of the cookies do you want? We have a chocolate cookie or a sugar cookie."

Child: "The chocolate one."

Can teachers really make a difference in the level and quality of children's language development? Very significant correlations have been found between both the frequency of informative staff talk, the frequency with which the staff answered the children, and the language comprehension scores of the children. Interaction does require teachers to "wonder out loud." They express their own curiosity while at the same time noticing each child's quest to find out what makes others tick and what the world is all about. How can teachers interact skillfully?

- Expand topics in which the child shows interest.

- Realize that children are likely to learn more when they are attentive and interested.

- Add depth to information on topics of interest.

- Answer and clarify children's questions.

- Help children sort out features of events, problems, and experiences, reducing confusion.

- Urge children to put what is newly learned or discovered into words.

- Cue children into routinely attending to times when the adult and child are learning and discovering together through discussion of daily events.

6-5c Dealing with Children's Past Experiences

A teacher encounters a wide range of children's perceptions concerning the way children think they should communicate with adults. A child's family or past child care arrangements may have taught the child to behave in a certain way. With this in mind, the teacher can almost envision what it means to be a conversationalist in a particular family or societal group. Some families expect children to interrupt; others expect respectful manners. Wild, excited gesturing and weaving body movements are characteristic of some children, whereas motionless, barely audible whispering is typical of others. Teachers working with newly arrived children from other cultures may see sharp contrasts in communication styles. Some children verbally seek help, whereas others find this extremely difficult. Some speak their feelings openly; others rarely express them. To promote child learning, a teacher needs to consider how she, their teacher, will interface to help each child understand that school may be very different than home.

Past child care experiences may have left their mark. A four-year-old child named Perry seemed to give one teacher insight into how speech can be dramatically affected by past undesirable child care arrangements. The following is that teacher's observations and conclusions:

> Perry sat quietly near the preschool's front door ignoring all play opportunities, and holding his blanket until his mom's return on his first day at school. He only spoke or looked up when teachers tried repeatedly to engage him in conversation and activities. He sat on adults' laps silently when they tried to comfort him, and ate food quickly and then returned to his waiting place near the door. The real Perry emerged a few weeks later as a talkative, socially vigorous child.
>
> Our verbal statements and actions concentrated on rebuilding trust with adults and other children; only later was language-developing interaction possible.

It can be difficult for a child to engage an adult in conversation, as was the case with Perry. Seeking the availability of a teacher or caregiver and ensuring one's right to her attention and reply often calls for persistence and ingenuity in a poor-quality child care situation. Perry may have long before given up trying, and decided it was best to "just stay out of the way."

In all roles, the teacher needs to maintain a balance. This means

- giving, but withholding when self-discovery is practical and possible.
- interacting, but not interfering with or dominating the child's train of thought or actions.
- giving support, but not hovering.
- talking, but not over talking.
- listening, but remaining responsive.
- providing many opportunities for the child to speak.
- being patient and understanding.

As is most often the case, when adults know the answer, many may find it difficult to be patient so children can figure out the answer for

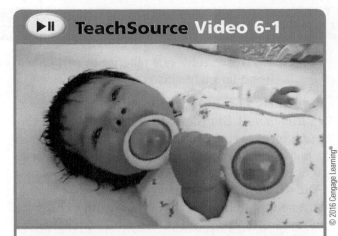

© 2016 Cengage Learning®

▶❚❚ TeachSource Video 6-1

0–2 Years: Module for Infants and Toddlers

Skip past the first segment with the crying infant and focus on the three caregivers comparing their vocal comments to the child who is exploring one or more play objects.

1. Which of the caregivers is providing a running commentary on what the child is doing at particular moments?

2. Which caregiver names objects and seems to encourage exploration, but does not direct the child's attention to toy features? Would you recommend pointing out toy features to the child? Why or why not?

3. Which of the three caregivers seems to have more enthusiasm and involvement with her child? What makes you think so?

themselves. The teacher orally reflects and guards against being overly invasive and didactic. There is an old story about two preschool boys who discover a worm in the play yard.

First child:	"Boy it tickles! Look at him!" (He holds the worm up to be seen.)
Second child:	"Let's show it to teacher."
First child:	"No way—she'll want us to draw a picture of it and make us print 'worm'!"

Teachers thoughtfully screen their comments and conversation to ensure they are free of sexist or biased attitudes or stereotypes. If a teacher is talking about a stuffed teddy bear or the school's pet guinea pig (whose sex is yet to be discovered), use of the pronoun "it," rather than "he" or "she," is recommended.

Summary

6-1   List three roles of a teacher in early childhood language instruction.

The early childhood language teacher serves as a *model* of Standard English usage, is a *provider* of experiences, activities, and materials, is a *facilitator* who shares experiences and encourages and promotes word usage and conversation. A teacher is also an *observer* who supports problem solving, child discovery, and the expression of children's ideas and concerns. The teacher can be described as a *balancer* who guards against overly invasive and didactic approaches. Every day decisions are made that affect children's language learning opportunities.

6-2   Discuss ways teachers model positive language behaviors.

Teachers model Standard English and correct child errors in subtle ways. Their manner words, such as please and thank you are often copied by children. They also model dictionary use, listening skill, the use of gestures, good print form, and proper book care besides modeling positive attitudes toward reading, writing, listening, speaking and the enjoyment of the literacy-building activities. They continually model the functional usefulness of language in daily living.

6-3   State three reasons why teachers should use specific and detailed speech.

Specific, accurate, and detailed teacher talk builds children's vocabulary and increases a child's knowledge. The teacher offers words a little more advanced but related to the words the child already knows, and provides visual and physical examples of word meanings when possible. Specific words a teacher purposefully uses may be key words or root words found in early readers. This prepares and promotes initial reading success when reading instruction begins.

6-4   Describe how and why a teacher uses extension techniques to build child language.

A teacher using extension builds upon child statements to purposefully add information, factual data, meaning, and vocabulary, and to promote the child's further elaboration of his/her comment. This technique can clarify or personalize some aspect or concept associated with the child's topic. It creates a more remembered learning while the child is focused and interested.

6-5   Discuss two ways that a teacher acts as a balancer.

Balancing may include giving teacher information immediately or prompting child discovery, interacting rather than interfering, providing support without stopping the child's ingenuity to solve his own problems, being responsive rather than talking excessively, and being patient rather than in a hurry or pushy.

Additional Resources

Readings

Bloom, P. (2000). *How Children Learn the Meanings of Words.* Cambridge: MIT Press.

Burman, L. (2009). *Are You Iistening? Fostering Conversations that Help Young Children Learn.* St. Paul, MN: Redleaf Press.

Neuman, S., & Wright, T. S. (2013). *All About Words: Increasing Vocabulary in Common Core Classrooms.* Pre-K-2. New York: Teacher's College Press.

Helpful Websites

National Association for the Education of Young Children
http://www.naeyc.org

Provides articles, publications, and other information.

National Council for Social Studies
http://www.social-studies.org

Search for early childhood topics.

Objectives

After reading this chapter, you should be able to:

7-1   List four types of listening.

7-2   Identify two recommended teacher interaction habits that aid young children's listening.

7-3   Define auditory perception and describe two activities to promote it.

7-4   Create a lesson plan to promote a phonemic awareness skill.

naeyc NAEYC Program Standards

3F04   Teaching staffs help children understand spoken language by using body language and physical cues.

2D03   Children have varied opportunities to develop competence in verbal and nonverbal communication.

2F08   Children are provided varied opportunities and materials that help them recognize and name repeating patterns.

2E06   Children are regularly provided multiple and varied opportunities to develop phonological awareness and to play with sounds, syllables, and word families.

DAP Developmentally Appropriate Practice (DAP) Preschoolers

2B5   Teachers recognize the importance of both child-guided and adult-guided learning experiences.

2C2   Teachers take into account children's capabilities as listeners, recognizing that preschooler's skills of recall and focused attention are still developing.

2C2   Teachers communicate information in small units, tie new information to what the children already know, check for understanding, and invite questions or comments to engage their interest.

3H13   Teachers understand the typical trajectory of phonological skill development for preschool children: rhyming, alliteration, syllable segmenting, onset/rime blending, and segmenting.

COMMON CORE Common Core State Standards for English Language Arts and Literacy

SL.CCR. 2   Integrate and evaluate information presented in diverse media and formats including visually, quantitatively, and orally.

Unexpected Answer

Claire, an early childhood teacher, circled her classroom of four-year-olds during the first week of school, trying to make conversation and listen intently to each child at free choice time. When she noticed Anna painting at the easel, Claire stood by and admired her work before saying "I can see many different colors in your painting. There is blue paint and an alphabet letter, too. It looks like an 'a.'" Anna, a tiny child, barely able to reach the top of the paper with her paint brush, responded, "Actually, it is a lower case 'a' that makes a long vowel sound, and this color is aquamarine."

Questions to Ponder

1. When children know more than you expect them to know, what is a prudent course of action?
2. How should Claire respond to being corrected by Anna?
3. Anna has told the teacher a lot about herself, including . . . ?

Listening skill is the first language arts skill learned, and it develops before a child speaks. Many children develop the ability to listen carefully to the speech of others during infancy and early childhood; others do not. Because language growth has been described as a receiving process followed by a sending process, a child's listening ability is important to speaking and future reading and writing success. **DAP naeyc**

Hearing and listening are quite different. **Hearing** is a process involving nerves and muscles that reach adult efficiency by age four to five. Listening is a learned behavior, a mental process that is concerned with hearing, attending, discriminating, understanding, and remembering. It can be improved with practice. Listening affects social interactions, one's level of functioning, and perhaps one's overall success in life (Photo 7-1). Researchers estimate that we listen to 50 percent of what we hear and comprehend only 25 percent of that.

Listening skill can be described as passive and receptive, but it involves active thinking and interpretation. Lively conversations between adults and young children who feel free to verbalize reactions to life's happenings promote listening and speaking. Children offer more verbal comments in school settings in small, relaxed groups in which comments are accepted and appreciated. Young children sometimes learn that it is best to keep quiet in some classrooms. In other classrooms, every child's opinion counts and classroom discussions are frequent and animated.

There are usually many opportunities to listen in early childhood centers. Teacher-planned or child-created play is a source of many sounds. A quality program sharpens a child's listening and offers a variety of experiences. Listening is not left to chance; planned programs develop skills.

Although listening skill is a critical dimension of language learning, it remains one of the least understood processes (Osada, 2004). Brown (1987) observed that in some schools listening is regarded as the least important language skill. A good number of teachers still expected children to develop listening skills naturally through experience without instructional help Mendelsohn reported in 1994. Research increased dramatically and focused on listening comprehension and active listening skills during the 1990s (Morley, 2001). Listening has been given more attention and

Photo 7-1 The teacher bends and listens intently to understand what the boys are requesting.

© 2015 Cengage Learning®

---

listening — a mental process that includes attending, hearing, discriminating, understanding, and remembering.

hearing — the facility or sense by which sound is perceived.

is considered an active skill involving many processes (Osada, 2004).

Direct instruction in listening skill is effective, according to early studies conducted in the 1950s and 1960s. Listening instruction produced measurable gains in listening comprehension. For many years most early childhood centers have incorporated research suggestions into their language arts program planning and have endeavored to promote and plan activities to develop listening abilities. Children's active involvement during and following listening activities is a built-in feature of many planned activities.

Listening is not a discrete skill or generalized ability, but a cluster of specific abilities closely related to those needed in the reading task. Early childhood professionals should be aware of the early development of a child's **listening comprehension level**. Thompson (1995) points out that the cognitive tasks involved in child listening are considerable. Children must comprehend as they listen, retain information in memory—integrated with what follows—and continually adjust their understanding of what they hear in light of prior knowledge and incoming information. Because young children can lose concentration quite quickly, reading material is selected to suit their developmental level and experiential background, and to hold and maintain their attention.

7-1 Types of Listening COMMON CORE

Listening occurs in many ways. A person does not always listen for knowledge, but may listen to a sound because it is pleasing. The first time children discover the sounds made by pots and pans, they are fascinated. Preschoolers often make their own pleasurable or rhythmic sounds with whatever is available.

The human voice can be interesting, threatening, or monotonous to a child, depending on past experience. Silence has also meaning. Sometimes teachers suspect that a child has a hearing problem, only to find that the child was inattentive for other reasons.

Children may listen but not understand. They may miss sound differences or listen without evaluating what they hear. Listening involves a variety of skills and levels. To provide growth opportunities, teachers should be aware of various listening skills, as shown in Figure 7-1. A child may rely on a combination of the skills described.

The goal of a good program in early childhood language arts is to guide the young child toward development of these listening levels. The listening process contains three stages the child moves through in efficient listening (Figure 7-2). When a sound occurs, it is remembered by thinking about its features: location, pitches, intensity, newness, and so on.

7-1a Toddler Listening Experiences

Families and center staff members can engage toddlers in a number of activities to stimulate listening. Body-action play of the old "coochee-coo" variety, "This Little Piggy," and simple rhymes and repetitions are recommended. Connecting noises and sounds with toys and objects and encouraging the child to imitate

Figure 7-1 Some of the ways a child listens.

Appreciative listening. The child finds pleasure and entertainment in hearing music, poems, and stories. It is best to begin with this type of listening because it is passive, but personal, for each child.

Purposeful listening. The child follows directions and gives responses.

Discriminative listening. The child becomes aware of changes in pitch and loudness. Sounds become differentiated in the environment. Eventually, the child is able to discriminate the speech sounds.

Creative listening. The child's imagination and emotions are stimulated by her listening experiences. Thoughts are expressed spontaneously and freely through words or actions, or both.

Critical listening. The child understands, evaluates, makes decisions, and formulates opinions. To encourage this critical listening, the teacher may pose such questions as "What happens when we all talk at once?" or "What if everyone wanted to play in the playhouse at the same time?" The child must think through the responses, decide the most logical solution to the problem, and present a point of view.

listening comprehension level — the highest grade level of material that can be comprehended well when it is read aloud to a child.

Figure 7-2 Stages of the listening process.

Responding to Stimuli	Organizing the Stimuli	Understanding the Meaning
awareness	sequencing and	(classification;
focus	synthesizing	integration;
figure-ground	scanning	monitoring)
discrimination		

←————————————Memory————————————→

Stage 1—Responding to stimuli. Was there sound? Where was it? Which sound was it? Was there more than one sound? Were the sounds the same?

Stage 2—Organizing the stimuli. What was the sequence of the sounds? What was the length of time between sounds? Have I heard that sound before? Where have I heard it?

Stage 3—Understanding the meaning. What do the sounds and words mean?

---

show the child that joy and sound making go hand in hand. Rhythmic clapping, tapping, and pan beating in sequence or patterns can be enjoyable (Photo 7-2). Musical toys and recordings add variety and listening pleasure. Encouraging children to watch facial expressions as different human sounds are produced and locating environmental sounds together are techniques in developing children's listening skills. Adults should exercise care in classroom sound volume and quality; at all age levels, extra loud, shrill, vibrating, or emergency alert sounds can be frightening.

7-1b Purposeful Listening Activities

The intent of purposeful listening practice is to increase the child's ability to follow directions

Photo 7-2 Josh listens closely to understand his teacher's comments.

© 2015 Cengage Learning®

and instructions, perform tasks, and respond appropriately in some fashion. Teachers can use a three-step method to help very young preschoolers gain skill in this type of listening. They tell children what they are going to tell them. Next, they say it; and last, they tell children what they told them.

Example:

1. "I'm going to give you an envelope and tell you where to take it."

2. "Take the envelope to the cook, Mrs. Corelli, and then come back to our classroom."

3. "You took the envelope to Mrs. Corelli just as I said and returned. Thank you."

If you were attempting to tell a story to promote children's purposeful listening ability, you might start by saying, "I'm going to tell you a story about my dog. He is a very funny looking dog who makes people laugh. Laughing happens when people see my dog or hear his name. If you listen, you'll find out about Picasso. That is his name. When my story is finished, see if you can tell me one thing that Picasso does that makes people laugh."

Purposeful, attentive listening takes concentration. Teachers can perfect a "what I'm saying next is important" tone and consequently create a desire in children to listen. Statements such as "You might want to know how" or "You can listen closely to find out" or "If you'd like a turn, watch and listen" may also provide the motivation to listen closely. Suggesting children keep their eyes on a speaker even if it means turning their heads is a good idea along with suggesting that children are quiet while another is speaking. A teacher can use her hands to gesture toward a speaker to aid children's ability turn in the speaker's direction.

Planned, purposeful listening activities can include activities that encourage children to listen in order to

- do something for themselves.
- tell another how to do something.
- operate some type of toy or equipment.
- carry a message.
- recall details.
- put objects in a special order or sequence.
- see how many names or facts they can remember.
- learn new skills, such as singing new songs or chanting or doing finger plays.

7-1c Appreciative Listening Activities

Appreciative listening deals with light listening when enjoyment or pleasure is paramount. A wide variety of recorded and live appreciative listening experiences is possible. Background music can accompany favorite preschool pursuits. Chanting a remembered selection of words gives the children a double treat of hearing voices in unison and feeling part of a group. Some appreciative listening builds moods, touches emotions, and adds another dimension to experience. The world is full of beautiful and not-so-beautiful sounds. Programs attempt to offer listening experiences that are aesthetically pleasing environmental sounds, such as familiar home and community sounds plus pleasant sounds found in nature.

Possible appreciative listening activities include:

- moving to music.
- discussing music, rhythms, and sounds.
- talking about favorite sounds.
- talking about happy, sad, or funny feelings that sounds produce.
- tapping, clapping, or moving to music or rhythmic speech.

As is mentioned in previous chapters, there are multiple benefits to introducing a music

curriculum to young children. Music offers another means of expression for children. It can build vocabulary, establish a sense of internal rhythm, develop an awareness of pitch and intonation in voice, and create an understanding of language concepts such as loud, soft, fast, and slow. Singing promotes the development of syntax and memorization skills.

There is a predictable pattern in children's learning of any song. Movements or words are learned first, then rhythms and other elements. Traditional nursery songs are plentiful, are appropriately pitched, and contain repetition of melodic and rhythmic patterns. Music is a "language builder."

Favorite Children's Classics and Traditional Songs. A few classics and traditional American children's songs include *Old MacDonald Had a Farm*, *Dinah*, *Teddy Bear*, *Eensy, Weensy Spider*, and *I'm a Little Teapot*. Educators try to uncover traditional songs in children's home language and offer these tunes also. The song *Ten Little Indians* sung in Spanish is frequently used.

Music or a song may involve more than one of these learning opportunities—vocabulary development, predictable features in a story line or sequence, rhyming features, repetitions that reinforce, cultural literacy significance, concept development, appreciative listening features, purposeful listening aspects, discriminative listening opportunities, and creative listening experiences. Often, a coordination of words with physical movement also occurs in children's music.

7-1d Critical Listening Activities

Critical listening requires the children's evaluation of what is heard and comprehended. It requires contemplation and reflection, and some preschoolers develop considerable skill in this area and use it frequently. These children seem able to weigh the new against what they already know and feel, and they are eager to discuss differences. Other children seem rarely to hold any opinion or particular viewpoint and are reticent to share thoughts. Activities that involve critical thinking can be ones in which

- a problem is discussed and solutions are offered and evaluated.
- a probable outcome or guess is prompted.

- a real or make-believe feature is pinpointed using some criteria.
- personal preferences or dislikes are discussed.
- group votes are reviewed and outcomes are anticipated.
- errors of some type are discovered or detected.
- feelings of others are predicted.
- inconsistencies are discovered.

Activity tips that aid children's comprehension follow.

- Listening comprehension is facilitated if children are familiar in some way with the content being discussed or read. Teacher might mention a bridge to children's past experience.
- Visual aids can aid listening comprehension.
- Repetitions of material increases listening comprehension and especially repetition of key points.
- Presenting a short synopsis of what is to come in a listening activity facilitates comprehension.
- Teacher talking about listening strategies, such as turning toward a speaker or removing distractions before beginning, is a good idea.
- Planning diverse (different types of) listening experiences where listening is required is suggested.
- Slower pace of speaking or when reading aids children whose listening skill is just developing or lagging.

7-1e Discriminative Listening Activities

Discriminative listening has gained increased attention as a result of current research and because of national legislative efforts to improve American children's reading abilities. To discern whether a sound or sound pattern is the same or different, one uses discriminative listening skill. This skill is necessary when a child attempts to decode words in early reading.

The preschool teacher who plans a "Listening Detective" activity in which preschoolers catch the teacher in a mistake—such as "he huffed and he puffed and he blew the *tree* down" after the group is well acquainted with *The Three Little Pigs*—is presenting a discriminative

listening exercise. Imitating a clapping pattern is another, as is finding rhyming sounds or matching xylophone notes.

7-2 Promoting Good Listening Habits

Many classroom literacy activities create an emotional response or reaction. Discussion after a read-aloud picture book or other literacy event may reveal children's feelings and imaginative ideas. Children may then be encouraged to recreate their feelings and ideas in subsequent art, drama, or other forms of expression.

Creative listening has been used as a strategy to unleash creative potential. Who among us hasn't had an "aha" or "light bulb turning on" experience when listening, or had a mental picture form while experiencing a piece of music or hearing a great storyteller? Good listening habits are especially important in school situations. Teachers need to assess their own listening habits and abilities in their daily work with children. Jalongo (2009) has developed a listening skill assessment exercise for teachers. See Figure 7-3.

If teachers expect undivided attention from children, educators must also give undivided attention to them. Most of us have been told in teacher training to bend or lower ourselves to child eye level when we speak to children. How often do we do this when we listen to them?

Two factors may decrease teachers' abilities to listen and model listening behavior: (1) they may not have had experienced teachers in their own schooling (including college professors) who listened with care and valued inquiry and/or (2) they are so busy imparting information that they miss the profound questions and comments of children. This type of interactive style teaches children to sit passively and withdraw. It teaches most vividly what the teachers least suspect they have transmitted.

Instructions from teachers should be clear and simple, with a sequence of what comes first, next, and last. Usually, instructions need not be repeated when given clearly and simply. Often, when the attention of the group is required, a signal is used. Any distinctive, easy-to-hear, pleasant sound or visual signal can alert children that it is time to listen. The silent pause before beginning an activity can be used effectively to focus attention on listening.

Figure 7-3 Do you listen to all kinds of children?

Ask Yourself these questions to help you reflect on your habits as a listener in an inclusive classroom:

- How do I deal with children who seldom talk or are very soft-spoken? Do I encourage them to remain quiet to keep the level of children's talk in the classroom low, or do I make a genuine attempt to draw them into conversation?

- How do I deal with children who are exceptionally talkative or loud? Do I make assumptions about them and their families? Do my assumptions differ based on gender, race, or culture?

- Do I listen patiently to children who have difficulty expressing their ideas and struggle to be understood, or do I quickly move on? Do I make opportunities for them to be heard, not only by me but also by their peers?

- What do I do when children who have asked for a chance to speak fall silent when their turn comes? Am I sensitive to the fact that young children can forget what they were about to say, and do I ensure they have another chance to speak?

- How about when children's behavior is challenging—does everyone get treated fairly, or does the child skilled in verbal expression (e.g., a "smooth talker") avoid consequences more often?

- Do I ask many different types of questions, allowing more children chances to contribute, or do I play the "read the teacher's mind" game much of the time?

- When children say something of questionable accuracy, how do I handle it? Do I pounce on the statement as a "lie," or do I try to get further clarification? If I know it to be untrue or inaccurate, do I lose respect for the child, or remember that the line between fantasy and reality for young children is a dotted one? Do I consider that children sometimes express wishes as fact, and acknowledge this sensitively, with a comment such as, "Yes, wouldn't it be nice if we could . . . "

- How do I respond if a child shares something that makes me uncomfortable (e.g., "My cat got runned over by a car" . . . "My dad promised to take me camping, but I waited all weekend and he never came to get me")? Do I quickly move on, or do I acknowledge the feelings that underlie the message ("It is so sad to lose our pets" . . . "You were upset that a promise was broken")?

Digital Download

In dealing with preschoolers with hearing loss, there are a number of factors and features teachers should consider:

- Seek the child's best seating position and location to see and hear at group times: usually front and center. This might mean using a small chair for the child at times.

- Use visuals or photos in activities and point to the topic, item, or example while speaking.

- Use a natural tone of voice and volume.

- Check the classroom environment for background noises that may interfere with hearing.

- Consult a sound technician for clues on room acoustics.

- Use clear, shortened sentences when giving directions.

- Monitor child comprehension to be sure of the child's level of understanding.

- Use gestures and/or pointing that provide clues to what is being discussed and who is speaking.

Teachers sometimes use a short song, finger play, or body-movement activity to stimulate interest and draw the group together (Photo 7-3).

Photo 7-3 Starting a circle time with a "clapping song" can focus and engage the group.

This helps children focus on what is to follow. Focused attention is the key to hearing well.

Encouragement and smiles at any time of the day can reward individual listening. Positive, specific statements, such as, "Ramon, you listened to what Jan had to say before you started talking," or "It's quiet, and now we can all hear the beginning of the story," give children feedback on expected listening behavior. The following are sample teacher statements, which can promote a group's ability to listen.

1. Pre-Activity Suggestions

- "When I see everyone's eyes, I'll know you're ready to hear about . . ."
- "It seems everyone is listening; it's time to begin."
- "We take turns speaking. Skye is first, then . . ."

2. During the Activity

- "Wyatt had his hand up. Would you like to tell us about your idea?"
- "We can hear better when just one person is talking. Louis, you go first, then Cristalee."
- "Ethan, it's hard to wait when you want to talk. Khesia is talking now; you can be next." (Later add, "Ethan, thank you for waiting for Khesia to finish. Now we will hear what you wanted to tell us.")

3. Post-Activity

- "We listened so quietly. We all heard every word of that story."
- "Everyone listened to what their friends said."
- "We listened and found out a lot about . . ."

Additional examples of teacher talk that promotes listening are as follows:

- "We are going to do two things right now."
- "Eyes open. Lips closed. It's listening time."
- "I can't hear when everyone is talking. Mario, it is your turn."
- "It's Adrian's time to talk now. That means no one else is talking."
- "Let's wait until it is quiet, then we are all ready to listen to the story."

- "When I see everyone's eyes looking in my eyes, I'll know you are ready to listen."
- "That was attentive listening. Everyone was quiet while Joni told us about her painting."
- "Josh has something important to say. Let's listen so that we all hear what he is going to tell us."

Figure 7-4 Rachel's group activity.

A Group Activity

At group time, Rachel, a preschool teacher, gathered the children, and silently waited while they settled in before beginning. "Let's see who is with us today. If you hear your name, give me one clap. Gage." Gage claps one time. "Gage heard his name, and I heard one clap. I'll whisper the next name. If you hear your name give me two claps." Two claps are heard. "Good listening, Mara." Rachel continues until all in the group have been recognized by name.

Rachel then reaches for a story book. "In this book there is something Nathan and Nicholas Alexander want, but they can't see it. Let's look at the book's cover and I will read its title. Then I think you can guess." She places her hand under each word and reads *Nathan's Fishing Trip*. Children's hands shoot up, and Skylar guesses fish. Others agree. "Lulu Delacre wrote this story," Rachel continues. She turns to the title page and comments, "Look carefully at the pictures (illustrations), do you see Nicholas Alexander? He has a big two word name, but Nicholas Alexander is a very small mouse." She fans the book closer so that all can see. Rachel starts the story, but interrupts briefl y to show a large drawing of a hook and a few colored fishing lures. When the word "hook and lure" are mentioned on the third page, she traces the hook shape as she talks about its sharpness. The book reading proceeds to its conclusion.

A discussion includes confirming that fish was a good guess. Rachel mentions it was a particular fish, a trout. She asks why Nathan and Nicholas Alexander may have decided to free the trout. Children's ideas are offered and discussed. Rachel then says, "Nathan and Nicholas Alexander have names beginning with the letter 'N' just like Nicole." She makes a quick "N" on a sheet of paper and holds it up.

A fishing game with fish shapes follows. This was prepared by Rachel beforehand. She explains some of the fish in the plastic washtub have the letter "N" printed on them, while other do not. "If you want a turn with the fishing game raise your hand." Rachel says. A waiting list is printed by Rachel, who selects one child and asks, "Do you want to choose a friend to play with you?" The child indicates a friend. Rachel lines out their names on the waiting list, and points to and reads the next child's name who is to have the next turn.

- "I know it's hard to wait, Cleota, but Rick is talking now. Wait. It will be your turn next."
- "It is my turn to speak, and your turn to listen."

Rewarded behavior is usually repeated and becomes a habit. Teachers should consistently notice correct listening behavior and comment favorably about it to the children. How can one recognize good listening habits? Good listeners look at a speaker's face, filter out distractions, concentrate on a speaker's message, and can repeat back what was said. They rarely interrupt and may ask pertinent questions after mulling over what's been said. Examine Figure 7-4. It is an example of a teacher attempting to promote listening skills and other language development skills.

7-3 Auditory Perception

Ears respond to sound waves. These sounds go to the brain and become organized in relation to past experience. The same process is used in early childhood and later when the child learns to read. Language development depends on the auditory process.

Educational activities that give practice and help perfect auditory skills usually deal with the following objectives:

- sustaining attention span
- following directions or commands
- imitating sounds
- identifying and associating sounds
- using memory
- discriminating between sounds (intensity, pitch, tempo)

The intensity of a sound is its degree of force, strength, or energy. Pitch is the highness or lowness of sound. Tempo is the rate of speed of a sound, in other words, the rhythm of the sound that engages the attention.

A wide range of auditory activities can be planned. The following goals often serve as the basis for planning. Simple skills come before more difficult ones. **DAP naeyc**

- recognizing own name when spoken
- repeating two nonsense words, short sayings, chants, poems, finger plays, or any series of words
- reporting sounds heard at home
- imitating sounds of toys, animals, classrooms, rain, sirens, or bells

- telling whether a sound is near or far, loud or soft, fast or slow, high or low, same or different
- identifying people's voices
- identifying and repeating rhythms heard
- retelling a story, poem, or part of either
- trying to perform first one-part and then two-part directions
- recalling sounds in sequence
- coordinating listening skills with body movements in a requested way
- enjoying music, stories, poems, and many other language arts, both individually and in groups

7-3a Settings for Listening

When preparing listening activities, the teacher can plan for success by having activities take place in room areas with a minimum of distracting sounds or objects. Use screens, dividers, and bookcases if needed, check heating and lighting, and make sure comfortable seating is provided (Photo 7-4). Decisions concerning the size of a group are important. In general, the younger the children, the smaller

Photo 7-4 A quiet corner is a good place to read a book alone, so a chair has been placed there.

the group the teacher will attempt to instruct, and the shorter the length of the activity.

Listening cannot be forced, but experiences can be provided that create a desire to listen. Some schools offer children the choice of joining a group listening activity or playing quietly nearby. Teachers find that an interesting experience will attract children who are playing nearby. When activities are enjoyable and successful, the child who was hesitant may look forward to new experiences. A teacher may be able to turn on or turn off attention by ending, changing, or modifying activities when necessary. The teacher should watch carefully for feedback in children's gestures, actions, attentiveness, responsiveness, body position, eye focus, and other nonverbal clues. A skillful teacher will complete the learning activity before the group becomes restless. When an activity is planned for which listening is required, it is important to consider that an active preschooler may have to struggle to remain seated for any extended period.

7-3b Evaluating Teacher Behaviors

Hopefully, during your years of schooling you've experienced a memorable class or teacher whose class you loved to attend. Think about the factors that made that teacher or class special. Usually mentioned are the teacher's personality, her style of teaching, and techniques that the teacher used to make students feel special, competent, smart,

accepted, and so on. Also, often mentioned are the teacher's uses of the classroom's physical space, enjoyed activities, and perhaps other adults or children in the classroom. The author remembers vividly the grammar school teacher who always skillfully read an interesting and exciting book after recess. She read with great enthusiasm, animation, and pleasure. Consider also the following questions.

Why do children listen to an activity? A number of reasons are possible.

- The activity relates in some way to past experience.
- The children are curious about something new (Photo 7-5).
- There is a motivation to listen because of something the children want to know that personally affects them.
- The children enjoy the company of the people present.
- Something has happened to capture their attention.
- They can hear clearly without distractions and/or can easily see what is going on.
- They are physically comfortable.
- They have no physical, emotional, social, or personal distracting life situation upon which they are focused, such as hunger, lack of sleep, emotional pain, and so on.

Photo 7-5 Cracking an egg is a new experience for many children.

© 2015 Cengage Learning®

What teacher's behaviors, speech, or actions might influence child listening?

- enthusiasm
- animation (but not overly so)
- acceptance
- recognition of children by name
- establishment of a you-talk turn, I-talk turn interaction
- eye contact
- listening skill
- patience
- clear and appropriately paced and pitched speech
- panning of a group with the eyes to gauge children's avid or waning attention and adjusting accordingly
- voice variety
- appropriate voice volume
- eye-level contact
- planning for enough time so that there is not a rushed feeling
- elimination of distractions such as two children sitting together who might "act up" or other noises in the classroom that interfere with listening
- lowered voice volume to gain attention
- stating of rules about turn-taking behavior, hand raising, and interrupting
- use of an attention-getting, gathering activity at the beginning

If you watch, you will know when they are with you: "all ears," so to speak. It is one of the joys of teaching. The feeling of communion never grows old. Ask any practicing teacher.

Can I assess which children listen well and which need help developing listening skill? If you are watchful, yes. However, there are days when even the best listeners will be distracted.

7-3c Speak-Listen Group Times

Some kindergarten and early childhood programs offer older preschoolers "talking-listening" social skill groups. The goal of this activity is to give children who desire to speak the chance to discuss child- and teacher-selected topics in a social setting. This structured activity promotes active listening. In elementary school, this group experience is usually termed "active listening" time or "community circle."

Children are seated in a circle so they can look at the person speaking and easily hear everyone's comments. In preschools, the circle times ideally are kept short and intimate, with small groups of children. Teachers structure this type of talking-listening time as follows:

1. The teacher announces a talk-listen circle as a choice of activity.

2. The teacher names the topic or elicits one from the group. It might be cats because a picture book has been shared, or worms because one has been found, or it might be an open-ended statement like, "After school I like to go home and . . ."

3. A chart depicting expected talk-listen circle behavior is introduced or reviewed. "We'll be looking at the person speaking. We'll listen with our ears." The teacher may choose to introduce only looking at others that are speaking during children's first circle experience, and listening as other speak another time.

4. The teacher states, "Each of us will have a turn to speak. If you don't want a turn to speak, you can say 'Pass.'"

5. The teacher speaks first, modeling a short sentence—"My cat is gray and likes to sleep in a sunny window." Then she proceeds around the circle.

6. A very short group evaluation can take place when all have had a turn. Was it easy to wait for your turn? Did you see others' eyes while you were talking? (Children's answers are given in turn.)

Teachers may continue if discussion is still of interest with statements such as, "We've all had a turn. Raise your hand if you've something more to tell. Anyone can choose to leave our talking-listening time."

A number of common behaviors occur at preschool discussion times. An egg timer might have to be used with the child who drones on and on. The same children may pass day after day, or the same children may choose to participate in circle discussions. A child may not stick to the announced topic, but all comments are accepted and appreciated by the teacher.

Because listening closely and group discussion may be new to preschoolers and because individual developmental levels vary, the rate at which children grasp the social and listening skills offered will vary. To encourage listening and speaking in turn, some programs use cardboard cutouts of lips and ears attached to tongue depressors. The speaker holds the stick with the lips while listeners hold ear sticks.

7-3d Listening Centers

Special listening areas, sometimes called listening posts, can become a part of early childhood classrooms. Enjoying a time alone wearing headphones while listening to recordings fascinates some children. Headsets plugged into a jack or terminal help block out room noise. Partitions cut distractions. Clever listening places with large packing boxes, armchairs, a stack of pillows, or a climb-into bunk, nook, or loft where children can settle in quickly become favorite spots.

DVDs, CDs, videos, audio cassettes, photographs, picture sets, tablets, books, and other technologies offer added dimensions to listening centers. Recordings (sometimes called read-alongs) of the teacher reading a new or favorite story can be made available for children's use (Photo 7-6); they are also available from commercial sources. Their quality varies widely, so it is recommended that they be reviewed before they are purchased.

When teachers realize how much future educational experience depends on how well language is processed through children's listening, listening activities and listening centers gain importance. Many of today's children have passively listened to considerable electronic media, but they may be lacking in the practice of auditory analysis and logical sequential reasoning.

With adult help, children can record their own descriptions of special block constructions together with accompanying drawings or photos. "Why I like this book" talks can be recorded and made available to the whole class. Children can record comments about their pieces of art. A field-trip scrapbook may have a child's commentary with it. Recorded puppet scripts and flannel board stories can be enjoyed while the child moves the characters and listens. The child might explore small plastic animals while listening to a recorded story. Possibilities for recorded activities are limited only by preparation time, budget,

Photo 7-6 Listening with earphones puts this child into deep thought.

© 2015 Cengage Learning®

and staff interest. Children's ages are always a factor in the use of multimedia equipment. Listening centers usually need teacher introduction, direction, explanation, and supervision.

7-3e Recorded Media

Some companies specialize in recordings for children that are designed to improve listening skills. These recordings involve children in listening for a signal, listening to directions, or listening to sounds. Some recordings include body-movement activities along with listening skills.

Not all recordings contain appropriate subject matter for young children. Before purchasing, the teacher should evaluate content. Recording devices can fascinate children. They become valuable tools for listening activities. Under the teacher's supervision or after being given instructions for use, children can explore and enjoy a variety of audio material. Books with themes related to listening can also be good springboards to discussions about listening skills.

7-4 Phonological Awareness

Phonological awareness skills are believed to be predictive of a child's ease in learning to read. Researchers have begun to investigate how to enhance these skills before children enter kindergarten. Rhyming; segmenting morphemes and syllables in words; using discriminative and critical listening, phonemic contrasting, and phonemic games emphasizing beginning letter sounds in words; commenting on alphabet letter sounds; and engaging in other such sounds-of-language activities could all be categorized as phonological skill-building opportunities. These types of activities might aid all four- and five-year-olds and be particularly valuable for at-risk children. Although phonological skill is an auditory skill, research suggests that using visual representation is helpful in supporting learning and competence. Explicit instruction in phonological awareness can result in gains. An activity might include a game, alphabet play, or printing components. Making these activities relevant and interesting can be a teaching challenge. Activities can become an outgrowth of many daily planned and unplanned happenings.

Phonological awareness is developmental—it develops in stages, the first and easiest being the awareness that our language is composed of words (Figure 7-5). Language learners progress and become aware that words are made up of word parts (i.e., syllables), and in the last and most difficult stage, they become aware that syllables are made up of individual sounds (i.e., phonemes).

The 2006 National Reading Panel Report, *Teaching Children to Read*, indicated that phonemic awareness instruction was more effective with focused and explicit instruction on one or two skills, rather than a combination of skills (Cassidy, Valadez, & Garrett, 2010). Phonetic awareness instruction was recommended for classes and to suit the needs of individual children. Instruction, the report noted, is best presented in print-rich classrooms that engage children as readers and writers. It should offer oral and written language experiences and provide alphabetic principle exposure using a variety of strategies that entail authentic and purposeful uses of reading and writing.

Important research-based conclusions of the report concerning phonetic awareness instruction note that it is a critical foundational skill that boosts reading comprehension. Before plans and activities are instituted, educators take into account children's developmental levels. Activities can teach alphabet letter names, shapes, and sounds, and the manipulation and blending of phonemes in spoken words and syllables. Instructional recommendations include teaching the manipulation of phonemes with letters by focusing on one or two types of phonemes at a time with an individual or small group. Instruction should also explain to children how to employ phonetic (phonemic) awareness skills in reading and writing tasks (National Reading Panel, 2000).

Phonological awareness typically begins at approximately age three and improves gradually over many years. It refers to the general ability to attend to (listen to) the sounds of language as distinct from its meaning. A sub skill, **phonemic awareness**, can be defined as understanding that spoken language can be analyzed into strings of separate words and those words can be analyzed in sequences of syllables and phonemes within syllables. English consists of approximately 39 to 44 phonemes (experts differ) depending on the dialect (Ehri & Nunes, 2006). Few words have but one phoneme. Most words contain a blend of phonemes. In everyday speech, phonemes may interweave and not be individually distinguishable.

Figure 7-5 Phonological awareness and children's developing skills.

1. Realizes language is composed of words
2. Can hear syllables in words
3. Can separate syllables or clap syllables
4. Identifies rhyming words
5. Can create rhyming words
6. Can recognize words beginning with the same alphabet sound
7. Can recognize ending sounds in words and match words that end with the same sound
8. Is able to blend sounds into words
9. Can create words by substituting or moving sounds

Note: Children's developing skills tend to follow a common progression, but some children can display a unique, individual progression.

---

phonemic awareness — the insight that every spoken word can be conceived as a sequence of phonemes, and/or the awareness that spoken words are made up of sounds, and the ability to segment a word into its constituent sounds.

A phoneme, at times, may flow together with the phoneme that comes before it and the phoneme that comes after it. Factors such as a speaker's articulation speed and speech habits may affect a phoneme's sound.

Young children begin to notice sound similarities in the words they hear. They enjoy rhymes, language play with words, repeated syllables, and **alliteration**. Because children's books contain these features, close listening at story time is certainly one way to develop phonemic awareness.

Eventually, but usually not until kindergarten or early first grade, children can hear all of the sounds in a word and can segment a word into each of its sounds, or phonemes. Is there a sequence in the development of phonemic awareness? Most educators agree that simultaneous learning is more characteristic. Learning about phonemes is not new. What is new is the importance assigned to phonemes. There is great pressure on teachers to make sure that young children know how to use them to decode words.

Educators without a strong English language background need to be aware that phonemes are different from alphabet letters used in spelling words. Ehri and Nunes (2006) point out:

Phonemes are different from the letters that are used as written units symbolizing phonemes in the spelling of words (Venezky, 1970, 1999). Letters that perform this function are called **graphemes**. Graphemes may consist of one letter, for example: P, T, K, A, and N, or multiple letters, such as: CH, SH, TH, CK, EA, and IGH, each symbolizing one phoneme.

Graphemes and phonemes combine to form words. (p. 111)

And:

If you find it difficult to distinguish the separate phonemes in words, this is because there are no boundaries in speech marking where one phoneme ends and the next begins. Rather, phonemes are folded into each other and co-articulated to produce seamless speech. (p. 111)

Can an early childhood program include the goal of developing phonemic awareness? Is phonological awareness training helpful for four- to five-year-old preschoolers who are at risk for reading difficulties? Research evidence points to a "yes" answer to both questions. A study by Brady, Fowler, Stone, and Winbury (1994) describes what was included in one well-known phonemic awareness training program. Activities dealt with

- directing children's attention to rhyme
- segmenting morphemes and syllables (e.g., "Say a little bit of butterfly" and "Can you say 'butterfly' without the 'but'?")
- categorizing sounds (e.g., "Which word doesn't belong: mop, top, pop, can?")
- identifying syllables ("Do you hear 'doe' in window?")
- illustrating phonemic contrasts (e.g., /p/ vs. /b/)
- using segmentation and identification games at the phonemic level (e.g., "Say a bit of *boat*.")
- segmenting phonemes in two- and three-phoneme words using a "say it and move it" procedure

7-4a Phonemic Awareness Skill   naeyc DAP

A child with phonemic awareness may have phoneme segmentation skill, a skill that allows her to hear phoneme segments in a word. A phoneme is the smallest unit of speech distinguishing one utterance from another. Reading research findings support the idea that phonemic awareness predicts reading success. Research in this area is motivated by the accepted conclusion that a good number of children having difficulty learning to read cannot hear sound sequences in words.

One clever research team introduced a guessing game in which children listened to phonemic hints by a troll character concerning presents they would receive by guessing the word correctly. Hints were stretched-out phonemes in familiar words. In English, this might be done with *d-o-ll?*, *c-a-r?*, or other short words. No alphabet letters need to be mentioned in this kind of activity.

Hearing individual phonemes is not an easy task. Hearing the "separate" words in a sentence is also difficult for children, especially children whose home language is not English. When researchers and educators talk about developing

---

alliteration — the repetition of the initial sounds in neighboring words or stressed syllables, for example, "The foam flowed free and fizzy."

grapheme — the sum of all written letters and letter combinations that represent one phoneme.

children's phonemic awareness, they are talking about developing children's ability to hear such sounds, and particularly to analyze words into their separate sounds. Children hear and isolate letters with **continuant**, or sustainable, sounds first. The sounds articulated in the letters *a, e, i, o, u, f, l, m, n, r, s, u,* and *z* are easier to sustain than the stop sounds articulated in the letters *b, c, d, g, h, j, k, p, q, t,* and *x.* Therefore, it is easier for children to hear the continuant sounds in the word *mom* than the stop sounds in the word *bat.*

There is believed to be a series of level to level ascending steps that children achieve as they gain more and more phonemic awareness skill. It starts with a vague awareness of sounds most often connected to repeated rhyme and the rhythmic language of the nursery word play. The next step is reached when a child gains increased sensitivity to language sounds and then thinks about them, leading him to compare and contrast sounds, and to note similarities and differences. A higher step is accomplished when a child grasps the idea that words can be split into smaller units of sounds that are meaningless unless blended together to form words. In a yet higher step, the ability to segment, analyze, and juggle the phonemes in words can happen, but most often this is not fully accomplished in preschool programs.

Phonemic awareness is required to make connections between single alphabet letters and sounds. It is a beginning skill, on the road to learning to read. Some preschool children can and do read the printed names of classmates and may have a large number of words memorized by sight, but tackling other words they see and sounding them out is impossible without phonemic awareness skill. A few can read simple picture books.

In-depth teaching in this area would focus on a number of language features, including **rimes** and **onsets**, before single phonemes (other than onsets). In spoken syllables, onsets are any consonants before a vowel in a syllable; rimes are the vowel and any consonants after it in a syllable (Figure 7-6).

Several researchers have shown that young children are competent at analyzing spoken words into onsets and rimes but not into phonemes when onsets or rimes consist of more than one phoneme.

Figure 7-6 Onsets and rimes.

Onset	Rime
b-	-ack
st-	-ale
p-	-ick
s-	-ame
pl-	-ay
cl-	-ick

There is usually more than one phoneme in the onset, the rime, or both. An example of this is the fact that children can mentally analyze the word *smiles* into /sm/ and /ilz/, but not into /s/, /m/, /i/, /l/, and /z/. Educators have identified 500 primary-grade words that can be derived from a set of only 37 rimes. The fact that young children can split spoken words into onsets and rimes more easily than into phonemes (when phonemes are parts of onsets and rimes) raises the possibility that children use onsets and rimes rather than phonemes to pronounce new print words. Fisher and Frey (2013) define rimes as word families that are groups of rhyming words, which end with the same vowels and consonants. Onsets consist of the first consonant letters in front of the first vowel (p. 55).

"Wait just a moment!" some readers of this text are saying, "I work at an early childhood center, and this type of language instruction isn't taking place." What questions will early childhood staff members discuss at their worksite before providing phonetic instruction or phonemic awareness activities? (1) Most certainly, is it developmentally appropriate? (2) Do children typically develop phonemic knowledge and phonic knowledge without direct teaching? The answer is yes to both questions. If a program decides to proceed with phonemic awareness and phonic knowledge instruction another important question is "Is the staff skilled enough to model letter sounds? If so, all letter sounds or a select few?" The English alphabet letters, 26 of them, represent many more than 26 sounds. The letter 'a' alone makes it least six sounds (Pandey, 2012). In the Spanish language, each alphabet letter corresponds to a single sound. This can be a problem for English language learners and

---

continuant — a consonant or vowel that may be continued or prolonged without alteration during one emission of breath.

rimes — the vowel and any consonants after it in a syllable.

onsets — any consonants before a vowel in a syllable.

young native English speakers as well. English is also confusing in that single sounds may be represented by different alphabet letters. A good number of English words—though sounding alike—are spelled differently (write/right). All of this becomes a challenge as preschoolers attempt to write real or invented words.

Direct and explicit instruction does not have to be intensive and systematic to be effective for a majority of children. At least three-fourths of children typically develop phonemic knowledge and phonic knowledge without much direct teaching. Program directors may believe enrolled children would not profit from phonetic or phonemic instruction so may not offer it, or they may not feel they are able to do so, or they may not be aware of its benefits for at-risk preschoolers. There may be other reasons also. Other preschool directors test to ascertain how aware children are in this area to guide instruction.

Various sources suggest that somewhere between 15 and 20 percent of children show a need for such additional instruction, whether it be provided in the classroom or not. Instructional techniques that help children gain phonics knowledge and phonemic awareness can be planned in the context of meaningful activities and language play. Many educators and phonics advocates recommend the following:

1. Read and reread favorite nursery rhymes, and enjoy tongue twisters and other forms of language play together.

2. Reread favorite poems, songs, and stories; discuss alliteration and rhyme within them; and play with sound elements (e.g., starting with *cake*, remove the *c* and consider what different sounds could be added to make other words, like *take, make, lake*).

3. Read alphabet books to and with children, and make alphabet books together.

4. Discuss words and make lists, word banks, or books of such words that share interesting spelling-sound patterns.

5. Discuss similar sounds and letter-sound patterns in children's names.

6. Emphasize selected letter-sound relationships while writing with, for, or in front of children.

7. Encourage children to play with magnetic letters and to explore letter-sound relationships.

8. Help children write the sounds they hear in words.

9. When reading together, help children use prior knowledge and context plus initial consonants to predict what a word might be, then look at the rest of the word to confirm or correct. This is especially important for helping children orchestrate prior knowledge with context and letter/sound cues in order to not merely identify words but to construct meaning from texts, which, after all, is the primary purpose of reading.

Phonological awareness activities should be embedded within a rich literacy context that also integrates reading, writing, and literature with the use of oral language across the curriculum. It requires children to be thoughtful, which does not happen when they passively complete worksheets or engage in drill sessions.

7-4b More Phonemic Awareness Activities

Teachers of young children should recognize the important role they can play in contributing to young children's phonemic awareness and realize it can become a natural outgrowth of a wide variety of language-related activities rather than being relegated to a "one-time-a-day" status. These activities can take place in the daily context of a developmentally appropriate program. The goal of any phonemic awareness activity is to facilitate children's perception that speech is made up of a series of sounds. Activities that easily fall into the category of phoneme awareness activities are wordplay and word-game activities. Study the references found in the Additional Resources section at the end of this chapter and search for other resources to uncover how educators have developed awareness programs for young at-risk children.

Learning Alphabet Letter Names. Research evidence suggests teaching alphabet letter names and sounds simultaneously produces better results (Piasta & Wagner, 2010). Most English letter names include the phoneme the letter represents and knowing a letter sound increases the probability the child also knows its name. This is not an endorsement of planned group lessons in prekindergarten, but is rather to increase an educator's awareness of the instructional approach that tries to introduce or offer a letter sound with its name. With older preschoolers, especially when children have an interest during common daily interactions such as book sharing, printing attempts, sign reading, singing, roll call or other opportune moments, teaching a letter name and sound together may be more appropriate.

Using Book Discussions to Develop Phonemic Awareness. A teacher's comments about a book the teacher is reading aloud can explicitly point out and analyze phonemic features, for example, "Those words start with the same sound: listen—*cap, cape,* and *coat.*"

7-4c More Listening Activities

Chapter 13 gives a great deal of encouragement and helps you conduct circle or group activities. If you will be trying out activities from this chapter, it is best to skip ahead and read Chapter 13 first.

Every classroom has some signal that alerts children to a change in activities or a new opportunity. This can range from a few notes on a classroom musical instrument to more creative signals. Usually, a short invitational and attention-getting statement will be used to pique children's curiosity, such as:

- "Gail has a new game for you in the rug area today."
- "Time to finish what you are doing and join us."
- "Madelyn is in the story-time center with a book about Clifford, the big, red dog."
- "Our clapping song begins in two minutes."

In some centers, children are simply asked to finish up what they are doing and join their friends in a particular room area. The enjoyment of already-started finger plays, chants, songs, or movement captures their attention and they are drawn in. This is a great time to recognize all children by name, as in the following (to the tune of "She'll Be Coming Round the Mountain").

"Susie is here with us, yes, yes, yes." *(Clap on yes, yes, yes.)*

"Larry's here with us, yes, yes, yes." *(Continue until all children are recognized, and end with the following.)*

"We are sitting here together,

We are sitting here together,

We are sitting here together, yes, yes, yes."

Early childhood programs that promote poetry, child dictation, storytelling, and authorship can institute a listening and discussion activity centered on what is called "an author's chair." Usually, the child-sized chair is specially decorated and used at one time of the day, or a sign is affixed—Author's and/or Reader's Chair. Children are invited to share their own efforts or share a favorite or brought-to-school picture book. Teachers may find a need to establish time limits for ramblers or may allow audience members to choose to leave quietly when they wish.

Riddles and Rhymes. Riddles are another way to develop children's listening skills.

Rhyming Animal Riddles

A tail that's skinny and long,

At night he nibbles and gnaws

With teeth sharp and strong.

Beady eyes and tiny paws,

One called Mickey is very nice.

And when there's more than one

We call them _____. (Mice)

He has a head to pat.

But he's not a cat.

Sometimes he has a shiny coat.

It's not a hog, it's not a goat.

It's bigger than a frog.

I guess that it's a _____. (Dog)

No arms, no hands, no paws, but it can fly in the sky.

It sings a song

That you have heard.

So now you know

That it's a _____. (Bird)

Sharp claws and soft paws,

Big night eyes, and whiskers, too.

Likes to curl up in your lap,

Or catch a mouse or a rat.

Raise your hand if you know.

Now all together, let's whisper its name very slow _____. (Cat)

Riddle Game

(Children take turns calling on others with raised hands.)

I'll ask you some riddles.

Answer if you can.

If you think you know,

Please raise your hand.

Don't say it out loud

Till _____?_____ calls your name.

That's how we'll play this riddling game.

Guessing Game

A beautiful flower we smell with our nose.

Its special name is not pansy but a _____. (Rose)

I shine when you're playing and having fun.

I'm up in the sky and I'm called the _____. (Sun)

If you listen closely you can tell, I ring and chime because I'm a _____. (Bell)

You've got 10 of me, I suppose, I'm on your feet and I'm your _____. (Toes)

I'm down on your feet, both one and two

Brown, black, blue, or red, I'm a _____. (Shoe)

I sit on the stove and cook what I can.

They pour stuff in me, I'm a frying _____. (Pan)

It is helpful to have magazine pictures of a rose, the sun, toes, shoes, and a pan, plus a real bell to ring behind you as you speak. Riddles appropriate for young children who have little experience with rhyming follow.

Body Parts Riddle

If a bird you want to hear,

You have to listen with your _____. (Ear)

If you want to dig in sand,

Hold the shovel in your _____. (Hand)

To see an airplane as it flies, look up and open up your _____. (Eyes)

To smell a pansy or a rose,

You sniff its smell with your _____. (Nose)

When you walk across the street you use two things you call your _____. (Feet)

If a beautiful song you've sung, you used your mouth and your _____. (Tongue)

All these parts you can feel and see are parts of your _____. (Body)

Tracing hands or drawing any body part they choose (on a picture with missing hands, feet, and so forth) is a fun follow-up activity for four and a half-year-olds.

Stories and Activities. The following stories and games also can be used to enhance listening skills. These activities help specifically with the skill of listening and following directions.

Sit-Down/Stand-Up Story and Activity

Say to the children, "Let's see if you can stand *up* and sit *down* when I say the words 'Listen: Stand *up!*' You all are standing. Sit *down!* Good listening; we're ready to start." Then, tell the children the following story.

When I woke *up* this morning, I reached *down* to the floor for my slippers. Then I stood *up* and slipped them on. Next, I went *downstairs* to the kitchen. I opened the refrigerator, picked *up* the milk, and sat *down* to drink. When I finished drinking, I tried to stand *up*, but I was stuck in the chair. I pulled and pulled, but I was still sitting.

"Don't sit on the chairs," my dad called from upstairs. "I painted them."

"It's too late! I'm sitting *down*," I answered.

"Hurry and help me."

Dad pulled and pulled, but I didn't come *up*.

"I'll go get our neighbor, Mr. Green. Maybe he can help pull you, too," Dad said. Dad and Mr. Green pulled and pulled.

"What'll I do?" I said. "The children will be waiting at school for me." Then I got an idea. "Go get the shovel," I said. Well, that worked. They pushed the shovel handle *down* and I came *up*.

You know, I think I'm stuck in this chair, too. Look, I am. _____ (child's name) and _____ (child's name), please help me.

Everyone else please sit.

Now, let's see if everyone can show how they can stretch way up with their hands and curl into a ball down on the floor.

A good follow-up is to talk about what can be seen in the room that is up above the children's heads and down below their knees, or say this poem together:

When you're up—you're up,

And when you're down—you're down.

But when you're halfway in between,

You're neither up nor down.

Digital Download

"Can You Say It As I Do?" Activity

Purpose: To imitate sounds

Materials: None

Procedure: The teacher says, "Can you change your voice the way I can?"

"My name is (teacher softly whispers her name)." With changes of voice, speed, and pitch, the teacher illustrates with a loud, low, or high voice, speaking fast or slow, with mouth nearly closed or wide open, when holding nose, and so on.

The teacher then asks for a volunteer who would like to speak in a new or funny way. "Now, let's see if we can change our voices the way Kurt does. Do it any way you want, Kurt. We'll try to copy you."

The teacher then gives others a turn. This activity may be followed up with a finger play with voice changes.

Digital Download

"Listen, Oops A Mistake!—Interrupt Me Please" Activity

Purpose: To associate and discriminate among word sounds and objects; to listen for inconsistencies

Materials: Four or five common school objects (such as a pencil, crayon, block, toy, cup, and doll) and a low table, or photographs or drawings of objects

Procedure: Talk about calling things by the wrong name, being sure to discuss how everyone makes mistakes at times. Begin with something like, "Have you ever called your friend by the wrong name?"

Teacher: When you call your friend by the wrong name, you've made a mistake. Look at the things on the table.

I am going to name each of them. (Teacher names them correctly.) All right, now see if you can hear my mistakes. This time I'm going to point to them, too. If you hear a mistake, raise your hand and say, "Oops, a mistake!" Let's say that together once: "Oops, a mistake!" Are you ready? Listen: *crayon, ball, doll, cup.*

Change objects, and give the children a chance to make mistakes while others listen. This activity can later be followed with the story *Moptop* (by Don Freeman, Children's Press), about a long-haired, redheaded boy who is mistaken for a mop.

Digital Download

Errand Game Activity

Purpose: To follow verbal commands

Materials: None

Procedure: Start a discussion about doing helpful things for family members. Include getting objects from other rooms, from neighbors, and so on. Tell the children you are going to play a game in which each person looks for something another has asked for.

Teacher: "Get a book for me, please." Or say, "Can you find a leaf?"

Items to ask for include a rock, a blade of grass, a piece of paper, a block, a doll, a crayon, a toy car, a sweater, a hat, clothes, a hanger, a blanket, and so forth. Send children off one at a time. As they return, talk to each about where the item was found.

While the group waits for all members to return, the group can name the returned items. Put them in a row, ask children to cover their eyes while one is hidden, and then ask the children to guess which item was removed.

If interest is still high, the teacher can make a request that the items be returned and repeat the game by sending the children for new items.

Digital Download

Jack-In-The-Box Activity

Purpose: To discriminate sounds by listening for a signal and responding to it

Materials: None

Procedure: Recite the following rhyme in a whispered voice until the word pop is reached. Use hand gestures or hide your thumb in your fist and let it pop up each time the word pop is said.

Jack-in-the-box, jack-in-the-box, where can you be?

Hiding inside where I can't see? If you jump up, you won't scare me. Pop! Pop! Pop!

Suggest that children squat and pretend to be jack-in-the-boxes. Ask them to listen and jump up only when they hear the word pop. Try a second verse if the group seems willing.

Jack-in-the-box, jack-in-the-box, you like to play.

Down in the box you won't stay. There's only one word I have to say. Pop! Pop! Pop!

Digital Download

Pin-On Sound Cards Activity

Purpose: To associate and imitate sounds and use auditory memory

Materials: Safety pins or masking tape; file cards (three-by-five) or self-stick memo paper with pictures of birds and animals (gummed stickers of animals and birds are available in stationery stores and from supply houses); suggestions: duck, rooster, chick, owl, goose, woodpecker, horse, cow, cat, dog, sheep, lion, mouse, turkey, bee, frog, donkey, seal

Procedure: Have a card pinned on your blouse or shirt before the children enter the room. This will start questions. Talk about the sound that the animal pictured on your card makes. Practice it with the children. Ask who would like a card. Talk about the animal and the sound it makes. Imitate each sound with the group. Have children imitate animal noises, and ask the child with the right card to raise her hand or stand up. Then prompt the child to finish "That's me; I'm a . . . ?" Children usually like to wear the cards the rest of the day and take them home, if possible.

Digital Download

See If You Can Activity

Collect objects from around the classroom (for example, scissors, ruler, eraser, cup, chalk). Put them on a small table or on the floor on a large piece of paper. Say, "I'm going to talk about one of the things you see on the table (floor). See if you can tell me what object I am talking about and say its name. Raise your hand if you know." (Keep giving hints until the children guess.)

"What has two circles for two fingers?" (Scissors)

"It's long and thin with numbers printed on one side." (Ruler)

"What makes pencil marks disappear?" (Eraser)

"You can fill it with milk." (Cup)

"What's white and small and writes on the chalkboard?" (Chalk)

Digital Download

What Has Changed Game Or Can You Keep A Secret? Activity

Purpose: To listen for the purpose of correctly identifying a missing object or item.

Materials: A bag with hats, scarves, belts, pins, socks, gloves, shoes, and so on

Procedure: The teacher can ask a group to examine her closely because something is going to change or look different. The teacher asks the children to close their eyes or look down, or the teacher can turn her back to the children and quickly slip on one item from the bag. Begin by making changes obvious, then more subtle as they gain skill. "If you know what looks different or has changed, raise your hand. Keep it a secret, but you can give clues like "It is small and shiny." Teacher or child gives clues until the change is guessed. Child volunteers can be used to change things themselves after the game is learned.

Digital Download

Summary

7-1   List four types of listening.

The types of listening discussed in the chapter were appreciative, purposeful, discriminative, creative, and critical.

7-2   Identify two recommended teacher interaction habits that aid young children's listening.

A teacher's style of interacting can encourage children's feelings of specialness, competence, and acceptance.

The physical space of the classroom is designed by the teacher to take advantage of space for educational purposes and allows for ease in children's hearing.

A teacher displays enthusiasm and pleasure in language developing activities.

Frequent eye contact is maintained and the teacher bends or stoops when necessary to listen.

A teacher gives undivided attention to children's speech.

Gaining attention before speaking to children is a teacher skill. Teachers know signals can be used to gain attention.

The teacher's speech is clear and distinct and has an appropriate pace.

7-3   Define auditory perception and describe two activities to promote it.

Auditory perception involves sound (waves) reaching the brain and being organized in relationship to past experience. Planned auditory perception activities are designed to provide practice and to increase children's auditory skill. They can include activities that help children sustain attention to sound, follow directions, imitate sounds, identify sounds and associate them to similar or different sounds, and discriminate sound intensity, pitch, or tempo. Auditory activities' instructional goals can include promoting children's ability to repeat words, sayings, short verses, poems, etc., or to repeat rhymes, recall sequences of sounds, or coordinate body movements with sounds or words.

7-4   Create a lesson plan to promote a phonemic awareness skill.

A phonemic awareness activity plan's goal could be to promote phoneme recognition or segmentation or to hear a sequence of sounds in a word. An activity may also encourage recognition of sounds articulated by individual alphabet letters. Hearing and recognizing rhyming sounds or identifying alliteration in spoken words also involves phonemic awareness and skill. Many other suggested activities are found in the text.

Additional Resources

Children's Books with Listening Themes

Fisher, A. & Sandin, J. (1988). *The House of a Mouse: Poems.* New York: Harper and Row. (Mouse poems can be read in a tiny teacher voice. It is full of rhyming text.)

Glazer, T. (1982). *On Top of Spaghetti.* New York: Doubleday. (Teacher sings a silly story.)

Glass, B. & Lubner, S. (2005). *Noises at Night.* New York: Henry N. Abrams. (Discusses listening to noises in bed at night.)

Lord, C. (2010) *Hot Rod Hamster.* New York: Scholastic. (Promotes listening to make a choice, and prompts discussion.)

McDonnell, P. (2008). *South.* New York: Little, Brown. (Bird falls asleep and doesn't listen.)

Novak, M. (1986). *Rolling.* Riverside, NJ: Bradbury Press. (The sounds of a storm dominate this story.)

Showers, P. (1991). *The Listening Walk.* New York: HarperCollins. (Good book to share before adventuring on a sound walk.)

Spier, P. (1971). *Gobble, Growl, Grunt.* New York: Doubleday. (Lots of variety in animal sounds, with brilliant illustrations included.)

Zolotow, C. (2002). *If You Listen.* Philadelphia: Running Press. (This is a touching tale of a child who, missing her father, turns to listening.)

Children's Books Promoting Phonemic Awareness

Bayer, J. (1992). *A, My Name Is Alice.* New York: Dutton. (Alliteration.)

Brown, M. W. (1991). *Good Night Moon.* New York: Harper. (Rhyming.)

Carle, E. (1994). *The Very Hungry Caterpillar.* New York: Scholastic. (Blending and segmenting.)

Christelow, E. (2000). *Five Little Monkeys Jumping on the Bed.* New York: Clarion. (Rhyming.)

Guarino, D. (1997). *Is Your Mama a Llama?* New York: Scholastic. (Rhyming.)

Hutchins, P. (1986). *The Doorbell Rang.* New York: William Morrow. (Blending and segmenting.)

Martin, B., Jr. (1997). *Polar Bear, Polar Bear, What Do You Hear?* New York: Henry Holt. (Blending and segmenting.)

Peek, M. (1985). *Mary Wore Her Red Dress and Henry Wore His Green Sneakers.* New York: Clarion. (Rhyming.)

Trapani, I. (1997). *I'm a Little Teapot.* Watertown, MA: Charlesbridge. (Rhyming.)

Urbanovic, J. (2007). *Duck at the Door.* New York: HarperCollins. (The "d" sound repeats.)

Readings

Dickinson, D. K., & Porche, M. V. (2011). Relationships between language experiences in preschool classrooms and children's kindergarten and fourth-grade language and reading abilities. *Child Development* (82), 870–886.

Lonigan, C. J., Driscoll, K., Phillips, E. M., Cantor, B. G., Anthony, J. L., & Goldstein, H. (2003). A computer-assisted phonological sensitivity program for preschool children at risk for reading problems. *Journal of Early Intervention* (25), 248–262.

McGee, J. M., & Ukrainetz T. A. (2009). Using scaffolding to teach phonemic awareness in preschool and kindergarten. *The Reading Teacher* 62(7): 599–603.

Readings on Phonological Awareness

Ellery, V. (2009). *Creating Strategic Readers: Techniques for Developing Competency in Phonemic Awareness.* Newark, DE: International Reading Association.

Opitz, M. F. (2000). *Rhymes and Reasons: Literature & Language Play for Phonological Awareness.* Portsmouth, NH: Heinemann.

Yopp, H. K., & Yopp, R. H. (2000). *Oo-pples and Bonoo-noos: Songs and Activities for Phonemic Awareness.* Orlando: Harcourt School.

Helpful Websites

International Reading Association

http://www.reading.org/

Read a joint position statement on foundational instruction.

National Child Care Information Center

http://npin.org

Features child literacy and early phonetic awareness information.

8 Children and Books

Objectives

After reading this chapter, you should be able to:

8-1 Describe the contents of children's books that existed before 1900.

8-2 Name four different categories of books for preschoolers.

8-3 Discuss criteria used to select read aloud books.

8-4 Discuss suggested techniques for reading a book to a group of children.

8-5 Describe an after-book reading discussion to promote child comprehension.

8-6 Name two reasons teacher- or child-authored books might be valuable additions to a classroom's book collection.

8-7 List three suggestions for features and furnishings of a book (library) center.

naeyc NAEYC Program Standards

2E08 Children have access to books and writing materials throughout the classroom.

2E04 Children have varied opportunities to read books in an engaging manner in groups or individualized settings at least twice a day in full-time programs.

2E04 Children have various opportunities and access to various types of books including storybooks, factual books, books with rhymes, alphabet books, and wordless books.

DAP Developmentally Appropriate Practice (DAP) Preschoolers

3H21 Teachers draw children's attention to print conventions.

3H22 To broaden children's knowledge and vocabulary, teachers use a variety of strategies, such as reading stories and informational books rich in new concepts, information, and vocabulary.

3H23 Teachers engage children with questions and comments to help them recall and comprehend what is happening in a story and make connections between the book and their own life experiences.

COMMON CORE Common Core State Standards for English Language Arts and Literacy

R.CCR.1 Read closely to determine what the text says explicitly and to make logical inferences from it, cite specific textual evidence when writing or speaking to support conclusions drawn from text.

R.CCR.2 Determine central ideas or themes of a text and analyze their development; summarize the key supporting details and ideas.

R.CCR.3 Analyze how and why individuals, events, and ideas develop and interact over the course of a text.

A Volunteer Reader

Mr. Mead, LaVon's grandfather, arrives in the four-year-old's classroom shortly after nap time and goes to the rocking chair. There is a small commotion in the book center as a few children dash for the reading shelf. A line of children clutching one book forms. The first in line peeks at Mr. Mead, who is reading a book and already has a child curled up on his lap, the child's face registering the intent of enjoying every minute. There is an air of magic and hopeful anticipation on the waiting children's faces. Mrs. Rex, the teacher, moves a few chairs in a row for the "waiters."

Questions to Ponder

1. One can hear Mr. Mead's laughter and a child's giggle. What would you like to know about Mr. Mead's reading technique?

2. What children's attitudes are being formed, and how might these affect their future academic success?

Picture books are an important beginning step on a child's path to literacy, as well as an excellent source of listening activities for the young child. Seeing, touching, and interacting with books is part of a good-quality program in early childhood education. Books play an important role in language development.

A child's first being-read-to experience can be thought of as his first curriculum. It is a curriculum rich in pleasant associations: a soft lap, a warm bath, and a snugly bed. This initial literature curriculum uses common words in uncommon ways, titillates the senses, nurtures curiosities, adds to the memory, and stretches the imagination. When handled with care, reading experiences at home and at school can create positive attitudes toward literature and can help motivate the child to learn to read. Attitudes toward literacy are most easily established early in life.

Many families read to their children; others do not. Mothers with no high school diplomas may read to their preschoolers less than a few times a month (Dionne, Mimeau, & Mathieu, 2014). Children from low-income families are often more dependent on school experiences for their literacy development than middle-class children. In fact, a teacher may offer some children their first contact with stories and books. Teacher and child can share the joy of this very pleasant experience. Many believe next to giving a child a hug, reading aloud is probably the longest-lasting experience that families can put into a child's life. Reading aloud is important for all of the reasons that talking to children is important—to inspire them, to guide them, to educate them, to bond with them, and to communicate feelings, hopes, and fears. In the beginning, the child is usually more interested in the reader than in the book or story.

Teachers know book-sharing time is an opportune time for teachers to help children build vocabulary, extend phonological awareness, and develop familiarity with literate forms (Photo 8-1). Reading books aloud to children exposes them to grammatical forms of written language and displays literate discourse rules in ways that conversation cannot. Discussions can encourage children to analyze the text, and these discussions can

Photo 8-1 Children often want to share with their teacher something they've found in a book.

have a powerful effect on the development of complex oral language, vocabulary, and story understanding—all critical abilities that young children will need when faced with later literacy tasks.

Early childhood teachers agree that book-sharing sessions are among their favorite times with children. Teachers introduce each new group of children to favorite books that never seem to lose their magic. There will be times when young children are rapt with enjoyment during picture-book readings and, at such times, the lucky reader will understand the power of literature and realize his responsibility as the sharer of a vast treasure. The value of offering thoughtfully selected books in a skilled way will be readily apparent.

What, exactly, do picture books offer young children? They open the door to literacy and create the opportunity to influence attitudes, broaden understanding, savor diversity, vicariously experience drama, expand the imagination, gain vocabulary and information, hear the rhythm of language and words, and enjoy the visual and aesthetic variety in illustrations. Another advantage is that young children learn to respond to the messages in children's stories that are told or read to them and in doing this they use the kind of language and thought processes that they will use in learning to read.

As you read through this chapter, other benefits of reading aloud to children will occur to you, and you will clarify your thoughts about the benefits you consider of primary and secondary importance. You will become acquainted with the cultural universals of story structure and form, which help us remember by providing meaningful frameworks. Stories make events memorable.

A special kind of language is found in books. Oral language differs from written language in important ways. Although many young children communicate well and have adequate vocabularies, they do not construct sentences in the same manner found in their picture books. Knowing the way books "talk" makes children better predictors of words they will discover in their early reading attempts.

Each child gets his own meaning from picture-book experiences. Books cannot be used as substitutes for the child's real-life experiences, interactions, and discoveries, because these are what help make books understandable. Books add another dimension and source of information and enjoyment to children's lives.

Careful consideration should be given to selecting books that are appropriate to the child's age and ability. Children younger than three (and many older than this age) enjoy physical closeness, the visual changes of

illustrations, and the sound of the human voice reading text. The rhythms and poetry of picture books intrigue them. Experts point out that very young children's "syntactic dependence" is displayed by their obvious delight in recognized word order. The sounds of language in picture books may be far more important than the meanings conveyed to the very young child. Teachers of two- and three-year-olds may notice this by observing which books children select most often. Four-year-olds are more concerned with content and **characterization**, in addition to what they previously enjoyed in picture books. Fantasy, **realism**, human emotions, **nonfiction**, and books with a variety of other features attract and hold them.

8-1 History to Present Time—Children's Literature

The idea that children need or deserve entertainment and amusement is a relatively new development. Until the mid-eighteenth century, books for children instructed and aimed to improve young children, particularly their moral and spiritual natures.

Folktales were sung and told in primitive times, and stories of human experience were shared. Storytellers often attempted to reduce anxieties, satisfy human needs, fire the imagination, and increase human survival, among other aims. Orally passed down, tales appeared in most of the world's geographical locations and cultures. Much of today's **fiction** reflects elements of these old tales and traditional stories.

Early American children's literature was heavily influenced by English and Puritan beliefs and practices. Books that existed before William Caxton's development of printing in fifteenth-century England were hand-copied adult books that children happened to encounter in private wealthy households. Caxton translated *Aesop's Fables* (1484) from a French version and printed other adult books that literate English children found interesting. *Aesop's Fables* is considered the first printing of talking animal stories. Themes of other books in Victorian England included

---

characterization — the way an author presents a character by describing character verbalizations, actions, or thinking, or by what other characters say, think, or do about the character.

realism — presents experience without embellishment to convey life as it appears in a natural world limited by the senses and reason.

nonfiction — prose that explains, argues, or describes; usually factual.

fiction — imaginative narrative in any form of presentation that is designed to entertain, as distinguished from that which is designed primarily to explain, argue, or merely describe.

romances of chivalry and adventure, knights in shining armor, battles with giants, and rescues of lovely princesses and other victims of oppression.

Victorian families read to their children, and minstrels and troubadours were paid to sing narrative verses to the families of rich patrons. The English Puritans were dedicated to a revolution founded on the deep conviction that religious beliefs form the basis for the whole of human life. Writers such as Bunyan, author of *A Book for Boys and Girls* (1686), were intent on saving children's souls.

Chapbooks (paper booklets) appeared in England after 1641. Initially, they were intended for adults, but eventually they fell into children's hands. They included tiny woodcuts as decoration, and later woodcuts were used to illustrate the text. Salesmen (chapmen) traveled England selling these small, four-by-two and a half-inch editions to the less affluent. Chapbooks written to entertain and instruct children followed, as sales and popularity increased. Titles included *The Tragical Death of an Apple Pie* and *The History of Jack and the Giants.*

John Newbery and Thomas Boreman are recognized as the first publishers of children's books in England. Chapbooks, although pre-dated, are considered booklets. Most of these newly printed books were instructional, but titles like *A Little Pretty Pocket-Book* (Newbery, 1744) were advertised as children's amusement books (Figure 8-1). In 1765, Newbery published *The Renowned History of Little Goody Two Shoes, Otherwise Called Mrs. Margery Two Shoes.* The book chronicles Goody's rise from poverty to wealth. Newbery prospered. Other publishers followed with their own juvenile editions, many with themes designed to help children reason and use moral judgment to select socially correct courses of action. Books used as school readers in early America contained subject matter of both a religious and a moral nature.

During the earliest years of our nation, many children had no schooling and could not read. Those few who could read often read works intended for adults, such as Jonathan Swift's *Gulliver's Travels* (1726). Reading was considered unimportant for children in agricultural society. Only the need for a literate workforce in the new industrialized society of the 1800s caused time to be set aside for children's education and more attention to be paid to books intended for children.

By the mid-1800s, adventure stories for older boys gained popularity with Mark Twain's *Adventures of Tom Sawyer*, published in 1876. Louisa May Alcott created *Little Women* in 1868 as a girl's volume. Toward the end of the nineteenth century,

Figure 8-1 Excerpts from *A Little Pretty Pocket-Book*, published by John Newbery, 1744.

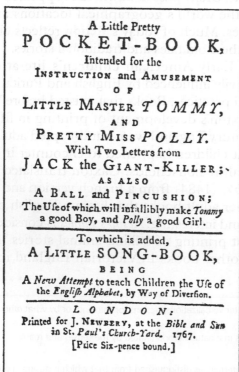

some picture books became artistic. English and French publishers produced colorful illustrations of charm, quality, and detail. The books of Randolph Caldecott, Maurice Boutet de Monvel, and Kate Greenway had captivating drawings that overshadowed the drab illustrations that were typically found in American picture books.

Although not intended or recommended for children, comic picture sequences, like those of A. B. Frost, appeared in American magazines from 1880 to 1890. Their humor was shared by families. Two American picture books resembling Frost's slapstick humor gained acceptance from American librarians: Gelett Burgess's *New Goops and How to Know Them* (Lippincott, 1928) and Palmer Cox's *Brownies* (1927).

E. Boyd Smith, an American, created illustrations for *The Story of Noah's Ark* (Houghton Mifflin, 1905), which are described as both artistic and humorous. The books Smith created delighted children and adults with colorful panoramic illustrations. Librarians speaking of Smith's illustrative work described it as honest, true, "better than any done by an American artist." The cost of full-color printing escalated, and illustrative color in picture books was not to reappear in the United States and become widely affordable until the later 1920s and 1930s. Little Golden Books became popular, and European books with colorful illustrative art were imported to the United States for those who could afford them.

Lynch-Brown and Tomlinson (1998) believe the establishment of book awards improved American picture books.

> By the 1920s a class of professional writers devoted solely or almost solely to writing literature for children—as opposed to moral reformers, teachers, and clerics as authors—produced a larger quantity and better variety and quality of children's books than had been seen to that point. This development was hastened by the establishment in 1922, under the auspices of the American Library Association, of the first of the great American children's book awards, the Newbery Medal. In 1938, with the establishment by ALA of the Caldecott Medal for illustration, more and better artists were encouraged to enter the field of children's books as well. For the remainder of the 20th century, book award programs were effectively used to create interest in children's books generally and to promote awareness of specific types of books. Competition for the most prestigious awards resulted in better, more original works. (p. 124)

American picture books for children began to reflect a worldview of children's literature. Colorful illustrations appeared in school readers. Stories for young children set in foreign countries were widely acclaimed during the 1930s. *Madeline* (Simon & Schuster, 1939) by Ludwig Bemelmans, is still found on most suggested early childhood reading lists.

The child-study movement and research at numerous universities and institutions during the late 1920s and 1930s led some well-known researchers to believe that young children's interests focused on "the-here-and-now." This was translated as home objects and environments, community settings, airplanes, trains, local workers and professionals, and "everyday matters." Approved and recommended book lists guided parents' selection of preschool books as early as 1913.

It is thought that Russian information and "how-to" books of the 1940s and 1950s increased nonfiction picture-book production in the United States. Books concerning machines and how they worked, insects, and science concepts became abundant. Photographs were used along with illustrations.

The Cat in the Hat (1957), by Geisel (Dr. Seuss), celebrated its 50th anniversary in 2007. Beloved by a generation of now baby boomers and enjoyed by succeeding generations of children, it is believed to have been written and illustrated by Geisel to allay his worry that basal readers were not aiding children's learning to read and that they also featured idealized illustrations depicting overly courteous and unnaturally spotlessly clean boys and girls (Freeman, 2007).

Geisel is thought to have developed his story line by intentionally maximizing the repetition of easily read rhyming words. He secured a beginning reading word list from a primary grade teacher and then attempted to incorporate as many list words as possible into his creation. Freeman notes virtually everyone in the English-speaking world who learned to read in the last 55 years is familiar with *The Cat in the Hat*.

Some of the changes in picture-book publishing during the 1960s occurred because several individuals spotlighted the lack of African-Americans in story lines and illustrations. The civil rights movement affected the social consciousness of many teachers and families. Ezra Jack Keats (1969) brought a new perspective to picture book illustration with the publication of his *The Snowy Day*, which featured an African-American protagonist. His use of authentic multicultural characters and urban settings in illustrations was a merging of collage and paint (*Wall Street Journal*, 2012).

Only a few research surveys conducted in the 1970s and 1980s attempted to pinpoint the numbers of picture-book representations for Mexican-Americans, Asian-Americans, or Native Americans. It is reasonable to say they were minimal in number.

Although published multicultural literature for young children increased and became an important part of language arts education, cultural accuracy that helps young children gain a "true" sense of the culture depicted (a so-called insider's view) is a relatively recent development. This type of picture book is eagerly sought by most early childhood educators.

The current trend toward publishing more multicultural literature to compensate for the almost total absence of it as recently as 35 years ago will continue as schools become more diverse and society becomes more accepting of different voices and viewpoints.

Picture books dealing with the reality of young children's daily lives, their families, and living problems (such as stress, fear, moving, and appearance) began appearing in larger numbers in the 1970s and 1980s, broadening subject matter believed appropriate and of interest to children. These books, many classified as "therapeutic," often attempted to build self-esteem or help young children cope in difficult situations. Characters in picture books always had problems to be solved by creative thinking and self-insight, but these new stories dealt more frequently with life situations children could not change themselves.

Literacy concerns and the whole-language movement (1980s to 1990s) have dramatically increased educators' ideas of the importance of quality literature in early childhood curriculum. More and more activities are based on children's reactions to books and language arts activities offered by their teachers.

Creative technology, including e-books, has interactive features not previously possible. New digital products capture attention and attempt to teach and entertain preschoolers. Yet most young children still enjoy traditional read-alouds with the special people in their lives. Today's picture books have historical roots. Some have outlived the generation of children for whom they were produced and are classics of quality. It is those that you, as a teacher of young children, will endeavor to find and share along with the "classics of the future."

8-1a Present Time Book Selection for Your Classroom

Each teacher should develop a personal collection. Librarians and bookstore salespeople can offer valuable suggestions and advice. Judging quality means reading and viewing a picture book to find out whether it contains something memorable or valuable. For every good book you discover, you may wade through a stack that makes you wonder whether the authors have any experience at all with young children. Each book you select may have one or more of the following desirable and valuable features:

- character development (such as *Madeline* by Ludwig Bemelmans, the wolf in *Goldilocks and the Three Bears*, or *Beady Bear* by Don Freeman)
- color (*Little Blue and Yellow* by Leo Lionni)
- an example of human courage, cleverness, or grit (such as *Peter Rabbit*, created by Beatrix Potter)
- aesthetic appeal (*Rain Rain Rivers* by Uri Shulevitz)
- wordplay (*Tikki Tikki Tembo* by Arlene Mosel)
- listening pleasure (*Make Way for Ducklings* by Robert McCloskey)
- nonsense (*What Do You Do with a Kangaroo?* by Mercer Mayer)
- onomatopoeia (the naming of a thing or action by a vocal imitation of the sound associated with it, as in *buzz* and *hiss*)
- suspense (*Deep in the Forest* by Brinton Turkle)
- humor or wit (*Nothing Ever Happens on My Block* by Ellen Raskin)
- fantasy (*Where the Wild Things Are* by Maurice Sendak)
- surprise (*Harry the Dirty Dog* by Eugene Zion)
- repetition (*The Little Engine That Could* by Mabel Bragg)
- hope (*The Carrot Seed* by Ruth Krauss)
- charm (*George and Martha* by James Marshall)

- sensitivity (*The Tenth Good Thing about Barney* by Judith Viorst)
- realistic dialogue (*Can I Keep Him? By Steven Kellogg*)
- cultural insight (*On a Hot, Hot Day* by Nicki Weiss)
- action (*Caps for Sale* by Esphyr Slobodkina)
- predictability (*Brown Bear, Brown Bear, What Do You See?* by William Martin)

Of course, this is only a partial listing. A book can excel in many different ways. An outstanding feature of many good stories is that they can cause the reader or listener to smile with recognition and think, "life is like that" or "I've been there myself." This promotes a positive feeling of connectedness.

- The theme of respect for individual differences in Bill Peet's *Huge Harold*, the gentleness of Uri Shulevitz's *Dawn*, or the tenderness of Charlotte Zolotow's *My Grandson Lew* may fit your criteria of quality. Or you may prefer the runaway fantasy of Frank Asch's *Popcorn* and Tomie de Paola's *Strega Nona*.

- The panoramic scenes of Mitsumasa Anno's *Anno's Counting Book*, the patterns and contrasts in Ezra Jack Keats' *The Snowy Day*, or the fun of discovery in Janet and Allan Ahlberg's *Each Peach Pear Plum* might help a book become one of your favorites because of visual appeal.

- For humor and wit, you might choose Steven Kellogg's *There Was an Old Woman*, Leah Komaiko's *Annie Bananie*, Robert Kraus's *Leo the Late Bloomer*, James Marshall's *Yummers*, Mercer Mayer's *Frog, Where Are You?*, or a selection of others that may make you laugh. You might never forget the way you trip over your tongue while reading about Jack, Kack, Lack, Mack, Nack, Ouack, Pack, and Quack in Robert McCloskey's *Make Way for Ducklings* or Arlene Mosel's *Tikki Tikki Tembo*. If you enjoy surprise or an ending with a twist, you might be delighted by Brinton Turkle's *Deep in the Forest* or Jimmy Kennedy's *The Teddy Bears' Picnic*. The sound pleasure in Wanda Gág's *Millions of Cats* or the onomatopoeia in Mabel Bragg's *The Little Engine That Could* might make these books memorable.

You might relive your experience of city living in *Tell Me a Mitzi* by Lore Segal. Perhaps discovering the facts through the colorful, precise artwork in Ruth Heller's *Chickens Aren't the Only Ones* will attract you to the world of nonfiction. You may look for books to promote children's phonological awareness, like Bill Martin Jr. and John Archambault's *Chicka Chicka Boom Boom* or Cheryl Hudson's *Afro-Bets ABC Book*. Unforgettable characters like Leo Lionni's *Frederick*, Don Freeman's *Corduroy* and *Dandelion*, Eugene Zion's *Harry by the Sea*, or Ludwig Bemelmans's demure individualist *Madeline* may be counted among your friends as you search for quality. Jewels will stand out, and you will be anxious to share them with children.

You will be looking for fascinating, captivating books. Some captivate by presenting believable characters. Character-drawing is like a tremendous, complicated conjuring trick. Appealing to imagination and goodwill, diverting attention by sheer power of technique, the writer persuades us (for the period of reading and sometimes for long afterward) to accept the identity of certain people who exist between the covers of his book. Some picture books fascinate to the extent that worries are forgotten, and the child lives in the fantasy world of the story during its reading and beyond.

Speaking about a true literature-based curriculum, teachers need to watch for stories that "catch on," stories that fulfill some deep understanding of human intentions, or express a developmental concern, or arouse our curiosity: these are the stories that should lead a curriculum of hearing stories, knowing them, and—if they appeal—reliving them through writing, drama, or retelling.

You will want to choose classics so that from the very beginning, the child has a chance to appreciate literature. Not everyone will agree as to what is a modern-day classic. *Where the Wild Things Are*, by Maurice Sendak, continues to cause arguments among adults about whether it is truly a classic. Teachers observe that some adults don't like it very much, but nearly all children respond to it. Many people think that Sendak is very much attuned to kids' wavelengths.

Knowing about family lifestyles, home language, and community individuality aids book selection and planning. Some schools order 50 percent of their books in the children's home language. The relevance of a farm book is bound to be different for children who have grown up on a farm, yet the human universality depicted may make it an attractive choice for urban children.

8-1b Award-Winning Books

Each year, the Association for Library Services to Children (American Library Association) recognizes the artist it believes has produced "the most distinguished American picture book for children" with the Caldecott Medal and Honor awards. Early childhood educators look for these and other award-winning books. Other awards given to books include the following:

- Newbery Medals
- International Reading Association Children's Book Awards
- The Parent Choice Awards
- Coretta Scott King Awards
- National Jewish Book Awards
- Catholic Book Awards
- The Children's Africana Book Award
- The McElderry Picture Book Prize (awards books by previously unpublished authors)
- The Ezra Jack Keats New Writer Award
- newspaper awards
- magazine reviews and recognitions found in *Book Links* (American Library Association) and *Language Arts* (National Council of Teachers of English)
- local public library awards or recognitions

8-1c Illustrations

In many quality picture books, the story stands well by itself. The illustrations simply visualize what is written. In others, illustrations play a dominant role and are an integral part of the entire action. Educators scrutinize illustrations to judge the amount of story support they offer and their connection and relationship to the text (Gaffney, Ostrosky, & Hemmeter, 2008). In some instances more information is conveyed in illustrations than is present in the text. One such picture book, *Love You Forever*, by Robert Munsch (1986, 2011) and illustrated by Sheila McGraw, depicts a toddler about to flush his mother's watch down the toilet. This is stated in the text. What isn't stated is the toddler has also pulled toilet paper across the room, squeezed toothpaste from a tube, and spilled liquid and cotton balls on the bathroom floor. A teacher reading this book aloud has an opportunity discuss the toddler's actions and the mother's emotions and reactions to more fully understand the story.

Picture books can be defined as books that rely on a combination of illustrations and **narrative,** with both being integral to the complete work. Fortunately, many picture-book illustrations are created by highly talented individuals. Justice and Lankford (2002) point out that about 95 percent of children's visual attention during storybook sharing is focused on the book's illustrations.

Young children may or may not have grasped the idea that book illustrations are drawn, created, or photographed by real people. The following happened to a student teacher at Evergreen Valley College Child Development Center.

> During a book reading activity the student teacher displayed the cover of the book *The Wide-Mouthed Frog*, and then read the title, the author's name, and said "This book's pictures were drawn for us by Jonathan Lambert." One four-year-old girl queried "Was it the frog or a people?" The book's cover has a large colorful green frog illustration.

A wide range of artistic styles exists in picture-book illustration, including line drawings, woodcuts, water colors, collage, crayon, pastels, oil paint, and photography. The style of art can be representational, impressionistic, expressionistic, cartoon, abstract, stylized, surrealistic, or a style that defies categorization. The true artist is one who is able to enter the realm that his work evokes and move as freely there as if it were the kingdom of his birth. As a consequence, the artist can show us things that we would not have seen as mere visitors.

Zielinski & Zielinski (2006) point out what they and many practicing educators believe:

> We are in a golden era of children's picture book illustration. There has never been a period where the number of high quality children's book illustrators has been so plentiful. But without question, active today, the quantity of quality book illustrators is without parallel. (p. 6)

Illustrations help give words reality. For young children, illustrations promote visual literacy. Additional benefits follow.

---

narrative — in general, a story, actual or fictional, expressed orally or in writing.

- provision of pleasure
- nourishment of the imagination
- promotion of creative expression
- development of imagery
- presentation and exploration of various styles and forms for the communication of ideas
- awareness of the functions of languages
- acquisition of metalinguistic awareness (defined as a sense of what printed language is all about)

Picture-book illustrations are often familiar objects in lifelike settings, and publishers are careful to emphasize figures rather than backgrounds. In addition to the simple, true-to-life depictions preferred by young preschoolers, illustrations of pure fantasy and illustrations that contain more detail appeal to older preschoolers.

Many possible teacher opportunities for child-book involvement occur during read-aloud activities. Among the interactive behaviors research has identified in read-aloud activities connected to both the book's illustrations and print are questioning, scaffolding dialogue and responses, offering praise or positive reinforcement, giving or extending information, clarifying information, restating information, directing discussion, sharing personal reactions, suggesting physical movement or repeating speech mentioned in the narrative, and relating concepts to life experiences. A teacher reading this list can

Photo 8-2 Schools provide as many one-on-one readings as staff and time allow.

never again believe that read-aloud book times are the simplest, easiest time of the day, although they will probably remain one of the teacher's favorite times (Photo 8-2). Children will have spontaneous and unconscious responses to books, including thoughts that agree or disagree, and other feelings and attitudes. At times children's responses to read-alouds are unexpected, immediately voiced, and can make the act of reading to young children a delightful experience because the teacher shares the excitement, concentration, joy, and laughter.

After studying young children's responses to read-aloud picture books, McVicker (2007) identified a wide variety of uninhibited and spontaneous verbal and nonverbal reactions. As children savor joyful language, meet interesting characters, or encounter personally significant story lines, teachers see evidence of the book's impact and effect. Just as adults are eager to share an interesting book with others, young children share their reactions with their teachers and peers.

8-1d Format and Genre

A book's format is defined as its overall and general character, that is, the way the book is put together. Decisions concerning format by book publishers and author/illustrators include the size and shape of the cover and interior pages, paper quality, printing colors, typesetting, content of each page, and binding. A book's format can enhance its narrative, appeal, and subsequent enjoyment, or it can confuse, frustrate, and alienate the reader. A book can reflect a thoughtful attempt to create a classic volume of enduring worth and value or represent a sacrifice of quality for the sake of quick profit.

Genre, another way of categorizing books, concentrates on a book's content. Narrative is either poetry or prose. Prose can be further classified as fiction or nonfiction. The category of fiction includes excursions into sheer fantasy as well as more plausible stories about people or situations that could be, could have been, or might be. The latter group is classified as realistic fiction. Most educators are eager to learn more about new children's books and are already quite knowledgeable. Picking books for a specific child's interest and then selecting books to suit some unique classroom situation or event are ongoing teacher tasks.

---

genre — a category used to classify literary works, usually by form, technique, or content.

8-1e If Only They Would Choose Books and Book-Related Activities

Many early childhood teachers are worried that busy, money-tight families do not have the time or resources to make books part of children's lives. Consequently, they are expending extra effort and attention to books and book-related activities. Early childhood educators have been alerted to the idea that preschoolers who are read to and who are interested in stories and books are more successful students in the beginning years of elementary school and in accomplishing reading. They monitor how many children select classroom book-related activities and library areas and also monitor the amount of time each child is so engaged (Photo 8-3).

Teacher planning and thoughtful analysis can increase child interest. Thinking of classroom schedules and book-reading times more critically can initiate change and creative and imaginative presentation of activities. Time spent reading to children can be viewed as only one part of a book's introduction. What precedes and what follows are equally important. Practitioners need to ask themselves the following: How is this book relevant to children's lives? What can I do to increase child involvement and interest? What will make children eager to be part of story times? How can I discover child thoughts about what has been read and then build in further experiences? What can follow this story time, and

will children give me clues? In other words, how can this book become part of their lives and at the same time be highly enjoyed? After attempting to answer these and other teacher questions, one can see that simply reading to children may not be enough to reach a teacher's true goals. Teachers spend considerable time in the classroom library (book center) themselves. One teacher technique is to introduce a new book or other printed material every day. Teachers think seriously about book variety, availability, child comfort, and adequate lighting. They determine a plan to "sell" the books they introduce.

8-2 Reading A Variety of Books to Young Children for A Variety of Purposes

Because children can gain so much from books, the teacher's way of presenting them is very important. The primary goal of a read-aloud event is the construction of meaning that develops in the interactive process between adult and child and the development of children's positive attitudes toward the activity. Becoming this type of teacher requires the teacher to view children as active, individual learners. In previewing Tomie de Paola's picture book *Strega Nona* (1975) for a group reading, a teacher might think as follows:

Photo 8-3 This classroom has been able to promote child self-selection of books.

© 2015 Cengage Learning®

What past experiences has this group had with pasta?

What follow-up, extending activities could be planned?

What teacher questions would guide a discussion that probes children's feelings and ideas?

How can I make the "overflowing," "too much" concept a real experience?

The teacher's goal should be to lead each child to understand that books can be fun and interesting, can hold new experiences, and can be enjoyed alone or in the company of others (Photo 8-4).

Children who enjoy read-alouds usually seek out other books. Preschool teachers think of the preschool years as a critical period for children to become "addicted" to books, when urges are felt as irresistible and objects that gratify the urge are also experienced as irresistible. The educator who wishes to capture a young child needs to ensure that early and repeated gratification from book-reading times exists.

In a diverse society, offering multicultural and ethnically representative literature is a must for young children. Although age-recommended lists are available, most teachers actively pursue additional publications. Librarians, publishers, and children's bookstores are excellent resources. Anti-bias themes and sex-equity themes are also eagerly sought to ensure book models give young children every chance to value themselves as individuals.

Not every child in preschool is interested in books or sees them as something to enjoy. Although children cannot be forced to like books, they can acquire positive feelings for them. Some of the positive feelings depend on whether children feel successful and competent during reading time. This, in turn, depends on whether a bond of trust and a teacher-child caring relationship has been established and how skillfully the teacher acts and reacts and how well the book sessions are planned. The key is to draw reluctant children into the story by making story times so attractive and vital that children simply cannot bear to stay away.

An important additional goal in reading books to children is the presentation of knowledge. Books can acquaint the child with new words, ideas, facts, feelings, and happenings. These are experienced in a different form than spoken

Photo 8-4 Creating enjoyment and interest when sharing big books involves promoting the children's positive interest toward books.

© 2015 Cengage Learning®

conversation. In books, sentences are complete; in conversation, they may not be. Stories and illustrations follow a logical sequence in books.

Teachers ought to be concerned with whether the child comprehends what is read. To ensure comprehension, the books must offer significant content, something that relates to the child's everyday experience. Humor and fantasy, for example, are common in favorite picture books. Usually, these books are not merely frivolous. A closer reading will often reveal that they deal with universal human emotions or imaginations. Comprehension is aided by open discussion. Children should be free to ask questions that will help them connect the book's happenings to their own past experiences. The more outgoing and talkative children often clear up misunderstandings of the whole group when books are discussed. Those who work with young children often notice children's innate tendency to try to make sense and derive meaning from the happenings in their lives.

Teachers can show that books may also be used as resources. When a child wants to find out about certain things, teachers can refer to dictionaries, encyclopedias, computers, or books on specialized subjects. The teacher can model the use of books to find facts. When a child asks the teacher a question about some subject of special interest and the teacher says, "I don't know, but I know where we can find out," the teacher can demonstrate how books and other resources can be used for finding answers. The teacher tells where to look and follows through by showing the child how the information is found. The joy of discovery is shared, and this opens the door to seeking more answers.

Many children pick up reading knowledge and reading skills as they become more familiar with book features. They will see regularities and differences in the book's illustrations and text that will aid them in their eventual desire to break the code of reading. An early type of reading has been witnessed by all experienced early childhood teachers. It is called imitative reading, and is defined as the child's reading the story from pictures, and sometimes speaking remembered text. Certain techniques can be used to encourage imitative reading. Reading and rereading favorites and reliving enjoyed sections helps. Giving attention and listening is positive encouragement for the child. A teacher can expect to hear some creative deviation from the book's original text, but correcting isn't advised. Instead, suggest other ways to read the picture book such as reading what is happening in each illustration in sequence. Consider children's imitative reading to be a mini-milestone.

Some preschoolers may begin to understand that the teacher is not telling a story or just reading illustrations but instead the teacher is reading the print (marks) in the book from left to right. The print may first look like strange rows of marks. As knowledge of the marks expands, the child may learn that the marks are single or grouped alphabet letters forming words, and that those words have spaces between them. Eventually the idea that alphabet letters represent sounds may become clear and then children may realize that the reader (teacher/adult) knows these sounds and can therefore "read" and speak words aloud. Many preschoolers recognize single words in books, particularly those that have been read and reread to them often. Some preschoolers develop a small sight word vocabulary and a few become actual readers of simple text. Eventually children come to know that readers use different parts of the text—such as words, photographs and illustrations, graphs, visual images, and the context of reading—to discern meaning.

Educators encourage children to learn how to care for books and where and how they can be used. Attitudes about books as valuable personal possessions should be instilled during early childhood. A number of emerging behaviors and skills will be noticed as children become fond of books. Learning to read is a complex skill that depends on smaller skills, some of which children develop during story times and by browsing through books on their own.

8-2a Common Core State Standards (CCSS)

Early childhood educators have become masterful "multitaskers" during read alouds. They select high-quality fiction and informational picture books and try to instill a joy, and hopefully a love, of picture book experiences. But educators also recognize a skilled reader can at the same time further children's literacy growth skills. By using planned and thoughtful strategies before, during, and after readings, they can achieve additional instructional goals. *Common Core State Standards for English Language Arts* (CCSS) (2010) sets specific expectations for kindergarten children in the areas of phonological awareness, print awareness, phonics, vocabulary, and comprehension. This text provides information on using read alouds to address these key literacy skills at preschool level.

8-2b Using Literature to Aid Conflict-Resolution Skills and Problem Solving

Concerned with rising levels of violence in our society, early childhood teachers are attempting to use picture books and stories to help children identify and define problems, a first step in conflict resolution. Books can be a valuable tool. Illustrations and book text may help children learn the conflict-resolution skills of **visualization** and empathy by providing nonviolent resolution to story-line disputes, portraying different types of conflicts, and giving examples of peacemaking at work.

Should early childhood educators use literature to help young children deal with their emotions and develop positive character traits? Kara-Soteriou & Rose (2008) point out that some picture books can encourage children's formulation of right and wrong. Many picture books depict good and bad behavior, whether teachers decide to discuss these themes is up to the school.

8-2c Selecting Book Collections for a Particular Classroom's Goals and Needs

Teachers are responsible for selecting quality books that meet the school's stated goals; often, teachers are asked to select new books for the school's collection. Book selection is not an easy task for teachers. When choosing books, educators must give much thought to each book's content and its relevance to particular children (Figure 8-2). They must be sensitive to how children might personalize a story. Teachers keep in mind family situations, cultures, religions, and social biases when they select. Some books may fill the needs completely; others may only partially meet the goals of instruction. The local library offers the opportunity to borrow books that can help keep storytelling time fresh and interesting, and children's librarians can be valuable resources.

Even when careful thought has been put into selecting a book, one child may like a book that another child does not. Some stories appeal more to one group than to another. Stories that are enjoyed most often become old favorites. Children who know the story often look forward to a familiar part or character. Selected books should match the children's needs, and their changing interests. They need books that range from simple to more difficult. They need books that are relevant and reflect the social and cultural reality of their daily lives.

Professional books and journals abound with ideas concerning the types of books that children like best. Some writers believe that simple fairy-tale picture books with animal characters that possess lifelike characteristics are preferred. Others mention that certain children want "true" stories. Most writers agree the success of any book for young children depends on its presentation of basic human tasks, needs, and concerns based on children's perceptions, and at a level at which they can respond. Condescending books that trivialize their concerns and efforts and present easy answers to complex problems are discarded for meaningful ones. Books that have intergeneration representations need to have realistic and sensitive depictions free of stereotypes of the old, young, teenagers, or any other age group.

Many families and educators have concerns about the violent nature of some folk and **fairy tales**. Others believe that children already know the world can be a dangerous and sometimes cruel place. Many old stories involve justice— good things happening to people with good behavior and bad things happening to people with bad behavior. Individual teachers and staff groups may decide that some folk tales are too violent, gory, or inappropriate for the age or living circumstances of attending children. Each book needs examination. It is likely that, at times, staff opinions will differ.

Some beginning teachers worry about book characters such as talking bears and rabbits.

---

visualization — the process, or result, of mentally picturing objects or events that are normally experienced directly.

fairy tales — folk stories about real-life problems, usually with imaginary characters and magical events.

Figure 8-2 Form for analyzing children's books.

Name _____ Date _____
Name of Book _____
Author _____
Illustrator _____
Story Line _____
1. What is the book's message? _____
_____
_____

2. Does the theme build the child's self-image or self-esteem? How? _____
_____
_____
_____

3. Are male and female or ethnic groups stereotyped? _____
_____

4. Why do you consider this book quality literature? _____
_____
_____
_____

Illustrations _____
1. Fantasy? True to life? _____
2. Do they add to the book's enjoyment? _____
_____

General Considerations
Could you read this book enthusiastically? Why?
How could you involve children in the book (besides looking and listening)?
How could you "categorize" this book? (e.g., firefighter, alphabet book, concept development, emotions,
    and so on)
On a scale of 1–10 (1—little value to 10—of great value to the young child) rate this book. _____

Digital Download

Make-believe during preschool years is an ever-increasing play pursuit. Most educators are not concerned if bears talk if the message of their speech is something with which children can identify. But they reject other stories that may seem more realistic if the problems the characters face have little to do with children's emotional lives.

The clear-cut story lines in many folk and fairy tales have stood the test of time and are recommended for a teacher's first attempts at reading to preschoolers. Good literature has something of meaning to offer any reader of any age, although on different levels of comprehension and appreciation. Each child will interpret and react to each book from an individual point of view, based on his unique experience.

Early childhood educators should include books depicting people with disabilities so that children can understand and accept people with varying abilities. This group of individuals has been overlooked and inadequately presented in children's books. It is prudent to be on the lookout for this type of depiction of physical differences in picture books.

You will want to introduce books with excellent language usage, ones that enchant and create beautiful images using the best grammatical structure, vocabulary, and imaginative style—in other words, memorable quality books.

8-2d Selecting Books for Specific Purposes

One might select a particular picture book because it increases children's knowledge on a certain subject or topic or its text includes a number of content-related words. Carle's (1969), *The Very Hungry Caterpillar*, is an excellent example of this, for it offers the life cycle of a caterpillar with many scientific and accurate content words. Other picture books support a wide range of teaching goals such as alphabet letter recognition, letter-sound correspondence, mathematical concepts, rhyming, wordplay, challenging vocabulary, graphics, technical illustrations, and so on. Books can be full of examples of cause and effect, classification, sorting, similarities and differences, action and reaction, or can involve predicting consequences. All of these features can promote intellectual growth if discussed and understood. There can be multiple reasons for sharing a book, rather than just one outstanding feature.

8-2e Reading Different Kinds (Categories) of Books

Children's book publishing is a booming business. Many types of books are available, as illustrated in Figure 8-3, which lists various categories in the left column. The figure identifies the major genre classifications and formats of children's books used in preschool classrooms, but it excludes poetry, which is discussed in another chapter. Many books do not fit neatly into a single category; some books may fit into two or more categories.

A vast and surprising variety of novelty books are also in print: floating books for bath time; soft, huggable books for bedtime; pocket-sized books; jumbo board and easel books (Scholastic); lift-the-flap books; flipbooks (Little, Brown & Co.); books that glow in the dark; sing-a-story books (Bantam); potty-training books (Barron's); and even books within books.

Figure 8-3 Categories of children's books.

TYPES	FEATURES TEACHERS LIKE	FEATURES CHILDREN LIKE
Storybooks (picture books) • family and home • folktales and fables • fanciful stories • fairy tales • animal stories • others	sharing moments seeing children enthusiastic and attentive making characters' voices introducing human truths and imaginative adventures sharing favorites easy for child to identify with small creatures	imagination and fantasy identification with characters' humanness wish and need fulfillment adventure excitement action self-realization visual variety word pleasure
Nonfiction books (informational) also referred to as *content books*	expand individual and group interests develop "reading-to-know" attitudes encourage finding out together provide accurate facts contain scientific content	provide facts; allow for discovery of information and ideas discuss reality and how things work and function answer "why" and "how" supply new words and new meanings
Wordless books	promote child speech, creativity, and imagination	provide opportunity to supply their own words to tell the story promote discovery of meanings include color, action, and visual variety
Interaction books (books with active child participation built in)	keep children involved and attentive build listening for directions skills	provide for movement and group feeling promote individual creativity and expression appeal to senses have manipulatable features
Concept books (books with central concepts or themes that include specific and reinforcing examples)	promote categorization present opportunities to know about and develop concepts many examples	add to knowledge visually present abstractions

Figure 8-3 *(continued)*

TYPES	FEATURES TEACHERS LIKE	FEATURES CHILDREN LIKE
Predictable books (books with repetitions and reinforcement)	permit successful guessing build child's confidence promote ideas that books make sense	provide opportunity to read along are repetitive build feelings of competence
Reference books (picture dictionaries, encyclopedias, special subject books)	provide opportunity to look up questions with the child promote individualized learning	provide answers are used with teacher (shared time) are resources that answer their questions
Alphabet and word books (word books have name of object printed near or on top of object)	supply letters and word models pair words and objects are useful for child with avid interest in alphabet letters and words can include letter and word play	discover meanings and alphabet letters and words see names of what is illustrated
Novelty books (pop-ups, fold-outs, electronic books, stamp and pasting books, activity books, puzzle books, scratch-andsniff books, hidden objects in illustrations, talking books) *Paperback books and magazines* (Golden Books, *Humpty Dumpty Magazine*)	add sense-exploring variety stimulate creativity come in many different sizes and shapes motor involvement for child many include humor are inexpensive come in a wide variety many classics available	encourage exploring, touching, moving, feeling, smelling, painting, drawing, coloring, cutting, gluing, acting upon, listening to a mechanical voice, and getting instant feedback include activity pages
Teacher- and child-made books	reinforce class learnings build understanding of authorship allow creative expression record individual, group projects, field trips, parties promote child expression of concerns and ideas build child's self-esteem	allow child to see own name in print provide opportunity to share ideas with others are self-rewarding
Therapeutic books (books helping children cope with and understand things such as divorce, death, jealousy)	present life realistically offer positive solutions and insights present diverse family groups deal with life's hard-to-deal-with subjects	help children discuss real feelings
Seasonal and holiday books	accompany child interest may help child understand underlying reasons for celebration	build pleasant expectations add details
Books and audiovisual combinations (read-alongs)	add variety offer group and individual experiencing opportunities stimulate interest in books	project large illustrations can be enjoyed individually
Toddler books and board books (durable pages)	resist wear and tear	are easy to use (ease in page-turning)
Multicultural and cross-cultural books (culturally conscious books)	increase positive attitudes concerning diversity and similarity	introduce a variety of people
Oversized books (big books)	emphasize the realities in our society have extra large text and illustrations	are easy-to-see in groups have giant book characters

Oversized Books (Big Books). Big, giant, and jumbo (20-by-30 or 24-by-36 inches) are descriptors used to identify oversized books. Publishers are mass producing this size book because of their increased popularity with both early childhood educators and whole-language curriculum advocates. Because they are easily viewed by groups of children, oversized books have been added to teacher curriculum collections. New and classic titles abound. Because the text is large, it is not overlooked by young children. Found in soft and hard cover versions with brilliant-colored illustrations, some have accompanying CDs and small book editions. Teachers use chalkboard gutters or art easels as book holders. Enlarged texts (Big Books) allow groups of children to see and react to the printed page. Active participation and unison participation can be encouraged. Using a hand to underline words while reading, the teacher can focus attention on print and its directionality.

Alphabet Books. Singing and learning the "Alphabet Song" is often a child's first introduction to the alphabet, one that precedes and promotes an interest in alphabet books. For a further discussion of alphabet books and print awareness, see Chapter 14.

Nonfiction Books. Teachers may encounter and share nonfiction books that answer children's questions, are related to a curriculum theme, or serve another teaching purpose, such as providing pictorial information. Nonfiction books can teach concepts and terms associated with various topics, people, places, and things children may never encounter in real life. A book with a simplified explanation of how water comes out of a faucet serves as an example. Nonfiction (books) may be perceived as more appropriate for older grades, and a real revolution has occurred in recent years in the writing and production of nonfiction books for young children. Much of the knowledge of our society, and many other societies, is accumulated in our nonfiction text (Duke, 2007). Duke notes:

- Using nonfiction reference materials in the classroom allows children to see one important and common reason that people read.

- For some children, reading nonfiction reference materials may be an especially compelling reason to read.

- Reading nonfiction reference materials may help deepen concepts of print and genre knowledge.

- Reading nonfiction reference materials provides a forum for building computer literacy.

- Reading nonfiction for reference provides another tool for developing comprehension and world knowledge. (p. 13)

Early childhood educators' attitudes concerning fiction and nonfiction books are changing due to the academic standards being adopted in most states. Common Core State Standards (2010) clearly position reading as the centerpiece of learning (Neuman and Roskos, 2012). The standards promote a more prominent exposure to nonfiction (informational) books. Nonfiction picture books may contain interesting storylines, narrative text and considerable vocabulary that is important to understand presented concepts and information on specific topics or themes. This does not mean that fictional picture books are not as valuable as before, for they also convey ideas and concepts through story, besides offering literary and literacy elements (Fisher and Frey, 2013).

Pentimonti et al. (2010) use the term *informational genres* to refer to two distinct types of text: expository texts (nonfiction) and mixed texts. Mixed texts are hybrids that blur the lines between genre categories. They contain features typical of both narrative and **expository** genres (Donavan and Smolkin, 2002).

Additional benefits for sharing nonfiction books can include introducing *technical* vocabulary and mathematics and science concepts. Nonfiction books may better suit the needs and interests of attending boys and girls who want answers to real-world questions. Nonfiction picture book illustrations can often aid vocabulary development, especially if they accurately depict word meanings. Teachers may believe nonfiction will not hold children's attention. They may not know that many are related in cumulative story form, some are wordless, and others have rhythmic features or include poetry. Most cover interesting topics, pique curiosity, and offer a

---

expository — provides accurate verifiable information about the social or natural world.

Figure 8-4 Tips for selecting informational texts.

LANGUAGE

Does the material:
- use simple, straightforward vocabulary?
- include some specific scientific or technical terms?
- present special or technical terms or context?
- use short, direct sentences?

IDEAS AND ORGANIZATION

Does the material:
- present one idea at a time?
- provide specific and concrete information?
- show relationships among ideas that are explicit and simple (e.g., sequence, cause-effect, descriptions)?
- use short paragraphs that begin with a clear topic sentence followed by details?
- use bold titles and headings?

GRAPHICS AND FORMAT

Does the material use:
- illustrations and graphics to support and provide content?
- clear relationship between text and illustrations?
- illustrations that elaborate and clarify the written text?
- type size that is 14 point or larger?

Digital Download

closer look at the world. Figure 8-4 offers tips on selecting quality nonfiction titles.

Early childhood teachers who are rediscovering informational texts find they often lead to projects, specimen collections, producing simple graphs, mapmaking, child interviewing activities, child reporting activities, documenting and recording activities, and interesting classroom displays. Best of all a "let's find out about it together" search can make a school day more exciting and rewarding.

Teachers realize that photographs, realistic drawings, paintings, collages, and other images should be accurate because young readers attend most directly to illustrations. If informational books sacrifice this, reject them.

A nonfiction book may be one or more people's opinion rather than widely accepted fact. Elementary school teachers purposely offer conflicting readings to promote discussion and critical thinking. At the preschool level, critical analysis is more commonly promoted during oral discussions.

Given a choice of reading materials, young children are as likely to state a preference for informational picture books as for fictional ones. The effects of immersing young children in non-fiction picture books are not fully documented in research. Most practicing teachers know children readily use and consult them. Examples of classroom nonfiction books follow.

Falk, L. (2009). This is the way we go to school: A book about children around the world. New York: Scholastic.

Hatkoff, J., Hatkoff, I., & Hatkoff, C. (2009). Winter's tail: How one little dolphin learns to swim again. New York: Scholastic.

Taus-Bolstad, S. (2013). From wheat to bread. New York: Lerner.

Kirby, P. F. (2009). *What bluebirds do.* Honesdale, PA: Boyds Mills.

After conducting a study of informational picture book read-alouds in early childhood classrooms, Pentimonti et al. (2010) suggest educators take several steps to begin to integrate informational nonfiction books into daily read-alouds. The steps include selecting books relevant to standards and preparing for discussions on key points. Identifying words that need clarification is also recommended. Book follow up activities might be planned for learning centers.

A growing number of favorite books put to music, and favorite songs published as books, are available. An adult sings as pages are turned. Teachers can introduce this literary experience and encourage children to join in. The added advantage of visual representations helps induce the child to sing. The novelty of a teacher singing a book also offers a possible incentive for the child to select this type of book because of his familiarity with an already memorized and perhaps enjoyed song. Word recognition is sometimes readily accomplished. Popular books of this type include the following:

de Paola, T. (1984). *Mary had a little lamb.* New York: Holiday House.

Kovalski, M. (1987). *The wheels on the bus.* Boston: Little, Brown & Co.

McNalley, D. (1991). *In a cabin in a wood.* New York: Cobblehill/Dutton.

Books With Nonviolent Themes. A good number of educators are offering picture books whose story lines include conflict resolution. These can lead to group discussion. Because many stories involve a conflict to overcome, it is not difficult to find positive models of character's actions, words, and behaviors in picture books.

8-2f Reading Books to Boys

Studies by Zambo (2007) and other researchers suggest preschool boys may have already formed a gender stereotype, believing that books and reading are an activity thought to be primarily associated females. When reading instruction begins, boys have more reading problems, take longer to learn, express less enthusiasm for reading, and, generally speaking, don't perform as well as girls on all types of standardized reading tests. Many educators attribute these boy behaviors to two crucial elements: motivation and attitude (Boltz, 2007). Early childhood educators realize they may build a positive attitude toward books in boys in many ways. Some of the most common are to provide read alouds with lots of action, overlook boys fidgetiness at reading time due to a boy's high energy level, help boys maintain attentiveness, watch the length of sitting necessary, select book subjects of particular interest to males, suggest acting out words or story parts, and promoting boys' confidence that their ideas and their oral statements concerning the book's content are accepted and appreciated. The wise teacher obtains individual interest books for individual boys. Extra efforts to engage African-American boys is critically prudent to attempt to mitigate and change the undeniable achievement gap that separates some young black males and their peers in elementary school classrooms in reading ability and achievement.

8-2g Interactive Technology

Technology and young children's books have been combined by companies like LeapFrog, Fisher-Price, and Publications International. With a touch of the finger or a stylus, a young child can flip pages, hear any particular word pronounced, hear a book read by a clear voice, select the reader's pace, play games, hear word definitions, and take quizzes. Some models have light attachments and a microphone. Some teach phonics; encourage children to pronounce phonemes, words, and sentences; and prompt children to record their names, which are then put into stories. Some models focus on writing skills

and enable children to trace alphabet letters, work mazes, or engage in dot-to-dot activities or handwriting exercises. Individual companies have developed over 70 children's book titles that use technology.

Families are lured by educative features, and some preschools are adding electronic books to their book collections. Prices vary, but they usually are not prohibitive for the average center.

The terms digital book and e-book are sometimes used interchangeably and considered to be the same thing, even though e-books are usually static while digital books have multimedia features such as sound or other elements. An original digital book is specifically created to be read on a digital device. Other digital books were first published books and then turned into digital formats. There is an increasing use of e-books. A good number of young children have experienced them. Preschool figures are yet unavailable. Quality has become an issue with educators as both self-published e-books and digital bookstores grow. Educators are beginning to recognize high-quality digital publishing companies and are using websites that conduct e-book and digital book reviews. They are also conducting their own research and designing screening procedures to gain knowledge and the ability to assist parents and families in digital and e-book selection for children.

Educators do know that besides print and graphics, e-books can include multimodal features, such as sounds, music, animation, and videos. E-books most often are read with minimal adult involvement. What is unknown is whether e-books support or impede child comprehension. A few researchers believe e-books' features can be alternately beneficial and problematic (Verhallen, Bus, dejong, 2006). Other researchers theorize multimedia features may support children's ability to make inferences about characters' actions and feelings; but multimedia overload may concurrently inhibit and tax children's working memory. Another unknown is whether a child e-book reader is game playing, listening, or actually reading the text and what percentage of the child's time is given to each activity. Although controversial and unsubstantiated, some researchers believe distracting information embedded in an e-book's text may divert the reader away from main or key ideas and book meaning by focusing the child on clever but unimportant story details.

8-3 Criteria for Read-Alouds

Consider the attention span, maturity, interests, personality, and age of children you are targeting when selecting books. Developing broad literary and artistic tastes is another important idea. The following is a series of questions a teacher could use when choosing a child's book to read aloud.

1. Could I read this book enthusiastically, really enjoying the story?

2. Are the contents of the book appropriate for the children with whom I work?

   a. Can the children relate some parts to their lives and past experiences?

   b. Can the children identify with one or more of the characters?

   Look at some children's classics, such as *Mother Goose*. Almost all of the stories have a well-defined character with which children share some common feature. Teachers find that different children identify with different characters—the wolf instead of one of the pigs in *The Three Little Pigs*, for example.

3. Does the book have directly quoted conversation?

   a. If it does, this can add interest; for example, "Are you my mother?" he said to the cow.

4. Will the child benefit from attitudes and models found in the book? Many books model behaviors that are unsuitable for the young child. Also, consider the following questions when analyzing a book for unfavorable racial stereotypes or sexism.

5. Who are the "doers" and "inactive observers"?

6. Are characters' achievements based on their own initiative, insights, or intelligence?

7. Who performs the brave and important deeds?

8. Are value and worth connected to skin color and economic resources?

9. Does language or setting ridicule or demean a specific group of individuals?

   a. Are individuals treated as such rather than as one of a group?

   b. Are ethnic groups or individuals treated as though everyone in that group has the same human talent, ability, food preference, and hairstyle, taste in clothing, or human weakness or characteristic?

   c. Do illustrations capture natural-looking ethnic variations?

10. Does this book broaden the cross-cultural element in the multicultural selection of books offered at my school?

    a. Is the book accurate and authentic in its portrayal of individuals and groups?

11. Was the book written with an understanding of preschool age-level characteristics?

    a. Is the text too long to sit through? Are there too many words?

    b. Are there enough colorful or action-packed pictures or illustrations to hold attention?

    c. Is the size of the book suitable for easy handling in groups or for individual viewing?

    d. Can the child participate in the story by speaking or making actions?

    e. Is the fairy tale or folktale too complex, symbolic, and confusing to have meaning?

12. Is the author's style enjoyable?

    a. Is the book written clearly with a vocabulary and sequence the children can understand?

    b. Are memorable words or phrases found in the book?

    c. Are repetitions of words, actions, rhymes, or story parts used? (Anticipated repetition is part of the young child's enjoyment of stories. Molly Bang's *Ten, Nine, Eight* contains this feature.)

13. Does the story develop and end with a satisfying climax of events?

14. Are there humorous parts and silly names? The young child's humor is often slapstick in nature (pie-in-the-face, all-fall-down type rather than play on words). The ridiculous and farfetched often tickle them. Tomie de Paola's *Pancakes for Breakfast* (Harcourt, Brace, Jovanovich) is a wordless book.

15. Does it have educational value? (See Photo 8-5.)

    a. Could you use it to expand knowledge in any special way? Maureen Roffey's

Photo 8-5 Color words are easily learned with this book and adjacent real leaves.

Home, Sweet Home (Coward) depicts animal living quarters in a delightful way.

   b. Does it offer new vocabulary? Does it increase or broaden understanding? Masayuki Yabuuchi's *Animals Sleeping* (Philomel) is an example.

16. Do pictures (illustrations) explain and coordinate well with the text? Jane Miller's *Farm Counting Book* (Prentice Hall) has both of these features.

Some books meet most criteria of the established standards; others meet only a few. The age of attending children makes some criteria more important than others. Schools often select copies of accepted old classics. These titles are considered part of our cultural heritage, ones that most American preschoolers know and have experienced (Figure 8-5). Many classics have been handed down through the oral tradition of storytelling and can contain archaic words, such as *stile* and *sixpence*. *Green Eggs and Ham* by Dr. Seuss (Random House) is a recognized classic and is frequently mentioned in surveys of children's favorites. Most teachers try to offer the best in children's literature and a wide variety of book types

Anderson (2007) points out that much of children's literature is moralistic but may also contain excellent literature that is pleasurable to young children. If a book contains a moral or important human truth, look to see if it also shies away from an obvious, overdone attempt to teach.

8-3a Reading Aloud Culturally Conscious and Culturally Diverse Books

Multicultural literature can be defined as children's literature that represents any distinct cultural group through accurate portrayal and rich detail. Educators urge teachers to evaluate multicultural children's literature by examining both literary quality and cultural consciousness before reading them to groups. A different definition of multicultural literature states that

Figure 8-5 Stories, songs, rhymes, and poems considered classics for preschoolers.

A PARTIAL LISTING

"Ba, Ba, Black Sheep"	"Little Girl with a Curl"	"Row, Row, Row Your Boat"
Chicken Little	"Little Jack Horner"	"Silent Night"
"There Was a Crooked Man"	"Little Miss Muffet"	"Simple Simon"
Goldilocks and the Three Bears	*The Little Red Hen*	"Sing a Song of Sixpence"
"Here We Go Round the Mulberry Bush"	"Little Robin Redbreast"	"Take Me Out to the Ball Game"
"Hey Diddle, Diddle (the Cat and the Fiddle)"	"London Bridge Is Falling Down"	*The Three Bears*
	"Mary Had a Little Lamb"	*The Three Billy Goats Gruff*
"Hickory, Dickory, Dock"	"Mary, Mary, Quite Contrary"	"The Three Blind Mice"
"Humpty Dumpty"	"Old King Cole"	*The Three Little Pigs*
"Jack and Jill"	"Old Mother Hubbard"	"To Market, to Market"
Jack and the Beanstalk	"The Old Woman Who Lived in a Shoe"	"Twinkle, Twinkle, Little Star"
"Jack Be Nimble"	"Peter Piper"	*Ugly Duckling*
"Jack Sprat"	"Pop Goes the Weasel"	"You Are My Sunshine"
"Little Bo Peep"	"Ride a Cock Horse (Banbury Cross)"	
"Little Boy Blue"	"Rock-a-Bye Baby"	

multicultural literature is about some identifiable "other," a person or group, that differs in some way (e.g., racially, linguistically, ethnically, culturally) from the Caucasian-American cultural group. Publishers are beginning to create books depicting gay and lesbian families in loving relationships, such as *Molly's Family* (2004). When a center is selecting books, staff members will need to discuss whether books depicting gay and lesbian families fit into their book collection.

The question of authenticity or, more correctly, what constitutes an accurate portrayal of a culture, has plagued educators for years. Teachers try hard to present an authentic portrayal of cultural reality in the books they select. Multicultural books offer opportunities for children to learn to recognize similarities, value differences, and also respect common humanity. Children need literature that serves as a window into lives and experiences that are different from their own, and literature that serves as a mirror reflecting themselves and their cultural values, attitudes, and behaviors.

The books listed in the Additional Resources section at the end of this chapter include not only African-Americans, Asian-Americans, Hispanic Americans/Latinos, and Native Americans, but also subgroups of different and distinct groups under each heading. Other world groups are also included.

When offering multicultural and multiethnic books to young children, no attempt to give these books special status is suggested. Children's questions and comments that arise are discussed as all interesting books are discussed. These books are not shared only at certain times of year or for recognized celebrations but are included as regular, standard classroom fare.

Multicultural picture books may help a child from a diverse background by validating and affirming his life experiences as being part of a larger American culture (Oslick, 2013). This is especially true if a book mirrors and reflects similar looking living conditions, a family's cultural and ethnic characteristics, family structure, and community settings, in other words, the child's own circumstances. It also aids and promotes a child's development of a positive attitude toward books and book reading, especially if the story is enjoyed and the child identifies with a book's character who finds a solution to a recognizable life problem.

Hispanic children's literature does not refer to one culture but rather a conglomerate of Central and South American cultures. Hispanics have been poorly represented in children's literature until recently. Books that existed were often folktales or remembrances of an author's childhood.

In picture books classified as depicting the Asian culture, one may find Chinese, Japanese, Korean, Taiwanese, Laotian, Vietnamese, Cambodian, and Filipino cultural experiences depicted. Increasingly, published books about Asians deal with Asian assimilation into the American mainstream. One can find numerous books dealing with Asian folktales. Yet to be written are plentiful picture books from the Vietnamese, Cambodian, and Laotian cultures, but they are slowly appearing.

Books concerning Native Americans can be easier to locate. Most are folktales, but some deal with rituals, ceremony, everyday life, family joys, and problems. Books depicting Middle Eastern cultures are scarce. Again, the teacher needs to screen for stereotypical characteristics.

8-3b Bibliotherapy

Bibliotherapy, literally translated, means book therapy. Teachers, at times, may seek to help children with life problems, questions, fears, and pain. Some professionals believe that books can help children cope with emotional concerns. At some point during childhood, children may deal with rejection by friends, ambivalence toward a new baby, divorce, grief, or death, along with other strong emotions.

Fairy tales can reveal the existence of strife and calamity in a form that permits children to deal with these situations without trauma. These tales can be shared in a reassuring, supportive setting that provides a therapeutic experience. A small sampling of books considered to be therapeutic in nature follows.

> Gershator, P. (2004). *The babysitter sings.* New York: Henry Holt. (Separation.)
>
> Le Tord, B. (1987). *My Grandma Leonie.* New York: Bradbury Press. (Death.)
>
> Mayer, M. (1968). *There's a nightmare in my closet.* New York: Dial. (Fear.)
>
> Parr, T. (2001). *It's okay to be different.* Boston: Little Brown. (Rejection.)
>
> Viorst, J. (1973). *The tenth good thing about Barney.* New York: Atheneum. (Death of a pet.)

8-4 Teacher Skills, Techniques, and Strategies When Reading naeyc DAP

Teachers read books in both indoor and outdoor settings, to one child or to many. Koralek (2007) suggests that teachers look beyond the library corner as the only place to display, share, and read books with young children. Books can be linked to all areas of the curriculum, she feels. Her recommendations include carrying books outdoors, placing them near discovery tables, and displaying them alongside dress-up clothes. Other suggested areas are block areas, housekeeping areas, window seats where natural outdoor settings can be viewed, theme and display areas, and room settings where counting or number concepts are explored. Other room areas with comfortable seating should not be overlooked.

Mem Fox (2001) reveals the gift and opportunity teachers (and all adults) have when they participate in the act of reading aloud to young children.

> Engaging in this kind of conspiracy with children is perhaps the greatest benefit of reading aloud to them. As we share the words and pictures, the ideas and viewpoints, the rhythms and rhymes, the pain and comfort, and the hopes and fears and big issues of life that we encounter together in the pages of a book, we connect together in the pages of a book, we connect through minds and hearts with our children and bond closely in a secret society associated with books we have shared. The fire of literacy is created by the emotional sparks between a child, a book, and the person reading. It isn't achieved by the book alone, or by the adult who is reading aloud—it's the relationship winding between all three, bringing them together in easy harmony. (p. 10)

Teachers need to assess their ability to make books and book-reading times exciting and personally relevant and rewarding to each young child. In successful classrooms, observable child behaviors include eager attendance at book-reading times, joyous participation, active dialogue, and self-selected investigation and time spent in the classroom library.

How the teacher achieves this is critical. Most of us have seen well-meaning adults use reading techniques that are questionable and defeat the adult's purpose in reading. Your goals should include making reading aloud times an activity of intrinsic interest to the children, adding to children's comprehension of the world, and stimulating children's imagination. Some educators encourage the storybook reader to make comments and ask questions during the reading experience to increase child comprehension. Others believe maintaining the flow and tempo of the story to be paramount so that the story's literary quality remains intact. The first story readers might query factual details, child opinions, or during the reading ask children to infer, label, evaluate, summarize, elaborate, and predict. They might also make comments that point out, explain, or build bridges to children's experiences during story reading. While others, following the second method would instead save teacher comments and questions for an after-story discussion. A beginning teacher can attempt to ascertain if either approach is at work at their center. Or perhaps both approaches are used or the center has its own unique approach to reading aloud.

The burden of making reading interesting falls on the teacher. A teacher must also strive to make the book's content relevant to each child. This means relating and connecting story elements to children's lives and their past experiences whenever possible. This can be likened to building a bridge to the world of books—a bridge that children will be eager to cross because books are pleasurable and emotionally satisfying. Building these positive attitudes takes skill. A step-by-step outline is helpful in conducting group story times.

Step 1: *Think about the age, interests, and special interests of the child group and consider the selection criteria mentioned in this chapter.* If you are required to write a lesson plan for sharing a particular book, identify possible unfamiliar vocabulary and what child comprehension goals you are planning to achieve. Read the book to yourself enough times to develop a feeling for characters and the story line. Practice dialogue so that it will roll smoothly. For example, you might not be able to read *The House That Jack Built* unless you have practiced the incremental refrain. In other words, analyze, select, practice, and prepare.

Step 2: *Arrange a setting with the children's and teacher's comfort in mind.* The illustrations should be at children's eye level, and the teacher should face the audience as she speaks. A setting should provide comfortable seating while the book is being read. Some teachers prefer small chairs for both children and teachers; others prefer rug areas. Avoid traffic paths and noise interruptions by finding a quiet spot in the classroom. Cutting down visual distractions may mean using room dividers, curtains, or furniture arrangements.

Preschoolers who are read to in small groups make greater language gains than when they are read to in larger groups. Some classrooms use "instant replays" of storybook readings when adult supervision affects group size.

Step 3: *Make a motivational introductory statement.* The statement should create a desire to listen or encourage listening: "There's a boy in this book who wants to give his mother a birthday present"; "Monkeys can be funny, and they are funny in this book"; "Have you ever wondered where animals go at night to sleep?"; "On the last page of this book is a picture of a friendly monster." Then briefly introduce the author and illustrator.

Anderson (2007) suggests starting by showing the book's cover or first illustration and asking the group to predict book content using questions such as "What do you think might happen in this book?" Serafini (2012) challenges the wisdom of overusing this kind of book beginning and suggests using an alternate strategy, such as asking both what the children notice on the cover, and what they know about it before asking for prediction. This elicits a focus upon what is at hand as much as what is coming next.

Step 4: *Hold the book to either your left or right side or beneath the bottom centerfold.* With your hand in place, make both sides of the page visible. Keep the book at the children's eye level.

Step 5: *Begin reading.* Try to glance at the sentences and turn to meet the children's eyes as often as possible so that your voice goes to the children. Also watch for children's body reactions, including facial expressions, and try to ascertain whether children are engaged and understanding or have quizzical looks. Speak clearly with adequate volume, using a rate of speed that enables the children to both look at illustrations and hear what you are reading. Enjoy the story with the children by being enthusiastic. Dramatize and emphasize key parts of the story, but not to the degree that the children are watching you and not the book. Change your voice to suit the characters, if you feel comfortable doing so. A good story will hold attention and often

stimulate comments or questions. Savor it and deliver each word. Try not to rush unless it adds to the drama in places.

Step 6: *Answer and discuss questions approvingly, and if necessary or prudent increase child interaction by guessing about or labeling character actions.* If you feel that interruptions are decreasing the enjoyment for other children, ask a child to wait until the end when you will be glad to discuss it. Then do it. If, on the other hand, most of the group is interested, take the time to discuss an idea, but be careful to resist the temptation of making a lengthy comment that will disrupt the story. Sometimes, children suck their thumbs or act sleepy during reading times. They seem to connect books with bedtime; many parents read to their children at this time. By watching closely while reading, you will be able to tell whether you still have the children's attention. You can sometimes draw a child back to the book with a direct question like, "Debbie, can you see the cat's tail?" or by increasing your animation or varying voice volume. Wondering out loud about what might happen next may help. For help in promoting child comprehension and analysis, read An Approach to Promote Comprehension that appears later in this chapter.

Step 7: You may want to ask a number of previously planned questions that deal with the book's story problem or probe the comprehension of main book elements. Creating questions that help clarify what the children newly understand about the story and how this relates to their lives and experiences is helpful. Open ended questions are okay when your goal is to encourage children to share their ideas and oral opinions. Keep questions spontaneous and natural—avoiding testing questions. Questions can clear up ideas, encourage use of vocabulary words, and pinpoint parts that were especially enjoyed. "Does anyone have a question about the fire truck?"

If you have initially asked for story predictions, this is the time to follow up with "Was your prediction about what was going to happen in this book correct?"

You will have to decide whether to read more than one book at one time. It helps remember how long the group of children can sit before getting restless. Story times should end on an enthusiastic note, with the children looking forward to another story. Some books may end on such a satisfying or thoughtful note that discussion clearly is not appropriate; a short pause of silence seems more in order. Other times, there may be a barrage of child comments and lively discussion.

Many children's comments incorporate the story into their own personal vision of things and indicate that the text has meaning for them. Personal meanings are confirmed, extended, and refined as children share their interpretations with others. The focus in after-book discussions is on meaning, and the goal is to "make sense of the text." If one wished to ascertain whether comprehension of certain story elements was achieved, one might ask about problems faced by the main characters, problem-solving solutions attempted, feelings characters displayed, or some other probe that refers to the main content of the book.

Judging oneself on the ability to capture and hold children's attention during group reading times is critical. Many factors can account for children's attention wandering, so analyze what can or did interfere with classroom focus. Factors to consider include group size, seating comfort, temperature, the way the light shines on the book, the child who cannot sit next to a friend without talking or touching, and so on, and, of course, the teacher's presentation skills. One teacher who hated distractions created a sign that read, "Story time; please wait to enter our room." The book itself may also need closer scrutiny.

Your personality will no doubt permeate your individual reading-aloud style. There is no exact right way (Fox, 2001). Become aware of your facial and body language, especially your expressiveness, your vocal variety, and animation at times. Hopefully, children will sense it is an especially enjoyable and looked-forward-to time as special for you as you wish it to be for them.

Teachers should examine daily programs to ensure that children have time to pursue favorite books and new selections (Photo 8-6). It is ridiculous to motivate then not allow self-selection or time for children to spend looking at and examining introduced books page by page at their own pace.

Additional Book-Reading Tips

- Check to make sure all of the children have a clear view of the book before beginning.
- Watch for combinations of children sitting side-by-side that may cause either child to be distracted. Rearrange seating before starting.
- Pause a short while to allow children to focus at the start.
- If one child seems to be unable to concentrate, a teacher can quietly suggest an alternative activity to the child. Clear understanding of alternatives or lack of them needs to be established with the entire staff.
- If one points to or makes references to print on a page occasionally, children will take notice, make more comments about print, and ask questions about it more frequently (Ezell & Justice, 2000).

Photo 8-6 There should be plenty of time to enjoy books with a friend.

© 2015 Cengage Learning®

- Moving a distracted child closer to the book, or onto a teacher's lap, sometimes works to improve attention.

- When an outside distraction occurs, recapture attention and make a transitional statement leading back to the story: "We all heard that loud noise. There's a different noise made by the steam shovel in our story. Listen and you'll hear the steam shovel's noise."

- Personalize books when appropriate: "Have you lost something and not been able to find it?"

- Shedd and Duke (2008) recommend teacher picture book reading discussions should go beyond the classroom and relate a book's feature to past or future happenings, if possible.

- Skip ahead in books, when the book can obviously not maintain interest, by quickly reading pictures and concluding the experience. It is a good idea to have a backup selection close by.

- Children often want to handle a book just read. Make a quick waiting list for all who wish to go over the book by themselves.

- Plan reading sessions at relaxed rather than rushed or hectic times of day.

- Handle books gently and carefully.

- At times when a new word with multiple syllables appears, repeat it, emphasizing syllables. Clap word syllables such as *festival* (fes-ti-val) and *interpreter* (in-ter-pret-er). This technique is primarily used with children nearing kindergarten age.

- Lower or raise your voice and quicken or slow your pace as appropriate to the text. Lengthen your dramatic pauses, and let your listeners savor the words and ideas.

- Introduce vocabulary words associated with the book sharing experience—*cover, title, author, illustrator, front, first page, beginning, print, middle, ending, turn, words, pictures, last page, ending, back cover.*

- Read a book a child has brought to school before you read it aloud to children. Share suitable "parts" only if necessary.

- Handle a child comment such as, "I've heard it before," with a recognizing comment such as, "Don't tell how it ends" or "See if you see something different this time."

- Savor new words as you introduce them. Think of them as words that are new friends entering the child's repertoire.

- Support and accept children's ideas without correcting or challenging.

- Unusual and fun-to-say words can be pronounced a few times for emphasis and either defined or looked up in the dictionary with children.

- Encourage children to talk about illustrations.

- Suggest children act out action verbs.

- Discuss what feeling illustrations arouse.

- After a book is familiar to children, reread it pausing and asking periodically, "What happens next?" Or "Then Beady Bear ___?" At the end ask, "Who knows how our story started?" "Then what happened?" Discuss making an event map together with children.

8-4a Clarifying the Act of Reading With Children

Teachers who want to enhance children's understanding of a book can elicit children's ideas about what might happen in a new book by examining its cover or interior illustrations. They might also focus on print (little marks in a row) or the title page, or the authors' or illustrators' names, or the first word in the story and where that word is found on the page, or the last word in the book, or the book's back cover. They can encourage children to "read" a book by using cover to cover illustrations.

Many teachers are more interested in building a love of books during preschool years than talking about book characteristics. But others believe that they are able to add to children's knowledge of books without diminishing children's enjoyment. What may preschoolers know about books?

- They contain stories and information.

- They can be read by adults and older children.

- A book has an author, and maybe an illustrator.

- The name of an author is usually printed on the book cover.

- Books have a front and back cover and first page.

- Adults read a page starting at the top left and read horizontally across the line of words.

- The last word on a page is usually printed on the right bottom corner.

- There are spaces between words.

- Words are made of alphabet letters.
- Letters are printed in capitals and small letters.

This is not a complete listing. Some children may know much more, including letter sounds, punctuation marks, and other print features.

8-4b Finger-Point Reading and Hand Underlining

Teachers often wonder if using a flat hand to underline words being read is appropriate. It is, but it depends upon the circumstances and the teacher. With chart reading or big book reading, one hand can easily do so because of print size. With most picture books, hand underlining would be awkward, block large portions of illustrations, and may distract the listeners.

Finger point reading is an accepted practice and is another technique to focus attention to the separate identity of words in a sentence while reading. Richgels (2013) suggests it is just one of a number of strategies used in reading and writing instruction. With both techniques it becomes a matter of teacher preference. There is meager research to confirm its value but some individual teachers have a strong conviction that it works.

8-4c Paraphrasing Stories

Paraphrasing means putting an author's text into one's own words, and this is done when some teachers realize the book or some other factor is interfering with children's ability to maintain attention. It brings the book to a speedy conclusion. By tampering with the text, the teacher may interfere with a book's intent, message, and style. Many professionals find this objectionable and urge teachers to read stories exactly as they are written, taking no liberties, respecting the author's original text. Other educators feel that when a book does not hold the interest of its audience, it should be saved for another time and place, perhaps another group. Some teachers believe that maintaining children's interest and preserving children's positive attitudes about books supersedes objections to occasional paraphrasing.

8-4d Targeting Words for Vocabulary Development and Building Participation

A recommended technique used to promote vocabulary development during book-sharing is referred to as targeting. The teacher attempts to ask open-ended questions during a book's re-reading, which allows the teacher to determine unfamiliar vocabulary words and then explain them. Explicit explanations are deemed best. Later, purposeful teacher use of the unfamiliar (target) words during daily or weekly activities takes place, therefore providing additional child exposure and deeper word understanding. To do this the teacher needs to guess which words her class may not know beforehand by scanning the book(s) to be shared.

When a picture book is identified as having the ability to reinforce or aid children's comprehension of theme-related concepts, teachers can decide which vocabulary words are salient to children's understanding. These then can be given particular teacher attention and emphasis during reading while teacher watches children's faces to assess their level of understanding. Teacher conversations in follow up activities can purposely include these vocabulary words to again connect, reinforce, and prompt child usage.

Words fit into a conceptual framework that surrounds any given topic selected for instruction or discussion. For example, if the topic is transportation, a conceptual framework includes the major concepts and realities of the topic. In the case of transportation, a short listing of some of these follows.

- People and **machines** may **transport** things from one **place** to another.
- There are many ways to do so. They are called **modes** of **transportation**.
- Forces of nature can **move** objects also.
- There can be different advantages and disadvantages for using one mode of transportation compared to another.
- People may own **vehicles**; machines or **tools** that help them transport things.

Often identified concepts of a topic can become goals for instruction and one can identify a set of vocabulary words used in any discussion of the topic. These are called set, key, or topic words. Identifying a listing of major concepts and realities of a topic can help a teacher identify significant set vocabulary words. They are the bold words above, but remember this was but a short example.

Children love to be part of the telling of a story. Good teachers plan for child participation when choosing stories to read. Often, books are read for the first time, and then immediately re-read, with the teacher promoting as much participation as possible. Some books hold children spellbound and usually take many readings before the teacher feels that it is the right time for active involvement other than listening. Listening skills are encouraged when children contribute to read-aloud sessions and become active, participating listeners. Three-year-olds take awhile to settle into appropriate and expected story-time behaviors. A young group may heartily enjoy the physical participation opportunities that a teacher plans ahead of time. This is possible if she has recognized portions of the about-to-be-read picture book where children can chime in, make movements or sounds, or in other ways mirror or duplicate something in the story.

Nonfiction books may not provide many opportunities for child involvement. Examining them closely may give the teacher ideas for children's active participation. Many of the benefits young children derive from adult-child readings come through adult reading strategies such as prompting responses, modeling responses for them to copy, asking children to relate responses to real experiences, asking questions, and offering positive reinforcement for children's participation.

The following is a list of additional ways to promote child participation and active listening.

- Invite children to speak a familiar character's dialogue or book sounds. This is easily done in repeated sequences: "I don't care," said Pierre.
- Pantomime actions: "Let's knock on the door."
- Use closure: "The cup fell on the . . ." (floor). When using closure, if children end the statement differently, try saying "It could have fallen on the rug, but the cup in the story fell on the floor."
- Predict outcomes: "Do you think Hector will open the box?"
- Ask opinions: "What's your favorite pie?"
- Recall previous story parts: "What did Mr. Bear say to Petra?"

- Probe related experiences: "Emil, isn't your dog's name Clifford?"
- Dramatize enjoyed parts or wholes.

Younger preschoolers, as a rule, find sitting without active motor and/or verbal involvement more demanding than older children.

8-4e Sharing Your Thoughts

A strategy suggested by Dori (2007) for use with preschoolers and kindergartners involves thinking aloud during read-alouds and during other teaching moments.

> When teachers think aloud, they stop whatever is going on and signal in some way (for example, I point to my head) that their next words will describe thoughts that normally are not spoken aloud. Then they talk through their thought processes. (p. 101)

And Dori describes the results:

> It's easy to see the effectiveness of think-alouds, because the children's voices begin to chime in as they add their own ideas to the adult's thinking. (p. 103)

Two teaching goals promoted by using this strategy are (1) encouraging children's self-initiated active thinking and (2) encouraging metacognition, the act of thinking about one's own thinking. At kindergarten level, it also helps create thoughtful readers.

8-4f A Read-Aloud Approach Designed to Promote Child Comprehension

McGee and Schickedanz (2010), after reviewing research on the value of reading aloud to children age three to six years, conclude studies suggest that merely reading books aloud is not sufficient for accelerating children's oral vocabulary development and listening comprehension. It is the *way* books are shared that matters. Teacher's conversation during read-alouds can enhance understanding when her comments include predictions or connect story happenings or prompt children's engagement in analytical thinking. This is considered crucial to child comprehension. It can also be done by modeling thinking aloud during a reading or asking thoughtful questions. Other teacher strategies that increase the value of reading books aloud are teacher comments that promote preschoolers retelling or dramatizing stories. Many reading experts feel that reading aloud in a way that engages children in dialogue is essential to building comprehension and expressive language.

Comprehension is defined as the process of deriving meaning from text and includes the objects, settings, events, interactions, and speech integral to the story. It involves understanding the connections and relationships among sets of people, actions, words, and ideas. In this discussion, it pertains to children's making sense of the storybook's narrative and/or illustrations. This is accomplished when children gain knowledge through gathering and remembering data and using it to make inferences and conjectures that make "sense" to them.

Educators believe the comprehension of stories is a progressive process beginning in preschool and continuing through life as one encounters stories of increasing depth and complexity. Children's early comments when being read to can seem somewhat unrelated to the book's narrative, but as they age comments are connected in some fashion. Then children grasp and talk about some story specifics and details and move on to relate them to past experiences. At this point, some children develop the ability to create their own narratives, and their stories resemble some of the features they've learned about in storybooks.

McGee and Schickedanz (2010) have identified four suggested *preparatory* teacher actions (techniques) to help build a stronger understanding of a to-be-read book. These are planning a book introduction, using planned vocabulary support techniques, identifying possible teacher analytical comments and questions, and planning an after reading "why" question. This is a systematic approach that also includes attention to vocabulary development that is—words that are critical to the story and are needed to analyze the story problem and/or character's motivation and traits. These words are defined succinctly during the read-aloud.

To try these comprehension building techniques, let's look at preparing to read a picture book titled *Best Best Friends*.* First, one would need to read the book and clarify what features of book or story problem one wants to help

*Chodos-Irvine, M. (2006). *Best Best Friends*, New York: Harcourt.

children infer in order to better comprehend the story and understand what human characteristics are involved. A brief synopsis of the book follows.

> Mary and Clare are best friends. But watching her best friend in a frilly pink dress receive special attention and treatment at preschool, including a pink-saturated birthday party, Clare is angry and envious. When the snack time party is over Clare has had enough. "Yellow is prettier than plain old pink," she declares, and before long both children are yelling at each other. Mary loudly screams, "YOU ARE NOT MY FRIEND!" and stalks off. After a cooling off period and nap time, all ends happily with the girls making up and becoming best friends again.

A planned book introduction of this book to a child audience might be "In this book Clare is having an unhappy day at school. She has some strong feelings and says some angry words to her best friend. Let's find out why." From this introduction you suspect the teacher feels this story and illustrations can generate a subsequent discussion leading perhaps to an in-depth comprehension of either jealousy, unfairness, feeling special, or anger and its relationship to children's lives. Before actually reading the book, the teacher is certainly going to prepare a definition of which feeling or feelings are certain to enter the planned discussion and examine which other book words are necessary to understand character feelings. She will also check which illustrations visually depict these feelings. At this point the teacher might develop a simplified and age appropriate definition of jealous such as "Jealous is how you feel when you want something someone has but you don't have. You may think that is not fair and you're unhappy." Then identifying possible analytical comments and questions comes next and might include the following.

"Does Clare look unhappy or upset?"

"Can you tell if all the children are enjoying the party?"

"I think Mary is feeling special."

"What might be making Clare feel jealous?"

"Has there been a time when you felt special?"

"I feel it is unfair when everyone else is eating a cookie, and I don't have one, do you?"

"Do you think Clare really means what she is saying when she says, 'You are not my friend.'?"

"Have you been angry with one of your friends?"

"Have you felt left out when others don't pay attention to you?"

"Why do you think this book ended happily with Mary and Clare best friends again?"

"Does pink really look 'old'?"

Of course, many other thought-provoking questions are possible. When using this approach, one would preplan an ending "why" question or questions. It could be some of the ones that follow or others that might be more thought-provoking or age appropriate for a particular group of children. "Why did Clare feel jealous?" "Why did Mary forgive her?" "Why do people say things they don't mean sometimes?" "Was feeling jealous a good way to feel or could Clare have handled this situation in a better way?" "Why do best friends like each other but at times have angry feelings?"

What can a teacher do when children display some misconceptions during an after story conversation? (1) She can help children reconsider their initial misinterpretation by explaining and providing further information about the story or text; (2) help a child by prompting the use of the child's background knowledge; (3) by rereading or referring to relevant text passages, (4) by using teacher modeling of her own reasoning; and (5) by supporting the child's attempt to reason things out himself. These strategies have the potential to increase storybook comprehension and vocabulary, and to develop skills for early reading success.

Preschool teachers choosing to increase child comprehension during read-alouds would keep in mind the developmentally appropriateness of these strategies. And also, they would think about whether they could execute all of their preplanned actions, questions, and targeted vocabulary, and still be able to remain a spontaneous and enthusiastic companion enjoying the act of reading aloud.

Teachers without aides and/or volunteers in their classroom may never have undivided time to share books with individual children. One-on-one readings can be the most beneficial and literacy-developing times of all. The dialogue and the personalized attention exceed what is possible in group readings. In large groups, some children are reluctant to speak and consequently receive less appreciation and feedback. (Small groups are recommended.)

Busy families tend to rely on schools to offer books. Many centers have been clever in promoting home reading. Bulletin boards, lending arrangements, and mandating family classroom volunteering are among the most common tactics.

It is not the simple "I-read-you-listen" type of adult-child interaction with books that really counts. It is the wide-ranging verbal dialogue the adult permits and encourages that gives children their best opportunity to construct a full knowledge of how people use books. Schools consequently include and share reading techniques in their communications with parents.

Teachers plan times to be in the classroom's book center, book corner, library, or book-reading area (whatever it is called). A teacher's presence models interest and allows for individual child readings, questions, and interactions other than at planned group book times.

8-4g Rereading Stories

It never ceases to amaze teachers and families when preschoolers beg to hear a book read over and over. Beginning teachers take this statement to mean that they have done a good job, and even veteran teachers confess it still feels good. A teacher who can read the same book over and over again with believable enthusiasm, as if it were his first delighted reading, has admirable technique and dedication. Children often ask to have stories reread because, by knowing what comes next, they feel competent, or they simply want to stretch out what is enjoyable. The decisions that teachers make about fulfilling the request depend on many factors, including class schedules and children's lack of capacity to sit through a second reading (despite their expressed desire to hear it). It is suggested that books be reread often and that teacher statements such as, "I'd like to read it again, but . . ." are followed by statements such as, "After lunch, I'll be under the tree in the yard, if you want to hear the story again."

Requests to "read it again" arise as a natural developmental demand of high significance and an integral part of book exposure. The child's behavior alerts adults to which books hold and preoccupy them. Teachers can think of the behavior as children selecting their own course of study. Multiple copies of favorite books and fresh, new books that extend individual children's "course of study" are provided by alert teachers.

A curious response may occur when the same storybooks are read and reread to four-year-olds. Children may be able to make more detailed comments centering on characters, events, titles, story themes, settings, and the book's language with rereading. Experienced teachers have noticed that as children understand particular aspects of stories (gained through numerous rereadings), they shift focus and attend to additional story dimensions overlooked in initial readings.

Early childhood educators with any experience have met children who want to "read" to teachers or peers. Teachers often smile, hypothesizing that the child is using rote memory, but often find that the child is telling his own version of the story. Researchers suggest this indicates a child has displayed a deep understanding and response to the story's meaning.

Teachers decide to introduce books with objects or other visuals for a number of reasons. A chef's hat worn by a teacher certainly gets attention and may motivate a group to hear more about the chef in the picture book. A head of lettuce or horseshoe may clarify some feature of a story. The possibilities are almost limitless. With theme or unit approaches to instruction, a picture book may expand or elaborate a field of study or topic that has already been introduced. If so, some new feature mentioned in a book may be emphasized by using a visual.

When the teacher wears an article of clothing, such as the hat mentioned previously, it may help him get into character. Because children like to act out story lines or scenes, items that help promote this activity can be introduced at the end of the story. Previewing a picture book may make it easier to find an object or person who could add to the storytelling experience.

8-5 After-Reading Discussions and Activities

How soon after a story is read should discussion, which promotes comprehension of stories, take place? Some educators believe it is obvious that a discussion might ruin the afterglow that occurs after certain books are shared. Teachers are sometimes understandably reluctant to mar the magic of the moment.

The teacher's role during storybook readings is to act as a "mediator" who assists children in two ways: (1) by helping them learn to take knowledge they had gained outside of book-reading experience and use this knowledge to understand the text and (2) by helping them apply the meanings and messages gained from books to their own lives.

What can early childhood teachers expect when children make comments or have questions after book reading? Ezell and Justice (2000) suggest that book illustrations or book concepts account for approximately 95 percent of children's comments during shared readings. Children's questions about meaning can be less common, and their questions about alphabet letters, words, or letter sounds are infrequent, as are questions concerning the author, illustrator, title, or book's format.

The teacher's focus in asking questions in an after-book discussion may not be to check children's knowledge but rather to learn from the child, build comprehension, and promote oral dialogue. A preschool teacher's story-reading discussions can be described as negotiated, unfocused interactions in which teachers become aware of the "sense making" children express. The process depends on what children say about their confusions and interpretations and what they understand, together with the teacher's response to the meaning the group seemed to make of the story.

Early childhood teachers could at times consider asking questions that draw attention to major elements of characterization and plot and the moral or deeper implications of a story, if appropriate, as was discussed previously. The solution that some teachers favor rather than a planned and systematic approach is to wait until children seem eager to comment, discuss, and perhaps disagree, and only then act as a guide to further comprehension. All present are given the opportunity to respond or add comments and cite personal experiences. Teachers using after-book discussions believe book content, word meanings, and ideas are best remembered if talked about.

Some centers designate a time after a story is read as "story time talk time." It is described as a time when children's ideas may be recorded by the teacher on a "language chart" made of chart paper or large sized paper. This activity gives importance to children's ideas. Writing the children's names by their contributions affords additional status. Children's art related to the book can be appended. Other book follow up activities can include making a basket collection of inexpensive small plastic (or other material) figures of story characters, animals, houses, story objects, and so on, to go along with a book. These are so popular one teacher made home-sewn story dolls for the school basket collection.

Discussions can promote print knowledge and include the idea that books are held in a certain way, and pages are turned from front to back. They learn about beginnings and endings of stories, about title pages, authors, and illustrators. They discover that teachers and other adults read print rather than pictures. Children also acquire concepts about print directionality—in English, print is read from left to right and top to bottom—as well as concepts about letters and words—words are made up of letters and are marked by spaces on either side.

8-5a Story or Book Dramatization

Some early childhood educators encourage child dramatization of favorite picture books and stories. Young children's recollection of literal story details and their comprehension of story features are enhanced if enactment takes place. Planning for book enactment means teachers start with simple short stories and display various props, objects, costumes, and so forth, to serve as motivator and "get-into-character" aids. In previewing picture books or oral stories for story times, teachers become accustomed to looking for material with repeated words, sentences, or actions. These are the books or story parts that are easy to learn. In the telling of *the three little pigs*, most children will join in after just a few readings with "then I'll huff, and I'll puff, and I'll blow your house down!"

8-5b Picture Books as the Basis for Theme Instruction

Some early childhood centers experiment with using picture books as the basis for theme program planning (Photo 8-7). Under this approach to program planning, instruction branches out from the concepts and vocabulary present in the book. Usually, the meaning of the story is emphasized, and a number of different directions of study and activities that are in some way connected to the book are conducted.

Photo 8-7 Many books for children have a train theme.

The classroom setting can be transformed into the cabbage patch that Peter Rabbit was so fond of exploring. Activities such as counting buttons on jackets, singing songs about rabbits or gardens, taking field trips to vegetable gardens, and engaging in science experiences in vegetable growing are a few examples of associated activities. A "Stuffed Toy Animal Day" when children bring their own favorite to class might follow the reading of Frank Asch's picture book *Popcorn*. The book *Fast Food* by Freymann and Effers could initiate a study of restaurants. Memorable experiences connected to classic books can aid literacy development, and an increasing number of early childhood centers are using this approach.

8-5c From Books to Flannel (Felt) Boards and Beyond

Teachers find that a number of books can be made into flannel board stories relatively easily; Chapter 11 is devoted to these activities. Some books that are particular favorites have been adapted for flannel board presentation, such as

- *The Very Hungry Caterpillar* by Eric Carle
- *The Carrot Seed* by Ruth Krauss
- *Johnny and His Drum* by Maggie Duff
- *My Five Senses* by Aliki
- *Brown Bear, Brown Bear, What Do You See?* by William Martin

Teachers have attempted to advertise particular books in creative ways. Enlarged book characters might be displayed, or displays of the book of the week or book of the day may be placed in a special spot in a classroom. An attending child's family member may be a special story-time book reader. During a morning greeting to children, a teacher might say, "I have a new book in my lap. See the cover," so she can create excitement for story time.

A visit to the local library is often planned for preschoolers. Librarian-presented story hours often result in the children's awareness of the library as a resource. Selecting and checking out one's choice can be an exciting and important milestone. Most early childhood centers also do their best to encourage this family-child activity. Many libraries have well-developed collections and enthusiastic and creative children's librarians who plan a number of activities to promote literacy. Along with books, you may find computers, language-development computer programs, CDs, DVDs, book and electronic media combinations, children's encyclopedias, foreign language editions, pamphlet collections, puzzles, and other language-related materials.

Finding out more about the authors of children's books can help provide teachers with added insights and background data. One goal of language arts instruction should be to alert children to the idea that books are created by real people. Most children find a photograph of an author or illustrator interesting, as well as stories concerning an author's childhood or reasons for writing a particular picture book.

Becoming more familiar with authors such as Margaret Wise Brown, often called the "Laureate of the Nursery," helps a reader appreciate the simplicity, directness, humor, and the sense of the importance of life that are found in her writings. Identifying and researching the authors of your children's classroom favorites is a good idea and prompts discussion of authors' individuality.

Websites that give information about children's book authors and illustrators are helpful, and librarians can guide you to books with autobiographical and biographical information.

Some early childhood centers set up author displays, celebrate author/illustrator birthdays, and encourage guest authors and illustrators. Letters or emails to authors might be written with child input.

8-6 Child- and Teacher-Authored Books

Books authored by children or their teachers have many values. They

- promote interest in the classroom book collection.
- help children see connections between spoken and written words.
- contain material based on child and teacher interests.
- personalize book reading.
- prompt self-expression.
- stimulate creativity.
- build feelings of competence and self-worth.

Hostetler (2000) describes child-authored books in her classroom.

> The children in my class who are four and five years old love to dictate text and illustrate the pictures for our handmade books. These books become treasures. The first book the children usually write is about our field trip to the farm. (p. 34)

She suggests creating a group-produced classroom book in which each child has a page. The teacher suggests a focal point subject, such as something the children would like to have in their pocket or some family-related topic. Another idea is to ask older four-year-olds who will be going to kindergarten soon to help make a book for children coming into their four-year-olds' classroom. The book will give the new children advice about the good things that might happen at preschool, tips on how to play with others, and so on. Many teachers make an alphabet book as an ongoing class project. When too many "A" pages are collected, a separate "A" book is developed.

Ray and Glover extended the invitation to make books (picture books) to a group of preschoolers and the experience led to their authored book for teachers in *Already Ready* (2008). They developed a profound respect for the capacity of children to thoughtfully compose and create.

Teachers involved in their study and project made time, space, and materials available for "bookmaking." When child reticence or tentativeness happened after a child was offered a bookmaking opportunity, teachers explained it was an okay feeling. They stressed that three- and four-year-olds weren't expected to know everything about drawing or writing words. Instead, children were urged to do the best they could. Children were supported and came to see themselves as writers.

If a child-authored book is one of the school's books, the book corner becomes a place where the child's accomplishment is exhibited. Teachers can alert the entire group to new book titles as the books arrive and make a point to describe them before they are put on the shelves.

Child-made books require teacher preparation and help. A variety of book shapes and sizes add interest and motivation (Figure 8-6). But size should be large enough to accommodate children's degree of small muscle control. Covers made of wallpaper or contact paper over cardboard are durable. The pages of the books combine child art and child-dictated words, usually on lined print script paper, or print is enlarged with computer help. Staples, rings, yarn (string), or brads can bind pages together (Figure 8-7). Child dictation is taken word for word with no or little teacher editing.

Figure 8-6 Book shapes.

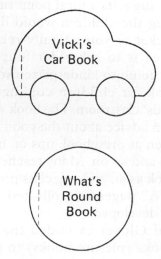

Figure 8-7 One way to bind pages.

BOOKBINDING

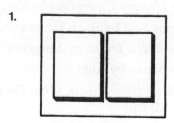

1.

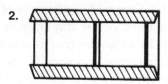

2.

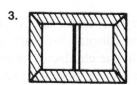

3.

One stitch on outside fold.

4.

Two stitches on inside fold.

5.

Masking tape with adhesive facing cover boards.

The following book, dictated by a four-year-old, illustrates one child's authorship.

THE WINDOW

Page 1: Once upon a time the little girl was looking out the window.

Page 2: Child's art.

Page 3: And the flowers were showing.

Page 4: Child's art.

Page 5: And the water was flushing down and she did not know it.

Page 6: Child's art.

Teacher-authored books can share a teacher's creativity and individuality. Favorite themes and enjoyed experiences can be repeatedly relived. Books containing pets' names are popular. Photographs of familiar school, neighborhood, or family settings are great conversation stimulators. Field trips and special occasions can be captured in book form.

Some educators suggest using what they call caption books with young children. Their caption books carefully place the print at the top left of the page; include photographs that give clues to the print message on the same page; and use short, meaningful sentences that repeat on succeeding pages. These writers also suggest teacher-made books that record nature walks, seasonal events, and holiday celebrations. Urging children to illustrate their favorite stories with their own art is recommended.

8-7 Book Areas and Centers

Classrooms with inviting book storage areas beckon curious browsers. Teachers have become exceptionally clever at devising eye-catching, comfortable, well-lighted, inviting, visually stimulating book-browsing classroom areas. If an educator is trying to attract children to the book collection or book display area, thought and effort may be necessary to sell the "look-at-books" activity. Use your creativity and use what is at hand, whether it is a sunny interior wall, a tabletop, an old bookcase, or an unused corner. Thematic and seasonal displays, potted plants, spotlights, and lamps have been used to lure children. Displays in or near the book center can broadcast, lure, shout, reach out, and grab the eyes and ears of passersby, forcing them to stop and pay attention.

Books should be at the child's eye level with book front covers in sight. Book-jacket wall displays and life-size book characters (drawings made by using overhead projectors to increase size, then tracing on large sheets of paper) have their own appeal. Comfort and color attract. Softly textured rugs and pillows, comfortable seating, and sprawling spaces prolong time spent

▶❚❚ **TeachSource Video 8-1**

© 2016 Cengage Learning®

Parent Involvement in School Culture: A Literacy Project

1. Linda Schwerty, a literacy specialist, is conducting a parent meeting. Parents are invited to publish a four-page book for their children's elementary school. If a similar project was undertaken at an early childhood center, how might it be planned?

2. Would you suggest using parent or child illustrations or photographs or another strategy?

3. How would you explain to parents interested in a book making project what features in a self-created picture book might capture attention and delight preschoolers? Would it be a good idea if the books became part of the classroom library? Would you add a photograph of both parent and child to the book's inside cover?

in book areas. Low round tables and plump pillows used as seating can also be inviting. Quiet, private spaces that are shielded from outside distractions and sounds and that have good lighting increase the child's ability to stay focused. Hideaways where friends can escape together and experience a book that has captured their attention are ideal.

Guidelines that outline the rules and responsibilities of book handling can be developed by the school. Rules should be designed to encourage children to return books to shelves, turn pages carefully, and respect the quietness of the area. Well-defined boundaries of library centers help books stay put. Teachers should promote the idea that using the area is a privilege and should monitor book centers frequently when younger preschoolers, who may have had little past experience with book collections and libraries, enter the area.

Rotating books by removing and storing some books from time to time and providing a different, previously stored set of books will make the area more interesting. Some centers categorize and store related books together and label them with a sign, identified picture, or drawing (such as animals, trains, things that are blue, and so on). Library books supplement the school's collection and may have special classroom-handling rules. Seasonal and holiday books are provided when possible. Paperbacks round out some collections, and multiple copies are considered for younger preschoolers' classrooms. Constant book repair is necessary in most classrooms because of heavy use. A classroom "Book Hospital" box reflects teachers' concern and esteem for books.

Teachers should browse in book centers, modeling both interest and enthusiasm when time and supervision duties permit. It is sad to think of curious children wandering into the book area, selecting a book, trying to grasp meaning from illustrations, wondering how teachers find a story within, and giving up after studying the book closely. Many teachers set up a system so that the story (or nonfiction) can be heard by using an "I-want-to-know-about-this-book" box. Children's name cards are adjacent. The child can select his book, slip his card inside, and place the card in the box. Younger children can find a name card with their picture and do the same. This system works well only if the staff finds the time to share the child-chosen book.

8-7a Group Settings

Most classrooms have areas suitable for picture-book reading in groups, besides areas for individual, self-selected browsing and places where children can be in the company of a few others. If these areas are not available, staff members can create them. The reading area should be comfortable and well lit and as far removed from interruptions and distractions as possible. Generally, lighting that comes from behind the children is preferred. Intense, bright light coming from behind the book can make it hard to see. During group readings, one center put a floor lamp in the reading area and dimmed the overhead lights. This setup worked well to cut distractions and focus the group on the reading. Another teacher brought a large packing case into the classroom with a light inside, added comfortable pillows, made a door, and called it the "Reading Box." A large, horseshoe-shaped floor pillow can increase child comfort. Many centers use small carpet sample squares for comfort and to outline individual space.

The number of children in groups is an important consideration; as the size of the group increases, intimacy, the child's ease of viewing, and the teacher's ability to be physically close to and respond to each child decreases (Photo 8-8). The ideal group size for story time ranges from five to 10 children. Unfortunately, staffing ratios may mandate a much larger group size. Some early childhood centers do "instant replays"—they have many small reading groups in succession, rather than large group reading sessions.

Most centers have developed rules about what behavior is expected from the child, whether the child chooses either to come or not come to a book-reading time, and whether a child can leave before the book's end. If the staff decides to give children a choice, usually the rule is stated thusly, "You need to find a quiet activity inside our classroom until story time is over."

By setting an example and making clear statements about handling books, the teacher can help children form good book-care habits. However, with time and use, even the sturdiest books will show wear. Teachers should be quick to show their sadness when a favorite book is torn, crayoned, or used as a building block. Some classrooms have signs reading "Books Are Friends—Handle with Care" or "Books are for looking, talking about, and sharing." Teachers need to verbally appreciate children who turn pages gently and return books to shelves or storage areas.

8-7b Resources for Finding Reading Materials

Many children's book stores carry popular new and older titles, but they are disappearing as online ordering becomes preferred. At teacher

Photo 8-8 Group size is an important consideration.

© 2015 Cengage Learning®

supply houses and school supply stores, a wide selection is often stocked, sometimes at discount prices. Teachers can contact children's book publishers for free catalogs with listings of new titles and summaries of contents or can find this information online.

Book clubs offer monthly selections of a wide variety of titles. These clubs usually reward schools with free books and teacher gifts that include posters and teaching visuals. Enough order forms for each child's parents are sent on a monthly basis. This offers parents an easy way to order books for their children by having school personnel send and receive orders.

Since 1919, the Children's Book Council has sponsored National Children's Book Week to promote reading and encourage children's enjoyment of books. A Digital Toolkit that aids teachers is often included on the Children's Book Week website. In addition, preschools that have overnight and weekend book-borrowing privileges promote book use and home enjoyment of books. The Additional Resources section at the chapter's end provides a list of books that are young children's favorites. You can help children learn the value of reading, first by falling in love with picture books yourself and then by developing your repertoire for sharing that enjoyment with children.

Summary

8-1   Describe the contents of children's books that existed before 1900.

Early books were printed to promote and improve children's moral and spiritual natures. Early American children's literature reflected English and Puritan messages. European fables contained animal stories and a few fables. In Victorian England, literature for children dealt with kings, knights, princesses, and oppressed victims.

8-2   Name four different categories of books for preschoolers.

Fiction and nonfiction are major book categories. Other book types include folk and fairy tales, poetry books, novelty books, oversized books, story songs, wordless books, concept books, predictable books, resource and reference books, alphabet books, therapeutic books, seasonal books, antibias themed books, infant and toddler books, board books, and multicultural books. Many preschool books fit into more than one category.

8-3   Discuss criteria used to select read aloud books

Many different criteria are considered when selecting read aloud books. Book features such as: is quality, has redeeming social value, contains specific child interests, offers multicultural and ethnically appropriate content, has significant and accurate content knowledge, matches children's everyday experiences, contains elements of familiarity, offers humor and fantasy, deals with universal human emotions, has desirable illustrations, includes interesting characters, may all be considered when selecting. A teacher might select a particular book for a particular teaching purpose or because the teacher can read it with enthusiasm.

8-4 Discuss suggested techniques or strategies for reading a book to a group of children.

The teacher begins with a book appropriate to classroom's particular children, and their age and interests. Instructional goals are considered. Then she arranges for comfortable seating and starts with a motivational introduction. The book is displayed so that whole pages are visible and at eye level. When reading the teacher makes eye contact, watches for feedback, speaks clearly, uses adequate volume, paces herself, and allows for children's proper hearing and ability to see. During the reading words or passages may be emphasized, key parts may be pointed out, and the teacher continually ascertains if she is holding children's attention and focus. The teacher acknowledges and discusses child remarks and questions and makes pertinent remarks moving along so as not to lose the thread of the storyline for children. If child interaction with the book is appropriate, it takes place. She makes time for ending discussion and clears up ideas, if necessary, and gives children the time to personalize what they have seen and heard.

8-5 Describe an after-book reading discussion to promote child comprehension.

Teacher behavior includes probing and asking questions that involve promoting children's deriving meaning from book features integral to the basic story. This promotes thinking about and understanding connections and relationships between people, actions, words, and ideas. Teachers help children make sense of the story by promoting knowledge and gathering, finding, or pointing out stated material in the text. She helps children remember data used to make inferences and conjectures.

8-6 Name two reasons teacher- or child-authored books might be valuable additions to a classroom book collection.

Books authored by children and their teachers can accomplish many goals, including enhancing child interest in books authored by someone he/she knows, and giving status to authorship. Authored books may contain material of mutual and familiar interest. It personalizes books, prompts going to the book collection library area, and can build a child author's confidence and feelings of self-worth. It also promotes child motivation and authorship, promotes an interest in bookmaking, allows for child creativity and expression. Authored books may contain concept knowledge and include material that forwards teaching goals.

8-7 List three suggestions for features and furnishings of a book (library) center.

A teacher, when creating an inviting book or library center, starts with considering comfortable seating, lighting, heating, and eye-catching features. The center will need adequate eye-level storage. Thematic related or seasonal displays may be added. Books are rotated from time to time as necessary and kept in good condition. Teachers develop necessary guidelines or rules concerning book handling and center use. A well-defined center with boundaries is a good idea and can be accomplished by furniture placement. The teacher becomes a resource person in book centers at times and models an interest in books. Personal individual space for children to read by themselves can be a plus feature.

Additional Resources

Children's Big Books

Crowley, J. (1986). *Mrs. Wishy Washy*. Bothell, WA: Wright Group. (Humorous.)

Hoberman, M. A. (1986). *A House Is a House for Me*. Ontario: Scholastic-TAB (Rhythm and rhyme.)

O'Donnell, E. L. (1995). *I Can't Get My Turtle to Move*. New York: Harcourt Brace School Publishers. (Predictive, colorful, and a drama enactment opportunity.)

Trumbauer, L. (1998). *Sink or Float*? Delran, NJ: Newbridge Educational Publishing. (Nonfiction, color photo illustrations.)

Tullet, H. (2007). *Juego De Colores*. Barcelona: Kokinos. (Colorful, interactive, and in Spanish.)

Multiethnic and Multicultural Children's Books

Ashley, B. (1991). *Cleversticks*. New York: Crown. (Multiracial class with Chinese-American child who questions his capabilities.)

Bruchac, J., & Ross, G. (1995). *The Story of the Milky Way*. New York: Dial Books. (Presents a Cherokee legend with colorful illustrations.)

Buchanan, K. (1994). *This House Is Made of Mud/Esta Casa Está Hecha De Lodo*. Flagstaff, AZ: Northland. (In both Spanish and English, poetic language about a home made of mud.)

Cave, K. (2003). *One Child, One Seed: A South African Counting Book*. New York: Henry Holt.

Chen, C. (2007). *On My Way to Buy Eggs*. New York: Kane/Miller. (Asian tale with an everyday problem that a child solves.)

Dale, P. (1987). *Bet You Can't*. Philadelphia: Lippincott. (African-American brother and sister clean room at bedtime.)

Garden, N. (2004). *Molly's Family*. New York: Farrar, Straus, and Giroux. (Nontraditional family.)

Garza, C. L. (2005). *Family Pictures*. San Francisco: Children's Book Press. (Multicultural families.)

Greenspun, A. A. (1991). *Daddies*. New York: Philomel. (Photographs of dads and children of diverse cultures.)

Hale, I. (1992). *How I Found a Friend*. New York: Viking. (Interracial friendship.)

Hamanka, S. (1994). *All the Colors of the Earth*. New York: Morrow Junior Books. (An exuberant, lovingly illustrated book celebrating the beauty of diverse people.)

Hoffman, M. (1987). *Nancy No-Size*. New York: Oxford University Press. (A middle child's self-concept in an urban African-American family is examined.)

Hutchins, P. (1993). *My Best Friend*. New York: Greenwillow. (Friendship between African-American children.)

Keats, E. J. (1964). *Whistle for Willie*. New York: Viking Press. (A well-known classic featuring an African-American child.)

Keller, H. (1995). *Horace*. New York: Mulberry. (About a spotted leopard who feels out of place in his adopted family of striped tigers.)

Kleven, E. (1996). *Hooray, a Pinata*. New York: Dutton. (A diverse way to celebrate birthdays and other special days.)

Machado, A. M. (1996). *Nina Bonita*. New York: Kane/Miller. (A fanciful story about a rabbit and a dark-skinned Brazilian girl.)

Marcellino, F. (1996). *The Story of Little Baboji*. New York: Harper Collins/Michael di Capua. (An authentic tale set in India.)

Morris, A. (1992). *Tools*. New York: Lothrop, Lee and Shepard Books. (Around the world encountering tool use.)

Perez, A. I. (2000). *My Very Own Room*. San Francisco: Children's Book Press. (A dream for private space.)

Pinkwater, D. M. (1997). *The Big Orange Splot*. New York: Hastings House. (Showcases diversity and pressures to conform.)

Roe, E. (1991). *Con Mi Hermano/With My Brother*. New York: Bradbury Press. (A loving relationship between Mexican-American brothers.)

Rosen, M. (1996). *This Is Our House*. Cambridge, MA: Candlewick Press. (Opens discussion concerning exclusion.)

Russo, M. (1992). *Alex Is My Friend*. New York: Greenwillow. (Child's disability handled with feeling.)

Samton, S. W. (1991). *Jenny's Journey*. New York: Viking Penguin. (Interracial friendship.)

Schaefer, C. L. (1996). *The Squiggle*. New York: Crown. (Asian child delights in imaginative play.)

Spinelli, E., & Iwai, M. (2000). *Night Shift Daddy*. New York: Hyperion Books. (Ethnic family relationships.)

Waters, K., & Slovenz-Low, M. (1990). *Lion Dancer: Ernie Wan's Chinese New Year*. New York: Scholastic. (Color photographs capture a Chinese New Year celebration in New York.)

Williams, V. B. (1990) *"More More More," Said the Baby*. New York: Greenwillow. (Love and life with multiethnic families with babies. Caldecott Honor winner.)

Zalben, J. (1988). *Beni's First Chanukah*. New York: Henry Holt. (Family traditions are experienced by a small child.)

Volumes Listing Multiethnic and Multicultural Children's Books

Bhattacharyya, R. (2010). *The Castle in the Classroom: Story As a Springboard for Early Literacy*. Portland, M. E.: Stenhouse.

Jenkins, E. C., & Austin, M. C. (1987). *Literature for Children About Asians and Asian Americans*. New York: Greenwood Press.

National Black Child Development Institute. (1995). *Young Children and African American Literature*. Washington, DC: National Association for the Education of Young Children.

Rand, D., Parker, T., & Foster, S. (1998). *Black Books Galore! Guide to Great African American Children's Books*. New York: John Wiley and Sons.

Schon, I. (1978). *Books in Spanish for Children and Adults: An Annotated Guide*. Metuchen, NJ: Scarecrow Press.

Favorite Children's Books

Aylesworth, J. (2003). *Goldilocks and the Three Bears*. New York: Scholastic. (An inquisitive child encounters problems; repetitive dialogue; a classic tale.)

Brown, M. W. (1938, 1965). *The Dead Bird*. New York: Young Scott Books. (Deals tenderly with the death of a bird.)

Carle, E. (1984). *The Very Hungry Caterpillar*. New York: Penguin-Putnam. (The hungry caterpillar eats through the pictures and emerges as a butterfly on the last page.)

Chorao, K. (1977). *Lester's Overnight*. New York: E. P. Dutton. (Family humor about a child's overnight plans and his teddy bear.)

Ets, M. H. (1955). *Play with Me*. New York: Viking Press. (A lesson to learn on the nature of animals.)

Flack, M. (1932). *Ask Mr. Bear*. New York: Macmillan. (The search for just the right birthday present for a loved one.)

Freeman, D. (1954). *Beady Bear*. New York: Viking Press. (Meet Beady and his courage, independence, and frailty.)

Freeman, D. (1968). *Corduroy*. New York: Viking Press. (The department store teddy who longs for love.)

Freymann, S., & Elffers, J. (2006). *Fast Food*. New York: Arthur A. Levine. (Contemporary life.)

Gag, W. (1928). *Millions of Cats*. New York: Coward-McCann. (Word pleasure and magic—a favorite with both teachers and children.)

Greene, R. G. (2003). *At Grandma's*. New York: Henry Holt. (Grandma's house can be a special place.)

Guilfoile, E. (1957). *Nobody Listens to Andrew*. New York: Scholastic Book Services. (An "adults often-ignore-what-children-say" theme.)

Hazen, B. S. (1974). *The Gorilla Did It*. New York: Atheneum Press. (A mother's patience with a fantasizing child. Humorous.)

Henkes, K. (2005). *Chrysanthemum*. New York: Scholastic (A new classic.)

Hoban, R. (1964). *A Baby Sister for Frances*. New York: Harper and Row. (Frances, "so human," deals with the new arrival.)

Hutchins, P. (1968). *Rosie's Walk*. New York: Macmillan. (A fox is outsmarted.)

Hutchins, P. (1971). *Changes, Changes*. New York: Macmillan. (Illustrations of block constructions tell a wordless story of the infinite changes in forms.)

Hutchins, P. (1976). *Goodnight Owl!* New York: Macmillan. (Riddled with repetitive dialogue; a delightful tale of bedtime.)

Jenkins, S., & Page, R. (2003). *What Do You Do With a Tail Like This?* Boston: Houghton Mifflin. (Humor.)

Keats, E. J. (1967). *Peter's Chair.* New York: Harper and Row. (A delightful tale of family life.)

Kennedy, J. (1987). *The Teddy Bears' Picnic.* New York: Peter Bedrick Books. (A delight for the child who has his own teddy bear.)

Kraus, R. (1973). *Leo the Late Bloomer.* New York: Dutton. (Wonderful color illustrations and a theme that emphasizes individual development.)

Krauss, R. (1945). *The Carrot Seed.* New York: Harper and Row. (The stick-to-it-tiveness of a child's faith makes this story charming.)

Leonni, L. (1949). *Little Blue and Little Yellow.* New York: Astor-Honor. (A classic. Collages of torn paper introduce children to surprising color transformations, blended with a story of friendship.)

McCloskey, R. (1948). *Blueberries for Sal.* New York: Viking Press. (The young of the two species meet.)

Mosel, A. (1968). *Tiki Tiki Tembo.* New York: Holt, Rinehart and Winston. (A folktale that tickles the tongue in its telling. Repetitive.)

Potter, B. (1987). *Peter Rabbit's ABC.* Bergenfield, NJ: Frederick Warne. (Clever alphabet letter presentation.)

Provensen, A. (2003). *A Day in the Life of Murphy.* New York: Holiday House. (A memorable animal story for children who own pets.)

Raskin, E. (1975). *Nothing Ever Happens on My Block.* New York: Atheneum Press. (The child discovers a multitude of happenings in illustrations.)

Scott, A. H. (1972). *On Mother's Lap.* New York: McGraw-Hill. (There's no place like mother's lap!)

Segal, L. (1970). *Tell Me a Mitzi.* New York: Farrar. (New York City life.)

Shulevitz, U. (1969). *Rain Rain Rivers.* New York: Farrar, Straus and Giroux. (Illustrative fine art.)

Slobodkina, E. (1947). *Caps for Sale.* New York: William R. Scott. (A tale of a peddler, some monkeys, and their monkey business. Word play and gentle humor.)

Stevens, J. (1987). *The Town Mouse and the Country Mouse.* New York: Holiday House. (One's own house is best.)

Stone, J. (1971). *The Monster at the End of This Book.* Racine, WI: Western Publishing Co. (Suspense and surprise.)

Viorst, J. (1971). *The Tenth Good Thing About Barney.* New York: Atheneum. (Loss of family pet and positive remembrances.)

Viorst, J. (1976). *Alexander and the Terrible, Horrible, No Good, Very Bad Day.* New York: Atheneum Press. (Everyone relates to the "everything-can-go-wrong" theme.)

Zion, G. (1956). *Harry the Dirty Dog.* New York: Harper and Row. (Poor lost Harry gets so dirty his family does not recognize him.)

Finding Recommended and Award-Winning Books

American Library Association. (2003). *The Newbery and Caldecott Awards: A Guide to Medal and Honor Books.* Chicago: Author.

Deeds, S. (2001). *The New Books Kids Like.* Chicago: American Library Association.

Gillespie, J. T. (2002). *Best Books for Children: Preschool Through Grade 6.* New Providence, NJ: R. R. Bowker.

Children's Books Cited in This Chapter

Ahlberg, J., & Ahlberg, A. (1979). *Each Peach Pear Plum: An "I Spy" Story.* New York: Viking Press.

Aliki. (1962). *My Five Senses.* New York: Crowell.

Anno, M. (1975). *Anno's Counting Book.* New York: Crowell.

Asch, F. (1979). *Popcorn: A Frank Asch Bear Story.* New York: Parents Magazine Press.

Bragg, M. C. (1930). *The Little Engine That Could.* New York: Platt & Munk.

Chodos-Irvine, M. (2008). *Best, Best Friends.* New York: Harcourt.

de Paola, T. (1978). *Pancakes for Breakfast.* New York: Harcourt Brace Jovanovich.

Duff, M. K. (1972). *Johnny and His Drum.* New York: H. Z. Walck.

Gág, W. (1928). *Millions of Cats.* New York: Coward-McCann.

Garden, N. (2004). *Molly's Family.* New York: Farrar, Straus and Giroux.

Heller, R. (1981). *Chickens Aren't the Only Ones.* New York: Grosset & Dunlap.

Hudson, C. W. (1987). *Afro-Bets ABC Book.* Orange, NJ: Just Us Books.

Keats, E. J. (1962). *The Snowy Day.* New York: Viking Press.

Kellogg, S. (1971). *Can I Keep Him?* New York: Dial Press.

Kennedy, J. (1987). *The Teddy Bears' Picnic.* New York: Bedrick Books.

Komaiko, L. (1987). *Annie Bananie.* New York: Harper and Row.

Marshall, J. (1972). *George and Martha.* Boston: Houghton Mifflin.

Martin, B., & Carle, E. (1970). *Brown Bear, Brown Bear, What Do You See?* New York: Holt, Rinehart and Winston.

Martin, B., Jr., & Archambault, J. (1989). *Chicka Chicka Boom Boom.* New York: Simon & Schuster.

Mayer, M. (1974). *What Do You Do With a Kangaroo?* New York: Four Winds Press.

McCloskey, R. (1941). *Make Way for Ducklings.* New York: Viking Press.

Miller, J. (1983). *Farm Counting Book.* Englewood Cliffs, NJ: Prentice Hall.

Munsch, R. (1986, 2011). *Love You Forever.* New York: Firefly books.

Peet, B. (1961). *Huge Harold.* Boston: Houghton Mifflin.

Roffey, M. (1983). *Home Sweet Home.* New York: Coward-McCann.

Sendak, M. (1963). *Where the Wild Things Are.* New York: Harper and Row.

Turkle, B. (1976). *Deep in the Forest.* New York: Dutton.

Yabuuchi, M. (1983). *Animals Sleeping.* New York: Philomel Books.

Zolotow, C. (1974). *My Grandson Lew.* New York: Harper and Row.

Readings

Anderson, N. A. (2007). *What Should I Read Aloud? A Guide to 200 Best Selling Picture Books.* Newark, DE: International Reading Association.

Bang, M. (2000). *Picture This: How Picture Books Work.* New York: Chronicle.

Jalongo, M. R. (2009). *Learning to Listen, Listening to Learn.* Washington, DC: National Association for the Education of Young Children.

Keifer, B. Z., & Tyson, C. A. (2010). *Charlotte Huck's Children's Literature.* New York: McGraw-Hill.

Schon, I. (2001, March). Los ninos y los libros: Noteworthy books in Spanish for the very young. *Young Children, 56*(2), 94–95.

Temple, C. A., Martinez, M., & Yokota, J. (2010). *Children's Books in Children's Hands.* Boston: Allyn and Bacon.

Mantzicopoulos P., & Patrick, H. (2010). The seesaw is the machine that goes up and down: Young children's narrative responses to science-related informational text. *Early Education and Development: 21*(3): 412–444.

Trelease, J. (1995.2008). *The Read-Aloud Handbook.* New York: Viking-Penguin.

Helpful Websites

Miami University

http://dlp.lib.miamioh.edu

Contains information concerning 5000 abstracts of picture books for preschool through grade 3.

American Library Association

http://www.ala.org

Publications and awards of interest to teachers.

International Reading Association

http://www.reading.org

Download Children's Choices or IRA Choices reading lists.

Parents Magazine

http://parents.com

Search for best books by age.

9 > Storytelling

Objectives

After reading this chapter, you should be able to:

9.1 Describe how storytelling can help language growth.

9.2 Identify three suggested story selection criteria.

9.3 Discuss types of stories commonly used for preschool storytelling.

9.4 List reasons to practice stories before telling.

9.5 Describe two teaching aids that might be used in a storytelling activity.

9.6 Describe the value of promoting child dictation stories.

naeyc NAEYC Program Standards

3G14 Teachers demonstrate their knowledge of content and developmental areas by creating experiences that engage children in purposeful and meaning learning related to key curriculum concepts.

3G01 Teachers have and use a variety of teaching strategies that include a broad range of approaches and responses.

2E04 Children have varied opportunities to retell and reenact events in storybooks.

DAP Developmentally Appropriate Practice (DAP)

3M1 Teachers give children daily opportunities for creative expression and aesthetic appreciation.

3M5 Teachers do not provide a model that they expect children to copy. However, they demonstrate new techniques or uses of materials to expand children's options.

3H7 Teachers help children use communication and language as tools for thinking and learning.

COMMON CORE Common Core State Standards for English Language Arts and Literacy

W.CCR.9 Draw evidence from literary or informational texts to support analysis, reflection, and research.

W.CCR.3 Write narratives to develop real or imagined experiences or events using effective techniques, well-chosen details, and well-structured event sequences.

Hey! Godzilla!

A tree in our yard was perfect for climbing, with a smooth trunk and a thick layer of tan bark underneath. I watched as Fenton climbed up and out on a limb. He was hanging on the limb with both hands, feet dangling a foot or so above the ground. He seemed unable to let go and unable to swing his legs back up on the limb. As I walked closer to help him, he yelled, "Godzilla help me." Other boys, closer than I, grabbed his legs. He let go, knocking them down with him. They rolled on the ground unhurt. Then Pierre jumped up and said, "My turn," and he headed up the tree.

Questions to Ponder

1. Could you create a short story with a beginning, middle, and end about a boy stuck in a tree?

2. How would you describe this tree to give listeners a vivid mental image?

Storytelling is a medium that an early childhood teacher can develop and use to increase a child's enjoyment of language. When good stories are told by a skilled storyteller, the child listens intently; mental images may be formed.

Storytelling enables teachers to share their life experiences and create and tell stories in their own way. It is a teacher's gift of time and imagination. Your style of storytelling will be individual and unique, and you will be free to improvise. Beginning teachers do not worry that their version of a favorite story differs from others.

Storytelling can be defined as the seemingly easy, spontaneous, intimate sharing of a narrative with one or many persons. The storyteller relates, pictures, imagines, builds what happens, and crafts characters, all of which is manifested through the storyteller's voice and body. Storytelling is the act that essentially makes humans human. It defines us as a species. We are shaped by the stories we hear. In storytelling, children leave the "here and now" and go beyond what is seen and at hand. They experience the symbolic potential of language with words themselves, the main source of meaning independent of the time and place they are spoken. Children

create imaginative scenarios quickly and easily in everyday play situations.

Early childhood teachers recognize the importance of storytelling in a full language arts curriculum. Good stories that are well told have fascinated young listeners since ancient times. Storytelling is a form of expressive artistry, and storytelling remains one of the oldest and most effective art forms. The oral story, be it aesthetic or pedagogical, has great value. It seems to be a part of the human personality to use it and want it. The art of the storyteller is an important, valuable ingredient in the lives of children.

America is rediscovering the magic of storytelling. Storytelling festivals are now held throughout the United States. There's also a National Storytelling Festival, which is a three-day storytelling celebration in Jonesborough, Tennessee. Regional, intergenerational, multicultural, and multiethnic story themes delight audiences.

In many cultures, oral stories have passed on the customs, accumulated wisdom, traditions, songs, and legends. Storytelling is as old as language itself. Storytellers in the ancient world often traveled from village to village enlightening and entertaining. They gained status as "the keepers" of the groups' treasured oral history and unwritten stories.

How could one describe skilled storytellers? They are gloriously alive, live close to the heart of things, have known solitude and silence, and have felt deeply. They have come to know the power of the spoken word. They can remember incredible details about a good story that interests them. Preschool teachers may know silence only at nap times, but they indeed live close to the heart of young children's forming character, personality, and growing intellect. When books or pictures are not used to tell a story, teachers tell a story with their face, gestures, words, and voice. The child pictures the story in her mind as the plot unfolds.

9-1 Storytelling and Literacy

The promotion of oral literacy is an important consideration for preschool program planners. Oral literacy involves a shared background and knowledge of orally told stories plus a level of competence. Being able to tell a story well depends on a number of factors, including observation of techniques. Natural storytellers, if they exist, are overshadowed by storytellers who have practiced the art. Some adult job hunters find telling a story is a requested part of their job interview and is used to assess intelligence, communication ability, and literacy.

Preschools are sure to offer picture-book readings, but storytelling may be neglected. Some teachers shy away from the activity for a variety of reasons, including not feeling like they can hold their child audience's attention. Teachers can increase their own storytelling skills by observing practiced storytellers, taking classes, or engaging in self-study (Photo 9-1). The best suggestion for a teacher wishing to develop her storytelling skills is to start by relating short, significant happenings from daily life. Keep it lively. Four-year-olds make a better audience for the beginning storyteller than do younger children.

As children observe and listen to the teacher's storytelling, they notice common elements, including beginnings, middles, and story endings. They discover some stories vary little between tellers. They imitate techniques using hand and body gesturing, facial expression, and vocal variation; they speak in character **dialogue,** and they may even copy dramatic pause. They also may attempt to make their audience laugh or add suspense to their stories.

Acredolo and Goodwyn (2000) suggest how young children begin to get "the idea of story":

> . . . They hear important people in their lives talking about the past: "Remember what we did today? We went to the zoo! And do you remember

what animals we saw?" What's more it's clear that these people are especially pleased when the children themselves also remember. The implication is clear. Adults literally teach their children about beginnings, middles, and endings by structuring their own narratives in an organized way: "Remember we saw the flamingos when we first went though the gate? And then we went into the snake house and we got scared." (p. 16)

Sharing oral stories and verbally putting daily happenings into words can be cherished for what they are—the building blocks of thinking and imagining, describing, creating, expressing ideas, and later achieving writing and reading skill. Gallas (2003) suggests that not only is the storyteller absorbed in thought during the storytelling experience, but the audience is as well.

> Over the years as I have watched successive classes create stories for sharing time, I have seen that the storytelling child does one kind of imaginative, synthesizing work that takes skill and thought. The listening children, however, do another kind of imaginative, synthesizing work in order to become part of the story. That work is personal, social, and intellectual. (p. 176)

Educators try daily to really engage children in talk and to celebrate its occurrence. Forget quiet classrooms; strive for talk-filled rooms balanced with quiet times! Children attempt to make sense of the stories they hear and try to fit

Photo 9-1 Watching a skilled storyteller may increase teacher skill.

dialogue — a conversation between two or more persons or between a person and something else.

them into their lives. Stories can give meaning to events by making connections between them and the real world. The content of stories can have a lasting effect on children.

One benefit that is fostered by teacher storytelling is child story making. Other possible child competencies and understandings promoted by storytelling experiences include developing a sense of oral power and group inclusion. A child may understand he has personal stories to tell and becomes curious about others' stories. His sense of drama grows and storytelling may heighten his awareness of phonetic and phonemic elements in words. He may get the idea that gestures can enhance storytelling by influencing audience moods and feelings and also help clarify ideas. If exposed to multicultural stories, he may more fully realize cultural similarities and differences.

Much research encourages teachers to promote each child's oral development and the dictation of child-created stories and subsequent dramatization. The teacher then reads the child's work to child groups. Besides the obvious benefits of the speaking and writing involvement in this activity, it is based on child-relevant material. Experts believe that this kind of activity primes children's inner feelings and thinking processes for change and growth, and increases self-awareness and awareness of self in relation to others. All in all, it is a powerful language arts approach.

Gainsley (2003) describes a teacher dictation activity that took place before a firehouse field trip. Children were asked what they might see. The teacher made a list that was checked off during the trip. Later the teacher and the children discussed the things they saw that were on the list, along with other things children observed and recalled. The same approach could be used before, during, and after a storytelling experience. If the teacher said, "I've a story about a beach called Surfer's Cove. What do you think might be talked about in a story about a surfer's beach?" Other teacher dictation ideas cited by Gainsley were creating grocery lists, creating new verses for songs, and writing letters and cards.

9-1a Telling Stories Without Books

Chapter 8 described the merits and uses of picture books with young children. Storytelling without books has its own unique set of enjoyed language pleasures. Storytelling is direct, intimate conversation. The well-told story's power to hold children spellbound is widely recognized. It is the intimate, personal quality of storytelling as well as the power of the story itself that accomplishes these minor miracles. Yet in order to work this spell, a story must be learned, remembered, and so delightfully told that it catches and holds the attention of the most inveterate wrigglers.

Teachers observe children's reactions as they tell a story. A quizzical look on a child's face can help the teacher know when to clarify or rephrase for understanding. A teacher's voice can increase the story's drama in parts when children are deeply absorbed.

Many educators have noted how quickly and easily ideas and new words are grasped through storytelling (Photo 9-2). This is an additional benefit. Stories are told to acquaint young children with this enjoyable oral language art. Obvious moralizing or attempts to teach facts by using stories usually turn children away.

Storytelling may occur at almost any time during the course of the day, inside or outside. No books or props are necessary, but use of them may focus attention and add to the child's enjoyment. Teachers are free to relate stories in their own words and manner. Children show by their actions what parts of the story are of high interest. The storyteller can increase children's enjoyment by emphasizing these features.

9-1b Storytelling Goals

A teacher seeks to become a skilled storyteller so that she can model storytelling skill while providing another avenue to the development of oral competence. Another goal is to acquire a repertoire of stories that offer children a variety of experiences. The teacher's goals also include:

- increasing children's enjoyment of oral language.
- making young children familiar with oral storytelling.
- encouraging children's storytelling and authorship.
- increasing children's vocabulary.
- increasing children's confidence as speakers.
- increasing children's awareness of story sequence and structure.

Photo 9-2 A story about a singer prompts children to use cylinder blocks.

© 2015 Cengage Learning®

- increasing children's story comprehension and higher level thinking skills.
- promoting oral skill, use, and expression of ideas.

Mathias (2006) would add these goals:

- helping children gain listening skills.
- extending young children's knowledge of facts and fantasy.
- stimulating listener's imagination.
- creating an appetite for words.
- introducing audience experiences.

Storytelling is a wonderful way to promote understanding of audience behaviors and performer behaviors. Teachers experience rewarding feelings when their technique and story combine to produce audience enjoyment and pleasure. Child storytellers gain tremendous insights into the performing arts, their own abilities, and the power of orally related stories. Most reading experts agree that oral competence enhances ease in learning to read and promotes understanding of what is read.

Thoughtful writers have questioned the wisdom of always exposing children to illustrations at story time. By not allowing children to develop mental images, they believe we have possibly distracted children from attaining personal meaning. On the other hand, discussing what children see in a photograph or drawing and conjecturing with them about what is happening, the details they notice, the feelings that they or the person pictured might be having, and what might happen next can be both a visual literacy experience and a motivational strategy to encourage child storytelling. There are benefits children can accrue from both "with visuals" and "without visuals" literacy experiences.

9-1c Using Picture Books for Storytelling

At times, a picture book is the source for storytelling. The teacher later introduces the book and makes it available in the classroom's book center for individual follow-up. Used this way, storytelling motivates interest in books. Many picture books, however, do not lend themselves to storytelling form because illustrations are such an integral part of the experience (Photo 9-3). Books that have been successfully used as the basis for storytelling can be handled in unique ways. An experienced teacher using professional presentation skills in a storytelling experience using *Caps for Sale* by Esphyr Slobodkina would make it an audience participation story and would shake a fist at the monkeys. The audience, with only the slightest encouragement, might shake its fists at the peddler.

Photo 9-3 Some picture books are not good sources for oral storytelling.

The following books are recommended for teacher storytelling:

Asbjornsen, P. C. (1972). *The three billy goats gruff.* New York: Harcourt, Brace, Jovanovich.

Fleming, D. (2006). *The cow who clucked.* New York: Henry Holt.

Galdone, P. (1961). *The old woman and her pig.* New York: McGraw-Hill.

Martin. D. (2006). *All for pie, pie for all.* Cambridge, MA: Candlewick Press.

During and After Storytelling Discussion. Storybook discussions can aid children's narrative abilities. Justice and Pence (2006) urge teachers to help children master narrative skills and to use literate language. Literate language, as they define it, is a specific type of language that is highly precise and is necessary when little context is available—such as telling about an incident or happening in the past without a visual. Justice and Pence suggest that the following discussion activities are aligned to the objectives that characterize important early achievement in narrative knowledge.

1. to discuss the sequence of events in a story

2. to discuss what happens to characters in a story

3. to discuss the location or setting of a story

4. to discuss reported speech used by characters in a story

5. to identify the high point of a story (pp. 72–73)

9-1d Multicultural Story Resources

An increasing number of multicultural picture books are in print as publishers strive to react to America's changing and diverse school populations. The following are suggested as storytelling sources.

Escardo, M. (2006). *The three little pigs/Los tres cerditos.* San Francisco: Chronicle Books.

Hudson, C. (1999). *Glo goes shopping.* East Orange, NJ: Just Us Books.

Rylant, C. (2007). *Alligator boy.* New York: Harcourt.

Rocco, J. (2007). *Wolf! Wolf!* New York: Hyperion.

Tsubakiyama, M. (1999). *Mei-Mei loves the morning.* Morton Grove, IL: Albert Whitman & Co.

An increasing number of classrooms promote acting out stories after they are read. Immediately following this acting experience, children are urged to create their own stories. These can be taped and later written by adults. These child stories can also be enacted with the story's author or teacher selecting her actors or with actor volunteers.

9-1e Other Story Sources

Story ideas can be found in collections, anthologies, resource books, children's magazines, films, or story recordings. A story idea can also be self-created. Teachers shouldn't overlook nonfiction books, nursery rhymes, poetry, story songs, or stories created by other teachers or their families (Soderman, Clevenger, Kent, 2013). A teacher-created story can fill a void. In any group of young children there are special interests and problems. Stories can expand interest and give children more information on a subject. Problems can possibly be solved by the stories and conversations that take place.

New teachers may not yet have confidence in their storytelling abilities, so learning some basic techniques for selecting, creating, and telling stories can help build confidence. This, together with the experience gained by presenting the stories to children, should convince the teacher that storytelling is enjoyable for preschoolers and rewarding to the teacher.

Teachers telling children personal stories about their lives actually "model" storytelling. They also let children know that their actions and words are the stuff of stories too. Gestures, facial expressions, body language, and variety in tone of voice are observed. This type of storytelling is a natural part of social interaction. With young children, short anecdotes and humorous life incidents work well. "News of the Day Time" is often included in daily schedules.

Many stories can be introduced through song. Some may know of the delightful folk story song that begins "A fox went out on a chilly night" and tells of the animal's adventures. These types of songs may include opportunities for children's oral, physical, and creative expression or for child involvement in the storytelling. A creative teacher can use story songs to complement, extend, and reinforce a multitude of classroom activities. Vocabulary meanings are often more apparent to children when learned in the context of a story song.

Simple, quick definitions by teachers are offered in a conversational tone. Imagine the fun involved in a story song about the saga of a lump of dough becoming a loaf of bread: ". . . and they pushed and pulled me. Oh, how they pushed and pulled" or "It's warm in here. I'm getting hot. Look at me. I'm growing and turning golden brown."

9-2 Story Selection

The selection of a story is as important as the selection of a book because stories seem to have individual personalities. Searching for a story that appeals to the teller and that can be eagerly shared is well worth the time. A few well-chosen and well-prepared stories suiting the individual teacher almost always ensure a successful experience for all. The following selection criteria are commonly used.

1. Age-Level Appropriateness

Is the story told in simple, easily understood words? Is it familiar in light of the child's life experiences? Is it frightening? Can the child profit from traits of the characters?

2. Plot

Does the setting create a stage for what is to come? Is there action? Is there something of interest to resolve? Does the story begin with some action or event? Does it build to a climax with some suspense? Does it have a timely, satisfying conclusion? Are characters introduced as they appear?

The stories you will be searching for will have one central **plot**; a secondary plot may confuse children. Action-packed stories where one event successfully builds to another hold audience attention.

3. Style

Does the story use repetition, rhyme, or silly words? Does it have a surprise ending? Does it include directly quoted conversations or child involvement with speaking or movements? Does the mood help the plot develop?

4. Values

Are the values and models presented appropriate for today's children? Screen for ethnic, cultural, and gender stereotypes that would lead you to exclude the story or discuss the issue with children.

---

plot — the structure of the action of a story.

5. Memorable Characters

Look for a small number of colorful characters who are distinct entities in contrast to the main character and each other. One should be able to identify and recognize character traits.

6. Sensory and Visual Images

The visual and sensory images evoked by stories add interest. For example, phrases like "gingerbread cookies, warm and golden" rather than "cookie" and the "velvet soft fur" rather than "fur" create different mental images. Taste, smell, sight, sound, and tactile descriptions create richness and depth.

7. Additional Selection Criteria

Elements that make stories strong candidates for young children include stories with an economy of words, a polished quality, and tales with a universal truth, suspense, or surprise.

8. Themes and Story Structure

Many well-known and loved stories concern a problem that is insightfully solved by the main character. They begin by introducing a setting and characters and have a body of events that moves the story forward to a quick, satisfying conclusion. The story line is strong, clear, and logical. One category of stories described as cautionary seems to have been designed to keep children safe by teaching a truth or moral, consequently helping children make wise decisions. Tales can be selected based upon their versatility and the perceived needs of an individual child or a particular group of children.

> Storytellers are the direct medium between the story and the audience, able to change pace, alter or explain a difficult point, dramatize or play down an event, according to the needs of those listening. (Mathias, 2006, p. 9)

Teachers intent on increasing the vocabulary have the opportunity to introduce, emphasize, define, and weave in specific words of their choice into stories. **DAP**

9. Storyteller Enthusiasm

Is the story well liked by the teller? Does the teller feel comfortable with it? Is it a story the teller will be eager to share?

Finding a story you love may make it easier for the child to enjoy the story you tell. The easiest door to open for a child is one that leads to something you love yourself. All good teachers know this. And all good teachers know the ultimate reward: the marvelous moment when the spark you are breathing bursts into a flame that henceforth will burn brightly on its own (Photo 9-4).

Photo 9-4 A classroom prop can introduce a teacher's story.

© 2016 Cengage Learning®

MacDonald (1996) advises:

Just jump in. Storytelling is like swimming. You can't do it by sitting on the bank. You have to jump in and start dog paddling. You take a story that you love and think would be fun to tell, and you just start telling it. You keep on doing it until you get good at it. It's that simple, but you've got to start. You'll never do it sitting on the bank. (p. 13)

9-3 Types of Stories

Some stories, particularly folktales and fairy tales, have been polished to near perfection through generations of use. Classic tales and folktales may contain dated words and phrases, but these might be important story parts that add to the story's charm. In retelling the story to young children, a brief explanation of these types of terms may be necessary. A **fable** is a simple story in which animals frequently point out lessons (morals), which are contained in the fable's last line.

Many great stories, called **participation stories**, have opportunities for active child involvement and the use of props. Props, such as pictures, costumes, and other objects, may spark and hold interest. An old cowboy hat worn by the teacher during the telling of a Western tale may add to the mood and can later be worn by children in play or during a child's attempt at storytelling.

Repetitive phrases or word rhythms are used in all types of stories, and chanting or singing may be necessary in the telling. If these aren't present, the teacher can create them and add them. Some tales, such as the adventures of Anansi, a spider of African origin, have a rhythm and cadence found in no other stories. Anansi stories, researchers believe, exist today because of an African oral storytelling tradition.

Stories of children of color are a natural part of the curriculum. Teachers should try to avoid the tendency to just look for stories in their own cultural and ethnic background. The right story, regardless of the characters' ethnicity, will fit emotionally, intellectually, and physically.

9-3a Story Ideas

Almost any life adventure or happening and any classroom-inspired story works well when it has a touch of drama. Don't be afraid to tell stories

other teachers find unsuccessful, and borrow their good ones, too!

Classic Tales

Goldilocks and the Three Bears

Little Red Riding Hood

The Three Little Pigs

The Billy Goats Gruff

The Little Red Hen

The Gingerbread Boy

From Aesop's Fables

The Lion and the Mouse

The Hare and the Tortoise

The Ant and the Grasshopper

Traditional Stories

Hans Christian Andersen, *Ugly Duckling*

Arlene Mosel, *Tikki Tikki Tembo*

Florence Heide, *Sebastian*

Beatrix Potter, *Tale of Peter Rabbit*

It is wise for beginning teachers to not waste their time on material that does not inspire them to feel, "I can't wait to tell this!" You are sure to find such stories if you look.

9-4 Practice and Preparation

When a teacher has selected a story, a few careful readings are in order. Try to determine the story's main message and meaning. Next, look closely at the introduction that describes the setting and characters. Study Figure 9-1 and analyze how the selected story fits this pattern. The initial setting besides describing location and characters often sets up a problem or dilemma. The story can be outlined on a four-by-six-inch (or larger) cue card to jog your memory during practice sessions (Figure 9-2). Memorizing beginning and ending lines and interior chants or songs is suggested. Once the story rolls out effortlessly, the storyteller fine-tunes it by practicing

---

fable — a short tale in prose or verse that teaches a moral, usually with talking animals or inanimate objects as main characters.

participation stories — stories with some feature children can enact through physical movements, verbal expression, or both.

Figure 9-1 Common and classic story pattern form.

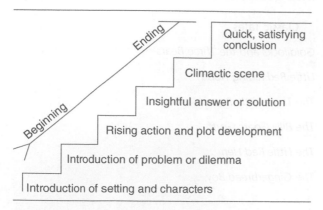

- Ending — Quick, satisfying conclusion
- Climactic scene
- Insightful answer or solution
- Beginning — Rising action and plot development
- Introduction of problem or dilemma
- Introduction of setting and characters

dialogue, and identifying pauses, gesturing, and facial expressions. Particular attention should be given to the rising action in the story's body so that one event builds on another until a quick, satisfying conclusion is reached.

In many cultural rituals, an air of magic, soft flickering embers, were part of the storytelling experience. African storytellers would begin, "A story, a story, let it come, let it go." Ritual can mean entering a particular "distraction-free" classroom area, lighting a candle, wearing a special teacher hat, dimming the lights, saying a chant, or engaging in a special finger play that

Figure 9-2 Cue and file card example.

Intro. "Once upon a time, there were four little rabbits, Flopsy, Mopsy, Cottontail, and Peter. They lived with their mother in a sand-bank, underneath the root of a very big fir tree."

Theme. Mind your mother.

Problem. Peter disobeys and goes into McGregor's garden.

Rising action.

Peter squeezes under garden gate and eats a lot.

McGregor sees him.

McGregor chases him, and he loses a shoe.

Peter gets caught in a gooseberry net and loses his jacket.

Peter hides in the tool shed in a can full of water.

Peter sneezes, almost gets caught, but jumps out a window.

Peter cries and sees cat (another danger).

Peter makes a dash for the gate and gets free.

Peter gets home without clothes and shoes, goes to sleep, and misses dinner. Mother serves him tea.

Ending lines.

"But Flopsy, Mopsy, and Cottontail had bread and milk and blackberries for supper. And that's the end of the Tale of Peter Rabbit!"

settles and brings anticipation. One clever teacher created a story sack and reached inside and slowly raised her hand to her mouth before beginning. Another teacher found only short, action-packed stories containing many move-the-body features appealed to his group of three-year-olds.

Use the following steps in preparing a story: The first step is to divide the story into units of action. As you read the story, you will notice that most divide into an easily definable series of actions, scenes, or episodes; these can be summarized in brief form, and then the sequence can be learned. The second task is to identify those sections that do need to be memorized verbatim. This may include some words, some repeated phrases, or perhaps some larger sections. A discerning storyteller learns verbatim these repeated sections, because the repetition encourages children to join in as the teller recites the lines. As you tell a story, your eyes might be constantly roaming the group, touching every face and drawing each listener back into the story over and over again. Many stories come to life and grab attention; you will notice changes in the children's behavior.

Select a setting with few distractions where everyone can hear and seating is comfortable. Do not begin until listeners are ready. Be at a level to maintain eye contact and prepare an introduction that piques children's interest. Use a prop, or tell something about the story's source or author, or discuss a related event, or ask a question to focus attention (Photo 9-5). Your opening phrase is your bridge between the world of ordinary conversation and the world of the story, and this crossing is best when both magical and deliberate.

9-4a Additional Techniques

The following storytelling techniques and tips should be kept in mind.

- Guard against sounding mechanical. Tell the story in your own personal way.
- Develop story sequence pictures. These can be mental images.
- Practice before a mirror or with another staff member.
- Use gestures.
- Maintain eye contact by scanning the group during the telling; watch for children's interest or restlessness.

Photo 9-5 Using pictures or photos to introduce the setting in your story is sometimes successful.

© 2015 Cengage Learning®

- The teacher should pace the storytelling by going faster during exciting or fast-action parts and slower in serious parts. Adventure stories may feature the unknown or unexpected and include elements of excitement and surprise.

- Use a clear, firm voice. Try changing voice volume and tone to fit the story; in some parts of the story a whisper may be most effective. Change your voice to fit the characters when they speak, if you feel comfortable doing so.

- Learn to lengthen or shorten a story for maximum effect and involvement of the audience (Mathias, 2006).

- Interrupt the story if necessary to explain some item, event, or action that does not seem clear to the audience.

- Don't worry about retelling a story exactly as before, but stick to the sequence of story events.

- Involve the children often, especially with repetitions, rhymes or actions, silly words, or appropriate questions, if the story lends itself to this.

- Sit close to the group; make sure all are comfortable before beginning.

- Include teacher's and children's names and familiar places in the community.

- Start by telling little personal stories about your family, pets, and daily happenings, if you are a novice; move on to simple stories with lots of repetition.

- Seek out talented storytellers in your community to observe your storytelling or to appear as guest storytellers in your classroom.

- Become very familiar with any pronunciations, including proper names and foreign or unfamiliar terms in stories.

- Use dramatic pauses to build suspense, after an exclamation, or to facilitate transitions between story events.

- Try to communicate characters' attitudes and motivations.

- Consider the flavor and language of the particular tradition from which the story comes.

- Let the story unfold as you picture scenes in your mind.

- Slow down. Some tales are best shared when spoken at half of normal conversation speed.

- Move your body with your story.

A storyteller who sees that children are losing interest in a story is free to make changes in it, based on intuition and knowledge of the group. Others would disagree with changing well-known, classic tales, but they do advise changing one's style, pace, or voice volume to draw listeners back to the story. It is important to remember that even the best storytellers have an occasional flop. If the storyteller is not able to draw the children back to the story, the story may be ended very quickly and tried at a later time, using a revised version.

9-4b Teacher-Created Stories

Many teachers find that they have a talent for creating stories and find that a popular character in one story can have further adventures in the next. Remember that "bad guys" in stories are enjoyed as much as "good guys." Whenever a teacher cannot find a story that seems tailor-made for a particular group of children, she can create one. Take care that themes do not always revolve around "mother knows best" episodes, and watch for sexism and stereotypes when creating a story.

9-4c Telling Stories for an Educational Purpose

If the story includes an important concept, *content* needs to be creatively conceived and made interesting. It can be made interesting by relating it to children's lives. *Motivation* is enhanced when children identify with some story element. Interactive storytelling, where children have some part in the telling, engages unmotivated learners.

Timing involves telling a story in a progression from beginning, to middle, to end. Pacing, at the right speed, holds attention. **Semiotics** considers cultural and cognitive differences. A story set in an imaginary preschool classroom similar to the children's own classroom and the inclusion of familiar words like block area or bicycle path will help children connect.

The writings of Vivian Paley (1990, 1994) are full of examples of purposeful educative storytelling, and show how one dedicated teacher used storytelling to change and enhance children's lives in and out of school.

9-4d Child-Created and Child Dictated Stories

Storytelling is probably the first situation in which the child must sustain a **monologue** without the support of a conversational partner. It is a complex cognitive endeavor that involves a kind of "story sense" and "story grammar." To be coherent, a child's story needs to be more than an unrelated series of events, as is often the case with beginning child storytellers. Teachers should realize that for some preschoolers, including those from low-income homes and minority backgrounds, personal storytelling may be their area of strength and giftedness.

As children are exposed to stories told and stories read, they construct their own ideas about the linguistic features of narrative storytelling. They use their stories as a way of expressing certain emotionally important themes that preoccupy them and of symbolically managing or resolving these underlying themes.

Many educators believe that despite our best efforts, we just do not reach young children on the inside, where they hide their stories. They think that teachers fail, at times, to consider children's individual and developmental histories—in other words, who they are and how they think. Watching children's dramatic play, teachers will see stories "acted out" rather than told. They will be spontaneous, creative, natural, and seemingly much easier and enjoyable than the act of child storytelling. Teachers can appreciate child actors in dramatic play situations, for they create their own script, improvise, and develop characters in the roles they have chosen or been assigned. At times, dramatic play may seem a series of unrelated events, but surprisingly, the teacher will witness many logically flowing scenarios, such as stories in action or preschool "soaps."

Encouraging child authorship and child storytelling goes hand-in-hand with teacher storytelling. It is an excellent way to develop fluency and elaborated language. Children's sense of "I am a story creator" is often incorporated into their self-concept. This helps children form the skills an author needs. It is a good idea to offer activities in which pictures or props are used as motivators. Children's attempts are not edited or criticized but simply accepted. Logic should not be questioned, nor should the sequence of events be corrected. Each story is special. Teachers can think of child-dictated stories as print-awareness activities. Young children may have had limited experiences with adults printing their ideas (Photo 9-6). Child story dictation presents another use of print—a personal important use. Beginning writers do not write because they have something they want to say; they write in order to discover what they have to say, just as they played with blocks and discovered what they could create. This is why dictation is so valuable to the young storyteller. Subtly and, over time,

---

monologue — literally "speaking alone."

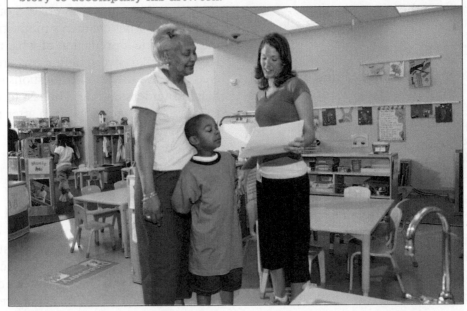

Photo 9-6 The teacher explains that Tray has dictated a short story to accompany his artwork.

dictation helps teach the child-author that a written story is merely an oral story put into print.

If recorded or dictated, the story should be taken verbatim. Discussions that allow the children to tell what they liked best about a story can alert children to desirable story features. Egg timers may be useful if rambling, long-winded children leave little time for others. Asking for child volunteers to retell stories to other children works in some programs; an announcement may be made that Mark or Susie will be sitting in the storyteller's chair after snack. Teachers tactfully remind children before the volunteer starts her story that questions or comments will be saved until the story is over. An adjacent box of storytelling props may help a child get into character. If the teacher has told *Goldilocks and the Three Bears* using three stuffed bears, a yellow-haired doll, three doll beds, and three dollhouse chairs, chances are children will want to use the same props for their own telling of the story.

Clipboards can be used to list the stories that are created throughout the day. The creation of stories is given status, and sharing these stories is a daily occurrence. Sharing takes place with the child's permission, and the child chooses whether she or the teacher will present the story to the group.

Children's first storytelling attempts often lack sequence, have unclear plots, ramble, and involve long, disconnected events; as children mature and are exposed to stories and books, authorship improves. The goal is not to produce child storytellers but to encourage a love for and positive attitudes toward oral storytelling. The development of child storytelling seems to follow a sequence beginning with children's use of language to create a special or private world. This is believed to be a forerunner to the child's use of language to create a world of make-believe. It leads to the gradual acquisition of the specific conventions that constitute a sense of story. Jones (2011) points out that children's imaginative play involves making conscious choices. She proposes that when a child is engaged in mastering play skills, either constructive or dramatic, the child is practicing storytelling by recreating a plot, motive, character, and setting. As children mature, their stories increase in length and complexity. Children gradually acquire greater control over the events in their stories, moving from a loose collection of related and unrelated events to a tightly structured narrative that links a set of events to each other and to a common theme.

Children's Artworks and Storytelling. When a class conversation focuses upon a child's piece of art that depicts a real life event, the child usually becomes an eager translator and communicator. Not only is verbal fluency involved, but also child emotion. Many times higher-level thinking skills become apparent. Each individual child's story can offer new insights and the joy of realizing others have the same emotions.

9-4e Working on Comprehension

One important goal in formal reading instruction is promoting children's **story** comprehension. Another goal is to help children organize and understand the ideas, events, and feelings the story produced. Children get practice in using logic when they think about story sequence, cause and effect, emotions felt, fantasy versus reality, incongruities, and other story elements. After-story discussion led by the teacher might focus on

- making a visual graph of some story element (whether the monkeys ate grapes, bananas, melons, etc.).
- asking if anyone has a question about the story.
- listing on a chart what information about alligators was present.
- asking if someone heard a new word or name.
- asking about story noises or actions.
- discussing how children might change something a character did.
- having the children make up a different way to end the story.
- discussing how the children might have solved a problem in the story.
- asking the children if they could show the story in pictures and what would come first and last.
- making a **story map** showing the travels of a story character.
- asking the children's opinion of a story character's behavior as being good or bad—and why,
- asking about a character's possible emotions during story events.

Teachers wanting to use a storytelling activity to promote children's story comprehension, vocabulary, and analytic ability; and higher level thinking skills can use the same steps used with read alouds discussed in Chapter 8. This preplanned approach includes analyzing the story to be told for its story content, character development, and identifying the vocabulary words necessary for children's deeper level of understanding. A preplanned story introduction is then created offering a mini-overview to whet children's motivation to listen. It might include a prediction of what might happen. Key vocabulary word definitions are then considered and also the teacher questions and comments that aid understanding. The last teacher planning task involves a story question after the story ends that aids additional comprehension.

9-5 Teaching Aids

Encourage young children to tell a story while using pictures, photographs, or other visuals supplied by the teacher. Visuals stimulate both creative thinking and visual literacy skills. What is so interesting to teachers is the diverseness of stories a group of children may relate from the same visual images. Picture files are useful in many language arts activities and are well worth the time spent collecting, mounting, and protecting them with clear contact paper.

Story sequence cards are popular teaching aids. These are made for children's viewing and use rather than teacher practice cards. Children can see that stories progress from a beginning to an end, with events, actions, and happenings occurring in a sequence. Children can use them for storytelling and retelling by lining or propping them up in sequence to "picture read." Cards can be made from two picture books, teacher tracings, or photo copies pasted on cardboard, with or without adjoining print. Examine Figure 9-3, which displays picture sequence cards for a story found at the chapter's end called *It Was My Idea.* Elster (2008) notes:

> Storytelling through a sequence of pictures without words is an old and varied genre, appearing on church walls and American Indian Winter Counts (Native American tribal chronicles painted on animal skins), and in wordless comic strips. (p. 25)

One teacher offered storytelling using a clothesline activity. A new story scene was added to the clothesline each day until the story was complete. Children were asked to suggest and decide what might happen next after teacher pinned up each new scene. Only limited teacher

story — an imaginative tale with a plot, characters, and setting.

story map — a timeline showing an ordered sequence of events.

Figure 9-3 Story sequence cards.

Two snow geese flying

Geese by lake

Turtle

Geese with turtle
flying together

Farmer

Turtle falling
into haystack

art ability was necessary, for the children readily accepted her drawings. The teacher added a short printscript story sentence on each new scene after a group discussion took place.

9-6 Successful Dictation and Special Concerns

Teachers act in the dual role of scribe and facilitator when taking dictation of a child's story. Asking questions to clarify and help the child express ideas is deemed appropriate. Younger children seem to run out of steam after 10 minutes or more of storytelling, and some are done in less than two minutes.

Statements that help children start dictating stories follow.

- "Tell me the words you want me to write down on the paper."
- "Do you have a story to tell?"

"Let's write down what you said about your new puppy."

During dictation a teacher may guide a child toward developing the sequence of a story or help the child find the story's beginning and end. When working with a child who is more advanced, the teacher might encourage the child's use of dialogue or the child's development of descriptive language. The decisions children make mentally during dictation are complex. The child may pause, start, and stop, all of which reflect the child's attention to the task at hand.

Preschool classrooms that announce that the teacher or volunteers are available and start a waiting list for a child-dictated storytelling time find that children accept and look forward to the opportunity. The success of the dictation activity may rely on the promise of dramatization. Linking dictation to children's opportunity to jointly act out before peers what the children have written is believed to be the key (Figure 9-4). Young children's interest in a concrete representation of their stories (the drama or action) coincides with young children's emotional need to establish their individual identity within the group.

Teachers experienced in recording dictated stories frequently find differences in boys' and girls' tales. Boys' stories are far less likely than girls' to have either a stable cast of characters or a well-articulated plot. Their action-packed themes are often not developed in a realistic progression of events. Girls' stories usually maintain a more sequential storyline and depict events in family life. Boys' stories focus on generating adventure and excitement. Boys' main characters are often big, powerful, frightening, wild, scary, and violent while girls may create animals that are soft, cute, and cuddly. Bathroom-type stories

Figure 9-4 Example of a child's story dramatization.

Teacher:	Alexandra's story goes like this: (Paraphrasing) "The lady knocked on the door. Her dog was big and fluffly. The lady said, "Do you want to buy my cookies?" The girl in the house told the lady "yes" if the lady could sing a song that would make her dog bark. She did. They had cookies and lemonade under the tree in the yard."
Teacher:	(to Alexandra) Who do you choose to be the lady with the dog and the cookies? (Alexandra chooses Dana.)
Teacher:	Dana will you be the lady? (Dana nods "yes.")
Teacher:	Alexandra choose your dog. (Alexandra chooses Patrick.)
Teacher:	Patrick can you be a dog that barks? (Patrick says, "Okay.")
Teacher:	Now we need a girl in the house. Who do you choose Alexandra? ("Maria," she answers.)
Teacher:	Maria would you play the girl in Alexandra's story? (Maria nods "yes.")
Teacher:	Dana, Patrick, and Maria, please come up here in front. Everyone else can move to where they can see and sit down. Alexandra's play is going to start. (Children move and sit.)
Teacher:	Dana and Patrick, let's start with you moving to the door of Maria's house. "The lady knocked on the door." "Do you want to buy my cookies?"
Teacher:	"I will if you sing a song and your dog barks."
Teacher:	Dana if you don't know a song to sing you can just sing la, la, la. "The dog barks." The teacher and the children finish the play sequence. Maria improvises giving Dana coins.
Teacher:	Good acting. Dana really sang a song. Patrick, what a good job of pretending to be a dog. You walked like a dog. Maria that was a good idea—giving money for cookies. A class discussion follows. Children decide to ask Alexandra if the story can be "acted" again.

or gory stories appear at times in child dictation and should be censored if inappropriate.

9-6a Early Writing Skill and Teacher Dictation

Should early childhood educators help children with *relating skills*? Relating skills would include the ability to speak and later write ideas clearly. To do so when dictating a story, the child needs some beginning idea of story structure: what comes first, next, etc. If they are giving a report of something experienced, they need some idea of a sequence of happenings. If they are providing directions that help someone accomplish a task, they will need to have some sequence of actions in mind. If they are dictating a note or message, children will need to identify what facts or information they want the receiver to know.

Early childhood teachers use picture-book readings, storytelling, flannel board stories, story songs, poetry, and other literary activities to provide young children with opportunities to acquire an understanding of story structure. They point out story sequence in picture-book discussions. Many other preschool activities deal with a sequence of time, actions, and steps needed to complete a task. Teachers gently promote children's clarification of ideas by accepting statements and children's ideas and their opinions. When a teacher makes comments such as "Jacob thinks we should have snack after recess" or "Ethan wants to know if the hamster has been fed," the teacher is restating what she thinks a child has said and this let's the child know she has been either understood or misunderstood. It gives the child the opportunity to correct and try again to express herself more clearly.

What early childhood teacher actions, strategies, and techniques encourage children's dictation of stories and other types of written communication? Some suggestions follow.

- Don't pressure the child to dictate. This is a child-choice activity.
- Encourage children to dictate their ideas concerning a real and present happening such as how they made a drawing or block structure, or how a problem was solved, or how a project was completed. They can also be encouraged to relate an important experience or happening or a message they want to send, or to dictate a sign for a dramatic play area, and so on.

- Listen raptly at the child's eye level.
- Probe for intent.
- Help the child articulate what she is trying to communicate.
- Help the child begin if necessary.
- Recap by reading what the child has already contributed after dictation starts.
- Give a short teacher example, when prudent.
- Talk about what you are doing as you take dictation.

- Date the child's work, and encourage creation of a title, if the child wishes.
- Compliment what story structures or features you can.
- Comment on descriptive word use that adds clarity and interest.
- Suggest that the child may want a visual to accompany her words—such as a drawing, etc.
- Post the child's work and/or encourage the child share the writing with others. (Teachers can read

Figure 9-5 Teacher dictation statements.

1. Probing for intent:
- "Those are scary words—monster, ghost, and devil. You are trying to tell a scary story, is that right?"
- "Your kitten's fur is soft and you are saying you like to feel the soft fur."
- "In your story something is going to happen to this very small mouse and you have used the words *little* and *tiny* to describe the mouse."

2. Commending children's efforts:
- "You've decided on an interesting title for your story. It tells me your story will be about a cat."
- "Your message begins with telling your mom something you want her to know. Is there something else you want to tell her?"
- "That's a good start. Now I know you are in a park when your story begins."
- "You've said three words—see, here they are."

3. Getting the ball rolling:
- "Lots of stories start with 'Once upon a time.' "
- "Is your story about a zoo, and airplane, a clown, or something else?"
- "Your first word is . . ."
- "Your story is about . . ."

4. Providing a short story or another writing example:
- "I wrote a story about how I locked myself out of my car yesterday."
- "I wrote a story about my horse, Captain, and how he jumped over a high fence."
- "When I write a note, I think about the important things I want the person to know."
- "Sometimes just one word in a sign says what I want others to know, like 'danger' or 'hot.' "

5. Talking about what you are doing as you are doing it:
- "I'm listening to hear your words."
- "I'm starting in the left-hand corner."
- "I'm printing the word _____."
- "It starts with a 'B.' "
- "That word has two syllables: 'door' and 'way.' "
- "Joseph is his name, so I printed a capital (big) 'J.' "

6. Giving compliments:
- "You told me three things about your dog. That's neat, because now I know more about him." (content)
- "Your story had a beginning, a middle part, and an end. All good stories have those, too." (appropriate story sequence)
- "You talked until you were finished and didn't stop to play—good going." (staying focused)
- "I liked that word you used. The word was *gigantic*. It's a big word that describes large objects like elephants, skyscrapers, and monster trucks." (vocabulary)

7. Commenting on the use of descriptive words:
- "You used the word *spotted* to tell me how your dog looks. That tells me he looks different from my dog."
- "When you said your favorite cookie was chocolate chip, I knew exactly what kind of cookie it was."
- "Your description of the snow floating to the ground told me it was a certain kind of snow."
- "When you said you ran very fast, I knew you were in a hurry."

and talk about the child's dictation, after asking the child if she wishes the teacher to do so.)

- Develop a classroom writing file where children's dictation is kept and explain that all will go home at the end of the week unless the child wants it to go home sooner.

Figure 9-5 gives examples of additional teacher statements that relate to the dictation suggestions in the above list.

9-6b Reaching Reluctant Storytellers

Educators may be faced with some young children who seem unable to initiate stories or who are reluctant interactive audience members. Reaching these children can be a challenge. Telling one's own story involves an element of risk. Becoming comfortable speaking before a group may be difficult for some children in light of their innate nature, home culture, or past experience. A classroom alive with "story," dramatization, and performance may slowly reach these children, as the fun, excitement, and "social connectedness" of storytelling become part of their classroom lives. Most child groups have a number of enthusiastic story presenters, who are learning which of their presenter skills or created story parts are enjoyed by their audience. These are willing and eager models.

Some children feel comfortable using active body movements and dance, and it has become integral to their storytelling style. The early childhood educator who introduces storytelling discovers that wild fantasy and vivid imagination are alive and well in most young children.

Limited-English Children. Pantomimes of eating dinner, going to bed, dressing, washing one's face and brushing teeth, opening a door with a key, rocking a baby to sleep, and other activities intrigue limited-English speakers. Pantomimes can include words in English and other languages enacted by children and adults. Props are sometimes useful. Guessing is half the fun. Using pantomimes can introduce and enhance the world of storytelling.

9-6c A Cut-and-Tell Story

Clever teachers have created cut-and-tell stories that readily capture children's attention, but these take practice so that a teacher's cutting

while telling does not dim the story line. A surprise at the story's ending usually delights. While telling these stories, the teacher cuts a paper shape relating to the story line. *The Boy in the Boat*, an example, follows.

Preparation

Step 1: Fold a piece of 9-by-12-inch (or larger) paper in half.

Step 2: Fold top corners of the folded side down toward the middle.

Step 3: Fold single sheet up over triangles.

Step 4: Turn over and fold single sheet up.

Those who know how to fold a sailor's hat will recognize the pattern. Tell the story with scissors handy.

Once there was a boy (or girl) who wanted to be a sailor. He had a sailor's hat. (Show hat shape.) And he had a boat. (Turn the hat so it becomes a boat.) One day he climbed in his boat and floated to the middle of a big lake. It was very hot, for the sun was bright. He took off his shirt and pants and threw them into the water. He had a swimming suit on under his clothes, and he felt much cooler. His boat hit a large rock and the front of his boat fell off. (Cut off front of boat.)

Then a giant fish took a bite out of the bottom of the boat. (Cut off the bottom.) It is best to use the scissors here. Cut a bite shape (half circle).

The back of the boat came off when a big bird flew down and sat on it. (Cut off the back of the boat.)

The boy didn't have but a little boat left and water was reaching his toes, so he jumped overboard and swam to the shore. He watched his boat sink. Then he saw something white floating toward him. What do you think it could be? (Unfold what's left of the boat.)

His shirt! (Using large newspaper sheets works also.)

9-6d Parents, Volunteers, and Community Storytellers

It is surprising how many family members, volunteers, and community elementary school-aged children, high school students, and adults will rise

Figure 9-6 Letter to parents and guardians about storytelling

Dear Parents/Guardians,

This letter is written to you to encourage you to tell personal and created stories to your children. The benefits of your storytelling are multiple. Every parent, family member, and grandparent can be a vast treasure chest of stories about real-life adventures. Families are unique resources and may possess knowledge of family heritage, stories of past family happenings, and contain family viewpoints. These stories will be lost if adults don't recall and share them.

You've probably already told a few stories to your children. Maybe you prefer to tell stories in a quiet private place or at a certain time of day. Building anticipation is a great idea. Opportunities present themselves frequently such as on car trips, and during waiting times. These are part of daily life. The more frequently you are with children the more opportunities present themselves.

If you can remember family stories told to you as a child, or stories told by your teachers or others, you probably remember how fascinating and appealing the stories were, and how they led you to ask for more and eventually to reading books. Some of us were very fortunate to have had a beloved storyteller in our childhood, and carry pleasant memories of the mental pictures that were conjured up.

It won't really take a lot of energy or effort because most of your stories are already in your head. Every story you tell makes you a better teller, that is, if you monitor the reaction you see in your listener's behavior. If you like to ham it up, you may have the makings of a great storyteller. If you don't that's fine because every storyteller has his own style and just being yourself, being natural, works very well.

Most storytellers take into account the age and interests of their child listeners and modify stories to fit. The goal is to make the experience enjoyable, pleasant, and stop before the child's ability to focus is exhausted. It's best to stop with the child still eagerly hear more, than to fall into the trap of overdoing it!

Sincerely,

Your Child's Teachers

Digital Download

---

to the occasion when asked to tell fictional stories or stories concerning significant life experiences. Grandparents and other seniors might relate stories from their own unique childhoods and backgrounds. Stories about contemporary happenings are also valuable. Many of these stories might involve a rich array of multicultural and multigenerational themes and offer wisdom accumulated through many years of living. Stories might also be told in the authentic language of the storyteller. Many individuals and groups work hard to preserve cultural and ethnic stories and techniques.

Many cities have storytelling clubs and associations. One well-known resource is the National Storytelling Association. Be sure to provide visiting storytellers guidelines regarding story suitability, time length, child seating arrangements, and fielding children's questions (Figure 9-6).

It Was My Idea

One winter two snow geese were on their way south flying high in the sky. They looked down and saw a beautiful lake. They were tired and hungry, so they landed together, splashing across the sparkling water. There were seeds and bugs everywhere, and they ate their fill. A talkative turtle poked his head up from the water, and talked, and talked, and talked. "We'll get no rest here," said one goose to the other. The turtle overheard, and said, "I want to see the world. Take me with you. Will you? Will you? Will you?" The geese laughed. "Now, how can we take you with us?" they said. "I'll get a stick. If you both hold it in your beaks, I can clamp down in the middle with my strong snapping mouth," explained the turtle. "It won't work turtle, you couldn't stop talking that long," laughed a goose. The turtle talked, and talked, and talked. Finally, the geese said, "Yes," just to shut him up. The three took off together with turtle biting the stick and hanging between them. Soon they flew over a farm. A farmer in the field looked up. He had never seen such a sight. He called to his wife, "Look at those clever birds, aren't they smart?" Turtle called back as he fell from the sky, "It was my idea." Turtle was very lucky to fall into a giant haystack. He was happy and ready to start a new adventure on the farm.

(This is a "bare bones" version of this tale. The author suggests you embellish it by adding descriptive words and developing further characterization. Invoke color and use sounds. Add details suiting your own personal style.)

Summary

9-1 Describe how storytelling can help language growth.

Through storytelling, children begin to realize the power and potential of the words they speak. Storytelling adds new words to their vocabulary and promotes their oral speech development and output. Children's listening behavior sharpens after hearing a number of stories. This adds to their recognition of common story elements and structure: beginnings, middles, and endings. Understanding how a speaker's gestures, facial expressions, body positions, and movements communicate meaning is also experienced. Storytelling offers children the opportunity to use words creatively and mentally form images that combine words and actions. Cultural traditions and classic themes are often presented through storytelling. This promotes additional cultural literacy understandings. Storytelling can prompt children's authorship, increase self-confidence, and improve their precision in their expression of ideas.

9-2 Identify three suggested story selection criteria.

Recommendations for the selection of a story to be told by a beginning teacher include:

- Choose stories that appeal to the teacher.
- Judge stories' age level appropriateness.
- Decide if children can relate to the story in light of their past life experiences.
- Judge if the story has a valuable or redeeming feature that adds to the children's knowledge and lives.
- Decide if the story transmits appropriate values.
- Decide if the story is too frightening.
- Choose a story that is well plotted and clear.
- Choose action-packed stories that involve the children in some physical or oral way.
- Successful stories often use repetition, rhyme, silliness, directly quoted conversation, and end in an engaging or satisfactory way.

- Cultural stories that include traditions and stories with classic themes can lead to additional literacy understandings.
- Choose stories that promote child authorship, self-confidence, and more precise vocabulary.

9-3 Discuss types of stories commonly used for preschool storytelling.

The variety of story types is large. Classic tales and folktales have been enjoyed by generations of young children. Some fables can be told. A story that invites child participation or uses props adds to child enjoyment and language learning. Repetitive phrases, chanting, or singing increase child pleasure. Cultural stories enlarge the child's base of experience and can increase vocabulary. Stories with a touch of drama are suitable and often sought. Teacher-created stories can be used for a specific teaching objective.

9-4 List reasons to practice stories before telling.

Practice first involves determining a story's meaning and message so that a teacher's actions and speech are appropriate and reflect intentions. A story's setting introduces a story's particular location and characters. When a story is understood and practiced, the teacher is able to prepare the child audience to begin to grasp what might follow and take place. This sets the stage for learning. Preparing cue cards helps the teacher remain confident and relaxed in her telling and also be better able to watch the children's reactions instead of concentrating on her own words and actions. Cards can display opening and ending lines when prepared beforehand. Teaching aids enhance the storytelling experience because they can jog the teacher's memory for details and dialogue. Gestures will better reflect story happenings when they are well in mind through both practice and preparation. With a story well prepared, the teller remembers a series of sequential scenes. As the story unfolds, the teacher can better gauge what pace, pause, or volume is necessary. When prepared, the teacher can choose the best possible classroom telling site suiting the story.

9-5 Describe two teaching aids that might be used in a storytelling activity.

Teaching aids are visuals that enhance the storytelling experience for they connect words and actions to representations. Pictures, photographs, picture files, story sequence cards and teacher drawings were mentioned. Objects and other items that are mentioned in the story can also be used.

9-6 Describe the value of promoting child dictation stories.

Children engaged in telling a story dictated to their teacher can come to understand stories have sequential happenings, dialogue, and descriptive language. They mentally make complex decisions about what words best relate their intentions. Story structure becomes clearer. Their story may lead to its enactment and increase their individual identity and confidence within their peer group. Children can gain the realization that their words are powerful and can entertain and elicit different audience reactions. Child dictation also benefits early print (writing) skill development.

Additional Resources

Readings

Bennett, T. (2013). *The Power of Storytelling: The Art of Influential Communication*. American Fork, UT: Sound Concepts, Inc.

Buvala, K.B. (2012). *How to Be a Storyteller*. Tolleson, AZ: Creation Company Consultants.

Cooper, P. M. (2009). *The Classrooms All Children Need: Lessons in Teaching from Vivian Paley*. Chicago, IL: The University of Chicago Press.

Christie, I., Raines, S., & Waites, W. (2000). *Tell It Again 2*. Beltsville, MD: Gryphon House.

Gottschail, J. (2012). *The Story Telling Animal: How Stories Make Us Human*. New York: Houghton Mifflin Harcourt Publishing Company.

Hamilton, M., & Weiss, M. (1996). *Stories in My Pocket: Tales Kids Can Tell*. Golden, CO: Fulcrum Publishing.

Simmons, A. (2001, 2006). *The Story Factor*. New York: Basic Books.

Vierra, J., & Gorbachev, V. (2002). *Silly and Sillier: Read-Aloud Tales from Around the World*. New York: Random House.

Helpful Websites

National Storytelling Network
www.storynet.org
Offers teacher storytelling resources.

The Internet Public Library
http://www.ipl.org
Includes some story text. Click "For Kids," then Story Hour.

Reading Is Fundamental
http://www.rifnet.org
Reviews storytelling history and benefits.

10 Poetry

Objectives

After reading this chapter, you should be able to:

10-1 Discuss what learning objectives poetry activities may promote.

10-2 Describe poetry selection criteria for preschoolers.

10-3 List three teacher techniques that improve poetry presentation.

10-4 Name two good sources for children's poetry.

naeyc NAEYC Program Standards

2E06 Children are helped to recognize and produce words that have the same beginning or ending sounds.

2E06 Children are encouraged to play with sounds of language, including syllables, word families, and phonemes using rhymes.

2E04 Children have varied opportunities to access books with rhymes.

DAP Developmentally Appropriate Practice (DAP) Preschoolers

3H12 Teachers introduce engaging oral language experiences that include rhyming and alliteration.

3H12 Teachers encourage children to add their own verses and variations.

2D1 Teachers consistently plan learning experiences that children find highly interesting, engaging, and comfortable.

2.3 Use a wide range of texts including poetry.

COMMON CORE Common Core State Standards, K-3

SL.CCR. 2 Integrate and evaluate information presented in diverse media and formats including visually, quantitatively, and orally.

Freckles

I notice Yolanda staring at my arm one day. She was new and had moved here from Arizona. She asked, "What are those?" It was summer, and my freckles really stood out. "They are called freckles," I said. She answered, "Have you tried to get them off?" I replied, "I tried buttermilk one time because someone told me buttermilk would make them go away. But it didn't work." She thought about that for a moment and said, "Have you tried soap and water?" I laughed, and told her that soap and water did not work either. Later that day, Yolanda walked by saying, "Sprinkles, speckles, freckles," while smiling up at me. "That's a rhyme, Yolanda," I answered.

Questions to Ponder

1. What do you think about Yolanda's logic?
2. Would freckles or Yolanda's created rhyme be something to talk about with children at a sharing time?
3. Were the teacher's verbal responses appropriate?

Children's poetry is an enjoyable vehicle for developing listening skills and oral language. Activities that involve poetry hold many opportunities to promote the association between pleasure and words. Poetry has a condensed quality that makes every word important. It prompts imagery through its sensory descriptions and can introduce enchanting rhyming tales. Nonsense verse appeals to the preschoolers' appreciation for slapstick.

The repetitive format of rhymes makes them "memorable." Expectancies are set up and gloriously materialize. Children's desire to hear more is intensified. The language of rhyme becomes easily remembered; it can become part of a child's linguistic and intellectual resources for life. naeyc DAP

Photo 10-1 Poetry can hold a child's attention.

© 2015 Cengage Learning®

Poetry is a perfect test for what language can do; it is full of wordplay. Poets have always used language in special ways, and in poetry, we have a vehicle for looking at the use of words; that is, the choosing of the one special word that fits perfectly. We need to share with children words that "taste good"—that tickle the tongue, tease the ear, create images in the mind's eye, delight us with their trickery, and amuse us with their puzzles and complexities.

Appropriate children's poetry is plentiful and varied. In addition to fast action and mood building, there is the joy of the rhythm of the words in many **poems**. Some rhythms in classic rhymes are so strong that they can motivate children to move their bodies or clap. The nursery rhymes "Jack and Jill," "Twinkle, Twinkle, Little Star," and "The Little Turtle" are good examples. Rhythm encourages children to join in orally, experiment with language, and listen to the rhythmic sounds. Some poems appeal to the emotions; others, to the intellect (Photo 10-1).

A preschool child with beginning literacy might be described as a child familiar with Mother Goose rhymes and other contemporary and classic poems, and one who knows that rhyming words sound alike. Three-year-olds delight in silly and playful poetry.

---

poems — metrical forms of composition in which word images are selected and expressed to create powerful, often beautiful, impressions in the listener and/or enjoyable rhythmic responses in young children.

10-1 Learning Opportunities

Poetry provides an opportunity for a child to learn new vocabulary, ideas, and attitudes and to experience life through the eyes of the poet. To remember how many days there are in a month, many people still recite a simple poem learned as a child. If you are asked to say the alphabet, the classic ABC song of childhood may come to mind. If you are a child trying to remember how to turn a water faucet on one might recite, "Left is hot, right is not."

Poetry has form and order. It is dependable, which makes it easy to learn. Simple rhymes are picked up quickly, as most families know from their children's ability to remember television jingles. Children in early-childhood centers enjoy the accomplishment of memorizing short **verses**. They may ask to share the poems they have learned with the teacher, just as they ask to sing songs they know (which are often poems set to music).

The teacher provides encouragement, attention, and positive comments to the child who responds to poetry. As with picture book reading, storytelling, and other language activities, the goal of the teacher in regard to poetry is to offer children pleasure and enjoyment of the language arts while expanding their knowledge and interest.

Poetry, then, is used for a variety of reasons, including the following.

- familiarizing and exposing children to classic and contemporary poetry that is considered part of our literary heritage
- training children to hearing sounds
- providing enjoyment through the use of poems with silly words and humor
- stimulating children's imaginations
- increasing vocabulary and knowledge
- building self-worth and self-confidence
- encouraging an understanding of rhyming
- alerting children to rimes (word families) is a productive way to explore an element of phonics (Rasinki & Zimmerman, 2013).

McNair (2012) points out that hearing and becoming familiar with poetry benefits children. Poetry often includes new vocabulary exposure. It increases attention and focus on language and wordplay, and offers insights about self, others, and the world in general. Literacy experts, such as Temple et al. (2010), suggest poetry encourages children's celebration of what is clear, precise, beautiful, artful, and true in our language.

10-1a Poetry and Early Reading Ability

Poems, rhymes, and chants acquaint young children with language in repeated pleasant patterns and with catchy rhythms, such as "The Grand Old Duke of York." Drop the words in this rhyming chant. Use da-Da, da-Da, da-Da, etc., and see how easy it is to isolate and sense the accented words and syllables. Pointing out rhyming words helps teach a child that different words share some of the same sounds.

Experts believe children's ability to discriminate, create rhyming words, and sense the rhythm of words is closely related to early reading ability. Playing sound-based word games with rhyming features help prepare children for ease in early reading (Dehaene, 2009). Educators agree that a great deal of evidence indicates that both early awareness of rhyme and nursery rhyme knowledge facilitate literacy acquisition. It is a significant predictor of later progress in reading and spelling. A relationship exists between early rhyme awareness and later phonological skills.

Nursery rhyme knowledge is a strong predictor of word attack and word identification skills when children begin early reading. The connection between rhyme awareness and the child's subsequent acquisition of literacy-related skill demonstrates that a developmental pathway to reading involves rhyme. Repetition of consonant sounds in the lyrics of **nursery rhymes** like "cock-a-doodle-doo, dee-doodle-dee doodle-dee doodle-dee-doo" certainly demonstrates rhyme and **alliteration.**

Children develop skill in identifying rhyme at an early age. The relationship between rime units

---

verses — lines of a poem or poetry without imaginative or conceptual power.

nursery rhymes — folk sayings with rhyming words for very young children

alliteration — repetition of beginning consonant sounds.

and words that rhyme is obvious: words that rhyme share the same rime unit. Refer back to the discussion of phonemic awareness and rimes in Chapter 7. Children's knowledge of nursery rhymes is believed to be predictive of their success in spelling two to three years later.

10-2 Selection

Poetry introduces children to characters with fun-to-say names such as:

- "Jonathan Bing" by Beatrice Curtis Brown.
- "Mrs. Peck Pigeon" by Eleanor Farjeon.
- "Godfrey Gordon Gustavos Gore" by William Rands.

The characters can live in familiar and farfetched settings, such as.

- under the toadstool, from "The Elf and the Dormouse" by Oliver Herford.
- the animal store, from "The Animal Store" by Rachel Field.
- in a little crooked house, from *Mother Goose*.

And they have various adventures and difficulties.

- "The kids are ten feet tall," from "Grown-Up-Down Town" by Bobbi Katz
- "Christopher Robin had wheezles and sneezles," from "Sneezles" by A. A. Milne
- "Listen, my children, this must be stopped," from "The Grasshoppers" by Dorothy Aldis

Teachers select poetry that they can present eagerly and that they believe children will like. Delight in words is a natural outcome when the poem suits the audience. Teachers look for poems of quality and merit. Three elements exist in good poetry: (1) distinguished **diction**, (2) carefully chosen words and phrases with rich sensory and associated meanings, and (3) significant content. Much of classic poetry has a song quality and a melody of its own. Poetry can say something to children, titillate them, recall happy occasions or events, or encourage them to explore.

Teachers have found traditional eighteenth-century nursery rhymes are still popular with today's children. Favorite rhymes with strong

four-beat **couplets** ("Humpty Dumpty" and others) were repeated with the teacher exaggerating the beat (as children do). This technique held group interest. Categories of verse popular with most preschoolers have one or more of the following characteristics:

- simple story line ("Jack Be Nimble").
- simple story line with finger play ("This Little Piggy").
- story in song with repeated chorus ("London Bridge").
- verse/story with nonsense words ("Hey, Diddle, Diddle").
- descriptions of daily actions ("Little Jack Horner").
- choral reading in which youngsters could join in with rhymed words ("To Market, to Market").

No child should miss the fun, wit, and wisdom of Mother Goose. Literacy, in part, depends on a child's exposure to cultural tradition. Mother Goose is an American tradition with origins in Europe. Make a list of Mother Goose characters. You will be surprised at how many you remember.

Practicing teachers recommend the following poetry selection criteria. Begin with poems that are sure to please. Select poems that have strong rhythm and rhyme. Find poems that play with sound or are humorous. And, look for content that is familiar to children's lives and experience. Once children have been bitten by the poetry bug, focus on rhythm and rhyme, and explore how various poets use sound devices such as alliteration or onomatopoeia.

10-2a Types of Poetry

There are several types of poetry:

- lyric melodic is descriptive poetry that often has a song quality.
- narrative poetry tells a story or describes an event or happening.
- limerick is a poem with five lines of verse set in a specific rhyming pattern that is usually humorous.
- free verse poetry does not rhyme.
- nonsense poetry is often ridiculous and whimsical (Figure 10-1).

---

diction — clarity of speech; enunciation.

couplets — stanzas of two rhyming lines.

Figure 10-1 A whimsical poem.

"What's did you do?" said the shoe.

"I sat on the hog," answered the dog.

"Is he dead?" asked the bread.

"That is not funny!" said the bunny.

"Is that a hat?" said the cat.

"No, it is not," replied the clock.

"Well, what is it then?" asked the hen.

"Stop. This poem is too silly!" said Uncle Willy.

10-2b Poetry Elements

A particular poem's rhythm is influenced by sounds, stress, pitch, and accented and unaccented syllables. Manipulation of one or all of these features creates a particular idea, feeling, or message. Some rhythms are regular; others are not. The enjoyable quality of the Mother Goose rhymes stems from their strong rhythm and cadence. In poetry, authors use rhythm to emphasize words or phrases, consequently capturing children's immediate focus. Exciting, dramatic rhythms and relaxed, soothing rhythms can be included in the same poem. Poetry's rhythm is capable of making children feel that they are actively participating, rather than merely listening.

Children's literature is full of rhyming words and rhyming names (Photo 10-2). Poetic rhyme can occur within sentences or at line endings. Children often rhyme spontaneously, during play. Nonsense rhymes have given joy to generations of children; sayings like stomper-chomper, icky-sticky, and Dan, Dan, elephant man, can spread immediately among children.

Alliteration (defined as the occurrence of two or more words having the same initial sounds, **assonance**, or vowel sounds) is often used in poetry. All types of repetition are characteristic of children's poetry. Visual images are stimulated

Photo 10-2 Children often recognize rhyming words in their favorite digital and print books.

© 2016 Cengage Learning®

---

assonance — the repetition of words of identical or similar vowel sounds followed by different consonant sounds.

by the poet's use of sensory words and **figurative language** (nonliteral meanings). A poet may provide a new way of looking at things by comparing previously unconnected objects or events. **Similes** (direct comparisons between two things that have something in common but are essentially different) or **metaphors** (implied comparisons between two things that have something in common but are essentially different) are often found in poetry. Giving human characteristics and emotions to inanimate objects and animals **(personification)** is also commonplace, and talking dishes, trains, birds, bears, and pancakes are plentiful in children's poems.

The format of printed poetry (type size and style, page layout, punctuation, and capitalization) has been used to heighten enjoyment and highlight the subject matter. One can find poems printed in the shape of a tree or in a long, narrow column of single words.

10-3 Teacher Techniques

naeyc DAP

If a poem is read or recited in a conversational manner, rather than in a singsong fashion, the rhyme is subtle and enjoyable. Singsong reading and recitation may become tiresome and difficult to understand. Teachers know that reciting from memory requires practice, so the poems they memorize are a few favorites. However, memorization can create a mechanical quality, as the teacher focuses on remembering rather than enjoyment.

Often, poetry is shared through teacher readings from lap cards. A poem should be read smoothly without uncalled-for hesitation. This means the teacher has to prepare by reading the poem enough times for it to roll off the tongue with ease, savoring the words in the telling.

The enjoyment of poetry, like other types of literature, can be increased by an enthusiastic adult. Careful reading of poetry is necessary because of poetry's compactness, and tendency to make every word count. When encouraging children to join in and speak favorite poetry lines, sensitive handling is in order. A teacher can suggest, "Let's say it together" or "Join me in saying this poem if you like." A child should not be

singled out or asked to recite without volunteering. Some gregarious children will want to share poems they have learned. A number of repetitions of a favorite verse may be needed before it is totally remembered. Children usually start with a few words or phrases.

Giving careful attention to both pitch and stress is important. Another important element when reading poetry aloud is juncture, where one makes the breaks in the poem. Your awareness of juncture will make or break your presentation. The natural tendency is to break at the end of the printed line, which may lead to artificial segmenting, not intended by the poet. Look at Figure 10-2. Read the first two lines as one sentence without pausing at the word *tree*. Now, read the poem stopping at each line's end and you'll see what artificial segmenting means.

A technique that works well for a change of pace is to use music without lyrics but with a strong repeated beat as a backdrop for poems or

Figure 10-2 A rhyming chart.

I am a pine tree growing on a hill. I can stand so very, very still. All at once the wind begins to blow. I bend to and fro, to and fro, to and fro.

---

figurative language — language enriched by word images and figures of speech.

similes — comparisons of two things that are unlike, usually using the words *like* or *as*. Example: "Love is like a red, red rose."

metaphors — figures of speech in which a comparison is implied by analogy but is not stated.

personification — a metaphorical figure of speech in which animals, ideas, things, etc., are represented as having human qualities.

teacher-created rhymed lines. The result is chant-like or rap-like and promotes children's joining in and at times also clapping. Being playful with rhyme is another strategy that can draw attention to the sounds in rhyming words. Teacher might say, "Let's say it again with an 's' sound and make it *'Swinkle, swinkle, little star.'*" Or try something fun like *"Pondon Pridge is Palling Pown."*

Poetry charts displayed on a stand next to the teacher are a helpful device for capturing attention and freeing a teacher's eyes to meet those of the children. When reading from a chart, quickly glance at a line and then turn so that the words are transmitted to the children. The school poetry chart referred to earlier (Figure 10-2) contains print and illustration. For Figure 10-3, children were encouraged to think of a poem that a book might say about book care and handling. The teacher printed the child-dictated poems and identified them with the authors' names.

Preschool children sometimes create rhymes during play. The teacher can jot them down for

Figure 10-3 If books could talk, what would they say?

A POETRY CHART

Be gentle Turn pages slow I don't want to Rip you know! <div align="right">by Ashad</div>	Sticky hands Make a mess When I'm clean I look my best. <div align="right">by Carla</div>
I fall apart In the rain Pages crinkle It's a pain! <div align="right">by Ling</div>	My printed words Will make you laugh This book's about A funny giraffe. <div align="right">by Hensie</div>
If after you hold me You put me back Others will find me On the book rack. <div align="right">by Rena</div>	Don't walk away I'm lonely today Look at me Before you play. <div align="right">by Lori</div>
Inside my cover A story hides Pick me up And look inside. <div align="right">by Juan</div>	When you hold me In your hands And turn my pages I feel grand. <div align="right">by Omar</div>
If you've never Been to the zoo Animals inside Might frighten you. <div align="right">by Sierra</div>	I'm not safe On the floor Where feet kick And make me sore. <div align="right">by Bradford</div>

display or to be taken home by the children. A child's "Amber, pamber, big fat bamber," was of great interest to other children. The teacher who recorded it shared it at group time as a rhyme created by a playmate.

Poems dictated by children should be recorded verbatim, with no editing or teacher suggestions. Each creation is regarded as special. Lionni's *Frederick*, a wonderful picture book, helps children understand rhyming. This book's last two lines read:

"But Frederick," they said, "you are a poet!"

Frederick blushed, took a bow, and said shyly, "I know it."

10-3a Ways to Introduce Children to Poetry

- Posting poems in conspicuous places may help create interest, particularly if pictures or illustrations are placed adjacent to the poems.

- A poetry tree, made by placing a smooth tree limb in plaster of Paris, can have paper leaves with poems on the back that can be selected at group times.

- A poem of the day (or week) bulletin board has worked well in some classrooms.

- The Academy of American Poets sponsors a *Poem in Your Pocket Day* and encourages teachers to share their pocketed poems in celebration of poetry.

- Pictures and flannel boards can be used in poetry presentation to interest and help children focus on words. Other props or costumes that relate to the poem (such as a teddy bear or police officer's hat) will gain attention. Some of the best collections of poems have no pictures; others have an illustration for each poem.

- A poem can be enjoyed indoors or outdoors, or between activities as a "fill-in" when the teacher or children are waiting.

- Mounting cut magazine pictures and trying to think up words that rhyme with what is pictured is a rhyming activity many teachers favor. Teachers can hold up a picture and say, "Here's a toy. Let's give it to a . . . "

Nursery songs emphasize rhyme, rhythm, alliteration, and playful enjoyment. Classic nursery and preschool songs are listed in Figure 10-4.

Figure 10-4 Nursery songs—old and new classics.

OLD CLASSICS

"Here We Go 'Round The Mulberry Bush"

"London Bridge Is Falling Down"

"Rock-a-Bye Baby"

"Row, Row, Row Your Boat"

"Sing a Song of Sixpence"

"Three Blind Mice"

"Twinkle, Twinkle Little Star"

"I'm a Little Teapot"

"Pop Goes the Weasel"

NEW CLASSICS

"You Are My Sunshine"

"Take Me out to the Ball Game"

"Blue-Tailed Fly"

10-4 Sources

A fine line divides finger plays, body and movement games, chants, songs, and poems. All can involve rhyme and rhythm. Poems presented later in this chapter are primarily the type that children would merely listen to as they were being recited, although many do contain opportunities for child participation. Many fine picture books contain rhymed verse and can enhance a center's poetry program. Collections, anthologies, and books of children's poetry are available at the public library, bookstores, online booksellers, and school supply stores, as well as in children's and teachers' magazines.

Teachers also can create poetry from their own experiences. The following suggestions for authoring poems for young children help the teacher-poet by pointing out the special features found in older classics and quality contemporary poetry.

- Include mental images in every line.
- Use strong rhythms that bring out an urge to chant, move, or sing.
- Use frequent rhyming.
- Use action verbs often.
- Make each line an independent thought.
- Change the rhythm.
- Use words that are within the children's level of understanding.

- Use themes and subjects that are familiar to the young child.

Teacher-created poems promote child-created poems.

Many teachers search for ethnic poems that allow them to offer multicultural variety. No one cultural group has a corner on imagination, creativity, poetic quality, or philosophic outlook. Each has made important contributions to the total culture of the country and the world.

Recalling the poems and verses of one's own childhood may lead a teacher to research poems by a particular poet. Remembering appealing poetry elements may also help a teacher find poetry that may delight today's young child. Poetry collections are cited in the Additional Resources section at the end of this chapter.

10-4a Suggested Poems

The poems that follow are examples of the type that appeal to young children.

If I Were an Apple

If I were an apple

And grew on a tree,

I think I'd drop down

On a nice boy like me.

I wouldn't stay there

Giving nobody joy;

I'd fall down at once

And say, "Eat me, my boy!"

Old Rhyme

Animal Crackers

Animal crackers, and cocoa to drink,

That is the finest of suppers, I think;

When I'm grown up and can have what I please

I think I shall always insist upon these.

What do you choose when you're offered a treat?

When Mother says, "What would you like best to eat?"

Is it waffles and syrup, or cinnamon toast?

It's cocoa and animals that I love the most!

The kitchen's the coziest place that I know:

The kettle is singing, the stove is aglow,

And there in the twilight, how jolly to see

The cocoa and animals waiting for me.

Daddy and Mother dine later in state,

With Mary to cook for them, Susan to wait;

But they don't have nearly as much fun as I

Who eat in the kitchen with Nurse standing by:

Having cocoa and animals once more for tea!

"Animal Crackers," © 1917, 1945 by Christopher Morley. From *Chimneysmoke* by Christopher Morley. Reprinted by permission of Harper and Row Publishers, Inc.

One Stormy Night

Two little kittens,

One stormy night

Began to quarrel,

And then to fight.

One had a mouse,

The other had none;

And that's the way

The quarrel begun.

"I'll have that mouse,"

Said the bigger cat.

"You'll have that mouse?

We'll see about that!"

"I will have that mouse,"

Said the eldest son.

"You shan't have the mouse,"

Said the little one.

The old woman seized

Her sweeping broom,

And swept both kittens

Right out of the room.

The ground was covered

With frost and snow,

And the two little kittens

Had nowhere to go.

They lay and shivered

On a mat at the door,

While the old woman

Was sweeping the floor.

And then they crept in

As quiet as mice,

All wet with the snow,

And as cold as ice.

And found it much better

That stormy night,

To lie by the fire,

Than to quarrel and fight.

Traditional

Whisky Frisky

Whisky frisky,

Hipperty hop,

Up he goes

To the tree top!

Whirly, twirly,

Round and round,

Down he scampers

To the ground.

Furly, curly,

What a tail,

Tall as a feather,

Broad as a sail.

Where's his supper?

In the shell.

Snappy, cracky,

Out it fell.

Anonymous

To Market

To market, to market,

To buy a fat pig,

Home again, home again,

Jiggety jig.

To market, to market,

To buy a fat hog,

Home again, home again,

Jiggety jog.

To market, to market,

To buy a plum bun,

Home again, home again,

Market is done.

Mother Goose

Secrets

Can you keep a secret?

I don't suppose you can,

You mustn't laugh or giggle

While I tickle your hand.

Anonymous

Oliver Twist

Oliver-Oliver-Oliver Twist

Bet you a penny you can't do this:

Number one—touch your tongue

Number two—touch your shoe

Number three—touch your knee

Number four—touch the floor

Number five—take a dive

Number six—wiggle your hips

Number seven—say number eleven

Number eight—bang the gate

Number nine—walk the line

Number ten—start again.

Traditional

Raindrops

"Splash," said a raindrop

As it fell upon my hat;

"Splash," said another

As it trickled down my back.

"You are very rude," I said

As I looked up to the sky;

Then another raindrop splashed

Right into my eye!

Anonymous

Pretending

I'd like to be a jumping jack

And jump out from a box!

I'd like to be a rocking horse

And rock and rock and rock.

I'd like to be a spinning top

And twirl around and round.

I'd like to be a rubber ball

And bounce way up and down.

I'd like to be a big fast train

Whose wheels fly round and round.

I'd like to be a pony small

And trot along the ground.

I'd like to be so many things

A growly, scowly bear.

But really I'm a little child

Who sits upon a chair.

Anonymous

Slow Turtle, Fast Rabbit

Turtle and Rabbit went walking each day.

They moved along in the funniest way.

Turtle talked s-l-o-w-l-y but he listened well.

Rabbit hopped fast and had much to tell.

He hopped in circles around turtle slow.

He talked and talked about all he did know.

Rabbit, of course, knew of every disaster

And he spoke out in spurts like a TV forecaster.

"Molefellinahole." "Roosterflewintoapole."

Words shot out of his mouth like an arrow in flight.

Turtle, a good listener, understood them all right.

Turtle answered, "T-o-o b-a-d t-h-a-t i-s s-o s-a-d."

Rabbit went on to relate,

"Snakeateawholecakegottastomachache."

"Bearlosthercub."

"Antwasswallowedbyabigyellowbug."

Turtle said, "N-o h-a-p-p-y n-e-w-s t-o-d-a-y?"

"Ohsurelknowsomething," he did say.

"Skunkfellinthewellandhelosthissmell!"

J.M.M.

The Island of a Million Trees

I took my ship and put out to sea

Sailing to the Island of a Million Trees.

Lucky Duck flew on the deck

There was Happy Me, and Lucky Duck sailing free.

To Million Tree Island we sailed our ship.

Neal the Seal asked to join our trip.

The ship was big so we said, "yes."

Happy Me, Lucky Duck, Neal the Seal, our new guest.

The wind did blow and along we flew

Sailing, playing, eating lunch, too.

We heard a meow from a floating raft

And rescued a kitty named Sweet Little Taff.

There was Happy Me, Lucky Duck, Neal the Seal, and Sweet
 Little Taff.

Sailing free to the Island of a Million Trees.

We drifted east and drifted west.

A storm stirred the waves, we could not rest.

A voice cried out from the gray fog

And over the side climbed Sailor Bob.

There was Happy Me, Lucky Duck, Neal the Seal,

Sweet Little Taff and Sailor Bob.

Off to the Island of a Million Trees.

Off in the distance we spotted land

With a million trees and mile of sand.

Closer and closer our boat did go.

Hands on the oars we started to row.

There was Happy Me, Lucky Duck, Neal the Seal,

Sweet Little Taff, and Sailor Bob.

Stepping onto the Island of a Million Trees.

Danielle Tracy

Permission granted by Danielle Tracy, 2008.

Harry T. Bear Learns To Rhyme

Harry T. Bear says he can rhyme.

"Harry," I say. "Rhyme the word game."

He says, "Game rhymes with door."

I say, "Game rhymes with name."

"Give me a better word," says he.

"Well then try to rhyme the word bug."

Harry T. says, "Bug rhymes with bear."

"They start with the 'B' sound that's true

But Harry T. no rhyme is there."

He smiles and says, "Rhymes I can do!

Bug rhymes with rug, jug and mug, too."

"Harry T. you've got it hurray!"

That was the start of a very bad day

He could only talk in rhyme you see

His awful rhymes were bothering me.

When I said, "It's time to eat."

He said, "Meat, feet, sweet, tweet and seat."

I said, "I am going to bed."

He said, "Dead, lead and read."

"Stop please." I said "This is hurting my head!"

"But I can say rhymes anytime"

"Enough already," I then cried.

"Please take your rhymes and go outside."

Away he went out the door

My head ached I wanted no more.

As Harry T. Bear walked out of sight

I heard him say light, kite and bite.

Then his voice disappeared into the night.

He'll be back on my bed when I awake

I hope he has no other rhymes to make.

Danielle Tracy

Permission granted by Danielle Tracy, 2008

Harry T. Bear Says He Can Read

At night Harry says "Is it time?"

He puts on pajamas when I put on mine

Harry T. Bear hides books in my bed

Under the pillow where I lay my head.

"See," Harry T. says "Black marks

In a straight row

Are alphabet letters

Making words that I know!"

Harry says, "I CAN read books

But you read them best"

He sits and looks

While I read his requests.

Harry picks books 'bout caves and honey,

Or silver fish swimming in streams.

I like books that are funny,

Or have birthday parties with chocolate ice cream.

Together we sit all snuggled tight.

I read the pictures by the lamp's golden light.

Harry T. Bear says, "Please read it again."

But I fall asleep before the book's end.

That's when Harry T. Bear says he reads to me.

Danielle Tracy

Permission granted by Danielle Tracy, 2008.

I Bought Me a Rooster

I bought me a rooster and the rooster pleased me.

I fed my rooster on the bayberry tree,

*My little rooster goes cock-a-doodle-doo, dee-doodle-dee
doodle dee doodle dee doo!*

I bought me a cat and the cat pleased me.

I fed my cat on the bayberry tree,

My little cat goes meow, meow, meow.

*My little rooster goes cock-a-doodle-doo, dee-doodle-dee
doodle dee doodle dee doo!*

I bought me a dog and the dog pleased me.

I fed my dog on the bayberry tree,

My little dog goes bark, bark, bark.

My little cat goes meow, meow, meow.

*My little rooster goes cock-a-doodle-doo, dee-doodle-dee
doodle dee doodle dee doo!*

Traditional

Note: This is a cumulative poem that takes teacher practice; additional verses include as many animals as you wish.

The Chickens

Said the first little chicken,

With a queer little squirm,

"I wish I could find

A fat little worm!"

Said the next little chicken,

With an odd little shrug:

"I wish I could find

A fat little bug!"

Said the third little chicken

With a small sign of grief:

"I wish I could find

A green little leaf!"

Said the fourth little chicken,

With a faint little moan:

"I wish I could find

A wee gravel stone!"

"Now see here!" said the mother,

From the green garden patch,

"If you want any breakfast,

Just come here and scratch!"

Anonymous

Talking Animals

"Meow," says cat.

"Bow-wow," says dog.

"Oink," says pig.

"Croak," says frog.

Hen says, "Cluck."

Lamb says, "Ba."

Cow says, "Moo."

and babies "Wah."

Lion says, "Roar."

Mouse says, "Squeak."

Snake says, "Ssssis."

Chick says, "Peep."

Pig says, "Squeal."

Owl says, "Hoot who."

Toad says, "Ree deep."

Cuckoo says, "Cuckoo."

Donkey says, "Hee Haw."

Horse says, "Neigh Neigh."

Turkey says, "Gobble."

And we all say, "HOORAY!"

J. M. M.

Note: Last line can also read, "And we say 'Happy Birthday!'"

Here Comes the Bus

Lights flashing, gravel crunching, the big yellow door
   swings open swooshing the air.

Big kids make faces in the windows and the driver smiles
   down the stairs.

When I climb in that bus I'm a big kid too

With my snack in my backpack and my new shiny shoes.

I'll wave to mom and kiss the glass. Today I'll be a
   kindergartner—at last.

I'll make new friends and run and play. There are things to
   do like blocks and clay.

I'm going to learn to draw and write, and spell and make
   my numbers right.

Mom says to share, be kind and good for the teacher has
   rules to tell.

I'll sit or stand like teacher says and listen for the bell.

Since I'm five, I know a lot like alphabet letters, left, right,
   and stop.

I can print my name and say colors, too. I'm a big kindergartner and that is new.

J. M. M.

Over in the Meadow

Over in the meadow, in the sand in the sun,

Lived an old mother frog and her little froggie one.

"Croak!" said the mother; "I croak," said the one,

So they croaked and were glad in the sand in the sun.

Over in the meadow in a pond so blue

Lived an old mother duck and her little ducks two.

"Quack!" said the mother; "We quack," said the two,

So they quacked and were glad in the pond so blue.

Over in the meadow, in a hole in a tree,

Lived an old mother robin and her little birds three.

"Chirp!" said the mother; "We chirp," said the three,

So they chirped and were glad in the hole in a tree.

Over in the meadow, on a rock by the shore,

Lived an old mother snake and her little snakes four.

"Hiss!" said the mother; "We hiss," said the four,

So they hissed and were glad on a rock by the shore.

Over in the meadow, in a big beehive,

Lived an old mother bee and her little bees five.

"Buzz!" said the mother; "We buzz," said the five,

So they buzzed and were glad in the big beehive.

Little Boy Blue

Little Boy Blue,

Come, blow your horn!

The sheep's in the meadow,

The cow's in the corn.

Where's the little boy

That looks after the sheep? Under the haystack, fast asleep!

Traditional

The Cat and the Fiddle

Hey, diddle, diddle!

The cat and the fiddle,

The cow jumped over the moon;

The little dog laughed

To see such sport,

And the dish ran away

With the spoon.

Mother Goose

The Little Girl with the Curl

There was a little girl

Who had a little curl

Right in the middle of her forehead;

When she was good

She was very, very good,

And when she was bad she was horrid.

Mother Goose

Summary

10-1 Discuss what learning objectives poetry activities may promote.

Early childhood language learning objectives attempted with poetry sharing can include connecting literature with pleasure and interest in words and the way words sound. Both listening skill and oral language development are encouraged. Children can gain a sense of poetry's rhythm, predictability, and patterns. Poetry introduces children to cultural classics and increases children's common literary heritage. Phonological sound play is a pre-reading activity, and the power of words to provoke emotions may be better understood. Vocabulary development often happens and poetry memorization can increase child self-confidence.

10-2 Describe poetry selection criteria for preschoolers.

Poetry selection criteria can include selecting poetry that a teacher can read with enthusiasm, content quality and value is assessed, diction is judged, strong rhythmic content is appropriate, variety in poetic verse can be a plus, and content that relates to young children's lives is sought.

10-3 List three teacher techniques that improve poetry presentation.

Teacher techniques when presenting poetry include reading in a conversational manner, memorizing but a few favorites while avoiding mechanical presentation, using lap cards, preparing by practicing beforehand, reading with enthusiasm, suggesting children join in, adjusting pitch and stress to suit words and phrases, considering juncture (natural breaks), drawing child attention to rhyming words, and reading from poetry charts.

10-4 Name two good sources for children's poetry.

Sources for poetry suggestions in the text were books of children's poetry collections and/or anthologies, public and professional libraries, bookstores, online booksellers, school supply stores, and children's or professional teachers' journals or magazines. Self-authored poems were encouraged.

Additional Resources

Readings

Cole, B. (1990). *The Silly Book.* New York: Doubleday.

Crews, N. (2004). *The Neighborhood Mother Goose.* New York: Harper Collins.

Elliott, D. (2010). *In the Wild.* Cambridge, MA: Candlewick.

Rovetch, L. (2001). *Ook the Book and Other Silly Rhymes.* San Francisco: Chronicle Books.

Yolen, J., & Peters, A. F. (2010). *Switching on the Moon: A Very First Book of Bedtime Poems.* Cambridge, MA: Candlewick.

Yolen, J., & Peters, A. F. (2007). *Here's a Little Poem: A Very First Book of Poetry.* Cambridge, MA: Candlewick.

To find multicultural poetry for young children using an Internet search, use the key words *Multicultural Poetry, African-American Children's Poetry, Hispanic Children's Poetry,* and so on.

Read-Aloud Rhyming Picture Books

Christelow, E. (1998). *Five Little Monkeys Jumping on the Bed.* Boston: Houghton Mifflin.

Collins, H. (2003). *Little Miss Muffet.* Toronto: Kids Can Press.

Guarino, D. (1997). *Is Your Mama a Llama?* New York: Scholastic.

Lansky, B. (2004). *Mary Had a Little Jam.* New York: Meadowbrook Press.

Miranda, A. (1997). *To Market, to Market.* San Diego: Harcourt.

Mosel, A. (1988). *Tikki Tikki Tembo.* New York: Henry Holt.

Shannon, G. (2006) *Busy in the Garden.* New York: Greenwillow

Seuss, Dr. (1960). *One Fish, Two Fish, Red Fish, Blue Fish.* New York: Random House.

Stead, P. C. (2010). *A Sick Day for Amos McGee.* New York: Roaring Book Press.

Poetry Collections

Brown, M. (1985). *Hand Rhymes*. New York: E. P. Dutton.

Brown, M. (1998). *Party Rhymes*. New York: Dutton.

Ghigna, C. (1995). *Riddle Rhymes*. New York: Hyperion.

Kennedy, C. (2005). *A Family of Poems. My Favorite Poetry for Children*. New York: Hyperion.

Moore, H. H. (1997). *A Poem a Day*. New York: Scholastic.

Prelusky, J. (2000). *It's Raining Pigs and Noodles*. New York: Greenwillow Books.

Roemer, H. (2004). *Come to My Party and Other Shape Poems*. New York: Henry Holt.

Schlein, M. (1997). *Sleep Safe, Little Whale*. New York: Greenwillow.

Trapani, I. (1997). *I'm a Little Teapot*. Watertown, MA: Charlesbridge Publishing.

Helpful Websites

The Academy of American Poets

http://www.poets.org

Select "For Educators" link.

Poetry Foundation

http://poetryfoundation.org

Articles about poetry for teachers.

11 Language Growth Through Flannel Boards,

Objectives

After reading this chapter, you should be able to:

11-1 Describe three features of flannel board activities that promote language growth.

11-2 Identify four important teacher skills in flannel board presentations.

11-3 Discuss how puppet use may increase children's language skills.

11-4 Describe four types of puppets used with children.

11-5 Discuss the role of the teacher in encouraging pretend play and simple dramatization.

11-6 Describe teacher planning that takes place before a drama production.

naeyc NAEYC Program Standards

2J05 Children are provided many and varied opportunities to develop and widen their repertoire of skills that support artistic expression.

2J06 Children are provided many and varied opportunities and materials to express themselves creatively.

2J07 Children have the opportunities to respond to the art of other children and adults.

DAP Developmentally Appropriate Practice (DAP) Preschoolers

3M5 Teachers demonstrate new techniques or uses of material to expand children's options.

3M2 Teachers introduce concepts and vocabulary to extend children's experiences in the arts.

3H7 Teachers help children use communication and language as tools for thinking and learning.

COMMON CORE Common Core State Standards, K-3

W.CCR.8 Gather relevant information from multiple print and digital sources, assess the credibility and accuracy of each source, and integrate the information.

Santa Puppet

Blaine, a student teacher, was pleased to be invited to a classroom Christmas party. Blaine's cupcake had a small, inch-and-a-half-high Santa Claus decoration. Other cupcakes had trees, bells, wreathes, and snowmen, but he was served the only one with a Santa. He slipped the small decoration on his little finger and playfully uttered, "Ho, ho, ho, Santa's here." Every child near was interested and wanted to talk to Santa. Blaine could not believe such a tiny finger puppet could hold their attention. The activity went on until all who wanted to talk to Santa did so. Blaine was amazed at the young children's ability to so quickly accept the fantasy. He then remembered that children don't seem to put together the differences in the various Santa representations they see: the red coat, hat, and beard seem to be enough.

Questions to Ponder

1. Was Blaine's activity appropriate? Why or why not?
2. Could you make up a quick, simple poem Santa might say or a simple song Santa might sing that emphasizes the alphabet letter "H"?
3. Can you think of a way that children could create a Santa puppet?

11-1 Flannel Board Experiences and Activities

A flannel (or felt) board activity is a rewarding experience for both the child and the teacher. Because the attention of young children is easily captured by the visual and movement aspects of these activities, the teacher finds the use of flannel board activities very popular and effective. Children are highly attentive during this type of activity—straining to see and hear—looking forward to the next piece to be placed on the flannel board. Learning occurs through the visual representations being paired with words. **naeyc DAP**

> The occipital lobe (part of the brain) is located in the middle back of the brain and is primarily responsible for vision. Connect visual areas to language areas, and you can see what you hear and say. That's part of the essence of reading—high visual–auditory connectivity. (Jensen, 2008, p. 16)

Stories to be used with flannel board activities are selected using many of the same criteria as one would for picture books and storytelling. Quality and instructional goals are kept in mind. In addition to stories, nonfiction, poetry, songs, and a wide range of listening, language, and learning activities can be presented using the flannel board. The practice of telling a story or passing along information while drawing a visual in the sand, dirt, or on another surface is a very old one. Early man used it to communicate with comrades the location of food, water, predators, or game.

11-1a Flannel Board Construction

Boards of different sizes, shapes, and designs are used, depending on the needs of the center. However, consider making or purchasing a flannel board no smaller than 24- by 30- inches. Boards can be covered on both sides in different colors or scenes. Many are made by covering a sheet of heavy cardboard, display board, plywood, Styrofoam, or a pre-stretched artist's canvas (Figure 11-1) with a piece of solid-colored flannel or felt (Figure 11-2). The material is pulled smooth and held by tacks, tape, glue, or wood staples, depending on the board material. Sometimes an under padding is added. Putting wire mesh or a sheet of metal between the under padding and the covering material makes flannel board set pieces with attached magnets adhere. Because all metal does not attract magnets, the

Figure 11-1 Directions for artist's canvas flannel board.

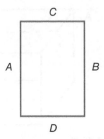

A prestretched *artist canvas* can be obtained at an art and craft store or through artist's supply catalogs. Flannel or felt is available in navy blue or black in 45" widths.

Purchase ¾ yard of 45" yardage to cover a 24" x 36" canvas. Place the flannel or felt on a flat surface, and place the artist canvas face down on the material. Fold over and staple material onto the wood frame in this manner: First, staple side A. Pull the material snugly, and staple side B, then sides C and D making four hospital corners. Trim.

Figure 11-2 Freestanding boards.

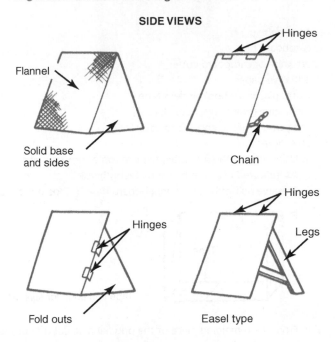

mesh or metal needs to be tested before construction or purchase. Decisions on which materials to use in flannel board construction are often based on the intended use of the flannel board, material cost, and tools or skills needed in construction.

A tabletop flannel board can be made from a cardboard box (see instructions and necessary materials in Figure 11-3). One clever idea is to use a secondhand attaché case. Using a case that opens to a 90-degree angle, glue a large piece of flannel to the inside of the top lid. When the lid is open the flannel will be in view. The case is used for storing sets and the handle makes it easy to carry. The attaché case could be used for individual child's play or for small groups, but it may be too small for larger groups.

Styrofoam is a good choice if having a lightweight board is important; however, wood-based boards are more durable. Stores and companies that sell school supplies have premade boards in various price ranges. Many options exist online. Some of them are listed in the Additional Resources at the end of this chapter.

Although flannel and felt are popular coverings for boards, other materials also work well. Almost all fuzzy textured material is usable. The nap can be raised on a flannel or felt by brushing it with a stiff brush. It is a good idea to press a small piece of felt or pellon (fabric interfacing) to a fabric to see how well it sticks before buying the fabric. Display fabrics, which three-dimensional objects will adhere to, are also available. Special adhesives and tapes are needed for this type of flannel board and set pieces. Most centers obtain or construct both an instructional flannel board that may also be used for child use at times and a staff flannel board for staff instructional use only.

Some boards have pockets in the back so that flannel pieces can be lined up and ready for use (Figure 11-4). Some early childhood centers have parts of walls, dividers, and backs of pieces of furniture covered with flannel or felt. Making a board that tilts backward at a slight angle is an important consideration for a freestanding flannel board because pieces applied to a slanted board stick more securely. A simple homemade freestanding board holder is shown in Figure 11-5.

11-1b Flannel Board Activity Sets

Many schools make or purchase flannel board activity sets for teacher use and to accompany children's favorite books and to use in other flannel board activities. Before making or purchasing set pieces, teachers consider what

Figure 11-3 Tabletop cardboard box flannel board.

Materials:
cardboard box
art knife or cardboard cutter
adhesive paper
cloth, plastic, or bookbinder's tape
tacky glue (or white school glue)
felt yardage (large enough to cover box)

Directions:
1. Using the cardboard cutter, remove top of box so that only the four sides and bottom remain.
2. As indicated in *A*, cut box in half lengthwise.
3. Preserve half of box for flannel-board base *B*. Tape bottom of box for support. Cut sides diagonally, as shown in *C*.

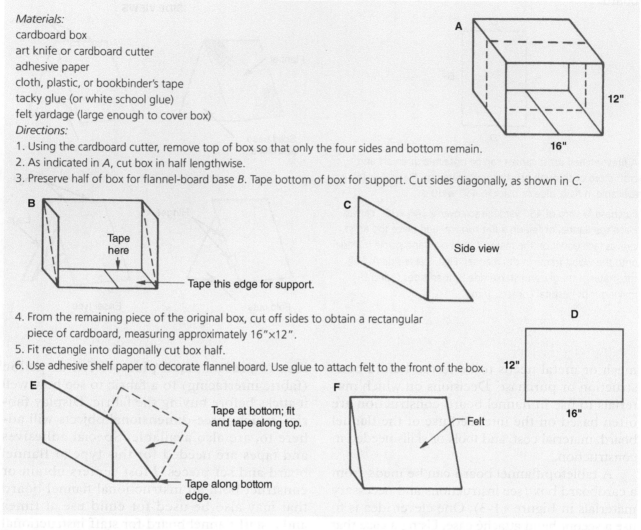

4. From the remaining piece of the original box, cut off sides to obtain a rectangular piece of cardboard, measuring approximately 16″×12″.
5. Fit rectangle into diagonally cut box half.
6. Use adhesive shelf paper to decorate flannel board. Use glue to attach felt to the front of the box.

Figure 11-4 Pocket chart.

Construction:

Obtain a piece of cardboard, of the size you desire for the back of your flannel board, and a large sheet of flannel or heavy wrapping paper. The flannel (or paper) should be several inches wider than the cardboard and about twice as long as the finished chart size. One-inch deep with a back three inches high is a good pocket size.

Measure and mark both sides of flannel (paper) at intervals of three inches and one inch, alternating. Using accordion folds, the first one-inch section is creased and folded forward over the second three-inch section, and so on. Pull tight and secure ends.

A pocket chart conveniently holds set pieces in sequence for flannel-board stories and can be useful in other child activities with flannel set pieces.

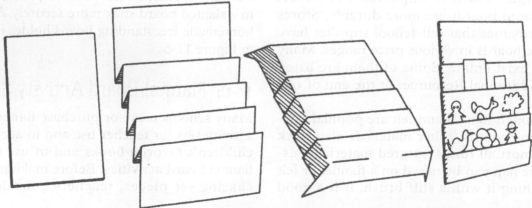

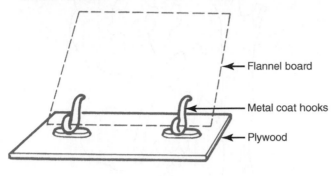

Figure 11-5 Two metal coat hooks screwed to a piece of heavy plywood make a good flannel board holder.

← Flannel board

← Metal coat hooks

← Plywood

pieces are central to the story or activity. In telling a story with the flannel board, teachers and children in free play will decide how set pieces are to be placed on the board. Teachers attempt to increase audience understanding and also select what visual pieces are essential in each scene. They choose words that coordinate with the visuals during presentations. In stories involving "running away" set pieces, teachers often move a piece in a running movement across the board before attaching it. Stories with rabbits keep teachers hopping! When a child imitates teacher's telling a tale, his or her version may resemble or creatively deviate from the teacher's presentation. Considerable visual literacy thinking is taking place. It is easy to understand why teachers of second language learners find flannel board presentations to be an excellent instructional tool. They not only hold children's attention but also pair words with actions and visuals. An example of a story and accompanying flannel board pieces in reduced size follows.

The Lion and the Mouse

Author Unknown (a classic story)

Pieces

lion, sleeping	rope
lion awake	mouse
tree	two hunters

(On the board, place the sleeping lion next to the tree. Place the mouse near the lion's back, moving it slowly toward the lion while speaking in a soft voice.)

There once was a little mouse that saw a big lion sleeping by a tree. "Oh, it would be fun to climb on top of the lion and slide down his tail," thought the mouse. So—quietly, he tiptoed close to the lion. When he climbed on the lion's back, the fur felt so soft and warm between his toes that he began running up and down the lion's back.

The lion awoke. He felt a tickle upon his back. He opened one eye and saw the little mouse, which he then caught in his paw. (Move mouse under lion's paw.)

"Let me go—please!" said the mouse.

"I'm sorry I woke you from your nap. Let me go, and I'll never bother you again. Maybe you and I could be friends—friends help each other, you know."

This made the lion laugh. "A little mouse like you, help me? I'm big, I'm strong, and I'm brave!" Then the lion laughed again, and he let the mouse go.

(Take the mouse off the board.)

The mouse ran away, and he didn't see the lion for a long time. But, one day when the mouse was out looking for seeds for dinner, he saw the lion tied to a tree with a rope, and two hunters near him. (Remove sleeping lion. Add awake lion, placing it next to tree, with rope on top. Put the two hunters on the other side of the tree.)

One hunter said, "Well, this rope will hold the lion until we can go get our truck and take him to the zoo." So the hunters walked away.

(Remove the hunters.)

The mouse ran up to the lion as soon as the hunters were out of sight. He said, "Hello, lion."

(Add mouse.)

The lion answered, "Well, I guess it's your turn to laugh at me tied to this tree."

"I'm not going to laugh," said the mouse, as he quickly started to chew on the rope.

(Move mouse close to rope.)

The mouse chewed, and chewed, and chewed. The rope fell apart, and the lion was free.

(Remove rope.)

"You are a good friend," said the lion.

"Hop on my back and hold on. Let's get away from here before those two hunters come back." (Place lion in running position with mouse on lion's back.)

"OK," said the mouse. "I'd like that."

So you see, sometimes little friends can help big friends. The size of a friend isn't really too important.

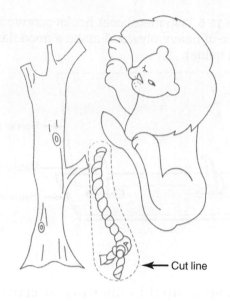

← Cut line

11-1c Activity Set Construction

Pieces for flannel board activity sets can be made in a number of ways and from a number of fabrics and papers. Pellon and felt, because of their low cost and durability, are probably the most popular. Heavy paper figures with flannel backing or felt tape also stick well. Commercial tape, sandpaper, fuzzy velour flocked wallpaper, Velcro, and used foam laundry softener sheets are other possibilities for backing pieces. Premade flannel or felt board sets are available at school supply stores and at most teacher conferences.

Shapes and figures for the flannel board activity sets can be traced from books, magazines, or coloring books; self drawn and created; or borrowed from other sources. Tracing paper is helpful for this purpose. Tracing can be done simply by covering the back of a paper pattern with a heavy layer of pencil lead. Soft art pencils work best. The pattern is then turned over and traced. Another method is cutting the object out, tracing its outline, and then drawing details freehand. Tracing pencils and pens are commercially available and come with directions for use; they can be found at craft stores.

Color can be added to set pieces with felt markers, oil pastels, acrylic or poster paint, embroidery pens, crayons, paints, and colored pencils. Remember strong vivid colors that contrast with the background are recommended by brain researchers and learning advocates. Sets take time to make but are well worth the effort. Favorites will be presented over and over again. Pieces can be covered with clear contact paper or can be laminated (fronts only) for durability but it cuts down on their brilliance. Teachers can be creative with flannel board activity sets by decorating pieces with layered felt, wiggly eyes (commercially available at variety stores), hand-stitched character clothing, imitation fur fabric, glittery materials, and commercial fluorescent paint or crayons.

Most copy machines have the ability to enlarge or shrink figures. Activity set pieces that are too small are difficult to handle and see. Narrow parts on set pieces should be avoided because they tend to tear with use. Also, try to preserve the size relationships between characters (such as between a mouse and a human figure) as well as the cultural and ethnic diversity of characters.

Pattern transfer books are plentiful and available from craft and sewing stores, as well as on the Internet. Patterns can be ironed on cloth quickly and it is possible to obtain multiple copies. Some schools buy inexpensive picture books and use the illustrations as flannel board set pieces. After the pieces are cut, they are glued to oak tag and backed with some of the materials mentioned earlier.

Proper storage and care will preserve pieces and prolong their usefulness. A flat box or mailing envelope or a manila folder is practical for storage. If pieces become bent, a warm iron can often be used to flatten the pieces. Sets can be stored in plastic page protectors used in three-ring binders (available in stationery stores). Large sealed plastic household bags, as well as plastic envelopes available at teacher supply stores, can also be used to protect pieces.

Teachers should periodically check to see if a set has all of its pieces, particularly in large centers where many staff members use the same sets. If pieces are missing or damaged, a teacher or volunteer can make new pieces. New sets are always appreciated by the entire staff and can be developed to meet the needs, interests, and developmental level of a particular group of children or to accomplish the goals or standards of the program.

11-1d Nonfiction Sets

You will find that young children are just as interested in nonfiction topics as they are in narrative stories. Educators attempt to build on recognized child interest and construct their own nonfiction flannel board sets or use ones commercially manufactured related to a child's topic. A true representation of detailed subjects is best. Library or computer research can secure accurate images. Textbooks for elementary schools are another good resource. A robin activity set piece should look like a robin: not just a bird in general. The same goes for other set figures. Distinguishing features should be depicted accurately. Nonfiction set pieces can also be easily woven into other designed activities, such as categorizing animals by color or number of legs. Referring back to the discussion in Chapter 8 on nonfiction book selection will be helpful.

11-2 Presentation Skills

As is the case with most listening activities, a semi-secluded, comfortable setting for child hearing and seeing should be chosen for presentation of flannel board activities. The activity begins with introductory comments; then the teacher starts to place pieces on the board in proper sequence as the story or activity unfolds. In many cases pieces that identify a particular story setting or location come first. Always focusing on the children's reactions and feedback, the teacher may change the pace of her speech or modify it in some way. In this activity, as in many others described in this text, the teacher is presenting but also watching simultaneously to increase educational opportunity and enjoyment. Because pieces are usually added to the board one at a time at children's eye level, they should be kept in an open flat box, folder in the teacher's lap, or, better yet, behind the board, stacked in the order they will appear. The teacher's presentation flows smoothly when the activity or story is well in mind and pre-practiced when necessary.

Steps recommended for a beginning teacher presenting a flannel board activity for the first time include:

1. becoming familiar with the sequence of a story or activity and practicing until a smooth coordination of words and placement of pieces is achieved.

2. deciding on a desirable room location and placing set pieces in order.

3. deciding on group size and considering intimacy and the conversational aspects of small groups (two presentations may be better than one).

4. gathering children and making seating adjustments according to children's needs.

5. making an opening statement that builds a desire to listen.

6. telling the story or presenting the activity.

7. speaking in characters' voices while moving pieces across the board's surface, if appropriate.

8. creating drama and suspense or using pauses.

9. initiating an after-activity group discussion or comprehension check in which teacher questions can probe particulars and elicit children's ideas and comments.

Many times children wish to do their own retelling on the flannel board and teacher may need to create a waiting list for children who wish to do so. This can involve moving children to an appropriate room area. Critiquing one's own presentation skill is a necessary last consideration.

11-2a Suggested Stories and Activities

There are many resources for story ideas, including: using songs, poetry activities, and other curricular domains such as number activities. Stories created by teachers can be enjoyed as much as commercial sets and classic stories. Sets can enhance vocabulary and concept development often within one activity. A child's picture book can be presented as a flannel board activity before the book becomes part of the school's books collection. Even children's self created stories can become an activity set with the teacher's help. Many centers include flannel boards and their sets in their language centers along with alphabet letter cutouts. If so, this then becomes a free choice activity during the day when remembered words, lines, and whole stories or their adaptations can be relived in children's play. Children often go beyond the story or activity devising their own events and characters. A flannel board with the word *closed* attached may be used to block entrance to a play area or section. A few suggested picture books that lend themselves to flannel board presentations are included in the Additional Resources section.

11-3 Puppetry

Puppets provide countless opportunities for children's speech growth. They match and fulfill many of the preschooler's developmental needs, besides being of high interest. Imagine a lifeless puppet lying on a table. Suddenly, a child slips his hand into the puppet and it awakens to a life and personality of its own. Magic happens and the world of make-believe begins. Children love to pretend and puppetry allows them to create their own magic.

When used by a child, puppets can be:

- moved and controlled by the child (Photo 11-1).
- a challenge because of the need to coordinate speech and movement.
- talked to as an accepting companion.
- used individually and in group play.
- used to create and fantasize.
- used to explore another's personality.
- used as a way to release pent-up emotions.
- used to relive and imitate experiences.
- seen as an adult-like activity.
- used to entertain others.
- constructed by children.

Many of these uses build and develop children's confidence in their own speaking ability. There are many ways the teacher can use puppetry in language development activities. When used by a teacher, puppets can motivate, gain, and hold attention and provide variety in the presentation of ideas and words. They are models to imitate when used to tell stories. Child creativity and pretending is promoted when the puppet is slipped on the hand and motor-skill becomes necessary. Puppets can be instructional tools that introduce new information. A positive attitude toward speaking and dramatizing may result from puppet use. They can be used to build children's audience skills and enhance the enjoyment of teacher presentations. Besides

Photo 11-1 Controlling puppet actions can be great fun.

these numerous teacher uses, children's vocabularies grow and their expression of ideas increases. naeyc DAP

What can puppets offer both children and their teachers? For the child, the introduction of puppets can create fresh and creative learning opportunities. Young children can usually accept the puppet as a nonthreatening, sympathetic friend with whom they can share their thoughts and feelings without fear of ridicule, rejection, or reprimand. This friend is privy to the child's inner world and able also to communicate with the outer world as an intermediary. It is perhaps here that the teacher finds in puppetry its most valuable asset for contributing to the process of education. A skillful teacher can take advantage of special moments of puppet-inspired communication to tune in to the child's thinking and to open up new avenues for learning. Fortunately, a wide variety of puppet personalities can be created to suit different teaching situations.

Crepeau and Richards (2003) explain how puppets can become an extra pair of teacher's hands.

> Hands that could tell a gripping story, get children excited about cleanup, excite the imagination, or explain a complicated lesson on why eating apples is good? What if these extra hands were willing to work for free, never ate anything, never spoke out of turn, and were willing to sleep in a shoe box. If that all sounds too good to be true, then you haven't thought enough about bringing puppets into your classroom. (p. 1)

▶❚❚ **TeachSource Video 11-1**

Language Development: Oral and Literacy Related Activities in an Early Childhood Setting (Bonus Video 2)

View Bonus Video 2, in which a child recreates a picture book story with objects she is attaching to a flannel board, and then answer the following questions.

1. What materials, objects, or equipment would you need to implement this strategy?

2. This chapter includes tips for creating flannel board set pieces from a picture book without destroying the book. Describe a few ways to do this.

11-3a Teacher Modeling of Appropriate Handling and Care

Educators introduce puppets to children before they become free choice classroom objects. This teacher modeling of use promotes proper puppet handling, manipulation, care, and storage. It is easy for a teacher to demonstrate a few simple puppet movements and use speech. With prior planning, a teacher can give a new puppet individual character, personality, and voice. A child volunteer might be asked to slip a hand inside, and with help, wave to the group or make the puppet say words. The classroom area for puppet storage can be explained. Teacher decides whether it is appropriate to mention inappropriate puppet behaviors that children may not have yet considered (Crepeau & Richards, 2003). Crepeau and Richards point out some puppets may lend themselves to inevitable misuse.

Teachers encourage **audience** skills through discussion and modeling. Clapping after performances is recommended. Listening and being a quiet audience is verbally appreciated. Teachers and staff need to decide whether a child in the audience can leave during a performance. Most schools adopt this plan of action, and the child is expected to leave silently and choose a quiet play activity that does not disturb others.

During a teacher demonstration, it is a good idea to separate reality and make-believe by sharing the fact that the teacher is pretending and the puppet is a toy that seems to come to life with teacher's help. The puppet only moves, acts, and speaks through the teacher's handling and voice. It is similar to the pretending that takes place when someone gives movement or speech to dolls or stuffed animals or toys. Some young children may believe that if an object moves it must be alive. This is a logical conclusion for young children. If a child says, "That is not a real alligator!" The teacher answers "You are correct. I am just pretending it is alive and real."

Teachers can expand children's experiences with puppets by finding other community resources, such as puppeteer groups, children's theater groups, high school and elementary classes, and skilled individuals. Puppets should be displayed and stored invitingly in the classroom and puppet theaters and props made available. It also helps to keep puppets in good condition. Think about supplying new ones periodically. A puppet carried in a teacher's pocket can be useful in a variety of teaching situations, as mentioned previously. Children imitate the teacher's use of puppets, and this leads to creative play.

11-3b Teacher Puppetry

Children sit, excited and enthralled, and watch simple skits and dialogues performed by the teacher. Continually amazed by young children's rapt attention and obvious pleasure, most teachers find puppetry a valuable teaching skill (Photo 11-2). Prerecording puppet dialogue (or attaching puppet speeches inside the puppet stage) helps beginning teacher puppeteers. With practice, performance skills increase and puppet coordination can then become the main teacher task. naeyc DAP

Many books are available that provide valuable suggestions for increasing teacher puppetry skill, including tips on developing a puppet voice and personality. Some teacher puppeteers advise becoming skilled at giving puppets a voice that contrasts to your own and looking at the puppet to see what characteristics its physical features suggest. A deep commanding voice, for example, may be appropriate for a large mouth while sleepy eyes may connote a slow, tired voice. Become fully involved with the character and experiment freely. A puppet's personality can evolve over time, but a name should be stable. It is sometimes easier to pattern a puppet's personality and character after a real person than to fashion an imaginary one. Naturally, puppet **characters** in plays or from printed sources already have built-in personalities, but a teacher's daily puppets have no such script and challenge teacher creativity.

Planning and performing simple puppet plays requires time and effort. The plays are selected for suitability and then practiced until the scene-by-scene sequence is firmly in mind. Good

---

audience — a group of people attending a performance such as a play and/or dramatic presentation, or a group of listeners or spectators attending an event.

characters — persons (or puppets) represented in or acting in a story or drama.

Photo 11-2 A teacher delights this child with impromptu puppet interaction.

preparation helps ensure a smooth performance and adds to children's enjoyment. Several related helpful tips follow.

- A dark net peep-hole enables performers to watch audience reactions and helps dialogue pacing.
- Puppets with strong, identifiable personality traits that stay in character are well received. Another way to enhance a puppet's personality is to give it an idiosyncrasy that sets it apart.
- Plan your puppet's personality in advance and stick to it. For example, Happy Mabel has the following characteristics: she is always laughing; says "Hot Potatoes!" often; likes to talk about her cat, Christobel; lives on a farm; is an optimist; speaks in a high-pitched voice; lives alone; and likes young visitors.
- Use your favorite puppet in at least one activity weekly.
- Practice keeping the puppet's mouth shut between words.
- Realize that many human speech actions can enliven puppet talk including laughing, yawning, sneezing, giggling, snoring, hiccupping, yawning, whispering, and slowing or speeding voice tempo.

Storage and Theaters. Store puppets in an inviting way, face up, begging for handling; shoe racks, wall pockets, or upright pegs within the child's reach are suggested. An adjacent puppet theater tempts children's use. Old television cabinets (with insides removed and open backs) make durable theaters that the children can climb into. Other theaters can be constructed by the teacher using large packing crates that can be painted and decorated by the children. For additional ideas, see Figure 11-6. In most early childhood centers, rules are set for using puppets. The puppets should stay in certain designated areas and should be handled with care.

11-3c Child Activities

Child participation with puppets can be increased when planned puppet activities are performed. The following are a few of the many possible puppet play activities.

1. Invite children to use puppets (with arms) and act out that a puppet is sleepy, hungry, dancing, crying, laughing, whispering, saying "hello" to a friend, climbing a ladder, waving good-bye, and shaking hands. (A large mirror helps children build skill.)

2. Ask two volunteers to use puppets and act out a situation in which a mother and child are waking up in the morning. The teacher creates both speaking parts, and then prompts two children to continue on their

Figure 11-6 Ideas for puppet theaters.

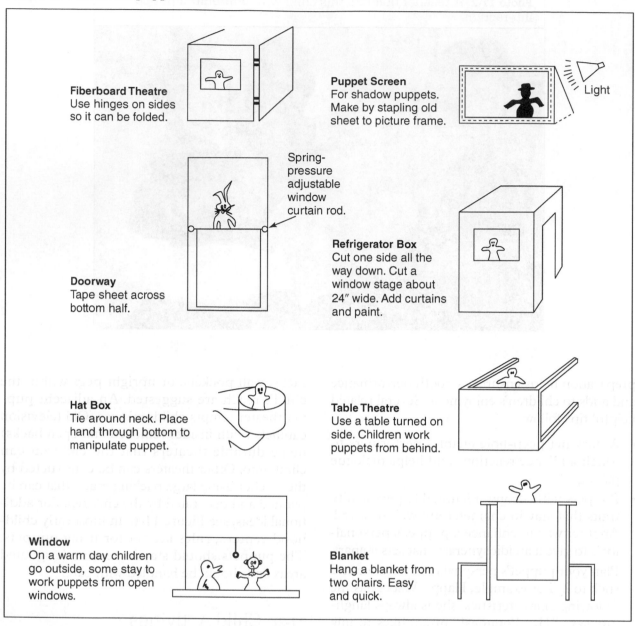

own. Other situations include a telephone conversation, a child requesting money from a parent to buy an ice cream cone, and a puppet inviting another to a party.

3. Urge children to answer the teacher's puppet. For example:

Teacher: "Hi! My name is Mr. Singing Sam. I can sing any song you ask me to sing. Just ask me!"
or
Teacher: "I'm the cook. What shall we have for dinner?"
or

Teacher: "My name is Randy Rabbit. Who are you? Where am I?"

4. Record simple puppet directions (such as the following) and have a large mirror available so that the children can see their actions.

- Make your puppet touch his nose.
- Have your puppet clap.
- Kiss your hand, puppet.
- Rub your eyes, puppet.
- Reach for the stars, puppet.
- Hold your stomach.

Photo 11-3 These puppeteers have a rapt audience.

© Cengage Learning®

5. Record simple puppet **dramas**. After a teacher demonstration, make them available to children on a free-choice basis. Familiar and favorite stories make good puppet dramas. Many contain simple, repetitive lines that most of the children know from memory. Children will often stray from familiar dialogues in stories, however, adding their own lines, actions, or settings. Older preschoolers speak through puppets easily; younger children may be more interested in manipulating alone or simple imitating (Photo 11-3). Wooden spoons with cutout felt details can be created for use in *The Three Billy Goats Gruff* reenactments.

6. Let children speak for a puppet that has not learned to talk.

7. Give one special puppet the role of the teacher's helper. This puppet gives directions, rings the clean-up or snack-time bell, and introduces new children.

8. Invent a singing puppet that sings new songs or sings to pieces of music karaoke-style.

9. Have puppets say character lines in a simple drama.

10. Have a puppet read a picture book.

11. Make a set of alphabet letter stick puppets that sing the alphabet song. (It is best to line these up beforehand in an upright position on a foam block.)

12. Many centers create a "visiting puppet." This puppet is sent to children's homes in a tote bag containing a pen and pad for a family to record the child's account of what the puppet did during its visit. During group time, when the puppet returns to school, the teacher reads the family's comments and invites the visited children and/or other children to elaborate on the puppet's adventures. naeyc DAP

11-3d Other Puppetry Tips

• Some children are fearful of puppets. They may even think that a puppet has died when they see the puppet limp on the shelf. With reassurance and additional exposure to teacher puppet use, fear subsides.

• The act of becoming the puppet's persona (such as an alligator or wolf, for example) may be frightening to three-year-olds.

dramas — plays; stories in dramatic form, typically emphasizing conflict in and among key characters.

Aggressive puppet play of the "Punch and Judy" type should be avoided. Having puppets punch and hit is common behavior in traditional Punch and Judy shows, and consequently is not presented to young children in school settings. Any modeling of excessive aggressive and violent behavior in puppetry is inappropriate, for it is quickly imitated by some children. This does not mean bad behavior in a drama can't be offered. In most stories bad behavior receives its rightful consequences. Unfortunately, because of violence in society, young children may attempt to use puppets roughly. If child misuse or unintended accidents damage a puppet, it may need repair or replacement. Teachers then express dismay as they would with any other classroom equipment.

- Teacher resources to keep in mind concerning puppets and puppetry are public libraries with occasional puppet plays, parents, and families with free or inexpensive materials for puppet making, commercial school supply companies, and elementary or high school drama classes.

11-4 Puppet Construction

Puppets can be divided into two general categories—those worked with the hands and fingers and those that dangle on strings. Hand puppets are popular in the preschool because they are so versatile and practical. Teacher-made, child-made, and commercially manufactured hand puppets are an essential part of most centers. Actually, almost any object of the right size given eyes can become a puppet! Bleach bottle puppets are common. Moving arms and pliable faces on puppets increase the possibilities for characterization and action. Rubber, plastic, and papier-mâché puppet heads are durable. Cloth faces often permit more expressive facial expressions. Following is a variety of ideas for teacher-constructed or child-made puppets, depending on the age and ability of the children.

11-4a Papier-Mâché Puppet Heads

Materials

- Styrofoam egg or ball (a little smaller than the size you want for the completed head), soft enough to have a holder inserted into it
- neck tube (made from cardboard—about one and one-half inches wide by five inches

long, rolled into a circle and taped closed, or plastic hair roller)
- bottle (to put the head on while it is being created and to hold it during drying)
- instant papier-mâché (from a craft store)
- paints (poster-paint variety)
- spray-gloss coat (optional)
- white glue

(Use instant papier-mâché in well-ventilated teacher work areas.)

Construction Procedure

1. Mix instant papier-mâché with water (a little at a time) until it is like clay—moist, but not too wet or dry.
2. Place Styrofoam egg on neck tube (or roller) securely. Then place egg (or ball) on bottle so that it is steady.
3. Put papier-mâché all over head and half way down neck tube. Coating should be about a half-inch thick.
4. Begin making the facial features, starting with the cheeks, eyebrows, and chin. Then add eyes, nose, mouth, and ears.
5. When you are satisfied with the head, allow it to dry for at least 24 hours in a well-ventilated place.
6. When the head is dry, paint the face with poster paint. When that is dry, coat it with spray gloss finish to seal paint (optional).
7. Glue is useful for adding yarn hair, if desired.

11-4b Sock Puppets

Materials

- old sock
- pink felt
- sewing machine

Construction Procedure (Figure 11-7)

1. Use a wool sock or other thick sock. Turn it inside out and spread it out with the heel on top.
2. Cut around the edge of the toe (about three inches on each side).
3. Fold the mouth material (pink felt) inside the open part of the sock and draw the shape. Cut the mouth piece out and sew into position.
4. Turn the sock right side out and sew on the features.

Figure 11-7 Sock puppet construction.

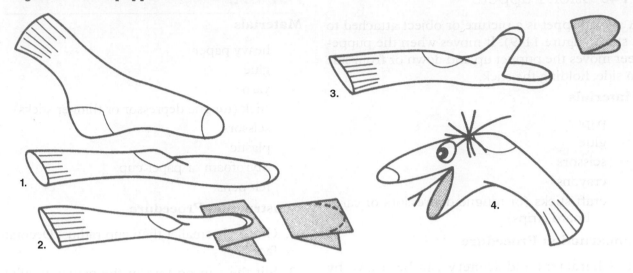

11-4c Easy Puppet

Obtain a stuffed animal. Try yard sales or outgrown shops. Cut a slit in the back of the animal large enough to insert a hand and remove the stuffing from the upper half. Use stiff cardboard or paper folded and cut for the animal's mouth. A sock or soft glove can be sewn to the slit opening to prevent stuffing escape.

Note: Choose a stuffed animal with a cloth instead of molded face.

11-4d Paper-Bag Puppets

Materials

- paper bags
- scissors
- crayons or marking pens
- paste
- yarn or paper scraps
- paint (if desired)

Construction Procedure

1. Making paper-bag puppets is quick and easy. Give each child a small paper sack.
2. Show the children how the mouth works and let them color or paste features on the sack (Figure 11-8a).
3. You may wish to have the children paste a circle on for the face. Paste it on the flap part of the bag and then cut the circle on the flap portion so the mouth can move again.
4. Children may want to add special features to their paper-bag puppets, for example, eyes, tail, or ears (see Figure 11-8b). Another puppet face pattern is shown in Figure 11-8c.

Figure 11-8 a–c Paper-bag puppets.

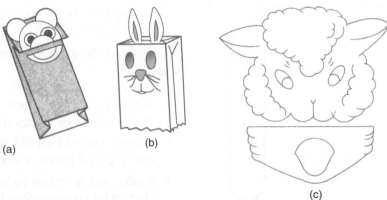

(a)   (b)

(c)

11-4e Stick Puppets

A stick puppet is a picture or object attached to a stick (Figure 11-9). It moves when the puppeteer moves the puppet up and down or from side to side, holding the stick.

Materials

    paper
    glue
    scissors
    crayons
    craft sticks (or tongue depressors or cardboard strips)

Construction Procedure

1. Characters and scenery can be drawn by children or can be pre-outlined. Depending on the age of the children, the characters and scenery can then be colored or both colored and cut out.

2. Older children may want to create their own figures.

3. Stick puppets with verse pasted or written on their backs can introduce a poem. Stick puppets are easily made by tracing book characters or coloring-book figures, cutting them out, adding a stiff backing, and attaching a tongue depressor.

Figure 11-9 Stick puppets.

POP-UPS

Materials

    heavy paper
    glue
    yarn
    stick (tongue depressor or thinner sticks)
    scissors
    plastic
    Styrofoam or paper cup
    felt pens

Construction Procedure

1. Cut circle smaller than cup radius. Decorate face.

2. Slit the cup bottom in the center to allow sticks to move up and down.

3. Glue the face to the stick. Glue on yarn hair.

4. Slip puppet in the cup with stick through cup bottom so that the puppet disappears and can pop up.

11-4f Shadow Puppets

Shadow puppets are easy to construct. Simple shapes made of stiff paper allow the audience to see the puppet's mass.

Materials

    stiff paper
    scissors
    doweling sticks (hardware store)
    tape
    fabric
    staple gun or thumb tacks
    large picture frame (thrift store)

Construction Procedure

1. Cut puppet.
2. Attach rods using heavy tape (adhesive or electrical).
3. Stretch fabric over frame using a staple gun.

Hints

• When purchasing fabric, take a flashlight to make sure light shines through it.

• Fabric, such as an old sheet, can be stretched and secured across a doorway.

• Make sure a strong light source is available. It should be strong enough to shine on the back

Figure 11-10 Shadow puppets.

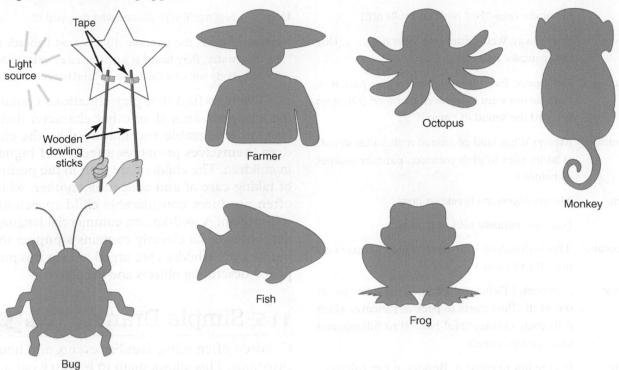

Additional puppet ideas

- plastic-bottle-head puppet
- dust-mop-head puppet
- favorite-television-character puppet
- stuffed paper puppet
- decorated paper bag puppets
- stuffed cloth puppet
- finger puppets
- jumping jack puppet
- box puppet
- garden-glove puppets (different faces can be snapped on or attached with Velcro)
- hang an old thrift store stuffed animal from stick or small paddle. Add beads to feet to provide sound effects. Dangle over a surface.

11-4g Teacher Puppet Presentation Possibilities

Many simple stories can be shared with children through teacher puppetry. The following story is an example of a tale that lends itself to a puppet presentation. Teachers can create their own stories that appeal to the interests of the children with whom they work.

The Pancake

Narrator: Once upon a time, an old woman made a pancake. When it was nice and golden brown, it hopped out of the frying pan and began rolling down the road, saying:

Pancake: Whee! I'm free! Nobody will ever eat me! What a nice day! I'll just roll along till—hey! I wonder what that funny looking round thing is by the river!

Narrator: He didn't know it, but it was a bridge.

Pancake: I'll bet I can roll over that thing. Watch this! I'll just get a head start back here—(backs up) one . . . two . . . three! (As the pancake starts over the bridge, frog comes up and grabs it.)

Pancake: Let me go! Let me go!

Frog: I want to eat you! I love pancakes! (Pancake pulls away and rolls out of sight.)

Frog: Oh, dear . . . it got away . . .

(Frog down. Bridge down. Pancake rolls in.)

Pancake: That was a close one! I hope I do not meet any other—(Off stage is heard the sound of barking . . .)

Pancake: What's that sound? I do not think I like it . . . (Dog in, tries to grab pancake.)

Dog:	I want a bite! I love pancakes!
	(Pancake cries "No! No!" and rolls off.)
Dog:	It got away. Well, better luck next time . . . (Dog out, pancake rolls in.)
Pancake:	Goodness! Everybody seems to love pancakes, but I do not want to be loved that way! (Off stage is heard the sound of "meow!")
Pancake:	Meow? What kind of animal makes that sound? (Cat in, tries to grab pancake, pancake escapes as before.)
Cat:	Meow? Meow, no breakfast now!
	(Cat out, pancake rolls in panting.)
Pancake:	This is dreadful! Everybody I meet wants to eat me! (Bird flies in.)
Bird:	A pancake! Delicious! I'll just peck a few pieces out of it! (Bird starts to peck at pancake, which rolls away crying, "No! No!" Bird follows, and then returns alone.)
Bird:	It's too hot to chase it. Besides, it can roll faster than I can fly.
	(Bird out. Put bridge up again.)
Narrator:	And all day long the pancake rolled until it finally found itself back at the same bridge. (The pancake rolls in.)
Pancake:	(Wearily) Oh, dear . . . here I am again, back at the same bridge . . . I must have been rolling around in circles. And I'm too tired to roll another inch. I must rest. I'll just lie down here next to this round thing over the river . . .
	(Pancake lies down flat, or leans against the bridge, if possible.)
	(Now puppeteer has two free hands to put on frog and dog. But before they come in, we hear their voices.)
Frog's Voice:	(half-whisper) It's mine!
Dog's Voice:	(half-whisper) No, it's mine. I saw it first!
Frog's Voice:	(same) You did not! I saw it first!
Dog's Voice:	(same) Who cares—I'm going to eat it! (Dog and Frog enter and grab the pancake between them.)
Pancake:	Let me go! Let me go! (Frog and dog tussle, drop pancake out of sight, look after it.)

Frog:	Oh no! You dropped it in the water!
Dog:	Not me! You're the one who dropped it!
Narrator:	And as the pancake disappeared beneath the water, they heard it say, (far away voice) "Nobody will ever catch me . . ." and nobody ever did.

Teachers find that play situations containing a puppet, animal, or other character that is less knowledgeable and mature than the children themselves promotes a feeling of bigness in children. The children are then in the position of taking care of and educating another, which often produces considerable child speech and self-esteem. A well-known commercial language development kit cleverly contains a puppet that has no eyes. Children are urged to help this puppet by describing objects and events.

11-5 Simple Drama naeyc DAP

Children often relive familiar events and home situations. This allows them to both try out and work out elements of past experiences that they remember for one reason or another. Their playacting can be an exact imitation or something created by their active imaginations.

Much of children's imaginative play (pretend play) reenacts life situations and leads to creative embellishment (Photo 11-4). It happens all of the time in preschool. Children often need only a jumping-off place provided by a room setting, real or toy telephone, story, or teacher suggestion. Picture what might happen if a teacher says:

Photo 11-4 In today's world, almost everyone has a telephone.

© Cengage Learning®

"Here comes the parade, let's join it and march."

"A kitten is lost in the play yard, what can we do? Where can we look?"

"The bus just stopped at the gate. Let's go places. Where will we go first? First we need to step up inside and pay our money."

"The astronauts' rocket ship crashed on the moon. Our rocket ship is here. Let's get on and rescue them."

"Let's pretend we're hummingbirds searching for sweet nectar in all of the brightly colored flowers."

"My goodness, teddy bear has fallen out of the bed. His leg is hurt. What can we do?"

The teacher will be amazed at children's ingenuity. The astronauts will be rescued and returned to earth, the kitten will be found, and the bus ride will lead to adventures without difficulties. In creative drama, the teacher's role is to be a fellow participant that follows children's creative lead. The benefits of creative drama experiences are multiple—social, intellectual, linguistic, and sometimes therapeutic. Creative language use is a natural outcome.

Four-year-olds, because of their ability to conceptualize and fantasize, are prime candidates for beginning exposure to this literary form. They pick up both acting skill and audience skill quickly. Three-year-olds enjoy drama presentations and are good audiences. They profit from exposure, but can have a difficult time with the acting role. Imitative, pretend play, and **pantomime** suit their developmental level. Pantomime becomes the foundation on which four-year-olds build their acting skills for created and scripted parts. In both drama and pantomime, children can act out all of the joy, anger, fear, and surprise of their favorite characters. This gives children the opportunity to become someone else for a few minutes and to release their frustration and energy in an acceptable way.

Young preschoolers will need teacher prompting and suggestions for acting out. Teachers can ask children how someone might feel or act under certain circumstances. They can also ask children to think about what takes place in their homes, at school, at various times of the day, or in other life settings and situations to determine possible acting scenarios. Positive, appreciative teacher and peer comments concerning convincing or appropriate acting behavior provide additional pointers.

After young children become familiar with stories, they thoroughly enjoy reenacting or dramatizing them. By using both physical motions and verbal comments, children bring the words and actions of the stories to life. Because most stories deal with a character with a problem, decision, or challenge, part of the draw of drama for young children is their interest in figuring out how the characters are going to resolve their dilemmas.

11-5a Playacting Tips

Children will act out parts from favorite stories as well as scenes from real life. The teacher sets the stage, keeping some points in mind.

- The children must be familiar with the story to know what happens first, next, and last.
- Activities in which the children pretend to perform certain actions, to be certain animals, or to copy the actions of another help prepare them for simple drama.
- Recorded plays and films are good motivators.
- A first step is to act without words or while listening to a good story.
- The teacher can be the narrator, while the children are the actors.
- Children should be encouraged to volunteer for parts.
- Props and settings can be simple. Ask, "What can be used for a bridge?" or a similar question so that children can use their creativity.
- Any of the children's imaginative acts should be accepted, whether or not they are a part of the original story, unless they endanger others.
- Individual and group dramatizations should be appreciated and encouraged.
- Every child who wishes a turn playing the parts should be accommodated.
- No-touching guidelines are necessary when vigorous acts are part of dramas.
- With large groups, the teacher can limit acting roles to a manageable number to prevent chaos.

---

pantomime — creative communication done with nonverbal physical actions.

- In child-authored dramas, the teacher may need to clarify the child's intent in story sequences.

- Reenacting stories with different children playing parts is usually done with popular stories.

- Include multicultural stories when possible.

Some classic stories that can be used for playacting (drama) include:

- *Goldilocks and the Three Bears*
- *The Three Little Pigs*
- *The Little Red Hen*
- *The Gingerbread Boy*
- *Little Red Riding Hood*
- *Little Miss Muffet*

Fast-action and simple story lines are best for the young child. Playacting presents many opportunities for children to develop self-expression and coordination of actions and words. It promotes creativity, builds confidence, and sharpens listening skill during social interaction.

As mentioned in Chapter 9, children's own dictated stories are excellent vehicles for dramatization. In child-authored stories, the most popular procedure is for the child-author to choose the role he would like to play, and then which classmates will play the rest of the characters. Teachers read previously dictated stories before and as children act the roles.

11-5b Teacher-Created Problem-Solving Drama

Early childhood practitioners may want to try problem-solving dramas with older preschoolers. Imaginary problem-solving situations are suggested by the teacher and are then enacted creatively by children working toward a solution. Children are not given words to say, but character parts are assigned. Sample problems might include the following.

- While at the zoo on a preschool field trip, the class learns that a giraffe is loose. The teacher asks a group of children to guess where a giraffe might hide. Characters include a zookeeper, police officer, four children, and their preschool teacher.

Teachers trying this type of creative drama may need to slip in and out of the dramatization, serving as a confidant, collaborator, and helpful—but not dominating—coach.

11-5c Drama from Picture Books

A seasoned teacher tells a funny story about children's love of dramatization. Because picture books are often enacted at her center, a child who readily identifies with a particular book character often speaks up, saying, "I want to be the rabbit," long before the reading session is finished.

In enacting stories from books or storytelling sources, the teacher may have to read the book or tell the story many times so that it is digested and becomes familiar to the children. A discussion of the story can promote children's expression of opinions about enjoyed parts, the feelings of characters, and what might be similar in their own lives. The teacher can then ask, "Who's good at crying and can go 'Boo-hoo'?" or "Who can act mad and stomp around the floor?" Most child groups have one or more children ready to volunteer. The teacher can play one of the parts occasionally.

The following is a step-by-step teacher guide for child enactment of a book.

- Start by keeping dramatization simple. Forget props or rehearsing. Props can be added later after subsequent readings or when highly enjoyed enactments are identified.

- Read the book (or child's dictated book or story).

- Announce that you will reread the book and that children can pretend to be book characters by acting out what happens in the story.

- Select roles from volunteers by asking questions such as, "Who can bark like a big red dog?"

- Then ask the selected children to stand together in front of the group to the side of the teacher or in any classroom space that lends itself to drama production.

- Reread the story more slowly than before.

- Feel free to interrupt the text and give clues to actors, such as, "Beady Bear was surprised. How might his face look?"

- Promote audience skills, such as clapping, and cast skills, such as holding hands and taking bows.

- Time permitting, if child attentiveness hasn't waned, go through a second enactment, giving all children a chance to act or change characters.

- Think about asking another group or class in as an audience occasionally.

Many action- and dialogue-packed picture books, such as the following, lend themselves to child reenactment.

Carle, E. (1996). *The grouchy ladybug.* New York: HarperCollins.

Gág, W. (2003). *The funny thing.* Minneapolis: University of Minnesota Press.

Galdone, P. (1975). *The gingerbread boy.* New York: Houghton Mifflin Company.

Keats, E. J. (1998). *Peter's chair.* New York: Penguin Putnam Inc.

Krauss, R. (1945). *The carrot seed.* New York: Harper & Row Publishers.

Rylant, C. (1987). *Birthday presents.* New York: Orchard Books.

A number of well-known children's songs and popular poems set to music can also be enacted, including:

Aliki. (1996). *Go tell Aunt Rhody.* New York: Aladdin Paperbacks.

Cauley, L. B. (1992). *Clap your hands.* New York: G.P. Putnam's Sons.

Oxenbury, H. (1999). *Clap hands.* New York: Simon & Schuster.

Oxenbury, H. (1999). *Say goodnight.* New York: Simon & Schuster.

11-5d Dramatizing Fairy Tales and Folktales

A number of educators urge teachers to dramatize classic fairy tales and folktales.

For two and one-half and three-year-olds:

The Three Little Pigs

The Three Billy Goats Gruff

Goldilocks and the Three Bears

For four-year-olds:

Cinderella

Jack and the Beanstalk

The Wolf and the Seven Little Kids

The Shoemaker and the Elves

Some teachers are reluctant to offer children many of these classic tales because of their inherent violence, but other educators try to persuade them to do so. Their argument for using these books is based in their belief that in order to solve life's problems one must not only take risks, but one must confront the worst that might happen. Children, like the rest of us, ruminate and worry about these worst things. Fairy tales confront them. This is the chief reason some adults won't buy or share fairy tales. They think they can protect children from the hard realities of life. Children think about death, separation, and divorce. None of us wants to think about these painful possibilities, yet we must. Teaching staffs decide whether fairy and folk tales are appropriate for their group of children and consult parent's attitudes toward them.

Nonfiction books can also be dramatized. Content such as bears hibernating in their dens or dinosaurs moving through swamps, for example, might lend itself to dramatization. When acting, children appear to be thoroughly absorbed and enjoying themselves. At play they may retain more of the information presented than during the book's reading. Nonfiction books should not be overlooked by early childhood teachers when looking for dramatization possibilities.

11-5e Progressive Skill

Dramatizing a familiar story involves a number of language skills—listening, auditory and visual memory of actions and characters' speech lines, and remembered sequence of events—as well as audience skills. Simple pantomime or imitation requires less maturity. Activities that use actions alone are good as a first step toward building children's playacting skills. Children have imitated others' actions since infancy, and—as always—the joy of being able to do what they see others do brings a feeling of self-confidence. The children's individuality is preserved if differences in ways of acting out a familiar story are valued in preschool settings.

11-5f Pantomime

Among the all-time favorites for pantomime is the following.

The Bear Hunt

We're going on a bear hunt

We're going where?

We're going on a bear hunt.

OK, let's go! I'm not afraid!

Look over there!

What do you see?

A big deep river.

Can't go around it.

Can't go under it.

Have to swim across it.

OK, let's go. I'm not afraid!

What's this tall stuff?

What do you see?

Tall, tall grass.

Can't go around it.

Can't go under it.

Got to go through it.

OK, let's go. I'm not afraid!

Hey, look ahead.

What do you see?

A rickety old bridge.

Can't go around it.

Can't go under it.

Got to go across it.

OK, let's go. I'm not afraid!

Now what's this ahead.

It's a tall, tall tree.

Can't go under it.

Can't go over it.

Have to climb it.

OK, let's go. I'm not afraid!

Do you see what I see?

What a giant mountain!

Can't go around it.

Can't go under it.

Got to climb over it.

OK, let's go. I'm not afraid!

Oh, look at that dark cave.

Let's go inside.

It sure is dark in here.

I think I feel something.

I think it's a nose.

And two furry ears.

HELP! It's a bear!!!!!!!!!!!!!!

Let's get out of here . . . I'm afraid.

(Pretend to climb back over the mountain and down the tree, run across the bridge, swish through the tall grass, swim the river, open the door, run in, slam the door, and collapse in a heap.)

Whew . . . Home at last . . . I was afraid!

11-6 Creative Drama Productions

Starting a language program that includes creative drama productions requires planning. Props and play materials must be supplied for children to explore. When children see simple plays performed by teachers, other children, and adult groups, they are provided with a model and a stimulus. Some drama activity ideas for the older preschool child that provide experience in performance skills include

- **pantomiming action words and phrases:** tiptoe, crawl, riding a horse, and using a rolling pin.
- **pantomiming words that describe a physical state:** cold, hot, and sleepy.
- **pantomiming feeling words:** happy, sad, hurt, holding a favorite teddy bear lovingly, feeling surprise.
- **acting out imaginary life situations:** such as opening a door with a key, climbing in and out of a car, helping to set the table.
- **acting familiar character parts in well-known stories:** "She covered her mouth so the clown couldn't see her laugh." "The rabbit dug a big hole and buried the carrot." "He tiptoed to the window, raised the shade, and opened it."
- **saying familiar lines from known stories or from a play script:** "And he huffed and he puffed, and he blew the house down."
- **playing a character in a short story or song that involves both spoken lines and actions.**
- **pantomiming actions of a character in a short, familiar story that the teacher reads (or from a teacher-recorded story tape).** There are a vast number of commercially recorded stories available at school-supply stores.

• **making story sequence cards for a favorite book.**

The following pantomimes for young children are good initial exercises.

• Drink a glass of water. "Oh! It turned into hot soup and burned your mouth!"
• Pick a flower. Smell it.
• Eat a bowl of spaghetti.
• Row a boat.
• Bounce a ball.
• Pour your milk from the carton to a glass. Drink it.
• Play the piano, trumpet, drums, or guitar.
• Shoo away a fly.
• Chew a piece of bubble gum and blow a bubble. It gets bigger, bigger, and bigger. Suddenly it breaks.
• Blow up a small paper bag, and then pop it.
• "You and your grandmother are in a supermarket. Suddenly, you cannot find her and you feel scared. You look up and down all of the aisles trying to find her. There she is. You see her."

11-6a Costumes, Props, and Stages

Imagination and inexpensive, easy-to-make costumes are great performing incentives. Accessories such as aprons, shirts, canes, and gloves can be used in a variety of play and drama situations, and hats are popular when head lice problems do not exist. A "stage" area can be a semi-permanent part of the classrooms. Comfortable audience seating and viewing should be considered.

Cutout art board (or cardboard) heads and figures held by the child quickly aid his ability to step into character (Figure 11-11). (Make sure that the board is lightweight and the hand holes are comfortable.) Older children may be able to draw their own patterns, or patterns for figures can be found in children's books and can be enlarged with the use of an opaque projector. These props allow children to put their faces into the spaces cut out of the characters' faces and are useful in child dramatization. However, some teachers feel that these props are physically awkward and prefer, instead, simple costumes.

Figure 11-11 Story character boards.

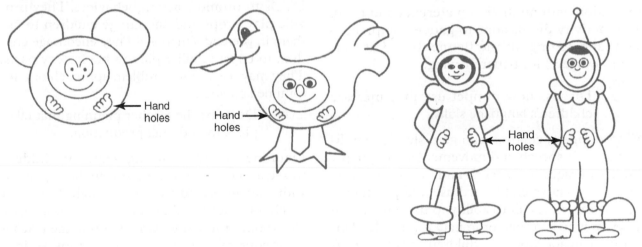

11-1 Describe three features of flannel board activities that promote language growth.

Flannel board activities connect spoken language to visual representations. They promote pre-reading skills, and hold child attention with a combination of words, visuals, and actions. Activities prompt children's comments and their retelling of stories, thus increasing their verbal output. Activities can contain new concepts, experiences, adventures, problem-solving exercises, and new knowledge in many domains. They can also sharpen listening skills. Flannel board activities are vocabulary builders.

11-2 Identify four important teacher skills in flannel board presentations.

Important teaching skills include the ability to adjust child seating before beginning; coordinating movements with words and actions for a smooth presentation; observing child feedback to enhance learning; monitoring story sequence and maintaining eye contact; presenting age level appropriate activities; increasing enjoyment with language by building drama when appropriate; providing vocabulary, accuracy, and detailed information with nonfiction material; conducting after activity discussions to gauge comprehension; and setting up the flannel board at children's eye level for better viewing.

11-3 Discuss how puppet use may increase children's language skills.

With puppets, children can gain skill in coordinating their speech and movements, and puppet use encourages oral speech and output. Puppets promote creative child word use and pretending opportunities. A child's ability to use language in a new way to entertain or imitate is possible. Puppet use can add words to children's vocabulary. A puppet can also add to a child's store of information and knowledge. It prompts close listening skill.

11-4 Describe four types of puppets used with children.

Puppet types mentioned in the text include hand and finger manipulated ones and ones that dangle on strings. Homemade, child-made, or commercially manufactured types were also discussed. Puppets might also be constructed of rubber, plastic, papier-mâché, or cloth, and it's possible to make puppets from used kitchen bottles or boxes. Shadow, stick, paper bag, sock, pop-up, finger, and glove puppets were also suggested.

11-5 Discuss the role of the teacher in encouraging pretend play and simple dramatization.

Pretend play and simple dramatization is encouraged when teachers design classrooms with pretend play settings or areas. It is the role of the teacher to make pretend play suggestions and also, at times, become a fellow participant while following children's lead. Teachers can prompt children's expression of feelings and acting these feelings out. They support appropriate acting behaviors. Teachers also provide play materials. At times they may model pretending themselves. Teachers plan activities in which children imitate or copy the actions of others or the speech of others. Teachers sometimes show videos or DVDs to promote acting behaviors. They provide play props and encourage children to use them in pretend situations. They encourage children to enact familiar picture book story parts. They may use a story problem approach or pantomime activities.

11-6 Describe the teacher planning that takes place for a drama production.

Planning includes finding ways for children to see a performed drama production, play, or short scenes acted by others, including their teachers or older children. In planning for a classroom production with children, the teacher must consider space for a stage, props, scripts, costumes, and audience seating. Child experience with pantomiming and reenacting parts of picture books helps prepare them for a drama with a script. Practice sessions and introducing children to the newness of saying lines that accompany physical actions are performance essentials.

Additional Resources

Picture books for Flannel Board Sets

Hobson, S. (1994). *Chicken Little*. New York: Simon & Schuster.

Stevens, J. (1995). *Tops and Bottoms*. New York: Harcourt.

Young, E. (1992). *Seven Blind Mice*. New York: Philomel Books.

Suggestions for Flannel Board Readings

Wilmes, L., Wilmes, D., & McDonnell, C. (2001). *Felt Board Stories*. Building Blocks.

Carlson, A., & Carlson, M. (2005). *Flannel Board Stories for Infants and Toddlers*. American Library Association (Bilingual edition available).

Vaughn, G. G., Taylor, S., & Morris, L. J. (2012). *The Flannel Board Story Book*. Green Dragon Publishing Group.

Sources for Flannel boards, Puppets, Dress-ups

Flannel Boards: Online Kaplan Toys

Dress-Ups, Furniture, Storage: Online at Kaplan Early Learning Company

Felt Puppets: Online at The Puppet Store

Puppet Patterns: Online at Puppet Patterns

Books for Creative Dramatization

DePaola, T. (1975). *Strega Nona*. New York: Aladdin Paperbacks.

Hutchins, P. (1986). *The Doorbell Rang*. New York: Greenwillow Books.

Keats, E. J. (1966). *Jennie's Hat*. New York: Harper and Row.

Lionni, L. (1969). *Alexander and the Wind-Up Mouse*. New York: Pantheon.

Mayer, M. (1968). *There's a Nightmare in My Closet*. New York: The Dial Press.

McGovern, A. (1976). *Too Much Noise*. New York: Houghton Mifflin Company.

Slobodkina, E. (1968). *Caps for Sale*. New York: William R. Scott Inc.

Readings

Breyer, M. A., & Seho, R. (1999). *A Guide for Using the Master Puppeteer in the Classroom*. Westminster, CA: Teacher Created Materials.

Crepeau, I. M., & Richards, M. A. (2006). *A Show of Hands: Using Puppets with Young Children*. St. Paul, MN: Redleaf Press.

Fox, M. (1987). *Teaching Drama to Young Children*. Portsmouth, NH: Heinemann.

Helpful Websites

Empowered by Play

http://www.empoweredbyplay.org

Helps families and teachers protect and promote imaginative play.

12 Realizing Speaking Goals

Objectives

After reading this chapter, you should be able to:

12-1 State four goals of planned preschool speech activities.

12-2 Describe professional techniques used in daily conversations with children.

12-3 Explain how teachers support and enrich children's dramatic play.

naeyc NAEYC Program Standards

2D04 Children have varied opportunities to develop vocabulary through conversations.

2D06 Children have varied opportunities and materials that encourage them to have discussions to solve problems related to the physical world.

2D07 Children are provided with opportunities and materials that encourage them to engage in discussions with one another.

DAP Developmentally Appropriate Practice (DAP) Preschoolers

3H7 Teachers help children use communication and language as tools for thinking and learning.

3H4 Teachers engage the child more frequently in sustained conversations and make extra efforts to help them comprehend.

3H2 Teachers provide frequent opportunities for children to talk to each other, so children also get modeling from their more skilled peers.

COMMON CORE Common Core State Standards, K-3

SL.CCR.1 Prepare for and participate effectively in a range of conversations and collaborations with diverse partners, building on others' ideas and expressing their own clearly and persuasively.

SL.CCR.6 Adapt speech to a variety of contexts and communicative tasks, demonstrating command of formal English when indicated or appropriate.

Sword Play

Two four-year-old boys were pretending to fence with paper swords. One kept saying "mustard" as he wielded his. After saying it a few more times, the other boy said, "hot dog" in response. They thought this was hysterical. I didn't get it until later, when I realized the first child must have observed someone saying "en garde" while fencing.

Questions to Ponder

1. Is this a type of dramatic play?
2. Do you have any other examples of young children copying words they have heard but not understood?

In a well-planned classroom, a child has many opportunities to speak without underlying stress attached to doing so. Oral language is the foundation of literacy learning. Although some activities are planned, others just happen. Classroom discussion is paramount. Aim for a dynamic room where action and discussion reign. In this type of atmosphere, true literacy emerges. Help children see the uses of speaking in social interactions in their daily lives and tie speech to print and reading activities when possible. Preschool children do a wonderful job of learning to communicate, and the more they talk, the more their talking improves.

Activities can be divided into three groups: structured, unstructured, and child-initiated. Structured activities are those that the teacher plans and prepares. The teacher may be, for a while, at the center of all action—motivating, presenting ideas, giving demonstrations, eliciting child ideas and comments, and promoting conversation. Care is taken to remove any environmental factor that couples speaking with increased anxiety. Unstructured activities, on the other hand, may still be prepared by the teacher, but the children decide the action through self-directed play, and the teacher is cast primarily in the role of cohort, confidant, and interested party (Photo 12-1). The teacher remains conversational and supportive. For optimal child learning, teachers need to appreciate and offer authentic dialogue and real human communication in a reciprocal relationship between learner and teacher rooted in equality, respect, and trust. Educators who are skilled in responsive involvement and responsive conversation make a difference in children's lives. Warm, sensitive, observant, interested listeners, are those who encourage, make suggestions, and promote child verbal expression. At times, educators are playful companions of the language arts that definitely contribute to the quality of children's experiences.

Photo 12-1 Teachers often become "coexplorers" who offer pertinent and language-expanding comments.

Child-initiated activities are those that follow children's interests and exploration. The teacher may provide materials or activities to further child opportunities. He may act as a resource, someone to share ideas with, someone to discuss discovery, and may also provide help in recording the child's research (Photo 12-2). Teachers take every possible avenue to increase and promote children's expression of ideas. They avoid calling on learners unless they volunteer, but rather tactfully invite their comments. Overt comparisons of children's speech or statements are not made, and teachers guard against saying or doing anything that causes children embarrassment.

DAP

Educators understand that during a part of the school day they will use a didactic teaching style that provides young children with information. If they are serious about improving children's oral language ability, that portion of the day will be relatively small compared to the amount of time devoted to the use of scaffolded teaching approaches. This teaching style—which includes responsive teacher conversation, open-ended questioning, and the facilitation of children's initiatives—provides children with opportunities to talk about what they have heard, experienced, learned, and understood and gives children a chance to link their present learning to previous knowledge and life experiences. Realizing the importance of a child's oral language skill developing at an early age because of its implication for later reading and academic achievement, educators strive to provide the time and teaching style that typifies best practice for both dual language children and native English speakers.

12-1 Program Goals

Each early childhood center contains a unique group of children and adults. A center has its own geography and its children come from different segments of society, so the goals and priorities of one program may differ from others. There are, however, some common factors among centers. The following goals are acceptable to most programs. They give the teacher a basis for planning speaking activities and daily conversational exchanges. Each child should be helped to attain:

- confidence in the ability to use speech with others.
- enjoyment in speaking experiences in play, conversations, and groups.
- acceptance of the idea that another's speech may be different.
- a higher level of interest in the meaning of new words.

COMMON CORE

In addition, each child should be helped increase his skill in:

- using speech for ideas, feelings, and needs.
- using speech to solve problems.
- using speech creatively in play situations.
- coordinating speech and body actions.
- waiting for a turn to speak.

Photo 12-2 Talking over children's discoveries with them is a recommended practice.

© 2016 Cengage Learning®

Teachers realize the importance of children's **discourse skills** that go beyond basic conversation. Discourse skills involve children's use of language in structured ways, like telling a story about a past event, explaining how something works, building a fantasy world with words, explaining classroom rules to a peer, and dictating a "made up" poem. Thought-provoking and open-ended adult–child conversations support children's discourse efforts.

The overall goal in the development of speech communication in language arts is to increase each child's ability to use the speech he already possesses and to help the child move, when ready, toward the use of Standard English. Program goals can be realized mainly through the planning of daily activities, daily staff–child and child–child interaction, and the use of equipment and materials.

Kindergarten teachers agree that speaking and listening skills have a profound effect on children's success during their first few months at school. Children who know how to express themselves are prepared. Those who listen carefully to others are likely to adjust more readily to changing situations within the classroom.

A wide variety of different experiences can provide many learning opportunities. An activity can follow, review, and add depth to a previous one. One has to consider how much practice time is available. The special interests or needs of each child are considered when planning daily programs. Programs then become more valuable and meaningful.

Dr. Frederick Zimmerman et al. (2007) note that pediatricians should encourage families to provide their young children with language input through picture book reading, storytelling, and simple narration of daily events. After conducting research, these researchers report although this is sound advice, this form of input may not place enough emphasis on children's role in daily conversational exchanges or highlight the importance of prompting children to speak their mind as much as possible. Engaging children in basic daily conversations could be up to six times more effective than just reading to them, these researchers believe. (p. 690)

12-1a Daily Conversations

Daily teacher–child conversations become amazingly easy when teachers focus on the "children's agenda." When classrooms seem always to be too hectic to get eye to eye with the child and listen to and pursue the child's interests, the program, environment, and teaching situation need to be evaluated and overhauled, for intimate conversations are severely limited and infrequent. At the other extreme, teachers defeat their purpose when the objective is always to teach or add a new word to the child's vocabulary. The key is to identify the child's interests; words then become meaningful. When the child is engrossed, he will connect the teacher's words with what has fascinated him.

Excellent teachers make their students feel valuable, competent, and worthwhile. The following are the attitudes and behaviors teachers should cultivate in conversation.

- concern for each child's well-being
- an unwillingness to interrupt a child's conversation to respond to an adult
- a willingness to share the small moments of child accomplishment, sometimes even recognizing a child's achievement in a nonverbal way across a busy classroom
- consideration of children's verbal comments as worthy contributions,
- respect for individual opinions
- recognition of each child's potential
- special regard for children as future leaders and discoverers

Teacher actions, questions, or statements that indicate the listener's genuine interest elicit a wealth of oral language (Photo 12-3). Johnson et al. (2012) believe that nothing a teacher can say is more important than the teacher listening carefully once a conversation has started. Teachers should carefully guard and protect each child's self-confidence. By waiting patiently and reading nonverbal clues, teachers become understanding listeners. Every effort should be made to give a logical response, showing the child that the teacher finds value in the communication. Offering a reassuring arm or hand and giving one's whole attention to the child often seems to relax the child and increase speech production.

---

discourse skills — refers to using language in structured ways to go beyond basic conversation, for example, telling a story, explaining a procedure, creating a fantasy, dictating ideas, and elaborating to provide greater understanding.

Children are more willing to speak when the proper classroom atmosphere is maintained. Characteristics of a classroom that is conducive to children's speaking opportunities includes:

- a warm and relaxed room environment where children have choices to speak or not.
- groups are kept small whenever possible.
- children's efforts and accomplishments are recognized.
- activities hold children's attention. Some of the best activities happen when the teacher notices what the child or group is focusing on and uses the opportunity to expand interest, knowledge, and enjoyment. A rainbow, a delivery truck, or any chance happening can become the central topic of active speaking by the children.
- A teacher's willingness to engage in light-hearted dialogue may make the child more open to talking for the fun of it. When the mood is set for discovery, the teacher becomes active in the quest for answers, carefully guiding children through their exploration and expression.

Adults who emphasize the reasons for events and who take a questioning, thoughtful, and systematic approach to problems become model explorers. Thinking out loud while sharing activities is a useful device. "I wonder what would happen if you put the block there?" a teacher might ask. In their speech, young children often deal with the reality of what is happening around them; teachers' speech should also be based on this concept.

In reacting to young children's sometimes awkward, fractured, or incorrect speech, adults intuitively provide useful corrective feedback in a casual tone so the child does not sense she is being corrected. The child's "posta put in" would automatically be accepted and corrected with, "Yes, the blocks go on the shelf." Seasoned teachers listen for content and the ideas behind words and matter-of-factly model correct usage so smoothly that the child is not made to feel that his speech usage was in any way deficient. The teacher must know how to make alert, sensitive comments that ensure that the children will continue to see the teacher as a responsive, accepting adult.

Educators and researchers have classified different "functions" of human speech. Some classifications follow. Teachers observing children will notice the young child's increasing use of different speech functions in social situations:

- *Instrumental* speech satisfies wants and needs. "I want to be next."
- *Regulatory speech* helps children control others. "Don't drop the cup because it will break into a zillion pieces."

- *Interactional* speech establishes and maintains contact with others.

  "M," that's my letter. I'm Monroe." (A child is pointing to an alphabet chart with a friend.)

- *Personal function* speech expresses and asserts individuality.

  "Let's push it under, and make it stay down." (Child statements made during water play.)

- *Heuristic function* speech helps children learn and describe.

  "You're the baby, who goes wah, wah, wah."

- *Imaginative function* speech creates images and aids pretending.

  "Look, I'm flying."

- *Representational* speech informs.

  "I don't like bananas."

The California State Department of Education (2009) has also identified key functions of language children use to demonstrate communicative competence.

1. Imparting and seeking factual information.
2. Expressing and finding out intellectual attitudes (agreement, disagreement, declining or accepting, giving and seeking permission).
3. Expressing and finding out emotional attitudes (words, desires, likes, interests, preferences, intentions, surprise, hope, satisfaction, fear, worry, sympathy and their opposites).
4. Expressing and finding out moral attitudes (forgiving, apologizing, approval and disapproval, appreciation, regret, indifference).
5. Getting things done (course of action, asking, inviting, advising, instructing, directing, offering, helping).
6. Socializing (social small talk, hello, goodbye, and other social conventions). (p. 24)

Teachers trying to facilitate children's use of different speech classifications will want to study Figure 12-1. All of these speech functions are present in the average preschool classroom.

Children have their own feelings, views, and opinions about the world around them. As their social contact increases, they exchange their ideas with other children. When they become older preschoolers, they typically engage in criticism, commands, requests, threats, and questions and answers. As a teacher listens to child-to-child conversations, he can make out both self-interest speech and speech that indicates social–intellectual involvement. Quite a lot of child conversation reflects the child's active, exploring, questioning mind and attempts to try, test, manipulate, control, and discover what speech can do for him. Flights of fantasy and make-believe are also evident.

Certain teacher behaviors and planned programs enhance children's speaking abilities. Are there factors that work counter to the realization of goals? Some child centers lack or minimize language stimulation. Children spent most of their time in teacher-directed large-group activities. Their language behavior can be described as primarily receptive, such as listening to and following teachers' directions. Although their teachers might provide adequate oral language models, they may not be active listeners, nor do they encourage children's curiosity. Teacher's language may not spontaneously expand children's vocabulary or concepts or use professionally accepted practice.

During interactions, children need their conversational partners to provide them with information that relates to the topic of the conversation and is relevant and appropriate to their language level so that they can use it to build upon what they already know. Teachers should try to *avoid* inappropriate behaviors because they discourage healthy speech development. These include making inappropriate or irrelevant comments, talking at rather than with, using a controlling or commanding mode of interaction, and repeating unnecessarily.

A New York study paired a proficient "talker" with a less proficient preschooler. At a special table, the "talk table," the study authors provided sets of categorized miniature figures and furnishings (Woodward, Haskins, Schaefer, & Smolen, 2004). Rules limited the table to one pair of children for 15 minutes of uninterrupted talk-time play per day. The miniature toys were not to be moved away. Each new set of toys was introduced with vocabulary. Children were urged to "use your words" at the talk table. During the 10-week study, teachers expended efforts to stimulate oral language through interactions and additional literacy activities. Test scores showed statistically significant oral improvement. The authors of the study believe the project clearly indicates that when an assessment suggests that a child has an expressive speech problem, concerned and innovative teachers can do something about it (Woodward et al., 2004). [DAP]

Figure 12-1 Suggested teacher strategies to promote child speech in differing classifications of human speech.

Personal Speech Expressing Individual Ideas, Feelings, Concerns

Teacher actions include:

1. providing time and opportunity for adult-child and child-adult sharing of personal thoughts and feelings.
2. eye-level listening and impromptu conversations throughout the school day.
3. accepting individual child ideas and feelings and expressing your own.
4. encouraging family visitation, participation, and interaction in classroom activities and affairs.
5. sharing literature that elicits children's personal speech responses.

Speech Helping Children Obtain and Satisfy Wants and Needs

Teacher actions include:

1. listening and responding to children's requests.
2. encouraging children's ability to ask for wants and needs.
3. increasing children's opportunities to help other children by giving verbal directions.
4. explaining in step-by-step fashion the sequence needed to obtain desired results (e.g., how to get a turn with a favorite bike).

Speech That Promotes and Maintains

InteractionTeacher actions include:

1. planning for shared use of materials, areas, or adult help.
2. planning for small group discussion and problem solving.
3. including a mix of child ages and genders in planned activities.
4. celebrating and socializing between children and adults in classrooms.
5. devising activities in which self-worth and diversity are valued.
6. devising activities in which negotiating and compromise are possible.

Speech That Expresses Imaginative Ideas

Teacher actions include:

1. planning for creative individual child and group response.
2. designing activities to promote pretending.
3. prompting child description of creative ideas, actions, and solutions.
4. offering dramatizing, play acting, and role-playing classroom opportunities and providing areas and furnishings.

5. being playful with language and appreciating children's playful language.
6. encouraging children's creative play by providing props and giving teacher attention.
7. using audio or visual taping or group enactment of child creativity to preserve, give status, and promote discussion and provoke additional creativity.

Speech That Enhances Children's Verbal Descriptions and Learning

Teacher actions include:

1. providing child activities to capture child interest and spark curiosity.
2. creating child and group verbal problem-solving opportunities.
3. putting phrases such as the following in daily teacher speech:
   "I wonder what . . ."
   "What would happen if . . ."
   "Let's see if . . ."
   "That's one way, can anyone think of another?"
   "What do we know about . . ."
   "Can we try a new way?"
   "What did we see when . . ."
4. suggesting real rather than contrived problems to solve.
5. listening closely to child discoveries and prompting children to put ideas into words.
6. noticing child interests. Building interest by following up with further activities.

Speech That Is Representational or Informative

Teacher actions include:

1. keeping record charts with children.
2. planning activities that involve observing carefully and analyzing or drawing conclusions.
3. eliciting additional or more precise information from children.
4. recording memorable classroom events, celebrations, and other happenings.
5. posting child birthdays, individual attributes, milestones, or other facts and data enhancing child self-worth or dignity.
6. graphing class composition factors (e.g., height and weight, food preference). Or presenting simple mapping activities involving school or neighborhood.
7. comparing time-related classroom factors.
8. providing activities that report individual child experiences to the group.

12-1b Children's Conversational Styles

Early childhood educators need to observe and notice children's conversational styles. Young children vary in their ability to approach others and speak to them and then respond. Conversational styles grow out of children's past experiences and conversations with others. Children form their own views of themselves as communicators and "the right" style (Photo 12-4). From your own experience with young children, what types of communication styles have you noticed? Have you encountered children that are eager, shy, self-conscious, self-confident, articulate, silent, questioning, repetitive, loud, advanced, and others? One child may need multiple descriptors, being social yet unclear, or shy but verbal when approached, for example. As one works daily with young children, one makes mental notes (or written ones) to help one decide what possible activities and adult interactions will provide opportunities for speech growth. Beginning teachers need to be aware of teacher tendencies to converse and spend time with children with whom they feel comfortable, perhaps because of that child's particular conversational style, cultural background, ethnic origin, or personality.

12-1c Sign Systems

Early childhood educators are aware that young children express themselves in a number of ways. Teachers realize that words are but one of the multiple systems young children use to construct and express meaning. Sign systems, like music, drama, and mathematics, are uniquely different from language, yet related. Words often accompany sign systems in both adults' and children's activities. Nonverbal signs, such as gestures, encountered in children's personal experience become associated with particular meanings that may differ widely for individual children. Teachers may encounter young children who are better able to express themselves in movement, art, or drama than with words. Actions can sometimes convey more than a child's language ability allows. Planned activities that encourage singing, dramatic expression, or use of art media to express what children know and feel expand the "confines" of language and are commonplace in most programs.

Almost all activities involve communication and expression. It is the teacher's job to see that words are prompted or supplied as a natural part of adult–child interaction so that consequent vocabulary growth is possible. Discussion between teachers and children in all curriculum areas can add and expand meaning to what is jointly experienced. For example, the statement, "You found out two cars can fit on the flat bed truck," puts into words the child's discovery. "Joylyn is showing us with her body how she feels about the doll she brought to sharing time" is another example. Early childhood educators need to be aware of their ability to be a model of rich, descriptive language and also their ability to use explicit, accurate, and appropriate vocabulary words in daily exchanges. They also should define words in easily understood terms, provide examples if necessary, and allow plenty of time to let their comments sink in.

Photo 12-4 Anna uses specific terms and mentions small details as she converses with others.

© 2015 Cengage Learning®

12-1d The Authentic Teacher

"Authentic" teachers are quick to issue appreciative comments about a child's persistence at tasks, creative or new elements in child activities, solutions to problems encountered, or other features of children's actions or behaviors. They are good at spotting every child's advances and accomplishments. They also provide honest comments when necessary, and this can be done with specific, detailed words that expand children's understanding. They promote children's ability to put their own feelings into words daily in conflict situations, empowering children in the process.

The goal of enhancing children's development by helping them feel like what they say has worth and value is of prime concern. Teachers work daily toward this. They attempt to stretch language skills and realize a confident child will converse freely and risk new experiences. It is obvious to teachers that many young children seek validation of their abilities. Children's "Look at me" or "Look what I did" requests can be answered in ways that are both language expanding and self-worth building. "Oh, that's nice" or "Yes, I see" are weak adult statements. A specific comment is more effective: "Your long blocks are standing on their small ends. You built your bridge very carefully" or "To make your cat's tail you had to cut a long thin piece of paper. It looks like a cat's tail because it comes to a small point on the end." These are valuable teacher comments. In social conflict situations, teachers channel child problems back to the conflicting parties so that verbal solutions between children are possible (Photo 12-5). They quietly stand near; hoping confrontations can come to satisfactory solutions, and intercede only when child communication breaks down.

12-1e Integrating Children into Social Groups

Because adults know children are teachers of other children, they want all children to obtain skills in social interaction. Teachers promote child friendships. The fragile friendships of two- and three-year-olds blossom and stabilize at about age four. The conversation of children in group play is a joy to overhear. A reluctant child is encouraged. Books, puppets, and other language arts media can offer friendship themes and empathy-building models. The story *The Lion and the Mouse* is a good example and usually increases child comments concerning what it means to be a friend. The story ends with ". . . little friends can help big friends. The size of a friend isn't really too important."

Common interests often bring individual children together in some pursuit or play. Observant teachers can create activities in which boys and girls share and enjoy each other's company. This can encourage them to seek former companions for later play and learning experiences (Manaster & Jobe, 2012). Language development is bound to be involved and can also aid the integration of children slow to make friends. Manaster and Jobe suggest teachers can take action by making simple changes in an activity to orient children to one another and provide opportunities to interact and collaborate (p. 16).

12-2 Suggested Interaction Guides

A teacher is a speech model for children. Because preschoolers range in abilities, the following guides for teachers in daily verbal conversations

Photo 12-5 Teachers often remind children to use their words if they wish others to give them a turn.

are based on understanding the level of each child. These guidelines help develop speaking ability when dealing with young nonverbal, or slightly verbal, children.

- Let the child see your face and mouth clearly, bend your knees, and talk and listen at the child's eye level.

- Use simple hand gestures that show meanings.

- Watch for nonverbal reactions.

- Talk to the nonverbal child slowly, stressing key words such as nouns and verbs.

- If you cannot understand a word, repeat it back to the child in a relaxed way.

- If a child says "lellow," say, "Yes, the paint is yellow." Articulation will improve with age and good speech modeling.

- Answer **expressive jargon** (groups of sounds without recognizable words) or jabbering with suitable statements such as "You're telling me."

- Play games in which the child copies sounds or words.

- Watch for the child's lead. If he is interested in some activity or object, talk about it in simple sentences.

- Make directions simple. Indicate actions as you say the words.

- Encourage the child's imitations, whether verbal or nonverbal. Show that the effort is appreciated.

- Pause and wait patiently for the child's response.

The following guidelines help children who speak in one-word phrases or simple sentences develop speaking ability.

- Enlarge a child's one-word sentences into meaningful simple sentences, for example, "ball" to "The ball bounces."

- Use naming words to describe objects and actions: "The red ball is round."

- Use conjunctions (*and*, *but*, *so*, *also*, *or*), possessives (*mine*, *theirs*, *ours*, *Billy's*, *yours*, *his*, *hers*), and negatives (*is not*, *will not*, *do not*, *isn't*, *don't*, *won't*, *am not*).

- Help the child talk about his feelings.

- Use previously learned words with new words: "The black candy is called licorice." "Your dog is a poodle; this dog is a beagle." "It's a kind of hat called a baseball cap."

- Ask simple questions that help the child find out and discover while his interest is high: "Where did you find that round rock?"

- Play labeling games with pictures and objects.

- Correct speech errors such as "wented" or "goed" by matter-of-factly saying the correct word in a sentence: "Yesterday you went to the store." (Omit any corrective tone of voice.) The child may answer by saying it the same as before, but you have modeled correct usage, and in time it will be copied.

- Accept hesitant speech and stuttering in a patient, interested way. When a child is excited or under stress, ideas may not develop into words properly.

- Wait patiently while a child tries to speak; silently hold eye contact. The thought may get lost, but if you are a good listener, and if you respond with interest to what is said, the child will try again.

When the child speaks in sentences and comes close to mature speech, the teacher should

- include appropriate classifications or categories in sentences to help children form concepts: "Dogs and cats are animals."

- ask questions that help the child pinpoint identifying characteristics: "Does it have a tail?"

- ask questions that help the child see what is alike and what is different.

- after modeling a sentence pattern in conversation, ask a simple question so that the child can imitate the proper form while it is still fresh in his mind: "I think this lemon tastes sour. How does the lemon taste to you?"

- help the child keep ideas in order. What happened first? What happened next? What came last?

- state instructions clearly, building from one- to two- or three-part directions: "First wash your hands; then you can choose a cracker."

- use prepositions in speech. Say them with gestures: "Put the toy on the shelf. Thank you.

---

expressive jargon — a term describing a child's first attempts at combining words into narration that results in a mimic of adult speech.

The blocks go inside the box." (Use your hand to show position as you speak.)

- use adjectives (*big*, *little*, *bright*, *red*, *soft*, and so forth) and comparatives (*more*, *less*, *lighter*, *heavier*, *shorter*, *tallest*): "Tell me about the rubber doll." "Yes, this pink doll is bigger" (Photo 12-6).

- ask the child to take simple verbal messages to another staff member: "Tell Mrs. Brown it's time to fix the snack." Alert other staff members to the fact that you are trying to promote verbal memory and self-confidence.

- help the child discover cause and effect: "Teacher, I'm afraid of bugs." "Why do bugs make you afraid, Billy?"

- remember that what is said in response to the child helps the child in many ways. Really listen. Answer every child if possible. When children talk at the same time, say, "I want to hear each one." "Mary, please say it again." "John, you can tell us next."

- give ownership to the ideas children contribute: "Yesterday Nancy told us . . ." "Kate's idea is . . ."

Teachers use a technique in adult–child conversation called **recasting**. This is very similar to expansion and feedback, previously mentioned.

Recasting fills in what is missing or gently makes a change in the child's incorrect usage in the adult's answering comment and extends the child's idea. If a child says, "I like apples," for example, the teacher could respond with, "Apples taste good. Some are red or green." or "I like green ones, don't you?"

When teachers actively listen and observe, questions and teacher responses can better suit individual children. Teachers can grow to understand speech and conceptual errors, miscues, misconceptions, and the ways certain children express themselves with greater depth. With close observation, teachers begin to build a personal and cultural history of attending children. Some preschool children may have traveled extensively, whereas others have never left their neighborhoods. Both can have rich, full vocabularies but completely different fields of reference. In a conversation about tree blossoms brought into the classroom, the teacher might ask, "Where have you seen trees blossom in your neighborhood?" or "Tell me how the blossoms feel when you rub them gently on your cheek like this" or "What do you see if you look very closely at the blossom in your hand?" A number of teacher options for extending child conversations can be found in Figure 12-2.

Photo 12-6 "Is this how long you want to make it?"

© 2015 Cengage Learning®

recasting — a teaching technique that involves a teacher who supplies children's missing words or gently models correct usage of words or extends the child's idea following the child's verbal statement.

Figure 12-2 Teacher options and ways to extend child conversations.

When a child's attention or focus is upon an object, action, event, animal, person, and so on, try the following:

- *Probe* with comments using your five senses.
  Discuss visual attributes (color, shiny, round, etc.).
  Comment on tactile qualities (soft, smooth, etc.).
  Make sound observations (loud, clang, thud, etc.).
  Describe smell or taste, if present.

- *Suggest* that the child "describe" using his senses.

- *Provide* data or information that is pertinent.

- *Comment* on significant facts and features, such as function, usefulness, category or class, novelty, origin, timeliness, parts, details, construction, mobility, weight, height, bulk, dimension, movement, and so forth.

- *Compare* it with something similar.

- *Relate* it to present, past, or future.

- *Probe* its relationship to other things.

- *Make guesses* in reference to what has captured the child's attention.

- *Discuss* opinions, impressions, conclusions, and problems that are possible or apparent.

- *Mention* likes and dislikes.

- *Fantasize*, imagine, pretend, or dream out loud.

- *Talk* about humorous, ridiculous, or incongruent features.

To assess your skill:

The child is observing a large ice cube melt in the outside yard. Return to the above and generate extending teacher comments.

Digital Download

12-2a Research Related Strategies

 COMMON CORE

Strategies for oral vocabulary development based upon current research are being explored and implemented by early childhood educators who want to adopt a more systematic approach. This approach enhances academic thinking abilities and the size and quality of children's vocabularies recommended by new state standards. These strategies reflect recognition that intervention is necessary for children falling behind. Strategies include the following.

1. Teacher plans for more repetition, practice, and usage of words just entering children's oral vocabulary by

   - increasing the frequency at which the words are encountered. Research suggests hearing a word repeated more frequently helps it to be retrieved and remembered.

   - playing games with new vocabulary words. "I'm holding a picture of something we talked about at story time. It's a...?"

   - going back and reviewing new and older vocabulary words. "Remember yesterday we discovered that plants *shrivel* when they don't get enough water?"

   - questioning. "Our puppet can help us to know where to put our foot on a *rung* on a ladder if the puppet points to the *rung*, is that correct?"

   - using visuals or other media that prompt a discussion that connects or uses a new word in another context. For example, if the new word is *magnet*, photos of other things that cling together such as stamps, stickers, tape, and post-it notes, might be discussed.

2. Teachers target new vocabulary words by

   - introducing words necessary for a firm understanding of an important storybook message before the book is read aloud, or by quickly identifying key topic words that come up in random discussions.

   - defining words accurately, clearly, and with a rich explanation or example tailored to children's past experience.

   - offering a slightly more sophisticated or advanced word than the child is using.

   - acting out new words with the child or group.

   - suggesting children listen closely to give a signal of recognition when a word is read aloud or heard.

3. Teachers intentionally select new vocabulary words because of their instructional value. These might be key words and/or

concept-related words critical for developing knowledge in subject areas such as science, number and measurement, and so on. Teachers choose new vocabulary words, which are useful in helping children more accurately and closely describe, compare, and contrast their discoveries and concepts by

- offering more technically advanced vocabulary, such as in a study of my body including ankle, wrist, abdomen, elbow, knee, nostrils, thumb, etc.
- using nonfiction picture books with accurately detailed illustrations.

4. The teacher purposefully builds vocabulary word clusters from a group of words associated with a concept or category by

- introducing interesting and child-selected courses of study, such as units, themes, projects, and by offering a specific or rich technical vocabulary that is necessary to understand and discuss the topic as fully as possible.
- by providing activities and experiences that make connections, contrasts, or comparisons between diverse objects, experiences, or happenings.
- by charting or listing categories, such as things with wheels, people who help in emergencies, or kinds of vegetables.
- by designing and conducting comparison activities when similarities and differences exist.

5. Teachers create classrooms where words are savored and collected by

- modeling enthusiasm for new and ever more descriptive and precise words.
- by game playing and clapping 'extra long' syllable words.
- by making individual child word boxes or lists of fun to say words, such as chickadee, bumbershoot, cummerbund, dragonfly, etc.
- by giving definitions that relate the words to children's lives when possible.
- by introducing teacher's fun or strange word(s) of the day.
- by using multimedia and music to introduce vocabulary words.

- by making word cards for games.
- by making job (helper) cards on lanyards.

12-2b Awareness of Intelligent Behavior

Over time, a number of researchers have tried to identify effective thinking and intelligent behavior indicators. Would-be teachers observe children and conjecture how young children "come to know" rather than remember or state what they already know. Most classrooms enroll children whom teachers would call "successful students." By closely observing children, teachers can note behaviors that indicate children's reasoning abilities, insightfulness, strategies, perseverance, creativity, and craftsmanship.

Many indicators are best observed in children's speech behavior. Costa's classic study (1991) outlines intelligent behavior characteristics, but also notes that the listing may be incomplete.

1. Persistence in Tasks: Persevering when a solution to a problem is not immediately apparent. In preschool, some children ask abundant questions, others try various and different approaches to reach goals. A child might ask all other teachers in a room if one teacher admits he/she doesn't know the answer to the question. Many children probe the reasons behind happenings and are persistent in getting more and more data to explain happenings.

2. Decreasing impulsiveness: A thoughtful pause rather than a quick answer or action may be observed in some preschoolers.

3. Listening to others with understanding and empathy: Some young children hear others' points-of-view and can paraphrase another's ideas. Others may not be able to "overcome ego-centrism" at this age as Piaget observes. Both groups are displaying developmentally appropriate behavior. The first group has achieved a maturity in thinking processes, and is usually slow to ridicule, laugh at, or put down other children's ideas.

4. Flexibility in thinking: No matter what a teacher or parent tells a child on a certain subject, the child may not believe or accept the information. This isn't flexibility in

thinking. As children age, however, many will at least consider new possibilities and doubt their previous ideas. Some check out new ideas with others with questions like "Do daddies cook?"

5. Metacognition: Awareness of one's own thinking: Preschoolers may be able to describe the steps they took to achieve some desired outcome, but rarely can they put into words what went on inside their heads or describe their strategies. More often when asked "How did you do that?" they will be silent or say "I just did it." This is a developmentally appropriate answer.

6. Checking for accuracy and precision: The child who shows a printed form to teacher saying "I made an A" may be simply stating a truth as he sees it. With another child who says "That's not an A. Is it, teacher?" The child is checking for accuracy. In discussions, a child may seek a correction. Many teachers have learned this lesson with the child who's a dinosaur buff for the child has learned the distinguishing characteristics of each dinosaur well, and may be better informed than the teacher.

7. Questioning and problem posing: This is a characteristic of many preschoolers who inquire about the "whys" of things and are alert to discrepancies and uncommon phenomena.

8. Drawing on past knowledge and applying it to new situations: At times, teachers have difficulty trying to understand what common element in a present situation the child is connecting to the past. Other connections are readily apparent as when a child reacts negatively to a worker dressed in white.

9. Precision of language and thought: Young children use an increasing number of descriptive words and analogous comments when exposed to adult language that is not vague or imprecise.

10. Using all of the senses: Young children readily probe, manipulate, and savor the sensory opportunities presented to them.

11. Ingenuity, originality, insightfulness, and creativity: Early childhood professionals treasure child attempts and behaviors in this area, and most teachers can immediately cite examples they've observed.

12. Wonderment, inquisitiveness, curiosity, and enjoyment of problem solving—a sense of efficacy as a thinker: Child attitudes toward problems, thinking games, guessing, and obstacles can enhance or impede their quest for knowledge and solutions. Adults may model attitudes of "giving up" or "it's too hard" or "I'll never get it right" rather than the preferred "let's find out," "let's see what we can do." Adults can also model enjoyment when in the pursuit of solving some task or dilemma (p. 203).

In considering the sixth item in Costa's list, the teacher may consider a child saying, "Sudeh didn't drink her juice," as checking to see if a rule about juice-finishing exists, rather than tattling. The teacher might reply, "At school we can choose to drink as much juice as we want, but everyone should drink all that he pours in his cup."

How can early childhood teachers support children's emerging intellectual abilities? From Costa's list, there are many clues. A teacher begins by having faith in the ability and intelligence of all children and acknowledges that not all children's homes (or all teachers) value intelligent behavior. Intelligent child behavior can be recognized and appreciated.

Children can absorb the idea that often there is more than one solution or answer or way of doing something and that pausing, gathering more data, and "thinking things over" are good strategies. Children can be asked to share their plans and outcomes on chosen activities. Day-to-day happenings and real dilemmas can be talked about and problems solved through actions and discussions in which every child's ideas are valued.

The teacher can rig classroom activities to promote children's thinking, problem solving, creative ideas, and imagination. Children can develop the attitude that what they contribute is worthwhile. When teachers listen, paraphrase children's comments, clarify, and try out student ideas, children feel that what they say is meaningful. "Maybe the school's pet bird does eat paper, or maybe it just tears it up. If we watch carefully we can find out, can't we?"

Providing a continually interesting classroom full of exploring opportunities is a must. Classrooms that are rich in first-hand manipulative experiences and are staffed with responsive adults can make this happen. One of the chief causes for failure in formal education is that we begin with language rather than with real and material action. At the preschool level this means that some teachers have a tendency to tell children about reality rather than "providing" reality—real exploring experiences encountered together. Teachers also need to model their own intelligent behaviors and enthusiasm for learning. Nothing works as well as an example.

12-2c Settings for Preplanned Speaking Activities naeyc DAP

Speaking activities occur when children are inside or outside the classroom or when they are on the move. Preplanned activities are more successful when both children and teachers are comfortable and unhurried and when there are no distractions. Peers will be a valuable source of words and meanings.

Close attention should be given to group size and the seating space between children at group times. It is easier to create an atmosphere of inclusion and intimacy in a small discussion group than in a large group, thereby promoting children's willingness to share thoughts. Lighting and heating in the room must also be considered. Soft textures and rugs add warmth and comfort. A half-circle seating arrangement, with the teacher in the center, provides a good view of both the teacher and what is to be seen. Ease of viewing depends on eye level and seating arrangement. When possible, the objects children are to look at should be at their eye level. Teachers often sit in child-sized chairs while conducting language arts experiences. Screens, dividers, and bookcases can help lessen distractions.

One inventive teacher thought of a way to promote child speech during a family–child "Back to School" night. Children were asked to draw self-portraits. A large mirror was set up beside various drawing supplies and paper. They were asked not to write their names on their self-portraits. Before the meeting, child drawings were posted under signs reading, "Can you find me?" Signs were done in the home languages of attending children. The activity promoted the children's verbal identification of their artwork and their classmates' drawings and highlighted the children's role as a verbal classroom guide for families.

TeachSource Video 12-1

Language Development: Oral and Literacy Related Activities in Early Childhood Settings

1. This teacher stated she used both recall and open-ended questions to stimulate children's oral expression and language growth. Could you estimate a percentage of each type of question used during this segment? And estimate the total number of questions asked?

2. Comment about the number of "low quality" teacher questions asked. Check the text section under the heading Questioning Skills for help in doing so.

12-2d Questioning Skills

A teacher's questions often prompt children to ponder and wonder. Questions checking whether the teacher has understood the child's comment are common. They provide the child feedback concerning the teacher's attention and interest and clarify whether the child's intended message was understood. This gives the child the opportunity to correct the teacher and send further data or explanation or to clear up miscommunication. Questions can also help keep conversations afloat and show that the teacher is interested in the child's pursuits.

Questions can help children see the details they would otherwise have missed. Sometimes questions help a child form relationships between objects and ideas; they may prompt the child to speak about both feelings and thoughts;

they can lead the child to a new interest. Skill in questioning is an important teaching ability. Questions asked by a teacher can often lead children to discovery.

Many experts suggest that teachers need help and specific training in questioning strategies so that they can aid children's ability to see contradictions, move them toward rethinking, and assist concept development. Teachers need to ask questions that are readily understood and require easy responses from the very young child and more challenging, thoughtful responses from language-capable preschoolers. This means modifying questions depending on language levels. Asking questions may be "the most fragile" of all conversation starters. Teachers can make questions less threatening by asking about a child's activities or interests and by using familiar expressions.

In a situation in a classroom when a door has blown shut and one of the children says, "Someone shut that door, teacher!" a skillful question such as "Is anyone standing near the door?" or "Could anyone reach that door from where they are in the room?" or "Can you think of something else that might cause the door to slam shut, something that could push it? These questions could lead the child to a new conclusion.

The following example illustrates the teacher's role in stimulating the thought process that emerges from play. The teacher, who has created the climate for learning by supplying and arranging the equipment, sees a child playing with cars on ramps that he has constructed with blocks. She knows that if a car is placed on a slope made with blocks, the speed with which it descends and the distance it goes are affected by the slope and length of the ramp. The teacher asks, "Did the blue car go farther than all the others?" or "What might happen if you built your ramp higher?" The teacher also introduces new words to the child's vocabulary—*slant, ramp, slow, faster, above, below, under, tall, smaller than*—and uses and elicits this vocabulary in conversation.

Teachers need to be sensitive to the anxiety that some children may have. In past experiences, if a child's answers have been overcorrected, or if adults' questions are associated with punishment, teachers' questions can cause children to be silent and tense. Teachers use "choice" questions at times. This allows them to slip specific, descriptive words into their speech while the child is focused: "Do you want the red paint (pointing) or the blue paint (pointing)?"

Also important in asking questions is the teacher's acceptance of the child's answers. Because each child answers a question based on his own experience, children may give very different answers. The following conversation (observed at the San Jose City College Child Development Center) shows how a teacher handled an unexpected answer. (The conversation had centered on television sets.)

Teacher: "Where could we go to buy a television set?"

Chase: "Macy's."

Chloe: "At a pear store."

Vanda: "The TV store."

Teacher: "Chase says Macy's sells television sets. Chloe thinks we could buy one at a 'pear' store. Vanda thought at a TV store. Maybe we could go to three places to buy one. Chloe, have you seen television sets at the 'pear' store?"

Chloe: "The pear store has lots of 'em'."

Teacher: "You've been to a 'pear' store?"

Chloe: "Our TV broke, and we took it to the 'pear' store."

Teacher: "The repair shop fixed my broken television set, too. Yes, sets can be for sale at a repair shop."

The teacher must view the incorrect answer as a starting point to gain insight into the child's instructional needs (Enz & Morrow, 2009).

The teacher's task is to keep the speech and answers coming, encouraging each child's expression of ideas. Sometimes a question can be answered with a question. When a child says, "What does a rabbit eat?" the teacher might say, "How could we find out?" The teacher knows that a real experience is better than a quick answer.

When using questions, the level of difficulty should be recognized. Early childhood teachers can use carefully asked questions to find the child's level of understanding. Teachers try to help each child succeed in activities while offering a challenge at the same time. Even snack time can be a time to learn new language skills.

Open-ended questions are very useful, and teachers try to increase their ability to ask them. Open-ended questions are defined as questions with many possible answers. Some teachers are so intent on imparting information to children that they forget to assess the ways it may be assimilated. Thus answers to open-ended questions—"Can you tell me about what you see on the table. . . ?" "What do you think about . . . ?"—are often more revealing than answers to questions with a more specific focus. An example of a specific focus question like, "How many blocks are on the table?" may only be answered by one word.

Wasik (2010) explains how children may benefit when open-ended questions are asked.

> . . . children who are asked open-ended questions, encouraged to expand on their language, and provided with feedback to their comments and questions have more opportunities to talk and use language, and therefore are more likely to develop language. (p. 624)

Almost all teacher questions can be classified into eight main types.

1. **Recall**: Asks the child to remember information, names, words, and so forth. Recall questions are the type most often asked. Many studies report that about 60 percent of teachers' questions require students to recall facts, about 20 percent require students to think, and the remaining 20 percent are procedural. Teachers emphasize fact questions, whereas research indicates an emphasis on higher, cognitive questions would be more effective.

2. *Convergent thinking:* Asks the child to compare or contrast similarities or differences and seek relationships. Example: How are these two toy cars alike?

3. *Divergent thinking:* Asks the child to predict or theorize. Example: If the boy steps on the marble, what might happen?

4. **Evaluation**: Asks the child for a personal opinion or judgment or asks the child to explore feelings. Example: What would be on your plate if you could have your favorite food?

5. **Observation**: Asks the child to watch or describe what he senses. Example: What is happening to the ant on the window sill?

6. **Explanation**: Asks the child to state cause and effect, reasons, and/or descriptions. Example: The clay feels different today. What do you think happened to it?

7. **Action**: Asks the child to move his body or perform a physical task. Example: Can you show us how to walk like a duck?

8. **Open-ended**: Many answers are possible. Example: How do children get from their homes to their school in the morning?

Certain types of teacher questions promote children's thinking processes. These include questions seeking children's opinions, questions calling for a verbalized choice, questions promoting a hypothesis, questions asking for cause-and-effect explanations, and questions seeking solutions. Teachers can question children's past happenings in light of present happenings to help children form relationships.

Teachers should limit "low-quality" questions that center on isolated bits of knowledge and are designed to test what is learned or remembered. Unfortunately, many adults link the words *teacher* and *test* and doggedly ask continual questions of children, believing this is age-old and appropriate behavior for all "good" teachers. When an adult approaches a young child playing in the sandbox with questions such as "What are you doing?" or "What are you making?" the child may wonder why the adult cannot see for himself or whether he is supposed to be making something. It may be hard for this adult to really focus on the child's activity and make pertinent comments, such as "That's a big mountain of sand you've just made," or to pick up a sand toy cup and say, "Please pour some sand in my cup."

Preschool teachers have many opportunities through questioning to explore children's imaginative responses to books, events, and classroom happenings. Their questions can be child-centered, promoting creative and interpretive child responses. Teachers can improve their ability to stop, listen, and learn from what their charges are saying.

The way questions are phrased may produce short or longer answers. Questions using "what" or "where" usually receive one-word or short-phrase answers. Many questions, such as *Do you? Did you? Can you? Will you? Have you? Would you?* are answered by *yes* or *no*. This type of question fits the level of the very young.

Questions that help a child compare or connect ideas may begin as follows:

---

convergent thinking — the process of analyzing and integrating ideas to infer reasonable conclusions or specific solutions from given information.

divergent thinking — the process of elaborating on ideas to generate new ideas or alternative interpretations of given information.

What would happen if . . . ?

Which one is longer?

How are these two alike?

Why did you say these were different?

What happened next?

If it fell off the table, what would happen to it?

Can you guess which one will be first?

Could this ball fit inside this can?

I wonder why the dog is sniffing?

What do you think is happening?

The following are examples of questions that encourage <u>problem solving</u> or <u>stimulate creative thought.</u>

If you had a handful of pennies, what would you buy?

Could you tell me what you are going to do when you're as big as your dad?

Can you think of a way to open this coconut?

How could we find out where this ant lives?

These questions can be answered by the more mature speakers. Through close listening and observation, the teacher can form questions that the child will want to answer.

12-3 Speech in Play and Routines

Children's play opportunities in early childhood centers are planned for, promoted, and wide ranging. An examination of whether an early childhood center has built conversation and discussion times into its daily schedule can reflect a staff's efforts to encourage child talk and oral expression. A conversational lunch period is an example of a routinely planned "small talk time."

In play, children can symbolize ideas and feelings through gestures and speech and can collaborate with friends. Children reexamine life experiences, adding their imagination and at times manipulating happenings, settings, and people (Photo 12-7). Play stimulates much child-to-child conversation, and some kinds of play promote talking more than others. Quiet activities such as painting or working puzzles may tend to limit speech while the child is deeply absorbed.

If teachers observe children's play sequences, they will note many child-initiated play situations that involve print, acting, drawing, "reading," and "writing." Props are improvised as dramas unfold. With writing, art, or construction materials handy, children will incorporate these into child-created and child-directed situations. Teachers plan opportunities for children to play by themselves and with others in small and large groups. Toddlers may play near each other in a nonverbal, imitative manner using sounds, squeals, and sometimes screams. Interaction with other children promotes the growth of speaking ability.

Studies of children with nonsocial or withdrawn play behavior during preschool found this behavior was a strong predictor of peer rejection, social anxiety, loneliness, depression, and

Photo 12-7 Look how intent and careful this child is while she is play ironing.

© 2015 Cengage Learning®

negative self-esteem in later childhood. Extra teacher help and encouragement may be necessary. A child case study by staff, conferencing, and referral to diagnostic experts may be needed if the school is unsuccessful in encouraging a child to engage in more social play behavior.

Early in life, children act out and repeat the words and actions of others. During preschool years this is called **dramatic play**, and the staff in early childhood centers plans and prepares for it. Dramatic play is believed to have important benefits for children and holds many learning opportunities. Young children's engagement in high-level make-believe play contributes to the development of underlying cognitive skills, such as symbolic thinking and self-regulation (Bodrova & Leong, 2012). Make-believe play occurs when children create roles in joint imaginary scenarios with pretend characters using imaginary or symbolic props, tailored language, and symbolic gestures. It helps children develop conversational skills and puts ideas in words (Photo 12-8). It is terrific for building an understanding of the feelings, roles, or work of others. Dramatic play combines words and actions and builds vocabulary. In social interactions, child creativity flowers. It also can be therapeutic and may develop leadership skills. The development of social skills and self-regulation give literacy a boost.

With a rising emphasis on prereading skill development crowding out free play time, some educators may need to justify offering children a curriculum with rich and generous dramatic play time. Hatcher and Petty (2004) suggest that teachers observe and document children's use of cognitive skills during play episodes; they believe that teachers will find plenty of examples of symbolic representation, cognitive flexibility, problem solving, make-believe, divergent thinking, and perspective taking. With close observation, educators can see considerable language growth and learning taking place, including new word use, concept development, linguistic awareness, and language practice. In a research study reported by Marcon (2007), children's later school success appears to have been enhanced by more active, child-initiated early learning experiences, but their progress may have been slowed by overly academic preschool experiences that introduced formalized learning experiences too early for most children's development status.

Pretend play is no easy task, even though it may look to be to the uninitiated observer. It is actually a milestone in development. It requires the ability to transform events and objects symbolically. Pretend play is full of interactive social dialogue and negotiation involving role taking, script knowledge, and improvisation. For example, when playing house, the child can start

Photo 12-8 Pretend photographers need cameras.

---

dramatic play — acting out experiences or creating drama episodes during play.

out as the grandfather and end up as the baby or the family dog. In each role, the child mixes real and pretend factors simultaneously; acts out thoughts, speech, and actions; and may portray emotions appropriate to the play scenario. Joint planning and problem solving using linguistic skill also takes place during play.

In trying to identify children's vocabulary during dramatic play, some educators have cleverly recorded children's dramatic play. From recordings they developed word and comment lists. These were later shared with children during daily recap meetings. One tea party word list included *tea, teapot, cup, spoon, saucer, plate, pour, spill,* and *please*; "No, thank you" and "What a beautiful hat!" were on a comment list. This teacher technique is especially helpful for second-language learners when word list words and actions are accompanied by demonstrations.

Teachers watch dramatic play develop from the simple imitative actions of toddlers and younger preschoolers to the elaborate dramatic play of four-year-olds, in whom language use blossoms. Teachers support each step along the way by providing the necessary objects and materials that enhance dramatic episodes and by offering assistance (Photo 12-8). Effective teachers must observe and be aware of the adult actions and situations that capture child interest enough to prompt reenactment. One surprised student teacher who dreamed up a shaving activity, complete with mirrors, shaving cream, and bladeless razors, found that the boys rolled up their pants legs and shaved their legs. This brings up two interesting items: first, the wisdom of letting razors, even bladeless ones, become play items, and second, how dramatic play often enlightens teachers. Child safety is always the first criterion used to evaluate whether an activity is appropriate.

Four-year-olds engage vigorously in superhero play. As cowboys, good guys and bad guys, or monster or ghost enactments have captured the imaginations of past generations of American children, new heroes such as talent show stars along with cartoon or video and movie characters have appeared. Robots and space creatures are common dramatic play themes for four-year-olds. The children mimic the chosen power figures in actions and words.

Many teachers feel ambivalent when they witness the violence enacted in some of these play episodes, which can require special handling and decisions to intercede to keep children safe. Most teachers set up times for group dialogue about superheroes so that reality and fantasy come under group discussion; such discussions can provide learning opportunities for the entire class or group. Other teachers worry about the perceived lack of child creativity in this type of play because the same theme and action are generally repeated over and over. Some educators believe a positive benefit exists. It may diminish fears associated with scary experiences, powerful people, or fictional media characters. Play may be children's attempt to give themselves extraordinary abilities and strengths.

Rich home and school experiences (going places and doing things) serve as building blocks for dramatic play. One would have a difficult time playing "restaurant" or "wedding" if there had been no previous experience with either. Early childhood centers can provide activities and objects that promote dramatic play, such as field trips, discussions, and readings by visitors and guest speakers; books, discussions based on pictures, films, videos, filmstrips, and slides; teacher-made kits (boxed sets), play equipment, and room settings; and career presentations made by family members.

In dramatic play, children often use symbols and language to represent objects that are not actually present. An oblong block may become a baby bottle; a pie plate, the kitchen clock; and so on. The enactment of role-appropriate behavior in a make-believe situation is a major step toward literacy. A significant relationship exists between kindergartners' symbolic play and reading achievement. Children with symbolic dramatic play skills seem to have increased ability to comprehend words and understand a variety of syntactic structures.

Dramatic play fosters children's growth in many areas, including verbalization, vocabulary, language comprehension, attention span, imaginativeness, concentration, impulse control, curiosity, problem-solving strategies, cooperation, empathy, group participation, and intellectual development. In play, the child is often behaving beyond his age and above his usual everyday behavior. Much time and effort are devoted to dramatic play in childhood. The child engages in this type of activity often and is able to slide easily from the real world into the make-believe world.

12-3a Dramatic Play Settings

A playhouse area with a child-size stove, refrigerator, table, and chairs encourages dramatic play. An old boat, a service station pump, and a telephone booth are examples of other pieces of equipment that children enjoy using in their play. Furniture found at early childhood centers can be moved into room arrangements that suggest a bus, a house, a tunnel, or a store. Large cardboard boxes may become a variety of different props with, or without, word labels. Large paper bags, ropes, blankets, and discarded work clothes or dress-up clothing also stimulate the child to pretend. Items for dramatic play can be obtained from commercial school-supply companies, secondhand stores, flea market sales, garage sales, and other sources.

12-3b Dramatic Play Kits

Items that go together and suggest the same type of play can be boxed together, ready for use. A shoe-shine kit, complete with cans of natural shoe polish, a soft cloth, a shoe brush, play money, and a newspaper or a magazine, is very popular. Functional print items can also be added and are a good way to develop print awareness. Children catch on to the activity quickly. Unfortunately, many may not have seen a shoe-shine stand or a family member polishing their shoes, so a teacher demonstration of this kit may be necessary.

Community theme prop boxes, such as bakery, flower shop, bank, car repair shop, and so forth, are suggested. Children using them make decisions about what community people think and do. Incorporating writing materials natural to the play theme promotes an additional language arts dimension.

Ideas for kits to be used in dramatic play follow.

Post Office. Large index cards, used postcards and letters, stamp pads, stamp blocks, stationery, envelopes, greeting cards, crayons or pencils, stamps (Christmas or wildlife seals), mailboxes (shoe box with slot cut in front and name clearly printed), old shoulder bag purses for mailbags, and men's and women's shirts.

Cleaning Set. Several brooms, mops, sponge mops, dust cloths, dustpans, sponges, shirts with logos, aprons, plastic bottles and spray bottles with water, and paper towels for windows.

Tea Party. Set of cups and saucers, plastic pitchers, napkins, vase, tablecloth, plastic spoons, placemats, place cards, teapot, invitations, small empty food packages such as cereal boxes, and clay or plastic cookies or biscuits.

Hospital and Doctor. Stethoscope, bandages, masking tape, red stickers for play wounds, tongue depressors, play thermometer, medical exam checklist, paper pad and pencil for prescriptions, billing forms for bill, adhesive tape, cotton balls, armband with a red cross on it, bag to carry, paper hospital gowns, white shirt, and photographs of culturally diverse doctors of both sexes.

Teacher. Notebooks, pencils, plastic glasses, chalk, bell, chalkboard, attendance book, photographs of a variety of teachers' desks, chairs, rulers, books, flannel board with sets, book about the first day at school.

Washing the Car. Towels, spray bottles with soapy water, sponges, buckets, cut hose lengths, window squeegees, old plastic raincoats, feather dusters, window cleaner spray bottles with blue-colored water, wax cans, drying line with clothes pins for wet towels, an old car. (A warm, sunny day in an outside grass area works best.)

Supermarket. Cash register, play money, newspaper ads, paper pads and pencils or crayons, hole punch, store name tags, shopping list, paper sacks, empty food cartons, wax fruit, play grocery cart or rolling laundry cart, purse, cell phone, and wallet.

Hair Salon. Plastic brushes, combs, cotton balls, powder, scarves, colored water in nail polish bottles, old hair dryer (no cord or plug), curlers, water spray bottle, hairpins, book of male and female hairstyles, and mirror.

Service Station. Tire pump, pliers, cans, sponges and bucket, short length of hose and cylinder (for gas pump), hat, plastic charge cards, squirt bottle, paper towels, paper and pencil, and a "Gas for Sale" sign.

Fishing. Hats, bamboo lengths (about 3 feet) with string and magnet at the end, fishing box, a basin, and small metal objects such as paper clips for the fish or cutouts for fish shapes with a paper clip attached to each (to attract the magnet), and bucket.

Gift Wrap. Old wallpaper books, assorted empty boxes or blocks to wrap, used bows, tape, scissors, gift cards, ribbon, crayons, and calendar.

Camping. Old pots and pans, plastic dishes, backpacks, blankets, sleeping bags, foam pads, flashlight, short lengths of logs, red cellophane, large box or tent, food boxes, card table and chairs, old camp stove, canteen, cell phone, portable radio, pretend child-safe sun tan or protection lotion in plastic bottles, and sunglasses.

Airplane. Chairs in rows, trays, plastic utensils, play food, headphones, little pillows, blankets, tickets, magazines, rolling cart, cups, plastic bottles, napkins, airline attendant clothing, backpack, and snack packages.

More kits can be made for the following careers and settings—repair person, baker, painter, picnic, restaurant, wedding, police officer, construction worker, mail carrier, firefighter, pilot, circus, birthday party, astronaut, airport, and plumber. This does not list all possibilities. Families are good sources for kit items.

Collecting props for favorite stories and putting them in a storage bag or container that has a picture or illustration of the story on its front is another idea. For example, for the story *Stone Soup*, the following props could be collected: large pot, large stone, long-handled spoon, assorted vegetables, aprons for cooks, hats for travelers, three-cornered hats for soldiers.

12-3c Costumes

Costumes and clothing props let a child step into a character quickly. Strong, sturdy, child-manageable ties and snaps encourage self-help. Elastic waistbands slip on and off with ease. Clothing that is cut down to size (so that it does not drag) can be worn for a longer time. Items that children enjoy are:

- hats of all types. (*Note*: The use of hats, wigs, and headgear may not be possible in some programs where head lice have occurred.)

- shoes, boots, and slippers.
- uniforms
- accessories, such as ties, scarves, purses, wallets, old jewelry, aprons, badges, and key rings.
- discarded fur jackets, soft fabrics, and fancy fabric clothing.
- wigs.
- work clothes.

A clever idea for a child-made costume is using a large-handled shopping bag. Once the bottom of the bag is cut out, the child can step into it, using the bag handles as shoulder straps. The child can decorate the bag and use it as a play prop.

12-3d The Teacher's Role in Dramatic Play

Dramatic play is child-directed instead of teacher-directed. Play ideas come from the child's imagination and experience. Teachers can motivate dramatic play before they withdraw to remain in the background. They are watchful but do not hover. Sometimes a new play direction is suggested by a teacher to divert the children away from unsafe or violent play. The flow of play preferably is decided by the children. Teachers' close presence and words can stop or change behavior when the situation becomes unsafe or gets out of hand. If things go smoothly, the ideas, words, and dramatic play actions are those of the children. Periodic suggestions by the teacher and introduction of material may extend and enrich play. Care is taken not to dominate, but rather to be available as a friendly resource.

Play is where reading and writing begin. In dramatic play, children understand its pretend or make-believe nature (although, in certain play situations, a child occasionally may confuse play with reality). Older preschoolers' dramatic play becomes increasingly mature, involved, complex, and riddled with abstract symbolic representations.

Pioneering attempts to train children who were less able to engage in appropriate pretend play have occurred. Teacher modeling, teacher assuming a play role in reenactments of real-life experiences, and teacher interventions such as suggestions, giving directions, asking questions, and clarifying behavior took place. Study children were encouraged to engage in and sustain sociodramatic play. Teachers let children decide play direction and content. Teachers' actions, it was found, *aided* child elaboration of child- play themes.

Some educators believe a few children without adult support may never reach what they describe as a fully developed dramatic play status. They recommend teachers spend more time in adult directed dramatic play activities such as providing scaffolding that targets the most critical components of play, and take actions to increase children's ability to maintain play roles. Prairie's (2013) suggestions include a more planned and opportunistic educational approach to children's dramatic play. She encourages teachers to talk with forming playgroups about their chosen play theme and what events might happen, what play roles will be assumed, and what real and imaginary props might be used. She urges teachers to provide detailed information about the children's chosen theme and ask questions and provide suggestions. Teachers might also encourage children to think about what is involved in playing a particular role, for instance, "the doctor." She suggests a teacher can be involved as an eager nonplayer observer or assume but a minor playacting role in the child-directed play scenario.

Traditionally, teachers have been advised to limit or omit adult interaction and domination of young children's dramatic play. The teacher might be involved by briefly modeling equipment use or making quick statements suggesting children's options—for example, writing a note, selecting menu items, or looking at signs. If children are playing with old cell phones, the teacher might remark, "It says *talk* and *send* on your cell phone buttons," while pointing out the buttons on the phone. Teacher behavior of zooming in and out is believed appropriate. This involves adding to the child's ideas and giving choices for the child to consider without directing or dominating the flow of the child's ideas and play except when child safety is concerned.

When teachers observe dramatic play, lots of language use is occurring, and teachers may be able to provide materials, equipment, or additional play items that facilitate even more language usage. Many times this is done by connecting language in some way to the children's play themes, such as by providing signs, old cell phones, or paper and writing tools so something can be written down, recorded, created, or composed with or without teacher assistance. Teachers try to determine what can be supplied that is naturally connected to the children's play scenarios. By observing closely, they can gain insights into individual children's ability and play skills.

12-3e Dramatic Play as an Intellectual Reaction to Book Events

Children's dramatic play and role-playing are ways to synthesize and connect what has been presented in picture books and in their own lives. Any observant teacher knows children's dramatic play mirrors their significant life experiences. The child who first says, "Did you bring home any money?" in a play scenario in which the child playing father enters the play situation has observed or experienced a background event.

What then could be the benefit of playacting a book? Besides the recreating (retelling) of book parts or themes, the experience offers a number of intellectual and literary benefits. Deeper or clearer meaning might be achieved. Early childhood practitioners can conclude that this activity helps children construct knowledge on a number of levels.

Wanerman (2010) believes story drama using a favorite picture book is an ideal curriculum approach with young preschoolers. He explains:

> Underneath this basic premise, however, lie opportunities to promote a complex web of language skills—negotiating roles promotes self-advocacy and negotiation, exploring character and theme helps children articulate and explore emotions and gain self-knowledge, navigating the narrative thread develops sequential thinking and discussing possible story outcomes involves abstract concepts and language. (p. 25)

Children often retell more detailed and complex stories when they are supplied with simple props, such as small objects or pictures. Practicing teachers suggest using a story clothesline tied between two pieces of furniture with 6 to 10 pictures (created or selected) to depict major story or book events. "Story collars," which represent the clothing story characters might wear, such as a farmer's work shirt collar or a faux fur collar for an animal character, were also suggested.

Props like hats, clothes, and objects and settings connected to the picture book can be created using teacher ingenuity. A teacher can examine a book before presenting it for features that lead to easy enactment; for example, if using *The Three Billy Goats Gruff*, it would be easy to set up a bridge with the materials and equipment found in most preschools. When children reenact a picture book with a teacher's help, the teacher may be surprised because as children reenact they will usually insert objects and events from their own lives into the story context.

The following books lend themselves to child reenactment:

Battersby, K. (2011). *Squish rabbit*. New York: Viking.

Eastman, P. (1960/1993). *Are you my mother?* New York: HarperCollins.

Flack, M. (1971). *Ask Mr. Bear*. New York: Young Readers Press.

Marshall, J. (1997). *Goldilocks and the three bears*. New York: Putnam.

Preschoolers and kindergartners who frequently engage in thematic fantasy play (in which children act out stories that have been read aloud to them) have better vocabularies, use more complex language, and have better story comprehension than children who only draw or talk about stories. McGee (2003) notes that children are more likely to enact stories when teachers repeatedly read them.

12-3f Daily Routines

Periods designed especially for conversation are included in the program of an early childhood center. A gathering or group time at the start of the day is used to encourage individual recognition and speaking. Snack and lunch periods are set up to promote pleasant conversation while eating. Activities are planned and structured to provide for as much child talk as possible.

12-3g Show-and-Tell

One of the most common daily routines is show-and-tell time. It must be noted here that some early childhood educators believe that this routine is outdated and overused and prefer to eliminate it from their daily schedules. In contrast, show-and-tell advocates believe that this activity encourages children to talk about their special interests in front of others. The

child can bring something from home or share something made or accomplished at school. Following are some helpful hints for conducting show-and-tell.

- Encourage, do not force, children to speak.
- If they do not want to talk, they can just show what they brought.
- Let the child who is showing something to the group stand or sit near the teacher. A friendly arm around the child's shoulders may help.
- Stimulate the other children to ask the child questions: "Mark, you seem to want to ask Gustavo about his blue marble."
- Limit the time for overly talkative children by using an egg timer.
- Limit the time for the activity so that the children do not become bored.
- Thank each child for his participation.
- Try something new such as the following:

  a. Display all articles and have the group guess who brought each.

  b. Have children swap (if possible) what they have brought so that they can talk about each other's items.

  c. Bring in a surprise item to share with the children.

  d. Make a caption for each item and display it on a table (for example, "Betty's Green Rock").

  e. Have the child hide the object behind his back while describing it to the others. Then the other children can guess what the object is.

  f. Be sensitive to ethnic and cultural communication styles.

Show-and-tell times can be tedious and stressful, but when well-conducted and varied in clever ways, they can also be the highlight of the day. Show-and-tell items are usually kept out of children's reach to prevent the loss of a valued or favorite toy. The teacher can divide the class into groups and name the days on which each group can bring in items or the teacher may prefer to allow the children to share whenever they wish. Show-and-tell helps children develop vocabulary, responsibility, and the ability to speak in front of others.

When making these goals known to parents, teachers explain that the children have choices in these sharing times and that items do not have to be brought to school on a daily or regular basis. Asking a parent group if show-and-tell is causing a home problem or child stress can be a wise move. Sharing-time objects can be related to a classroom theme, if families are alerted beforehand. Children who bring in objects unrelated to the topic could be given time after topic-centered sharing.

12-3h The Daily News or Recap Times

Many centers engage in daily news or recap group time that focuses on important or interesting events of the day. Teachers and children gather to share news, anecdotes, and happenings in both their home and school life. The teacher can initiate this activity with statements such as "Keith told me about something new at his house. Would you like to share your news, Keith?"

At group times, the teacher must be aware of group reaction and response. On some days, there may be excited response and conversation; on others, there may be little response, and the activity should be kept brief. To give children an opportunity to talk about problems and their solutions, recap times can be partially devoted to children's verbalizing success or lack of it in proposed courses of action and projects.

12-3i Promoting Daily Oral Language Use

The following are suggestions that can promote more child speech in daily programs.

- Have children give verbal messages or directions to other children often: "Petey, please show Flynn our dustpan and hand broom. Tell him how we empty it." (Then follow through by thanking him.)
- Let children describe daily projects.
- Relate present ideas and happenings to the children's past when possible: "Shane had a new puppy at his house, too. Did your puppy cry at night? What did you do to help it stop? Kathy has a new puppy who cries at night."
- Promote child explanations: "Who can tell us what happens after we finish our lunch?"
- Promote teacher–child conversations in which the teacher records children's words on artwork, constructions, or any happenings or projects.
- Periodically make pin-on badges (for teachers and interested children) like the ones shown in Figure 12-3.
- Play "explaining games" by setting up a group of related items on a table and having the children explain how the items can be used. For example, three groups of items might be (1) a mirror, comb, brush, washcloth, soap, and

Figure 12-3 Pin-on badges.

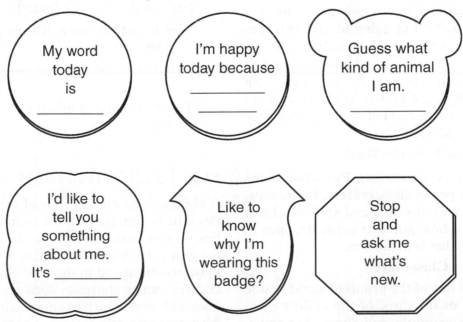

basin of water; (2) shoes, white shoe polish, and new shoelaces; and (3) nuts, a nutcracker, and two bowls. Encourage child volunteers to explain and demonstrate the use of the items by facing the group from the other side of the table. Other possibilities include items to demonstrate peeling an orange, making a sandwich with two spreads, or making a telephone call.

- Design and create games that encourage children to speak.

Games Promoting Speech.

1. Suitcase Game

Teacher: I'm going on a vacation trip. I'm putting suntan oil in my suitcase. What will you put in your suitcase?

Child: A swimming suit.

Child: Candy.

Teacher: (After the group has had an opportunity to contribute.) Let's see how many items we can remember that people wanted to bring on vacation.

2. Grocery Store Game

Have a bag handy with lots of grocery items. Pull one out yourself and describe it. Have the children take turns pulling out an item and describing it. The teacher can make a shopping list of items named and explain a shopping list's use.

3. Letter Game

Provide a large bag of letters. Pull one letter out. Talk about a letter you are going to send to a child in the group. "I'm going to give this pretend letter to Frankie and tell him about my new car" or "I want to send this thank-you card to Janelle because she always helps me when I ask for cleanup helpers. Who would like to pull out a letter from this bag and tell us the person they would like to send it to?"

4. Guess What Is in the Box

Collect small boxes with lids. Put small items inside, such as paper clips, erasers, bottle tops, plastic toys, leaves, flowers, and so forth. Have a child choose a box, guess its contents, open it, and talk about what is in the box.

5. Describe a Classmate

Choose a child out of the group to stand beside you. Describe or list three of the child's characteristics, for example, red shoes, big smile, and one hand in pocket. Ask who would like to choose another classmate and tell three things about that person.

6. Guessing Photograph Happenings

Use photographs showing a sequence of actions. Help children express their ideas of what is depicted. Examples: digging in the garden, planting bulbs, a flowering tulip, and mixing pancake batter, frying pancakes, eating pancakes.

7. The Mystery Bag

An activity children enjoy in small groups is called the mystery bag. The teacher collects a series of common objects. Turning away from the group, the teacher puts one of the objects in another bag. The game starts when a child reaches (without looking inside) into the second bag and describes the object. It is then pulled out of the bag and discussed: "What can we do with it? Has it a name? It's the same color as what else in the room?" The group should be small, because it is hard for a young child to wait for a turn. Examples of objects that could be used include a rock, comb, orange, pancake turner, feather, plastic cup, sponge, hole punch, flower, toy animal, and whistle.

8. Parts-of-the-Body Guessing Game

I can see you with my ___ (eyes).

I can smell you with my ___ (nose).

I can chew with my ___ (teeth).

I can hear with my ___ (ears).

I can clap with my ___ (hands).

I walk on my ___ (feet).

I put food in my ___ (mouth).

This is not my nose; it's my ___ (point to ears).

This is not my eye; it's my ___ (point to nose).

This is not my mouth; it's my ___ (point to eye).

12-3j Leading Activities

A child can be chosen to lead others in activities if he is familiar with the routines and activities. One or more children can be at the front of the group, leading songs or finger plays. (Finger plays are discussed in the next chapter.) Often, children can be chosen as speakers to direct routines with words such as announcing snack time. Also, teachers can promote speaking by asking one child to tell another child something: "Tell Billy when you want him to pass the wastebasket to you." or "If you're finished, ask Georgette whether she wants a turn, please." It is helpful during group times to point out that the teacher and the other children want to hear what everyone says, and because of this, children should take turns speaking.

Summary

12-1 State four goals of planned preschool speech activities.

Some goals of planned activities that promote preschool speech include building child confidence, increasing enjoyment in speaking, promoting the understanding that other's speech may be different, building childen's interest in word meanings, encouraging children to use speech to express feelings, desires, and needs, using speech to solve problems, and also using speech creatively and increasing children's ability to coordinate words with body actions. Other goals involve encouraging children's discourse skills and exercising the speech children already possess while moving toward Standard English usage.

12-2 Describe professional techniques used in daily conversations with children.

Many professional teacher techniques to promote children's speaking abilities were mentioned including focusing on children's agenda, identifying children's interests and conversing about them, recognizing child achievement and discussing it, respecting individual child opinions and contributions in discussions, using a variety of questioning types, providing logical responses in conversational exchanges, offering reassurance when necessary, focusing total attention on children's statements and comments, and creating and developing a classroom atmosphere conducive to child speaking opportunities.

12-3 Explain how teachers support and enrich children's dramatic play.

Teachers value dramatic play, for many learning experiences are possible. Teachers provide time, space, materials, and teacher energy. They follow child interest and support it when it takes place. Classrooms have designed areas that encourage children to plan and play their own scenarios. Planned kits are collected and stored for use. These include safe costumes, props, visuals, and real objects. Teachers motivate, monitor, and withdraw, except when needed. Children decide the flow of play. Teachers extend and enrich play without dominating it. They serve as a friendly resource that observes and encourages and sometimes steps in if play becomes unsafe.

Additional Resources

Adams, M. J. (2013) *ABC Foundations for Young Children: A Classroom Curriculum.* New York: Brookes Publishing.

Hyson, M. (2008). *Enthusiastic and Engaged Learners.* New York: Teachers College Press.

Resnick, L. B, & Snow, C. E. (2009). *Speaking and Listening for Preschool Through Third Grade.* Newark, DE: International Reading Association.

Wanerman, T. (2010, March). Using story drama with young preschoolers. *Young Children* 65(2) 20–28.

Helpful Websites

NAEYC National Association for the Education of Young Children
http://www.naeyc.org

Includes links to articles and publications.

13 Group Times

Objectives

After reading this chapter, you should be able to:

13-1 Describe professional and successful circle (group) time features.

13-2 List three factors to be considered when planning to lead a group time.

13-3 Discuss goals for group times and circle time.

13-4 Describe what a child might gain when learning a finger play or a body action play.

naeyc NAEYC Program Standards

2E06 Children are encouraged to play with sounds in finger plays.

2A10 The curriculum guides teachers to incorporate content, concepts, and activities that foster social, emotional, physical, language, and cognitive development and that integrate key areas of content including literacy.

2A11 The schedule provides children learning activities in large groups, small groups, and child-initiated activity.

DAP Developmentally Appropriate Practice (DAP) Preschoolers

3H6 Teachers are especially attentive to helping English language learners grasp word meanings.

3H28 Teachers are comfortable with slight diversions that occur when children share connections that are relevant to them.

3M8 Teachers encourage children to engage in full body activities that require rhythm and timing, such as swinging; Teachers join them in such movement.

3H7 Teachers provide ways for every child to talk during group time.

COMMON CORE Common Core State Standards, K-3

L.CCR.1 Demonstrate command of the conventions of Standard English grammar and usage when writing or speaking.

Mr. Fuzz

At a group time, Billy Jay was sharing what had happened to the classroom's visiting teddy over the weekend. Each child in the class has a turn to take Mr. Fuzz home, and Billy Jay had just done so. It was expected that the child taking Mr. Fuzz would then relate some important weekend happenings at Monday morning's circle time. So far, Mr. Fuzz had been hidden by the family dog, accidentally washed in the washing machine, taken up in an airplane, and thrown out of a window on his previous excursions to the children's homes. Billy Jay was excited when he told the group that Mr. Fuzz went to "Three and one." This puzzling statement was soon cleared up when Billy Jay said, "And he likes Jamoca Almond Fudge just like my mom."

Questions to Ponder

1. Would it be a good idea to make a book of Mr. Fuzz's adventures for the library corner?

2. Can you think of other literacy activities that could also grow out of the use of Mr. Fuzz?

3. Billy Jay is obviously aware of numbers on signs. Could this lead to a sign recognition activity for the whole class? If yes, identify one.

The activities in this chapter give children many language opportunities. Children involved in the activities have the opportunity to imitate speech, to use creative speech, and to express their own ideas and feelings. However, you should realize that it is difficult to categorize activities as listening or speaking activities because they often overlap.

13-1 Group and Circle Time

Group time and **circle time** offer a time of day when children develop understandings about themselves as group members. They enjoy language together by using familiar songs, favorite finger plays, chants, and a wide variety of activities. Children gain self-confidence, feelings of personal worth, and group spirit (Photo 13-1). Group times are often conducted as both instructional and "sharing times" within programs that are

Photo 13-1 At lunchtime a child feels he is part of the group.

© 2016 Cengage Learning®

---

circle time — an early childhood term describing a planned gathering of children, usually seated in a half-circle configuration, led by a teacher.

designed for an abundance of child-selected and child-initiated activities.

School administrators and teachers need to clarify their priorities concerning group times. You already know intimacy declines as group size grows. Many schools prefer working with small groups of children so that conversations can flourish. However, decisions regarding group size may hinge on staffing considerations. Sometimes large groups can be temporarily divided so that there can be "instant replays" of activities for smaller groups.

Whole group instruction, if planned instead of recommended small group instruction, can include read-aloud time, interactive writing, phonological awareness activities, and letter knowledge activities or other literacy activities and other curriculum area content. Interactions during group time can also include (1) explicit instructional content to which all children should be exposed; (2) intentional instruction that builds on stated curriculum goals; and (3) interactions used diagnostically to determine the need for individual and small group follow-up instruction. When teacher directed instruction takes place, teachers plan to relate content to what the children are familiar with. It should provide an overview of what will be learned or will take place and proceed in a planned progression that allows for practice and/or a recap of what was learned.

Many educators are debating the value of larger group activities, especially programs that attempt to teach the bulk of the school's curriculum in that manner. Educators also doubt its developmental appropriateness. Large group times used for news, announcements, morning welcome, a quick class discussion, or closing wrap-up are a different story and may be part of the established school routine. Nemeth (2009) suggests having group meetings with second language learners at the beginning of the day. Teachers can then probe children's ideas and describe planned events and activities. In this way routines might be modified to incorporate children's ideas or needs into the schedule.

When presenting new material during small group sessions, teachers should allow time to receive and react to children's comments and questions. One pitfall in conducting group activities is the tendency for teachers to remain the center of attention, assuming the role of the great dispenser of knowledge. When this occurs, child feedback can be ignored.

Beginning teachers may be unskilled in drawing conversation from children in large group and small group discussions. Discussion becomes the teacher asking questions and calling on children for answers. If this happens children learn very little about what it means to "talk things over" with a group. Other questionable teacher skills and behaviors are discussed under the heading "Circle-Time Pitfalls" later in this chapter.

In group settings with four-year-olds, early childhood teachers become acutely aware of children who are having difficulty paying attention, following directions, getting along, and controlling emotions. These children usually will do less well in school. Research on early schooling suggests that the relationships children build with peers and teachers are based on their ability to react in social versus antisocial ways; behaviors can help or hurt academic performance (Raver, 2003). At group times, teachers make every effort to keep children focused and involved in language arts activities. Educators develop teaching strategies that help children take turns, listen patiently, and remember directions.

Language activities add sparkle and liveliness to circle times. The following is a list of words used to describe a successful group experience.

- **active**—Children's participation includes motor and speech involvement.
- **enthusiastic**—The teacher's commitment in making a presentation is communicated by the teacher's facial expressions and manner.
- **prepared**—All the necessary materials are at the teacher's fingertips and are used with smooth verbal presentations.
- **accepting**—The teacher is open to children's ideas and feelings and is appreciative of children's contributions.
- **appropriate**—The activity suits the particular group.
- **clear**—The teacher provides purposeful clarification of new concepts.
- **comfortable**—The seating and light source are appropriate.
- **familiar**—The activity includes previously learned and enjoyed material.
- **novel**—New ideas and material are presented.
- **relaxed**—The activity does not stress, pressure, or threaten children.
- **sharing**—All children are invited to take turns participating in the activity.

TeachSource Video 13-1

Language Development: Oral and Literacy Related Activities in Early Childhood Settings (Bonus Video 1)

After viewing Bonus Video One, respond to the following questions.

1. Discuss what you felt were positive features of the circle time viewed. It used circle time to transition children to their next classroom activity.

2. Were there any aspects of the teacher's teaching style or behavior that you'd like to discuss with your training group? If so, list them. If not, instead comment on any teacher behaviors you especially admired.

3. Did you view any child skills that would be important assets for the child's success in kindergarten?

© 2016 Cengage Learning®

13-1a Important Skills for Entering Kindergarten

Gamel-McCormick (2000) surveyed kindergarten teachers asking them to rate the importance of a set of skills desirable in entering kindergartners. Two communication-related skills appeared in their top 10 choices: (1) communicates needs and preferences and (2) attends to peer or adult talking. The number one teacher selection was "exhibits self-control." Kindergarten teachers were also asked for a written definition of readiness. A summary of their answers follows.

- Teachers included components of all domains in their definitions except children's physical skills.

- Definitions that mentioned social and behavioral skills and skills that allow students to function independently were given a top priority.

- Teachers included some academic skills in their definitions.

- For most teachers, the definitions focused on children's abilities to successfully interact with peers and adults.

Blair (2003) reports similar results in a nationally represented sample of kindergarten teachers who cited child self-regulation as being essential to school readiness. This included a child's being able to communicate needs, wants, and thoughts verbally; sustain attention; and be enthusiastic and curious in new activities. It also mentioned children's ability to inhibit impulses, follow directions, and take turns and be sensitive to other children's feelings.

COMMON CORE

What can early childhood educators learn from these studies? Foremost is that the work undertaken at the preschool level to promote children's self-help, independence, social interaction, cooperation, and group participation skills is highly valued by kindergarten teachers. The child's ability to recognize alphabet letters and write her name was also cited by kindergarten teachers, but these choices followed skills concerned with child self-control and self-help. To build these skills in four-year-olds, early childhood programs make sure teachers spend considerable time in small group or circle-time activities that strongly encourage and reinforce group expectations (rules for group behavior). Skills pinpointed include turn taking, listening with focus, appropriate social interaction, and cooperation.

13-1b Groups of Younger Preschoolers

Two- and three-year-olds participating in group times are learning social interaction sometimes for the first time. Their group participation may depend on their feelings of trust and security. After adjustments to seating comfort are made, the teacher welcomes each child by stating or singing their names, or the teacher starts a simple song or finger play. The teacher watches for child focus and involvement. Often, active participation grows slowly as watchers become doers. In well-conducted circle times, children can choose their own level of participation. Teacher flexibility and preplanning, together with the teacher's obvious enthusiasm and delight in each child's presence, breed social acceptance and success. Time will determine whether a teacher decides to expand highly enjoyed circles or cut others short because of children's feedback signals.

Because younger children's classrooms usually are staffed with adults, volunteers, and assisting adults, these adults can sit near or beside children to encourage child participation. An inviting group time may draw in all attending children after it is in progress. Some schools employ a visual sign (reminder) that listening is expected. Teachers might use a paddle-shaped card with a drawing of an ear or a drawing of closed lips to cue children to attend while others are speaking.

Group time for very young preschoolers can be described as "loose and light" formations or groupings. Children choose to be present and choose their level of involvement. Teachers count on child curiosity and desire to be part of the action. Think of yourself in a new social situation: Wouldn't you watch briefly before entering conversations with strangers and approach those who seem most open and welcoming? And wouldn't you move on if conversations were boring, irrelevant, or obtuse?

13-2 Planning Small Group Times

After considering child capacity to remain involved, a group for either younger or older preschoolers can be planned to occupy a specific time period. What happens and when it happens is roughly outlined. A gathering-together activity can be a song, a finger play, or a recording followed by any number and type of activities. A planned closing and transition ends the experience and moves the group in an orderly fashion onto other classroom pursuits. If group time is of considerable length, then standing and moving activities are interspersed with seated ones. Try creating finger play motions for any of the following:

Pizza

Let's make a pizza big and round

Take tomato sauce and spread it around.

Onions, olives, peppers, and cheese

Add mushrooms, sausage if you please.

Put it in the oven. Careful it's hot!

Bake 'til a warm brown crust you've got.

It's bubbly, spicy, and tastes so nice.

Raise your hand if you'd like a slice.

Taking Off

The airplane taxis down the field

And heads into the breeze.

It lifts its wheels above the ground.

It skims above the trees

It rises high and higher

Away up toward the sun.

It's just a speck against the sky and now—

and now—it's gone.

Little House

I'm going to build a little house (Fingers form a roof.)

With windows big and bright. (Make square with hands.)

With chimney tall and curling smoke (Arm up in the air—waving in spiral.)

Drifting out of sight

In winter, when the snowflakes fall (Hands flutter down.)

Or when I hear a storm (Cup hand to ear.)

I'll go sit in my little house (Stand, then sit down.)

Where I'll be nice and warm. (Hug chest.)

This Is The Mountain

This is the mountain up so high, (Form a triangle.)

And this is the moon that sails through the sky. (Make a circle with thumbs and index fingers.)

These are the stars that twinkle so bright. (Make a small circle with thumb and index finger, other three fingers moving.)

These are the clouds that pass through the night. (Make fists.)

This is the window through which I peep, (Make a square with thumb and index.)

And here am I, fast asleep. (Close eyes.)

Clap Your Hands

Clap your hands high,

Clap your hands low,

Pat your head lightly,

And down you go.

I'll touch my hair, my lips, my eyes,

I'll sit up straight, and then I'll rise.

I'll touch my ears, my nose, my chin,

Then quietly, sit down again.

Butterfly

Roly-poly caterpillar

Into a corner crept.

Spun around himself a blanket

Then for a long time slept.

A long time passed (Whisper.)

Roly-poly caterpillar wakened by and by.

Found himself with beautiful wings

Changed to a butterfly.

Sleepy Time

Open wide your little hands,

Now squeeze them very tight.

Shake them, shake them very loose,

With all your might.

Climb them slowly to the sky.

Drop down like gentle rain.

Go to sleep my little hands,

I'll wake you once again.

A Funny One

'Round the house

'Round the house (Put fingers around the face.)

Peep in the window (Open eyes wide.)

Listen at the door (Cup hand behind ear.)

Knock at the door (Knock on head.)

Lift up the latch (Push up nose.)

And walk in (Stick out tongue and walk fingers in mouth.)

—I caught you! (Bite gently down on fingers.)

Two Little Apples

Two little apples hanging on a tree, (Put hand by eyes.)

Two little apples smiling at me. (Smile.)

I shook that tree as hard as I could. (Shake tree.)

Down came the apples. (Make falling motions.)

Mmmm—they were good. (Rub stomach.)

Peanut Butter And Jelly

First you take the peanuts and you crunch them and you crunch them. (Repeat.)

Peanut butter—jelly! Peanut butter— jelly! Then you take the grapes and you squish them and you squish them. (Repeat.)

Peanut butter—jelly! Peanut butter—jelly! Then you take the bread and you spread it and you spread it. (Repeat.) Peanut butter—jelly! Peanut butter—jelly!

Then you take the sandwich and you eat it and you eat it. (Repeat. Then with your mouth closed hum the refrain as if you had a mouth full of sandwich.)

Peanut butter—jelly! Peanut butter— jelly!

("Peanut butter" is said in the following fashion: "Pea"[medium pitch] "nut"[low pitch] "but"[medium] "ter"[high pitch with hands above head, fingers shaking to side in Vaudeville-type motion]. "Jelly" is said in a low, throaty voice, accompanied by hands to opposite side shaking at knee level.)

Five Little Astronauts

Five little astronauts (Hold up fingers on one hand.)

Ready for outer space.

The first one said, "Let's have a race."

The second one said, "The weather's too rough."

The third one said, "Oh, don't be gruff."

The fourth one said, "I'm ready enough."

The fifth one said, "Let's Blast Off!"

10, 9, 8, 7, 6, 5, 4, 3, 2, 1, (Start with 10 fingers and pull one down with each number.)

BLAST OFF!!! (Clap loudly with "Blast Off!")

Be sure to take into consideration the seating arrangement during small group times because it can play a role in a child's wandering attention. If a large rug is used for circle time and children are asked to sit on the periphery or edge at a distance from the teacher, then intimacy and the ability to see visuals and hear well may be lost. Teachers may need to break up child combinations in seating when children are seated in a "pack." The teacher's physical closeness is part of the "circle-time" experience. In other words, circle time does not necessarily mean children must sit in a circle. A half-circle or arc is a common seating arrangement.

13-2a Group Activities

A group activity is begun by capturing group attention. A signal or daily routine can be used. To make sure all children are focused, a short silence (pause) adds a feeling of anticipation and expectation. Occasionally varying the signals keeps one signal from becoming old hat. A visual signal, a xylophone ripple, a tap on a musical triangle, an attention-getting record, a puppet announcing a group activity, or reminder stickers placed on children's hands related to the theme of the activity are a few alternatives.

A musical recording can set the mood as children form a group. Singing can serve as a magnet that pulls the group together, and a quiet song is a great means of relaxing and bonding a group. Opening activities that recognize each child help build group spirit. Such recognition is a way of communicating to each child that "You're an important person; we're happy to have you with us." The children can then begin group activities on the right note.

Arranging small group times so they follow a period of physical activity is a good technique for enhancing children's ability to sustain focus and attention. Teachers using this planned strategy use calming circle starters or finger plays as beginning group time settlers.

13-2b Group Projects and Common Core State Standards

Since the adoption of language arts curriculums based upon common core state standards, more programs emphasize grouping children and promoting project work. This promotes child collaboration, planning, joint decision making, and can involve children's use of clear and persuasive speech. This reflects a serious effort to build children's listening, speaking and conversational skills with peers and also prompts each child's expression of ideas.

The project approach has been widely used in elementary schools and was recommended to early childhood educators by Katz and Chard in 1993. It was adopted by many preschools at that time and is currently being given more attention by others influenced by common core recommendations.

A project is usually defined as an in-depth investigation of a topic selected by a small group within a class. A key feature of participating in a project is the child's opportunity to pursue a subject of interest jointly with others, collaborate, and share results. It can also involve subsequent projects along the same or a related course of group study. It is currently being used by enthusiastic early childhood educators who believe in young children's innate ability to gather information, create solutions, and discover information and answers with teacher assistance. A teacher supplies needed materials that aid children's pursuit of knowledge.

A child might play a number of roles as a member of a project team. He might serve as a coach, a tutor, a companion, a guide, a play pal, or translator, to name but a few possible roles. Project work not only encourages interaction, conversation, collaboration, friendship, and the expression of children's ideas, it promotes social acceptance and the social integration of a newcomer into the group.

Of course, there are many variations of how projects work in individual classrooms. The means by which teachers and staffs will achieve the child outcomes spelled out in the common core state standards has been left to the ingenuity and expertise of teachers and schools. Project work is but one promising course of action.

Objectives:

new vocabulary—*plain, feather, wobble*

new concepts—bird sounds, teaching "threes," leading, and following

Other possibilities—Make the following into a flannel board set or dramatize with a group.

Six Little Ducks (Good with younger preschoolers)

Six little ducks that I once knew

Fat ones, skinny ones, plain ones, too.

But the one little duck with the feather on his back

He led the others with a quack, quack, quack!

Down by the river they would go,

Wibble wobble, wibble wobble, to and fro

But the one little duck with the feather on his back

He led the others with the quack, quack, quack!

Home from the river they would come,

Wibble wobble, wibble wobble, Ho hum hum.

But the one little duck with the feather on his back

He led the others with a quack, quack, quack!

Child participation opportunities

1. For the feather on his back the teacher makes a hand into a fist and with the other hand points it up behind the fist symbolizing a feather.

2. Saying quack, quack, quack in unison.

3. Standing with hands at waist and wiggling the hips to the words wibble, wobble, wibble wobble.

Traditional Stories Can Still Delight/Portfolio Item— classic stories.

13-2c Leading Groups

The following is one teacher's internal dialogue while leading a group of children: Are they going to understand this? Should I rephrase this question? How can I get Tyrell or Sue to participate? Antonio looks sleepy. To the outside observer, a skilled teacher leading and interacting with a group may look like a relaxed, interested individual. Under the surface of the teacher's enthusiastic manner, many decisions are being made. Reciprocal interchange is happening; there's internal dialogue going on. The teacher may be watching the clock for time length, watching for both interested and restless behavior, or listening intently for child comments and framing appropriate verbal interaction. With all this going on, many beginning teachers are sometimes not able to truly relax.

In many schools circle time often starts with a few children, and others join as they finish chosen pursuits and/or become attracted to circle activities. This practice may have been adopted because the school's staff believed that when a child chooses to be at circle time he will be more focused, making it easier for the teacher to hold interest. Early childhood centers differ in philosophy or practice concerning required child presence at circle. Staffing may influence their decision.

13-2d Circle Starters

Many educators suggest using opening and closing circle time with special "hello" and "good-bye" songs. Teachers take the time to recognize each child by name, welcoming them. Singing can quiet the children, allow latecomers to enter the group unobtrusively, and meld into the ongoing action. Children may be individually touched and eye contact is maintained.

The following activities are circle-time starters, attention getters, socializers, and wiggle reducers.

Circle Time

I've just come in from outside.

I'm tired as can be.

I'll cross my legs

And fold my hands,

I WILL NOT MOVE.

My head won't move.

My toes are still.

I'll put my hands on my chin,

And when it's quiet, we'll begin!

Who's That?

(Chant or sing to tune of Ten Little Indians.)

Who's that _____ in the _____

            (boy, girl, lady, man)   (red, blue, etc.)

_____?

     (shirt, pants, shoes, etc.)

(Repeat twice.)

Oh, _____ is_____ name, oh.

(child or adult gives name) (his/her)

(Teacher supplies name when child is hesitant.)

Friendship Song

(Sing or chant the song The More We Get Together using hand movements.)

The more we get together, together, together,

(Hug yourself.)

The more we get together, the happier we'll be. (Pull up cheeks in a smile.)

'Cause your friends are my friends, (Point around the circle.)

And my friends are your friends.

The more we get together, the happier we'll be. (Pull up cheeks in a smile.)

A Phonemic Awareness Version

(same melody)

We can find a "t," a "t," a "t"

(Hold up a print "t.")

We can find a "t," if we just look around.

(Hand by side of eye panning room.)

There's your "t," and my "t," (Pointing.)

And my "t," and your "t," (Pointing.)

We can find a "t," if we just look around.

There is tongue (Touch.)

And t-shirt, (Point; substitute attending children's names when possible.)

And table, (Point.)

And teacher, (Point.)

We can find a "t" word, if we just look around.

Wiggles

I'll wiggle my fingers

And wiggle my toes.

I'll wiggle my arms

And wiggle my nose.

And now that all the wiggle's out,

We'll listen to what circle's about.

Clapping Startv

Turn around and face the wall. Clap, Clap, Clap.

Down upon your knees now fall. Clap, Clap, Clap.

Up again and turn around. Clap, Clap, Clap.

Turn around and then sit down. Clap, Clap, Clap.

Not a sound.

Where Are Your ___?

Where are your eyes? Show me eyes that see.

Where are your eyes? Shut them quietly.

Where is your nose? A nose that blows.

Where is your nose? Show me your nose and wiggle it so.

Where is your mouth? Open it wide.

Where is your mouth? With teeth inside.

Smile—Smile—Smile.

If You're Happy And You Know It

If you're happy and you know it, clap your hands.

If you're happy and you know it, clap your hands.

If you're happy and you know it, then your face will surely show it.

If you're happy and you know it, clap your hands.

Additional verses:

If you're sad and you know it, wipe your eyes.

If you're mad and you know it, pound your fist.

If you're hungry and you know it, rub your stomach.

If you're silly and you know it, go tee hee.

If you're cold and you know it, rub your arms.

If you're hot and you know it, wipe your brow.

If you're sleepy and you know it, go to sleep . . . snore, snore.

Hands On Shoulders

Hands on shoulders, hands on knees.

Hands behind you, if you please.

Touch your shoulders, now your nose.

Now your ear and now your toes.

Hands up high into the air.

Down at your sides then touch your hair.

Hands up high as before.

Now clap your hands,

One, two, three, four.

Ball Rolling Circle

The ball will roll across our circle.

Touch toes with your neighbors.

Here comes the ball, Susie. "I roll the ball to Susie."

(Teacher says: "Susie, roll the ball across the circle and say your friend's name.")

"I roll the ball to ___"

I Like You

(Chant or sing.)

I like you.

There's no doubt about it.

I like you.

There's no doubt about it.

I am your good friend.

You like me.

There's no doubt about it.

You like me.

There's no doubt about it.

You are my good friend.

There's my friend (child's name), and my friend

(child's name).

(Continue around circle.)

Oh Here We Are Together

(Chant or sing.)

Oh here we are together, together, together,

Oh here we are together

At (school name) Preschool

*There's (child's name) and (child's name) and (names of all
    children).*

Oh here we are together to have a good day.

We're Waiting

(Circle starter.)

We're waiting, we're waiting, we're waiting for (child's name).

(Repeat until group is formed.)

*We're here, because we're here, because we're here,
    because we're here.*

And my name is ___, and my name is ___. (Around the circle.)

Hello

Hello (child's name). Hello, hello, hello.

Shake my hand and around we'll go.

Hello (child's name). Hello, hello, hello.

Shake my hand and around we'll go.

*(Teacher starts; children continue around the circle chanting
until all are recognized.)*

Secret

I've got something in my pocket

That belongs across my face.

I keep it very close at hand

In a most convenient place.

I know you couldn't guess it

If you guessed a long, long while.

So I'll take it out and put it on

It's a great big friendly SMILE!

Ten Fingers

I have ten little fingers

And they all belong to me.

I can make them do things.

Would you like to see?

I can shut them up tight

Or open them wide.

I can put them together

Or make them all hide.

I can make them jump high.

I can make them jump low,

I can fold them quietly

And hold them just so.

Everybody Do This

Refrain:

Everybody do this, do this, do this.

Everybody do this just like me.

Actions:

Open and close fists

Roll fists around

Touch elbows

Spider fingers

Pat head, rub tummy

Wink

Wave hand good-bye

(Ask children to create others.)

The Carrot Seed Will Grow

Carrots grow from carrot seeds,

I'll plant this seed and grow one.

I won't be disappointed if my seed doesn't grow.

What makes seeds grow? I don't know!

So I won't be disappointed if my seed doesn't grow.

My brother said "Na, na. It won't come up. Na, na. It won't come up.

Na, na. It won't come up. Your carrot won't come up."

(Repeat above, ending with the following.)

Oh, carrots grow from carrot seeds.

I planted one, it grew. I watered it. I pulled the weeds.

No matter what he said.

Carrots grow from carrot seeds.

13-3 Circle Time Activities and Features

A circle group keeps its liveliness and social enjoyment when well planned. The activities that follow involve both language and coordinated physical movement.

13-3a Passing Games

Arrange children in a circle. Have the children pass a small object around the circle. Start the game by having the children pass the object in front of themselves, then behind, then overhead, and then under their legs. Directions can be changed on command of the teacher, such as "pass it to your left, pass it to your right," and so on. Ask the children for suggestions for other ways to pass the object. Passing a toy microphone can also promote a child's verbal contribution. When a child is done, she passes the microphone to the next child.

Teddy Bear Circle Pass

(Have bear in bag behind leader.)

Love somebody, yes, I do.

Love somebody, yes, I do.

Love somebody, yes, I do.

Love somebody, but I won't tell who.

(Shake head sideways.)

Love somebody, yes, I do.

Love somebody, yes, I do.

Love somebody, yes, I do.

Now I'll show (him or her) to you!

Here's a hug—Pass it on.

(Group continues to chant as each child hugs and hands teddy to next child. When teddy returns to leader, last verse is repeated, ending with the following line.)

Now back in the bag; our hugs are through!

13-3b Taking Turns and Directing Attention

During circle times, conversations, and other group activities, the following teacher statements are helpful in emphasizing to children the importance of taking turns.

- "It's Monica's turn now."
- "Barry's turn to talk, and everyone's turn to listen."
- "Listen to Bonnie. Bonnie's lips are moving, and ours are resting."
- "Just one person talks at a time."
- "I am guessing that you really want to say something, Jason, but that you are waiting for your turn."
- "Sierra was telling us a story, so it's her turn. What happened next, Sierra?"
- "It is time to give Angel a turn to talk, Aki. Angel, you live in an apartment house and I think you wanted to tell us about something that happened there."
- "Hiko is answering my question now. Wait and you can answer next, Bradford."
- "Raise your hand if you're waiting to tell us about your pet. I see four hands up— September, Ariel, Xander, and Alwin. You will all have a turn. Alwin, it's your turn now."
- "Wait, Collette, Rio hasn't finished his turn."
- "My turn to talk, Elias; your turn to listen."

Being a member of a group provides children with two conditions essential for learning: a sense of security and opportunities for social interaction.

13-3c Closing Group Activities

Exciting circles and other group activities sometimes need a quiet, settling closing. The following can be used to wind down group activities and prepare excited children for the change to another activity or play.

Up And Down

Up and down,

Up and down,

Clap your hands and turn around.

Up and down,

Up and down,

Clap your hands and sit down.

Rag Doll

I'm just a limp rag doll.

My arms are limp.

My legs are limp.

My head is limp.

I'm just a limp rag doll.

Up, Down, And Rest

Up and down,

Up and down,

Round, round, round,

Up and down.

I stretch, I stretch, I yawn.

I rest and then I start again.

Up and down

(Second time—"I rest, I rest, I rest" is the fifth and ending line.)

Going To Grandma's House

Wash the face.

Wash the hands.

Put on a jacket.

Shoes to lace.

Down the stairs

Open the door.

Shut the door.

Jump in the car.

It's not far.

Good-bye.

13-3d Transitions

Disbanding a circle or group at an activity's ending calls for a planned approach. If the group is large, you will need to excuse a few children at a time. When carpet squares are to be picked up and stacked or small chairs returned to tables, a reminder is in order: "When you hear your name, pick up your carpet square and carry it to the stack."

Transitional statements that relate to the just-completed activity work well: "Crawl like Victor the Boa Constrictor to the block center" or "Let the wind blow you slowly to the water table like it blew in the little tree."

Transition Poem

Wiggle both ears.

Touch your nose.

Wiggle your fingers.

Stamp your toes.

Point to your eyes.

Your mouth open wide.

Stick out your tongue.

Put it inside.

Trace your lips.

Go "shh!" Don't speak.

Hands on your neck.

Touch both cheeks.

Shake your hands.

Now let them sleep.

Bend your knees.

---

transitional statements — teacher statements made to disperse students in small groups or in an orderly fashion.

Sit on your feet.

Now we finished with this play,

Take your feet and walk away!

Going To Line Up

(To the tune of "The Bear Went over the Mountain.")

_____ *is going over to line up.*

(1st child's name)

_____ *is going over to line up.*

(1st child's name)

_____ *is going over to line up.*

(1st child's name)

And _____ *is going next.*

(2nd child's name)

_____ *went over to line up*

(1st child's name)

_____ *went over to line up*

(2nd child's name)

_____ *is going over to line up*

(3rd child's name)

And _____ *is going next.*

(4th child's name)

(Last line when all have gone:)

And all are standing tall.

Additional Transitions. A fun way to move children one by one is to recite the rhyme "Jack Be Nimble," substituting the child's name for "Jack": "(Child's name) be nimble, (child's name) be quick, (child's name) jump over the candlestick." (Children clap for the child who jumps or steps over a small plastic candleholder and unlit candle stub.) Another way to disband a group is to make a "tickler" from a three-foot-long dowel and some yarn. Say to the children, "Close your eyes. When you feel a tickle on your head, it's time to stand and walk carefully through your friends to the . . ." Some statements that are helpful in moving a group of children in an orderly fashion are listed here. Many identify language concepts and serve a dual purpose.

- "Everyone with brown shoes stand up. Now it's time to . . ."
- If your favorite sandwich is peanut butter and jelly (ham, cheese, tuna, and so forth) raise your hand. If your hand is up, please tiptoe to the . . ."

- "Richie is the engine on a slow, slow train. Richie, chug chug slowly to the . . ." "Darlene is the coal car on a slow, slow train." (The last child is, naturally, the caboose.)

Thelen and Klifman (2011) suggest using visual clues for transitions. This might include a visual sign or sequence strip, a drawing, a photo, or a symbol that could alert a group to the activity that is coming next. It could also include a cleanup or pickup responsibility directive before disbanding, and also depict the expected physical exit behavior, such as skipping to leave the area. A pictorial representation of the type of activity or activities that will be available next in the daily schedule is also an idea. The use of schedules, these authors point out, makes transitions less stressful for children and helps children learn to manage their time and build self-regulation skills.

13-3e Multicultural Considerations and Activities

If second-language learners are present, circle times need to include special considerations. Routines that recognize each of the group's children by name will help children feel accepted and included. Activities within circle times that are repeated each day add predictability and promote children's successful participation. The words to songs can be introduced without music before singing them. This gives children a better opportunity to catch on and join in. Second-language learners frequently "find their voice" or "go public" for the first time in their new language as they sing, chant, or say words in connection to physical motions or actions.

The inclusion of multicultural and multiethnic aspects to group activities is not a new idea. Songs and finger plays in the native languages of attending children promote acceptance of diversity. Teachers may need family help in discovering literary material or for translation. Children usually eagerly learn motions and translated words presented with catchy rhythms. Introduce the name of the language when presenting: "This is a song with Russian words. Gregory's mom taught me how to sing it." As with multicultural and multiethnic picture books, stories, and poetry, these activities are not given extra or special status but are everyday, standard activities—ones that many teachers do not wish to neglect. The problem, at times, is finding them when teacher resources abound with "Anglo-intense" examples.

13-3f Circle Time Goals

There are many possible goals that teachers hope to achieve during circle time. Pawlina and Stanford (2011) describe a preschool circle time routine they have conceived that aims to promote children's focus on problem solving and children's recognition of their growing developing abilities. These authors hope to foster children's knowledge that they are in control of their actions and that they are competent and capable. These educators plan and conduct an ending circle time recap period. Each day a question is suggested by the teacher such as, "What challenge did you work on today?" The teacher then would effectively comment on each child's effort. If a child offers that they have been working on how to ride a bike, the teacher's comment might include how last week the child could only peddle the bike for a small distance. Pawlina and Stanford also suggest saying," When we practice something we get better at it and it feels good inside." (p. 30) Pawlina and Stanford's circle time routine also encourages children to put their thinking and actions into words before a group of their peers.

13-3g Hints for Successful Circle Times

Before you conduct your circle

- review your goals for circle times periodically.
- plan for active child participation and involvement.
- make proposed circle-time duration appropriate to the group's age.
- practice language games and activities so that you can focus on the children.
- think about group size and settings.
- remember that it is better to stop before enthusiasm wanes.
- consider child comfort.
- identify possible room distractions.
- keep rules simple, clear, and at a minimum.
- plan how your are going to gain children's attention. Novel stimuli including the unusual, unpredictable, and distinctive are powerful ways to harness attention (Medina, 2008). A moving object also can capture children's eyes. A funny noise, flashlight, or putting a large feather behind your ear are examples of brain-based learning suggestions (although they may be considered silly by more sedate teachers).

- realize that when listening to a speaker, attention plummets at about nine minutes for adults, and this can happen within a shorter interval for young children. Alternate circle time activities with passive and active movement or involvement.
- recapture attention by saying something that triggers a positive child emotion, or make a funny remark or try a quick anecdote. Positive emotions can be elicited with humor, praise, and recalling past pleasant events or memories or happenings.

Note that some centers also institute the word *pass* as a circle-time signal that the child does not want to contribute during a discussion, but more commonly teachers wait for raised hands (and celebrate inside when a child's hand goes up for the first time). This releases pressure to talk when a child cannot think of a response or chooses not to share her ideas. Additional circle time hints follow.

- focus children at the beginning (Photo 13-2).
- state what you expect early, if necessary: "Sit where you can see."
- try to be unhurried.
- think about including activities that promote child decisions, guessing, voting, creativity, expression of personal preferences, problem solving, and prediction making.
- stop the rambling child speaker with "It's time for your friends' turn now, Clyde."
- make eye contact with all children.
- reduce waiting times.
- remember that your skill increases with experience.

Most teachers realize that children aren't being rebellious by moving around. They are just moving because they need to do it. At the same time, educators will always have children, particularly very young preschoolers or culturally diverse preschoolers, who do not readily choose to participate with speech or actions at group times. The preschool years are a time of rapid language development.

Photo 13-2 An active song activity can settle and focus children.

Occasionally one child's silliness or mimicking behavior can lead to circle-time disruption as the attention-getting child's behavior challenges the teacher's hold on group focus. It can seem to teacher that a power struggle is in progress as the "cut up" attempts to divert attention to him or herself. Teacher restatement of a circle-time rule may be necessary followed by a teacher comment that reengages child interest. Usually when disruptive behavior occurs, it is just one child; if more than one, the teacher needs to examine whether the activity itself or some other factor is causing the disconnect. Aides or volunteers attending a circle time need to be alert to child distractions. Moving closer to or between two children may be helpful, or quietly suggesting an alternative activity to a disinterested child can aid the teacher leader.

13-3h Circle-Time Pitfalls

Circle times can fall apart for a number of reasons. An examination of the teacher's goals and planning decisions prior to conducting a circle time may clarify what caused child disinterest or lack of enthusiasm. When circles go poorly, the children's behavior may be focused away from the circle's theme and action.

Before examining teacher behaviors, other factors should be reviewed, such as the setting, length, and age-level appropriateness of the activity. Then examine whether the children enjoyed and participated enthusiastically in the activity and how teacher behavior contributed to this. If the activity was not a success, the activity failed the children rather than vice versa.

A teacher whose goals include child conversation and involvement will not monopolize the activity with a constant up-front presentation. Unfortunately, some beginning teachers seem to possess an overwhelming desire to dispense information, eliminating children's conversation and reactions. When this happens, circle times become passive listening times.

The size of the circle has also been discussed in this chapter. Teachers attempt large circle times for various reasons. They may be more comfortable with their ability to maintain control when the whole group is involved in the same activity. They may want to be sure everyone in the group learns the same concepts and skills. Unfortunately, these teachers need to understand that large group instruction at the preschool level may cause group disinterest and restlessness by becoming impersonal.

Teachers should engage in spontaneous conversation at circle times given the importance of children's comments. Teachers can relax in not having to be overly reliant on following planned, step-by-step circle time routines or a lesson plan, which lacks back-and-forth flexibility. Newer teachers are careful and act intentionally so children aren't afraid to answer questions or share ideas. They realize a teacher who constantly asks rapid-fire questions to maintain child attention may defeat her purpose. Most adults remember from past school experiences how it felt when they failed to give an answer the teacher expected. Experienced teachers know that active and involved children stay focused (Photo 13-3). On the other hand, when children have to wait a long time for a turn to speak during circle time, children can become frustrated and tune-out.

Photo 13-3 Active and involved children who participate in circle time activities and discussions will stay more focused.

© 2016 Cengage Learning®

13-3i Watching Children's Participation Level

As teachers scan faces and observe child vocalization and movement during circle times, obvious differences in children's ability to focus, stay focused, and participate as fully functioning group members are apparent. Many conditions influence each child's ability to concentrate, actively contribute, and follow group activities—age, health, hunger, language deficiencies, weather, distractions, home problems, past experiences, disabilities, and a multitude of other factors may change child behavior at circle time on any given day. After a teacher has become familiar with her group and leads a few circle times, she mentally categorizes child behaviors. Often at circle time, teachers can tell who is having a bad day. Possible child-attending behavior will vary from not focused to fully engaged, with other behaviors between these two end points. A child may tune in and out, attend but not participate verbally or with body involvement, or attend and participate sporadically. Practicing teachers often notice windy days and wild weather affect children's ability to settle down.

Teachers become increasingly aware of how their teacher behaviors and verbalizations affect children. Ask any teacher about the teacher satisfaction felt at the conclusion of a well-planned and conducted group time during which child interest was held and maintained and something of educational quality or value was achieved. When a group is eager, engaged, responsive, enjoying the experience, and the teacher feels he or she is interacting skillfully, it is a moment of togetherness and elation.

13-4 Circle Time Chants and Choruses naeyc DAP

Throughout history, rhythmic **chants** and choruses have been used in group rituals and ceremonies. The individuals in the group gain a group identity as a result of their participation. Natural enjoyment of rhythmic word patterns can be seen in a child's involvement in group chants. The child and teacher can also playfully take part in call and response during the preschool day. "I made it, I made it," the child says. "I see it, I see it," the teacher answers, picking up the child's rhythm. This verbal play is common. Sounds in the community and on the school's playground can be brought to the children's attention by teachers who notice them and make comments.

Chants and choruses are mimicked, and sound and word patterns that have regularity and predictability are imitated. Choruses usually involve a

---

chants — rhythmic monotonous utterances

back-and-forth conversation (one individual alternating with another) and involve the rise and fall of accented sounds or syllables. Children need the teacher's examples and directions, such as, "When it's your turn, I'll point to you" or "Let's say it together," before they can perform the patterns on their own. Chants printed on charts with simple illustrations can enhance chanting and chorus times and tie the oral words to written ones.

Chanting promotes successful language experiences regardless of children's background or talent and helps children learn the importance of clear and expressive pronunciation. Teacher charts developed for chanting can be used over and over and are another way for children to discover the relationship of spoken words and print. Many strong-rhythm chants invite clapping, foot stomping, or a wide variety of other physical movements. Two picture books that are naturals for chanting include:

Sayre, A. P. (2012). *Go, go, grapes!: a fruit chant*. New York: Beach Lane Books.

Sayre, A. P. (2010). *Rah, rah, radishes!: a vegetable chant*. New York: Beach Lane Books.

The chants that follow are some tried-and-true favorites.

The Grand Old Duke Of York

The grand old Duke of York

He had forty thousand men.

He marched them up the hill.

He marched them down again.

And when you're up, you're up!

And when you're down, you're down.

And when you're half-way-in-between,

You're neither up nor down.

And It Was Me!

I looked in my soup, and who did I see?

Something wonderful . . . and it was me.

Additional verses:

I looked in the mirror, and who did I see?

I looked in the puddle . . .

I looked in a window . . .

I looked in the river . . .

I looked in the pond . . .

I looked at a snapshot . . .

I turned off the television . . .

Ending:

When I'm grown up, I'll still be there.

Right in reflections everywhere.

When I'm grown up, how will it be?

A wonderful world with you and me.

It's Raining, It's Pouring

It's raining, it's pouring.

The old man is snoring.

He went to bed and he bumped his head

And he couldn't get up in the morning.

Rain, rain go away—come again some other day.

Miss Mary Mack

Miss Mary Mack, Mack, Mack

All dressed in black, black, black

With silver buttons, buttons, buttons

All down her back, back, back.

She asked her mother, mother, mother

For fifteen cents, cents, cents

To see the elephants, elephants, elephants

Jump the fence, fence, fence.

They jumped so high, high, high

They touched the sky, sky, sky

And never came back, back, back

Till the fourth of July, ly, ly.

July can't walk, walk, walk

July can't talk, talk, talk

July can't eat, eat, eat

With a knife and fork, fork, fork.

She went upstairs, stairs, stairs

To say her prayers, prayers, prayers

She made her bed, bed, bed

She hit her head, head, head

On a piece of corn bread, bread, bread.

Now she's asleep, sleep, sleep

She's snoring deep, deep, deep

No more to play, play, play

Until Friday, day, day

What can I say, say, say

Except hooray, ray, ray!

Additional Chants

Pancake

Mix a pancake.

Stir a pancake.

Pop it in the pan.

Fry a pancake.

Toss a pancake.

Catch it if you can.

The Big Clock

Slowly ticks the big clock

Chorus: Tick-tock, tick-tock (Repeat twice.)

But the cuckoo clock ticks double quick

Chorus: Tick-a-tock-a, tick-a-tock-a

Tick-a-tock-a, tick!

Little Brown Rabbit

Little brown rabbit went hoppity-hop,

All: Hoppity-hop, hoppity-hop!

Into a garden without any stop,

All: Hoppity-hop, hoppity-hop!

He ate for his supper a fresh carrot top,

All: Hoppity-hop, hoppity-hop!

Then home went the rabbit without any stop,

All: Hoppity-hop, hoppity-hop!

Who Ate The Cookies In The Cookie Jar

All: Who ate the cookies in the cookie jar?

All: (Child's or teacher's name) ate the cookies in the cookie jar.

(Teacher points to different child for each verse.)

Named person: Who me?

All: Yes you.

Named person: Couldn't be.

All: Then who?

Named person: (Child's or teacher's name) ate the cookies in the cookie jar.

Newly named person: Who me? (and so forth).

Lock And Key

(A back-and-forth chorus.)

I am a gold lock; I am a gold key.

I am a silver lock; I am a silver key.

I am a house lock; I am a house key.

I am a car lock; I am a car key.

I am a monk lock; I am a monk-key

(whoo, whoo, whoo).

Fill-In-The-Blank Poem

If I had a dollar,

I'll tell you what I'd do.

I'd spend it all on ice cream,

And I'd give it all to you.

'Cause that's how much I like you! (child's name)! (Originally, this ditty used 'Baby' instead of a child's name.)

(Child's name is said with a deep voice in vaudeville style.)

'Cause that's how much I like you, (child's name).

(Substitute other words for ice cream that children suggest, such as hamburgers, toys, and so on. Those not wishing to promote sugar can substitute vegetables or other items. Examples follow.)

a. If I had a bike

   I'll tell you what I'd do

   I'd pedal on the pedals

   And I'd give a ride to you

   'Cause that's how much I like you, Tracy

   'Cause that's how much I like you, Tracy.

b. If I had an elephant

   I'll tell you what I'd do

I'd put it on a truck

And take it to the zoo.

13-4a Using Accessories

Teachers often use accessories or props to go with chants and choruses used at circle time. The following example, "Little Things," uses accessories. It is a highly enjoyable activity that provokes giggles and "do-it-again" requests.

Little Things

(to the tune of "Oh My Darling" or chanted)

Little black things, little black things

Crawling up and down my arm.

I am not afraid of them

For they will do no harm.

(Substitute any color for black.)

Materials

The following colors of yarn are needed.

red	green	black	pink
orange	blue	brown	gray
yellow	purple	white	

Instructions

You will need to make a set of as many colored things as you choose for each child. Yarn works well. These can be stored easily in sealed sandwich bags.

Step 1: For each colored thing, cut five yarn pieces, each measuring eight inches long.

Step 2: Put one yarn piece aside and, keeping the other four together, fold them in half.

Step 3: Using the fifth piece of yarn, tie it around the other four, one inch from the folded ends; knot it well, to form a "head" and "legs." Fold the knotted ends down to form more legs.

Give each child a bag of "things." Let the children tell you what color to use. While chanting or singing, have the colored thing crawl up and down arms.

13-4b Clapping Songs and Rhymes

Batchelor and Bintz (2012) encourage teachers to include clapping songs and rhymes during group time. Besides being entertaining, clapping activities provide a kinesthetic and participatory experience. It may also enhance motivation and concept development. As a fun and engaging exercise, it can increase phonological awareness, phonemic manipulation, oral language development, and involve content area material. It's an educationally sound type of language play. Two books for clapping follow.

Hoberman, M. A. (1998). *Miss Mary Mack.* Boston: Little, Brown & Co.

Westcott, N. B. (1998). *The lady with the alligator purse.* Boston: Little, Brown & Co.

13-4c Finger Play

Finger play is a classic preschool group (or individual) activity that families have probably already introduced to children with "Peek-a-Boo" or "This Little Piggy." Finger plays use words and actions (usually finger motions) together. Early childhood play frequently goes beyond finger movements and often includes whole body actions.

When learning a finger play, the child usually practices and joins in the finger movements before learning the words. Words can be retained by doing the play over and over again. Finger plays are often done with rhymes. Easy-to-remember rhymes give the children pleasure in listening and a chance to feel competent because (1) they quickly become part of a group having fun and doing the same thing, and (2) they experience a feeling of social accomplishment when they are saying and doing what peers are doing in unison.

Teachers use finger plays to prepare children for sitting, to keep children active and interested while waiting, and as transitions between activities. Finger plays are also used for special purposes, such as quieting a group or getting toys back on the shelves. They can build vocabulary as well as teach facts and can help a child release pent-up energy.

Teachers should practice a finger play and memorize it beforehand to be sure of a clear and smooth presentation. It should be offered enthusiastically. As with other activities, the teacher can say, "Try it with me." The child who just watches will join in when ready. Watching comes first, one or two hand movements next, and then using words and actions together. Each child learns at her own rate of speed.

Finger plays can be found in many resource books or can be created by the teacher. The following are recommended because of their popularity with both children and teachers.

Hickory, Dickory, Dock

Hickory, dickory, dock! (Rest elbow in the palm of your other hand and swing up raised arm back and forth.)

The mouse ran up the clock; (Creep fingers up the arm to the palm of the other hand.)

The clock struck one. (Clap hands.)

The mouse ran down. (Creep fingers down to elbow.)

Hickory, dickory, dock! (Swing arm as before.)

Omitting Sounds Poem (Phonemic Awareness)

This is the "at" I like best. (Make pointed hat with hands on head.)

I mean my hat. (Make an "oh no" face.)

This is an "op," here on my chest. (Hands on chest.)

No, no, it's my top! (Make face.)

These are my "ants." (Touch pants.)

Oops, I meant pants. (Make face.)

This is my "hoe." (Push out shoe.)

No, its my shoe. (Make face.)

What's wrong with me today? (Hands on head.)

Letters left off words that I say. (Point to mouth.)

I think I better walk out and "lay." (Walk fingers up arm.)

I did it again, I meant play! (Make face.)

Choo! Choo!

Choo-o! Choo-o! Choo! Choo! (Run fingers along arm to shoulder slowly.)

This little train goes up the track.

Choo! Choo! Choo! Choo! (At shoulder, turn "train" and head down arm.)

But this little train comes quickly back.

Choo-choo-choo-choo! Choo-choo-choo-choo! (Repeat last line.) (Run fingers down arm quickly.)

Whoo-o! Whoo-o! Whoo-o! (Imitate train whistle.)

Where Is Thumbkin?

Where is thumbkin, where is thumbkin?(Hands behind back.)

Here I am, here I am. (One hand out, thumb up. Other hand out, thumb up.)

How are you today, sir? (First thumb bends up and down.)

Very well, I thank you. (Second thumb bends up and down.)

Run away, run away. (First thumb behind back; second thumb behind back.)

Repeat with:

Where is pointer? (Use first finger.)

Where is tall man? (Use middle finger.)

Where is ring man? (Use ring finger.)

Where is pinkie? (Use little finger.)

Where are all the men? (Use whole hand.)

Newer, less well-known but still popular and enjoyable finger plays appear in the Activities section at the end of this chapter

13-4d Body-Action Plays

Encourage children to move their bodies in rhythm to the first chant example while doing what the rhyme says. Use these for working out pent-up energy.

Head, Shoulders

Head, shoulders, knees, and toes (Stand; touch both hands to each part in order.)

Head, shoulders, knees, and toes.

Head, shoulders, knees, and toes. That's the way the story goes. (Clap this line.)

This is my head, this is not. (Hands on head, then feet.)

These are my shoulders, these are not.

(Hands on shoulders, then knees.)

Here are my knees; watch them wiggle,

(Wiggle knees.)

Touch my armpits and I giggle. (Hands under armpits with laugh.)

Head shoulders, knees, and toes. (Touch in order.)

That's the way the story goes. (Clap.)

Beat One Hammer

My mother told me to tell you

To beat one hammer (Pound one fist.)

Like you see me do.

My mother told me to tell you

To beat two hammers (Pound two fists.)

Like you see me do.

My mother told me to tell you

To beat three hammers (Pound two fists; stamp one foot.)

Like you see me do.

My mother told me to tell you

To beat four hammers (Pound two fists; stamp two feet.)

Like you see me do.

My mother told me to tell you

To beat five hammers (Add nodding head.)

Like you see me do.

My mother told me to tell you

To beat no hammers (Stop!)

Like you see me do.

Getting Out the Wiggles

Wave both hands

Then clap, clap, clap.

Clasp your hands together

In your lap, lap, lap.

Blink both eyes

Go blink, blink, blink.

Rub both thighs

Rub, rub, rub, then wink.

Pick up your feet

And jump, jump, jump.

Take your seat

And melt into a lump.

BINGO (The Song)

Preparation

Secure five 4 × 6 cards and attach tongue depressor handles. Print one different capital letter on each card using only the alphabet letters B, I, N, G, O. Print the word "clap" on the back of each card.

"This is the word bingo and I have a song about Bingo the dog."

There was a farmer had a dog

And Bingo was his name-o.

B-I-N-G-O, B-I-N-G-O, B-I-N-G-O,

And Bingo was his name-o.

When singing the song a second time, instead of saying the letter B in the third line, clap, and turn the tongue depressor to the printed word clap. Explain the print says clap.

The third time clap for both B & I.

The fourth time clap for B, I, and N.

The fifth time clap for B, I, N, and G.

The sixth time clap for all letters.

Practice this classic song (It can be chanted instead) activity before singing with children. Turn the letter cards over one at a time to clap when appropriate. When the song activity is well learned five children can stand in front—each with a letter card and be instructed to sit when the letter on his card is clapped rather than spoken.

Summary

13-1 Describe professional and successful circle (group) time features.

Successful circle time features include using small intimate groups and—when necessary—using whole group times for daily routine particulars and announcements and/or instruction. Other successful elements involve children's active participation, teacher enthusiasm and preparation, teacher acceptance of child oral communications, subject matter that is appropriate for a particular child group and its individuality, teacher clarity in introducing concepts, child comfort in seating, lighting and ability to adequately see what is presented, making teacher remarks that connect subject matter to what the teacher believes attending children already know, adding new or novel content, and creating a learning atmosphere that is stress free and unpressured and invites children to participate and share feelings and ideas.

13-2 List three factors to be considered when planning to lead a group time.

Considering the age and ability of children is of prime importance, the appropriate length of time is decided, a rough sequence of activity progression is devised, a gathering device or signal is planned, as well as a closing statement or event and a transition statement to move children to subsequent activities in an orderly fashion are all part of the planning process. Active and inactive group time is considered when group time is necessarily long. Teacher plans to adjust seating arrangements before beginning and to secure other adult help to provide adult physical closeness to some children when necessary.

13-3 Discuss goals group times and circle time.

Goals include promoting children's social enjoyment and social skills necessary for active involvement and behavior with a group of peers and a teacher, coordinating physical movement and words, child participation in group games, and promoting children's ability to take turns. The teacher's goals when offering a group time includes the teacher's ability to use calming activities after exciting ones, making effective transition statements, offering language-rich child participation activities and multicultural and multiethnic activities, increasing the children's knowledge and vocabulary, offering problem-solving experiences and learning challenges, offering opportunities for child verbal expression of ideas using words and movements, being able to digress from a lesson plan when appropriate, and working toward group participation skills that increase educational chances for children's success in future schooling.

13-4 Describe what a child might gain when learning a finger play or body action play.

A child might experience a familiarity with rhyming words, a feeling of competency having memorized a finger play or body action, listening pleasure, a feeling of inclusion as a member of a social group, practice in coordinating words with body actions, new vocabulary words, knowledge, and a release of pent-up energy.

Additional Resources

Finger Play Collections

Ellis, M. J. (2013). *Fingerplay Approach to Dramatization*. Whitefish, Montana: Literary Licensing, LLC.

Redleaf, R. (1997). *Busy Fingers, Growing Minds: Finger Plays, Verses and Activities for Whole Language Learning*. St. Paul, MN: Redleaf Press.

Phonemic Awareness Circle-Time Ideas

Jordano, K., & Callella, T. (2000). *Phonemic Awareness Songs and Rhymes*. Cypress, CA: Creative Teaching Press.

Readings

Denham, S. A., & Brown, C. (2010). Play nice with others: Social–emotional learning and academic success. *Early Education and Development 21*: 652–680.

Claycomb, P. (1998). *The Learning Circle: A Preschool Teacher's Guide to Circle Time*. Beltsville, MD: Gryphon House Inc.

Yifat, R., & Zaduniasky-Ehrlich, S. (2008). Teachers talk in preschools during circle time: The case for rejoicing. *Journal of Research in Childhood Education 23*: 211–227.

Helpful Websites

Early Head Start National Resource Center

http://www.ehsnrc.org

Provides tips concerning group instruction.

Gayle's Preschool Rainbow—Activity Central

http://www.preschoolrainbow.org

Click on Rhymes, Songs, and Finger Plays.

14 ▶ Print—Early Knowledge and Emerging Interest

Objectives

After reading this chapter, you should be able to:

14-1 Discuss young children's print awareness and child behaviors that reflect it.

14-2 Outline the probable sequence of events occurring before a child prints a first recognizable alphabet letter.

14-3 Name two goals of print instruction in preschool.

14-4 Discuss drawing experiences' relationship to prewriting instruction.

14-5 Describe five ways that a classroom can promote alphabet awareness.

14-6 Print both the lowercase and uppercase printscript alphabet without using a guide.

14-7 Name four kinds of instructional charts.

naeyc NAEYC Program Standards

2E05 Children have multiple and varied activities to write.

2E06 Children are helped to identify letters and the sounds they represent.

2E03 Children have opportunities to become familiar with print.

2E03 Teaching staff help children recognize print and connect it to spoken words.

DAP Developmentally Appropriate Practice (DAP) Preschoolers

3H19 Teachers create a print-rich environment in which lots of print not only is present, but is also used in ways that show print's many purposes.

3H14 Teachers plan activities that give children a motivation to engage in writing.

3H20 Teachers draw attention to letters and their sounds and use various strategies to help children grasp the alphabetic principle and relate print to spoken language.

COMMON CORE Common Core State Standards, K-3

W.CCR.4 Produce clear and coherent writing in which the development, organization, and style are appropriate to the task, audience, and purpose.

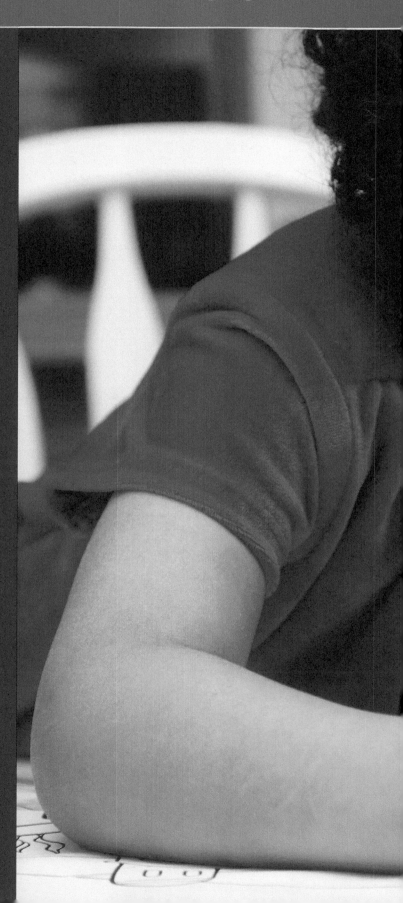

UPS

Cheney and Ong, four-year-olds, are busy stuffing toy animals into boxes provided by their teacher, Mr. Sanchez. They ask for tape, and their teacher supplies strips of masking tape. He watches them struggle to carry the box outside and then pretend to knock on the door. Mr. Sanchez goes to the door. "Well, hello. Is this for me?" he says. Cheney pretends to look at his hand and says, "Is this Cherrywood Preschool?" "Yes," the teacher answers. "Are you the deliverymen?" "No, we're from U-P-S," Ong says.

Questions to Ponder

1. What does this vignette tell you about Ong and Cheney?

2. Could the teacher turn this dramatic play into some kind of additional print-awareness learning?

3. What type of teacher-supplied materials could have added depth to the boys' play and print knowledge?

14-1 Printing in Preschool

Preschool teachers ask themselves two pertinent questions concerning print and teaching children to write in printscript:

1. Is it appropriate to offer lessons (activities) that teach print letter recognition and formation at this age?

2. How is instruction in printscript undertaken?

Resolving these questions is made easier by this chapter's discussion.

Current ideas about the child's development of **writing** (printing) skill have undergone a major change. Preschool children are seen as writers. Older ideas promoted the idea that teaching children to print and read should not be undertaken until children are in kindergarten or first grade. It was believed that at that stage children are mature enough or possess the readiness skills that would make these tasks much easier. Writing and reading skills were thought to be different from listening and speaking skills. Speech was accomplished without direct or formal teaching over a long period, beginning in infancy. Educators have revised their thoughts. naeyc DAP

The concept of early literacy suggests that the foundations of literacy develop from a child's early experiences with print before the onset of formal reading instruction. Educators take children's writing seriously, and they listen for their intended message and support writing development. They are aware early writing is one of the best predictors of children's successful reading (National Early Literacy Panel, 2008).

Symbol making is the essence of what it means to be human. Young children often talk about what they have done, constructed, and drawn, and they "read" meaning into their creations, a meaning they wish to communicate to others. Through talk with others, children invest their marks with meaning. Giving attention to children's work prompts children to translate their work's meaning to the interested adults. It is believed that this type of speech in children paves the way for their eventual use of written forms.

At some point, children gain the insight that print is categorically different from other kinds of visual patterns in their environment, and eventually they learn that print symbolizes spoken language and can be produced by anyone. Children also begin to realize that print holds information. Educators urge teachers to help children see that print holds ideas, observations, stories, and plans.

A review of current research with preschoolers shows that adult–child shared book reading, which stimulates verbal interaction, can enhance language (especially vocabulary) development and knowledge about concepts of print. In addition, activities that direct young children's attention to the sound structure within spoken words, and to the relationships between print and speech, can facilitate learning to read with greater ease.

Preschool children already know something about the world of print from their environment.

---

writing — the ability to use print to communicate with others.

Most children form primitive hypotheses about letters, words, and messages, both printed and handwritten. An estimated 40 percent of children entering kindergarten have a basic familiarity with print. It is a widely held view that learning to read and write will be easier for the child who has had rich home and preschool literacy experiences than for the child who has had little or limited literacy opportunities.

Much of young children's writing is a kind of exploratory play, common in the developmental beginnings of all symbolic media. **Print awareness** and beginning printing skill, and reading awareness and beginning reading skills are now viewed as developing at younger ages, simultaneously with children's growing understanding of a number of other symbol systems. Print awareness describes the child's sensitivity to the presence and use of print in the world around her. When supported by an educative environment, young children compose connected written discourse using emergent forms long before they hold conventional ideas about writing. Children's scribbling, drawing-used-as-writing, nonphonetic strings of letters, and invented spellings are now accepted and honored as reflecting underlying understandings about writing.

The clues have been there for some time. Early childhood educators have always had children that asked questions and displayed early attempts and interest in printing. Preschool children can respond to and learn about visual features of print, know some letters, write some words, make up pretend writings such as letters to people, and dictate stories they want written before they have begun to consider how the words they say may be coded into print, and in particular how the sounds of speech are coded in print. Through informal daily literacy events and adult–child interactions (such as making useful signs), children learn the many purposes and the power of print in their lives and in those of adults. Adults expect children to talk before they read, but they may not have noticed that children are interested in writing before they can read.

Alphabet letters appear in three- and four-year-olds' drawings. Young children go through the motions of reading books, and some have a keen interest in numbers and measurement. This supports the idea that children are attempting to make sense out of what they encounter and are expanding their understandings of symbol systems on a number of fronts (Photo 14-1). However, children do not leap from illiteracy to an understanding that our writing system is alphabetic. They may have hypothesized many conclusions, and they may have tried writing with a variety of their own inventions after puzzling over the relationship between print and speech.

Professional practice promotes teachers' supporting, welcoming, and recognizing children's efforts and accepting children's correct and incorrect conclusions about printing, just as they accepted and supported incorrect or incomplete speech and welcomed it. Teachers are encouraged to have faith in children's ability to discover and develop their own writing theories and symbol systems, as they did when they taught themselves to speak. This takes place in a print-rich environment with responsive adults. Some educators worry about providing too many literacy-focused activities, materials, and

Photo 14-1 Teachers promote interest by showing interest in children's printing attempts.

© 2016 Cengage Learning®

---

print awareness — in early literacy, the child's growing recognition of the conventions and characteristics of a written language. It includes recognition of directionality in reading (left to right and top to bottom), that print forms words corresponding to speech, and that spaces separate words and other features.

furnishings in classrooms, fearing that they may displace other toys and other curricula. This may turn children's play into literacy work.

Teachers must be willing to introduce, demonstrate, and discuss print's relationship and use it in daily activities to pique child interest. Optimal developmental opportunities can be missed in the very best equipped and print-prolific classroom environments. An environment conducive to a child's development of print awareness is a place where print is important and where interactions with print are a source of social and intellectual pleasure for individual children and the people who surround them. Preschoolers who observe and interact within a print-rich environment with sensitive, responsive teachers may discover that print is different from other kinds of visual marks and patterns, and it appears on all kinds of surfaces and objects in different locations (Photo 14-2). They may also notice adults read print materials aloud and silently. With further experience, children often conclude that print symbolizes oral language and holds information.

When preschoolers are read to frequently, they learn

- where one starts reading on a page.
- that reading moves from left to right.
- that at the end of a line, the reader returns to the left margin.
- that pages in a book are in a sequence usually starting with page 1.
- that there is a difference between letter, word, and sentence.

- that there are spaces between words.
- that there are marks, called punctuation marks, that have different names and meanings.
- that there are uppercase (big) and lowercase (little) letters.

Preschoolers will also discover a number of other print-related concepts. For example, they also may become aware that written language functions to label, communicate, remind, request, record, and create.

A child will not learn the name of the letter *B*, the sound of the letter *B*, or how to print it, simply by being with adults or by being with an adult who likes to read. Children learn these critical concepts because adults take the time and effort to teach them in an exciting, engaging, and understanding manner. Figure 14-1 is an example of a teaching assistant's approach.

Writing awareness and beginning writing attempts make more sense to children who have experienced an integrated language arts instructional approach. The areas of speaking, listening, reading, and writing are interrelated. The child's ability to see how these areas fit together is commonly mentioned in school goals. Adults in classrooms communicate with others daily—both orally and in written form. Written communication offers daily opportunities for teachers to point out print's usefulness.

Increased focus on children's early reading success in the United States has provided additional impetus for researching early writing and reading relationships. An increasing number

Photo 14-2 Print is at eye level and saturates this classroom area.

Figure 14-1 A teaching assistant helps a child print the word *Daddy*.

Child 1:	(three-year-old): I'm writing a letter to my daddy. How do you write "Daddy"?
Teacher:	Well, let's think about that. /d/, /d/, /d/. What letter do you think we might use to write /d/?
Child 2*:	[five-year-old]: D!
Teacher:	Yes. We do use D, but let's let Ana (fictitious) think about it. She's the one who is writing the word. If she needs help, I'll tell you and then you can tell me what your idea is.
Child 2:	OK.
Child 1*:	I can't make a D.
Child 2:	I can. I will show you. (*Gets up from his chair and puts his arm down next to the child's paper, indicating that he is ready to demonstrate.*)
Teacher:	Well, actually, wait just a minute. I'll grab the chart. (*Reaches toward an alphabet letter chart that is hanging from a hook on the side of the paper display shelf in the writing center.*)
Child 2:	But I know how. I can show her.
Teacher:	I know that you know how, but Ana might like to know how you learned it, and she might like to know that this chart can show us how, so we'll just take a quick look at it, and, Allen (fictitious), get another piece of paper. Let's not do our demonstration on Ana's paper. She'll write her own D after we show her how.
Child 2:	(*Draws a straight, vertical line, very deliberately on his paper.*)
Child 1:	(*Watches Child 2 with eyes wide and bright.*)
Teacher:	Ok, that's just great. Now, Ana, you make that part of the D on your paper. Where was it you thought you wanted to write "Daddy"?
Child 1:	(*Points to the middle of her paper.*)
Teacher:	Ok, you want it down here in the middle. OK, start a little over here (*gesturing to the left side of the paper, across from where the child had pointed*) so that you will have enough room for all of the letters we'll need to write "Daddy."
Child 1:	(*Moves to the spot indicated by the teacher's finger and draws a pretty good straight, vertical line.*) Now what?
Teacher:	Well, now, there's a curved line that comes out like this (*uses index finger to trace curved line in the D on the chart*), and then it goes back in to touch the line down here. Allen is going to show you how to do that on the D he is making on his paper.
Child 2:	(*Draws the curved line very carefully to complete the* D.)
Teacher:	OK, now you can add that curved line to finish your D. Start right up here at the top of the vertical line you have already drawn, and then move your marker out this way and then gradually down to touch the line down here (*uses finger to trace the path*).
Child 1:	(*Draws curved line.*) Now what?
Teacher:	Well, let's see. D /ae/, /ae/, Daddy. That's a really hard sound to know how to write.
Child 2:	No it isn't. My name starts with that sound.
Teacher:	That's right, it does, and you know what's really funny? Ana's name also starts with that sound, and the sound in her name is spelled with the same letter as the sound in your name. What a coincidence! (*Said as if she had just noticed this herself and thought that it was a remarkable discovery.*)
Child 2:	A!
Child 1:	A?
Teacher	Yes, A. Just as in (*says both names, one after the other, isolating the first vowel phoneme in each name before saying the rest of it.*)
Child 1:	I know how to write A! (*Proceeds to do it.*) Now, what is next?
Teacher:	Da /d/, /d/ . . .
Child 1:	D?
Teacher:	Yes, there are two of them.

Figure 14-1 *(countinued)*

Child 1:	I already did one.
Teacher:	Well, I mean there are two more in the middle.
Child 1:	*(Writes the two D's.)*
Teacher:	*(Offers verbal guidance to support recall of lines needed and their direction.)*
Child 1:	OK. Now what?
Teacher:	Daddy, Dadd /e/.
Child 1:	E! *(Child begins to position her marker to begin making an E.)*
Teacher:	Well, the sound is /i/, but we write it with the letter Y. Let me show you one on the chart. *(Same process as was used before is used to instruct Child 1 on making Y and then to help Child 1 to make one of her own.)* OK, that says "Daddy." *(Underlines it with her finger.)* Did you want to write something else?
Child 1:	No, I'm finished.

of experts believe children establish early ideas about printing (writing) that serve as a basis for early printing and reading attempts. Some children can print a word (or many words) the first day they enter kindergarten, and a good number of children come to school believing that they can write. Their first attempts to print concentrate on messages rather than perfection. Generations of children have been asked to learn the letters of the alphabet, sound and symbol correspondences, and a vocabulary of sight words before they learned to write or read. If the same were true of learning to speak, children would be asked to wait until all letter sounds were perfected at age seven or eight before attempting to speak. Early-on children begin to understand that reading means getting meaning from print, and they become increasingly aware of the different functions and uses of written language. Enri (2002) suggests there are four phases children traverse in learning to read words—prealphabetic, partial alphabetic, full alphabetic, and consolidated alphabetic. These phases combine to form a process that involves first using a whole word strategy that doesn't involve letter-sound connections. Children sight read known words and guess at others using picture (contextual) clues. As they become phonologically aware, they start using a partial decoding approach. Developing further they employ a full decoding strategy. According to Enri, they enter the consolidated phase in which they read words by grouping rimes, syllables, and morphemes together.

Based on the notion that the child constructs from within, piecing together from life experiences the rules of oral language, educators believe that if children are given time and supportive assistance, they can crack the writing and reading code by noticing regularities and incongruence, thus creating their own unique rules. Children progress at their own speed, doing what is important to them and what they see others doing. Without formal instruction, children experiment with and explore the various facets of the writing process. They decorate letters and invent their own symbols—sometimes reverting to their own inventions even after they are well into distinguishing and reproducing different, recognizable alphabet letters. Some children expect others to know what they have written, regardless of their coding system.

Evidence indicates that children have extensive knowledge of some aspects of written language. A few children may have developed both phonological awareness and phonemic awareness. Researchers report that roughly 15 percent of three- and four-year-old children can identify words that begin with a particular phoneme and about 25 percent can reliably identify rhyming words. Tests designed to measure print awareness have been found to predict future reading achievement.

The concept of writing readiness began with some important figures from the past that influenced the directions that early childhood education has taken. It became popular to talk about writing readiness as being that time when an average group of children acquired the capacity, skills, and knowledge to permit the group to accomplish the task. Figure 14-2 compares traditional, readiness, and "natural" instructional approaches. It would be difficult to find an early childhood center that does not use some elements of each of the three approaches in the instructional program.

Figure 14-2 Comparisons of instructional approaches in printing.

Traditional Approach

- providing play materials and free time
- supplying art materials, paper, writing tools, alphabet toys and games, chalkboard
- reading picture books
- planning program that excludes instruction in naming or forming alphabet letters
- providing incidental and spontaneous teaching about print

Readiness Approach

- providing writing materials and models
- planning program with introduction to tracing, naming alphabet letters, and naming shapes
- reading picture books
- providing a language arts classroom center
- channeling interested children into print and alphabet activities by offering supportive assistance

Natural Approach

- providing writing and reading materials and models
- planning program that emphasizes print in daily life
- promoting dramatic play themes that involve print, such as grocery store, restaurant, newspaper carrier, print shop, and office
- creating a writing center for the classroom
- supplying alphabet toys and models
- answering questions and supporting children's efforts
- making connections between reading and writing and speaking
- reading picture books

14-1a Starting from a Different Place

At about 16 to 20 months, some toddlers become interested in scribbling. One sees them grasp a drawing or marking tool in their fist and use it in sweeping, whole-arm motions to make marks. Motions can be vigorous, rhythmic, scrubbing, and repetitive and may include sharp stabs at the paper, which tears because of the pressure applied. Adults can wisely provide sturdy, large pieces of paper taped down onto a surface that can take the punishment. Large flattened brown grocery bags work well.

Scribbling involves decision making. It coincides with young children's emerging sense of autonomy. Children make decisions about line, color, and the placement of marks on the paper. They also use and gain control over the tools of their home and classroom—crayons, markers, pencils, paper and so on—if it is regarded as a valued activity.

Past opportunity may have dramatically molded the individual child's literacy behaviors and language competency. Teachers hope to expand language competencies that exist and introduce children to new activities and opportunities. Much of young children's writing is exploratory. Through personally motivated and personally directed trial and error—a necessary condition of their literacy development—children try out various aspects of the writing process. They sometimes interact and collaborate with peers who are more literate (Photo 14-3). Competent others provide help and eventually children function without supportive assistance.

Photo 14-3 Teachers promote both individual and collaborative printing activities.

© 2015 Cengage Learning®

TeachSource Video 14-1

Preschool: Communication through Language and Literacy Activities

1. Is the printscript displayed in the classroom functional and does it have a purpose for being there?

2. Do you think the classroom is well supplied with equipment that is useful for children's writing development? If yes, identify some of these items. If no, what do you think is missing?

3. Name some of the activities that promoted writing development.

14-1b Teaching Writing Tool Grip

Although somewhat controversial, some early childhood programs provide instruction for three- and four-year-olds on how to grip a writing tool. These programs purposefully provide broken crayons (ones of a short length that glide well) and promote young children's use of a finger gripping motion rather than whole hand grasping. Children are shown what these programs believe is the most efficient and comfortable finger gripping position. It is believed that this type of grip allows the best control of the writing tool and aids eventual speed in writing (printing). Children who have already found their own unique grip are shown a second way that they can choose to adopt. Program plans include enjoyable activities that promote small motor control with a finger pinching action, such as picking up small objects. Instructions for the "right" tool grip are as follows: hold the writing tool between a bent thumb and a first finger (index) pointed at the tool's marking tip, with the tool resting on the middle finger; the ring and little finger should be bent

inward toward the palm. Some educators are less enthusiastic about this instructional approach for many reasons, including research that points out that about half of all three-year-olds have already mastered the grip. Other educators feel that child motivation and interest is paramount before grip instruction takes place.

Advocates counter by describing a writing fundamentals curriculum that is without pressure, game-like, and uses songs with clever rhythms to introduce concepts and terms. Each early childhood program will decide how, or if grip instruction or writing fundamentals instruction, will be included in its program. Family members frequently demonstrate their own writing grip to children, and educators usually initiate instruction with a child who exhibits awkwardness or frustration. A right-handed teacher may find that demonstrating a writing grip is difficult with a left-handed child because the paper is slanted in a different direction than for right-handed children. Teachers routinely tape or secure writing paper to tables or large surfaces so the paper won't slip away from early writers, or they may show how holding the paper with the other hand solves the problem.

14-2 Research and Fundamentals in Writing Development

In *Literacy Before Schooling* (1982), researchers Ferreiro and Teberosky revolutionized educators' thinking about young children's development of print knowledge and writing. Subsequent research in children's self-constructed knowledge of alphabet forms and printing has followed, using anthropological, psychological, and other investigative approaches. Ferreiro and Teberosky identified three developmentally ordered levels.

1. **First Level**

In this level, children

- search for criteria to distinguish between drawing and writing. Example: "What's this?" referring to their artwork.

- realize that straight and curved lines and dots are present but organized differently in print. Example: Rows and rows of curved figures, lines, and/or dots in art.

- reach the conclusion that print forms are arbitrary and ordered in a linear fashion.

© 2016 Cengage Learning®

- accept the letter shapes in their environment rather than inventing new ones. Example: Rows of one letter appear in linear fashion in art.
- recognize from literacy-rich environments written marks as "substitute objects" during their third year. Example: "What does this say, teacher?" or "This says 'Mary.'"

2. Second Level

In this level, children

- look for objective differences in printed strings.
- do not realize that there is a relationship between sound patterns and print.

3. Third Level

In this level, children

- accept that a given string of letters represents their name and look for a rational explanation of this phenomenon.
- may create a syllabic hypothesis.
- may print letter forms as syllables heard in a word. Example: I C (I see).
- may develop knowledge about particular syllables and what letters might represent such a syllable.
- may look for similar letters to write similar pieces of sound.
- begin to understand that printing uses alphabet letters that represent sounds; consequently, to understand print, one must know the sound patterns of words.

What conclusions of this landmark research may affect language arts program planning and early educators' interaction techniques? Certainly, teachers will note attending children's active attempts to understand print. They will realize that each child constructs her own ideas and revises these understandings as more print is noticed and experienced. The seemingly strange questions children ask or off-the-wall answers some children give in classroom discussions about print may now be seen as reflecting their inner thoughts at crucial points in their print development. As teachers view children's artwork, they will more readily see early print forms, and they will continue their attempts to provide literacy-rich, print-rich classroom environments.

Some preschoolers demonstrate that they know the names and shapes of alphabet letters. They may also know letters form words and represent sounds. They might have grasped the idea that spoken words can be written and then read. They may be able to express daily uses of written words. Why would a young child write or pretend to write? It is not an easy motor task. Is it simple imitation or is it done for adult reaction? Do children do so because there is an inner drive to know or become competent? Research has yet to answer these questions. Teachers conjecture reasons with each young child they meet who has beginning printing skills. The reasons why children pretend to write are not the most important thing; what matters more are teachers' reactions and their commitment to providing additional opportunities to nourish and expand what already exists.

14-2a Young Children's Progress

Baker and Schiffer (2007) suggest that learning to write begins as children gain familiarity with the alphabet, learn about writing instruments, and recognize simple words in everyday places, such as *STOP* on the familiar red street sign. At some point, children learn that written marks have meaning. Just as they sought the names of things, they now seek the names of these marks and, later, the meanings of marks. Because each child is an individual, this may or may not happen during the preschool years. One child may try to make letters or numbers. Another child may have little interest in or knowledge of written forms. Many children are somewhere between these two examples.

Preschool children may recognize environmental print words before they know the name of any alphabet letters. This is termed **sight reading**, and some preschool children may recognize most of the children's names in their group if nametags are used. Quite a few researchers believe a period of time exists when a young child conceives of a certain alphabet letter as representing a person or object (for example, all "B" words remind the child of her own name). At that point, the child may say, "'B,' that's my name." A child may not understand that the alphabet is a complete set of letters representing speech sounds used in writing, but rather, she may have a partial

---

sight reading — the ability to immediately recognize a word as a whole without sounding it out.

Figure 14-3 The alphabetic principle.

The child may:
- understand that letters have different shapes.
- identify some letters by name.
- notice some words start with the same letter.
- realize letters make sounds.
- match some sounds to letters correctly.
- possess a sight word vocabulary—usually her own and peer's names.
- realize alphabet letters are a special category of print.

and beginning view of the **alphabetic principle**. Figure 14-3 displays possible child understandings concerning the alphabetic principle.

Writing (printscript) is complex. Many subcomponents of the process need to be understood. Development may occur at different rates, with spurts and lags in different knowledge areas. Besides the visual learning of letter features and forms, the ability to manually form shapes, and knowing that writing involves a message, a writer must listen to the sounds of her inner speech and find matching letters representing those sounds. Because letter follows letter in printing, the child needs to make continuous intellectual choices and decisions.

Many events happen between the ages of three and five. Children begin to vary their marks and move from imitation to creation. They produce a mixture of real letters, mock letters, and innovative symbols. A few written messages are readable. These actions signal several new behaviors and child discoveries. They are attending to the fine features of writing, noting shapes and specific letters, and they are developing an early concept of sign—the realization that symbols stand for something. Some children also see that there is variation in written language. Children refine and enlarge these concepts by experimenting with writing. They draw, trace, copy, and even invent marks and letter forms of their own.

Print awareness is usually developed in the following sequence:

1. The child notices adults making marks with writing tools.
2. The child notices print in books and on signs. When this time comes, a child is increasingly aware of all the print in the world around her—street signs, food labels, newspaper headlines, printing on cartons, books, billboards, everything. He may try to read everything. Already having a good foundation in translating spoken words to print, he may move on and try printing. If help is provided when he asks for it, he progresses. It can be a very exciting time for him.
3. The child realizes that certain distinguishable marks make her name.
4. The child learns the names of some of the marks—usually the first letter of her name. While building a sizable store of words recognized on sight, children will begin to make finer and finer distinctions about print by using more and more visual cues. They begin to pay attention to individual letters, particularly the first ones in words.

The child's imitation of written forms usually develops in the following sequence:

1. The child's scribbles are more like print than artwork or pure exploration (Figure 14-4).
2. Linear scribbles are generally horizontal with possible repeated forms. Children's knowledge of linear directionality may have been displayed in play in which they lined up alphabet blocks, cut out letters and pasted them in a row, or put magnetic board letters in left-to-right rows (Figure 14-5).
3. Individual shapes are created, usually closed shapes displaying purposeful lines (Photo 14-4).
4. Letter-like forms are created.
5. Recognizable alphabet letters are printed and may be mirror images or turned on sides, upside down, or in an upright position (Figure 14-6).
6. Words or groupings of alphabet letters with spaces between are formed.
7. **Invented spelling** appears; this may include pictured items along with alphabet letters (Figure 14-7).
8. Correctly spelled words with spaces separating words are produced.

---

alphabetic principle — the awareness that spoken language can be analyzed as strings of separate words and that words, in turn, can be analyzed as sequences of syllables and phonemes within syllables.

invented spelling — the result of an attempt to spell a word whose spelling is not already known, based on a writer's knowledge of the spelling system and how it works.

Figure 14-4 Scribbles are sometimes print-like.

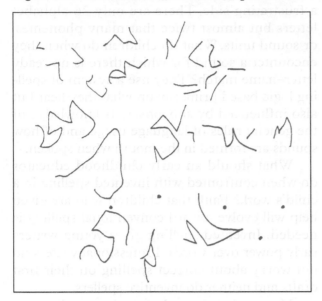

Figure 14-5 Linear scribbles.

Photo 14-4 This boy has just made a closed-shape letter with purposeful lines.

Figure 14-6 Recognizable alphabet letters.

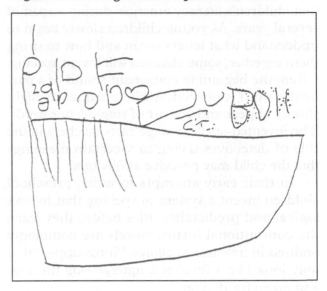

Figure 14-7 Child read as "Blast off rocket to the moon."

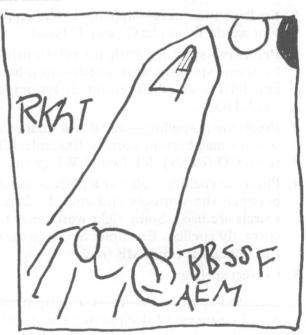

14-2b Invented Spelling (Developmental Spelling)

Invented spelling is something children do naturally. It is a temporary phenomenon that is later replaced with conventional spelling. Until the mid to late 1980s, teachers gave young children the idea that until they learned to read, they needed to write only those words they had memorized or copied. Research has changed educational philosophy and methods. It suggests that children's literacy emerges during a span of several years. As young children slowly begin to understand what letters mean and how to string them together, some children will invent spelling. Often, the beginning consonant sound of a particular word is printed. A whole sequence might shortly appear and consist of single-letter words. The invented-spelling stage casts teachers in the role of detectives trying to ascertain meanings that the child may perceive as obvious.

In their early attempts to write, preschool children invent a system of spelling that follows logical and predictable rules before they learn the conventional forms. Vowels are commonly omitted in invented spellings. Words appear that may look like a foreign language—*dg* for dog, and *jragin* for dragon.

Identifiable stages in invented spelling are followed by some children and are given here for teacher reference.

1. Spelling awareness—alphabet letters represent words. Example: C (see), U (you).

2. Primitive spelling with no relationship between spelling and words—numbers and letters are differentiated. Example: tsOlf..DO.

3. Prephonetic spelling—initial and final consonants may become correct. Example: KT (cat), CD (candy), RT (write), WF (with).

4. Phonetic spelling—almost a perfect match between the symbols and sounds. Some vowels are used. Some sight words may be correctly spelled. Example: SUM (some), LIK (like), MI (my), ME (me).

5. Correct spelling.

Invented spelling serves as an important stage in the process of deciphering the sound–symbol system of written language. It is believed that at this point, phonics becomes important to children. Early on, the child selects letters in her inventive spelling that have some relationship to how the word is pronounced. Large items such as "elephants" may be written in huge letters and with more letters than small objects, because the child is operating under the misconception that bigger necessitates more letters. A perfectly logical conclusion! The names of letters may words (*u* for you) or parts of words. Young writers' invented spelling uses personal logic rather than or in conjunction with standard spelling, and the

child's strategy of using a name of a letter has a frustrating side. There are only 26 alphabet letters but almost twice that many phonemes, or sound units. What do children do when they encounter a sound for which there is no ready letter–name match? They use a system of spelling logic based primarily on what they hear but also influenced by subconscious knowledge of the general rules of language usage and of how sounds are formed in the mouth when spoken.

What should an early childhood educator do when confronted with invented spelling in a child's work? Faith that children who are given help will evolve toward conventional spelling is needed. Invented spelling gives young writers early power over words. Professional writers do not worry about correct spelling on their first drafts and neither do inventive spellers.

Many primary teachers write out the standard spelling for words below a child's invented spelling. By doing so, teachers honor the original but provide further information so children can compare their spelling inventions with regular standard spellings. Inventive spellers who realize their spelling differs from text in books and the world around them may experience frustration and confusion. Teachers at this juncture may introduce phoneme spelling by "sounding out" words that they print.

Some educators recommend putting a small teacher translation on papers containing invented spelling. They record the child's intended message (or a translation of what the child has tried to write) using small letters on a remote corner of the page or on its back. This can be a satisfying arrangement if the child has no objection to the practice. It also gives the teacher the opportunity to observe and hear the child decode her message in her own words. In this way a family examining "take-home" papers can possibly understand the thought processes the child used to write the message and understand the child's great accomplishment. A family-teacher discussion is usually necessary for family to realize that beginning attempts are not immediately corrected. Teachers need to use these techniques carefully with older preschoolers, being mindful of the child's inventiveness and pride in her work. Many preschoolers object to teachers adding any marks on their papers.

When a child asks the teacher to write a specific word, the teacher has a chance to help the child with letter sounds (rather than letter names), saying *d-o-g* as she writes it. Time permitting, the teacher can add, "It starts with the alphabet letter d, like Dan, D-a-n."

14-3 Goals of Instruction

Providing experiences that match a child's interests and abilities is the goal of many early childhood centers. Most schools plan activities for those children who ask questions or seem ready and then proceed if the children are still interested. Others work with children on an individual basis. Yet others believe in providing a print-rich environment where the child will progress naturally with supportive adults who also model an interest in print and point out uses of print in daily activities. A fourth group of preschools identify a curriculum that includes emerging letter knowledge and print word recognition skills for their instruction program drawn from recognized standards, academic research, the findings of the National Early Literacy Panel (2008), or another professional group's recommendations. Most often these programs include phonemic and print awareness goals in their preschool program's goal statements. Specific proposed outcomes for a child attending their school are to be reached at the end of the year or another period of time and might look like the following. The child will

- Name most upper and lowercase alphabet letters in a fluent manner.
- Identify beginning letters in familiar words such as peer's names.
- Correctly match some sounds to letters.
- Identify words that rhyme.
- Create or remember a word that rhymes with a teacher's word.
- Stretch a three letter word and demonstrate he can hear the three sounds it contains.
- Clap syllables in one to three syllable words correctly.
- Substitute a new letter sound for a given word ending, therefore, creating a new word.
- Blend sounds in a few words.
- Print a number of recognizable alphabet letters using a printscript style that teacher has modeled.
- Dictate words for a teacher to print.
- Print in a lineal left to right direction.

- Make attempts to write a message.
- Use technology to print words when technology is available.
- Read a number of words by sight when requested.

Programs with at-risk students may design implicit and specific lessons that include selected alphabet and vocabulary instruction in common words that form the basis for successful early reading. Teachers plan activities involving authentic writing (printing), that is, writing done for the "real world" rather than for contrived school purposes. Research emphasizes that when planning printing activities, instruction should concentrate on using print in authentic activities that are meaningful and have a purpose and/or a reason in the child's daily life. An authentic written message may also involve a child's need or desire. It is possible to combine these approaches. A teacher might say, "Let's say the word you are trying to print very slowly, and stretch it out so we can hear its sounds."

As with other language abilities, goals include stimulating further interest and exploration. This should be done in such a way that the child is not confused by instruction that is either too advanced or boring. Most early childhood educators subscribe to the idea that teaching print concepts encountered during a read-aloud with a picture book should be kept to a minimum and used only when print in some way clarifies a main theme or feature in the book's format or story. Usually teachers concentrate primarily on children's understanding of a book's meaning and enjoyment.

As stated previously, an important goal concerning print awareness is relating writing to other language arts areas or other domains. It is almost impossible to not do so. Teachers are encouraged to consciously mention connections so that children will understand how writing fits in the whole of communicating. Figure 14-8 is a listing of both print and book awareness understandings that early childhood educators endeavor to promote before a child begins kindergarten.

Another important *teacher* goal would be having the ability to print every lowercase and uppercase alphabet letter in excellent form, so as to offer children the best model possible. A primary and overriding goal of early childhood educators involves basing their teacher–child

Figure 14-8 Print and book awareness goals.

Print and Book Awareness Goals

The child understands that:

- reading obtains information from books.
- writing communicates thoughts and ideas.
- print can carry messages.
- letters are different from numerals.
- book illustrations carry meaning.
- print can be read.
- books have authors who create books and their titles.
- print is read from left to right and top to bottom.
- alphabet letters in print can form words.
- alphabet letters have names.
- words are separated by spaces.
- spoken words can be written down.
- print has everyday functional uses (for example, shopping lists, messages, recipes, signs).
- one can follow print with one's eyes as it is read aloud.

interactions upon current research and best practices. Knowing that both young children's letter *name* knowledge and letter *sound* knowledge are recognized as important predictors of early reading competence, teachers work to promote each skill. Head Start centers are congressionally mandated to teach letter names to at-risk, low income children (U.S. Department of Health and Human Services, 2003). Research evidence points to the value of teaching letter names and sounds together. When children learn letter names it increases the possibility they know or will learn its sound. Most letter names include the phoneme the letter represents in the English language (Treiman & Kessler, 2003).

14-3a Coordination

Children's muscle control follows a timetable of its own. Control of a particular muscle depends on many factors—diet, exercise, inherited ability, and motivation, to name a few. A baby can control her neck and arms long before her legs. A child's muscle control grows in a head-to-toe fashion. Muscles closer to the center of the body can be controlled long before those of the hands and fingers. Large-muscle control comes before small-muscle control (Photo 14-5). Think of a toddler walking; the toddler's legs seem to swing from the hips. Just as each child starts walking and develops muscle control at different ages, so, too, does each child develop fine motor control, which influences her ability to control a writing tool. Under the right circumstances, fine motor skills can progress to very specific motor control at the fingertips. This is promoted by young children's access to developmentally appropriate activities and play materials that involve using the thumb and fingers and opposition or using pincher movements in play activities with tongs, tweezers, eyedroppers, or picking up small objects.

Photo 14-5 The small-muscle control Ria is using to trace a leaf will be needed when she begins to print.

© 2015 Cengage Learning®

Photo 14-6 This child displays her own unique finger-and-thumb grasp.

Precise writing is extremely difficult for some three- and four-year-olds, who grasp writing tools in their fists and guide them with movements started at the shoulder, elbow, or wrist. With the pivot and the writing tool point so far apart, children can't help but write large. Preschoolers' spatial skills are limited, and it can be difficult for them to construct and combine lines. Four-year-olds with more advanced fine motor skills can hold a pencil in a well-controlled finger and thumb grasp (Photo 14-6).

14-3b Cognitive Development

Mental growth, which allows a child to see similarities and differences in written symbols, comes before the ability to write. The child recognizes that a written mark is a shape made by the placement of lines. Seven prerequisite skill areas exist for handwriting. These are small-muscle development and coordination, eye-hand coordination, the ability to hold writing tools

properly, the ability to form basic strokes (circles and straight lines), letter perception, an orientation to printed language—which includes a desire to write and communicate—including the child's enjoyment of writing her own name, and left-to-right understanding. A number of these skills deal with the child's cognitive development. Through past experiences, including child's play, ideas about print and writing have been formed.

14-3c Boys' Writing Development

Whitmire (2010), author of *Why Boys Fail*, urges educators to take particular care to help young boys verbalize and receive skilled adult verbal feedback. He believes some boys fail elementary and high school and avoid college for diverse reasons. Among these are their verbal and vocabulary skill development and their inability to express themselves. The largest gender gap involves boys' writing skills. Teachers, especially early childhood ones, need to find books of interest to young boys, which might include ridiculous or goofy ones. Listening and watching closely for boys' enjoyment and engagement during teacher-chosen readings is important. Minority and low-income boys seem to struggle the most with academics (Marklein, 2010). Zambo (2007) suggests boys may need special teacher attention and guidance. She recommends using stories and literacy activities to increase skills.

> Hearing stories about male characters acting responsibly improves a boy's vocabulary, helps him understand story structure, and, at the same time, teaches him how responsibility looks, sounds, and feels. (p. 12)

and

> Make sure the book has rich language and a substantive plot that will capture boys' attention and keep them interested. (p. 13)

14-4 Play, Drawing, and Other Influences

Print, signs, and writing imaginary messages often become part of a dramatic play sequence. During play, children may pretend to read and write words, poems, stories, and songs, and they may actually make a series of marks on paper. Play encourages children to act as if they are already competent in and able to control the activity under consideration. Through pretend play, they may feel that they are already readers and writers; at least a beginning move toward eventual literacy takes place. Children observe families using reading and writing in their daily lives. These activities are given status. Early childhood teachers can build on children's early attitudes by modeling, demonstrating, and providing dramatic play opportunities involving print, which promote collaborative peer printing.

14-4a Drawing Experience

A young child scribbles if given paper and a marking tool. As the child grows, the scribbles are controlled into lines that she places where desired (Figure 14-9). Gradually, the child begins to draw circles, then a face, later a full figure, and so on. Children draw their own symbols representing what they see around them. Educators urge teachers to examine one child's drawings over a few weeks' time; they may discover that the child is working on a basic plan. Perhaps a child makes the same pattern or schema again and again. It may seem as if the child has learned a plan of action for producing the pattern or schema. This gives the child enough control over pencil and paper to play with variations, which often leads to new discoveries. The length of time it takes this process to develop differs with each child.

A profound connection exists between experience and ability in drawing and interest in and ability to write (Photo 14-7). Drawings and paintings not only communicate children's thinking (when they reach the level of drawing that is representative of the environment), but

Photo 14-7 Nontoxic felt-tip pens (markers) are standard preschool materials.

© 2015 Cengage Learning®

also often display early attempts to create symbols. Some of these symbols may be recognized by adults, but others seem to be unique and represent the world in the child's own way. Children often want to talk about their work and create stories to accompany graphics.

Because alphabet letters are more abstract than representative drawing, most educators suggest that drawing precedes writing. One research study identified a characteristic that was common to almost all children in the study who read early and continued to hold their lead in reading achievement. The children in the study were described by their parents as "pencil-and-paper kids," whose starting point of curiosity about written language was an interest in scribbling and drawing.

Figure 14-9 Children start writing by scribbling and, when older, drawing symbols of the world around them.

14-4b Writing and Exposure to Books

naeyc DAP

Probably the most common experience that promotes a child's interest in print is hearing and seeing picture books read over and over. Through repeated exposure, the child comes to expect the text to be near or on the same page as the object depicted. Two- and three-year-olds think that pictures in a book tell the story; as they gain more experience, they notice that the reader reads the print, not the pictures. Memorized story lines lead to children's questions about print on book pages. Once a word is recognized in print, copying that word onto another piece of paper or manipulating magnetic alphabet letters to form the word is a natural outgrowth. This activity usually leads to parent attention and approval and further attempts. Scribblers, doodlers, drawers, and pencil-and-paper kids are all labels researchers have used to describe children who have an early interest in writing, and much of what they do has been promoted by seeing print in their favorite books.

Stages of print recognition are believed to exist, starting with a stage in which the text and the picture are not differentiated. Then children begin to expect that the text is a label for the picture. In a third stage, the text is expected to provide cues with which to confirm predictions based on the picture. Some important concepts that young children gradually understand concerning print are: print tells a story along with illustrations, and alphabet letters can be printed. Other concepts to learn are: words are clusters of letters, words have first and last letters, and they are found in upper- and lowercase. Spaces between words happen and punctuation marks have meaning are additional understandings.

Children may notice the left-to-right and top-to-bottom direction of printing and also the left-page-first directional feature. It is important to promote the idea that there are different purposes for print and text, and that it appears in different forms depending on its purpose. Road signs have large block print and may be colorful and reflective to alert pedestrians and drivers both day and night. This fact is an example of both purpose and form. There are other examples in classrooms, such as hot and cold written on water handles. Lists of print words, newspapers, dictionaries, and poetry usually look different from picture book text, whose purpose usually is to tell a story.

The acquisition of skills in writing and reading and the development of the attitude that books are enjoyable involve more than academic or technical learning. These skills flourish with a warm physical and emotional base with shared enjoyment and intimacy. Most experts believe that considerable support exists for the notion that oral language provides a base for learning to write. The importance of emotionally satisfying adult–child interactions in all areas of language arts cannot be overestimated.

14-4c Alphabet Books

Children's books in print before the twentieth century were mostly informational and moralistic. Alphabet books suited the then prevailing public view that a good children's book should promote learning rather than pleasure. Presently, library collections for young children include a variety of alphabet books. Although many are in print and some are classic favorites, new titles continually appear. It is said that almost every author of young children's literature yearns to develop a unique alphabet book. The following are some recommended titles:

Bunting, E. (2002). *Girls A to Z*. Honesdale, PA: Boyd Mills Press. (A girl-can-be-anything theme.)

Fleming, D. (2002). *Alphabet under construction*. New York: Henry Holt and Company. (Suits toddlers and preschoolers, with colorful and playful illustrations.)

Sierra, J. (2009). *The sleepy little alphabet: A bedtime story from Alphabet town*. New York: Alfred Knoff (Upper and lower case alphabet letters that rhyme.)

Wood, A. (2006). *Alphabet rescue*. New York: Blue Sky Press. (A creative and charming way to learn letters.)

Wordless books with printed signs in their illustrations are great for focusing young children's attention on print, alphabet letters, and their purpose in daily life. A side benefit is that it channels attention to the concept of word. Words consist of a string of letters with spaces between them and this can also be recognized. Teachers can easily finger point and identify individual letter names and sounds. When children are asking for alphabet letter names, and when alphabet letters are appearing in their art or writing, alphabet books can become favorites. Teachers notice that a first interest in alphabet letters often appears when the child sees her printed name and then notices similar letters in friends' names.

Ideas for ways to build alphabet books into further classroom activities follow: (1) paint on a giant alphabet letter shape; (2) hide an alphabet letter in a large drawing and have children search for it; (3) make a class alphabet book by outlining large alphabet letters on pages and encouraging interested individual children to decorate a letter; (4) create a "Who looked at this book today?" chart. Add children's names to the chart if they browsed the book; and (5) create a personalized alphabet book for each child or suggest this to families.

Full understanding of the alphabet requires children to understand four separate yet interconnected components (Bradley & Jones, 2010). Those components are (a) letter-shape knowledge or letter recognition, (b) letter-name knowledge, (c) letter-sound knowledge, and (d) letter-writing ability. Each component is described more specifically as follows.

> (a) The ability to distinguish letters requires recognition of visual features, such as shape, orientation, and directionality and discerning key features presented in various sizes, fonts, cases, and handwriting styles.
>
> (b) The realization that alphabet letters are symbols, each with a given name that can appear in both upper- and lowercase.
>
> (c) The knowledge that letters represent different sounds, and sometimes multiple sounds, and
>
> (d) The ability to form written alphabet letters. (p. 76)

Bradley and Jones (2010) point out as young children have opportunities to learn and develop fluent knowledge of the alphabet, their ability to read and write will likely be facilitated. When assessing a child's alphabet knowledge, each of the above components is important. These authors suggest children benefit most from alphabet books when teachers are explicit when presenting them.

14-5 Planning a Program for Print Awareness and Printing Skill

Program planning is often done on an individual basis, but standards have been initiated and used as a basis for program planning in an increasing number of child development centers. If group instruction takes place, it deals with general background information concerning print use during the school day and how it relates to children's lives, including print use in the home and community. A great deal of spontaneous and incidental teaching takes place. Teachers capitalize on children's questions concerning mail, packages, signs, and labels. In most preschool settings, print is a natural part of living, and it has many interesting features that children can discover and notice when teachers focus attention on print.

A supportive classroom environment allows children to design their own route to further knowledge about print. It is critical for children to have a literacy-rich, risk-free environment that includes time to invent, to play, and to experiment with written language for meaningful purposes in an authentic context while interacting with knowledgeable others. Such experiences allow children to work through questions and perplexities, and to build conceptualizations and understandings in ways meaningful to them. As children compare their inventions with the written language around them, particularly their names, they deepen their understandings of the complexities of our written language system.

A discussion is necessary here concerning the practice of asking the child to form alphabet letters and practice letter forms. The dangers in planning an individual or group experience of this nature are multiple. One has to consider whether a child has the physical and mental capacity to be successful and whether the child has an interest in doing the exercise or is simply trying to please adults.

The logical progression in learning about letters is to first learn letter names and then learn letter shapes, but this can be reversed when a child has an interest in making letter form in artwork. The child then has a solid mnemonic peg on which to hang the concept of "letter" as the concept is learned. Activities such as singing the alphabet song, reading alphabet books, and playing with alphabet magnets or puzzles help preschoolers learn letters. The uppercase letters are larger and research suggests that they are the easiest forms for preschoolers to reproduce. Preschools often present "big" and "little" letters together in the school's visual environment. It is the uppercase letters that most children recognize when they enter kindergarten. Preschool and kindergarten teachers also print children's names with an uppercase first letter followed by lowercase letters in printscript.

Teachers encourage children to print ("write") their own names on their artwork when they believe children have an interest in printing. Any attempt is recognized and given attention. These teachers may also say, "May I write your name on the back? With two names, one on the front and one on the back, we will find your work quickly when it's time to leave school." Teachers print names on the upper left corner of the children's work because that is the spot reading starts on any given page written in English. (It is hoped that the child and/or child's family has been asked before enrollment what name the child prefers to be called at school.)

Early writing instruction is not a new idea. Maria Montessori (1967a) (a well-known educator and designer of teaching materials) and numerous other teachers have offered instruction in writing (or printing) to preschoolers. Montessori encouraged the child's tracing of letter forms using the first two fingers of the hand as a prewriting exercise. She observed that this type of light touching seemed to help youngsters when writing tools were later given to them. Montessori (1967a) designed special alphabet letter cutouts as one of a number of prewriting aids. These cutouts were thought to help exercise and develop small muscles and create sight-touch sensations, fixing the forms in memory.

In seventeenth- and eighteenth-century England, a gingerbread method of teaching alphabet letters was developed. As a child correctly named a letter-shaped cookie or a word formed by cookies, she was allowed to eat it (or them). This is offered here to point out past educators' practices rather than to recommend. Brain learning advocates would advise giving children concrete (real) letter forms to touch and manipulate while naming them (Jensen, 2008).

One prekindergarten teacher's print awareness plan is described by Kissel (2008). Each day a writer's workshop took place after a read-aloud. The teacher crafted a follow-up mini lesson in which she made a drawing related to the storybook on a large paper to represent her "writing."

> As the year progressed, she included initial-letter word sounds next to some of the central themes of her writing. Near the end of the year, she added simple words that the children helped her sound out as she wrote. She always included a picture (teacher drawing). This evolution mirrored the writing of the children. She gently scaffolded their writing development, introducing print, when most of the children were ready. (p. 28)

Her teaching strategy, she believed, was based on the writings of Vygotsky (1976, 1980, 1986), and the idea that when she drew her pictures in front of the class she demonstrated the use of images and symbols to convey messages. Children were able during writing workshop times to confer with her and other children. She added words and short sentences to her drawings near the end of the school year.

Another early childhood educator designed a year-long writing awareness program for her class based upon the belief that preschoolers possess a seemingly endless supply of personal stories. She observed that they required varying levels of teacher and classroom support to enable them to put them down on paper (King, 2012). King's approach to acquaint preschoolers with writing (printing) entailed using a four component classroom instructional strategy: (1) she presented many lessons about writing; (2) she initiated a child-centered, open-ended classroom writing time; (3) she started a teacher–student conference time; and (4) she scheduled a child sharing his/her work time (p. 393). Her approach also promoted child journal writing in teacher-made individual child booklets in which a child could express a chosen story topic in a drawing or words or use it for writing alphabet letters, writing their name or common words, or using a combination of these.

14-5a Learning Print Conventions

The sub skills of print conventions may be learned in a number of ways, including through daily interactions and exchanges in a classroom. These sub skills follow in the left column below. In the right column are sample teacher comments. The teacher's goal is not only to inform, but also to pass on the information enough times for children to recall it or display their knowledge with an action or comment.

Front cover of a book	"Right here on the book's *front cover* it says..."
Back cover	"On this book's *back cover* we see..."
Author or authorship	"A lady named Mary Smith made up this story and we will find out..."

Illustrator	"The pictures in our book were painted by…"
Illustration	"I like to look at this *illustration* on page 3 because…"
Photographer	"The pictures in our picture book were taken with…"
Title or title page	"When I read a book's *title page* I find out…"
Alphabet letters	"Anna, your name starts with the letter 'a' and ends…"
Letter form	"To make the letter B you start with a straight line and…"
Symbols, symbolic representation	"The arrow pointing down tells us to push down…"
Directionality & top left progression	"The first word to read on this page…"
Sign directionality	"This sign has three words 'Park bikes here.'"
Left to right progression	"Pogo is the first word. I have my hand beneath it and the next…"
Last word on page	"I've run out of words to read on this page. The last *word* is…"
Lines on a page	"This is a paper with lines across it, if I write…"
Words are printed using alphabet letters	"You want a sign for the playhouse to say…"

14-5b How to Make the ABCs Developmentally Appropriate

In a print-rich classroom environment, children are bound to see alphabet letters as a natural part of their world and to develop curiosity about them. Teachers examine activities and take advantage of teachable moments. Educators realize alphabet knowledge prompts phonemic awareness. Teachers promote children's fluency in naming alphabet letters. Fluency can be defined as speed and accuracy. Children

fluent in alphabet letter names can recognize and correctly name alphabet letters without hesitation, thereby indicating that letter names have been well learned. The following are samples of alphabet-related activities.

- **Name of the Day.** One child's name is chosen and discussed at circle time. The first alphabet letter in the child's name is named and searched for in room displays.

- **Alphabet Letter Sorting Game.** A teacher-made box with slots under alphabet letters is provided, along with a deck of teacher-made alphabet cards. A child (or children) decide what card is slotted, and then the box is lifted and the cards retrieved for the next child. The box can be a large cardboard box upended with letters on the box and adjacent cut slots. This game needs a simple introduction and demonstration.

- **Alphabet Chart Game.** The teacher posts large alphabet letters on large paper around the room. Child volunteers choose how to get to one letter from the starting place to touch the letter and then how to get to the next. (Every child gets a turn.) The teacher may have to start by saying, "Let's tiptoe to the letter C" or "Who can think of a way to get to 'M'"?

- **Designing Game Activities.** When designing games, remember that in developmentally appropriate games everyone gets a turn, clear directions (rules) are introduced, everyone wins, competition is inappropriate, cooperation is promoted, praise or prizes are omitted, and creating musical games is possible. Movement games are wiggle reducers if they end on a cooling-down note. Games are designed to include or give a turn to every child who wants to play, and game parts are sturdy and well made to eliminate frustration.

Remember also that these games can promote listening skills and problem solving. It is recommended that alphabet letters be introduced. Most early childhood program staffs specifically designate exactly which letter form they will offer first and affirm alphabet letters named by children in either uppercase or lowercase. Teaching the sounds of alphabet letters is an instructional decision based on children's age, interest, and ability. Schools decide if it is developmentally appropriate and whether it is done only on a one-to-one basis.

14-5c Seeing and Hearing Patterns

Infants, toddlers, and preschoolers have an innate capability to see and hear patterns (Vergano, 2009). Vergano notes this is something psychologists doubted for decades. Learning research, he suggests, urges educators to discover patterns with young children during their play. Doing so may aid brain development and sharpen children's ability to recognize environmental patterns. Print recognition, during the preschool period, will involve this skill. Recognizing patterns in the environment such as a special friend knocking on the door in a specific rhythm sequence, or understanding there is a sequence of routines during the school day that repeat the next day, or recognizing a friend's name on artwork because of a sequence of certain alphabet letters are examples of this skill.

14-6 Environment and Materials

Children's access to drawing tools—magic markers, chalk, pencils, crayons, brushes—is important so that children can make their own marks. It is suggested that teachers create a place where children can comfortably use these tools. The following early childhood materials help the child use and gain control of small arm and finger muscles in preparation for writing—puzzles, pegboards, small blocks, construction toys, scissors, and eyedroppers.

Most early childhood centers plan activities in which the child puts together, arranges, or manipulates small pieces. These are sometimes called tabletop activities and are available for play throughout the day. A teacher can encourage the use of tabletop activities by having the pieces arranged invitingly on tables or resting on adjacent shelves. The following are examples of materials common in print-immersion classrooms.

- labels—pictures or photographs accompanied by corresponding words
- charts and lists—charts that convey directions, serve as learning resources (pictures and names of children in alphabetical order), organize the class (attendance roster or class calendar), show written language as a reminder (children's sign-up lists)
- materials and activities—various materials, including alphabet toys, puzzles, stamps, magnetic

letters, and games, along with clever teacher-made materials (Photo 14-8) or commercial furnishings, such as blocks, stuffed alphabet-shaped pillows, alphabet rugs, and wall hangings

- books and other resources—a variety of books and magazines, poetry, newspapers, computer software, picture dictionaries, riddle and novelty books, and other printed material

Early childhood centers create rooms that are full of symbols, letters, and numbers in clear view of the child. Room print should reflect teacher and child interests. Many toys have circles, squares, triangles, alphabet letters, and other common shapes. Recommended letter and symbol size for preschool playroom display is at least two to two and one-half inches in height or larger.

14-6a Labeling

Labeling activities revolve around the purpose and function of labels and signs in daily life. One educator created handheld signs for use during daily scheduled activities, such as clean-up,

Photo 14-8 Making charts that alert children to print's usefulness is a common teacher task.

Figure 14-10 Large printscript letters are used to label boxes.

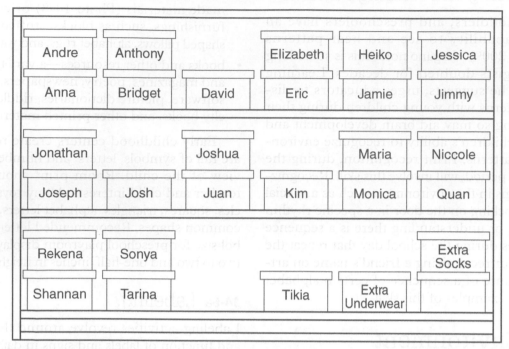

Andre	Anthony		Elizabeth	Heiko	Jessica
Anna	Bridget	David	Eric	Jamie	Jimmy
Jonathan		Joshua		Maria	Niccole
Joseph	Josh	Juan	Kim	Monica	Quan
Rekena	Sonya				Extra Socks
Shannan	Tarina		Tikia	Extra Underwear	

line-up, circle time, listening time, and washing hands. Each sign had printed words and a visual clue, such as a wastebasket for clean-up, an ear for listening time, and so on. In a classroom, many needs usually exist. A "Park bikes here" sign alerts bike riders to the proper storage area and may prevent yard accidents and be useful for a child looking for an available bike. A labeling activity initiated by a teacher to introduce the need for road signs and environmental signs can lead to an activity in which children decide the appropriate wording. Common classroom labeling includes the following: artwork, name tags, lockers and storage areas (Figure 14-10), belongings, common room objects, schoolroom areas, and place cards at eating times. Some educators believe labeling without a purpose is objectionable.

14-6b Display Areas

Display areas often include the following:

- magazine pictures with captions
- current interest displays, for example, "Rocks we found on our walk"
- bulletin boards and wall displays with words
- wall alphabet guides (Aa Bb . . .)
- charts
- child's work with explanations, such as "Josh's block tower" or "Penny's clay pancakes"
- folding table accordion display (Figure 14-11)
- signs for child activities, such as "store," "hospital," "wet paint," and "Tickets for Sale Here"

Figure 14-11 Folding table accordion.

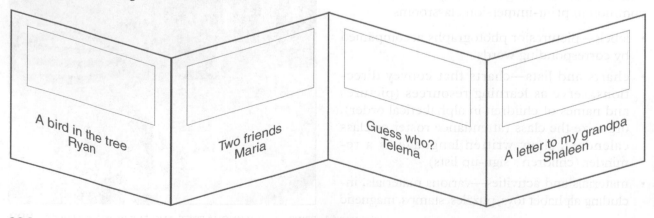

A bird in the tree
Ryan

Two friends
Maria

Guess who?
Telema

A letter to my grandpa
Shaleen

14-6c Message-Sending Aids

Classroom mailboxes, suggestion boxes, and message boards are motivational and useful. Writing short notes to children piques an interest about what is said. Large-sized stick-on notes are great for this purpose and can be attached to mirrors, plates, toys, and so on.

14-6d Writing Centers

Writing centers are planned, teacher-stocked areas where printing is promoted. A writing center can be a separate area of a room, or it can exist within a language arts center. Child comfort and proper lighting are essential, along with minimized distractions. Often, dividers or screens are used to reduce outside noise and activity. Supplies and storage areas are provided at children's fingertips so that children can help themselves. Teacher displays or bulletin board areas that motivate printing and have a listing of children's names can be close by. If water-based marking pens are provided, pens with distinct bright colors are preferred.

Through dialogue and exploration at a writing table or center, children are able to construct new ideas concerning print and meaning in a supportive mini-social setting. There should be a variety of paper and writing tools. Printing stamps and printing ink blocks, a hole punch, and brads are desirable. Old forms, catalogs, calendars, and computer paper may be inviting. Scratch paper (one side already used) or lined paper and crayons placed side-by-side invite use. Most local businesses or offices throw away enough scratch paper to supply a preschool center.

Colored or white chalk has an appeal of its own and can be used on paper, chalkboards, or cement. For variety, use brightly colored oil pastels or soft-lead pencils on paper. Most schools install a child-high chalkboard; table chalkboards are made quickly by using chalkboard paint obtained at hardware or paint stores and scrap wood pieces. Easels, unused wall areas, and backs of furniture can be made into chalkboards.

Computers capture interest. Shape books with blank pages and words to copy and trace appeal to some children, as do large rub-on letters or alphabet letter stickers (these can be made by teachers from press-on labels). Magnetic boards and magnetized letter sets are commonly mentioned as the favorite toy of children interested in alphabet letters and forming words.

Letters, words, and displays are placed for viewing on bulletin boards at children's eye level. Displays in writing centers often motivate and promote print. McNair (2007) suggests that young children are particularly fascinated by their own names. A name list or name cards can be used throughout the classroom.

14-6e First School Alphabets

In kindergarten or first grade, printing is done in printscript, sometimes called manuscript printing (Figure 14-12), or in a form called D'Nealian print (Figure 14-13). Centers should obtain guides from a local elementary school, because letter forms can vary from community to community.

Figure 14-12 Printscript alphabet.

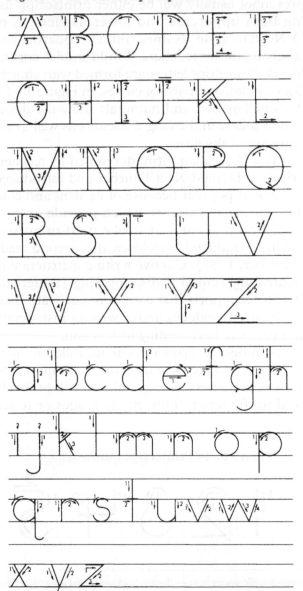

Figure 14-13 Samples of D'Nealian print and numerals.

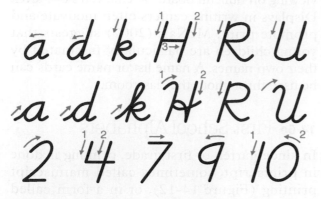

Teachers need to be familiar with printscript (or any other form used locally). It is easier for a child to learn the right way than to be retrained later. All printing seen by young children in a preschool usually will be either printscript, using both uppercase and lowercase letters, or D'Nealian style. Names, bulletin boards, and labels made by teachers should model correct forms. Printscript letters are formed with straight lines, circles, and parts of circles. In Figure 14-12, the small arrows and numerals show the direction to follow in forming the letters as well as the sequence of the lines.

The D'Nealian form, developed by teacher-principal Donald Neal Thurber and introduced in 1978, is popular because of its slant and continuous stroke features, which provide an easy transition to slant and stroke used in cursive writing introduced to children after second grade (Thurber, 1988). Cursive writing instruction in elementary school is disappearing (Bauerlein, 2013). He reports that common core state standards often neglect cursive writing instruction and promote keyboarding instruction.

Numbers in printed form are called numerals. Children may have used toys with numerals, such as block sets. Young children will probably hold up fingers to indicate their ages or to tell you they can count. They may start making number symbols before showing an interest in alphabet letters. Numeral forms (Figure 14-14) are also available from elementary schools. The numeral forms in one geographical area may also be slightly different from those of another town, city, or state.

14-6f Beginning Attempts

All children's attempts are recognized and appreciated by early childhood teachers as signs of the children's growing interest and ability. Figure 14-15 arranges alphabet letters in manuscript print from the easiest for children to manage and form to the most difficult. **Orthographic awareness** is the ability to notice and use critical features of the graphic symbols in written language. Children learn what makes a letter unique and that these features are often very finely drawn. The visual difference between the alphabet letters *n* and *m*, or *n* and *h*, are subtle, but many preschoolers have no difficulty. Educators realize that each child's knowledge is a very personal matter, with children finding their own ways of weaving understanding around a letter to help them remember it and reproduce it.

14-7 Planned Activities— Basic Understandings

Most planned activities in this language arts area, and most unplanned child–adult exchanges during the school day, involve basic understandings. Rules exist in this graphic art as they do in speech. Children form ideas about these rules. Print concerns the use of graphic symbols that represent sounds and sound combinations. Symbols combine and form words and sentences in a prescribed grammatical order. Alphabet letters are spaced and are in uppercase and lowercase form. They are written and read from left to

Figure 14-14 Printscript numerals.

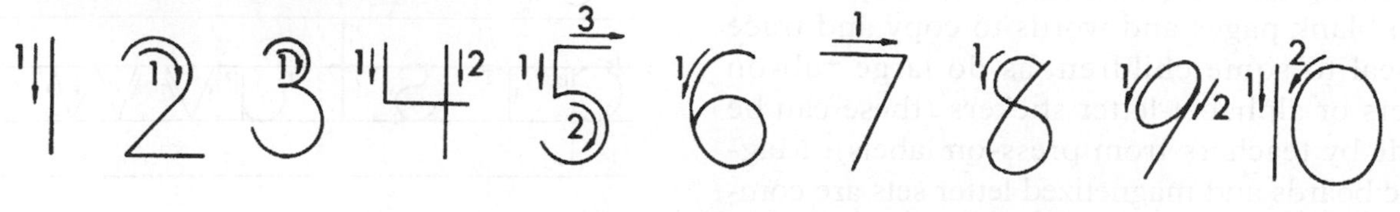

orthographic awareness — the ability to notice and use critical features of graphic symbols in written language.

1. I	14. V	27. Z	40. Y
2. o	15. c	28. t	41. d
3. L	16. x	29. B	42. R
4. O	17. T	30. Q	43. G
5. H	18. h	31. s	44. a
6. D	19. w	32. n	45. u
7. i	20. J	33. z	46. k
8. v	21. f	34. r	47. m
9. l	22. C	35. e	48. j
10. X	23. N	36. b	49. y
11. E	24. A	37. S	50. p
12. P	25. W	38. M	51. g
13. F	26. K	39. U	52. q

right across a page. Margins exist at beginnings and ends of lines and lines go from the top to bottom of pages. Punctuation marks end sentences, and indentations separate paragraphs. It is amazing how many rules of printing interested children discover on their own and with teacher help before they enter kindergarten.

Putting the children's names on their work is the most common daily use of printscript. The teacher asks the children whether they want their names on their work. Many young children feel their creations are their very own and may not want a name added. When a paper is lost because it has no name on it, children see the advantage of printing a name on belongings. All names are printed in the upper left corner of the paper, if possible, or on the back if the child requests. This is done to train the children to look at this spot as a preparation for reading and writing. Children's comments about their work can be jotted down at the bottom or on the back of their papers.

The teacher can be prepared to do this by having a dark crayon or felt-tip pen in a handy place or pocket. Dictation is written without major teacher editing or suggestions concerning the way it is said. The teacher can tell the child that the teacher will be writing down (printing) the child's ideas and then follow the child's word order as closely as possible. Some teachers prefer to print the statement, "Chou dictated these words to Mrs. Brownell on May 2, 2011," before or after the child's message. Most teachers would print the child's "mouses went in hole" as "mice went in the hole," which is minor editing. All child-dictated printing should be in printscript, using both uppercase and lowercase letters and proper punctuation.

When a child asks a teacher to print, the teacher stands behind the child and works over the child's shoulder (when possible). This allows the child to see the letters being formed in the correct position. If the teacher faces the child while printing, the child sees the letters upside down. Some teachers say the letter names as they print them. Letters or names written for the child should be large enough for the child to distinguish the different forms—more than one inch high. This may seem large to an adult (Figure 14-16).

Some schools encourage teachers to print examples on lined paper if a child says, "Make an *a*" or "Write my name." Others suggest that teachers blend letter sounds as they print words. Many centers expect teachers to respond to the child's request through conversation and by searching for letters on alphabet charts. This encourages the child to make her own copy before the teacher automatically prints it.

Teacher techniques often depend on the circumstances of a particular situation and knowledge of the individual child. One technique common to all centers is supportive assistance and voiced appreciation of children's efforts. Teachers can rejoice with a young child over approximations of intent in writing, just as we do with a toddler who makes an imprecise attempt to say a new word.

Children may show their printing attempts to the teacher or point out the names of letters they know. A positive statement to the child is appropriate: "Yes, that is an *a*" or "I can see an *a*, *t*, and *p*" (the teacher points to each) or

Figure 14-16 Letters should be large enough for the child to see easily.

Maryellen
Donald

"Marie, you did print the letters *a* and *t*." With these comments, the teacher encourages and recognizes the child's efforts. Often, the child may have the wrong name or form for a letter. The teacher can react by saying, "It looks like an alphabet letter. Let's go look at our wall alphabet and see which one" or may simply say, "Look. You made a *w*."

Encourage, welcome, and keep interest in print alive by providing attention. Children have many years ahead to perfect their skill; the most important thing at this early stage is that they are interested in the forms and are supplied with correct models and encouragement.

One technique is to have children who ask for letter forms trace over correct letter models or symbols. This can be done with crayons, felt-tip pens, or other writing tools. To explain the meaning of the word *trace*, the teacher gives the child a demonstration.

14-7a Environmental Print in Daily Life

A teacher of young children makes connections between print and daily classroom happenings. This is not difficult, but it does require teacher recognition and purposeful action. Print can be noticed starting with children's names and print on clothing, shoes, food, toys, and almost every object in the classroom, including light switches and faucet handles. Print is part of classroom life.

Children need to learn what print can do for them in satisfying personal needs. This makes print real. Children become aware of print by using it for real and meaningful purposes when they dictate and write stories, make signs for the block area, read names on a job chart, write messages, look for EXIT signs, follow recipes, have conversations and discussions, or listen to stories. Children may need teacher assistance in recognizing the usefulness of written messages. Many instances of sending or reading print messages are possible during a school day. For example, because print often protects one's safety, there are many opportunities to discuss and point out words that serve this function. Children's dramatic play offers many chances for teachers to support and suggest play actions and items that involve print use. See Figure 14-17.

Teachers look for functional use of print activities, such as:

- making necessary lists of children's names with children. Example: Teacher creates a waiting list.

- making holiday or special occasion cards.

- making group murals and labeling parts at a later date. Example: Teacher uses color words or children's ideas (Jane says, "This looks like a cat.").

- writing what-we-found-out activities. This can be done with many discovery experiences. Example: What floats, and what does not?

- classifying experiences. Example: "Shoes Are Different"—Teacher elicits from the group the kinds of shoes children see others wearing. It might be brown shoes, sandals, shoes with laces, and so on. Once these are listed across the top of the chart paper, children can choose under which headings their names should go.

- sharing the lunch or snack menu by discussing printed words on a chart or chalkboard.

- making classroom news announcements on a large sheet of paper posted at children's eye level. Examples follow: Enrico moved to a new apartment. Mrs. Quan is on a trip to Chicago.

Creating a large classroom journal will allow the teacher a daily or weekly opportunity to model writing a class-dictated sentence. The teacher can also talk aloud about her writing while using a large sheet of paper. The first step would be a joint discussion concerning what is to be written. The teacher can then "think aloud" as she writes, leveling her comments to the children's ability.

When working on the journal, the teacher may simply say, "We planted carrot seeds," and emphasize the number of words in the sentence by making three spaced lines. Or the teacher may say, "We will start by looking at the left side of the paper because the first word on a page is printed on the top left side of the page. We will put the first word of our sentence here." This can be repeated on other "journal days" before the teacher decides to think aloud about the names of the first letter in each word. No matter the journaling activity, the children will be watching their teacher form letters, use capital letters, form words, leave spaces between words, and end messages with a period. Depending on the class and its ability, the teacher may not think aloud about the sounds of the letters, but as journaling progresses she may choose to do so depending on the philosophy of the program.

Figure 14-17 Dramatic play themes and activities that promote print awareness and use.

Play Themes

Classroom Post Office
Suggested play items:
stamps (many come with magazine advertisements), old letters, envelopes, boxes to wrap for mailing, scale, canceling stamp, tape, string, play money, mailbag, mailbox with slots, alphabet strips, writing table, felt-tip pens, counter, postal-employee shirts, posters from post office, stamp-collector sheets, wet sponge, teacher-made chart that lists children by street address and zip codes, box with all children's names on printed individual strips, mailboxes for each child

Taco Stand
Suggested play items:
counter for customers, posted charts with prices and taco choices, play money, order pads, labeled baskets with colored paper taco items (including cheese, meat, lettuce, salsa, sour cream, avocado, shredded chicken, and onions), customer tables, trays, bell to ring for service, folded cards with numbers, receipt book for ordered tacos, plastic glasses and pitchers, cash register, napkins, tablecloth, plastic flowers in plastic vase, cook's jacket, waiter/waitress aprons, busperson suit and cleaning supplies, taped ethnic music, plastic utensils, soft pencils or felt-tip pens, line with clothespins to hang orders, paper plates
A hamburger stand or pizza parlor are other possibilities.

Grocery Shopping
Suggested items:
shopping-list paper, bookcase, pencils or felt-tip pens, chart with cut magazine pictures or labels from canned goods or vegetables labeled in print by teacher for children to copy if they desire, empty food cartons and cans, plastic food, shopping cart, purse and wallet, play money, brown bags, cash register on box, dress-up clothes for customers and store clerks

---

Print-Awareness Activities

Letter-Writing Classroom Center
(for writing to relatives and friends)

Classroom Newspaper
Make a class newspaper. Print children's dictated news or creative language after sharing a local paper with them. Child drawings on ditto master can be duplicated. Add teacher and parent news, poems, captions, drawings, and so forth. Some children may wish to print their own messages. These may range from scribble to recognizable forms and words.

T-Shirt Autograph Day
Each parent is asked to bring an old T-shirt (any size) to school for T-shirt autograph day. Permanent felt markers are used by children under teacher supervision. (Washable markers can also be used, but teachers must iron or put T-shirts in a clothes dryer for 5 minutes on a hot setting.) T-shirt forms are necessary and can be made of cardboard. Material must be stretched over a form so marks can be added easily. It is a good idea to have children wear plastic paint aprons to protect clothing from permanent markers. Children are free to autograph shirts in any manner they please. A display of T-shirts with writing usually prompts some children to add letters to their own shirts. Most teachers own or can borrow T-shirts with writing.

(Teachers using journaling must know how each alphabet letter is to be formed. Go back to Figure 14-12 and notice the small numbered arrows.)

Daily journal sheets can be bound with large metal rings to make a class big book. Child art is often attached to the blank area under the sentence on each page. Large sheets are used so large teacher print is easily observed by a group of children. See the Activities section at the end of this chapter for more ideas related to classroom journaling.

14-7b Writing Table or Area

Many classrooms include a writing table or area for children's daily free-choice exploration. Stocked with different paper types, a variety of writing instruments, alphabet letter stencils, letter stamps, and letter model displays, this type of setup makes daily access available and inviting. However, just providing a writing center is not enough. Teachers need to be in it daily, as motivators and resources. Some writing areas have considerable use. In other classrooms, teachers spend little or no time there (Smith, 2001). Whether a writing center appeals to children, grabs children's attention, and is child-functional depends on the ingenuity of teachers.

Recognizing that children need time as well as opportunity, teachers notice that individual children involve themselves in classroom literacy events based on their maturity and interest. When a child senses a reason and develops a personal interest in writing or reading, she acts on her own timetable. There seems to exist in the child at this point a desire to do something her own way; the child wants to retain ownership of early literacy behaviors. The child who examines a classroom alphabet chart and then copies letter forms may choose to share her marks with other children and avoid the teacher. Another child the same age may prefer to consult the teacher. Other children may ask, "What's this say?" or "What's this called?" In all situations, teachers aim to preserve and promote each child's idea of competency as a writer or reader.

14-7c Left-Handed Children

Left-handedness or right-handedness occurs as the child's nervous system matures. Preschool teachers notice hand preferences when children use writing tools. Some children seem to switch between hands as though hand preference has not been established. Most left-handers use their right hands more often than right-handers use their left hands. Writing surfaces in preschools should accommodate all children, and both right-handed and left-handed scissors should be available. Teachers should accept hand preference without attempting to change or even point out a natural choice. Seating left-handed children at the ends of tables (when possible) during activities or making sure left-handers are not crowded against right-handers is a prudent course of action.

14-7d Lined Paper

Some children acquire the necessary motor control and can use lined, printed paper (Figure 14-18), so some programs provide it. Lines can easily be drawn on a chalkboard by the teacher. This provides a large working surface and an opportunity for children to make large-size letters.

Figure 14-18 Example of a five-year-old kindergartener's printing accompanying art.

14-7e Chart Ideas

Printscript can be added to playrooms by posting charts that have been made by the teacher. Charts can be designed to encourage the child's active involvement and contain words in a child's home language. Pockets, parts that move, or pieces that can be added or removed add extra interest. Charts made on heavy chart board or cardboard last longer. Clear contact paper can be used to seal the surface. Chart ideas include:

- experience charts (Figure 14-19).
- color or number charts.
- large clock with movable hands.
- chart showing the four seasons.
- picture story sequence charts.
- calendars.
- room task charts ("helpers chart").
- texture charts (for children to feel).
- poetry charts (Figure 14-20).
- recipe charts using step-by-step illustrations.
- classification or matching-concepts charts.
- birthday charts.
- height and weight charts.
- alphabet charts.
- rebus charts (Figure 14-21).

Many teachers make "key word" charts. Key words can be words inspired by a picture-book title, character, and so forth; words solicited from children; or words taken from some classroom event or happening. The chosen word is printed by the teacher at the top of a chart. The teacher then asks a small group, "When I say this word, what

Figure 14-19 Experience chart.

The Picnic

We had lunch in the park. We sat on the grass.

Figure 14-20 Poetry chart.

Mix a pancake
  Stir a pancake
Pop it in a pan,
  Fry the pancake,
Toss the pancake,
  Catch it

If you   can!

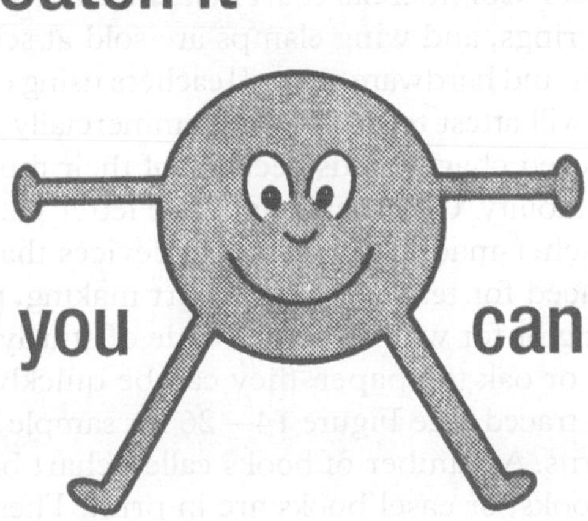

Figure 14-21 Rebus chart.

do you think of?" or "Salt and pepper go together. We see them in shakers sitting on the kitchen table. What goes with [key word]?" or "Tree is the word at the top of our chart. What can we say about the trees in our play yard?" or some such leading question. Children's offered answers are put below the key word on the chart. This activity suits some older four-year-olds, especially those asking, "What does this say?" while pointing to text.

Charts of songs or rhymes in the native languages of attending children have been used successfully in many classrooms. Parent volunteer translators are often pleased to help put new or favorite classics into their native tongue. "*Uno, Dos, Tres Inditos,*" a Spanish version of "Ten Little Indians," has been frequently enjoyed and learned quickly. A technique adopted in many schools involves using a color-code system when recording individual child contributions to a group-dictated chart. This enables a child to return to the chart and find her comments.

Think of all of the charts that can include a child's choice, vote, or decision! These charts are limitless. A child can indicate her individual selection under the diverse headings by making a mark, printing her name, using a rubber stamp and ink pad, or moving her printed name to a

Figure 14-22 Examples of charts.

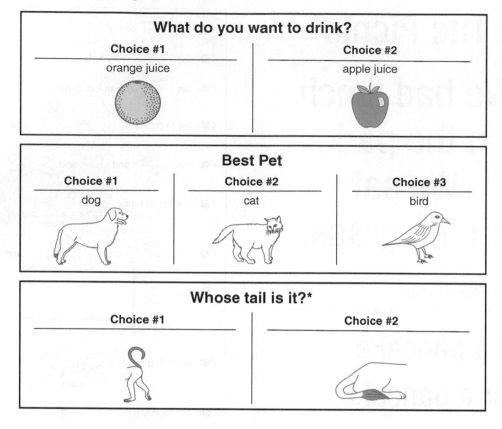

basket or pasting it onto the chart as shown in Figure 14-22. Child choices lead to discussions.

It is easy to see that placing pictures alongside print makes the task of choosing easier. Simple pictures are drawn by the teacher. This works well. The best charts relate to classroom themes or happenings. When making a chart, first draw sketches of the way words and pictures could be arranged. With a yardstick, lightly draw on guidelines with a pencil or use a chart liner (see Activities section). Then, add printscript words with a felt-tip pen or dark crayon. Magazines, old elementary school workbooks, old children's books, and photographs are good sources for pictures on charts. Brads or paper fasteners can be used for movable parts. Book pockets or heavy envelopes provide a storage place for items to be added later to the chart. The purpose of experience charts is to have children recognize that spoken words can be put in written form. Most centers keep large chart-making paper and felt-tip markers or thick black crayons in stock for chart making.

After an interesting activity, such as a field trip, visit by a special speaker, party, celebration, or cooking experience, the teacher can suggest that a story be written about the experience. A large sheet of paper or chart sheet is hung within the children's view, and the children dictate what happened. The teacher prints on the sheet, helping children sort out what happened first, next, and last. Figures 14-23 and 14-24 show examples of other word and picture charts.

Homemade chart stands can be made by teachers. Commercial chart holders, chart stands, chart rings, and wing clamps are sold at school-supply and hardware stores. Teachers using charts daily will attest to preferring commercially manufactured chart stands because of their mobility and stability. Commercially made letter patterns or teacher-made sets are useful devices that can be traced for teacher use in chart making, game making or for wall displays. Made of sturdy card stock or oak tag paper, they can be quickly and easily traced. See Figure 14 – 26 for sample letter patterns. A number of books called chart books, big books, or easel books are in print. These giant books are poster size and easily capture children's attention. The print stands out and cannot be missed. Creative teachers have produced their own versions with the help of overhead projectors that enlarge smaller artwork. Chart paper or poster board is used.

Figure 14-23 Rebus listening chart.

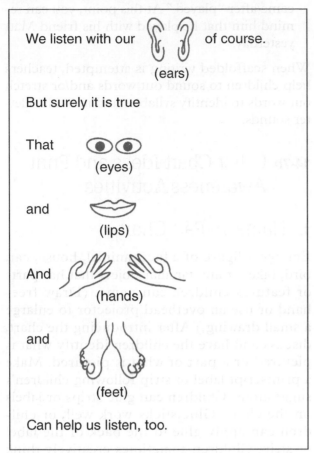

We listen with our 👂👂 of course.
(ears)

But surely it is true

That 👀 (eyes)

and 👄 (lips)

And 🖐🖐 (hands)

and 🦶🦶 (feet)

Can help us listen, too.

Figure 14-24 A chart using line drawings.

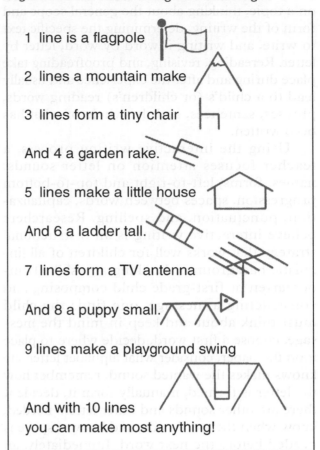

1 line is a flagpole

2 lines a mountain make

3 lines form a tiny chair

And 4 a garden rake.

5 lines make a little house

And 6 a ladder tall.

7 lines form a TV antenna

And 8 a puppy small.

9 lines make a playground swing

And with 10 lines
you can make most anything!

14-7f Generating Story Sentences

Story sentence activities are similar to chart activities. A child, or a small group of children, an author. After a classroom activity or experience, the teacher encourages generating a story (a written sentence). The activity is child-centered thereafter, with the teacher printing what the child or group suggests. The teacher can use a hand-wide space between words to emphasize the end of one word and spacing between words, and may talk about letters or letter sounds found at the beginning or end of children's names. It is not unusual for all children in a group of four-year-olds to recognize all of the names of other students in their class. Ideas and contributions from individual children are accepted, appreciated, and recognized by the teacher, and generated sentences are read and reread with the group. Long strips of chart paper or rolled paper can be used. Story sentences are posted at children's eye level.

14-7g Interactive and Scaffolded Writing

Interactive, or shared, **writing** times take place in many kindergartens and first-grade classrooms. They are described here to acquaint preschool practitioners with what lies ahead and what might be adapted, modified, or individualized for the few individual children who read (not memorize) simple text in picture books and write messages during their preschool years. Whether this strategy is adopted at a school where you are employed is the school's decision.

This kindergarten strategy is receiving an increased amount of use and attention from educators. Educators define interactive writing as an instructional context in which a teacher shares a pen—literally and figuratively—with a group of children as they collaboratively compose and construct a written message. Children participate

---

interactive writing — (1) an instructional strategy popular in American kindergartens; (2) a process involving a teacher who verbally stretches each word so that the child (children) can distinguish sounds and letters. This is also known as shared writing.

in every element of the writing process—deciding on a topic, thinking about the general scope and form of the writing, determining the specific text to write, and writing it word by word, letter by letter. Rereading, revising, and proofreading take place during and after the experience and usually lead to a child's (or children's) reading words, phrases, sentences, and the whole of what has been written.

Using the interactive writing process, a teacher focuses attention on letter sounds, names, forms, left-to-right and top-to-bottom progression, spaces between words, capitalization, punctuation, and spelling. Researchers believe interactive writing is an instructional strategy that works well for children of all linguistic backgrounds. Looking at a skilled kindergarten or first-grade child composing and constructing a message, one finds the child must think about and keep in mind the message, choose a first word, decide where to place it on the paper, consider what alphabet letter she knows makes the wanted sound, remember how the letter is formed, manually form it, decide if there are other sounds and other letters needed, know when the word ends, and know a space is needed before the next word. Immediately, an early childhood educator can see foundational understandings concerning writing must have been well learned.

Teachers who work individually with a child might define scaffolded writing as a process that involves supportive teacher assistance. Assistance by the teacher enables a child to do what she can't do by herself, but may be able to do if parts of the writing task are gradually handed over to the child. Bennett-Armistead, Duke, & Moses (2005) suggest that scaffolded writing consists of the following steps:

- Ask the child the message he would like to write. He may say something like "I played with my friend Matt yesterday."
- Repeat this message to the child.
- Draw one line for each word using a highlighter or ball point pen. Have the child write one "word" per line at the level that is most comfortable for the child.
- Read and reread the message together as necessary, as he writes, to help him remember the whole message. For instance, he may get

as far as "I played" and not remember what came after "played." At this point, you can remind him that he played with his friend Matt yesterday.

When scaffolded writing is attempted, teachers help children to sound out words and/or stretch out words to identify syllables and individual letter sounds.

14-7h Other Chart Ideas and Print Awareness Activities

1. Name-A-Part Chart

Enlarge a figure of a face, animal, house, car, bird, bike, or any familiar object that has parts or features children can name. (Draw freehand or use an overhead projector to enlarge a small drawing.) After introducing the chart, discuss and have the children identify what is pictured or a part of what is pictured. Make a printscript label or strip following children's suggestions. Children can glue strips or labels on the chart. Glue sticks work well, or children can apply glue to the back of the label or strip. Children sometimes creatively think up silly names, and that is part of the fun. At other times, they may discuss seriously what they believe are the correct labeling words. In a variation of this activity, the teacher draws an outline and parts are drawn as they are named by children.

2. Chart Liner Instructions

See Figure 14-25. Use Figure 14-26 for letter shapes if necessary.

3. A Word-a-Day Activity

Printing and defining just one word a day is a useful strategy for building vocabulary and promoting word recognition. Best if the word is drawn from the children at a group time, but teachers can add a word that might be encountered in the theme of study or for another purpose. A special display spot for word-of-the-day is recommended, and children can be asked when they might speak the word or how they might tell a short story using the word. Lots of activity possibilities exist.

Figure 14-25 Making a chart liner.

INSTRUCTIONS TO MAKE A CHART LINER

Cut a piece of Masonite® 12" by 36". Make 7 sawcuts 1½" apart, beginning and ending 1½" from either end. Then glue or nail 1½" square pieces of wood 12" long to each end.

Note: A teacher-made chart liner is a useful device that helps teachers make evenly spaced guidelines on charts that use lines of print. By placing the chart liner over chart paper, quick guidelines are accomplished by inserting a sharp pencil in sawcut slots.

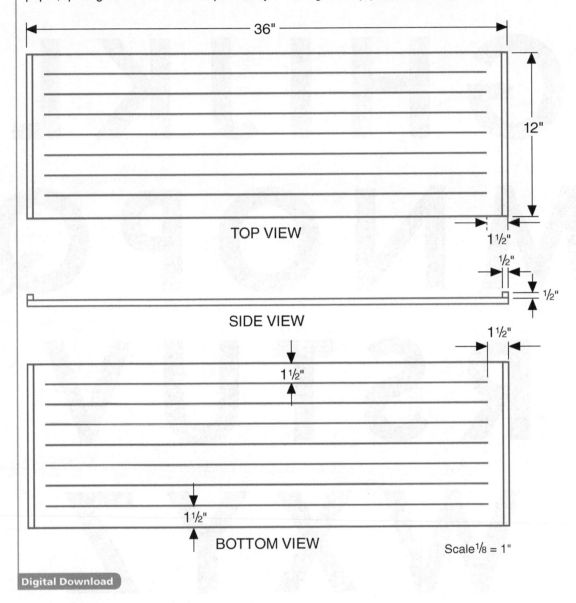

TOP VIEW

SIDE VIEW

BOTTOM VIEW

Scale ⅛ = 1"

4. Clay-On Patterns

These patterns can be used to enhance small, manipulative-muscle use and tracing skills. Materials needed include clay and 9 x 12-inch contact-covered cardboard sheets with patterns (Figure 14-27). The activity involves children making clay cylinders to form the patterns. The teacher demonstrates how to roll clay in cylinders and place them on patterns where clay can dry and later be painted.

Figure 14-26 Letter patterns.

A B C D E F
G H I J K L
M N O P Q
R S T U V
W X Y Z

Note: Letters will need to be enlarged for display in the classroom.

Figure 14-26 *(countinued)*

abcdef

ghijkl

mnopq

rstuv

wxyz

Figure 14-27 Patterns.

5. Sticker Pictures

The children are shown the relationship between objects and words.

Materials:
stickers
paper strips
felt markers

Activity: The teacher has each child choose a sticker for her paper strip. The child names the sticker, and if the child desires, the teacher writes the name of the sticker on back of the strip. The children can then decorate the sticker strips.

6. Alphabet Eaters

Large-muscle use and visual discrimination are enhanced.

Materials:
cards with printscript
alphabet letters (small enough to be slipped into animal's mouth)
sturdy boxes on which animal heads and alphabet strips are glued (holes are cut in the opposite sides of boxes so that children can reach in for cards)

Activity: A child selects a card and "feeds" it to the animal that has a similar alphabet letter on the strip under its mouth (Figure 14-28).

7. Tracers

Tracers can be used over and over again. Waxy crayons or felt markers wipe off with a soft cloth. They can be used to help children recognize and discriminate among symbols and enhance small-muscle coordination.

Materials:
acetate or clear vinyl sheets
cardboard
scissors
strapping or masking tape
paper
felt-tip pen or marker

Construction Procedure: Attach acetate to cardboard, leaving one side open to form a pocket. Make letter or word guide sheets. Simple pictures can also be used (Figure 14-29).

Activity: A child or the teacher selects a sheet and slips it into the tracer pocket. A wax crayon or marker is used by the child to trace the guide sheet. A soft cloth erases the crayon or marker.

8. Rebus Stories

Teachers can use drawings or photographs to encourage child participation during storytelling time. At a crucial point in the story, the teacher pauses and holds up a picture, and the children guess the next word in the story. Teachers can name the picture and resume the story if the children have not guessed the

Figure 14-28 Alphabet "eaters" and cards.

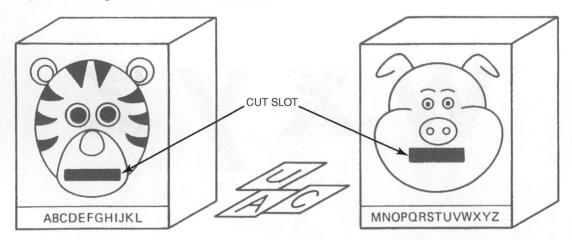

Figure 14-29 Tracers.

Open to slip in guide sheets

- Back cardboard
- Front acetate
- Masking tape

Guides for tracing

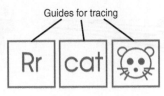

word. Any guess that is a close approximation is accepted; for example, "It is a truck, Josh, a fire truck." The rebus story in Figure 14-30 is an example of teacher authorship. Many additional teacher-created rebus stories are possible.

Figure 14-30 This rebus story, created by a teacher, uses computer-generated graphics

DUCK AND BEAR TAKE A TRIP

This is and this is his friend .

 cried one day and said, "Let's take a vacation!" had not

learned to fly. "I get tired walking," said . "Let's ask

wise old how we can take a trip when a won't walk

and a can't fly." Wise old said, "That's not a problem.

Both of you can ride your  to the airport. Buy a ticket

Figure 14-30 *(countinued)*

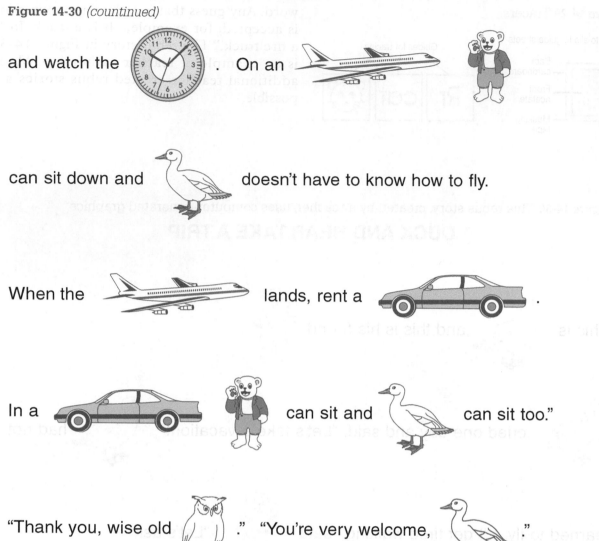

and watch the [clock]. On an [airplane] [bear]

can sit down and [duck] doesn't have to know how to fly.

When the [airplane] lands, rent a [car].

In a [car] [bear] can sit and [duck] can sit too."

"Thank you, wise old [owl]." "You're very welcome, [duck]."

"Now take along a [pencil] so you can write me a postcard," said [owl].

Summary

14-1 Discuss young children's print awareness and child behaviors that reflect it.

Print awareness instruction is offered in programs that believe foundational knowledge about print can be acquired through early experiences during preschool years before formal reading and writing instruction begin. Early writing attempts are supported. Young children often talk about what they have done, created, constructed, or drawn by attaching meaning to their work. This behavior paves the way toward children's beginning understandings about written form and symbol use. Young children begin to grasp that print holds information and that it symbolizes spoken language. Children develop primitive hypotheses about print and explore making marks playfully.

14-2 Outline the probable sequence of events occurring before a child prints a first recognizable alphabet letter.

Research suggests the following sequence of events before a child makes a recognizable alphabet letter. The child:

- asks questions about artwork and/or marks being made.
- experiments with straight and curved lines.
- realizes forms are arbitrary and written in a linear fashion.
- concentrates on environmental shapes (forms) in drawings or art.
- searches for differences in a string or group of letters/marks.
- believes a string of letters or marks represents their own name.
- may display an understanding of syllables.
- may print syllables to represent a word or part of a word.
- may look for similar letters to write pieces of sounds.
- uses alphabet letters to represent sounds.

At some point in this continuum, especially when the child concentrates on the symbol shapes in the classroom, a recognizable alphabet letter may appear. A good number of preschoolers have learned to copy alphabet letters in their homes before they attend preschool through the efforts and direct instruction of a family member.

14-3 Name two goals of print instruction in preschool.

Preschool goals for print instruction include providing instruction that matches children's interests and ability. Being responsive to children's curiosity concerning print and providing a print-rich environment are important goals. Emphasizing the functional use of print in activities that are meaningful and have a purpose in the classroom is another prime goal. A school's curriculum and goal statements include promoting emerging skills, letter knowledge, and word recognition. Often curriculum goals are based upon reaching recognized professional standards for different preschool age levels. Goals can encompass acting on recognized child needs that relate to a child's success when eventually learning to read.

14-4 Discuss drawing experiences' relationship to prewriting instruction.

Teachers notice children's art (drawing) moves from scribbles to controlled lines, curves, and circles. Children begin to make their own symbols representing their world. Drawings seem to be based on a child's plan and often repeated patterns become apparent. Drawings expose children's thinking and recognizable symbol-like figures appear. Educators believe that drawing activities are prewriting experiences, a starting place. Engaging children in conversations about their work and providing supportive teacher comments can lead children to a greater understanding concerning their art as a form of communication. This may also prompt the children's realization that print is a form of communication, especially when teachers print words reflecting children's comments about their work.

14-5 Describe five ways that a classroom can promote alphabet awareness.

Many ways to promote alphabet awareness are possible. Alphabet book reading and follow-up activities are an example. Activities can also be designed around a child's interest in a particular letter, such as the first letter of his/her name, a daily happening with environmental print, especially on signs and labels, singing the alphabet song, playing with alphabet magnets, alphabet puzzles, or alphabet games, planning times and opportunities for child dictation, by creating room centers with writing areas and writing tools and materials, posting alphabet letter guides or charts in a classroom, through child experiences with sensory alphabet-shaped objects, an alphabet letter of the day activity, and through creating classrooms full of displayed words.

14-6 Print both the lowercase and uppercase printscript alphabet without using a guide.

To ascertain whether you were able to reach this goal it is necessary to obtain an alphabet letter guide for printscript lettering particular to your geographic (local) location or to use the one provided in this chapter. You will need to have letter forms memorized when you aid a child who wishes to use an alphabet letter in some way.

Testing yourself or asking a peer to check your printing when you immediately produce both uppercase and lowercase printscript without a guide is advised.

14-7 Name four kinds of instructional charts.

Classroom charts vary based upon need and instructional goals and plans. Charts mentioned in the text include: lunch charts, classifying charts, classroom announcement charts, alphabet charts, active involvement charts, experience charts, color charts, number charts, seasonal charts, story sequence charts, experience charts, calendars, helper charts, recipe charts, texture charts, concept charts, poetry charts, birthday charts, height and weight charts, rebus charts, keyword charts, multicultural charts, song charts, dictated charts, picture charts, and book charts.

Additional Resources

Readings

Barone, D., & Taylor, J. (2006). *Improving Students' Writing K-8*. Thousand Oaks, CA: Corwin Press.

Stacey, S. (2011). *The Unscripted Classroom: Emergent Curriculum in Action*. St. Paul, MN: Redleaf Press.

Temple, C., Nathan, R., & Temple, C. (2012). *The Beginnings of Writing*. Upper Saddle River, NJ: Pearson.

Children's Books with Writing Themes

Ahlberg, J., & Ahlberg, A. (1986). *The Jolly Postman*. Waltham, MA: Little, Brown & Co. (Letter writing.)

Barton, B. (2001). *My Car*. New York: Greenwillow. (Discusses road signs and other functional print.)

de Groat, D. (1996). *Roses Are Pink, Your Feet Really Stink*. New York: HarperCollins. (Writing or dictating Valentine rhymes.)

Alphabet Books

Catalanotto, P. (2002). *Matthew A. B. C.* New York: Atheneum. (A child's adventures.)

Marzollo, J. (2000). *I Spy Little Letters*. New York: Scholastic. (Finding letter shapes.)

Paul, A. (1999). *Everything to Spend the Night from A to Z*. New York: DK Publishing. (The overnight bag brought for an overnight stay with Grandpa yields A to Z objects.

Satin, A. S. (2004). *Mrs. McTats and Her House Full of Cats*. New York: Simon & Schuster. (Alphabet cats.)

Helpful Websites

National Association for the Education of Young Children

http://www.naeyc.org

Read NAEYC Position Statements link.

International Reading Association

www.reading.org

Search for position statements on early writing.

Objectives

After reading this chapter, you should be able to:

15-1 Discuss current standards for reading instruction.

15-2 Describe factors promoting a few preschoolers to actually read before kindergarten.

15-3 Describe children's usual sequence of reading-like behaviors.

15-4 Name four recognized reading instruction methods used in elementary schools.

15-5 Describe ways centers involve parents in their child's prereading instruction.

naeyc NAEYC Program Standards

2E06 Children are regularly provided multiple and varied opportunities to develop phonological awareness.

2E06 Children are helped to identify letters and the sounds they represent.

2E06 Children's self-initiated efforts to write letters that represent sounds are supported.

DAP Developmentally Appropriate Practice (DAP) Preschoolers

3H8 Teachers promote children's engagement and comprehension using strategies such as reading with expression and asking questions.

3H13 Teachers assess and take into account where each child is in phonological awareness and tailor instruction accordingly.

3H14 Teachers focus on capturing children's ideas, recording their dictated words in charts, stories, or messages to parents or others then reading the dictation back (using their finger to indicate the words so that children can follow along).

COMMON CORE Common Core State Standards, K-3

R.CCR.4 Interpret words and phrases as they are used in a text, determining technical, connotative, and figurative meanings, and analyze how specific word choices shape meaning or tone.

R.CCR.1 Read closely to determine what the text says explicitly and to make logical inferences from it, cite specific textual evidence when writing or speaking to support conclusions drawn from the text.

Mackenzie's Ability

During group time, Mackenzie's teacher makes a discussion chart that reflects what the children in her class of three-year-olds "love to eat" at breakfast. Later, she notices the following poorly formed letters in Mackenzie's painting: BBRY PNKS.

Questions to Ponder

1. What does the teacher know about Mackenzie's literacy development?
2. Is this precocious behavior or just precious behavior?
3. What course of action should Mackenzie's teacher pursue?
4. Could it be assumed that Mackenzie may be reading a few words?

15-1 Reading

At one time, it was thought that there was a magic age when all children became ready for "sit-down" reading instruction. Now it is believed that early childhood teachers at every level must be considered teachers of reading, even if they do not offer formal reading instruction. Research and theory suggest that teachers of young children need to be actively engaged in providing experiences that will build children's language and eventually lead children to become readers. These experiences are deemed appropriate if they match the individual child's level of language development and promote new competence in oral and written language. When children learn to read, they use what they know about oral language to comprehend written language.

Anderson (2007), along with most other early childhood educators, believes that learning to read is a process that begins at birth when children first start to recognize speech sounds and the meanings the sounds represent. Later, children associate this early knowledge with alphabet letters and letter clusters within words. They discover words in books and/or printed signs in their environment and learn how to use pictures as clues to understand adjacent print.

A wide range of age-appropriate activities involving understanding oral language, awareness of print, intimate experiences with picture books, dramatization, listening, musical activities, and diverse kinds of language arts activities discussed in this text promote early literacy and prepare children for the discovery of reading. Neuman and Roskos (2007) remind educators of the importance of preschool children's quest for knowledge and discovery in all content areas that is the true foundation for reading success. A strong literacy (language arts) curriculum is thought to be tremendously valuable but in itself is not enough.

> Reading achievement in the earliest years may look like it's just about letters and sounds—but it's not. Successful reading, as will become abundantly clear by grades 3 and 4, consists of knowing a relatively small store of unconscious procedural skills, accompanied by a massive and slowly built-up store of conscious content knowledge. It is knowledge and the disposition to want to learn more that encourages children to question, discover, evaluate, and invent new ideas and that enables them to become successful readers. (p. 8)

Some children who are in early childhood centers and kindergartens can read. Some have picked up the skill on their own; others have spent time with an older brother or sister, parents, or others. Although reading is considered the fourth language art, this chapter does not intend to suggest reading instruction for groups of young children or even encourage formal instruction for the one to five percent of children who can read words during preschool years.

It is clear from research that the process of learning to read is a lengthy one that begins very early in life. A lot of teacher effort during preschool years involves setting up young children to learn to read with ease. Many experts have discussed children's disposition to read. This disposition can be defined as a desire; a positive attitude toward the act of reading; or a feeling that reading is worthwhile, enjoyable, and fun (Photo 15-1). It includes the knowledge that one can find helpful or important information if one can read.

If a child enters kindergarten with certain values, beliefs, and behaviors surrounding the act of reading, the child will have a definite

Photo 15-1 Children sometimes select books and carry them to their teachers to read them.

© 2016 Cengage Learning®

advantage. If the child possesses a feeling of pleasure in learning something new and that feeling is combined with feelings of competency and confidence concerning books, reading success has every chance of occurring. This is the kind of child who likes to spend time with a favorite book and has an intrinsic interest in books—meaning it is something the child selects for its own sake. This indicates certain things have happened in the child's past. A children's time in preschool presents a precious opportunity to teachers to build foundational values, beliefs, and promising behaviors. There is empirical evidence that differences in preliteracy experiences are associated with varied levels of reading achievement during the early years of elementary school. Children who begin school with few experiences in and less knowledge about literacy are unable to acquire the prerequisites quickly enough to keep up with formal reading instruction in the first grade.

Preschoolers who are given training in phonological awareness evince significant acceleration in their later acquisition of reading. Prereaders' letter knowledge and their ability to discriminate phonemes were found to be the best predictors of first-year reading achievement. In early reading instruction—besides recognizing each alphabet letter's name—children will need to be able to recall and possess a mental image of a letter's form when only presented with its name or sound.

Elkin (2012) defines reading as an extraordinarily complex cognitive skill acquired in a number of age-related stages that parallel stages in the construction of number as described by Jean Piaget (1952b). Elkin suggests the first reading stage, *nominal reading*, is simply the child's ability to recognize and name a word (sight word). One- and two-year-olds in this stage might communicate with gestures, hand, or body signals as well as beginning words. In the next stage, *ordinal reading* (ages two to four), a child names, uses, and joins words in grammatical order. Elkin explains that it is only after a child attains new mental abilities described by Piaget (1952, 1995) as *concrete operations*, that a child can make sense of phonics or *unit reading*. (p. 84) *Unit reading* involves understanding letters as units and realizing that one and the same letter can be sounded differently depending upon context. Once this happens, Elkin theorizes, a child can quickly move toward reading with comprehension. (p. 85) Children who will probably need additional support for early language and literacy development should receive it as early as possible. Preschool practitioners should be alert for signs that children are having difficulties.

15-1a Children Who May Need Special Help DAP maeyc

Research has identified children who are likely to begin school less prepared. Their characteristics include living in a low-income family or a poor neighborhood with an elementary school where reading achievement is chronically low. These children may have limited English proficiency or speak a dialect of English that differs substantially from one used in schools. Many at-risk children have specific cognitive deficiencies, hearing impairments, or early language impairments. The child's family members may have had a history of reading problems. This doesn't mean that only children with the aforementioned characteristics need special, early help. At-risk children can come from any segment of American society.

Early childhood educators are looking closely at what their individual language arts curricula contain and how to provide supportive assistance for those individual children and individual families they assume to be at risk. Research-derived indicators for potential problems include significant delays in expressive language, receptive vocabulary, or intellectual capacity during infancy; or delays during the preschool period, at kindergarten, or elementary school entry; or delays in a combination of abilities, such as the following:

- letter identification,
- understanding the functions of print,
- verbal memory for stories and sentences,
- phonological awareness,
- lexical skills, such as naming vocabulary,
- receptive language skills in the areas of syntax and morphology,
- expressive language, or
- overall language development.

Prior experiences necessary for young children to acquire reading skill development include early childhood circumstances that foster motivation and provide exposure to literacy in use. Gaining an understanding about the nature of print through opportunities to learn letters and to recognize the internal structure of spoken words is also important. Forming ideas about the contrasting nature of spoken and written language is considered critical. Optimal environments in preschool and kindergarten require teachers who are well prepared and highly knowledgeable and who receive ongoing administrative support. Forms of support can include in-service training, financial aid, tutoring or mentoring, administrative participation and communication, and other assistance.

15-1b Reading Instruction DAP naeyc

The language arts approach and whole-language approach to reading consider reading as one part of the communication process. The language arts are interrelated, instead of separate, isolated skills. The teacher is responsible for showing the relationship between the various areas of language arts. In other words, the goal is to help children understand that communication is a whole process in which speaking, listening, using written symbols, and reading those symbols are closely connected (Figure 15-1).

Figure 15-1 The four language arts are interrelated and interdependent. Note: Some educators accept a fifth language art—viewing and visual representation.

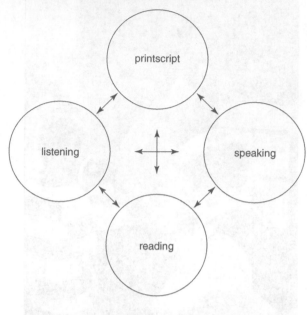

Early learning experiences in listening and speaking serve as a foundation for further language and communication. Children's beginning ideas about print, writing, and reading form concurrently, and children may display understanding and skill in all of these areas. Activities with young children can move easily from listening, speaking, viewing, or using printscript to beginning reading attempts: from passive to active participation. Many preschoolers are able to read most of the names of the children in their class.

15-1c Past and Current Thinking Concerning Early Reading Instruction

The National Reading Panel Report (2000) and the Elementary Education Act, which includes the No Child Left Behind Act passed in 2002, deal with ways to improve early literacy instruction and prepare young preschool children for school success. Early childhood educators are still taking these research-based suggestions to heart and are concerned about the approximately 30 to 40 percent of children who do not have an easy time learning to read in elementary school. Teachers are doing more assessment and documentation to help them identify children's individual needs and progress. Their efforts include attention to guidelines for developmentally appropriate practice and standards. They are planning a full and well-balanced early childhood language arts curriculum. This involves how children learn to read and write words and the unique structure of the English writing system. Ehri and Nunes (2006) point out that to remember how to decode new words, beginners must know how to blend phonemes; and to remember how to read individual words, beginners must be able to segment words into phonemes that match up to graphemes and phonemes and to store them in memory.

Concerns over national literacy and children's reading success have promoted study and discussion. Most states have adopted new standards for kindergarten. Experts in the past have recommended a literature-based program for both elementary school and preschool. Ideal classrooms were described as "language rich" or "literacy developing." Key ideas stress instruction offered in meaningful contexts with children developing strategies to achieve skills they view as useful to them. Other ideas of what should be included in preschool instruction are currently being developed because of common core state standards. These standards include more assessment of child progress and using the obtained data to guide instruction.

Early childhood professionals want to make sure that their programs or activities offer the best in children's literature, not watered-down versions of classics. There is thought to be both older and contemporary literature and language-related activities that have depth, meaning, and linguistic charm. Meaning and comprehension are aided by discussion and familiarity and can be guided by effective and sensitive teachers who also monitor the appropriateness of what is offered.

15-1d Pressure for Formal Reading Instruction in Preschools

Some families may hold the mistaken idea that their child will have an educational advantage if he receives formal reading instruction in preschool. Their rationale may be due to publicized research suggesting that science has misjudged infants' and preschoolers' innate capabilities. This idea is often expressed during initial enrollment interviews. Fortunately, early childhood educators can explain that foundational literacy experiences and activities are a standard part of a quality preschool curriculum, individual growth activities are planned for each child based on his developing capabilities, and research has not confirmed that reading at an early age is better or more advantageous. Durkin's research in the 1960s received considerable publicity, and subsequent studies by many others cite instances of young children reading before kindergarten. Well-advertised commercials on television and the Internet tout "We can teach your child to read" with programs and kits that are offered for sale. Some families and a few educators are intrigued by this idea and promote formal, sit-down instruction for three- and four-year-olds. Cullinan attempted to stem this practice and explained the error of this plan of action in the 1970s. Current educators often cite her position today. Some of Cullinan's views follow.

> . . . a major fallacy in basing programs on early reading studies is that children who learned to read early did not do so from exposure to formal reading instruction. Findings show that children who learned to read early were the ones who were read to, who showed interest in paper and pencil activities, and who were interested in visual distinctions in signs and labels. Their families valued reading as an activity.
>
> Someone answered their questions. Children learned messages encoded in writing can be decoded, or read, and that letters represented sounds used in speaking (Cullinan, 1977, p. 10)

In other words, typically children who learned to read while quite young did so by discovering decoding in responsive, literacy-enriched family situations. Most early childhood experts and educators fear that concentrating on early reading-skill instruction may reduce time for play and take away symbolic enrichment time. Play provides the interaction of imagery, imitation, and language, which builds a foundation necessary for learning to read. Chenfeld (2007) worries: "We have permitted developmentally *inappropriate* practices to become realities, squeezing the joy from children's early days in 'real school'" (p. 20). Widely recognized foundational skills and abilities are listed in Figure 15-2.

The pressure preschool administrators and staffs may feel to begin formal reading

Figure 15-2 Checklist for the foundations of reading.

Literacy skills that increase children's ability to learn to read with case and become successful readers include the ability to

- Maintain attention, focus, and fully engage.

- Display self-control and listening skills.

- Express ideas and feelings easily.

- Comprehend what is spoken or written.

- Be playful with engage and enjoy literacy activities.

- Recognize the symbolic relationships in pictures, images and icons (viewing).

- Understand concepts concerning print and its placement on a page and spacing between words.

- Conjure, predict, and interpret meanings from picture book reading and stories.

- Display phonemic awareness skill and alphabet letter fluency.

- Use art, building blocks, music, rhyme, dance, movement or another medium to express ideas and feelings.

Digital Download

instruction grates against the belief system that values the importance of play. Educators react to the tragedy of finding a number of children in a few preschools with worksheets to complete before they can play. Researchers have yet to find that early reading instruction is advantageous or better than later instruction. In fact, starting formal academics too early may do more harm than good. Studies show that children who are pushed to read early may not be such avid readers when they're older—which is when it matters—while their classmates who started slower may read often and spontaneously.

15-1e Standards, Benchmarks, and Behaviors

A standard is defined as a general statement that represents both the information and skills that a child (student) should understand or be able to perform by the end of his or her pre-K school experience. A benchmark is defined as a subcomponent of a standard. If your state has not developed prekindergarten standards for literacy instruction, samples of standards are available and can be obtained from states such as California, New Mexico, or Massachusetts or from one's state Office of Education. Another document that is research-based and has helped school curriculum planners identify standards for prekindergarten reading and writing

curriculum is based on work sponsored wholly, or in part, by the Office of Educational Research and Improvement (OERI). The publication is titled *A Framework for Early Literacy Instruction: Aligning Standards to Developmental Accomplishments and Student Behaviors: Pre-K through Kindergarten* (Bodrova et al., 2000).

COMMON CORE *Common Core State Standards for English Language Arts & Literacy in History/Social Studies, Science, and Technical Subjects* (2010) are now a prominent and somewhat controversial topic in the teaching of reading. Currently many state elementary school systems have adopted these new research-based standards and mandated that the standards guide all reading teachers. These Common Core State Standards were compiled through a joint effort of the National Governors Association Center for Best Practices and the Council of Chief State School Officers. It has already been adopted by 46 states and has become a standard reference for reading teachers. It is central in their planning of reading instruction. The few states that may not adopt the standards will not be forced to comply. Stern and Klein (2013) believe the common core standards represent a remarkable advance in rigor and academic content. Research on basal reading programs use has now cast doubt upon its effectiveness, yet Educational Market Research in 2010 found that 74 percent of schools and teachers were using basal readers fully or partially.

This is bound to change as other instructional practices used for teaching reading arise.

Producing efficient readers is mentioned in the standards. Efficient reading does not only require the ability to decode individual words in a sentence, but importantly also requires the ability to understand and comprehend meaning. Comprehending often involves gaining new ideas and information and fitting that into what one already knows and believes. When decoding skill is sketchy or time-consuming, a child often loses his train of thought. Child thoughtfulness is required to incorporate the new material into the mind's already stored data. A limited store of literary and literacy experience, a meager vocabulary, and reduced background knowledge affects child comprehension and reasoning. Background knowledge is defined as what a person (a child in this case) knows about the physical and social–emotional world. Think about what home and preschool conditions might curb a child's background knowledge. The Common Core State Standards are designed to promote children's comprehension skills with nonfiction material, stories, math materials, science, and technical reading materials. The goal of education is to produce more high school graduates able to enter the American workforce or college as thoughtful and efficient readers.

Prekindergarten educators and program planners are introducing more informational and nonfictional picture books. Some with story narrative and others with a more technical terminology and diverse vocabulary will be used. However, the standards do not prescribe how elementary school reading teachers should plan their program and teach to reach the outcomes that are specified in the standards for each grade level. More testing of student progress will take place to identify student growth or lack of it. Teachers will be free to adopt new reading methods and try new strategies in many schools. In others, administrators will do so. It is not only a time for innovation, but also a time when teachers and school administrators will be held accountable if outcomes are not accomplished.

15-1f Standards for Reading Teacher Preparation

Standards for Reading Professionals (2010), developed by the professional standards and ethics committee of the International Reading Association (IRA), is a reference used by community colleges, college and university faculties, and state departments of education. It is designed to guide the development of elementary school teacher preparation programs and the evaluation of teacher candidates and their training programs through the use of identified candidate performance-based assessments. The standards recognize seven categories of professionals: the *education support personnel paraprofessional* (two-year degree with specific course work), the Pre-K and elementary classroom teacher, the middle and high school content classroom teacher, the middle and high school reading classroom teacher, the reading specialist/literacy coach, the teacher educator, and the administrator.

Newly graduated reading professionals must demonstrate they can meet the needs of all students and that they possess the following capabilities or attitudes:

1. Candidates have knowledge of the foundations of reading and writing processes and instruction.

2. Candidates use a wide range of instructional practices, approaches, methods, and curriculum materials to support reading and writing.

3. Candidates use a variety of assessment tools and practices to plan and evaluate effective reading instruction.

4. Candidates create a literate environment that fosters reading and writing by integrating foundational knowledge, use of instructional practice, approaches and methods, curriculum materials, and the appropriate use of assessments.

5. Candidates view professional development as a career-long effort and responsibility.

The National Association for the Education of Young Children's 2010 *Standards for Initial and Advanced Early Childhood Professional Preparation Programs* may influence your training college's campus child center and the college's early childhood professional training degree program coursework. Your college may be seeking or may have been already granted NAEYC national certification. The initial standards describe expectations for graduates of early childhood teacher training from a two-year degree training program. Key elements of the standards include theoretical knowledge that when understood by a student leads to professional practice in classrooms. It also entails interactions with families and the community. The following lists NAEYC standards the author believes might affect your English language arts training classes and coursework.

<u>Standard 1. Promoting Child Development and Learning</u> prepares students to understand young children's characteristics and needs, to comprehend the multiple and interacting influences on their language and literacy growth and learning, and to create language and literacy environments that support and challenge each child.

<u>Standards 2. Building Family and Community Relationships</u> deals with successfully developing working family and community relationships to support and empower families to partner with educators in promoting their children's language arts listening, speaking, writing, and reading growth and development.

<u>Standard 3. Observing, Documenting, and Assessing to Support Young Children and Families</u> aims to ensure that child observation, documentation, and other forms of assessment will serve as a basis for program planning in the area of language arts. This includes using appropriate goals, curriculum, and teaching strategies to build individual and group experiences that promote positive outcomes for each child.

<u>Standard 4. Using Effective Approaches</u> involves the understanding and use of positive relationships and supportive interactions as the foundation for language and literacy instruction. It also encompasses relying on developmentally sound approaches, instructional strategies, and learning tools.

<u>Standard 5. Using Content Knowledge to Build Meaningful Curriculum</u> reinforces the idea that language and vocabulary is involved in the early study of content areas. The standards identify the content areas as language and literacy, the arts (music, creative movement, dance, drama, and visual arts), mathematics, science, physical education, health and safety, and social studies. It acknowledges that early childhood teachers become familiar and use the central concepts and inquiry tools while offering meaningful and challenging curriculum for each child.

<u>Standards 6 and 7</u> deal with professional teacher conduct and early childhood field experiences in a center or classroom rather than early childhood language arts instruction (NAEYC, 2011).

15-2 Teacher Awareness of Child Interest and Understanding

COMMON CORE

Each child will probably hold a totally different view concerning reading (Photo 15-2). Possible understandings a preschooler may have include:

- pictures and text have different functions.
- print contains the story.
- the words the reader says come from the pictures.
- stories tend to have some predictable segments and features.
- it is possible to write messages.
- there are words, and written words are made up of letters.
- letters are arranged from left to right.
- letters appear in linear fashion to represent the sequence of sounds in spoken words.
- spaces delineate word boundaries.

Photo 15-2 Teachers attempt to build children's positive attitudes toward books and the reading of them.

© 2016 Cengage Learning®

- letters come in capitals, in small print, and even in script, but they all have the same significance.

- some marks are used to show beginnings and ends of text.

The ability to read is present if the child understands and acts appropriately when he sees a printed word. In other words, the child must be able to understand the concept that (1) all "things" have a name, (2) the name of the thing can be a written word, (3) the two are interchangeable, and (4) the "word symbols" can be read.

Most teachers have had children "read" to them from a favorite, memorized storybook. Generally, a word from the book will not be recognized out of context and read by the child when seen elsewhere. However, this behavior—imitative reading—can be an indication of early literacy development. Early readers have a desire to read. Some have been moved toward reading because of an interest in printing (Photo 15-3). They may also have had interactions with others who have answered their questions and stimulated their interest. A few children will read between the ages of four and five, but many will not have the capability or interest to read until a later age. A teacher should be aware of each child's capabilities. Many other preschoolers read illustrations in storybooks and seek teachers who will listen to them read (Photo 15-4). In daily observations and conversations, a child's responses give valuable clues. The wrong answers are as important as the right ones.

Attempts to identify young children's emerging ideas about the act of reading have been undertaken. Children were asked what they knew about reading at age three, and the study continued through ages five or six. The following developmental sequence seemed apparent to the researchers.

DAP

Young children:

1. see reading as one aspect of social interaction. Children comment, look at illustrations, and observe page turning.

2. notice that readers eyes are on the book's pages, and if asked to read the book themselves will turn pages (front to back), and may read labeled objects or actions aloud. Some may talk to themselves—asking rhetorical questions—or speak memorized lines or words.

3. may show they realize a story has a meaningful sequence of actions or events that is reflected in the illustrations. Some children "read" from the pictures. Other children may mimic an adult's oral reading style.

4. may realize each book tells a unique story, and believe the reader has memorized it word for word.

5. grasp the idea that print tells the story and provides clues to the reader. The sounding out of simple words may begin.

Photo 15-3 An interest in printing can lead to an interest in reading.

© 2015 Cengage Learning®

Photo 15-4 "Reading" pictures (illustrations) is beginning reading.

© 2015 Cengage Learning®

6. use different and varied strategies to interpret the print. Medina (2008), an advocate of brain-based learning, notes data clearly show a word is unreadable unless the brain can separately identify simple features in letters. He points out the brain sees words as a series of little pictures.

Kindergarten teachers facing a wide range of enrolled children's language arts abilities often attempt to assess children's progress in letter identification, phonemic awareness (sound–symbol relationships), sight words, concepts of words, and printing skill. In a typical kindergarten class, children's literacy skills and functioning may span a five-year range; that is, some may possess skills typical of three-year-olds and others, those of eight-year-olds. Informal testing is common. Some common informal testing probes and questions follow.

1. Cards with an uppercase and lowercase printscript alphabet are displayed one by one.
   "What alphabet letter do you see?"
   "Can you tell me the sound it makes?"
   "Do you know a word that starts with this letter?"

2. The child is given paper and pencil.
   "Please write alphabet letters you know."
   "Tell me about the letters you've written."

3. The child is asked to write known words.
   "Write all the words you know."
   "Can you write your name?"

4. The child is presented a list of common sight words.
   "Do you know any of these words?"

5. The child is asked to describe/tell about his favorite book.

Individualized activities can become an easier task when assessment data have been gathered.

15-2a Child Knowledge of Alphabet Letters and Word Recognition

In comparing two children—one who knows the alphabet and reads a few words and one who crudely writes his own name and makes up barely understandable stories—one may conclude that the first child is bright. However, creativity and logic are important in literacy development, and the second child may be outdistancing the first by progressing at his own speed. Literacy at any age is more than merely naming letters or words. A child's fluency and ease at recognizing letters is important. The speed and accuracy of letter naming is an index of the thoroughness or confidence with which the letters' identities have been learned. Children's effortlessness may indicate an ability to see letters as "wholes" and then see words as patterns of letters.

Other educators suggest that it is other knowledge that is learned along with the ability to name letters that is crucial. More often than not, alphabet letter names are first encountered in the alphabet song (to the tune of "Twinkle, Twinkle Little Star") or in alphabet books at ages two, three, and four. Children usually memorize the oral names of a few alphabet letters. Children then develop a sense that different letter shapes have different names, and it is an easy jump to children understanding that their names are different in print than their friends' names. "That's my letter," a child may say when encountering a letter in the environment that is similar to or the same shape as the first letter of his first name.

Teachers and families need to understand that young children have two to four years to master the letter shapes before entering kindergarten. Instruction in letter recognition usually is begun during preschool years. The goal is to ensure that letter shapes are highly familiar and recognizable to the children before they are faced with the task of learning the letters' sounds or, more generally, of learning to read words. The sounds that letters make are commonly introduced after the names of the letters are well learned, but some programs choose to introduce the letter name and sound together. Still other programs follow the recommendation of McGuiness (1997) and call letters by their sounds.

Understanding the alphabetic principle involves the knowledge that there is a systematic relationship between letters and sounds. A child's grasp of the alphabetic principle may be the single most important step toward acquiring the code that eases early reading. Many prereaders figure this out without adult help. Letter-to-sound correspondence teaching has currently and historically been the subject of countless arguments and disputes among reading instruction professionals. Many teachers believe that knowing the names of letters helps some children remember sounds.

Increasingly, early childhood educators are finding or creating new ways to include more focus on alphabet letters by capitalizing on opportunities to point out print and its uses in classroom life, by saturating their classrooms with print, and by reading quality picture books with ABC themes These teachers are also busy relating the uses and functions of print to young children's lives.

The typical four-year-old relies on idiosyncratic cues to identify words, rather than intuitively making use of letter sounds. For example, when name tags are used with different types of stickers accompanying different children's names, the sticker is usually read (recognized) rather than the print.

▶❚❚ **TeachSource Video 15-1**

© 2016 Cengage Learning.

Language Development Activities in an Early Childhood Setting

In Bonus Video 4, the teacher and children are working with plastic upper- and lowercase alphabet letters in an activity in which children are constructing their names.

1. Would you consider this activity to be a prereading skill development exercise or was it simply a letter recognition activity? Explain the reasons for your answer.

2. Is there anything that might have helped these children to be more successful with the task at hand?

15-2b A Closer Look at Early Readers

Researchers studying both gifted children and early readers notice that families overwhelmingly report that they have read to their children from birth on or from the time the children learned to sit up. Research shows that early readers who learned to read without systematic instruction had one common experience, despite their different backgrounds: they were all introduced to books between the ages of three and five. Frequently, families also spend time with their young child using the computer or other kinds of electronic media—both educational program and entertainment varieties, and someone reads books aloud on a regular basis. Many reading experts believe that children who achieve at an outstanding level have families that did not impose their learning priorities upon their very young but instead followed the child's lead, emphasizing play and a rich, stimulating environment rather than formal instruction. Studies of the early reader indicate that the child was usually exposed to a variety of reading material and enjoyed watching educational television, spending close to equal time in both pursuits. An interest in print characterizes precocious readers, and their families were often described as responsive—noticing child interests and providing help when asked. Many child-centered family activities were part of the early reader's family lifestyle. These children seemed fascinated and obsessed with the alphabet, and families reported that they answered questions, read to the child, and engaged in play activities with letters and words but had not set out with a systematic plan to teach reading.

If we could examine parent–child storybook readings closely, simply reading aloud does not describe most parent actions accurately. Pointing out book features, relating book happenings to shared family experiences, defining words, engaging in turn-taking dialogue, prompting children's identification and naming of illustrations, listening to children's memorized "readings," and engaging in other parental interactions are all part of the experience (Photo 15-5). Educators use the same techniques.

They support efforts to ease children's difficulty in learning to read. These efforts can include:

- building children's oral language development.
- finding good books in which the pictures closely match the words.
- prompting, "Will you point to the words as you read them?"
- letting children ponder the problem that what they are saying does not match the number of words they are pointing to in the print and hoping children self-correct themselves.
- saying, "Great self-correcting," when it happens.
- watching for confusion and modeling the strategies readers use when they encounter problems. For example, pausing to see whether the child backs up and rereads on his own or saying, "Try it again, that's what I usually do."

The goal is for the black marks on the page to give the child enough feedback that the child can adjust his approximation. This marks a huge step in the process of learning to read.

Photo 15-5 When possible, teachers relate book features to children's past experiences.

© 2016 Cengage Learning®

Other effective strategies that early readers use to help themselves include:

- orienting themselves to a book as a whole.
- studying the pictures to heighten their sense of what the words say.
- guessing at what the print probably says.
- checking to confirm or disprove their guesses.
- pointing to words.

Bardige (2009) describes the possible last step on a child's journey toward becoming a reader.

The last of the steps from emergent to beginning reading is often referred to as 'cracking the code.' With all that children have learned about stories, print, words, sounds, and letters, they still need to associate specific letters with specific sounds, in the context of meaningful text. It's not enough for children to be able to figure out what a word says—they have to be able to decode the word and apprehend its meaning quickly and easily enough to turn their attention to the meaning of the sentence and of the larger story. In order to read fluently, children have to master some specific word recognition and word analysis skills—and to practice them until they become automatic. (p. 208)

For early readers in a preschool classroom, many experienced teachers recommend books with repetitive, patterned text and books with a jazzy, rhythmic phrase on every page that may change just a word or two as text moves ahead. Teachers watch out for and avoid books that consist of meaningless, silly ditties. Looking for logical books that are both interesting and tailored to a child's life and past experience is the prudent course of action. A list of suggested books follows.

Appelt, K. (2010). *Brand-new baby*. New York: HarperCollins Publishers.

Boelts, M. (2007). *Those shoes*. Cambridge, MA: Candlewick.

Bliss, H. (2011). *Bailey*. New York: Scholastic.

Crimi, C. (2011). *Rock 'n' roll mole*. New York: Dial Books.

Friedrich, M. (2004). *You're not my real mother*. New York: Little, Brown, & Co..

Kroll, S. (2011). *The biggest apple ever*. New York: Scholastic Inc.

What should happen when a child expects to learn to read the first day of school or kindergarten? Many kindergarten teachers suggest a teacher should "make it happen." The child should go home after the first day able to read a simple sentence such as "My name is ___." This enhances the child's perceptions that he can read. A big portion of the battle to improve children's self-esteem occurs and allows the child to believe in himself.

15-2c Shared Reading

Many prekindergartens, kindergartens, and lower elementary school classes conduct group reading activities called shared readings. Often, 14-by-17-inch or larger books, called Big Books, or teacher-made charts are introduced, discussed, and read. On a first reading, the book's cover and illustrations are examined. Predictions about the story or other content take place. Text is large, and colorful illustrations are directly connected to the text. Words are repeated frequently. After a first reading, children may be prompted to share something they noticed in the book. While reading, the teacher puts one hand under each word and moves from top to bottom and left to right or uses a pointer.

Shared reading promotes both letter and sound recognition, especially after repeated readings. In the course of shared reading, children query what a particular word says, notice that some words rhyme, and notice words with the same sound or letter. The teacher encourages discussion and children's touching or pointing to book features. Children may be asked to guess words or predict story outcomes. Pleasant attitudes toward the experience are built through accepting and appreciating each child's comments and ideas. It is easy to see that this exercise will result in children's efforts to point out letters, words, or rhymes that they know. Both fiction and nonfiction titles are used.

Borba (2009) describes the outcomes of shared reading as follows:

> With repeated readings of the same text over days and weeks, participation by the children grows and opportunities for teaching about the detail in print or the ideas in text increase. Early readings are done by the teacher while pointing to the text, but over time, the students join in reading the text. The connections between sounds and letters happen and making meaningful predictions are clearly modeled in the shared reading lesson. (p. 12)

15-2d Vocabulary and Early Readers

A child's vocabulary is strongly related to his comprehension and ease of learning to read. Reading comprehension involves applying letter–sound correspondence to a printed word and matching it to a known word in the reader's oral vocabulary. Oral vocabulary is a key in making the transition from oral to written forms. Many studies agree that reading ability and vocabulary size are related.

In trying to measure children's vocabulary, one finds that different vocabularies exist. Receptive vocabulary is seen in toddlers, who follow requests such as "get Grandpa's brown shoes" before they can say the words. Productive vocabulary is used when we speak or write to another. Oral vocabulary refers to words that are recognized in speaking or listening. For example, the toddler may bring Grandpa's black shoes because color words are not part of his oral vocabulary. Reading vocabulary refers to words that are used or recognized in print. Many young children can be described as having a reading vocabulary when they correctly recognize street signs and commercial fast-food symbols. Sight vocabulary is a subset of reading vocabulary. A sight word is immediately recognized and remembered as a whole and does not require word analysis for identification. Early childhood teachers rarely know the size of preschoolers' sight vocabularies unless they do assessments. When they do, they find some preschoolers have amazingly large ones.

Early childhood educators consciously promote and prompt vocabulary development. They relish and model an interest in words, their definitions, and dictionary use. New words enter children's vocabularies daily in a developmental environment. Teachers explain new words and relate them to children's experience by giving examples. Sight vocabulary words are composed of alphabet letters that can be named and sounded out, so-called teaching moment naturals. Kindergarten classrooms (and some preschools) have word charts, word lists, word walls, words used for labeling, and words in displays. Preschools have abundant alphabet letters and words used in functional ways.

Considerable study suggests that a small vocabulary is one major determinant of poor reading comprehension for Latino children and others who lag in readiness in the first grades of elementary school. Every effort in early childhood centers is made to aid children's oral vocabulary and work toward depth of understanding through firsthand experience, exposure to books, classroom discussion, play with peers, and the scheduling of frequent daily literacy events.

Some preschools develop a "Words I Know" file box for children who wish to have one. It can be taken home occasionally. Words are dictated by children then printed by the teacher. An oblong box with strips of sturdy paper works well. Printing with a wide-tip black marker is recommended. Strips can be used for tracing and other activities, when appropriate. Some preschoolers have sizable sight word vocabularies, as was mentioned. Sylvia Ashton-Warner (1963) believed, as do many other early childhood educators, that first words have intense meaning for a child. Ashton-Warner's conviction gave rise to her articulation of what she called the organic reading method, which used key vocabulary for teaching reading and writing.

15-3 Objectives

Differences exist in the objectives of instruction between (1) educators who believe in readiness activities and (2) educators who advocate natural self-discovery of reading skills. The first group hopes to facilitate learning and enjoyment of reading. The second group foresees the child's experimentation—creating ideas about reading, based on his notions of the use of writing and reading, and attempting to crack the code with supportive assistance. Both groups favor a print-rich classroom, and objectives in many programs are based on a consideration of a blending of the two positions. Both groups also agree that experiences with classic and quality literature and dramatic activity help children's early literacy.

Programs that choose to include reading readiness among their instructional goals and objectives plan activities that promote the following skills and attitudes.

- recognizing incongruities—the ability to see the inappropriateness of a situation or statement, such as "The mouse swallowed the elephant"
- recognizing context clues—realizing that pictures on the same page give visual clues to the words
- acquiring the ability to listen
- building vocabulary through firsthand experiences
- recognizing likenesses and differences
- identifying through sight and sound
- rhyming
- increasing memory span
- recalling sequence and content
- following directions
- increasing speech output
- developing attitudes of each child's ability and worth
- increasing imaginative and creative speech
- building critical thinking and problem solving with language
- identifying through clues
- classifying, sorting, and organizing
- developing concepts and recognizing relationships
- anticipating outcomes

- seeing cause-and-effect relationships
- developing self-confidence—attitudes of competence
- increasing interest and motivation through enjoyment of and success in language activities
- developing left and right awareness
- developing positive attitudes toward books and skills in book use such as turning pages and storing and handling books with care

Phonemic awareness, the awareness that words are composed of sounds, is important in facilitating learning to read. What can early childhood educators do to encourage phonemic awareness? Reading experts suggest literature that focuses on some kind of play with the sounds of language to help children "naturally" develop awareness. Books including alliteration, rhyme, repetition, and sound substitution fit this category.

Educators seriously consider each child's attitude development concerning reading times and reading in general. In both their actions and words, teachers convey their attitudes. If actions and words value reading and express enthusiasm (and joy) for finding out what enjoyment or information is possible in a book, young children also tend to adopt an "Oh boy, a book" orientation. They may then accept the idea that reading books can be a pleasurable pursuit—a treat, a door to adventure, fantasy, fun!

15-3a Sequence of Reading Behavior

In the absence of adult intervention that emphasizes another sequence, children generally seem to develop reading and writing abilities as follows:

1. The child develops an awareness of the functions and value of the reading and writing processes before becoming interested in acquiring specific knowledge and skills.
2. The child is likely to give greater attention to words and letters that have some personal significance, such as his name or the names of family, pets, and so forth.
3. The child develops both reading and writing skills simultaneously as complementary aspects of the same communication processes, rather than as separate sets of learning.
4. The child develops an awareness of words as separate entities (as evidenced when he dictates words slowly so that the teacher can keep pace in writing them down) before showing awareness or interest in how specific letters represent sounds.
5. The child becomes familiar with the appearance of many of the letters by visually examining them, playing games with them, and so forth, before trying to master their names, the sounds they represent, or their formation.
6. The child becomes aware of the sound similarities between high-interest words (such as significant names) and makes many comparisons between their component parts before showing any persistence in deciphering unfamiliar words by blending together the sounds of individual letters.

It is important for teachers to be able to help the child's existing reading abilities and actively plan for future reading skill.

15-3b The Transition to Kindergarten for Those with Special Needs

A relatively new entity, the **transitional kindergarten**, exists in some communities. It may have a curriculum designed to support each child's early skill or address at-risk status through special summer intervention classes and/or increased family and community participation in the child's learning. Its goal is to offer children a transitional period to enhance their effectiveness as prereaders. The goals of most transitional programs involve both child self-regulation and social interaction. Playing appropriately with others, collaborating, planning play directions, sharing, taking turns, approaching peers to play, and knowing some of the other children's names are social interaction skills. Self-regulation includes watching peers to find out what is expected, imitating behaviors, following classroom routines and rules, changing behavior when necessary,

---

transitional kindergarten — a relatively new feature of some elementary school districts that offers supportive literacy activities and classroom access (usually during the summer before the child is to enroll in kindergarten).

waiting, standing in line, and taking care of personal items. To perform some of these tasks the child needs to accept the teacher as an authority figure.

15-4 Reading Methods

Research studies conducted to try to pinpoint the one best **reading method** for teaching children to read have concluded there is no proven *best* method. The important factors seem to be the teacher's (1) enthusiasm for the method or technique used, and (2) understanding of the method used. The ideal situation for a child learning to read is a one-to-one child/teacher ratio, with the reading activity suited to the child's individual capacity, learning style, and individual interests. This is difficult to fulfill in an early childhood learning center because of the number of children per group and the many other duties required of a teacher. Other limitations can include the teacher's amount of training, knowledge of a variety of methods to teach reading, and ability to plan interesting and appropriate activities within a print-rich classroom. What preschool teachers need to understand is that advocates of many differing methods used to teach reading agree that a rich, strong base in quality children's literature and well-developed oral language and listening skill aid success in whatever reading method is eventually used.

15-4a The Natural Approach

Popular approaches to reading include what has been termed "natural" reading. The basic premise of this method centers on the idea that a child can learn to read as he learned to talk, that is, with adult attention and help with early skills. Advocates feel that children learn to read in a literate society the same way they learned to talk, walk, draw, and sing: by seeing and hearing reading modeled skillfully and by noticing and understanding that this is an interesting and useful thing to do. In the natural approach, an interest in print (words) leads to invented spelling and reading. "Organic" and natural reading systems propose that children learn to read by authoring from their own experiences, and by being exposed to great classic literature as well as child-authored literature.

Educators associated with natural reading also endorse a method called the language-experience approach. Stauffer (1970) points out the specific features of the language-experience approach, which he believes make it especially appropriate for young children.

- a base in children's language development and firsthand experiencing
- stress on children's interests, experiences, and cognitive and social development
- respect for children's need for activity and involvement
- requirement for meaningful learning experiences
- integration of school and public library resources with classroom reading materials
- encouragement of children's creative writing as a meaningful approach to using and practicing reading and writing skills

Johnson (1987), influenced by the work of Sylvia Ashton-Warner, recommends starting five-year-olds reading through a procedure that elicits children's images. The images are then connected to printed captions. Individual important images merge as meaningful words to be shared with others through sight reading. Slowly, visual discrimination, capitalization, sentence sense, phonetics, and punctuation are accomplished at each child's particular pace.

Sylvia Ashton-Warner's method of teaching reading inspired a whole generation of teachers during the 1960s. Thompson (2000) believes that Ashton-Warner gives today's teachers an early model for teaching multicultural children to read. Thompson describes Ashton-Warner's techniques.

> What she called her "scheme" for working in the New Zealand bicultural context may be, in some very basic ways, universally adaptable to intercultural or transcultural education for the new millennium. Organic teaching requires the teacher to listen to the pupils, to truly hear them and encourage what is important to them, and to use that as the working material for teaching and learning. This concept, Ashton-Warner asserts, embodies the kind of attitude necessary for building transcultural bridges for sharing understanding of cultures, ultimately a possible direction leading to peace in our shrinking global village. (p. 155)

---

reading method — any of several relatively specific procedures or steps for teaching one or more aspects of reading, each procedure embodying explicitly or implicitly some theory of how children learn and of the relationship between written and spoken language.

The author recommends, as do most teacher-training programs, the early childhood educator's reading of Ashton-Warner's book, *Teacher* (1963). It is as pertinent today as it was when it was first written.

To many people, the terms natural and organic methods and language-experience and language arts approaches are synonymous and describe the same or similar methods of reading instruction. Natural and organic approaches have lost favor. They are thought to be incomplete—good as far as they go, but not as systematic or explicit as they might be. Because no one reading method has been proved superior based on research data, teachers should be able to combine methods.

The language arts approach to reading instruction introduces children to written words through their own interest in play, through their enjoyment of speaking, and by listening to language. Often, children's first experience with written words comes from their own speech and actions. A sign that says "John's Block Tower" or "Free Kittens" may be the child's first exposure to reading. The emphasis is on the fact that words are part of daily living.

15-4b The Whole-Language Movement

Enthusiasm for a reading philosophy and approach called "whole language" is apparent in some elementary schools. Whole-language advocates believe in offering children meaningful and functional literature in full literary texts, rather than through worksheets or dittoed handouts. The approach emphasizes the interrelated nature of the language arts. It believes that learning in any one area of language arts helps learning in others.

The whole-language approach is a philosophy that suggests that children learn language skill by following the natural learning behavior that governs the way they learn to talk, and that writing, listening, reading, and speaking activities grow from a child's experiences and interests (Photo 15-6). The teacher directs natural curiosity into activities that develop skills.

All sorts of literature (instead of just basal readers) are used in whole-language classrooms, including posters, comics, classic literature, quality books, magazines, and newspapers, to mention a few. Poetry, songs, chants, and simple drama activities are among the language activities offered. The whole-language teacher

Photo 15-6 Because Evan has displayed an interest in a special topic, his teacher provides him with a related book.

© 2016 Cengage Learning®

presents opportunities for learning and development by relating activities to a single theme. Spontaneous conversational exchanges are typical and seen as enhancing and extending learning. Teachers using this approach draw attention to connections between speaking, writing, and reading by saying things like, "I heard you say *boat*. This is how you write that. Now let's read it." There are usually no ability-grouped reading circles, and classrooms are described as busy, active, and full of talk.

Critics point out that there are no formulas for planning, developing, organizing, and managing whole-language curriculum and that, consequently, whole-language teachers with similar philosophies may differ in what curriculum they present. Other criticism usually centers on the teacher's ability to assess each child's reading progress and the lack of instruction in phonics. Reading experts have predicted that the whole-language movement will survive but not dominate American public education. This has proved to be true. Exclusion of phonics instruction by some whole-language teachers and lower reading achievement test scores in California's whole-language classrooms in 1994 caused additional concern.

Many educators today believe that whole language has become a full-fledged, although still evolving, theory of learning and teaching. It exemplifies a constructionist view of learning, believing concepts and complex processes are constructs of the human brain; therefore, research suggests that the greater the intellectual and emotional involvement in learning, the more effectively the brain learns, uses, and retains what is learned.

15-4c Literature-Based Reading Programs

A literature-based reading curriculum has been adopted or recommended in many states. Au (2006) describes literature-based instruction as involving a continuum of strategies to be applied as children move up through the grades in elementary school: shared reading, guided reading, guided discussion, and literature discussion groups (also known as literature circles or book clubs). In addition, two strategies are used and considered important across the grade levels: teacher read-alouds and sustained silent reading.

Teachers using this approach to reading instruction usually fall into three groups (or types) depending on how "literature-based" is defined and carried out in their classrooms. The three types may vary somewhat with each teacher.

1. Literature-based readers. Basal reading programs that use literature content texts are adopted. In about 80 percent of these texts, the stories are faithful to the original writing. Books are based on selections of stories, not whole books. Teachers' guides and workbooks suggest fragmented kinds of word study and fill-in-the-blank exercises.

2. Basalization of literature. A literature-based reading program uses real books to study, but treats them as basal readers.

3. Comprehensive literature program. Literature permeates the curriculum. Teachers read aloud to children; they give children a choice of real books for their own reading; they make use of the fine informational books that we have today to use literature in every area of the curriculum; and they encourage children's response to books through discussion, drama, art, and writing. Their primary goal is to produce children who not only know how to read but also become readers.

Educators are examining New Zealand's literature-based reading approach because New Zealand has been recognized by some as the most literate country in the world. New Zealand's instructional approach is similar to whole-language theory put into practice. The instructional model was instituted after educational research pointed to the success of literature-based models. An influx of culturally diverse children who were not adequately progressing in reading prompted New Zealand's use of newer instructional methodology.

15-4d The Decoding or Phonetic Reading Approach

Decoding, using a phonetic approach to reading instruction, is based on teaching children the 38–44 (experts differ) language sounds (phonemes), which are 26 alphabet letters and combinations (graphemes). This approach assumes that to read, children first must be able to "decode"; that is, they must be able to pronounce the letter sequences they see on a page based on what they know about the link between spelling and sound. An underlying skill is phonemic awareness: the understanding that words, even simple ones like *cat*, are composed of individual sounds called phonemes, which make a difference in meaning. Only one phoneme makes the difference between rope and soap.

Although phonetic approaches differ widely, most users believe that when children know which sounds are represented by which letters or letter combinations, they can "attack" an unknown word and decode it. Some schools using this approach begin decoding sessions when all sounds have been learned; others expose children to select sounds and offer easily decoded words early. A few phonetic approach systems require teachers to use letter sounds exclusively and later introduce the individual letter names, such as *a*, *b*, *c*, and so forth. The following five "word-attack" (or decoding) skills are helpful in the complicated process of learning to read.

1. picture clues—using an adjacent picture (visual) to guess at a word near it (usually on the same page)

2. configuration clues—knowing a word because you remember its outline

3. context clues—guessing an unknown word by known words that surround it

4. phonetic clues—knowing the sound a symbol represents

5. structural clues—seeing similar parts of words and knowing what these symbols say and mean

Phonics may be most useful when a reader already has some general notion of what a word should be. A child trying to guess a word he does not know at the end of a sentence read by an adult, such as "the cup fell on the f____," might guess "fire." Such a guess would be phonetically reasonable, but a child relying on meaning would guess "floor."

Advocates of **phonetic instruction** are often critical and vocal about the exclusive use of any one reading approach that neglects phonics. Most teachers recognize that some children can learn to read with little or no phonetic instruction. They also note that many children may have difficulty without it. Fertig (2009), the author of *Why can't U teach me 2 read?* cites research suggesting intensive phonics (instruction) makes a significant difference in disadvantaged children's degree of early school success.

15-4e Look-and-Say Method

Many of the children who do read during preschool years have learned words through a "look-and-say" (whole-word) approach. That is, when they see the written letters of their name or a familiar word, they can identify the name or word. They have recognized and memorized that group of symbols. It is believed that children who learn words in this fashion have memorized the shape or configuration of the word. They often confuse words that have similar outlines, such as "Jane" for "June" or "saw" for "sew." They may not know the alphabet names of the letters or the sounds of each letter. This approach was prevalent in public school reading instruction in the twentieth century, but it is rarely used today. Children who are good at noticing slight differences and who have good memories seem to progress and become successful readers.

15-4f Other Approaches to Reading Instruction

Many elementary school districts emphasize that their approach to reading instruction is a combined or balanced approach. This approach offers a rich diet of quality literature and literary experiences, plus a sound foundation of phonics.

Cowen (2005) defines a balanced reading approach as follows:

> A *balanced reading approach* is research-based, assessment-based, comprehensive, integrated, and dynamic, in that it empowers teachers and specialists to respond to the individual assessed literacy needs of children as they relate to their appropriate instructional and developmental levels of decoding, vocabulary, reading comprehension, motivation, and sociocultural acquisition, with the purpose of learning to read meaning, understanding, and joy. (p. 10)

Scientific evidence-based reading research and brain-based instructional approaches are the hottest topics in literacy learning and reading methods.

15-4g Reading Instruction in Public Elementary Schools

An individual teacher's method of reading instruction is heavily influenced by many factors besides economics, including teacher experience regarding what works, politics, economics, and the popular wisdom of the day. Cunningham and Creamer (2003) note that reading instruction has experienced a "pendulum swing"—from whole language and silent reading in the middle to late 1990s to intensive phonics and oral reading.

Other eras are identified as follows:

- phonics era (1956–1964)
- language, literature, and discovery-learning era (1965–1974)
- individualized specific skills instruction era (1975–1986)
- language, literature, and discovery-learning era (1987–1995)
- phonics and oral reading era (1996–)

In a review of current reading instruction research, one finds the terms *balanced, eclectic, research-based, accountable, phonetic awareness, phonics instruction, fluency, comprehension,* and *alphabetics.* The field of reading instruction seems to lack consensus concerning what constitutes the best practices for the teaching of reading. Standards, assessment, and accountability are dominant factors in public school classrooms. National and state legislation and the state of the

---

phonetic instruction — instruction in phonics is instruction that stresses sound-symbol relationships. It is a strategy used in beginning reading instruction.

economy is driving change. Testing will take place, and the results will be published. Every effort is being made to make families and early childhood educators aware of the foundations of literacy necessary for successful participation in kindergarten.

15-5 Families' Role in Reading

Families often want to find ways to help their children succeed in reading. Because the ability to read is an important factor in early schooling, they may seek the advice of the teacher. Parents should be advised that almost everything that parents (families) do that includes language and books with their children can have a positive academic outcome. Lucky is the child whose caregivers are able to provide daily conversations, discussions, and experiences that offer learning and problem solving opportunities, Formal and informal, everyday family events and happenings can provide a world of background knowledge. Nurturing a child's sense of being capable and competent should be touched upon along with attempting to instill a love of learning. Many programs keep families informed of the school's agenda and goals and the children's progress. This will happen more frequently under new common core standards. An early childhood center's staff realizes that families and teachers working together can reinforce what children learn at home and at school. They also realize poverty, hunger, homelessness, and poor nutrition, and lack of hope contribute to children's school failure.

Summary

The fourth area of the language arts is reading.

15-1 Discuss current standards for reading instruction.

A reading standard is a general statement that includes information and skills that a child should be able to perform at a certain period in time. Reading standards are available from regulating entities, such as state offices of education or early childhood or other professional groups or agencies. Most standards are research-based. Current standards include common core state standards in reading used in the majority of public elementary and high schools. These standards are rigorous and academic and may affect preschools whose goals include preparing children to enter kindergarten with the prereading skills and abilities necessary to promote success in early instruction. Vocabulary development, the ability to comprehend what is read, decoding skills, and children's background knowledge are believed to be crucial, along with a thoughtful approach when children encounter nonfiction books, early mathematics, and science concepts.

15-2 Describe factors promoting a few preschoolers to actually read before kindergarten.

Factors that affect whether a child will actually read before kindergarten are multiple. They include children's past home language arts experience, children's understandings about illustrations, books, print, written words, and alphabet letters, and the preschool language arts programs that they have attended that offer activities and experience with literature and literacy. Early indicators that a particular child might accomplish the act of reading during preschool include: imitative reading behavior, interest in print, observed responses to storybooks, progress in alphabet letter identification, phonemic awareness skill, sight reading vocabulary, printing skill, understanding of the alphabetic principle, and also whether they were read books between the ages of three- and five-years-old on a regular basis. A last possible indication that a child may accomplish reading during the preschool period is the child's display of the ability to decode a word and comprehend its meaning.

15-3 Describe children's usual sequence of reading like behaviors.

A sequence of reading like behaviors includes:

1. developing an awareness of reading and writing processes.

2. paying attention to alphabet letters and words.

3. developing both prereading and writing skills.

4. knowing a word is a separate entity.

5. developing an awareness of alphabet letter shapes and their sounds.

15-4 Name four recognized reading instructional methods used in elementary schools.

Well-recognized reading methods include The Natural Approach, S. Ashton-Warner Reading Approach, Whole Language Instruction, Literature-Basal Reading Program, Look–Say Method, and the Balanced Reading Approach.

15-5 Describe ways centers involve parents in their child's prereading instruction.

Family involvement in a school's prereading efforts differs from school to school. Programs may attempt to advise families using a variety of planned outreach activities and communication vehicles. The extent of their efforts may be modified by a number of factors, including funding, parent interest and ability to attend, formal and informal events, and communication issues. Families are usually invited to afterschool sessions, meetings, or happenings, and the school attempts to keep families abreast of the educational agenda at school and also their child's progress through daily conversations. Schools usually transmit how instrumental families can be in promoting their child's school success by providing home conversation, discussions, activities and experiences, and problem-solving opportunities connected to the act of reading and child literature exposure.

Additional Resources

Readings

Ashton-Warner, S. (1963). *Teacher*. New York: Simon & Schuster.

Frey, N., & Fisher, D. (2010). Reading and the brain: What early childhood educators need to know. *Early Childhood Education Journal 38*(2),183–110.

Guthrie, J. T. (2011). Best practices in motivating students to read. In L. M. Morrow and L. B. Gambrell (Eds.) *Best Practices in Literacy Instruction* (pp. 177–198). New York: Guilford Press.

Morrow, L. M. (2005). *Literacy Development in the Early Years: Helping Children Read and Write*. Boston: Allyn and Bacon.

Neuman, S.B., & Dwyer, J. (2009). Missing in action: Vocabulary instruction in pre-K. *The Reading Teacher 62*(5), 384–392. doi:10.1598/RT.62.5.2

Wasik, B. A., & Hindman, A.H., & Jusczyk, A. M.(2009). Using curriculum-specific progress monitoring to assess Head Start children's vocabulary development, *NHSA Dialog 12*(3), 257–275.

Readings on Phonetic Instruction

Cunningham, P. M. (2000). *Phonics They Use: Words for Reading and Writing*. New York: Addison-Wesley/Longman.

Paris, S. G. (2005). Reinterpreting the development of reading skills. *Reading Research Quarterly 40*(2), 181–202.

Yopp, H. K., & Yopp, R. H. (2000). Supporting phonemic awareness development in the classroom. *The Reading Teacher 54*, 130–143.

Helpful Websites

PBS Kids.

http://pbskids.org/

Go to Teacher and Parent Resources for reports on research-based approaches to reading instruction.

Jumpstart

http://www.jstart.org

Provides information about Jumpstart, a national early education organization that matches children from low-income backgrounds with adults who focus on literacy.

National Center for Learning Disabilities

http://www.GetReadytoRead.org

Features screening tools, literacy activities, checklists, and games.

National Council of Teachers of English

http://www.ncte.org

Search for position papers titled *On Reading*, *Learning to Read*, and *Effective Reading Instruction*.

16 › Developing a Literacy Environment

Objectives

After reading this chapter, you should be able to:

16-1 List three suggestions for creating a print-rich classroom.

16-2 Describe the teacher's role in a language arts room center.

16-3 Discuss children's use of technology in a preschool classroom.

16-4 Describe a good location for a computer center and what it should contain.

naeyc NAEYC Program Standards

3A07 Teaching staff and children work together in predictable ways so children know where to find things and put them away.

3D03 Teachers provide time and materials for children to select their own activities.

2H02 All children have opportunities to access technology.

DAP Developmentally Appropriate Practice (DAP) Preschoolers

3H11 Teachers place books in an inviting, comfortable library area.

3K1 Teachers make thoughtful use of computers and other technology in the classroom, not to replace children's experience with objects and materials, but to expand the range of tools that children can use to seek information, solve problems, perform transformations, and learn at their own pace.

3K2 Teachers locate computers to foster shared learning and interaction.

3K3 Program provides enough equipment that a child can become engaged in a technology project in a sustained, deep way.

COMMON CORE Common Core State Standards, K-3

W.CCR. 6 Use technology including the Internet to produce and publish writing and to interact and collaborate with others.

"Can I Have Another Turn?"

Four-year-old Emma found computer use to be the high point of her day, and as her computer involvement grew her other interests narrowed. Her preschool teacher noticed she had lost interest in art projects, was socially less involved, spent less and less time with other children, and often tried to negotiate more time on the school's computer. Her teacher observed that Emma seemed distracted and restless, and she felt that Emma's gross-motor skills might be lagging. She also believed that Emma had shortened her attention span for everything else offered in class.

Emma's family noted that she immediately rushed to their home computer after school and had lost interest in playing with neighborhood friends. Most of them stopped dropping by to ask her to play. Emma's interest in toys also seemed diminished.

Questions to Ponder

1. Is it possible that a four-year-old could develop addictive behavior?
2. Emma's parents sought professional advice but wanted Emma to continue developing computer skills. What plan of action do you think might have been recommended to the parents?
3. What teacher plan of action would you suggest?

16-1 Print-Rich Classrooms

This text has emphasized the need to provide children with a variety of interesting classroom centers and areas, materials, objects, and furnishings. Such settings, equipment, and materials are important in keeping programs alive, fascinating, and challenging. The classroom environment can promote language skills in many ways, for it provides the reality behind words and ideas. It also supplies opportunities for sensory exploration and increases children's knowledge of relationships.

It gathers or creates materials that capture attention, motivate play, and build communication skills. Familiar and favorite materials and furnishings are enjoyed repeatedly with the child deciding how much time to devote to each. Materials and settings can isolate one or each room area and how each might promote and encourage more language or perceptual skills allowing for practice and accomplishment. Educators should clarify what goals of instruction and students' needs are to be served for engagement. One would hope a center would attract and provide the means for children to carry out their own self-chosen activities, as well as teacher-planned and directed ones.

In language arts centers, related instructional materials are located in one convenient and inviting area. Stocking, supervision, and maintenance of materials, furnishings, and equipment by the teaching staff are easily accomplished. The classroom can be a place to grow, expand, test ideas, predict outcomes, and ask questions. A prepared environment provides successful experiences for all children in a climate in which ideas and creative learning flourish.

The *physical* and *emotional comfort level* of classroom areas and spaces are central to the literacy learning of all students and, in particular, English language learners (Barone & Xu, 2008). Consequently, teachers consider this along with insuring children's health and safety. Rooms are planned to minimize the cultural discontinuity that may exist between home and school lives. Teachers recognize and support child differences. This might include classroom displays of diverse children's household items, cultural clothing, musical instruments, printed language examples, books, and photographs or other materials that help children maintain a healthy sense of identity at school.

A limited body of knowledge exists regarding how the physical features and equipment of a literacy-based classroom enhance learning.

A preliminary study examining the impact of literacy-enriched play areas (especially ones with meaningful print) found that preschool children who played in such areas spontaneously used almost twice as much print in their play. Consequently, teachers are urged to experiment and creatively design language arts centers and other play centers and monitor the effect of the room and its furnishings on children's language arts skill development. Reutzel and Clark (2011) suggest the first step in creating an effective literacy classroom involves taking an inventory of supplies, furnishings, literacy materials—including the classroom book collection—and the technology available. A rough "to scale" floor plan is then created that pinpoints the important center of an effective literacy classroom: the library/reading/book area.

16-1a Suggestions for Print-Rich Environments ▮naeyc▮

Suggestions for a print-rich classroom are abundant and depend on individual teacher innovation and creativity. Educators can label everything in the classroom that has a connection to current curriculum and post a picture or photo of the daily routine. Other ideas follow.

- Create a message center and classroom news bulletin where children can give and receive a message from teacher and vice versa.

- Create a slogan, caption, question, or new idea for each school day. Print it and talk to children about it and also print child reactions.

- Innovate with individual child tickets or cards bearing children's names that stick to a board or fit in a slot in a play area that accommodates only a certain number of children at any given time.

- Use print and numerals in games or use symbols.

- Have an attendance chart that allows children to take off their names from the chart and place them in a basket as they enter the classroom.

- Use graphing activities with children's names, physical features, or their selected preferences or choices.

- Add print to imaginative or dramatic play areas by monitoring conversation and suggesting labels.

- Highlight the functional use of print in daily classroom life by pointing it out to individuals or groups.

16-2 The Language Arts Center

Full of communication-motivating activities, every inch of floor and wall space of a language arts center is used. Small areas are enlarged by building upward with lofts or bunks to solve floor-space problems in crowded centers (Figure 16-1). Adding areas that children can climb into is another useful space-opening device.

A **language center** has three main functions: (1) it provides looking and listening activities for children, (2) it gives children an area for hands-on experiences with communication-developing materials, and (3) it provides a place to store materials. Barone and Xu (2008) suggest creating an inviting area that easily accommodates five to six children at one time.

Figure 16-1 Solving space problems.

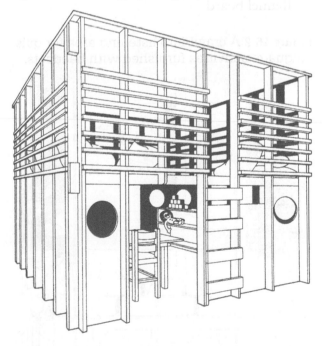

---

language center — a classroom area specifically set aside and equipped for language arts-related activities and child use.

The ideal area has comfortable, soft furnishings with ample work space, proper lighting, and screening to block out other areas of active classrooms. Teachers sometimes make centers cozy and inviting with pillows, a covered crib mattress, or a bean bag chair or two. The area can become a place of refuge for the child who needs to get away from the bustle of the group or the child who wants to interact with friends, and it can be a nice place for the teacher to spend time with children individually.

Language arts centers should be quiet places that are separated from the more vigorous activities of the average playroom. Suggested furnishings are listed by category.

General-Use Materials

one or more child-size tables and chairs

shelving dividers or screens

soft-cushioned rocker, easy chair, or couch

soft pillows

crawl-into hideaways, lined with carpet or fabric (Figure 16-2)

individual work space or study spots

audiovisuals and electrical outlets

book racks that display book covers

chalkboard

whiteboard/smartboard

storage cabinets

flannel board

Figure 16-2 A crawl-into listening area for quiet language activities furnished with headsets.

pocket chart

children's file box (Figure 16-3)

bookcase (Photo 16-1)

bulletin board

carpet, rug, or soft floor covering

chart stand or wall-mounted wing clamps

waste basket

Writing and Prewriting Materials

paper (scratch, lined, newsprint, and typing paper in a variety of sizes)

table

file or index cards

paper storage shelf

writing tools (crayons, nontoxic washable felt markers, and soft pencils in handy contact-covered containers. Additional writing tools include washable and dry erase crayons, markers, and window crayons.)

small, sturdy table or desk

word boxes

picture dictionary

wall-displayed alphabet guides

cutouts of colorful alphabet letters

tabletop chalkboards with chalk

blank book skeletons

scissors

tape

Figure 16-3 Children's work file box.

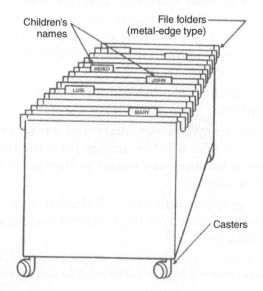

Children's names

File folders (metal-edge type)

HEIKO

JOHN

LUIS

MARY

Casters

Photo 16-1 Bookcases can be used as room area boundaries.

© 2015 Cengage Learning®

erasers

alphabet letter stamps and ink pads

tracing envelopes, patterns, wipe-off cloth

chart paper

magnet board with alphabet letters

hole punch

yarn

write-on, wipe-off boards

stick-on notes

notepads

pencil sharpener

envelopes, baskets, desk trays, and flat boxes

stationery

brass paper fasteners

set of printscript strips with attending children's and staff's names

stickers

glue sticks

stencils

Reading and Prereading Materials

books (including child-made examples)

book and audiovisual combinations (read-a-longs)

cutouts of favorite story characters

rebus story charts

an alphabetized chart of enrolled children's names

catalogs, television guides, and newspaper advertising (Barone & Xu, 2008).

Speech Materials

puppets and puppet theaters

flannel board sets

language games

Audiovisual Equipment

overhead projector

CD/DVD player; headsets; and jacks

story recordings

language master, recording cards

picture files

television screen and VCR/DVD player

computer and printer

video camera

digital camera

iPads, iPods, tablets

Schools with tight budgets are always on the lookout for free or donated books, materials, and furnishings. Quality is still monitored. Most centers try to obtain a wide, rich, and varied selection of titles and genres. Informational and nonfiction titles are sought more aggressively than before.

A school's collection aims to suit the needs of individual children besides the needs of the total group. There should be enough books to rotate them periodically so that something new is always happening in the book area to pique interest.

Adults usually supervise use of **audiovisual equipment** in a language center, and a number of the simpler machines can be operated by children after a brief training period. Tape recorders, CD/DVD players, electronic media, and headsets require careful introduction by the teacher.

16-2a The Teacher's Role in Language Centers

Teachers are congenial, interested companions for the children: sharing books; helping children with projects; recording children's dictation; playing and demonstrating language games; making words, word lists, signs, or charts (Photo 16-2 and Figure 16-4); and helping children use the center's equipment. Teachers slip in and out as needed and monitor equipment use. Vigorous or noisy play is diverted to other room areas or outside yard areas. Children who have been given clear introductions to a language center's materials and clear statements concerning expectations in use of the center's furnishings may need little help. It may be necessary, however, to set rules for the number of children who can use a language center at a given time. The teacher explains new materials that are to become part of the center's collection. Many materials are demonstrated before they are made available to the children.

Posting children's work on the center bulletin board and planning chalkboard activities and printing messages that may catch the children's attention motivate interest in and use of the center. Plants and occasional fresh flowers in vases add a pleasant touch. To help children use equipment, materials, and machines on their own, teachers have become inventive, using step-by-step picture charts posted above or near materials. Color-coded dots make buttons or dials stand out. Some centers control machine use by giving training sessions in which children obtain "licenses." Children without licenses need to have adult companions.

Another task the teacher may want to undertake is making read-along recordings to accompany favorite books. The popularity of

Photo 16-2 Stickers, words, or children's work may be added to charts.

---

audiovisual equipment — any mechanical or nonmechanical item useful in offering sight or hearing experience.

Figure 16-4 Language center chart.

Hurt no living thing:
Ladybug nor butterfly,
Nor moth with dusty wing,
Nor cricket chirping cheerily
Nor grasshopper
   so light of leap,
Nor dancing gnat,
Nor beetle fat,
Nor harmless worms
   that creep.

read-alongs cannot be denied, nor can the educational benefits. Children who use read-alongs are learning word recognition as well as some of the more advanced reading skills. For fun and pleasure, the lure of read-alongs makes them another gateway into the world of books. Teachers should consider the following when making recordings:

- A narrator's pacing is important. It cannot be too fast, or the child trying to follow along will be lost. If it is too slow, the child will become bored.

- The inflection and tone of the voice are also vital. The narrator cannot be condescending or patronizing; neither should there be an attempt to "act out" the story and run the risk of making the story secondary to the performance.

Besides these factors, a teacher needs to estimate audience attention span and use a pleasant page-turning signal. With story recordings, either on tape or CD (with or without a story visual), the child may be a passive listener or can be an active, responsive participant. Some commercial manufacturers and teachers have cleverly designed interactive features, but these, though enjoyable and educational, cannot match what is possible with a "live" book reading and are a second-best activity

16-2b Housekeeping and Block Areas

Educators emphasize the importance of housekeeping and block areas, both of which encourage large amounts of social interaction and the use of more mature, complex language. High levels of dramatic play interaction are also encouraged in theme (unit) centers. Teachers design spacious, well-defined, well-stocked (theme-related) partitioned room areas for block play and dramatic play.

16-2c Display and Bulletin Boards

Interesting eye-level wall and bulletin board displays capture the children's attention and promote discussion. Displaying children's work (with children's permission), names, and themes based on their interests increases their feelings of accomplishment and their senses of pride in their classroom. Displays that involve active child participation are suggested. Many can be designed to change daily or weekly.

Printscript is used on bulletin boards with objects, pictures, or patterns. Book pockets, picture hooks, one-quarter-inch elastic attached to clothespins, and sticky bulletin board strips allow pieces to be added and removed. Figure 16-5 shows one bulletin board idea. The child selects a spot to paste her picture (photo) and name. A colored line is drawn between the photo and name. Later, colored lines can be drawn, connecting friends' pictures.

Using classroom walls to teach is an old educational technique. Roskos and Neuman (2013) urge purposeful use of wall space, including displaying aspects of a story the children experience during a read-aloud. Many teachers have found when making displays with teachers and children working together to co-produce the display, it grabs more child attention. Clear and uncluttered displays with a printed sign, title, or

Figure 16-5 Bulletin board ideas.

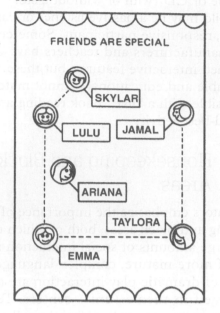

label added along with interesting graphics can stretch the display's educational value.

16-2d Chalkboard or White Board Activities

One of the most underutilized instructional items in early childhood centers can be the chalkboard or white board. The following chalkboard activities are suggested to help children's language development.

Tracing Templates and Colored Chalk. Using a sharp tool, cut large plastic coffee can lids into a variety of patterns (Figure 16-6). Suspend the patterns on cord or elastic with clothespins over the chalkboard.

Pattern Games. Draw Figure 16-7 on the chalkboard. Ask the children what shape comes next in the pattern. Then draw Figure 16-8 and see whether the children can make a line path from the dog to the doghouse.

Figure 16-6 Plastic lid chalkboard activities.

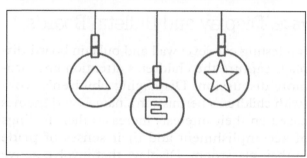

16-3 Audiovisual Equipment

Budgets often determine the availability of electronic items and materials in an early childhood center. Care of equipment and awareness of operating procedures are important. Special

Figure 16-7 What comes next in the pattern?

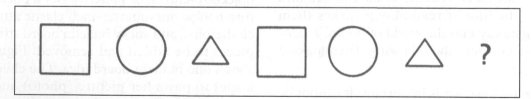

Figure 16-8 A left-to-right skill builder.

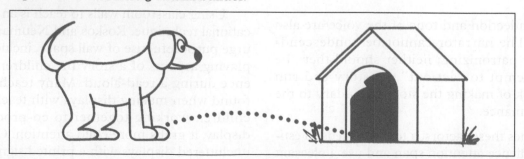

fundraising projects, rental agreements, borrowing arrangements, or donations have secured audiovisuals for some programs. The machine's or item's instruction manual should be studied for the proper care and maintenance necessary for efficient use.

The following audiovisual equipment enriches a center's language arts program activities.

- *Camera* (including cell phones and video cameras). A camera can be used to provide images and photos that are useful in speaking activities, displays, and games.
- *Projector and Screens.* Common home, school, field trip, and community scenes can be discussed, written about (experience stories), or used for storytelling.
- *Lite-bord™.* This is a special display board that uses nontoxic erasable crayons for making colorful drawings and words that glow.
- *Video Cameras.* Children enjoy being recorded while displaying and explaining their creations. It has multiple uses.
- *Overhead Projectors, Screens, and Transparencies.* Stories with silhouettes or numerous transparency activities can be designed. Small patterns and alphabet letters can be enlarged and copied by teachers for a variety of uses. A number of teachers have used drawings or have placed images on the screen while storytelling or reading poetry (for example, using a "Humpty Dumpty" picture sequence while reciting the rhyme). Meier (2004) recommends supplying children with overhead projector sheets, or other kinds of plastic sheets, so that they can project their images and words onto a large screen. Some, but not all, picture books work well with this instructional technique. If text and illustration appear on the same page, this type of sharing is recommended. Teachers may have access to equipment used to make transparencies. The author strongly recommends this type of alternative storybook reading. Illustrations can be enlarged and enjoyed. Text appears giant-sized.
- *Opaque Projector.* Pages of picture books can be projected on wall areas to offer a new way to read books. Guessing games are also possible. Characters from picture books can become life-size companions.

16-3a Listening Center Equipment

The following equipment is useful for the center's **listening center.**

- *Headsets and Jack Boxes.* Accommodating up to eight children at one time, they adapt to cassette and CD players. Volume control is set on the jack box.
- *CD Players.* Most centers have this piece of equipment. Commercial suppliers of story CDs are plentiful.
- *Digital Camera.* Classroom photographs can be displayed on the computer, and prints can be made for display. Photo printers are available from many manufacturers.
- *Digital Camcorder.* Classroom action photography can be displayed on television sets and computers, or prints can be made.
- *Pocket Wall Charts with Stands.* This handy teacher's aid displays alphabet letters, words, sentences, shapes, pictures, colors, names, and so on. It is easy to use. Teachers prefer see-through pocket styles. These can be teacher-made.
- *Big Book Storage Rack.* See-through individual hanging bags can be used for big books and oversized materials; this visual solves the problem of storing large items.
- *Write and Wipe Boards and Easels.* Colored markers glide on and wipe off quickly. They are useful for teacher activities or child use. They are made in free-standing or tabletop styles, and some are magnetic, so plastic alphabet letters and numerals with magnets will stick.
- *Computer.* Besides computer use with software programs and use as a word processor, the computer has become a versatile piece of equipment.
- *Tape Recorders.* This is still a popular audiovisual aid that is used in early childhood centers. The tape recorder opens up many activity ideas. Suggestions for language development activities with tape recorders follow.
- Record children's comments about their artwork or project. "Tell me about . . ." is a good starter. Put the tape and artwork together in the language center so that it is available for the children's use.

---

listening center — a classroom area designed to accommodate children's listening experiences.

- Let the children record their comments about a group of plastic cars, human figures, animals, and so on, after they arrange them as they wish.

- Have children discuss photographs or magazine pictures.

- Record a child's comments about a piece of fruit that she has selected from a basket of mixed fruit.

- Record a "reporter's" account of a recent field trip.

- Gather a group of common items, such as a mirror, comb, brush, and toothbrush. Let the child describe how these items are used.

- Record a child's description of peeling an orange or making a sandwich with common spreads and fillings.

- Record a child's comments about her block structures. Take a photo and make both tape and photo available in the listening and looking area.

- *Television Sets and VCRs/DVD players.* Children's classic literature is available. Active teacher–child discussion of what is viewed is recommended.

- *Discussion or Study Prints.* A collection of large posters, photographs, mounted magazine pictures, and life-size book characters can be used in activities. Visuals can increase child verbalization and serve as creative "jumping off" spots.

16-3b The Use of Picture Files

Picture files consisting of collections of drawings and photographs are made available to children in classroom language centers. Teachers find that they are invaluable motivators for many language-related child activities. Some of the most puzzling and outlandish images can get the most attention and discussion. Magazine photos and photos showing classroom scenes or attending children are popular with children. Images can be rotated and used to supplement a present course of study. Think about creating categories such as animals or fire engines and so on.

It is a good idea to start with enlarged photographs of each child and staff (affix to a firm backing). Resources for pictures include coloring books, shape books, inexpensive children's books, calendars, catalogs, trade journals, travel folders, and toy advertisements.

Suggested activities include:

- writing captions.
- storytelling from a series of pictures.
- giving names to animal pictures.
- finding hidden objects.
- categorizing pictures.
- finding objects that have alphabet letters printed on them.
- putting illustrations in a sequence and telling a story.
- matching pictures with related objects.
- finding alphabet letters in signs.
- identifying logos or outdoor signs from familiar fast-food restaurants or other local businesses.
- singing or creating a song to go with a picture.
- rhyming with pictures.
- finding things of the same shape, color, and category.
- classifying pictures by season.
- making a sound to fit a picture.
- writing a letter to someone shown in a picture.
- finding an object in the classroom that looks like something in a picture.
- choosing a favorite from a picture collection of food or other objects.
- labeling everything in a picture.
- finding things that start with the same alphabet letter sound.
- making an alphabet book as a group project or promoting each child's creation of an individual alphabet book.

A special column in NAEYC's *Young Children* reports on early childhood classrooms that are trying to integrate technology into their learning program. Following are described language arts ideas and suggestions for teachers interested in bookmaking activities.

- Create multimedia bookmaking centers.
- Promote child authored and illustrated books with scanned images of children's drawings combined with audio files of child storytelling.
- Use computer printouts of stories typed by teacher from children's dictation.

- Help children create blended stories featuring a combination of child-written text and dictated text with printed digital photographs taken by the child (NAEYC, 2008)

16-3c Technology, Electronic Equipment, and Literacy Learning naeyc

What do early childhood educators believe concerning the use of technology? Most will agree that machines, whether computers, audiovisuals, or other technology, can teach, support, assist, motivate, and be used for the practice and application of literacy skills. Technology cannot "be the teacher of literacy," but it can be a useful tool in assessing and tracking children's literacy skill development.

Following the recommendations of the American Academy of Pediatrics (2011) is a prudent course of action. After two years of age, screen time with all digital media that includes television, computer, handheld devices, or tablets, electronic games, or other digital screen devices, should be limited to brief periods and no more than about an hour per day for older preschoolers. These devices should also be mainly enjoyed with adult interaction (AAP, 2011). Screen time is defined as the total amount of time spent in front of any and all types of screens (Common Sense Media, 2011). Besides the television screen children may now have a growing body of screens to watch and interact with including computers, tablets, smart phones, handheld gaming devices, portable video players, digital cameras, video recordings and other new evolving technical devices.

If digital media are used with a preschool group, its cost and necessary staff time calls for both a generous budget and an analysis of its educational value. The amount of time spent by teachers in media program screening needs to be factored into the calculations. Surveying families will be important in determining an average of home screen time for enrolled children.

New products are building in features that encourage children's group play (e.g., Nintendo) and other features such as co-viewing. Websites such as Common Sense Media help families examine ratings of children's program titles. In early childhood classrooms, technology best fulfills its potential under certain conditions. These include an adult close by and available, and the teacher interacting professionally in a developmentally appropriate fashion. A school should also offer peer-to-peer learning opportunities for collaboration with comfortable settings. When working with children using technology, the teacher should have an opportunity to make comments that link program content to current classroom study. The setting of limits and rules when necessary will also be a teacher's chore.

One of a school's goals for children's technology use is increasing children's ability to work independently and confidently. It has become a tremendous challenge for early childhood educators to keep up with the growing number of digital tools, devices, and internet resources that may be used for language instruction. Early educators are aware that a recognizable shift from the printed word on a page to multiple modes of image, sound, movement, and text on a screen is a reality in today's society.

Carlsson-Paige (2012) points out that many companies that market electronic products claim they are educational, but research does not support their claims. She suggests additional research, including longitudinal studies, is needed to evaluate the impact of media and technology on young children's development. It is her belief that current research raises serious concerns and teachers should exercise caution concerning the use of screen technology.

A joint position statement of the National Association for the Education of Young Children and the Fred Rogers Center for Early Learning and Children's Media at St. Vincent College (2012) points out that early childhood educators need training, professional development opportunities, and examples of successful practice to develop the technology and media knowledge, skills, and experience that is needed to use technology and integrate it effectively into a preschool curriculum that is also developmentally appropriate. See the list of websites at the end of this chapter.

16-3d E-books

Families may consult early childhood educators for advice concerning e-books. Hsu (2011) notes e-book publishers are creating electronic picture books with illustrations that compromise the book's color and format. Some of the over 300 children's published e-book versions have a read-along component, sound effects, simple animations, games, and other features. Hsu suggests quality varies dramatically, so it is wise to preview e-books before purchasing them. An iPad app for young children is also available for some e-books. E-books are not recommended as substitutes for family book sharing times, but rather as a once-in-a while experience.

Teachers may field questions about game playing on electronic devises when families comment on the trancelike behavior they observe in their children or the whining and tantrums that can ensue after a game ends or parents limit use. Worthen (2012) reports that some iPad apps for children are designed to stimulate dopamine release in the brain. This encourages a child to keep playing. Some games offer rewards or exciting visuals so a child's feelings of withdrawal are bound to happen. Since game playing can be categorized as entertainment rather than an educational pursuit, and with contradictory research, teacher advice to families would be that there is no consensus concerning the value or negative effects of gaming for young children at the present time.

16-3e Technology and Dual Language Learners

The following are activity ideas for using existing classroom technology when working with dual language learners.

- Make books or games that contain key words in the children's home language. Translation programs are often available on tablets and smart phones.

- Make a class book with digital photos of the classroom's children and staff that parents or volunteers can translate into children's home languages.

- Download authentic music, rhythms, finger plays, and stories from diverse cultural groups.

- Research the internet to find images that are familiar to attending children and use these in various ways to promote conversations or to create additional child focus during learning activities.

16-4 Planning Language Centers and Computer Centers

Once rooms or areas are designated as language centers, staff members classify materials into "looking and listening" or "working with" categories (Photo 16-3). Display, storage, working space, and looking and listening areas are determined. Activities that require concentration are screened off when possible. Many different arrangements of materials and equipment within a language arts center are possible. Most centers rearrange furnishings until the most functional arrangement is found, but educators always have in mind the goal of having children grasp the interrelatedness of speaking, listening, reading, and writing. For sample arrangements with different functions, refer to Figure 16-9.

Many children like to escape noise with a favorite book or puppet. Most centers provide these quiet retreats within a language arts center.

Photo 16-3 Writing tools are always found in classroom language centers.

Writing utensils

© 2015 Cengage Learning®

Figure 16-9 Language arts center.

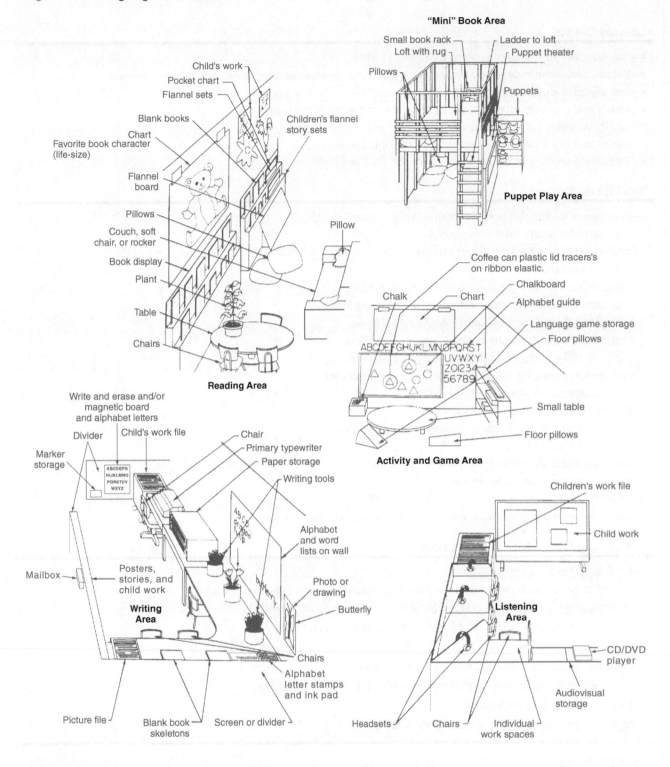

School staffs have found creative ways of providing private space. Old footed bathtubs with soft pillows, packing crates and barrels, pillow-lined closets with doors removed, tepees, tents, and screened-off couches and armchairs have been found workable in some classroom language arts areas. See Figure 16-10 for additional tips concerning creating a reading/library/book center.

With the fears mentioned earlier in this text concerning the overuse of television and videos, some educators see computer programs as offering a "cartoon world" rather than the real experiences and human interactions upon which real knowledge and literacy depends. Early childhood educators realize that computer skills and knowledge may be necessary in elementary school

Figure 16-10 Checklist for evaluating and improving the literacy environment.

Literacy Center

— manipulatives (roll movie or puppets with related books)

— children participate in designing the center (develop rules, select a name for center, and develop materials)

— area placed in a quiet section of the room

— visually and physically accessible, yet partitioned from the rest of the room

— rug, throw pillows, rocking chair, bean bag chair, and stuffed animals

— private spot in the corner, such as a box to crawl into and read

— the center uses 10% of the classroom space and fits 5 or 6 children

The Library Corner

— bookshelves for storing books with spines facing outward

— organizational system for shelving books

— open-faced bookshelves for featured books

— 5-8 books per child

— books represent 3 to 4 grade levels of the following types:

   (a) picture books, (b) picture storybooks, (c) traditional literature,

   (d) poetry, (e) realistic literature, (f) informational books,

   (g) biographies, (h) chapter books, (i) easy to read books,

   (j) riddle/joke books, (k) participation books, (l) series books,

   (m) textless books, (n) television-related books, (o) brochures,

   (p) magazines, (q) newspapers

— 20 new books circulated every 2 weeks

— check-out/check-in system for children to take out books daily

— headsets and taped stories

— felt board and story characters with the related books

— materials for constructing felt stories

— other story manipulatives

— system for recording books read (e.g., cards hooked onto a bulletin board)

The Writing Center (The Author's Spot)

— tables and chairs

— writing posters and a bulletin board for children to display their writing by themselves

— writing utensils (pens, pencils, crayons, felt-tipped markers, colored pencils)

— writing materials (many varieties of paper in all sizes, booklets, and pads)

— typewriter or computer

— materials for writing stories and making them into books

— a message board for children to post messages for the teacher and students

— a place to store "Very Own Words"

— folders for children to place samples of their writing

Digital Downloa

grades; however, they may be unsure about the best time to introduce them to young children.

Slowly but steadily, computer centers are becoming standard in three- and four-year-olds' preschool classrooms. Staffing, expense, and time for teacher preview of programs are important considerations. Many educators agree that computer centers are compatible with developmentally appropriate practice. Computers can offer problem-solving, creative experiences, and literacy opportunities. Benefits cited by many early childhood advocates of child computer use include child cooperation and turn taking and minimum need for supervision

Photo 16-4 One peer can often instruct another.

© 2016 Cengage Learning®

after child training on mechanics. Children can work at their own speed, and collaborate, mentor each other, negotiate, and problem solve alone or with a peer. The experience can build children's self-confidence and also feelings of independence.

Additional benefits children may experience when computers become part of classroom life that are related to language arts skills and development include children's:

- verbal interactions with a peer partner or others (Photo 16-4).

- experiences with alphabet letters, print, and words.

- ability to see uses of print, which include recording, informing, sending, and receiving messages.

- opportunity to create literary works that then can be recorded.

- experience in making greeting cards.

- exposure to rhyme.

- opportunity to match letters, patterns, rhymes, and words with pictorial representations.

- exposure to visual and interactive storybooks.

Teachers with computers in their classrooms will agree that it is appropriate to step in when children are frustrated or lack necessary user skills. They tend to offer minimal help if they believe that the child can work out a problem on her own, thereby allowing the child to experience mastery and the resulting feeling of accomplishment. Most teachers periodically join children at the computer to ask questions or make comments that encourage the expansion of skill.

Some educators are concerned about the fact that some elementary school children and adolescents have displayed obsessive and addictive behaviors, and have indulged in computer video game overuse. Some "gamers" have less social contact with peers and less interest in reading, which affects their school performance. Research on preschoolers' use of video games, handheld games, or similar recreational media is scarce and yet to be probed in a national study.

Technology in the classroom is a tool purchased to benefit children's education, but many believe that there may be hidden side effects. Technology can be used as an aid for instructional activities, child assessment, the storing or compiling of data, word processing, research, communication, or some other teaching or professional function. Whether digital or electronic, it cannot replace young children's real firsthand contact with the environment and human interaction. Scarce research suggests its use is beneficial for children less than three years of age. There is controversy about (1) the amount of time young children spend in front of screen media; (2) its value; (3) its possible power to affect children's brains; (4) its presentation of violence; and (5) early childhood educators' ability to recognize

TeachSource Video 16-1

Preschool: Appropriate Learning Environments and Room Arrangements

1. The computer center seemed to receive no child attention in the video with no children using or approaching it; what might have made it more appealing and inviting?

2. When the classroom was rearranged, the computer center had a few more positive features; can you identify one or more? Any less than desirable ones?

3. Could you suggest a better placement of the computers in this classroom?

inappropriate practice and identify questionable content. Many educators would rather err on the side of caution. They realize technology is definitely here to stay and already available in many children's homes. How many hours young children spend with it each day and what type of digital or electronic items they use becomes necessary information to secure from families.

Early childhood centers develop simple computer area rules that are appropriate to their classroom, children, and equipment. Rules usually involve clean hands, number of children allowed at one time, how to ask for help, taking turns, time allowed per turn, use of earphones, and what training is required before use.

Research seems to suggest that three- and four-year-old children who use computer programs that support and reinforce the major

objectives of their curricula have significantly greater developmental gains when compared with children who have not had computer experiences in similar classrooms. Among the gain areas researched were nonverbal skills, verbal skills, problem-solving, and conceptual skills.

Interestingly, computer program use has been found to improve the speech skills of children with dyslexia and other language-based learning disabilities. Researchers noted that language comprehension improved to normal, near-normal, or above normal in children who had been two to three years behind peers in speech skills. The findings are especially encouraging for children who have difficulty learning to talk (developmental dysphasia) or who have subsequent reading problems (developmental dyslexia). For preschool classrooms, educators recommend an initial training period; turn taking, cooperative learning in small groups, peer tutoring, hands-on experience, waiting lists, and a sufficient number of adults who make an "adult time" investment. **Software** variety should also be offered.

16-4a Software Selection

Developmentally appropriate integration begins with selecting hardware and **software** that will complement goals. The following is a list of software characteristics to check and consider.

- does not include violence
- provides positive verbal and visual cues and responses (feedback)
- allows the child to control pace and action
- allows the option of practicing a skill or moving on
- supports working alone or with others

When teachers provide open-ended software that encourages creativity, rather than drill-and-practice software, this is developmentally appropriate. Open-ended programs encourage children to explore and to extend their thinking. They spark children's interest as well as social and cognitive development. Other software features teachers need to examine include content, age appropriateness, pacing, child choices available, meaningful graphics and sound, clear directions for yet-to-read children, approaches to

---

software — a wide range of commercial programs developed for computer users' convenience, education, entertainment, and so on.

learning, and appropriate cost. The Children's Technology Review website is a good resource for help with evaluating technology products.

The integrity and craftsmanship in a software program determines its effectiveness and quality. Four critical steps to maximize children's learning through computer use follow.

1. selecting developmental software
2. selecting developmental websites
3. integrating these resources into the curriculum
4. selecting computers to support these learning experiences

Websites also may offer many rich educational opportunities and provide opportunities that appear to enhance problem solving, critical thinking skills, decision making, language skills, knowledge, research skills, the ability to integrate information, social skills, and self-esteem.

Reading Area Software Programs and Commercial Preschool Software. Medina (2008) reviewed a research program that combined a standard school reading class program and an individualized software program that analyzed a student's reading competencies and provided tailored exercises to strengthen reading deficiencies. In conjunction with the class, the software was wildly successful. The reading class experience alone or the software alone was not as effective (p. 68). Commercial preschool language development programs are plentiful. To find out whether software is effective or not, early childhood teachers will need to do their own classroom research while remembering every child's brain is individually wired. What promotes growth in one child may not in another.

16-4b Computer Location

The ideal classroom location for computers is a visible location where monitors can be seen throughout the classroom. This setting enables supervision and quick assistance. A computer center or activity area in a preschool or kindergarten classroom usually operates well with two or three computers and one or two printers.

Summary

16-1 List three suggestions for creating a print-rich classroom.

In creating a classroom with plentiful print present, many suggestions are recommended. These include creating classroom areas and settings that attract children and are challenging, motivating, build communication skills, encourage language use, are planned in accordance with the schools' language and literacy goals, allow for child-chosen activities, and are physically and emotionally comfortable areas that suit the needs of individual students and also culturally diverse ones. Specific print materials and language-related items recommended for the classroom include books, photographs, household items that are intended to strengthen children's individual cultural background and identity and also promote literacy. Print examples are encouraged for most room areas and are to be displayed on walls, tables, and other places. Displays featuring words, alphabet letters, printed signs and labels, and other symbols are recommended. Specific ideas mentioned are creating classroom message centers, using printed slogans and questions, developing games with printed words or symbols, creating name charts, using graphing materials and activities, and encouraging dramatic play with associated print or printing ideas. Educators are urged to highlight the functional use of print throughout the school day as they encounter print in the school environment.

16-2 Describe the teacher's role in a language arts room center.

A teacher's role (responsibilities) in a language arts room center includes providing language developing, looking and listening opportunities for children and also the necessary language and literacy items and materials to do so. The teacher's role also includes providing for hands-on experiences with communication-developing materials, furnishings, and equipment, making the language arts area comfortable, and providing for quiet rather than vigorous play activities. Teachers act as responsive companions and resources and may slip in and out of language centers to allow children privacy when teachers deem this best. They also monitor equipment use and children's need for assistance, and set rule expectations for area use when appropriate. A teacher may demonstrate new material use, give training sessions, introduce new books or other printed material, and provide operational help with equipment. Posting children's work, adding aesthetic touches, creating charts and other eye level displays of print, and creating educational media if necessary are also described as appropriate.

16-3 Discuss children's use of technology in a preschool classroom.

A wide variety of both digital and analog technology is available for use with young children. Educators are attempting to integrate developmentally appropriate and educationally sound content in a way that promotes young children's language growth and development in an enriching manner. Technology is seen as a useful tool requiring educator screening and evaluation. It can offer children an opportunity to practice and apply literacy skills, but it is not deemed appropriate for use with children less than two years of age. Educators are concerned with children's screen time and the need to professionally judge content value since research has raised serious concerns. Early childhood teachers are encouraged to gain additional training and knowledge so they can effectively use technology to young children's advantage.

16-4 Describe a good location for a computer center and what it should contain.

The functional arrangement of a computer center and its materials, software, and equipment is considered along with children's need to concentrate. A computer center is usually placed in a quiet screened off and "little trafficked" room area that also allows for teacher monitoring. The ease of child viewing and listening and children's comfort is given attention as is adequate lighting and seating. Display, storage, and working space is provided. Usually two or three computers and printers are suggested, along with display areas holding visual aids to machine use.

Additional Resources

Readings

Good, I. (2009). *Teaching and Learning with Digital Photography: Tips and Tools for Early Childhood Classrooms.* Thousand Oaks, CA: Corwin Press.

McManis, J. D. & Gunnewig, S. B. (2012). Finding the education in educational technology with early learners. *Young Children* 67(3), 14–24.

Puerling, B. (2012). *Teaching in the Digital Age: Smart Tools for Age 3 to Grade 3.* St. Paul, MN: Redleaf.

Schiller, P., & Willis, C. A. (2008, July). Using brain-based teaching strategies to create supportive early childhood environments that address learning standards. *Young Children* 63(4) 52–55.

Helpful Websites

NAEYC Technology & Young Children

http://www.techandyoungchildren.org

A special interest and discussion forum.

American Academy of Pediatrics

http://pediatrics.aappublications.org

Policy statements concerning media use for under two-year-olds.

TRUCE—Teachers Resisting Unhealthy Children's Media

http://www.truceteachers.org

Offers a guide, *What Do We Know About Children and Electronic Media?* It covers excessive screen time, viewing habits, talking to parents, and other links to explore.

NAEYC

http://www.naeyc.org/

Search files for a joint position statement with Fred Rogers Center for Early Learning and the Media Center at Saint Vincent College.

17 The Family-Center Partnership

Objectives

After reading this chapter, you should be able to:

17-1 Describe how programs and child centers build family–school partnerships.

17-2 List language art skills schools attempt to increase by working through families.

17-3 Describe a school's home visiting goals.

17-4 Name and describe two strategies used to facilitate family–school communication.

17-5 Discuss three ways families and volunteers might become resources for child language instruction.

naeyc NAEYC Program Standards

7A03 Program staff actively use information about families to adapt program environment, curriculum, and teacher methods.

7A05 Program staff provides support and information to family members legally responsible for the care and well-being of the child.

7A12 The program facilitates opportunities for families to meet with one another on projects to support the program and learn from and provide support for each other.

7.8.01 Program staff use a variety of mechanisms such as family conferences and home visits to provide dialogue with families.

DAP Developmentally Appropriate Practice (DAP) Preschoolers

5.1 Teachers actively work to create a partnership with each family, communicating regularly to build mutual understanding and trust and to ensure that children's learning and developmental needs are met.

5.2 Teachers and parents work together in making decisions about how best to support children's development and learning.

5.4 With parents who do not speak English, teachers/administrators seek strategies to facilitate communication.

The Power of Persistence

At pick-up time, when Martin's mother arrived, Mei Lin, Martin's teacher, observed a behavior she had not previously seen in Martin. Martin immediately started what Mei Lin would describe as vocal badgering. His verbal assault included a steady stream of, "But you promised . . . , I want one . . . , You said so . . . , I didn't have one yesterday . . . , I want it . . . , You told me I could . . . , I'm ready . . . , Let's go." His voice got louder and louder and didn't stop when his mother attempted to talk to Mei Lin. It continued as Martin and his mother exited to the porch. Mei Lin then heard Martin's mother say, "All right. We'll go to McDonalds!"

Questions to Ponder

1. What is happening here?

2. Should Mei Lin discuss the situation with Martin's mother? Why or why not?

3. Does this have anything to do with language development?

4. Is there anything positive about Martin's way with words?

17-1 Families and Child Literacy

Although families and teachers are partners in a child's education, a family is a child's foremost teacher and model, and the home is a child's first and most influential school (Photo 17-1). Many families are eager consumers of information about what is best for their offspring. Six in ten parents read books about parenting or early childhood development before their children were born and about 32 percent took classes for new parents.

Families are usually informed of the school's language and literacy curriculum during enrollment interviews. Most families want to find out how teachers interact with their children on a daily basis to realize their instructional goals. Educators find that some families will ask for advice concerning what to do in terms of their children's education and are vulnerable as a result. It is suggested that anxious families need reassurance and can be encouraged to trust their instincts.

Early childhood teachers can enhance their ability to work with the families of children in their classrooms. They should not make assumptions about a family's parenting practices. Within any cultural group—be it ethnic, racial, **socioeconomic**, or religious—individuals and

Photo 17-1 The child's foremost teachers and educators are the child's parents and family.

© 2015 Cengage Learning®

---

socioeconomic — relating to or involving a combination of social and economic factors.

families vary in their beliefs and adherence to the social conventions of their community.

Significant changes in family structure have occurred. More than 25 percent of all children and more than 55 percent of African-American children are living with an unmarried parent. Whatever family type exists, the family should be viewed by educators as having knowledge on a wide range of topics that might be accessed by schools and educators. Family members are experts concerning how the home supports their child's emerging literacy. Questions teachers ask during initial and later meetings and interviews can gather valuable information concerning family literacy goals and practices, home conversations with children, home literacy settings and materials—including books and other publications, and their children's particular preferences and developing interests. Information gathered can influence the classroom library book selection as well as individual and group instructional planning.

Early childhood teachers and centers examine a wide range of strategies to enhance their relationships with families. Researchers urge educators to consider a family-by-family approach. When reaching out to families, teachers are likely to find that intra-group differences may be as great as inter-group differences. Efforts could include hiring bicultural and bilingual staff to increase a program's ability to communicate and create trust. Trust, once established, can evolve into a collaborative partnership. This requires that teachers and their school administrators and enrolled families expend efforts to successfully communicate regularly with each other in a constructive manner—demonstrating mutual regard. School goals include learning from parents and families in discussions rather than primarily offering information.

Child literacy at home and school is influenced by three important factors: (1) setting, (2) models, and (3) planned and unplanned events. The setting involves what the home or school provides or makes available, including furnishings, space, materials and supplies, toys, books, and so forth. Family "connectedness" is crucial. Interactions with parents, siblings, grandparents, and other relatives enrich children's lives. Sharing hobbies, trips, chores,

mealtimes, community and neighborhood happenings, conversations, and stories are all language-development opportunities. Access to additional settings outside the home is also considered. Time allowed or spent in community settings can increase or decrease literacy.

Preschools planning to maintain the continued literacy development of attending children must face the fact that a home's low socioeconomic status often affects their children's literacy growth. Au (2006) notes that poverty appears to be the factor most highly associated with poor reading achievement in elementary school. Middle-class families usually offer their children the advantage of more home book reading, more library visits, and more print-related experiences. Families with low educational aspirations for their children and low motivation, which sometimes results from poverty, stress, fatigue, and other unfortunate living conditions, are the families who most need sensitive professional **outreach** from their children's teacher and school.

Family economics may determine the opportunities and materials that are available, but family ingenuity and know-how may overcome a lack of monetary resources. Most things that families can do to encourage reading and writing involve time, attention, and sensitivity, rather than money. All families can be instrumental in fostering literacy if they spend time doing so. The usefulness of speaking, writing, and reading can be emphasized in any home. Children's literature may be borrowed from public libraries and other sources in almost all communities.

Although preschools are not as programmed as elementary schools and much of the learning in preschools goes hand-in-hand with first-hand exploration, families still have a big edge over group programs in offering intimate, individualized adult—child learning opportunities. Family interactions during activities involve both the quality and quantity of communication (Photo 17-2). The supportive assistance given at home, the atmosphere of the home, family-child conversations, and joint ventures can greatly affect the child's literacy development. Educators take every opportunity in everyday conversations and in planned meetings to help families know how to turn ordinary home occurrences

---

outreach — an early childhood program's attempt to provide supportive assistance to attending children's families to promote their children's success in school and developmental growth.

Photo 17-2 Frequently, a family wants information concerning when to start book sharing with their children.

© 2015 Cengage Learning®

into young children's learning experiences. Trish Meegan (2009) has voiced what every teacher knows in her heart—"If we can't involve parents (families) in schools, then we do little to really impact the children we teach."

Successful families listen to what children say and respond to them. They interpret the child's language attempts and reply with related action accompanied by words and sentences. Learning is enhanced where children are supported by caring adults who share their world with them and enter into the children's worlds of play and talk, tuning in to their feelings and experiences. The essential element is the intimacy between child and the people in his life who share a common environment; this fosters the understanding of meanings and child curiosity.

Children who find their efforts and attempts at language received and valued develop the confidence to continue. Children's learning flourishes when they are allowed some degree of control over their own actions and when they interact with adults who are receptive, less concerned with the correctness of child speech, and more likely to respond in ways that stretch thinking. **DAP**

Early childhood centers design their own unique family involvement programs. With increased federal and state emphasis on early childhood educators' working jointly with parents and

families, educators working in publicly funded programs will need to clarify their goals and analyze their efforts. Most educators would agree any involvement must start with the development of a trusting relationship (Figure 17-1). NAEYC's Engaging Diverse Families (EDF) Project (2010) has researched and identified the family engagement practices of high-quality early childhood programs. They follow.

- Encourage family participation in decision making. (Programs have Boards of Directors with family representation, active committees, and regular parent–teacher conferences that encourage shared decision making concerning the program and individual children.)

- Facilitate consistent, two-way communication. (Programs communicate with families through the use of multiple formats and in the families' preferred language.)

- Seek out information about families' lifestyle and community and integrate this information into their curriculum. (Programs welcome family talents, interests, or family traditions into the classroom.)

- Support families' efforts to create home environments that value learning by connecting families with information and activities that enhance early learning. Announcements of community events, lending libraries, and

Figure 17-1 Parent involvement goals.

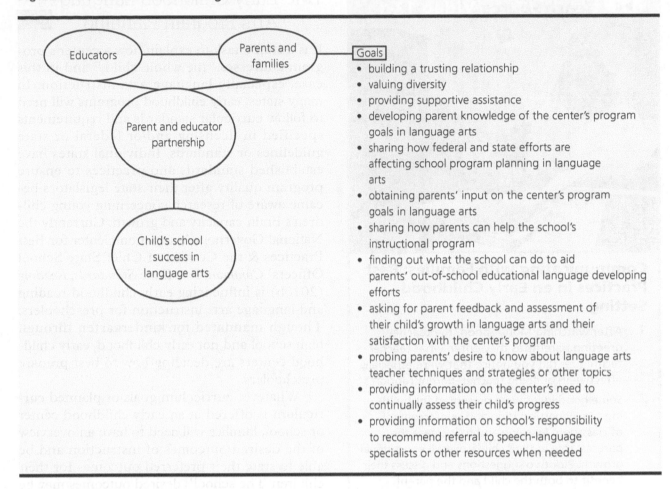

- **Educators** — **Parents and families**
- **Parent and educator partnership**
- **Child's school success in language arts**

Goals
- building a trusting relationship
- valuing diversity
- providing supportive assistance
- developing parent knowledge of the center's program goals in language arts
- sharing how federal and state efforts are affecting school program planning in language arts
- obtaining parents' input on the center's program goals in language arts
- sharing how parents can help the school's instructional program
- finding out what the school can do to aid parents' out-of-school educational language developing efforts
- asking for parent feedback and assessment of their child's growth in language arts and their satisfaction with the center's program
- probing parents' desire to know about language arts teacher techniques and strategies or other topics
- providing information on the center's need to continually assess their child's progress
- providing information on school's responsibility to recommend referral to speech-language specialists or other resources when needed

newsletter tips about child development are examples of how programs can extend the learning beyond the classroom.

- Develop a program supporting staff leadership and support dedicated and trained teachers in their efforts to reach out to and include families. (p. 8)

17-1a Developing Trust

Developing trust grows from family feelings of being respected, accepted, and valued for their individual and cultural diversity, and it also grows when staff members are sensitive to family economics. Educators need to be aware of what families' desire for their children. All of this starts the day family members walk through the school's door. What is on the walls and how they are welcomed and treated by staff are important. This calls for a consideration of comfort and requires staff preparation and planning. A clearly-labeled school entrance and an open classroom door should guide families on children's first day. Ideally, an adult who speaks their home language greets them or is immediately available. A welcoming letter should have reached homes beforehand that included a statement concerning whether a family member is welcome to stay if their child seems to need this, and also whether families are able to visit the classroom before opening session begins. Truly thoughtful administrators/teachers know if printed signs directing families to the school's office or classroom are necessary in parking areas and whether signs should be printed in more than one language.

17-1b Identifying Supportive Assistance

Identifying exactly what a center can offer in supportive assistance is a necessary task. A school's list can be long or short depending

TeachSource Video 17-1

Communicating with Families: Best Practices in an Early Childhood Setting

1. After watching Mona Sanon, the teacher greeting parents as they enter, what teacher techniques did you notice that were especially effective in building teacher–parent rapport?

2. Some good ideas were presented for building family participation and reinforcement of classroom learning and to increase the parents' role in their child's overall educational growth. Pick two suggestions and discuss their benefit to both the child and the parent.

3. "Make yourself available" was suggested to teachers. Does this in any way make you feel uneasy—or it's opposite—comfortable? Discuss this by writing a short paragraph or two.

17-1c Early Childhood Language Arts Program Planning **DAP**

It is a staff's task to explain how a center's program addresses "the whole child," and in this case, especially language arts instruction. In many states, early childhood programs will need to follow curricular standards and requirements specified in licensing and/or federal or state guidelines or standards. Individual states have established standards and practices to ensure program quality after their state legislators became aware of research concerning young children's brain capacity and growth. Currently the National Governors Association Center for Best Practices & the Council of Chief State School Officers' *Common Core State Standards: Reading* (2010b) is influencing early childhood reading and language arts instruction for preschoolers. Though mandated for kindergarten through high school and not early childhood, early childhood centers are deciding how to best prepare preschoolers.

Whatever curriculum goals or planned curriculum is offered at an early childhood center or school, families will need to have an overview of the desired outcomes of instruction and be able to state their preferred outcomes for their children. The school's desired outcomes may be difficult to explain to families without using specific examples over an extended period. Schools and centers that are *privately funded* may not use the same goals listed in national standards and instead may use other goals as the basis for their language arts instruction.

17-1d Obtaining Family Input

Schools have developed vehicles to ensure that family input is part of a school's operational plan. These include classroom mailboxes, parent advisory committees, and parent councils. Family questionnaires, surveys, and checklists often probe family ideas. Other efforts to reach out and communicate include e-mail, reading groups, home–school meetings, planning workshops, and on-the-fly daily contacts. An early childhood program that isn't aware of family member's special talents or their unique access to diverse resources that can in some way enhance a program's instruction or maintenance may be missing extraordinary opportunities. This might be a family member who can volunteer, or one who works

on the financial and human resources available. Some schools have generous budgets; others do not. Some have committed and dedicated staff members who realize working with and through parents and families is a priority. Most educators are familiar with data and research showing that a family's socioeconomic status, cultural and linguistic group membership, parenting style, and home literacy experiences correlate with the knowledge and skills that children bring to school. They realize that excellent instructional help will be necessary to prepare some children for kindergarten. The State of Kentucky (2009) has developed a valuable guide to facilitate home–school connections when working with other than English speaking families. See Figure 17-2.

Figure 17-2 Tips for strengthening the home–school connection with ELL families.

Since this may be the first opportunity that ELL families have with school contact, it's vital that they feel welcome. Below are some suggested activities that will assist in accomplishing this goal.

1. Host a back-to-school night with interpreters. Make accommodations for parent's schedules. offer transportation, food and childcare. Use this as an opportunity to find out how to establish and maintain regular contact with families. Also include information about adult education opportunities.
2. Find bilingual volunteers, parent liaisons, or staff assistants to translate or serve as interpreters.
3. Develop family learning activities (including multi-lingual activities.) Send home for the purpose of involving the family.
4. Consider sponsoring single parent and/or native language parent groups. Consider having meetings away from the school campus.
5. Involve language minority parents on advisory committees, councils, and key communicator groups.
6. Hold family nights on parenting issues, including child development, early math, writing, science and literacy, setting up a work area at home and goals for their children and family; provide translators.
7. Find bilingual volunteers, parent liaisons or staff assistants to bridge the gap between families and the school.
8. Offer ongoing interactive training sessions for parents on topics such as homework, school attendance, standards, report cards, and discipline.
9. Implement a bi-lingual hotline number where parents can get information on how to help their children at home.
10. Form a citizen advisory group that can advise the principal on how to improve services for students and families in poverty, singly parents, and those who do not speak English.

Digital Download

at a print shop, or a computer expert who might provide consultation services. Families may contain an ethnic storyteller or a teenager who can demonstrate a particular hobby or sport skill. This can't be discovered until a program sensitively asks or provides a probing take-home form or individual interview. Wouldn't it be a plus if teachers knew a public safety officer or dog groomer was available to discuss loose or stray dogs, or animal care, if a theme on dogs were planned?

Gaining insight into how families view their level of participation, volunteer work, and attendance at school meetings prior to scheduling these meetings is wise. Probing for information concerning how families feel about their role in their child's education is another area where acquired data can help a school's plan for parent outreach. Acquiring an understanding of a family's life situation and/or living conditions that may either facilitate or hinder a parent's ability to be involved at school can help prevent unfortunate misunderstandings.

What have schools done to gather such information? Some programs have hired a temporary community-school liaison person fluent in the family's language. Conducting in-community meetings in a conveniently located community setting has been tried. Other schools have scheduled home visits to newly enrolled families. Yet others collect data by surveying parents at initial enrollment. Questions dealing with the home's culture, language, and literacy activities are asked to give teachers additional insight into instructional planning. Teachers continually try to relate school learning to a child's past knowledge and experience. These connections strengthen understanding.

17-2 Family Guidelines for Literacy and Language Development

The techniques or actions recommended to help children's language and literacy development apply to both teachers and parents. A family may have different and more varied opportunities to use these techniques. The following guidelines have been gathered from various sources dealing primarily with family-child relations. Families can promote literacy when they spend time with their children every day. At school, the teacher has many children to attend to and may not be able to provide as much individual attention as a family can provide. Recommended family actions include:

- Create home activities in which a child matches buttons, beans, blocks, or toys by colors, shapes, sizes; this kind of categorizing is an important thinking skill.

- Sort groceries by categories (canned goods, vegetables, fruits, and so on) with children.

- Keep in mind that a child's early experiences with print, writing tools, alphabet letters, and books can be puzzling. When a child asks questions, answer while he is focused.

- Slip quickly in and out of children's play, encouraging child discovery. This type of on-the-move teaching is natural and different from sit-down structured teaching, to which a child may tune out as interest wanes.

- Offer what is just a little beyond what a child already knows using a supportive, enthusiastic, "let's-discover-together" attitude.

- Realize pressure and commands aimed at teaching language arts turn children off.

- Arrange things so that a child has opportunities to see operations from beginning to end. For example, make butter from whipping cream or applesauce from picked apples.

- Encourage accomplishment, success, or honest effort with approval or appreciation.

- Be available as a resource person. When a child asks questions that an adult cannot answer, do not hesitate to seek help from others or books.

- Help children feel secure and successful. Interactions can build feelings of self-worth—if children's ideas and opinions are valued.

- Realize that young children's self-control is developing. In preschool and kindergarten, behavioral expectations create the climate for learning. Families set home behavioral standards. Disciplined work habits promote school success.

- Believe that fantasy play (make-believe) is correlated with other positive attributes, such as being creative, understanding the perspective of others, and possessing greater social skills (Wang, 2009).

Henderson and Mapp (2002) suggest that parent's or a family's involvement in a child's academic success can lead to:

- a higher rate of school attendance.

- better social skills and behavior at school.

- higher grades and test scores.

- lower rates of retention and repeating grades.

- higher rates of high school graduation and college or further training.

17-2a How Parents Can Stimulate Speaking Abilities

- Talk to children naturally and clearly as you would a friend. Listen when children want to tell you something without overtly correcting speech errors.

- Read stories, poems, jingles, and riddles to children.

- Encourage play with puppets, bendable family dolls, dress-up clothes, play stores, doctor kits, and play telephones, letting the children act out various events.

- Encourage children to tell you stories.

- Increase your attempts to build vocabulary by including new and descriptive words.

- Give attention; listen for intent rather than correctness. Show children that what they say is important. Communicate with children at their eye level, when possible. Expand and tactfully extend children's comments; talk on the children's chosen subjects.

- Use your best speech model—Standard English, if it comes naturally. If you speak a language other than English, provide a good model of that language.

- If a member of a cultural or ethnic group, examine attitudes concerning adult–child verbal interactions being important.

- Become a skilled questioner by asking questions that promote thinking, predicting, and a number of possible correct answers based on children's viewpoints.

- Encourage children to talk about whatever they are making, without asking," What is it?"

- Talk frequently, give objects names, and describe the things you do—be specific.

- Talk about what children are interested in.

- Do things together and talk about them: trips to stores, the zoo, museums, and so on.

- Take photographs and urge children to take their own. Jointly label photos. Create stories or picture books with them for the family library. Let children dictate the text.

- Listen to your children so that you learn about them and show that you are interested.
- Talk with children to describe objects they see in a picture. Then hide the picture and see how many objects they can recall.
- Sing songs with rhyming words.
- Make up chants to give life to boring housekeeping jobs.

Parents should know that their child's expressive oral language vocabulary is associated with how well parent's verbal comments are contingently responsive to their children's interests and cues. Throughout any given day there are many parent opportunities to make real world connections with words. Parents who are "word conscious" produce children who are interested in words and gain satisfaction from using them and hearing others use them correctly (Neuman & Roskos, 2012). Parents should understand a slotted spoon is never just the spoon, but rather a slotted spoon that allows liquid to drain when talking with their child about it and that a poodle is a poodle because of certain characteristics that have been pointed out, named, and discussed in conversation. The bluish green color of a child's new shirt is identified by a parent as being turquoise, the color of a gem stone.

17-2b How Parents Can Build Print Awareness and Skill

- Provide literature and a language-rich setting in the home.
- Write down the things children tell you about their pictures. Make books of each child's work and photographs, and talk about the books.
- Read family letters and mail to children, along with circulars, junk mail, restaurant menus, wrappers and packaging, signs, labels, building identifications, catalogs, brand names, and calendars.
- Provide scrap paper and writing tools, and reserve an area in the home as a writing center for children's use.
- Make or buy alphabet letter toys or word books.
- Ask teachers for copies of the alphabet your children will use in kindergarten.
- Encourage scribbling and doodling.

- Write messages to children or make signs for their play, such as "Mark's tower."
- Talk about what you are writing and its use to you.
- Start sharing books in infancy. Promote a child's personal book collection.
- Help your child learn the rules of print, such as spaces separating words, reading left to right, and punctuation marks.
- Be a co-explorer of books who promotes critical thinking, discusses unfamiliar words, asks questions, predicts happenings, and discusses book characters and their actions.
- Encourage interest in paper-and-crayon activities by showing children their names in print. Give attention to their attempts to copy their names or write them from memory.
- For pretend play, provide bank forms, memo pads, school forms, store order pads, and ordering pads used in restaurants. This kind of play stretches children's imaginations and broadens their experiences.
- Help children in writing letters to grandparents, sick friends, book authors, or famous people.
- Put little notes in children's lunch boxes or backpacks. These can be picture notes or simple messages.
- Model writing for children; write private notes, grocery lists, and recipes with children.
- Praise preschool aged children's attempts to invent their own spelling when they are learning the relationship between print and speech. "Correct" spelling will follow later.
- Write down shared experiences or often-told family stories. Stories can help children anticipate a sequence of events or help children figure out words of personal importance.

Dokoupil (2009) points out families, especially those using government sponsored and funded preschool care, may unfortunately adopt parenting styles that over use verbal commands and directives. This practice offers less vocabulary and fewer language opportunities and can "short circuit" language growth. Dokoupil's recommendations are based upon a large research study of over 8,000 children with diverse Latino origins (Fuller, Bridges, Bein, Jang, Jung, Rabe-Hesketh, Halfon, & Kuo, 2009). Bardige (2009) suggests adult "business-like" talk about child behavior that directs, commands, and makes no-nonsense statements clarifying expected child actions and behaviors or states clear limits, isn't bad for young children. Business-like talk and adult–child play talk both have a place in young children's lives. Family talking, Bardige notes, adds an essential dimension, for it affects many aspects of development, including: relationships, creativity, exploration of self-concept, initiative, inquisitiveness, knowledge, grammar, vocabulary, expressive language, social skills, storytelling and literacy, imagination, thinking, and reasoning.

17-2c How Experiences Outside of the Home Can Promote Literacy

Taking trips to interesting places, such as a bowling alley, shoe-repair shop, bakery, zoo, farm, airport, or to different kinds of stores or on a train or bus trip is recommended. When the family returns, making drawings related to a trip can be encouraged. Discussing and reliving experiences and adventures promote expression of children's ideas. Remembrances might also be recorded or recreated using creative dramatizing. Effective trips can be quite simple ones like visiting community events such as 4-H fairs, craft shows, antique auto shows, etc. It is wise to find what learning destinations exist in a city. Accompanying family members on routine trips to the store, bank, post office, or park is also recommended. Families can plan many adventures that a school cannot duplicate.

Librarians and the internet can become invaluable resources for information and books along a child's particular passion or interest—be that bugs, baseball, electricity, or airplanes, etc. Wise adults help children pursue and discover the answers to their many questions. Preschool children, on average, ask their parents about 100 questions a day according to Bronson & Merryman (2010). By middle school, these authors believe children pretty much stop asking. It's no coincidence that this is the same time when student motivation and engagement in school plummets (p. 47).

Subotnik (2010), a researcher who has studied children's transitions into successful creative careers as adults, suggests children do better when they are allowed to develop deep passions and pursue them wholeheartedly during childhood. In the process, children may research their chosen topic, focus deeply, think creatively, and

communicate with others by various means, explaining what they have learned and discovered.

Families should be urged to choose worthwhile books for young children and should consider a book's vocabulary; its narrative connections; its possible print awareness opportunities; its ability to enhance children's alphabet letter and sound recognition; and its ability to help children's ability to follow words on a page.

17-2d How Parents Can Promote Listening Skills

Trying to teach children to listen to and identify sounds, such as the whine of car tires, bird calls, insect noises, and sounds of different kinds of doors closing in the house is something families can to do to increase skill. Recordings, television, and storybooks can also stimulate interest in listening. Experts also suggest adults pause before answering a child's questions to consider briefly what the child is really probing, and to wait patiently for children to formulate answers to the parent's questions.

17-2e How Families Can Promote an Interest in Reading

Some families create an environment that supports reading by making sure it is impossible to avoid books. They always bring a backpack full of books along on car rides, and keep books in the pockets of the back of car seats. These families understand that young children can make tremendous progress as readers while "just pretending." This happens when a child pretends to read books, read illustrations, or flips pages as he tells his own story or imitates the actions or voices of those who have read to him.

Families with positive attitudes about reading will usually find that their children are motivated, spend more time at reading, and expend more effort in learning to read. Put simply, parents who value reading have children with a greater interest in reading skills.

Reading is dependent on facility with oral language. Children who talk easily, handle words skillfully, ask questions, and look for answers usually become good readers. Families have more opportunities for one-on-one time with children compared with teachers who have groups of children to help. Skilled adults reading picture books

Figure 17-3 Predictable books.

AUTHORS	TITLES	PUBLISHERS
Arno, E.	*The Gingerbread Man*	Crowell
Bang, M.	*Ten, Nine, Eight*	Greenwillow
Baum, A., & Baum, J.	*One Bright Monday Morning*	Random House
Berenstain, S., & Berenstain, J.	*Bears in the Night*	Random House
Bonne, R., & Mill, A.	*I Know an Old Lady Who Swallowed a Fly*	Holiday House
Brown, M. W.	*Goodnight Moon*	Harper Festival
Charlip, R.	*What Good Luck! What Bad Luck!*	Scholastic
Charlip, R., & Supree, B.	*Mother Mother I Feel Sick Send for the Doctor Quick Quick Quick*	Tricycle Press
Flack, M.	*Ask Mr. Bear*	Simon & Schuster
Galdone, P.	*The Three Billy Goats Gruff*	Seabury
Graham, J.	*I Love You, Mouse*	Harcourt Brace
Hoban, T.	*Just Look*	Greenwillow
Hogrogian, N.	*One Fine Day*	Macmillan
Hutchins, P.	*The Surprise Party*	Simon & Schuster
	Rosie's Walk	Simon & Schuster
Isadora, R.	*Max*	Simon & Schuster
Langstaff, J.	*Oh, A-Hunting We Will Go*	Simon & Schuster
Martin, B., Jr.	*Brown Bear, Brown Bear, What Do You See?*	Holt
Mayer, M.	*What Do You Do with a Kangaroo?*	Macmillan
Sendak, M.	*Chicken Soup with Rice*	HarperCollins
Shaw, C. B.	*It Looked Like Spilt Milk*	HarperCollins
Slobodkina, E.	*Caps for Sale*	HarperCollins
Spier, P.	*The Fox Went out on a Chilly Night*	Doubleday
Stevenson, J.	*"Could Be Worse!"*	Morrow, William & Co.
Stover, J.	*If Everybody Did*	McKay
Thomas, P.	*"Stand Back," Said the Elephant, "I'm Going to Sneeze"*	HarperCollins
Viorst, J.	*Alexander and the Terrible, Horrible, No Good, Very Bad Day*	Simon & Schuster
Zolotow, C.	*If It Weren't for You*	HarperCollins

stop when a child has lost concentration. They try to obtain enthralling books. They restrain themselves and do not go overboard in their attempts to educate children. Instead they have fun, enjoy humor, and encourage questions. Literacy-promoting families read to children every day.

Many families consult librarians for help. See Figure 17-3 for a list of books with an element of predictability. Finding predictable picture books that include repetitive features enhances the child's feelings of being part of the telling. Competency increases when the child knows what comes next after a few readings. An appealing book selected by a parent can be read with enthusiasm and animation. Children enjoy active participation when chanting lines, pointing to illustrations, and speaking in characters' voices. Families can give reading status and importance; they can read recipes and directions with their children to show print's purpose.

Children will become readers when their emotions are engaged and their imaginations are stretched and stirred by what they find on the printed page. The truly literate are not those who know how to read, but those who read fluently, responsively, critically, and because they want to. It is wise to select from among the best books for even the youngest children. The best books are well designed with uncluttered pages, interesting text, and colorful pictures that stimulate young imaginations. When reading aloud from books, authors and illustrations can be discussed. Adult enjoyment should be apparent, and book happenings can be related to children's past experiences. Additional tips follow.

- Ask warm-up questions to set the stage and help children anticipate what will happen.
- Point as you read. For very young children, point to things in pictures as you talk about them. Pointing helps focus attention, thus lengthening the time children will sit still for a story. It also develops visual literacy—the idea that pictures have meaning.
- Try asking what the child expects the book to be about from looking at the cover.
- Look for ways to involve the child during readings.
- Stop and let the child supply words.
- Talk about words (unusual ones) the child may not understand.

Parents are able to connect book story features, not only to past happenings experienced together, but also to the unique characteristics of their child's personality, interests, desires, and abilities. They have an emotional bond that can connect book-reading times to "pleasantness." They can start book reading during infancy and make parent–child book time a special "together" time. Families can ask questions, point to objects in illustrations and hesitate to promote guessing, and prompt their child to see details and cause-and-effect relationships. All of these things will increase the child's literacy and vocabulary. Families can become active listeners who add information a little above what the child knows. When they accept their child's comments and ideas, parents reinforce the child's efforts and desire to share his ideas. Storybook illustrations can also be "read" and discussed in detail. Encouraging families to read in their native language is an important consideration. Schools enrolling other-than-English-speaking children include foreign language picture books in their classroom collection and often stock additional copies that parents can borrow. Local library staffers may be able to provide others. Family members who wish to rate themselves can use Figure 17-4. They may discover that they are

Figure 17-4 Family self-rating.

Use the following ratings: O = often, S = sometimes, I = infrequently, D = does not apply

Family attempts to:

_____ 1. initiate family discussions at mealtimes.	_____ 18. encourage child hobbies.
_____ 2. give full attention to child's comments.	_____ 19. answer questions readily.
_____ 3. add descriptive or new words in conversation.	_____ 20. discuss care and storage of books.
_____ 4. take child to library.	_____ 21. play word games or rhyme words playfully.
_____ 5. take time at post office to discuss letters and postage.	_____ 22. talk about how print is used in daily life.
_____ 6. discuss children's books.	_____ 23. find books on subjects of interest to child.
_____ 7. read to child daily.	_____ 24. consult with child's teacher.
_____ 8. point out print around the house.	_____ 25. give attention and notice accomplishments.
_____ 9. accept child's opinions.	_____ 26. take dictation from child.
_____ 10. use dictionary with child.	_____ 27. try not to interrupt child's speech frequently.
_____ 11. talk on the child's chosen subject.	_____ 28. initiate family reading times and family discussions of classics.
_____ 12. ask questions that promote child's descriptions or predictions.	_____ 29. establish a book center in the home.
_____ 13. listen patiently.	_____ 30. create child writing or art center in the home.
_____ 14. discuss television programs.	_____ 31. give books as gifts.
_____ 15. plan community outings.	_____ 32. provide different writing tools and scrap paper.
_____ 16. invite interesting people to home and promote interactions with child.	_____ 33. provide alphabet toys in the home.
_____ 17. correct child's speech casually with little attention to errors.	

already promoting child language and literacy in a number of ways.

Sladek (2012) comments about the difficulty of developing a passion for reading with today's often overstimulated and skeptical children. She believes a child's truly falling in love with literature takes parental action. Children, she suggests, need someone to discuss the books they have read such as asking about what emotions and thoughts the book evoked. Family members can be a safe sounding board if time is set aside to do so. Preschoolers enjoy sharing their ideas about books that are read to them.

Reach Out and Read, a pre-preschool program started over twenty years ago by two doctors, now touches four million low income children by providing them free books. Participating doctors, now over 12,000 in the United States, have distributed over six million books at doctor's offices. Studies published in pediatric journals report positive child outcomes. Important lessons learned over the long period of years the program has existed include the idea that parents, even those with their own educational deficiencies, must take responsibility and be vested in their child's success and understand there is no substitute for parent involvement in daily home book readings.

17-2f Family Storytelling

The magic of parental storytelling not only improves child listening, but also broadens child interests and opens new worlds of discovery. Following are tips from professional storytellers.

1. Select a story that will interest both you and the children. Your enthusiasm for a story is important in helping the children enjoy the story, too.

2. Practice the story several times before you share it with the children. Learn all you can about the characters, settings, and events within the story.

3. Decide how to animate the story. Practice some hand gestures, facial expressions, or body movements that will spice up the story for the children.

4. Practice different accents, voice inflections (angry, sad, joyous), and loud and soft speech patterns to help make characters come alive and to add drama to your presentation.

5. Create some simple puppets from common household objects such as wooden picnic spoons, paper plates, or lunch bags. Draw individual character features on each item and use them during your story.

6. Promote your storytelling time. Make an announcement about an upcoming story or design a simple "advertisement" for a story and post it in advance.

7. Design a simple prop for the children to use during the telling of a story: a paper boat for a sea story, a magnifying glass or camera for a mystery story, or a paper flower for a springtime story.

8. Have the children suggest new props, gestures, or voice qualities that would be appropriate for retelling of the story at a later date.

9. After telling a story, talk about it with the children. Ask them to tell you the most enjoyable or memorable parts.

10. Being a good storyteller takes a little practice, but the time invested can make a world of difference in helping children appreciate good literature.

Preschool educators are quick to inform the families of English language learners that they should continue to support the development of their child's home language. Research and educational experts confirm that the child's native language development aids the child's academic success in English. Leaving the child's home language behind is not the school's intent as some parents and families may believe (Nemeth, 2009). The advantage of learning two (or more) languages well is a desirable skill in any future career. Hearing stories in his home language is an experience no child should miss.

17-2g Families Can Build Children's Self-Regulation

Vanderkam (2009) defines self-regulation as the ability to stop, think, make a plan, and control impulses. Many educators believe these are important skills children need to do well in school. Vanderkam suggests self-regulation can be taught. Vanderkam notes educators are examining older studies, one of which is important research conducted in the 1960s and 70s by psychologist Walter Mischel. A description of a section of Mischel's research done by Vanderkam follows.

▶❚❚ TeachSource Video 17-2

© 2016 Cengage Learning.

Parent Involvement in School Culture: A Literacy Project

More than one parent in the video provided reasons for parents to be involved in their children's schooling.

1. Describe parent reasons and their suggestions for what a school or teacher should do to promote family involvement and school participation.

2. Linda Schwerty, the literacy specialist in the video, mentioned a number of ways she had tried to accommodate families so they could attend school meetings. Name a few.

. . . a researcher would place a marshmallow in front of a hungry four year old and tell the child that she could eat the marshmallow right then, or have two if she waited until the researcher returned. About a third of the children could distract themselves and wait. Followed for years, these highly disciplined kids had better school outcomes, and scored more than 200 points higher on the Scholastic Achievement Test (SAT) when older. (p. 9A)

A number of educational experts believe today's children are growing up with less practice in self-regulation. A good number have not demonstrated the ability to turn off the TV and other media to start homework, nor can they plan how to solve important daily problems or hurdle road blocks. Brown (2009) cites the conclusions of recent research that suggests certain kinds of fantasy (dramatic) play in which children plan the fantasy roles they are going to enact, can have a measurable effect on children's ability to control

their impulses. Some preschools are experimenting with planned activities and games that involve children's planning a course of action and then following through. Teacher's promotion of children's follow through plans is believed crucial. Games can be designed by teachers to promote (a) child's thinking first, and acting second, or (b) one where the child must control his/her impulses to be successful or complete the game.

Family advice to aid the development of children's self-control (regulation) development includes:

- playing games with rules that are enforced.
- promoting child help in household tasks that lead to successful task completion.
- setting time limits on TV or other electronic media especially during toddlerhood or preschool ages.
- limiting entertainment media viewing.
- letting a frustrated child think and plan his/her way out of a problem before jumping in with a solution or suggestion.
- coaching children to analyze and solve their own difficulties.
- promoting a child's work on a project and then expecting the child to complete to it.
- expecting a child to complete what activity he has chosen to start.
- increasing children's knowledge of process, such as understanding there is a beginning, middle, and a finishing end of a task.

The early predictors of children's academic success and future schooling may have never been discussed with families. School achievement is associated with a preschooler's ability to engage and participate in the classroom. Other behaviors, such as listening, working independently, following directions, planning, organizing, completing tasks, and cooperating with peers are also characteristics of students who achieve. A child's attitude toward school can also affect his school performance. A family's attitude that denigrates or plays down schooling or schooling's importance, worth, or value may be catching.

17-2h Home Reading and Writing Centers

Home reading centers are a lot like school reading areas. A comfortable, warm, private, well-lighted place free of distraction works best. Adjacent shelving and a chair for comfort is important for book-sharing times. Window seats and room dividers make cozy corners. Parents can get creative in selecting and furnishing reading centers.

Family book collections encourage children's positive attitudes concerning books as personal possessions and give books status. Homemade books often become children's favorite volumes. Families model appropriate storage and care in home reading centers. A special area with writing supplies, an alphabet chart, table, and chair should be suggested to parents. Families interested in purchasing books can be alerted to the opportunity to buy books through school-sponsored book clubs, local library book sales, used-book stores, thrift shops, and yard sales. Pointers should be shared concerning selecting quality books.

17-3 Home Visits and Outreach Efforts

In trying to understand attending children, especially "silent ones" or culturally diverse ones, a home visit may help plan for children's individual needs. Most early childhood centers with strong home-school partnerships schedule yearly visits to each family.

17-3a Families Who Speak Languages Other Than English

Early childhood centers have become increasingly sensitive to other-than-English-speaking families who are often eager to promote their child's literacy. Many children with limited English proficiency also have in common that their parents are poorly educated, that their family income is low, that they reside in communities in which many families are similarly struggling, and that they attend schools with student bodies that are predominantly minority and low achieving.

Family literacy programs attempt to break the cycle of intergenerational illiteracy by providing services to both family and child. Programs vary from community to community as each program tries to meet the needs of participants.

Participants are often parents who lack basic literacy skills and may need to acquire positive self-concepts to encourage their children's school success. Family literacy programs and adult literacy programs can be located through county Offices of Education or state agencies.

Family literacy programs have a greater chance of success and longevity when they attempt to tap into the wealth of background knowledge and experiences of the family (parent) participants (Ortiz & Ordonez-Jasis, 2010). Relevant themes in books by Latino authors urge families to preserve traditions, celebrate cultural richness and personal stories, value family heritage, and share family social issues and concerns (Ada, 2003). Directors and administrators can receive information and a multitude of resources concerning exemplary family literacy programs from the National Center for Family Literacy and the Division of Adult Education and Literacy, which is part of the U.S. Department of Education.

Early childhood centers can often locate family literacy programs and identify resources by contacting the Director of Adult Education in their state. A growing number of communities are instituting publicly funded family literacy programs. Many of these programs are designed to provide childcare, transportation, introduction to literacy-building home activities, access to community services, involvement in children's school activities, bilingual support, and the promotion of pride in language and culture.

Many education projects working with immigrant parents reject the idea that the best way to help families is to hold group parenting classes. They instead attempt to increase families' confidence in their teaching abilities by other means. They encourage family picture-book readings and after-book discussions in the child's native language. They provide books, book bags with suggested activities, or recorded books or may use other strategies.

17-3b African-American School Success

Murphy (2003) conducted case studies on four high-achieving elementary school children of African-American heritage. She points out the children's academic success was no accident

---

family literacy programs — community programs attempting to provide literacy-building opportunities and experiences for families. Services are available for both adults and children.

because all four benefited from the continuous, active involvement of their parents in guiding and influencing their school success (p. 17).

Murphy describes five factors that "maintained and sustained" these African-American families. They had a high-achievement orientation, strong kinship bonds, strong work orientation; displayed an adaptability of family roles; and had a religious orientation. Murphy also cites additional contributing family characteristics. These include individual family beliefs and values, the quality of the interactive behavior, placing an extraordinarily high value on education, and family maintenance of a social environment in which learning flourished.

Early childhood educators working with diverse groups of children will find this study interesting, for it alerts teachers to the strength, resolve, and commitment to education that exists in many American families. One of the four children that Murphy studied, a 10-year-old, was asked why he had done so well in school. He cited

> "great teachers, parents who cared about my schoolwork, friends who helped me with my schoolwork, and a great staff"; and about his parents, he said, "They helped me learn about the world and my environment"; and he added, "I'm special because God made me special. He sent me to this earth to have fun, get an education, and go to college." (p. 21)*

What child wouldn't do well with a similar attitude toward school, teachers, parents, and himself as a "learner"?

17-3c Family Education Projects— Working Together

The fact that many young families today may be less prepared to care for children than were their predecessors has not escaped educators. Nor has it escaped our national government. Government programs have helped state and local governments strengthen early learning for young children. Past initiatives have focused on young children's literacy and cognitive, social, and emotional development. In an effort to reduce the stark contrast some young children and their family members experience between home and school, family literacy programs and early

childhood programs currently are attempting to become aware of each enrolled child's family literacy proficiency, their culture-specific literacy practices, and family literacy knowledge. This type of collaboration and connection between home and school, it is felt, will promote better planning for school instruction and increase the school's ability to relate school activities to children's daily lives. Promoting home literacy events and activities— particularly storybook reading—is still an important goal, but collaborating and understanding what families know, what they do, and how they do it, has been given increased emphasis and attention.

Paratore and Edwards (2011) describe Project Flame (Family Literacy Aprendiendo, Mejorando, Educando) as follows:

> Although Project Flame is clearly based on teaching parents how to support their children in the acquisition of school-based literacy behaviors (including sessions on creating home library centers, book sharing, library visits, teaching the ABCs, and helping with homework), parents' personal perspectives and cultural knowledge provide an essential foundation for literacy conversation. This collaborative learning provides opportunities for participants to share the "multiple literacies'" of their home lives. (p. 59)

Current studies of Latino family's literacy practices confirm that there is considerable parent guidance, participation, assistance, and concern for their children's reading and writing development (Ortez & Ordonez-Jasis, 2010). These practices also result in children's higher scores, better school attendance, and children's stronger cognitive skills (Slavin, Madden, Karweit, Dolan, & Wasik, 1994). Numerous studies suggest that when children brought-home schoolwork, this often initiated family literacy interaction. Children sometimes served as teachers of other family members.

17-3d Screen Viewing and Young Children's Language Development

Parents often ask teachers about the value of television and other technologies, and about their child's viewing habits. A review of research generally supports the idea that children's television viewing casts children as "watchers" rather than active participants in language exchanges

*From Murphy, J. C. (2003, Nov.). Case studies in African-American school success and parenting behaviors. *Young Children* 58(6), 85, 89. Copyright © 2003 NAEYC. Used with permission.

with others. The effect of viewing on particular children differs. After children become readers, studies show that reading development is adversely affected when viewing is excessive.

Television programs for children older than age two that stress educational or informative material do not seem to have harmful potential. Again, the amount of viewing time is critical. Because research offers so many conflicting views, teachers cannot give definitive answers to families. Educators can express their concern that heavy television and video viewing rob a child of a literacy-rich home environment, one that is necessary for the child's optimal growth. Real first-hand experiences, exposure to books, and conversations with interested and responsive family members stack the odds in favor of early literacy and cannot be replaced by television or videos.

What is excessive viewing? Research suggests that more than 10 hours of viewing weekly is excessive. An increasing number of alarmed educators and researchers warn that excessive, unsupervised television and video viewing by young children promotes negative effects, including

- aggressive and violent behavior.
- decreased imagination, cooperation, and success in relationships.
- vulnerability to stimulus addiction, resulting in the child needing overstimulation to feel satisfied.
- immunity to vicarious emotional stresses, resulting in the inability to produce socially acceptable emotional responses.
- poor reading comprehension and inability to persevere to an outcome.
- listening problems.
- pronunciation difficulty.
- inability to make mental pictures (visual imagery).
- inability to remember or decipher meaning from what is viewed or heard because of the passive aspect of television viewing.
- hindered development of metalinguistic awareness (e.g., understanding that letters make up words, written words are linked together into meaningful sentences, a word is made from printed marks, one reads from left to right in English, and the meaning of terms such as *author, title, illustration*, etc.).★

★From Jane M. Healy, Ph.D. *Endangered Minds.*

- decreased verbal interactions with family.
- decreased opportunities to experience life and exercise verbal problem solving.

Very few research studies have attempted to reduce preschoolers' television watching. Dennison, Russo, Burdick, and Jenkins (2004) were successful in doing so. Their two-year study with 16 early childhood centers was funded in part by the National Institutes of Health. Intervention sessions emphasized reading and alternatives to television viewing. They also stressed the importance of families eating meals together. Children in the study group were rewarded with stickers for choosing television alternatives. A children's book, *The Berenstain Bears and Too Much TV*, featuring an anti-television theme, was introduced to children in the study. Results indicated that children in the study session reduced television watching time by 3.1 hours per week. Some studies suggest that children—even those who have been taught critical analysis skills—do not generate critical thinking during television commercials. Children and adults think differently, using different parts of their brain. In other words, they tend to believe the images they see!

What can parents do? They can place firm limits, participate in children's television viewing, discuss program content, turn off the set, and give substitute care providers clear instructions concerning screen time. Arden's family had another solution.

Arden's father explained to his child's teacher "I don't want the television or the computer to become the central focus of my home." His solution was to have each of his children select those television programs they wanted to watch during the next week on Sunday. Each program was to be one hour in length. Then designated viewing days and times were decided. Homework assignments had to be completed beforehand. Certain TV programs were off-limits. Child-selected programs were recorded or taped in advance if necessary and a schedule was posted. Computer time was also strictly regulated and varied with a child's age. The father also planned weekly family times. These included joint projects, discussions, field trips; library visits, social, cultural, and sports events, and other local education destinations. The time spent selecting and recording child programs was well worth the effort, Arden's parents believed (Machado, 2011).

17-4 Home–School Communication

Schools differ widely in both the amount of written home–school communication and the amount of time spent talking to or meeting with parents. Teachers are struggling, particularly in urban, coastal, and border states, to learn about family practices, beliefs, and educational needs and desires. They wish to find common ground and acknowledge parents' cultural values while also sharing their programs' philosophies and teaching techniques. That can be a challenging goal to achieve, particularly in areas with a diverse population. In places such as California's Silicon Valley, it is common to find children from as many as 10 to 29 different ethnic or culturally diverse groups in one elementary classroom.

Most preschool teachers desire more time and more conversations and additional written communication with families. This suits some families who seem to be seeking supportive assistance in child-rearing. Each parent group and center is unique, and consequently, tremendous differences exist in the degree to which preschool centers and families work together. Most centers try to provide some type of family assistance. Families who receive help and support feel more open to contribute to the school's activities.

Family–school contacts usually take place in at least seven ways—daily conversations, e-mails, written communications, family meetings, workshops, social events, and individual conferences. At the beginning of the child's school year, a telephone call or e-mail welcoming the family establishes communication. Weekly newsletters and personal notes from teachers maintain links thereafter.

Teachers have a good chance (time and duties permitting) to share children's interests and favorite school activities when families arrive to take their children home from the center; teachers can discuss with family such things as new interests, accomplishments, books, play objects, and child-created or constructed work. Children spend time with and talk about what excites them; the observant teacher can be aware of developing interests. Families are usually curious about what their children have shared about their home life and out-of-school activities.

Many schools use "family" bulletin boards as a communicative device. Schools may receive more announcements of literary happenings in their communities than do families. Language-developing local events and activities can be advertised so families can become aware of them when picking up or dropping off children. Short magazine and newspaper articles of interest can be posted at eye-catching levels.

The family language practices of English language learners can vary, yet similarities may exist. When teachers understand cultural differences in attending children's language use, it benefits their ability to plan instructional activities, converse, and respond. After a welcoming classroom environment is created for their English learning children, teachers monitor whether teacher language, gestures, or actions might convey meanings the educator had not intended.

Most experts suggest educators visit children's homes and observe family language interactions and also attend community functions in children's neighborhoods. Studying a family's culturally influenced communication style using a variety of methods and resources is also recommended. Family language practice may include (but is not limited to the following):

- storytelling frequently in family conversations.
- using particular hand gestures (both positive and objectionable) with specific implied meanings.
- using pantomime, role-playing, drama, or dance to express ideas.
- asking for child silence or listening during conversations.
- communicating fear and other emotions in uniquely different ways.
- using speech at a slower or faster pace than is customary in English.
- trying to avoid looking into a speaker's eyes during verbal exchanges.
- using direct instruction to teach children appropriate words to say in specific circumstances and situations.
- participating in many cooperative learning activities rather than independent learning ones.
- valuing artistic gestures as a means of expression.

Photo 17-3 Parents' wishes and concerns are often aired in parent–staff meetings.

17-4a Planned Meetings and Conferences

Planned meetings include individual and group gatherings (Photo 17-3). Conferences let families know what plans the school has in place to address their children's individual interests and growth, and whether their plans are working. When children have interests in alphabet letters, dramatizing, special-topic books, or other pursuits, families and teachers can discuss related school and home activities.

Preschool staff members prepare for home-based conferences with individual families by collecting child work samples, observation records, and assessments of social and academic progress. Discussions focus on child growth areas and then possible school and home planning to further growth. A portfolio, if developed, is shared and discussed. Families and teachers exchange perceptions of the child's unique needs and strengths while working together to plan and promote the child's full potential.

Teachers often gain insight into family goals, concerns, resources, and home environments during these conferences while families gain a deeper understanding of their children's progress and the families' role in being the child's first and ongoing teacher of language and literacy. Nemeth and Erdosi (2012) suggests using a thoughtful approach when conferencing with families with diverse language and cultural backgrounds. This includes reducing a teacher's messages to only the most critical and factual information and stating it briefly, simply, and clearly. Backing up teacher comments with a few examples or observations to explain a teacher's

concerns and preparing for a meeting well in advance is also recommended. A "talky" teacher would modify her style by saying a lot less than usual.

Galinsky (2012) describes how one Washington, D.C., early childhood center with mostly Spanish-speaking parents planned a meeting with teachers and parents learning together. The meeting involved study and discussion of photos and videos that captured young children listening, reading, in early writing activities, and using their oral language abilities. Short video clips taken at the children's center supported key ideas. This included children's learning through the five senses, and classroom situations honoring the importance of children's home language.

A meeting can be planned to take a closer look at the early childhood center's planned language program, materials, and language arts center. Families then get a first-hand look and an opportunity to explore what is at hand. Teachers often conduct sample activities and demonstrate material and equipment use. Families are able to ask questions about their children's use of or interest in a center's planned opportunities.

A family and parenting training effort developed by the National Latino Children's Institute (2008) blends child development research with traditional and community-based wisdom. Lessons highlight family relationships and child–adult interactions during the early years, especially language growth and development.

Other possible themes of study meetings might include the effects of television and other screen devices on young children's language development, bilingualism, or free and inexpensive toys that promote language or any other subjects selected by families from a list of possible topics.. Outside experts and speakers or films and other commercial media can present additional topics to be studied and discussed. Knowing what community and neighborhood issues exist that affect young children is important. This type of meeting helps inform all present. Differing views clarify everyone's thinking.

The following items are the author's high-priority topics. Many families show concern over their children's articulation and vocabulary, particularly children's pronunciation and speech errors. They may be worried when they notice that a child's language, which at three was apparently error-free and highly grammatical, becomes full of errors a year later. They need to know that this indicates progress. At each successive stage a child masters a limited range of simple speech structures. When more complicated structures are attempted due to his more mature thinking, his hypotheses are tested by whether he is understood or not. It is helpful to assure families that the school's staff monitors fluency and to share typical child speech characteristics. Such discussions often relax parents and dispel their fears. Hints concerning simple modeling of correct forms are well received by most families.

Sharing information on school interaction techniques used to increase children's speech by listening, following children's leads, and expanding interest in daily conversation is also very important. Families need to realize how influential they are in modeling an interest in and positive attitudes toward reading, writing, and speaking. Families profit when teachers share their goals and model their techniques and strategies for storybook read-alouds or other types of learning activities.

Family ability to listen closely to child ideas—rather than judging correctness of grammar—should be discussed. Alexander (2004) notes that research has found that before a child reaches age 14, parents are roughly twice as important as school is for a child's learning. Educators urge adults to engage in intellectually challenging conversations, offer new and increasingly descriptive words, and extend conversations with unpressured questioning. Another topic to discuss with families is the warm, unpressured social environments that promote family conversations. Discussing quality books and "advertising" books to children can perhaps combat electronic media dominance in the home. Analyzing books, pictures, text, and their messages is another great idea. The child's home access to creative materials, such as drawing and marking tools, is also important. Families have many questions about early reading and writing of alphabet letters. Both reading and writing acquisition is aided by a widely enriching home and preschool curriculum that preserves children's feelings of competence by offering that which is slightly above their level and related closely to their present interests.

Last on this list may be the most important topic teachers can discuss with families. A lot of language development is possible when family and other adults share activities they love—the ones they can speak about enthusiastically in detailed specific terms; the ones that are vital to them and for which they have a passionate interest. Examples are easy to find and role-play for a parent and family groups: the dad who does carpentry, the grandma who grows garden vegetables, the aunt who dances the flamenco, the mom who makes noodles from scratch, the brother who plays the flute, the sister who collects butterflies, and the uncle who restores motorcycles. So many times families do not see themselves as language and information resources and do not understand the power of shared experiences and conversations with their young child. Family members supply the daily experiences that give words meaning and depth, as do teachers, but they are more instrumental because of the amount of time spent with the child and their access to the world of children's lives out of school.

17-4b Fathers and Language Development

An increasing percentage of children do not live with their fathers (Child Care Bureau, 2004). The number of children in single parent homes has nearly tripled since 1960, and the percentage of men who call themselves stay-at-home dads has stalled below three percent (Romano & Dokoupil, 2010). For some young children, good fathering contributes to the development of emotional security, curiosity, and math and verbal skills, a national study concludes. Many preschools are rethinking their family involvement and planning ways to include children's male relatives to a greater degree. Some schools require "father classroom time," and family meetings are designed to cleverly interest and increase male attendance.

Fathers can play an important role in their children's school achievement, and the earlier they become involved with their children's learning and socialization, the better. Educational research suggests that a father's ability to support his child's learning can affect the child's engagement with books.

Could it be that a sizeable group of American men have been raised to feel incompetent at child rearing? Many people might say so. In Sweden in 1995, a simple but revolutionary law took effect, which helped Swedish fathers redefine their role in parenting. Romano and Dokoupil (2010) explain the law's effect in 2010.

> . . . now more than 80 percent of Swedish fathers take four months off for the birth of a new child,

up from four percent a decade ago. And a full 41 percent of companies now formally encourage fathers to go on parental leave, up from only two percent in 1993. Simply put men are expected to work less and father more. (p. 45)

If a man refuses time at home with kids, he faces questions from friends, family, and, yes, other guys. Policy changes produce personal changes—and then, slowly but surely, society changes as well (Hegedus, 2010, p. 46)

17-4c Explaining Phonemic Awareness to Families

Many families are well-read, but a definition of phonetic awareness and why it has become important is a good idea. Main points to transmit to families include: (1) Phonemic awareness is an essential skill in learning to read; (2) Preschoolers can become aware of and play with sounds, rhymes, and silly words; (3) Speech is composed of small units called phonemes (sounds); and (4) Lots of family word play with letter sounds can increase child skill.

School Lending Libraries. Increasingly, early childhood centers are aware of the benefits of maintaining a school lending library. Although extra time and effort are involved in this provision to families, centers are sensitive to the plight of families who are economically distressed and pressed for time. Lending libraries can also provide families with book-reading tips. Books in the first language of enrolled children are included in a center's book collection. Rules and procedures for checkout and return are prepared in print for families. Staff time, center budget, and staff availability are key factors in deciding whether a family lending library is a viable activity.

17-4d Working with Hard-to-Reach Families

Centers incorporate family dinners and provide child care to increase family attendance at home–school meetings. Every effort is made to make the center staff and facility as non-intimidating as possible and to convince every family that they can contribute to child literacy. The extra outreach efforts educators and school administrators make with hard-to-reach families can be crucial. Research confirms educator actions are instrumental in increasing levels of parent participation and involvement. Families have become diverse and unalike with an increasing number headed by a single parent. In 2009, an estimated 19 percent of children under age 18 lived in poverty with 15 percent residing in rural areas and 12 percent in urban ones. These types of circumstances may impede a school's outreach and communication efforts.

17-4e Daily and Written Contacts

Greeting both families and children as they arrive starts a warm, comfortable atmosphere; encourages talking; and sets the tone for conversation. Should a family member entering the classroom be ignored in the doorway or left to search for a staff person? Not in a school sensitive to the power of a personal greeting. Teachers should exchange comments, build family–school partnerships, and help children enter by offering choices of possible activities through statements such as, "We've put red play dough on the table by the door for you." Or "The matching game you told me you liked yesterday is waiting for you on the shelf near the bird cage."

Family mailboxes can hold daily teacher messages. Important milestones, such as the child's first interest in or attempt at printing alphabet letters or his name or his first created stories, should be shared. A short note from the teacher about a child's special events is appreciated by most families. A note about special daily happenings such as, "I think Toni would like to tell you about the worm she found in the garden" or "Saul has been asking many questions about airplanes," keeps families aware of their children's expanding interests.

Often, centers prepare informal letters, e-mails, or newsletters that describe school happenings or daily themes. Figures 17-5 and 17-6 are two examples of this type of teacher–family communication. A written communication may contain any information concerning child literacy and local services or events. If a school is trying to help families expand their children's experiences, newsletters can suggest family outings and excursions to local community events and low-cost and free entertainment. Dates, times, costs, telephone numbers, and simple maps can be included. It is suggested that newsletters be upbeat, with humor, quotes, and anecdotes scattered throughout the pages.

Figure 17-5 Sample of informal letter to parents to strengthen school learning. Note: Adding child drawings might create additional interest.

Dear Parents,

We are studying the size of things and will have many discussions this week comparing two or more objects or people. In similar discussions at home, emphasize the endings of size words (-er, -est).

Following are some activities you may wish to try in which size can be discussed. Note the words *big*, *bigger*, and *biggest* or *tall*, *taller*, *tallest*, or others could also be appropriately used.

1. Sort bottle caps, canned food cans, spoons, or crackers.
2. Discuss your pet's size in relation to a neighbor's pet.
3. Take a large piece of paper and cut into square pieces. Discuss small, smaller, and smallest.
4. Look for round rocks or pebbles and compare sizes. Ask the child to line them up from small to smallest.
5. Play games involving finding objects smaller than your shoe, finger, a coin, and so on, or smaller than a ball but larger than a marble.

You will find many opportunities to compare size in your neighborhood or on walks, or in the course of daily living.

Sincerely,

Your partner in your child's education

Your child's preschool teacher

Figure 17-6 A partnership letter.

Dear Family,

This week we have talked about many means of transportation—of how we use animals and machines to take us from one place to another.

We built things, painted things, and learned songs and heard stories about different vehicles such as bikes, cars, trucks, buses, boats, trains, airplanes, horses and wagons, etc., and we even took a bus ride.

Here are some suggested home activities to reinforce school learning.

• Talk about places you go together in your car.
• Save large cardboard boxes—line them up, and pretend they are railroad cars.
• Save old magazines. Let your child find "vehicles that move things from place to place." The child may want to find, cut, and paste pictures.
• Take a walk, and find all the moving vehicles you can.
• Sing a train song, "I've Been Working on the Railroad," or any other.
• Plan a ride on or in a vehicle that is new to the child.

As you enjoy life together, you may want to point out and talk about transportation.

Sincerely,

P.S. Here's a rebus poem to share.

 Sam wanted to go to the zoo.

The family wanted to go there too.

The 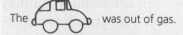 was out of gas.

And the  didn't go past

their 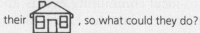 , so what could they do?

How could they get to the zoo?

17-5 Family Resources at School and Volunteering

Centers sometimes provide informational articles, magazines, and books that may be borrowed for short periods or available at the school's classroom parent library or office. Photocopied magazine articles in manila folders that have been advertised on the school's family bulletin board are a good resource for busy families. Family literacy packs are developed at some preschools to increase family engagement in children's learning and to build a positive link in home school. Early childhood teachers send home these packs that include literacy materials and suggested activities. The contained literacy material highlights young children's knowledge and learning (Hammack, Foote, Garretson, & Thompson, 2012). Packs can become a regular feature of a school's outreach and supportive assistance plan. It is possible to tailor pack items and activities to both classroom curriculum and a child's individual educational needs. A well-organized literacy pack might address specific learning goals and explain each material's purpose and use. A checklist can be included for families to record an activity's completion. An evaluation form solicits family comments.

Most centers feel that family literacy packs need a careful introduction and explanation before being initiated so families can understand they are not homework or a school's attempt to remediate a lagging child. Each center decides if literacy packs are to be introduced on a daily, weekly, monthly basis or otherwise. Families can opt in or out of their use.

A free public library card can be the smartest card in a family's wallet because the more children read, the better they do in school. Libraries offer a wide variety of services that promote child (and adult) literacy. Many public libraries offer the following: help locating material for children's homework assignments and/or research, books, magazines, periodicals, newspapers, videos, movie rentals, CDs, DVDs, internet access, laser printers, copy machines, photographs, audiobooks, and entertainment media. Libraries frequently sponsor and create children's programs and cultural events, bulletin boards post local happenings that promote learning opportunities, and they hold periodic used-book sales where inexpensive books and other literacy-promoting items can be obtained.

The role of families, relatives, neighbors, and community volunteers has changed. Family and community volunteers and resources are seen as vital parts of language arts instruction. The teacher's goal is to involve and invite resource people to participate in a relationship that urges them to become active participants in children's language learning and literacy. Some of the ways families can help and contribute include joining school efforts, being guest speakers, providing classroom demonstrations, joining class field trips, performing maintenance tasks, and spending time fundraising, or other types of assistance.

Some family members work in businesses in which useful language arts materials are discarded, such as scrap paper, cardboard, and so forth. The family is usually more than willing to obtain these previously discarded materials, especially if they are unable to volunteer. Some family volunteers enjoy making language games or keeping the school messageboard current. Art, photography, sewing, and carpentry talents lend themselves to creating and constructing many classroom materials. Repairing a school's books, flannel board sets, and puppet collections can be an ongoing task. Through the joint efforts of home and school, centers are able to cut costs and provide a wider range of language-developing experiences for attending children.

Summary

17-1 Describe how programs and child centers build family–school partnerships.

Schools build family–school partnerships by first building trust through actions that communicate the school's respect toward each family's educational values, economic resource level, and individual and cultural diversity. Families are welcome at school and treated sensitively. Educators try to become aware of each families' educational desires for their children. Usually a welcome letter is sent, a school tour is offered, and families are invited to stay children's first days. Schools develop plans to offer family supportive assistance.

Their efforts may include home–school activities, including different types of meetings, securing bilingual staff members or volunteers, offering family learning activity suggestions, and opening communication channels for aiding home–school connections. Schools strive to ensure family input is obtained in planning program goals and activities. Schools conduct various informational meetings and initiate communications that describe the school's philosophy, practices, and standards in both oral and written form

17-2 List language art skills schools attempt to increase by working through families.

Early childhood centers share their techniques and strategies to increase child language arts development and growth. Staff realizes families may have different views along with a greater opportunity to increase the language and literacy growth in their children's lives. The school encourages families to:

- spend time on language-developing activities.
- provide attention to child speech.
- offer home activities in matching items or characteristics.
- discuss color, shape, and size.
- sort household items.
- discuss and create categories of objects or happenings.
- provide writing tools, paper, etc.
- talk about alphabet letters and books.
- answer child questions and encourage child discovery.
- offer what is just beyond what the child knows.
- develop a "let us discover together" atmosphere.
- offer activities with a beginning and an ending process.
- recognize accomplishment and honest effort with verbal approval.
- create safe, secure environments in which children develop feelings of self-worth and feel valued for their ideas and opinions.
- encourage disciplined work habits.
- respect child fantasy play and make believe.

- stimulate child speaking abilities.
- attempt to add words to children's vocabulary.
- create an interest in print.
- encourage child social skills.
- provide outside of the home educational experiences and adventures.
- promote listening and prereading skills.
- offer storytelling.
- build child self-regulation skills.
- create home reading and writing centers.

17-3 Describe a school's home visiting goals.

Home visits are planned to help teachers understand children's individual needs and to cement home–school partnerships. Visits also help schools to assess the particular needs of children learning English and whether a family might be assisted by attending a family literacy program or by other kinds of services. Home visits enable staff members to gain an in-depth understanding concerning the culture of the home and its home literacy-encouraging activities. Visitors are better able to answer and react to family questions and concerns and also to discover child pursuits and interests at home and a child's particularly enjoyed language arts activity.

17-4 Name and describe two strategies used to facilitate family–school communication.

Strategies to facilitate family and school communication include written communication, spending time talking to or planning meetings with families, finding common concerns to discuss, offering information concerning program goals and teaching techniques, daily conversations, e-mails, workshops, social events, individual conferences, telephone calls, weekly newsletters, personal notes, family bulletin boards that include event announcements and local activities, posting articles of interest, and sharing with families topics that are of special interest or concern to individual staff members.

17-5 Discuss three ways families and volunteers might become resources for child language instruction.

Families and volunteers are seen as unique resources to a school's language instruction and a school's general operation. Schools encourage volunteering and active program participation by families and community volunteers. Becoming a guest speaker, providing classroom demonstrations on a variety of topics, joining in as an extra hand on field trips, performing volunteer maintenance task work, and raising operational funds is suggested. Securing useful language arts instructional supplies that were once discarded materials and making or constructing language games for classroom use or repairing classroom books, puppets, final sets, and other instructional materials is also suggested.

Additional Resources

Readings

Dunsmore, K. & Fisher, D. (Eds.) (2010). *Bringing Literacy Home*. Newark, DE: International Reading Association.

Fox, M. (2008). *Why Reading Aloud to Our Children Can Change Their Lives*. Orlando, FL: Harcourt.

Freeman, R. (2011). Home, school partnerships in family child care: Providers' relationships with their communities. *Early Child Development and Care 181*(6), 827–845.

Gonzales-Mena, J. (2008). *Diversity in Early Care and Education: Honoring Differences*. New York: McGraw-Hill.

McWilliam, R. A. (2010). *Working with Families of Young Children with Special Needs*. New York: Guilford Press.

Helpful Websites

American Academy of Pediatrics

http://www.aap.org

Position statements and pamphlets on media issues and age level recommendations.

International Reading Association

www.reading.org

Download related brochures and booklets.

National Center for Family and Community Connections with Schools

http://www.sedl.org/connections

Contains research and resources that encourage home–school partnerships.

National Child Care Information Center

http://nccic.org

A clearinghouse for information of interest to families and educators. Spanish-language resources are available. Select Publications link and request booklets.

NAEYC's Technology and Young Children

http://www.naeyc.org

A joint position statement on technology use with young children issued by the National Association for the Education of Young Children, and the Fred Rogers Center for Early Learning and Children's Media at Saint Vincent College.

Appendix

Resources for Education Standards Used in This Book

Education Standards Icons throughout the text alerted the reader to text sections that are related to standard's statements.

A complete set of the standards is found in the following references. Only areas in the standards pertaining to early childhood language and literacy are present in the text.

1. International Reading Association (2010). *Standards for Reading Professionals: A reference for the preparation of educators in the United States.* (Rev. ed.). Newark, DE: Author. (IRA Language and literacy standards are found on the inside of the front cover).

2. National Association for the Education of Young Children (2007). *NAEYC Early Childhood Program Standards and Accreditation Criteria: The Mark of Quality in Early Childhood Education.* Washington, DC: Author.

3. Copple, C., Bredekamp, S., Koralek, D., & Charner, K. (Eds.) (2013). *Developmentally Appropriate Practice in Early Childhood Programs: Focus on Infants and Toddlers.* Washington, DC: National Association for the Education of Young Children.

4. Copple, C., Bredekamp, S., Koralek, D., & Charner, K. (Eds.) (2013). *Developmentally Appropriate Practice: Focus on Preschoolers.* Washington, DC: National Association for the Education of Young Children.

5. National Governors Association Center for Best Practices and Council of Chief State School Officers (2010). *Common Core State Standards English Language Arts & literacy in history/social studies, science, and technical subjects.* Washington, DC: Authors.

Suggested Music (Chapters 2 and 7)

Suggested artists:

Tonja Evetts Weimer, Kathy Poelker, Raffi, Hap Palmer, Greg and Steve, L. Campbell Towel, Tom Glazer, J. Warren, J. Weissman, Fred Koch, and Ella Jenkins.

Commercial school supply resources for music/language play:

(All can be found online)

Lakeshore Learning Materials

Kaplan Early Learning Company

Discount School Supply

Rhythm Child Morphonix

Redleaf Press Curriculum Connections: Using Music to Help Children Learn, Moving and Learning across the Curriculum, and Rhymes, Songs, Homes, Fingerplays, and Chants.

Readings

A Report from the Early Child Summit

NAEYC

Finding Songs and Folk Music

The Teacher's Guide

Songs for Teaching

Contemplator's Child Ballad Website

ScoutSongs.org: Virtual Songbook—lyrics for Boy Scout's Songs, Girl Scout's Songs, and American Patriotic Songs

Author Recommended Activities and Experiences (Chapter 3)

The following program activities and experiences are recommended for children needing special instruction to equip them to enter a Common Core State Standards kindergarten.

Activities and experiences

- that encourage preschoolers to ask and answer questions about the details in picture books with teacher prompting and support.

- in which preschoolers gain listening skills and attempt to compare and contrast, make connections, or integrate new knowledge and ideas into what they already know and understand.

- that introduce foundational concepts and vocabulary in the content areas of mathematics, science, social studies, and other content areas mentioned in the Common Core State Standards.

- that introduce preschoolers to a wide range of types of children's literature and stories.

- that introduce preschoolers to the informational content found in nonfiction picture books and factual materials.

- that involve challenge and stretch what children already know by introducing new material just beyond what they possess.

- that point out the interrelatedness of reading, writing, listening, and speaking.

- that promote preschoolers' oral language and their participation in rich and varied conversational interactions in which children's ideas can be expressed.

- that involve print and the act of using printing for functional reasons and creative writing dictation.

- that are planned with built-in opportunities for preschoolers to use print to express themselves.

- in which explicit vocabulary development takes place and is repeated over time to promote the learning of new words.

- that offer preschoolers the opportunity to learn alphabet letter names, shapes, and sounds when developmentally appropriate.

- that offer access to developmentally appropriate technology and introduce basic operational procedures for child use with adult help and later self use.

These suggested recommendations are not meant to be a complete listing or a comprehensive language arts curriculum.

Assessment Tools (Chapter 5)

Ages and Stages Questionnaires, (A family checklist for 1 month to 66 months of age), Brookes Publishing Co.

Assessment of Literacy and Language (ALL), SEDL (www.sedl.org).

Boehm Test of Basic Concepts, Boehm-3-Preschool.

Bricker, D., Capt, B., Johnson, J., Pretti-Frontezak, K., Slentz, K., Straka, E., & Weddel, M. (2002). *Assessment, evaluation, and programming system for infants and children (AEPS)*. Baltimore, MD: Brookes Publishing Co.

Clay, M. (1996). *Observational survey of early literacy achievement*. Portsmouth, NH: Heinemann.

Early Language and Literacy Classroom Observation Toolkit (ELLCO). Baltimore, MD: Brookes Publishing Co.

ERA: Early Reading Assessment, PRO-ED.

PALS PreK: *Phonological Awareness Literacy Screening for Preschool*. (2002). Publisher: University of Virginia Press.

Preschool Language Scale (PLS-4).

Preschool Outcomes Checklist. Venn, E. C., & Jahn, M. C. (2004). *Teaching and learning in the preschool: Using individually appropriate practices in early childhood*. Newark, DE: International Reading Association (May be copied for classroom use.).

Reading Skills Competency Tests—Readiness Level. Publisher: The Writing Company.

Smith, M. W., Brady, J.P., & Anastasopoulas, L. (2009). *Early language & literacy classroom observation tool (ELLCO PreK)*. Baltimore, MD: Brookes Publishing Co.

TERA-3: Test of Early Reading Ability, 3rd ed., PRO-ED.

Test of Language Development (TOLD).

Test of Early Reading Ability (2001). Publisher: PRO-ED; ages: 3 to 10.

Test of Oral Language Development. Publisher: PRO-ED.

Test of Phonological Awareness. Publisher: PRO-ED; level: kindergarten.

TEWL-3: Test of Early Written Language, 3rd. Ed., PRO-ED.

TOPEL: Test of Preschool Early Literacy, PRO-ED.

Woodcock-Johnson Educational Battery. Publisher: Riverside Publishing; ages: 2 and above.

Woodcock-Johnson Reading Mastery. Publisher: American Guidance Services/Pearson AGS Globe; level: K–12.

Additional Story (Chapter 9)

The Crooked-Mouth Family

There are many versions of this action story. This one, however, appeals to young children and never fails to bring laughter and requests to have it repeated. Before the teacher begins the story, she can quietly light a candle—preferably a dripless one.

Once there was a family called The Crooked-Mouth Family.

The father had a mouth like this.
(Twist mouth to the right.)

The mother had a mouth like this.
(Twist mouth to the left.)

The Big Brother had a mouth like this.
(Bring lower lip over upper lip.)

The Big Sister had a mouth like this.
(Bring upper lip over lower lip.)

But the Baby Sister had a pretty mouth just like yours.
(Smile naturally.) (Repeat mouth positions as each character speaks.)

One night they forgot to blow the candle out when they went upstairs to bed. The father said, "I'd better go downstairs and blow that candle out."
(With mouth still twisted to the right, blow at the flame being careful not to blow it out.)

"What's the matter with this candle? It won't go out."
(Repeat blowing several times.)

"I guess I'd better call Mother. Mother!

Please come down and blow the candle out."

Mother said, "Why can't you blow the candle out? Anybody can blow a candle out. You just go like this."
(She blows at the flame, mouth still twisted to the left.)

"I can't blow it out either. We'd better call Big Brother."
(Change to father's mouth.)

"Brother! Please come down and blow the candle out."

Big Brother said, "That's easy. All you have to do is blow hard."
(With lower lip over upper, hold the candle low and blow.)

Father said, "See. You can't blow it out either. We'll have to call Big Sister.

Sister! Please come down and blow the candle out!"

Big Sister said, "I can blow it out. Watch me."
(With upper lip over lower, candle held high, blow several times.)

Father said, "That's a funny candle. I told you I couldn't blow it out." Mother said, "I couldn't blow it out, either." Big Brother said, "Neither could I." Big Sister said, "I tried and tried, and I couldn't blow it out."

Father said, "I guess we'll have to call Baby Sister. Baby Sister! Please come down and blow the candle out."

Baby Sister came downstairs, rubbing her eyes because she had been asleep. She asked, "What's the matter?" Father said, "I can't blow the candle out." Mother said, "I can't blow it out either." Big Brother said, "Neither can I." Big Sister said, "I can't either." Baby Sister said, "Anybody can blow a candle out. That's easy." And she did.

Author Unknown

Flannel Board Activity Sets (Chapter 11)

The Hare and the Tortoise

Pieces: rabbit, dog, rabbit running, rabbit sleeping, tree, finish line, lag, turtle, hen

One day the rabbit was talking to some of the other animals. "I am the fastest runner in the forest," he said. "I can beat anyone! Do you want to race?" "Not I," said the dog.

Put on turtle, dog, hen, and rabbit at left edge of board.

"Not I," said the hen.

"I will race with you," said the turtle.

"That's a good joke," said the rabbit. "I could dance around you all the way and still win."

"Still bragging about how fast you are," answered the turtle. "Come on, let's race. Do you see that flag over there? That will be the finish line. Hen, would you stand by the flag so you can tell who wins the race?"

Add finish-line flag on right edge of board. Move hen by flag.

Put on running rabbit. Remove standing rabbit.

"Dog, will you say the starting words—get on your mark, get ready, get set, go!"

"Stand there," said the dog. "Get on your mark, get ready, get set, go!"

The rabbit ran very fast. He looked over his shoulder and saw how slowly the turtle was running on his short little legs. Just then he saw a shady spot under a tree. He thought to himself—that turtle is so slow I have time to rest here under this tree. So he sat down on the cool grass, and before he knew it, he was fast asleep.

Add sleeping rabbit while removing running rabbit.

While he slept, the turtle was running. (Clump, Clump—Clump, Clump) He was not running very fast, but he kept on running. (Clump, Clump—Clump, Clump) Pretty soon the turtle came to the tree where the rabbit was sleeping. He went past and kept on running. (Clump, Clump—Clump, Clump) The turtle was almost to the finish line. The hen saw the turtle coming and said, "Turtle, keep on running. You've almost won the race." When the hen spoke, the rabbit awoke. He looked down by the finish line and saw the turtle was almost there. As fast as he could, the rabbit started running again. Just then he heard the hen say, "The turtle is the winner!"

Change sleeping rabbit to running rabbit.

"But I'm the fastest," said the rabbit.

"Not this time," said the hen. "Sometimes slow and steady wins the race."

The Big, Big Turnip

(Traditional)

Pieces:	farmer	turnip	daughter	mouse
	farmer's wife	large piece of ground	dog	cat.

A farmer once planted a turnip seed. And it grew, and it grew, and it grew. The farmer saw it was time to pull the turnip out of the ground. So he took hold of it and began to pull.

Place farmer on board. Cover turnip so only top is showing with ground piece, and place on board.

He pulled, and he pulled, and he pulled, and he pulled. But the turnip wouldn't come up. So the farmer called to his wife who was getting dinner.

Fe, fi, fo, fum.

I pulled the turnip,

But it wouldn't come up.

And the wife came running, and she took hold of the farmer, and they pulled, and they pulled, and they pulled, and they pulled. But the turnip wouldn't come up.

Move farmer next to turnip with hands on turnip top. Place wife behind farmer.

So the wife called to the daughter who was feeding the chickens nearby.

Fe, fi, fo, fum.

We pulled the turnip,

But it wouldn't come up.

And the daughter came running. The daughter took hold of the wife. The wife took hold of the farmer.

Place daughter behind farmer's wife.

The farmer took hold of the turnip. And they pulled, and they pulled, and they pulled, and they pulled. But the turnip wouldn't come up.

So the daughter called to the dog who was chewing a bone.

Fe, fi, fo, fum.

We pulled the turnip,

But it wouldn't come up.

And the dog came running. The dog took hold of the daughter. The daughter took hold of the wife. The wife took hold of the farmer. And the farmer took hold of the turnip. And they pulled, and they pulled, and they pulled. But the turnip wouldn't come up.

Place dog behind daughter.

The dog called to the cat that was chasing her tail. Fe, fi, fo, fum.

We pulled the turnip,

But it wouldn't come up.

And the cat came running. The cat took hold of the dog. The dog took hold of the daughter. The daughter took hold of the wife. The wife took hold of the farmer. The farmer took hold of the turnip. And they pulled, and they pulled, and they pulled. But the turnip wouldn't come up.

So the cat called the mouse that was nibbling spinach nearby.

Fe, fi, fo, fum.

We pulled the turnip,

But it wouldn't come up.

And the mouse came running.

"That little mouse can't help," said the dog. "He's too little." "Phooey," squeaked the mouse. "I could pull that turnip up myself, but since you have all been pulling, I'll let you help too."

So the mouse took hold of the cat. The cat took hold of the dog. The dog took hold of the daughter.

The daughter took hold of the wife. The wife took hold of the farmer. The farmer took hold of the turnip. And they pulled, and they pulled, and they pulled. And up came the turnip.

And the mouse squeaked, "I told you so!"

Place cat behind dog.

Place mouse behind cat.

Remove ground.

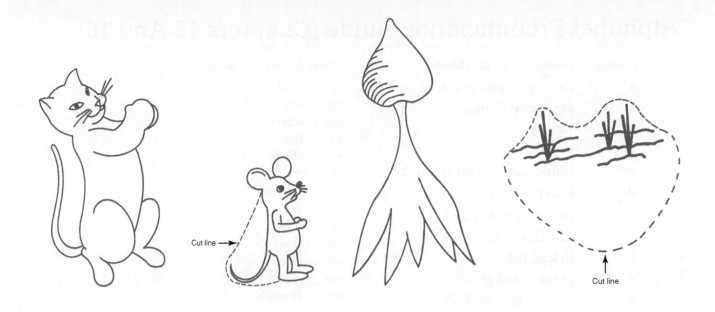

Cut line

Cut line

Alphabet Pronunciation Guide (Chapters 15 And 16)

Symbols	Sounds as in the Words
a	fat, apple, asks (short *a*)
ā	ate, name (long *a*)
b	rib, big
c	cereal (soft *c*)
c	traffic, cat, certain (hard *c*)
d	lid, end, feed
e	end, wet, pen (short *e*)
ē	me, Elaine, eat (long *e*)
f	if, leaf, full
g	grape (hard *g*)
g	rag, go, gem (soft *g*)
h	hat, how, high
i	it, individual, pin (short *i*)
i	piece, niece
ī	ice, while (long *i*)
j	jump, jeep
k	lick, kiss, milk
l	will, late, little
m	him, me, custom
n	sun, not, even
o	ox, on, not (short *o*)
ō	go, open, home (long *o*)
p	sip, pat
r	ran, rip, very
s	kiss, so, last, sugar
t	hit, top
u	up, rug, custom (short *u*)
ū	use, unite (long *u*)
v	give, have, very
w	we, win, watch
x	box
y	yea, you
ȳ	my, cry
z	zoo, fuzz

Vowel Digraph Sounds

ai . . . snail
ay . . . say
ea . . . lead
ea . . . tea
ee . . . sheep
ei . . . receive
ie . . . believe
ey . . . key
ey . . . they
oa . . . float
oe . . . hoe
ow . . . grow
ou . . . though

Vowel Diphthongs

oi . . . toil
ou . . . though
oy . . . soy
ue . . . sue
ew . . . new

Consonant Digraph Examples

ch as in chess
gh as in ghost
ph as in phonic
sh as in shoe
th as in thank

Short Vowels (one letter usually)

a   hat
e   net
i   pig
o   dog
u   duck

The Long Vowels

a   rain, pay, take, weigh, grey
e   feet, mean, she, chief
i   pipe, might, cry, mild
o   home, boat, slow, sold
u   cube
oo tube, boot, blue, blew

Glossary

A

accent — prominence or emphasis given to a word or syllable through one or more of the following factors: loudness, change of pitch, and longer duration.

accommodation — the process by which new experiences or events change existing ideas or thought patterns.

activity plans — written, detailed, step-by-step teaching plans, often including an evaluation section.

acuity — how well or clearly one uses the senses; the degree of perceptual sharpness.

affective sphere — the affectionate feelings (or lack of them) shaped through experience with others.

alliteration — the repetition of the initial sounds in neighboring words or stressed syllables, for example, "The foam flowed free and fizzy."

alphabetic principle — the awareness that spoken language can be analyzed as strings of separate words and words, in turn, as sequences of syllables and phonemes within syllables.

articulation — the adjustments and movements of the muscles of the mouth and jaw involved in producing clear oral communication.

assessment — a broad repertoire of behaviors involved in noticing, documenting, recording, and interpreting children's behaviors and performances. Testing is a subset of assessment behaviors in which performances are controlled and elicited in standardized conditions.

assimilation — the process that allows new experiences to merge with previously stored mental structures.

assonance — the repetition of words of identical or similar vowel sounds followed by different consonant sounds.

attachment — a two-way process formed through mutual gratification of needs and reciprocal communication influenced by the infant's growing cognitive abilities. It is sometimes referred to as bonding or a "love affair" relationship.

audience — a group of people attending a performance such as a play and/or dramatic presentation, or a group of listeners or spectators attending an event.

audiovisual equipment — any mechanical or nonmechanical item useful in offering sight or hearing experience.

auditory — relating to or experienced through hearing.

auditory processing — the full range of mental activity involved in reacting to auditory stimuli, especially speech sounds, and in considering their meanings in relation to past experience and to their future use.

B

babbling — an early language stage in sound production in which an infant engages in vocal play with vowel and consonant sounds, including some sounds not found in his or her language environment.

behaviorism — the theoretical viewpoint, espoused by theorists such as B. F. Skinner, that behavior is shaped by environmental forces, specifically in response to reward and punishment.

bilingual — refers to an individual with a language background other than English who has developed proficiency in the primary language and a degree of proficiency in English.

Black English — a language usually spoken in some economically depressed African-American homes. A dialect of non-Standard English having its own rules and patterns, it is also called African-American English.

C

chants — rhythmic utterances that may rhyme, be enjoyed, or become monotonous.

characterization — the way an author presents a character by describing character verbalizations, actions, or thinking, or by what other characters say, think, or do about the character.

characters — persons (or puppets) represented in or acting in a story or drama.

child-initiated curricula — a basic tenet underlying this type of curriculum is the belief that true growth occurs when children are free to develop intrinsic interests naturally.

circle time — an early childhood term describing a planned gathering of children, usually seated in a half-circle configuration, led by a teacher.

classify — the act of systematically grouping things according to identifiable common characteristics, for example, size.

closure — a conversation technique that prompts children to verbally guess and complete or fill in a teacher's sentence. The teacher pauses or hesitates, which prompts the child to finish a teacher verbalization.

cluttering — rapid, incomplete speech that is often jerky, slurred, spoken in bursts, and difficult to understand; nervous speech.

cognition — the process that creates mental images, concepts, and operations.

communication — the giving (sending) and receiving of information, signals, or messages.

concept — a commonly recognized element (or elements) that identifies groups or classes; usually has a given name.

consonant — (1) a speech sound made by partial or complete closure of the vocal tract, which obstructs air flow; (2) an alphabet letter used in representing any of these sounds.

constructivist theory — a theory such as that of Jean Piaget, based on the belief that children construct knowledge for themselves rather than having it conveyed to them by some external source.

continuant — a consonant or vowel that may be continued or prolonged without alteration during one emission of breath.

convergent thinking — the process of analyzing and integrating ideas to infer reasonable conclusions or specific solutions from given information.

cooing — an early stage during the prelinguistic period in which vowel sounds are repeated, particularly the *u-u-u* sound.

couplets — stanzas of two rhyming lines.

cues — prompts or hints that aid recognition, such as a parent pointing to and/or saying "teddy bear" when sharing a picture book illustration. This is done because the infant is familiar with his own teddy bear.

cultural literacy — literacy that reflects a culture's knowledge of significant ideas, events, values, and the essence of that culture's identity.

culture — all the activities and achievements of a society that individuals within that society pass from one generation to the next.

curriculum — an overall plan for the content of instruction to be offered in a program.

curriculum models — refers to a conceptual framework and organizational structure for decision making about educational priorities, administrative policies, instructional methods, and evaluation criteria.

D

deafness — hearing is so impaired that the individual is unable to process auditory linguistic information, with or without amplification.

deficit perspective — an attitude or belief that attributes children's school failures to children themselves, or to their family or culture.

dialect — a variety of spoken language unique to a geographical area or social group. Variations in dialect may include phonological or sound variations, syntactical variations, and lexical or vocabulary variations.

dialogue — a conversation between two or more persons or between a person and something else.

diction — clarity of speech; enunciation.

discourse skills — refers to using language in structured ways to go beyond basic conversation, for example, telling a story, explaining a procedure, creating a fantasy, dictating ideas, and elaborating to provide greater understanding.

divergent thinking — the process of elaborating on ideas to generate new ideas or alternative interpretations of given information.

dramas — plays; stories in dramatic form, typically emphasizing conflict in and among key characters.

dramatic play — acting out experiences or creating drama episodes during play.

dual coding — the belief that infants' experiences and emotions influence cognition.

E

early literacy — speaking, listening, print awareness and writing behaviors, reading of alphabet letters and words, and other skills that evolve and change over time, culminating in conventional literacy.

Ebonics — a nonstandard form of English, a dialect often called Black English that is characterized by not conjugating the verb "to be" and by dropping some final consonants from words.

echolalia — a characteristic of the babbling period. The child repeats (echoes) the same sounds over and over.

equilibrium — a balance attained with consistent care and satisfaction of needs that leads to a sense of security and lessens anxiety.

expansion — a teaching technique that includes the adult's (teacher's) modeling of words or grammar, filling in missing words in children's utterances, or suggesting ideas for child exploration.

explanatory talk — a type of conversation characterized by a speaker's attempt to create connections between objects, events, concepts, or conclusions to promote understanding in the listener.

expository — provides accurate verifiable information about the social or natural world.

expressive jargon — a term describing a child's first attempts at combining words into narration that result in a mimic of adult speech.

expressive (productive) vocabulary — the vocabulary a person uses in speaking and writing.

extension — a teaching strategy in which an adult expands the child's information by adding new, additional, related information or meaning.

F

fable — a short tale in prose or verse that teaches a moral, usually with talking animals or inanimate objects as main characters.

fairy tales — folk stories about real-life problems, usually with imaginary characters and magical events.

family literacy programs — community programs attempting to provide literacy-building opportunities and experiences for families. Services are available for both adults and children.

fiction — imaginative narrative in any form of presentation that is designed to entertain, as distinguished from that which is designed primarily to explain, argue, or merely describe.

figurative language — language enriched by word images and figures of speech.

G

gaze coupling — infant–mother extended eye contact.

genre — a category used to classify literary works, usually by form, technique, or content.

grammar — the rules of a specific language that include both written and spoken utterances and describe how that specific language works and the forms of speech that conform to the rules that well-schooled speakers and writers observe in any given language.

grapheme — the sum of all written letters and letter combinations that represent one phoneme.

H

hearing — the facility or sense by which sound is perceived.

hearing disabilities — characterized by an inability to hear sounds clearly. This may range from hearing speech sounds faintly or in a distorted way, to profound deafness.

holophrases — the expression of a whole idea in a single word. They are often found in the speech of children at about 12 to 18 months of age.

I

impulsive — quick to answer or react to either a simple or complex situation or problem.

inflections — the grammatical "markers," such as plurals. Also, a change in pitch or loudness of the voice.

inner speech — mentioned in Vygotsky's theory as private speech that becomes internalized and is useful in organizing ideas.

interactionists — those who adhere to the theory that language develops through a combination of inborn factors and environmental influences.

interactive writing — (1) an instructional strategy popular in American kindergartens; (2) a process involving a teacher who verbally stretches each word so that the child (children) can distinguish sounds and letters. This is also known as shared writing.

invented spelling — the result of an attempt to spell a word whose spelling is not already known, based on a writer's knowledge of the spelling system and how it works.

J

joint attention — child's awareness that he or she must gain and hold another's focus during communicational exchanges to get his or her message understood.

L

language — the systematic, conventional use of sounds, signs, or written symbols in a human society for communication and self-expression. It conveys meaning that is mutually understood.

language center — a classroom area specifically set aside and equipped for language arts–related activities and child use.

listening — a mental process that includes attending, hearing, discriminating, understanding, and remembering.

listening center — a classroom area designed to accommodate children's listening experiences.

listening comprehension level — the highest grade level of material that can be comprehended well when it is read aloud to a child.

literacy — involves complex cognitive interactions between readers and their texts and between background knowledge and new information. It involves both skill and knowledge and varies by task and setting. Different types of literacy are described — prose, document,

quantitative, academic, workplace, and functional. It is a distinct domain related to that of language and refers to the ability to produce and comprehend written language.

M

mental image — a "perceptual representation" or mental picture of a perceptual experience, remembered or imagined.

metalinguistic awareness — a conscious awareness on the part of a language user of language as an object in itself.

metalinguistic skills — the ability to think about language as a separate entity.

metaphors — figures of speech in which a comparison is implied by analogy but is not stated.

moderation level — an individual preferred state of arousal between bored and excited when learning and pleasure peak.

modifiers — words that give a special characteristic to a noun (for example, a large ball).

monologue — literally "speaking alone."

morpheme — the smallest unit in a language that by itself has a recognizable meaning.

morphology — the study of the units of meaning in a language.

N

narrative — in general, a story, actual or fictional, expressed orally or in writing.

nativists — those who adhere to the theory that children are born with biological dispositions for learning that unfold or mature in a natural way.

neurolinguistics — a branch of linguistics that studies the structure and function of the brain in relation to language acquisition, learning, and use.

nonfiction — prose that explains, argues, or describes; usually factual.

nursery rhymes — folk sayings with rhyming words for very young children.

nurturist — one who adheres to the theory that the minds of children are blank or unformed and need educational input or direct instruction to develop and "output" knowledge and appropriate behavior.

O

onsets — any consonants before a vowel in a syllable.

orthographic awareness — the ability to notice and use critical features of graphic symbols in written language.

otitis media — inflammation and/or infection of the middle ear.

outreach — an early childhood program's attempt to provide supportive assistance to attending children's families to promote their children's success in school and developmental growth.

overextension — in the early acquisition of words and their meanings, the application of a word to include other objects that share common features, such as "water" being used to describe any liquid.

overregularization — the tendency on the part of children to make the language regular, such as using past tenses like -ed on verb endings.

P

pantomime — creative communication done with nonverbal physical actions.

parentese — a high-pitched, rhythmic, singsong, crooning style of speech. It is also known as motherese or baby talk.

participation stories — stories with some feature children can enact through physical movements, verbal expression, or both.

perception — mental awareness of objects and other data gathered through the five senses.

personification — a metaphorical figure of speech in which animals, ideas, things, etc., are represented as having human qualities.

phonation — exhaled air passes the larynx's vibrating folds and produces "voice."

phoneme — the smallest unit of speech that distinguishes one utterance from another.

phonemic awareness — the insight that every spoken word can be conceived as a sequence of phonemes, and/or the awareness that spoken words are made up of sounds, and the ability to segment a word into its constituent sounds.

phonetic instruction — instruction in phonics is instruction that stresses sound–symbol relationships. It is a strategy used in beginning reading instruction.

phonetics — pertaining to representing the sounds of speech with a set of distinct symbols, each denoting a single sound.

phonological awareness — the whole spectrum from primitive awareness of speech sounds and rhythms to rhyme awareness and sound similarities; at the highest level, awareness of syllables or phonemes.

phonology — the sound system of a language and how it is represented with an alphabetic code.

plot — the structure of the action of a story.

poems — metrical forms of composition in which word images are selected and expressed to create powerful, often beautiful, impressions in the listener and/or enjoyable rhythmic responses in young children.

pragmatics — the study of how language is used effectively in a social context; varying speech patterns depending on social circumstances and the context of situations.

print awareness — in early literacy, the child's growing recognition of the conventions and characteristics of a written language. It includes recognition of directionality in reading (left to right and top to bottom), that print forms words corresponding to speech, and that spaces separate words and other features.

prosodic speech — the child's use of voice modulation and word stress to give special emphasis and meaning.

psychosocial theory — the branch of psychology founded by Erik Erikson; development is described in terms of eight stages that span childhood and adulthood.

R

reading method — any of several relatively specific procedures or steps for teaching one or more aspects of reading, each procedure embodying explicitly or implicitly some theory of how children learn and of the relationship between written and spoken language.

realism — presents experience without embellishment to convey life as it appears in a natural world limited by the senses and reason.

recasting — a teaching technique that involves a teacher who supplies children's missing words or gently models correct usage of words or extends the child's idea following the child's verbal statement.

receptive (comprehension) vocabulary — the comprehension vocabulary used by a person in listening (and silent reading).

regularization — a child's speech behavior that indicates the formation and internalization of a language rule (regularity).

resonation — amplification of laryngeal sounds using cavities of the mouth, nose, sinuses, and pharynx.

responsive mothers — mothers who are alert and timely in responding to and giving attention to infants' needs and communications.

rhythm — uniform or patterned recurrence of a beat, accent, or melody in speech.

rimes — the vowel and any consonants after it in a syllable.

S

scaffolding — a teaching technique helpful in promoting languages, understanding, and child solutions. It includes teacher-responsive conversation, open-ended questioning, and facilitation of children's initiatives. Also defined as instruction in which a teacher builds upon what the child already knows to help the child accomplish a task and/or suggests breaking a task down into simpler components to promote accomplishment.

selective (elective) mutism — a behavior that describes child silence or lack of speech in select surroundings and/or with certain individuals.

self-regulation — the extent to which children are able to control impulses and stop themselves from a reactive or habitual response.

semantics — the study of meanings associated with words and the acquisition of vocabulary.

sensory-motor development — the control and use of sense organs and the body's muscle structure.

sight reading — the ability to immediately recognize a word as a whole without sounding it out.

signing — a body positioning, sound, action, gesture, or combination of these undertaken by an infant in an effort to communicate a need, desire, or message.

similes — comparisons of two things that are unlike, usually using the words *like* or *as*. Example: "Love is like a red, red rose."

social connectedness — a term associated with the following human characteristics: is stable and secure, develops close relationships with others, has supportive family and friends, and is deemed a worthy individual by others. Often seen by others as able to transcend stress and possess an individual identity.

social constructivist theory — a theory involving ideas such as Vygotsky's emphasis on the importance of language and socially shared cognition in exchanges between adult and child when scaffolding is used, and encouraging children's use of private speech to aid problem solving.

socioeconomic — relating to or involving a combination of social and economic factors.

software — a wide range of commercial programs developed for computer users' convenience, education, entertainment, and so on.

spatial–temporal reasoning — the mental arrangement of ideas and/or images in a graphic pattern indicating their relationships over time.

speech and language disabilities — communication disorders that affect the way people talk and understand, ranging from simple sound substitutions to not being able to use speech and language at all.

Standard English — substantially uniform formal and informal speech and writing of educated people that is widely recognized as acceptable wherever English is spoken and understood.

story — an imaginative tale with a plot, characters, and setting.

story map — a timeline showing an ordered sequence of events.

subculture — an ethnic, regional, economic, or social group exhibiting characteristic patterns of behavior sufficient to distinguish it from others within an embracing culture or society.

symbols — things that stand for or suggest (such as pictures, models, word symbols, and so forth).

synapses — gap-like structures over which the axon of one neuron beams a signal to the dendrites of another, forming a connection in the human brain. They affect memory and learning.

syntax — the arrangement of words as elements in a sentence to show their relationship.

T

telegraphic speech — a characteristic of young children's sentences in which everything but the crucial word(s) is omitted, as if for a telegram.

transitional kindergarten — a relatively new feature of some elementary school districts that offers supportive literacy activities and classroom access (usually during the summer before the child is to enroll in kindergarten).

transitional statements — teacher statements made to disperse students in small groups or in an orderly fashion.

V

verses — lines of a poem or poetry without imaginative or conceptual power.

visualization — the process, or result, of mentally picturing objects or events that are normally experienced directly.

visual literacy — the ability to interpret and communicate with respect to visual symbols in media other than print.

vowel — (1) a voiced speech sound made without stoppage or friction of airflow as it passes through the vocal tract; (2) an alphabet letter used in representing any of these sounds.

W

webbing—a visual or graphic method of mapping a possible course of study.

writing—the ability to use print to communicate with others.

References

Acredolo, L., & Goodwyn, S. (1985). Symbolic gesturing in language development. *Human Development, 28,* 53–58.

Acredolo, L., & Goodwyn, S. (2000). *Baby minds: Brain-building games your baby will love to play.* New York: Bantam Books.

Ada, A. F. (2003). *A magical encounter: Latino children's literature in the classroom.* Boston: Allyn & Bacon.

Ainsworth, M. D. S., & Bell, S. M. (1972). Mother–infant interaction and development of competence. *ERIC Digest,* ED-065-180.

Alexander, L. (2004, Summer). Putting parents in charge. *Education next, 4*(3), 39–44.

American Academy of Pediatrics. (2011). Policy statement: Media use by children younger than two years. *Pediatrics, 128*(5), 1040–1045.

American Speech-Language-Hearing Association. (2001, 2004). *How does your child hear and talk?* [Brochure]. Rockville, MD: American Speech-Language-Hearing Association.

Anderson, N. A. (2007). *What should I read aloud? A guide to 200 best-selling picture books.* Newark, DE: International Reading Association.

Antonucci, M. (2003, October 29). Gaga over TV. *San Jose Mercury News,* pp. 1A, 5A.

Ashton-Warner, S. (1963). *Teacher.* New York: Simon & Schuster.

Au, K. H. (2006). Multicultural factors and the effective instruction of students of diverse backgrounds. In A. E. Farstrup & S. J. Samuels (Eds.), *What research has to say about reading instruction* (pp. 392–413). Newark, DE: International Reading Association.

August, D., & Shanahan, T. (2006). Introduction and methodology. In D. August & T. Shanahan (Eds.), *Developing literacy in second-language learners. Report of the National Literacy Panel on language-minority children and youth* (pp. 1–42). Mahwah, NJ: Lawrence Erlbaum Associates.

Baker, I., & Schiffer, M. B. (2007, May). The reading chair. *Young Children, 62*(3), 44–49.

Bardige, B. (2005). *At a loss for words: How America is failing our children and what we can do about it.* Philadelphia: Temple University Press.

Bardige, B. S. (2009). *Talk to me, baby!: How you can support young children's language development.* Baltimore, MD: Paul H. Brookes Publishing Co.

Barone, D. M., & Xu, S. H. (2008). *Literacy instruction for English language learners, Pre-K–2.* New York: The Guilford Press.

Barrett, J. (2003, November 10). Tune in or tune out? *Newsweek,* p. 71.

Batchelor, K. L, & Bintz, W. P. (2012, February). Hand–clap songs across the curriculum. *The Reading Teacher, 65*(5), 341–345.

Bauerlein, V. (2013, January 31). The new script for teaching handwriting is no script at all. *Wall Street Journal,* pp. A1, A3.

Begley, S. (2009, September 14). Pink brain, blue brain: Claims of sex differences fall apart. *Newsweek,* p. 28.

Begley, S. (2009, December 7). It's in our genes, so what? DNA takes you only so far. *Newsweek,* p. 36A.

Bennett-Armistead, V. S., Duke, N. K., & Moses, A. M. (2005). *Literacy and the youngest learner: Best practices for educators of children from birth to 5.* New York: Scholastic.

Bergren, D., Reid, R., & Torelli, L. (2001). *Educating and caring for very young children.* New York: Teachers College Press.

Bernstein, B. (1962). Social class, linguistic codes and grammatical elements. *Language and speech, 5,* 31–46.

Biemiller, A., & Slonim, N. (2001). Estimating root word vocabulary growth in normative and advantaged populations. *Journal of Education Psychology, 93,* 498–520.

Bintz, W. (2010, May). Singing across the curriculum. *The Reading Teacher, 63*(8), 683–686.

Birckmayer, J., Kennedy, A., & Stonehouse, A. (2009). *From lullabies to literature: Stories in the lives of infants and toddlers.* Castle Hill, Australia: Pademelon Press.

Birckmayer, J., Kennedy, A., & Stonehouse, A. (2010, January). Sharing spoken language: Sounds, conversations and told stories. *Young Children, 65*(1), 34–39.

Blair, C. (2003, July). Self-regulation and school readiness. *ERIC Digest,* EDO-PS-03-7.

Bodrova, E., & Leong, D. (1996). *Tools of the mind.* Englewood Cliffs, NJ: Prentice Hall.

Bodrova, E., & Leong. D. J. (2012). Scaffolding self-regulated learning in young children. In R. C. Pianta (Ed.), *Handbook of Early Childhood Education* (pp. 352–369), New York: Guilford Press.

Bodrova, E., Leong, D. J., Paynter, D., & Semenov, D. (2000). *A framework for early literacy instruction: Aligning standards to developmental accomplishments and student behaviors: Pre-K through kindergarten.* Aurora, CO: Mid-continent Research for Education and Learning.

Boltz, R. H. (2007). What we want: Boys and girls talk about reading. *School Library Media Research,* 10.

Borba, M. F. (2009, Fall). Shared Reading: A model for linking literacy instruction and informational text. *The California Reader, 43*(1), 11–17.

Boser, U. (2006, October). Say what? *Smithsonian, (37)*7, 84.

Bradley, B. A., & Jones, J. (2010). Sharing alphabet books in early childhood classrooms. In D. S. Strickland (Ed.), *Essential readings in early literacy* (pp. 70–82). Newark, DE: International Reading Association.

Brady, S., Fowler, A., Stone, B., & Winbury, S. (1994). Training phonological awareness: A study with inner-city kindergarten children. *Annals of Dyslexia, 44,* 27–59.

Bredekamp, S., & Copple, C. (1997). *Developmentally appropriate practice in early childhood programs* (Rev. ed.). Washington, DC: National Association for the Education of Young Children.

Bronson, P., & Merryman, A. (2010, July 19). The creativity crisis: For the first time, research shows that American creativity is declining, what went wrong—And how we can fix it. *Newsweek,* pp. 45–50.

Brown, E. (2009, November 21). The playtime's the thing. *The Washington Post.* Retrieved December 7, 2009 from http://www.washingtonpost.com/wp_dynlcontent/article/2009/11/20AR20091120039.html

Brown, G. (1987). Twenty-five years of teaching listening comprehension. *English Teaching Forum, 25*(1), 11–15.

Burman, L. (2009). *Are you listening? Fostering conversations that help children learn.* St. Paul, MN: Redleaf Press.

Burmark, L. (2002). *Visual literacy: Learn to see, see to learn.* Alexandria, VA: Association for Supervision and Curriculum Development.

California Department of Education (2009). *Preschool English Learners: Principles and practices to promote language, literacy and learning.* Sacramento, CA: Author.

Cambourne, B. (1988). *The whole story: Natural learning and the acquisition of literacy in the classroom.* New York: Ashton Scholastic.

Canada, G. (2010). Bringing change to scale: The next big reform challenge. In K. Weber (Ed.), *Waiting for Superman: How we can save Americas failing public schools* (pp. 189–200). New York: Perseus Books Group.

Carlsson-Paige, N. (2012, Winter). Media and technology in ECE. *Connections,* p. 26–27.

Cassidy, J., Valadez, C. M., & Garrett, S. D. (2010). Literacy trends and issues: A look at the five pillars and the cement that supports them. *The Reading Teacher, 63*(8), 644–655.

Center for Research on Education, Diversity & Excellence. (2001, Summer). Some program alternatives for English language learners, *Practitioners Brief #3.* Santa Cruz, CA: University of California.

Cheatham, G. A., & Ro, Y. E. (2010, July). Young English learner's inner language as context for language and early literacy development. *Young Children, 65*(4), 18–23.

Chenfeld, M. B. (2007, August/September). Handcuffed in the garden of thorns. *Reading Today, 25*(1), 20.

Child Care Bureau. (2004, May). *Promoting responsible fatherhood through childcare.* Washington, DC: U.S. Department of Health and Human Services, Administration for Children and Families, Administration on Children, Youth and Families.

Chomsky, N. (1968). *Language and mind.* New York: Harcourt, Brace, and World.

Christ, T., & Wang, X. C. (2010, July). Bridging the vocabulary gap: What research tells us about vocabulary instruction in early childhood. *Young Children, 65*(4), 84–91.

Christakis, D. A., & Zimmerman, F. J. (2007). Violent television viewing during preschool is associated with antisocial behavior during school age. *Pediatrics, 120,* 993–999. Retrieved January 23, 2008, from http://pediatrics.aapublication.org/egi/gca?aiich5&SEARCHED51&FULLTEXT5toddle.

Chukovsky, K. (1963). *From two to five.* Berkeley, CA: University of California.

Clay, M. (1993). *An observational survey of early literacy achievement.* Auckland, New Zealand: Heinemann.

Cohen, S. (2013, March 13). A preschool program conservatives can love. *Wall Street Journal,* p. A13.

Coles, G. (2004, January). Danger in the classroom: 'Brain glitch' research and learning to read. *Phi Delta Kappan,* pp. 344–351.

Colker, L. J. (2010, October/November). Teaching preschoolers to think optimistically. *TCY (Teaching young children/preschool), 4*(1), 20–23.

Collins, R., & Ribeiro, R. (2004). Toward an early care and education agenda for Hispanic children. *Early Childhood Research and Practice, 6*(2), 161–192.

Common Core State Standards Initiative. (2010). National Governors Association Center for Best Practices and Council of Chief State School Officers. Washington, DC: Authors.

Copple, C., & Bredekamp, S. (Eds.). (2009). *Developmentally appropriate practice in early childhood programs serving children from birth through age 8.* Washington, DC: National Association for the Education of Young Children.

Copple, C., Bredekamp, S., Koralek, D., & Charner, K. (Eds.). (2013a). *Developmentally appropriate practice: Focus on infants and toddlers.* Washington, DC: National Association for the Education of Young Children.

Copple, C., Bredekamp, S., Koralek, D., & Charner, K. (Eds.). (2013b). *Developmentally appropriate practice: Focus on preschoolers.* Washington, DC: National Association for the Education of Young Children.

Costa, A. L. (1991). The search for intelligent life. In *Developing minds: A resource book for teaching thinking.* Alexandria, VA: Association for Supervision and Curriculum Development.

Covey, S. R. (1989). *The seven habits of highly effective people.* New York: Simon & Schuster.

Cowen, J. E. (2005). *A balanced approach to beginning reading instruction.* Newark, DE: International Reading Association.

Cowley, G. (2000, Fall/Winter). For the love of language [Special Edition]. *Newsweek*, pp.12–15.

Cox, V. E. L. (1927). The literature curriculum. In L. Lamme (Ed.), *Learning to love literature* (pp. 1–12). Urbana, IL: National Council of Teachers of English.

Crawford, A. N. (2005). Communicative approaches to second-language acquisition: The bridge to second-language literacy. In G. G. Garcia (Ed.), *English learners: Reaching the highest level of English literacy* (pp. 152–181). Newark, DE: International Reading Association.

Crepeau, I. M., & Richards, M. A. (2003). *A show of hands. Using puppets with young children.* St. Paul, MN: Redleaf Press.

Cullinan, B. E. (1977). Books in the life of the young child. In B. E. Cullinan & C.W. Carmichael (Eds.), *Literature and young children* (pp. 1–16). Urbana, IL: National Council of Teachers of English.

Cummins, J. (2011, October). Literacy engagement: Fueling academic growth for English learners. *The Reading Teacher, 60*(2), 142–146.

Cunningham, J.W., & Creamer, K. H. (2003). Achieving best practices in literacy instruction. In L. M. Morrow, L. B. Gambrell, & M. Pressley (Eds.), *Best practices in literacy instruction* (pp. 333–346). New York: The Guilford Press.

Dale, E. & Chall, J. (1948). A formula for predicting readability. *Educational Research Bulletin, 27,* 11–20, 37–54.

Dangel, J. R., Durden, T. R., (2010, January). The nature of teacher talk during small group activities. *Young Children, 65*(1), 74–78, 80–81.

Darling-Kuria, N. (2010). *Brain-based early learning activities: Connecting theory and practice.* St. Paul, MN: Redleaf Press.

Dehaene, S. (2009). *Reading in the brain: The sense and evolution of a human invention.* New York: Penguin.

Delacre, L. (1988). *Nathan's fishing trip.* New York: Scholastic.

Delpit, L. (1995). *Other people's children: Cultural conflict in the classroom.* New York: The New Press.

Dennison, B. A., Russo, T. J., Burdick, P. A., & Jenkins, P. L. (2004, February). An intervention to reduce television viewing by preschool children. *The Archives of Pediatrics and Adolescent Medicine, 158,* 170–176.

dePaola, T. (1996). *Strega Nona.* New York: Scholastic.

Dewey, J. (1916). *Democracy and education.* New York: Free Press.

Dietrich, C., Swingley, D., & Werker, J. T. (2007, October 8). Native language governs interpretation of salient speech sound differences at 18 months.

PNAS, *104*(41), 16027–16031. (Proceedings of the National Academy of Sciences of the United States of America.)

Dionne, G., Mimeau, C., & Mathieu, E. (2014). The role of oral language development in promoting school readiness. In M. Boivin & K.L. Bierman (Eds.), *Promoting School Readiness and Early Learning* (pp. 105–132). New York: The Guilford Press.

Dokoupil, T. (2009, November 9). Let's be reasonable. *Newsweek*, p.19.

Dolch, E. W. (1948). *Problems in Reading.* Champaign IL: The Garrard Press.

Dolch Word List (1948). *Basic English Word List.* Retrieved from www.langmaker.com

Donovan, C. A., & Smolkin, L. B. (2002). Considering genre, content, and visual features in the selection of trade books for science instruction. *The Reading Teacher, 55*(6), 502–520.

Dooley, C. M. (2010, October). Young children's approaches to books: The emergence of comprehension. *The Reading Teacher, 64*(2) 120–130.

Dori, J. (2007, July). Think aloud! Increase your teaching power. *Young Children, 62*(4) 101–105.

Duke, N. K. (2007, May). Let's look in a book. *Young Children, 62*(3), 12–16.

Durkin, D. (1966). *Children who read early: Two longitudinal studies.* New York: Teachers College Press.

Dworak, M., Schierl, T., Bruns, T., & Struder, H. K. (2007, November). Impact of singular excessive computer game and television exposure on sleep patterns and memory performance of school-aged children. *Pediatrics, 120*(5), 978–985.

Eckhoff, A. (2010, January).Using games to explore visual art with young children. *Young Children, 65*(1): 18–22.

Education Market Research. (2010). *Elementary reading market: Teaching methods, textbooks/materials used and needed, and market size.* Rockaway Park, NY: Author.

Ehri, L. C. (2002). Phases of acquisition in learning to read words and implications for teaching. In R. Stainthorp & P. Tomlinson (Eds.), *Learning and teaching reading* (pp. 7–28). London: British Journal of Educational Psychology Monograph Series II.

Ehri, L. C., & Nunes, S. R. (2006). The role of phonemic awareness in learning to read. In A. E. Farstrup & S. J. Samuels (Eds.), *What research has to say about reading instruction* (pp. 110–139). Newark, DE: International Reading Association.

Eiserman, W. D., Shisler, L., Foust, T., Buhrmann, J., Winston, R., & White, K. R. (2007). Screening for hearing loss in early childhood programs. *Early Childhood Research Quarterly, 22*(1), 105–117.

Eliot, L. (2009). *Pink brain, blue brain: How small differences grow into troublesome gaps—And what we can do about it.* New York: Houghton Mifflin Harcourt.

Elkin, D. (2012, January). Knowing is not understanding: Fallacies and risks of early academic instruction. *Young Children, 67*(1), 84–87.

Elster, C. A. (2008, summer). Seven types of hybrids delight and challenge readers. *The California Reader, 42*(4) 19–26.

Enz, B. J., & Morrow, L. M. (2009). *Assessing preschool literacy development: Informal and formal measures to guide instruction.* Newark, DE: International Reading Association.

Erikson, E. (1950). *Childhood and society.* New York: W.W. Norton.

Ezell, H. K., & Justice, I. M. (2000). Increasing the print focus of shared reading through observational learning. *American Journal of Speech-Language Pathology, 9*, 36–47.

Ferreiro, E., & Teberosky, A. (1982). *Literacy before schooling.* Exeter, NH: Heinemann.

Fertig, B. (2009). *Why can't U teach me 2 read? Three students and a mayor put our schools to the test.* New York: Farrar, Strauss, & Giroux.

Fisher, D., & Frey, N. (2013). *Common Core English Language Arts in PLC at work.* Newark, DE: International Reading Association.

Foundation for Child Development. (2009, October). *How do families matter? Understanding how families strengthen their children's educational achievement.* New York: Author.

Fox, M. (2001). *Reading magic: Why reading aloud to our children will change their lives forever.* New York: Harcourt.

Fox, M. (2008, September). Usually, but not this time—Not with this book… *Young Children, 63*(5) 44–45.

Freedson-Gonzalez, M. (2008, September 12). Presentation at NJTESOL-NJBE Conference, Somerset, NJ.

Freeman, M. (2007, February/March). A wild restraint: Reading education and *The Cat in the Hat. Reading Today, 24*(4), 21.

Fuller, B., Bridges, M., Bein, E., Jang, H., Jung. S., Rabe-Hesketh, S. Halfon, N., & Kuo, A. (2009, November). The health and cognitive growth of Latino toddlers: At risk of immigrant paradox? *Maternal and Child Health Journal, 13*(6), 755–768.

Gaffney, J. S., Ostrosky, M. M. & Hemmeter, M. L. (2008, July). Books as natural support for young children's literacy learning. *Young Children, 63*(4), 87–93.

Gainsley, S. (2003, Summer). Write it down. *High/Scope Resource, 22*(2), 26–27.

Galinsky, E. (2010). *Mind in the making: The seven essential life skills every child needs.* New York: HarperCollins.

Galinsky, E. (2012, January). Learning communities: And emerging phenomenon. *Young Children, 67*(1), 20–27.

Gallagher, K.C., & Mayer, K. L. (2008, November). Enhancing development and learning through teacher–child relationships. *Young Children, 63*(6) 80–87.

Gallas, K. (2003). *Imagination and literacy: A teacher's search for the heart of learning.* New York: Teachers College Press.

Gamel-McCormick, M. (2000, November). Exploring teachers' expectations for children entering kindergarten and procedures for sharing information between pre-K and K programs. Conference presentation at the annual conference of the National Association for the Education of Young Children, Atlanta.

Garcia, E., & Jensen, B. (2009). The demographic imperative: Educating English language learners. *Educational Leadership, 66*(7), 9–13.

Gardner, H. (1993). *Multiple Intelligences.* New York: Basic Books.

Gardner, H. (1999). *Disciplined mind: What all students should understand.* New York: Simon & Schuster.

Gardner, H. (2000). *Intelligence reframed: Multiple intelligences for the 21st century.* New York: Basic Books.

Geist, K., & Geist, E. A. (2008, March). Do Re Mi, 1-2-3 that's how easy math can be: Using music to support emergent mathematics. *Young Children, 63*(2) 20–25.

Geist, K., Geist, E. A., & Kuznik, K. (2013). The patterns of music: Young children learning mathematics through beat, rhythm, and melody. In C. Copple, S. Bredekamp, D. Koralek, & K. Charner (Eds.), *Developmentally appropriate practice: Focus on preschoolers* (pp. 150–157). Washington, DC: National Association for the Education of Young Children.

Gerber, E. B., Whitebook, M., & Weinstein, R. S. (2007). At the heart of child care: Predictors of teacher sensitivity in center based care. *Early Childhood Research Quarterly, 22*, 327–346.

Gesell, A. (1940). *The first five years of life.* New York: Harper & Brothers.

Gillanders, C. (2007). An English-speaking prekindergarten teacher for young Latino children: Implications of the teacher–child relationship on second language learning. *Early Childhood Education Journal, 35*(1), 47–54.

Gilllespie, L., & Hunter, A. (2011, September). Creating healthy attachments to the babies in your care. *Young Children, 66*(5), 62–63.

Goldenberg, C., Rueda, R. S., & August, D. (2006), Synthesis; Sociocultural contexts and literacy development. In August, D., & Shanahan, T. (Eds.), *Developing literacy in second language learners: A report of the National Literacy Panel on language-minority children and youth* (pp. 249–268). Mahwah, NJ: Lawrence Erlbaum Associates.

Gopnik, A. (2013, Sunday June 15). Mind and matter: Wordsworth, the child psychologist. *Wall Street Journal,* p. C2.

Gopnik, A., Meltzoff, A., & Kuhl, P. (1999). *The scientist in the crib: Minds, brains, and how children learn.* New York: William Morrow and Company.

Gould, B. (2002). Stress and the developing brain. *Head Start Bulletin, 73,* 16–18.

Gowen, J.W. (1995, March). The early development of symbolic play. *Young Children, 50*(3), 75–84.

Greenspan, S. I. (1997). *The growth of the mind and the endangered origins of intelligence.* Reading, MA: Addison-Wesley.

Greenspan, S. I. (1999). *Building healthy minds: The six experiences that create intelligence and emotional growth in babies and young children.* Cambridge, MA: Perseus Books.

Guernsey, L. (2009, September 10). Kindergarten need not be a pressure cooker. *USA Today,* p. 11A.

Gurdon, M. C. (2012, January 7–8). Children's books: The book that broke the color line. *Wall Street Journal,* p. C10.

Hakuta, K., Goto Butler, Y., & Witt, D. (2000). How long does it take English learners to attain proficiency? Policy Report 2000-1. Berkeley. CA: University of California Linguistic Minority Research Institute.

Hammack, B. G., Foote, M. M., Garretson, S., & Thompson, J. (2012, May). Family literacy packs: Engaging teachers, families, and young children in quality activities to promote partnerships for learning. *Young Children, 67*(3)104–110.

Hatcher, B., & Petty, K. (2004, November). Visible thought in dramatic play. *Young Children, 59*(6), 79–82.

Heffernan, V. (2009, January 30). Click and Jane. *The New York Times Magazine.* Retrieved from http://www.nytimes.com/2009/02/02magazine/01wwwin-medium-t.html

Hegedus, N. (2010, September 27). Quoted in A. Romano & T. Dokoupil, Men's lib. *Newsweek,* pp. 43–49.

Henderson, A. T., & Mapp, K. (2002). *A new wave of evidence: The impact of school, family, and community connections on student achievement.* Austin, TX: National Center for Family and Community Connections with Schools.

Honig, A. S. (1999, March). The amazing brain. *Scholastic Early Childhood Today, 13*(6), 17–22.

Honig, A. S. (2002). *Secure environments: Nurturing infant/toddler attachments in child care settings.* Washington, DC: National Association for the Education of Young Children.

Honig, A. S. (2007, September). Play: Ten power boost for children's early learning. *Young Children, 62*(5), 72–78.

Honig, A. S. (2013). Keys to quality infant care: Nurturing every baby's life journey. In S. Copple, S. Bredekamp, D. Koralek & K. Charner (Eds.), *Developmentally appropriate practice: Focus on infants and toddlers* (pp. 93–100). Washington, DC: National Association for the Education of Young Children.

Horz, R. L. (2012, May 1). Attention: Why speaking two languages is better than one. *Wall Street Journal,* p. D2.

Hsu, M. (2011, November 10). Read me an E–book story? *Wall Street Journal,* p. D16.

Hunter, T. (2003, May). What about Mr. Baker? *Young Children, 58*(3), 77.

Hutchins, P. (1986). *The doorbell rang.* New York: HarperCollins Publishers.

Interlandi, J. (2007, August 20). Turn it off, baby. *Newsweek, CL,* 8/9, 14.

International Reading Association. (2008, April/May). Getting off to a good start. *Reading Today, 25*(5), 40.

International Reading Association. (2010). *Standards for reading professionals.* Newark, DE: Author.

International Reading Association. (2010, September). Toolbox: Remarkable retellings, super summaries. *The Reading Teacher, 64*(1), 61.

International Reading Association & The National Association for the Education of Young Children. (1999). *Learning to read and write: Developmentally appropriate practices for young children.* Washington, DC: National Association for the Education of Young Children.

International Visual Literacy Association. (2004). Retrieved July 23, 2004, from http://www.ivla.com.

Jalongo, M. R. (2004). *Young Children and picture books.* Washington, DC: National Association for the Education of Young Children.

Jalongo, M. R. (2009). *Learning to listen, listening to learn: Building essential skills in young children.* Washington, DC: National Association for the Education of Young Children.

Jensen, E. (2008). *Brain-based learning: The new paradigm of teaching.* Thousand Oaks, CA: Corwin Press.

Johnson, C. (2005, August 18). Quoted in P. Wingert & M. Brant, Reading your babies. *Newsweek,* pp. 32–38, 39.

Johnson, D. (2009). *The joy of children's literature.* Boston: Harcourt.

Johnson, K. (1987). *Doing words.* Boston, MA: Houghton Mifflin.

Johnson, P. H., Ivey, G., & Faulkner, A. (2012, January). Talking in class: Remembering what is important about classroom talk. *The Reading Teacher, 65*(4), 232–237.

Jones, E. (2011). Play across the life cycle: From initiative to integrity to transcendence. *Young Children, 66*(4), 84–91.

Jones, M. K., & Shue, P. L. (2013, March). Engaging prekindergarten dual language learners in projects. *Young Children, 68*(1), 28–33.

Justice, L. M., & Lankford, C. (2002). Preschool children's visual attention to print during storybook reading: Pilot findings. *Communication Disorders Quarterly, 24*(1), 11–21.

Justice, L. M., & Pence, K. L. (2006). *Scaffolding with storybooks: A guide for enhancing young children's language and literacy achievement.* Newark, DE: International Reading Association.

Kagan, J. (1971). *Change and community.* New York: John Wiley & Sons.

Kaiser Family Foundation Family Survey. (2003, 2006). Menlo Park, CA: Kaiser Family Foundation. Retrieved October 26, 2004, from http://www.kff.org and retrieved December 4, 2006, from http://www.kff.org

Kalmar, K. (2008, January). Let's give children something to talk about: Oral language and preschool literacy. *Young Children, 63*(1), 88–92.

Kantrowitz, B. (1997, Spring/Summer). Off to a good start [Special Edition]. *Newsweek,* pp. 5–8.

Kantrowitz, B. (2000, Fall/Winter). 21st century babies. [Special Edition]. *Newsweek,* pp. 4–7.

Kara-Soteriou, J., & Rose, H. (2008, July). A bat, a snake, a cockroach, and a fuzzhead: Using children's literature to teach about positive character traits. *Young Children, 63*(4) 30–35.

Katz, L., & Chard, S. (1993). *Engaging children's minds: The project approach.* Norwood, NJ: Ablex.

Katz, L., & Schery, T. K. (2006, January). Including children with hearing loss in early childhood programs. *Young Children, 61*(1), 86–95.

Keats, E. J. (1969). *The snowy day.* New York: Viking Press.

Kendall, J. S., & Marzano. R. J. (2004). *Content knowledge: A compendium of standards and benchmarks for K–12 education.* Aurora, CO: Mid-continent Research for Education and Learning. Retrieved from http://www.Mcrel.org/ standards-benchmarks

Kennedy, J. (1987). *The teddy bear's picnic.* New York: Peter Bedrick Books.

King, K. A. (2012, March). Writing workshop in preschool: Acknowledging children as writers. *The Reading Teacher, 65*(6), 392–401.

Kissel, B. T. (2008, March). Apples on train tracks: Observing young children re-envision their writing. *Young Children, 63*(2) 26–32.

Koralek, D. (2007, May). Incorporating books throughout the curriculum. *Young Children, 62*(3), 10–11.

Koralek, D. (2008, March). Integrating the curriculum in the early years and beyond. *Young Children, 63*(2) 10–11.

Kotulak, R. (1996). *Inside the brain: Revolutionary discoveries of how the mind works.* Kansas City, MO: Andrews and McMeel.

Kruger, J. (2013, July 29). The power of the bilingual brain. *Time, 182*(5), 42–47.

Kucan, L. (2007, November). Insights from teachers who analyzed transcripts of their own classroom discussions. *The Reading Teacher, 6*(13), 228–236.

Kucan, L. (2012, March). What is the most important to know about vocabulary? *The Reading Teacher, 65*(6), 360–366.

Kupetz, B. N., & Green, E. J. (1997, January). Sharing books with infants and toddlers: Facing the challenges. *Young Children, 52*(2), 22–27.

Lally, J. R. (1997). *Curriculum and lesson planning: A responsive approach.* Unpublished manuscript. Sausalito, CA: West Ed.

Leong, D. J., & Bodrova, E. (2012, January). Assessing and scaffolding make-believe play. *Young Children, 67*(1), 28–34.

Leong, D. J., & Bodrova, E. (2013). Assessing and scaffolding make-believe play. In S. Copple, S. Bredekamp, D. Koralek & K. Charner (Eds.), *Developmentally appropriate practice: Focus on preschoolers* (pp. 134–142). Washington, DC: National Association for the Education of Young Children.

Lloyd-Jones, L. (2002). Relationship as curriculum. *Head Start Bulletin, 73,* 10–12.

Lynch-Brown, C., & Tomlinson, C. (1998). Children's literature past and present: Is there a future? *Peabody Journal of Education, 73*(3), 228–252.

MacDonald, M. R. (1996). Quoted in B. Mooney & D. Holt, *The storyteller's guide.* Little Rock, AR: August House Publishers.

Machado, J. (2011, April 18). Recorded observation notes. Busy Bee Children's Center. Santa Clara, CA.

Machado, J., & Botnarescue, H. (2008, 2011). *Student teaching: Early childhood practicum guide.* Clifton Park, NY: Thomson Delmar Learning.

Magruder, E. S., Hayslip, W. W., Espinosa, L. M., & Matera, C. (2013, March). Many languages, one teacher: Supporting language and literacy development for preschool dual language learners. *Young Children, 68*(1), 8–15.

Manaster, H., & Jobe, M. (2012, November). Bringing boys and girls together: Supporting preschoolers' positive peer relationships. *Young Children, 67*(5), 12–17.

Mangione, P. (2010, November 4). Science of early brain development and how it informs our work. Presentation at the National Association for the Education of Young Children. Annual National Conference, Anaheim, CA.

Marcon, R. A. (2007, January/February). Quoted in S. J. Oliver & E. Klugman, Building a play research agenda: What do we know about play? *Exchange, 173,* 14–18.

Marian, V. (2009, May 20). Quoted in *Science Daily.* Exposure to two languages carries far-reaching

benefits. Retrieved from http://www.sciencedaily
.com/releases/2009/05/090519172157.htm

Marklein, M. B. (2010, February 9). Gender gap in college has far reaching consequences. *USA Today*, p. 4D.

Marzano, R. J. (2007). *The art and science of teaching: A comprehensive framework for effective instruction.* Alexandria, VA: Association for Supervision and Curriculum Development.

Mason, J. M. (1984). Early reading from a developmental perspective. In P. O. Pearson, R. Barr, M. L. Kamil, & P. Mosenthal (Eds.), *Handbook of reading research* (pp. 505–543). New York: Longman.

Mathews, J. (2010). What really makes a super school? In K. Weber (Ed.). *Waiting for Superman: How we can save America's failing schools* (pp. 167–186). New York: Perseus Books Group.

Mathias, B. (2006). The art of the storyteller. In T. P. Bicknell & F. Trotman (Eds.), *How to write and illustrate children's books and get them published.* Cincinnati, OH: Writer's Digest Books.

McCardle, P. (2006). Foreword. In D. August & T. Shanahan, *Developing literacy in second-language learners: Report of the National Literacy Panel on language-minority children and youth* (pp. ix–xi). Mahwah, NJ: Lawrence Erlbaum Associates.

McGee, C. D., & Hughes, C. E. (2011, July). Identifying and supporting young gifted learners. *Young Children, 66*(4), 100–105.

McGee, L. M. (2003). Book acting: Storytelling and drama in the early childhood classroom. In D. M. Barone & L. M. Morrow (Eds.), *Literacy and young children: Research-based practices* (pp. 157–172). New York: The Guilford Press.

McGee, L. M., & Richgels, D. J. (2003). *Designing early literacy programs: Strategies for at-risk preschool and kindergarten children.* New York: The Guilford Press.

McGee, L. M. & Shickedanz, J. A. (2010). Repeated interactive read-alouds in preschool and kindergarten. In D. S. Strickland (Ed.), *Essential readings on early literacy* (pp. 10–20). Newark, DE: International Reading Association.

McGuiness, D. (1997). *Why our children can't read and what we can do about it: A scientific revolution in reading.* New York: Free Press.

McMullen, M., & Dixon, S. (2006). Building on common ground: Unifying practices of infant toddler specialists through a mindful relationship-based approach. *Young Children, 61*(4), 46–52.

McMullen, M. B. (2013). Understanding development of infants and toddlers. In S. Copple, S. Bredekamp, D. Koralek & K. Charner (Eds.), *Developmentally appropriate practice: Focus on infants and toddlers* (pp. 23–50). Washington, DC:

National Association for the Education of Young Children.

McNair, J. C. (2007, September). Using children's names to enhance early literacy development. *Young Children, 62*(5), 84–89.

McNair, J. C. (2012, September). Poems about sandwich cookies, jelly and chocolate: Poetry in K–3 classrooms. *Young Children, 67*(4), 94–100.

McVicker, C. J. (2007, May). Young readers respond: The importance of child participation in emerging literacy. *Young Children, 62*(3), 18–22.

Medina, J. (2008). *Brain rules: Twelve principles for surviving and thriving at work, home and school.* Seattle, WA: Pear Press.

Meegan, T. (2009, October). Quoted in D. Russakoff, *How do families matter? Understanding how families strengthen their children's educational achievement.* New York: Foundation for Child Development.

Meier, D. R. (2004). *The young child's memory for words.* New York: Teacher's College Press.

Meltzoff, A., Kuhl. P., Movellan, J., & Sejnowski, T. (2009). Foundations for a new science of learning. *Science, 325*(5938), 284–288.

Mendelsohn, D. J. (1994). *Learning to listen: A strategy-based approach for the second language learner.* San Diego, CA: Dominie Press.

Mitchell, H. (2013, December 31). Burning question: Why does music aid memorization? *Wall Street Journal*, p. D3.

Montessori, M. (1967a). *The absorbent mind.* New York: Holt, Rinehart, and Winston.

Montessori, M. (1967b). *The discovery of the child.* New York: Holt, Rinehart, and Winston.

Morley, J. (2001). Annual comprehension instruction: Principles and practices. In M. Celce-Murcia (Ed.), *Teaching English as a second or foreign language* (pp. 69–85). Boston: Heine & Heinc Publishers.

Morphett, M. V., & Washburne, C. (1931). When should children begin to read? *Elementary School Journal, 31*, 496–508.

Morrow, L. M., & Asbury, E. (2003). Current practices in early childhood literacy development. In L. M. Morrow, D. H. Tracey, D. G. Woo & M. Pressley (1999), Characteristics of exemplary first grade literacy instruction. *Reading Teacher, 52*, 462–476.

Munir, K., & Rose, S. C. (2008, January 21). How to solve three puzzles. *Newsweek*, pp. 64–66.

Munsch, R. (2011). *Love you forever.* New York: Firefly Books.

Murphy, J. C. (2003, November). Case studies in African American school success and parenting behaviors. *Young Children, 58*(6), 85–89.

Narvaez, D. Quoted in J. Yardegaran (2012, January 15), Cry it out? Not so fast. *San José Mercury News*, pp. D1–D2.

National Assessment of Educational Progress. (1995). The NAEP reading: A first look—Findings from the National Assessment of Educational Progress. Washington, DC: U.S. Government Printing Office.

National Association for the Education of Young Children (NAEYC). (2007). *NAEYC Early childhood program standards and accreditation criteria: The mark of quality in early childhood education.* Washington, DC: Author.

National Association for the Education of Young Children. (2008, September). On our minds: Meaningful technology integration in early learning environments. *Young Children, 63*(5) 48–50.

National Association for the Education of Young Children. (2011). *2010 NAEYC Standards for initial and advanced early childhood professional preparation programs.* Washington, DC: Author.

National Association for the Education of Young Children. (2013). *Developmentally appropriate practice: Focus on infants and toddlers.* Washington, DC: Author.

National Association for the Education Young Children and the Fred Rogers Center for Early Learning and Children's Media at St. Vincent College. (2012). *Technology and interactive media as tools in early childhood programs serving children from birth through age 8.* Joint position statement. Retrieved from www.naeyc.org/content/technology-and-young children.

National Early Literacy Panel (NELP). (2008a). *Developing early literacy. Report of the National Early Literacy Panel.* Washington, DC: National Institute for Literacy.

National Early Literacy Panel (NELP). (2008b). *Developing early literacy: A scientific synthesis of early literacy development and implications for intervention.* Washington, DC: National Institute for Family Literacy and the National Center for Family Literacy.

National Education Association. (2005). *Children's favorite books.* Retrieved March 16, 2005, from www.nea.org/readacross/resources/kidsbooks.html.

National Governors Association Center for Best Practices & Council of Chief State School Officers. (2010). *Common Core State Standards for English Language arts & literacy in history/social studies, science, and technical subjects.* Washington, DC: Authors.

National Governors Association Center for Best Practices & Council of Chief State School Officers. (2010). *Common Core State Standards—Reading.* Washington, DC: Author.

National Institute of Child Health and Human Development. (2000). *Report of the National Reading Panel: Teaching children to read: An evidence-based assessment of the scientific research literature on reading and its implications for reading instruction.* (NIH Publication No. 00-4769). Washington, DC: U. S. Government Printing Office.

National Latino Children's Institute. (2008). *Words for the future—Creando el future.* Retrieved July 7, 2008, from http://www.nicl.org/kits/words%20intro.htm

National Reading Association. (2008, April/May). Getting off to a good start. *Reading Today, 25*(5) 40.

National Reading Panel. (2000). *Teaching children to read: An evidence-based assessment of the scientific research literature on reading and its implications for reading instruction* (NIH Publication No. 00-4769). Washington, DC: National Institute of Child Health and Human Development.

National Research Council. (2000). *How people learn: Brain, mind, experience and school.* Washington, DC: National Academy Press.

Neergaard, L. (2006, Thursday, May 26). Parents turn small fry on to the small screen. *Idaho Statesman,* p. 18.

Nelson, K., & Shaw, L. (2002). Developing a socially shared symbolic system. In E. Amsel & J. Byrnes (Eds.), *Language, literacy and cognitive development: The development and consequences of symbolic communication* (pp. 27–57). Mahwah, NJ: Erlbaum.

Nemeth, K. N. (2009). *Many languages, one classroom: Teaching dual and English language learners.* Beltsville, MD: Gryphon House, Inc.

Nemeth, K. N., & Erdosi, V. (2012, September). Enhancing practice with infants and toddlers from diverse language and cultural backgrounds. *Young Children, 67*(4), 49–57.

Nemeth, K. N., & Erdosi, V. (2013). Enhancing practice with infants and toddlers from diverse language and cultural backgrounds. In C. Copple, S. Bredekamp, D. Koralek & K. Charner (Eds.), *Developmentally appropriate practice: Focus on infants and toddlers.* (pp. 105–115). Washington, DC: National Association for the Education of Young Children.

Neuman, S. B., & Roskos, K. (2007). *Nurturing knowledge: Building a foundation for school success by linking early literacy to math, science, art, and social studies.* New York: Scholastic Inc.

Neuman, S. B. & Roskos, K. (2012). Helping children become more knowledgeable through text. *The Reading Teacher, 66*(8), 207–210.

Neuman, S. B., & Roskos, K. (2012, September). More than teachable moments: Enhancing oral vocabulary instruction in your classroom. *The Reading Teacher, 66*(1), 63–67.

Neuman, S. B., & Wright, T. S. (2013). *All about words: Increasing vocabulary in the Common Core Classroom, Pre-K–2.* New York: Teachers College Press.

New, R. S. (2002). Early literacy and developmentally appropriate practice: Rethinking the paradigm. In S. Neuman & D. Dickenson (Eds.), *Handbook of early literacy research* (pp. 254–262). New York: Guilford.

Ohl, J. (2002, Fall). Linking child care and early literacy: Building the foundation for success. *Child Care Bulletin, 27,* 1–4.

O'Leary, C., Newton, J., Lundz, D., Hall, M., O'Connell, R., Raby, C., & Czarnecka, M. (2002, June 1–4). Visual Communication Group ACM SIGGRAPH Workshop. Snowbird, UT.

On Campus. (2010, November/December). Mix it up. *30*(2) 2,. Author.

O'Neil, K. E. (2011, November). Reading pictures: Developing visual literacy for greater comprehension. *The Reading Teacher, 66*(3), 214–223.

Ortiz, R., & Ordonez-Jasis, R. (2010). Leyendo juntos (reading together): New directions for Latino parents' early literacy involvement. In D. S. Strickland (Ed.), *Essential readings on early literacy* (pp. 129–141). Newark, DE: International Reading Association.

Osada, N. (2004). Listening comprehension: A brief review of the past thirty years. *Dialogue, 3,* 53–66.

Oslick, M. E. (2013, April). Children's voices: Reactions to a criminal justice issue picture book. *The Reading Teacher, 66*(7), 543–552.

Paley, V. (1990). *The boy who would be a helicopter: The uses of storytelling in the classroom.* Cambridge, MA: Harvard University Press.

Paley, V. (1994). Princess Annabella and the black girls. In A. H. Dyson & C. Genishi (Eds.), *The need for story: Cultural diversity in classroom and community* (pp. 145–154). Urbana, IL: National Council of Teachers of English.

Pan, B. A., & Gleason, J. B. (1997). Semantic development: Learning the meanings of words. In J. Gleason (Ed.), *The development of language* (4th ed., pp. 311–331). Boston, MA: Allyn & Bacon.

Pandey, A. (2010). *The child language teacher: Intergenerational language and literary enhancement.* Mysore, India: Central Institute of Indian Language.

Pandey, A. (2012). *Language building blocks: Essential linguistics for early childhood educators.* New York: Teachers College Press.

Paratore, J. R., & Edwards, P. A. (2011). Parent–teacher partnerships that made a difference in children's literacy achievement. In L. M. Morrow & L. B. Gambrelle (Eds.), *Best practices in literacy instruction* (pp. 436–454). New York: Guilford Press.

Pawlina, S., & Stanford, C. (2011, September). Shifting mindsets for greater resiliency and better problem solving. *Young Children, 6*(3), 30–36.

Pense, K L., Justice, L. M., & Wiggins, A. K. (2008). Preschool teachers' fidelity in implementing a comprehensive language-rich curriculum. *Language, Speech, and Hearing Services in Schools, 39,* 329–341.

Pentimonti, J. M., Zucker, T. A., Justice, L. M., & Kadervek, J. N. (2010, May). Informational text use in preschool classroom read-alouds. *The Reading Teacher, 63*(8), 656–665.

Perry, J. (2000, February 17). Quoted in S. Steffens (Ed.), Preschool years give children the building blocks for learning. *San Jose Mercury News,* p. 1A.

Petersen, S., & Wittmer, D. (2008, May). Relationship-based infant care. *Young Children, 63*(3), 40–42.

Phillips, D. C., & Soltis, J. F. (2009). *Perspectives on learning.* New York: Teachers College Press.

Piaget, J. (1952, 1995). *Six psychological studies.* New York: Routledge.

Piaget, J. (1952a). *The language and thought of the child.* London: Routledge and Kegan Paul.

Piaget, J. (1952b). *The origins of intelligence in children.* New York: International Universities Press.

Piaget, J. (1970). *Science of education and the psychology of the child.* New York: Orion.

Piasta, S. B., & Wagner, R. K. (2010). Developing early literacy: A meta-analysis of alphabet learning and instruction. *Reading Research Quarterly, 45,* 8–38.

Pica, R. (2007). *Jump into literacy: active learning for preschool children.* Beltsville, MD: Gryphon House.

Poole, C. (1999, March). You've got to hand it to me! *Scholastic Early Childhood Today, 13*(6), 34–39.

Powell, D. R., & Diamond, K. E. (2012). Promoting early literacy and language development. In R. C. Pianta (Ed.), *Handbook of early childhood education.* (pp.194–216). New York: Guilford Press.

Prairie, A. P. (2013, May). Supporting socio-dramatic play in ways that enhance academic learning. *Young Children, 68*(2), 62–67.

Raftery, I. (2009, Tuesday, February 3). Infants learn earlier than thought. *The Seattle Times Health.* Retrieved from http://seattletimes.nwsource.com/html/health/2008700779_brains03.html

Rasinski, T., & Zimmerman, B. (2013, April/May). Try poetry! *Reading Today, 30*(5), 15–16.

Raymond, J. (2000, Fall/Winter). Kids, start your engines [Special Edition]. *Newsweek,* pp. 8–11.

Reutzel, D. R., & Clark, S. (2011, October). Organizing literacy classrooms for effective instruction. *The Reading Teacher, 65*(2), 95–109.

Richgels, D. J. (2013, February). Talk, right, read: A method for sampling emergent literacy skills. *The Reading Teacher, 66*(5), 380–389.

Rimm-Kaufman, S. E., Pianta, R. C., & Cox, M. J. (2000). Teachers' judgments of problems in the transition to kindergarten. *Early Childhood Research Quarterly, 15*(2), 147–166.

Risko, V. J. (2011, June/July). Celebrating teachers who teach with grit. *Reading Today, 28*(7), 26–27.

Rochman, B. (2013, February 25). Beyond counting sheep: Why math is the hot new bedtime reading. *Time, 18*(2), 52–53.

Romano, A., & Dokoupil, T. (2010, September 27). Men's lib. *Newsweek,* pp. 43–49.

Rones, N. (2004, August). Listen to this. *Parents,* 167–168.

Roskos, K., & Christie, J. (2007). Play and early literacy in these times. In B. J. Guzzetti (Ed.), Literacy for the new millennium. *Early literacy 1,* 201–12. Westport, CT: Preager.

Roskos, K., & Newman, S. B. (2013, March). Common core, commonplaces, and community in teaching reading. *Reading Teacher, 66*(6), 460–473.

Rubin, R. (2010, February 11). Gene mutations tied to stuttering. *USA Today,* p. 11B.

Sachs, J. (1997). Communication development in infancy. In J. Gleason (Ed.), *The development of language* (4th ed., pp. 261–282). Boston, MA: Allyn & Bacon.

Schmid, R. E. (2010, February 21). Studies find music may give voice to those who can't speak. *San Jose Mercury News,* p. A6.

Schwartz, C. (2011, August 15). Why it's smart to be bilingual: The brain's real superfood may be learning new languages. *Newsweek,* p. 26.

Schwartz, S. L., & Copeland, S. M. (2010). *Connecting emergent curriculum and standards in the early childhood classroom.* New York: Teachers College Press.

Seitz, H. (2008, March). The power of documentation in the early childhood classroom. *Young Children, 63*(2), 88–92.

Serafini, F. (2012). When bad things happen to good books. *The Reading Teacher, 65*(4), 238–241.

Shanahan, T. (2006). What reading research says: The promises and limitations of applying research to reading education. In A. E. Farstrup & S. J. Samuels (Eds.), *What research has to say about reading instruction* (pp. 8–24). Newark, DE: International Reading Association.

Sharapan, H. (2012, January). How early childhood educators can apply Fred Rogers' approach. *Young Children, 67*(1), 36–40.

Shedd, M. K., & Duke, N. K. (2008). The power of planning developing effective read-alouds. *Young Children, 63*(6) 22–27.

Singson, M., & Mann, V. A. (1999, April). *Precocious reading acquisition: Examining the roles of phonological and morphological awareness.* Paper presented at the 6th Annual Conference of the Society for the Scientific Study of Reading, Montréal, Canada.

Sladek, K. (2012, January). View from the chalkboard: Passing on a passion for reading to today's girls. *The Reading Teacher, 65*(4), 256.

Slavin, R. E., Madden, N. A., Karweit, N. L., Dolan, L. J., & Wasik, B. A. (1994). Success for all: Getting reading right the first time. In E H. Hiebert & B. M. Taylor (Eds.), *Get reading right from the start* (pp. 125–147). Boston: Allyn & Bacon.

Slobin, D. I. (1971). *Psycholinguistics.* Glenview, IL: Scott Foresman.

Smith, M. W. (2001). Children's experiences in preschool. In D. Dickinson & P. Tabors (Eds.), *Beginning literacy with language* (pp. 149–174). Baltimore, MD: Brookes.

Smith, R. G., Strand, P. J., Crowley, A., Colman, T., Robinson, C., & Swaim, M. (2011). *Gaining on the gap: Changing hearts, minds and practice.* Lanham, MD: Bowman and Littlefield.

Snider, M. (2008, Tuesday January 15). The digital download. *USA Today,* p. 7D.

Snow, K. (2011, July). A bridge between early childhood research and practice. *Young Children. 66*(4), 63–65.

Soderman, A. K., Clevenger, K. G., & Kent, I. G. (2013, March). Using stories to extinguish the hot spots in second language acquisition, Preschool to Grade 1. *Young Children, 68*(1) 34–41.

Spencer, P., & Stamm, P. (2008). *Bright from the start: The simple, science-backed way to nurture your child's developing mind.* New York: Gotham.

Spivak, L. (2000, Fall/Winter). In G. Cowley (Ed.), For the love of language [Special Edition]. *Newsweek,* pp. 12–15.

St. George, D. (2009, April 20). Study: Kids can get addicted to video games. *San Jose Mercury News,* p. 2A.

Stark, D. R., Chazen-Cohen, R., & Jerald, J. (2002). The infant mental health forum. *Head Start Bulletin, 73,* 46–47, 53.

Stauffer, R. C. (1970). *The language experience approach to the teaching of reading.* New York: Harper & Row.

Stern, S., & Klein, J. (2013, May 14). Conservatives and the common core. *Wall Street Journal,* p. A13.

Stieglitz, M. G. (2008). *The visual differential: An experimental study of the relation of varied experiences with visuals to shape discrimination.* Unpublished doctoral dissertation, University of Wisconsin.

Stoel-Gammon, C. (1997). Phonological development. In J. Gleason (Ed.), *The development of language* (4th ed., pp. 138–201). Boston, MA: Allyn & Bacon.

Strickland, D. (2010) *Essential readings on early literacy.* Newark, DE: International Reading Association.

Strickland, D. S., & Schickedanz, J. A. (2004). *Learning about print in preschool: Working with letters, words, and beginning links with phonemic awareness.* Newark, DE: International Reading Association.

Strickland, D. S., Shanahan, T., & Escamalia, K. (2004, November 12). *Laying the groundwork for literacy: The National Early Literacy Panel synthesis of research on early literacy education.* National Association for the Education of Young Children Annual Conference. Anaheim, CA.

Strickland, M. & Abbot, L. (2010, September). Enhancing the early reading experience: Books, strategies, and concepts. *The Reading Teacher, 64*(1) 66–68.

Subotnik, R. (2010, July 19). Quoted in P. Bronson & A. Merryman, The creativity crisis: For the first time, research shows that American creativity is declining, what went wrong—And how we can fix it. *Newsweek,* pp. 45–50.

Teachout, C., & Bright, A. (2007, July). Reading the pictures: A missing piece of the literacy puzzle. *Young Children, 62*(4), 106–107.

Temple, C., Martinez, M., & Yokota, J. (2010). *Children's books in children's hands: An introduction to their literature.* Boston: Allyn & Bacon.

Thelan, P., & Klifman, T. (2011, July). Using daily transition strategies to support all children. *Young Children, 66*(4), 92–95.

Thompson, I. (1995). Assessment of second/foreign language listening comprehension. In D. J. Mendelsohn & J. Rubin (Eds.), *A guide for the teaching of second language listening* (pp. 31–58). San Diego, CA: Dominie Press.

Thompson, N. S. (2000, January). Sylvia Ashton-Warner: Reclaiming personal meaning in literacy teaching. *English Journal, 89*(3), 90–96.

Thurber, D. (1988). *Teaching handwriting.* Glenview, IL: Scott Foresman.

Tomlinson, H. B., & Hyson, M. (2009). An overview. In C. Copple and S. Bredekamp (Eds.), *Developmentally appropriate practice in early childhood programs serving children birth through age 8* (p. 111–186). Washington, DC: National Association for the Education of Young Children.

Toppo, G. (2010a, January 20). Kids' digital day: Almost 8 hours. *USA Today,* p. 1A.

Toppo, G. (2010b, January 20). Plugged in but turned out. *USA Today,* p. 4D.

Toppo, G. (2010, March 25). Student's reading scores show little progress. *USA Today,* p. 11B.

Trautman, L. S. (2003, November/December). If your child stutters. *Parent & Child, 11*(3), 64–67.

Trawick-Smith, J. (2012). Teacher–child play interactions to achieve learning outcomes. In R. C. Pianta (Ed.), *Handbook of early childhood education* (pp. 259–277). New York: Guilford Press.

Treiman, T. A., & Kessler, B. (2003). The role of letter names in the acquisition of literacy. In R. V. Kail (Ed.), *Advances in child development and behavior 31,* 105–135. San Diego, CA: Academic Press.

Trelease, J. (2007). Quoted in S. B. Neuman & K. Roskos, *Nurturing knowledge: Building a foundation for school success by linking early literacy to math, science, art, and social studies.* (Forward). New York: Scholastic Inc.

Trousdale, A. M. (1990). Interactive storytelling: Scaffolding children's early narratives. *Language Arts, 69*(2), 164–173.

U.S. Department of Education. (2002). *The No Child Left Behind Act.* Washington, DC: Author. Retrieved June 17, 2003, from http://www.edgov /nclb/overview.

U.S. Department of Health and Human Services, Administration for Children and Families. (2003). *The Head Start leaders guide to positive child outcomes.* Washington, DC: Author.

U.S. Department of Health and Human Services. (2003). *The Head Start path to positive child outcomes.* [The Head Start Child Outcomes Framework]. Retrieved May 21, 2004, from http://www .hsnrc.org/CDI/outcontent.cfm.

Vanderkam, L. (2009, September 2). The secret of school success: Want your kids to master books? First they need to master themselves. Fortunately, new research is finding that self-control can be taught. *USA Today,* p. 9A.

Venezky, R. (1970). *The structure of English orthography.* The Hague, Netherlands: Mouton.

Venezky, R. (1999). *The American way of spelling.* New York: Guilford.

Vergano, D. (2009, July 22). New science of learning could reinvent teaching techniques. *USA Today,* p. 4D.

Verhallen, M .J., Bus, A. J., & deJong, M. T. (2006). The promise of multimedia stories for kindergarten children at risk. *Journal of Educational Psychology, 98*(2), 410–419.

Volk, D., & Long, S. (2005, November). Challenging myths of the deficit perspective: Honoring children's literacy resources. *Young Children, 60*(6), 12–19.

Vygotsky, L. S. (1976, 1978). *Mind and society: The development of higher psychological process.* Cambridge, MA: Harvard University Press.

Vygotsky, L. S. (1980). *Mind in society.* Cambridge, MA: Harvard University Press.

Vygotsky, L. S. (1986). *Thought and language.* Cambridge, MA: MIT Press.

Wall, J. (2009). *Half broke horses.* New York: Scribner.

Wall Street Journal. (2012, January 21). Review. Visualizer: Children's picture books,. C12, Author.

Walley, A. C., Metsala, J. L., & Garlock, V. M. (2003). Spoken vocabulary growth: Its role in the development of phoneme awareness and early reading ability. *Reading and Writing: An Interdisciplinary Journal, 16,* 5–20.

Wanerman, T. (2009). In D. R. Meier (Ed.), *Here's the story: Using narrative to promote young children's language and literacy learning.* New York: Teachers College Press.

Wanerman, T. (2010, March). Using story drama with young preschoolers. *Young Children, 65*(2) 20–28.

Wang, S. S. (2009, December 22). The power of magical thinking: Research shows the importance of make-believe in kids' development. *Wall Street Journal*, pp. D1–D4.

Wasik, B. A. (2006, November). Building vocabulary one word at a time. *Young Children, 61*(6), 70–78.

Wasik, B. A. (2010, May). What teachers can do to promote preschoolers' vocabulary development: Strategies from effective language and literacy professional development coaching model. *The Reading Teacher, 63*(8), 621–633.

Weber, K. (Ed.) (2010). *Waiting for superman. How we can save America's failing public schools.* New York: Perseus Books. (Participant Media)

Webley, K. (2012, January 12). Why it's time to replace No Child's Left Behind. *Time, 179*(3), 40–44.

Whitmire, R. (2010). *Why boys fail: Saving our sons from an educational system that's leaving them behind.* New York: Amacom Books.

Will, G. F. (2009, March 23). Calling the baby ugly. *Newsweek,* p. 64.

Williams, A. E. (2008, January). Exploring the natural world with infants and toddlers in an urban setting. *Young Children, 63*(1), 22–25.

Williams, K. C. (1997, September). What do you wonder? *Young Children, 52*(6), 78–81.

Wingert, P., & Brant, M. (2005, August 18). Reading your baby's mind. *Newsweek,* pp. 32–38, 39.

Winsler, A., Manfra, L., & Diaz, R. M. (2007). "Should I let them talk?" Private speech and task performance among preschool children with and without behavior problems. *Early Childhood Research Quarterly, 22,* 215–231.

Wittmer, D. S. (2008). *Focusing on peers: The importance of relationships in the early years.* Washington, DC: Zero to Three.

Wolf, J. (2000, March). Sharing songs with children. *Young Children, 55*(2), 19–31.

Woodward, C., Haskins, G., Schaefer, G., & Smolen, L. (2004, July). Let's talk: A different approach to oral language development. *Young Children, 59*(4), 92–95.

Worthen, B. (2012, May 22). What happens when toddlers zone out with an iPad: When toddlers are in the iPad zone. *Wall Street Journal,* pp. D1–2.

Youngquist, J., & Martinez-Griego, B. (2009, July). Learning English, Learning in Spanish. *Young Children, 64*(4) 92–99.

Zambo, D. (2007). Using picture books to provide arch types to young boys: Extending the ideas of William Brozo. *The Reading Teacher, 61*(2), 124–131.

Zambo, D. (2008, summer). Using picture books and literacy activities to help young boys develop literacy skills and positive traits. *The California Reader, 42*(4) 11–18.

Zambo, D., & Hansen, L. (2007). Love, language, and emergent literacy. *Young Children, 62*(3), 32–37.

Zaslow, M., & Martinez-Beck, I. (2006). *Critical issues in early childhood professional development.* Baltimore, MD.: Brookes Publishing Company.

Zielinski, L., & Zielinski, S. (2006). *Children's picture book price guide: Finding, assessing, & collecting contemporary illustrated books.* Park City, UT: Flying Mouse Books.

Zimmerman, F. J., & Christakis, A. (2007, November). Associations between content types of early media exposure and subsequent attentional problems. *Pediatrics, 120*(5), 986–992.

Index

Chapter	NAEYC Early Program Standards and Accreditation Criteria naeyc	Developmentally Appropriate Practices (DAP): Focus on Infants, Toddlers, and Preschoolers, 2013 DAP	Common Core Standards for English Language Arts & Literacy S
	1F02 Teaching staff help children use language to communicate needs. p. 68	**2B6** Teachers frequently engage children in planning or reflecting on their experiences, discussing past experiences, and working to represent them. p. 68	**R.CCR 7** Integrate and evaluate content presented in diverse media and format, including visually and quantitatively, as well as in words. p. 000
	2A10 The curriculum guides teachers to incorporate content, concepts, and activities that foster language and literacy. p. 68	**2B7** Teachers promote children collaborating to work through ideas and solutions. p. 68	
		2D2 Teachers use verbal encouragement and acknowledge effort with specific comments. p. 68	
		3G2 Teachers make sure that children have plenty of opportunities to use large muscles. p. 68	
		3G4 Teachers provide for fine-motor skill development. p. 68	
		4.1 Recognize, understand, and value the forms of diversity that exist in society and their importance in learning to read and write. p. 68	

SECTION 2, LANGUAGE AND LITERACY PROGRAMS: RECOGNIZING DIVERSE NEEDS AND GOALS			
Ch. 4, Understanding Differences	**2A02** The curriculum allows for adaptations and modifications to ensure access for all children. p. 98	**3H5** Teachers support dual language learners and their home language as well as promoting their English. p. 98	
	2D03 Children have varied opportunities to develop competence in verbal and nonverbal communications by responding to questions, communicating needs, thoughts, and experiences and describing things and events. p.98	**3H4** Teachers attend to the particular needs of dual language learners and children behind in vocabulary and other aspects of language learning. p. 98	
	2D04 Children have varied opportunities to develop vocabulary through conversations, experiences, field trips, and books. p. 98	**3H7** Teachers help children use communication and language as tools for thinking and learning. p. 98	
	2A04 The curriculum can be implemented in a manner that reflects responsiveness to family home values, beliefs, experiences, and language. p. 98		
	2D02 Children are provided opportunities to experience oral and written communications in a language their family uses or understands. p. 98		
Ch. 5, Achieving Language and Literacy Goals through Program Planning	**2A05** Curriculum goals and objectives guide teachers' ongoing assessment of children's progress. p. 130	**3A1** Curriculum addresses key goals in language and literacy. p. 130	**W.CCR. 7** Conduct short as well as more sustained research projects based on focused questions, demonstrating understanding of the subject under investigation. p. 130
	2G02 Children are provided varied opportunities to learn key concepts and principles in science. p. 130	**3A2** Curriculum is consistent with high-quality, achievable, and challenging early childhood learning standards and recommendations of the relevant professional organizations. p. 130	
	2G03 Children are provided varied opportunities and materials that encourage them to use the five senses to observe, explore, and experiment with scientific phenomena. p. 130	**3A5** Teachers integrate ideas and content from multiple domains and disciplines through themes, projects, play opportunities, and other learning experiences so that children are able to develop an understanding of concepts and make connections across content areas. p. 130	
	2J01 Children are provided varied opportunities to gain an appreciation of art, music, drama, and dance in ways that reflect cultural diversity. p. 130		

Chapter	NAEYC Early Program Standards and Accreditation Criteria naeyc	Developmentally Appropriate Practices (DAP): Focus on Infants, Toddlers, and Preschoolers, 2013 DAP	Common Core Standards for English Language Arts & Literacy
Ch. 6, Promoting Language and Literacy	**2a** Knowing about and understanding diverse family characteristics. p. 164		**SL.CCR 3** Evaluate a speaker's point of view, reasoning, and use of evidence in rhetoric. p. 164
Ch. 7, Developing Listening Skills	**3F04** Teaching staffs help children understand spoken language by using body language and physical cues. p. 190	**2B5** Teachers recognize the importance of both child-guided and adult-guided learning experiences. p. 000	**SL.CCR 2** Integrate and evaluate information presented in diverse media and formats including visually, quantitatively, and orally. p. 190
	2D03 Children have varied opportunities to develop competence in verbal and nonverbal communication. p. 190	**2C2** Teachers take into account children's capabilities as listeners, recognizing that preschooler's skills of recall and focused attention are still developing. p. 190	
	2F08 Children are provided varied opportunities and materials that help them recognize and name repeating patterns. p. 190	**2C2** Teachers communicate information in small units, tie new information to what the children already know, check for understanding, and invite questions or comments to engage their interest. p. 190	
	2E06 Children are regularly provided multiple and varied opportunities to develop phonological awareness and play with sounds, syllables, and word families. p. 190	**3H13** Teachers understand the typical trajectory of phonological skill development for preschool children: rhyming, alliteration, syllable segmenting, onset/rime blending, and segmenting. p. 190	

SECTION 3, LITERATURE AND OTHER LANGUAGE ARTS AREAS

Chapter	NAEYC	DAP	Common Core
Ch. 8, Children and Books	**2E08** Children have access to books and writing materials throughout the classroom. p. 214	**3H21** Teachers draw children's attention to print conventions. p. 214	**R.CCR 1** Read closely to determine what the text says explicitly and to make logical inferences from it, cite specific textual evidence when writing or speaking to support conclusions drawn from text. p. 214
	2E04 Children have varied opportunities to read books in an engaging manner in groups or individualized settings at least twice a day in full-time programs. p. 214	**3H22** To broaden children's knowledge and vocabulary, teachers use a variety of strategies such as reading stories and informational books rich in new concepts, information, and vocabulary. p. 214	**R.CCR 2** Determine central ideas or themes of a text and analyze their development; summarize the key supporting details and ideas. p. 214
	2E04 Children have various opportunities and access to various types of books including storybooks, factual books, books with rhymes, alphabet books and wordless books. p. 214	**3H23** Teachers engage children with questions and comments to help them recall and comprehend what is happening in a story and make connections between the book and their own life experiences. p. 214	**R.CCR 3** Analyze how and why individuals, events, and ideas develop and interact over the course of a text. p. 214
Ch. 9, Storytelling	**3G14** Teachers demonstrate their knowledge of content and developmental areas by creating experiences that engage children in purposeful and meaningful learning related to key curriculum concepts. p. 256	**3M1** Teachers give children daily opportunities for creative expression and aesthetic appreciation. p. 256	**W.CCR 9** Draw evidence from literary or informational texts to support analysis, reflection, and research. p. 256
	3G01 Teachers have and use a variety of teaching strategies that include a broad range of approaches and responses. p. 256	**3M5** Teachers do not provide a model that they expect children to copy. However, they demonstrate new techniques or uses of materials to expand children's options. p. 256	**W.CCR 3** Write narratives to develop real or imagined experiences or events using effective techniques, well-chosen details, and well-structured event sequences. p. 256
	2E04 Children have varied opportunities to retell and reenact events in storybooks. p. 256	**3 H7** Teachers help children use communication and language as tools for thinking and learning. p. 256	
Ch. 10, Poetry	**2E06** Children are helped to recognize and produce words that have the same beginning or ending sounds. p. 278	**3H12** Teachers introduce engaging oral language experiences that include rhyming and alliteration. p. 278	**SL CCR 2** Integrate and evaluate information presented in diverse media and formats including visually, quantitatively, and orally. p. 278

Chapter	NAEYC Early Program Standards and Accreditation Criteria naeyc	Developmentally Appropriate Practices (DAP): Focus on Infants, Toddlers, and Preschoolers, 2013 DAP	Common Core Standards for English Language Arts & Literacy
	2E06 Children are encouraged to play with sounds of language, including syllables, word families, and phonemes using rhymes. p. 278	3H12 Teachers encourage children to add their own verses and variations. p. 278	
	2E04 Children have varied opportunities to access books with rhymes. p. 278	2D1 Teachers consistently plan learning experiences that children find highly interesting, engaging, and comfortable. p. 278	
		2.3 Use a wide range of texts, including poetry. p. 278	
SECTION 4, THE GROWTH OF SPEECH AND EXPRESSION			
Ch. 11, Language Growth through Flannel Boards, Puppetry, and Dramatization	2J05 Children are provided many and varied opportunities to develop and widen their repertoire of skills that support artistic expression. p. 294	3M5 eachers demonstrate new techniques or uses of material to expand children's options. p. 294	W.CCR 8 Gather relevant information from multiple print and digital sources, assess the credibility and accuracy of each source, and integrate the information. p. 294
	2J06 Children are provided many and varied opportunities and materials to express themselves creatively. p. 294	3M2 Teachers introduce concepts and vocabulary to extend children's experiences in the arts. p. 294	
	2J07 Children have the opportunities to respond to the art of other children and adults. p. 294	3H7 Teachers help children use communication and language as tools for thinking and learning. p. 294	
Ch. 12, Realizing Speaking Goals	2D04 Children have varied opportunities to develop vocabulary through conversations. p. 320	3H7 Teachers help children use communication and language as tools for thinking and learning. p. 320	SL.CCR 1 Prepare for and participate effectively in a range of conversations and collaborations with diverse partners, building on others' ideas and expressing their own clearly and persuasively. p. 320
	2D06 Children have varied opportunities and materials that encourage them to have discussions to solve problems related to the physical world. p. 320	3H4 Teachers engage the child more frequently in sustained conversations and make extra efforts to help them comprehend. p. 320	SL CCR 6 Adapt speech to a variety of contexts and communicative tasks, demonstrating command of formal English when indicated or appropriate. p. 320
	2D07 Children are provided with opportunities and materials that encourage them to engage in discussions with one another. p. 320	3H2 Teachers provide frequent opportunities for children to talk to each other, so children also get modeling from their more skilled peers. p. 320	
Ch. 13, Group Times	2E06 Children are encouraged to play with sounds in finger plays. p. 348	3H6 Teachers are especially attentive to helping English language learners grasp word meanings. p. 348	L.CCR 1 Demonstrate command of the conventions of Standard English grammar and usage when writing or speaking. p. 348
	2A10 The curriculum guides teachers to incorporate content, concepts, and activities that foster social, emotional, physical, language, and cognitive development and that integrate key areas of content including literacy. p. 348	3H28 Teachers are comfortable with slight diversions that occur when children share connections that are relevant to them. p. 348	
	2A11 The schedule provides children learning activities in large groups, small groups, and child-initiated activity. p. 348	3M8 Teachers encourage children to engage in full body activities that require rhythm and timing, such as swinging; Teachers join them in such movement. p. 348	
		3H7 Teachers provide ways for every child to talk during group time. p. 348	
SECTION 5, WRITING AND READING: NATURAL COMPANIONS			
Ch. 14, Print—Early Knowledge and Emerging Interest	2E05 Children have multiple and varied activities to write. p. 372	3H19 Teachers create a print-rich environment in which lots of print not only is present but is also used in ways that show print's many purposes. p. 372	W.CCR 4 Produce clear and coherent writing in which the development, organization, and style are appropriate to the task, audience, and purpose. p. 372
	2E06 Children are helped to identify letters and the sounds they represent. p. 372	3H14 Teachers plan activities that give children a motivation to engage in writing. p. 372	